S0-AHY-483

Sunset

BEST HOME PLANS

500 Best-selling Home Plans

SUNSET BOOKS INC.

Director, Sales & Marketing:
  Richard A. Smeby
Editorial Director:
  Bob Doyle
Production Director:
  Lory Day
Group Marketing Manager:
  Becky Ellis
Art Director:
  Vasken Guiragossian
Consulting Editor:
  Don Vandervort

Cover: Pictured is plan E-2004 on page 160. Cover design by Vasken Guiragossian. Photography by Mark Englund/HomeStyles.

Third printing Febuary 1999

Copyright © 1997, Sunset Publishing Corp., Menlo Park, CA 94025.
First edition. All rights reserved, including the right of reproduction in whole or in part in any form. ISBN 0-376-01159-9. Library of Congress Catalog Card Number: 97-80068. Printed in the United States.

  For more information on Sunset's 500 *Best-selling Home Plans* or any other Sunset book, call (800) 526-5111.

2-00   # 38280068

What the Plans Include

Complete construction blueprints are available for every house shown in this book. Clear and concise, these detailed blueprints are designed by licensed architects or members of the American Institute of Building Design (AIBD). Each plan is designed to meet standards set down by nationally recognized building codes (the Uniform Building Code, Standard Building Code, or Basic Building Code) at the time and for the area where they were drawn.

Remember, however, that every state, county, and municipality has its own codes, zoning requirements, ordinances, and building regulations. Modifications may be necessary to comply with such local requirements as snow loads, energy codes, seismic zones, and flood areas.

Although blueprint sets vary depending on the size and complexity of the house and on the individual designer's style, each set may include the elements described below and shown at right.

■ **Exterior elevations** show the front, rear, and sides of the house, including exterior materials, details, and measurements.

■ **Foundation plans** include drawings for a full, partial, or daylight basement, crawlspace, pole, pier, or slab foundation. All necessary notations and dimensions are included. (Foundation options will vary for each plan. If the plan you choose doesn't have the type of foundation you desire, a generic conversion diagram is available.)

■ **Detailed floor plans** show the placement of interior walls and the dimensions of rooms, doors, windows, stairways, and similar elements for each level of the house.

■ **Cross sections** show details of the house as though it were cut in slices from the roof to the foundation. The cross sections give the home's construction, insulation, flooring, and roofing details.

■ **Interior elevations** show the specific details of cabinets (kitchen,

bathroom, and utility room), fireplaces, built-in units, and other special interior features.

■ **Roof details** give the layout of rafters, dormers, gables, and other roof elements, including clerestory windows and skylights. These details may be shown on the elevation sheet or on a separate diagram.

■ **Schematic electrical layouts** show the suggested locations for switches, fixtures, and outlets. These details may be shown on the floor plan or on a separate diagram.

■ **General specifications** provide instructions and information regarding excavation and grading, masonry and concrete work, carpentry and woodwork, thermal and moisture protection, drywall, tile, flooring, glazing, and caulking and sealants.

Other Helpful Building Aids

In addition to the construction information on every set of plans, you can buy the following guides.

■ **Reproducible sets** are helpful if you'll be making changes to the stock plan you've chosen. These blueprints are line drawings produced on erasable, reproducible paper for the purpose of modification. When alterations are complete, working copies can be made.

■ **Itemized materials list** details the quantity, type, and size of materials needed to build your home. (This list is extremely helpful in obtaining an accurate construction bid. It's not intended for use to order materials.)

■ **Mirror-reverse sets** are useful if you want to build your home in the reverse of the plan that's shown. Because the lettering and dimensions read backwards, be sure to buy at least one regular-reading set of blueprints.

■ **Description of materials** gives the type and quality of materials suggested for the home. This form may be required for obtaining FHA or VA financing.

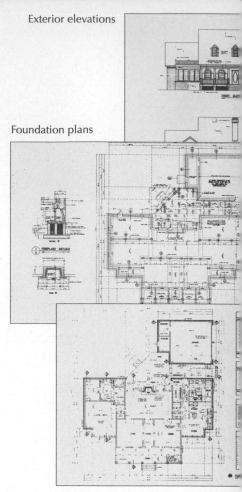

Exterior elevations

Foundation plans

Detailed floor plans

■ **How-to diagrams** for plumbing, wiring, solar heating, framing and foundation conversions show how to plumb, wire, install a solar heating system, convert plans with 2 by 4 exterior walls to 2 by 6 construction (or vice versa), and adapt a plan for a basement, crawlspace, or slab foundation. These diagrams are not specific to any one plan.

NOTE: Due to regional variations, local availability of materials, local codes, methods of installation, and individual preferences, detailed heating, plumbing, and electrical specifications are not included on plans. The duct work, venting, and other details will vary, depending on the heating and cooling system you use and the type of energy that operates it. These details and specifications are easily obtained from your builder or local supplier.

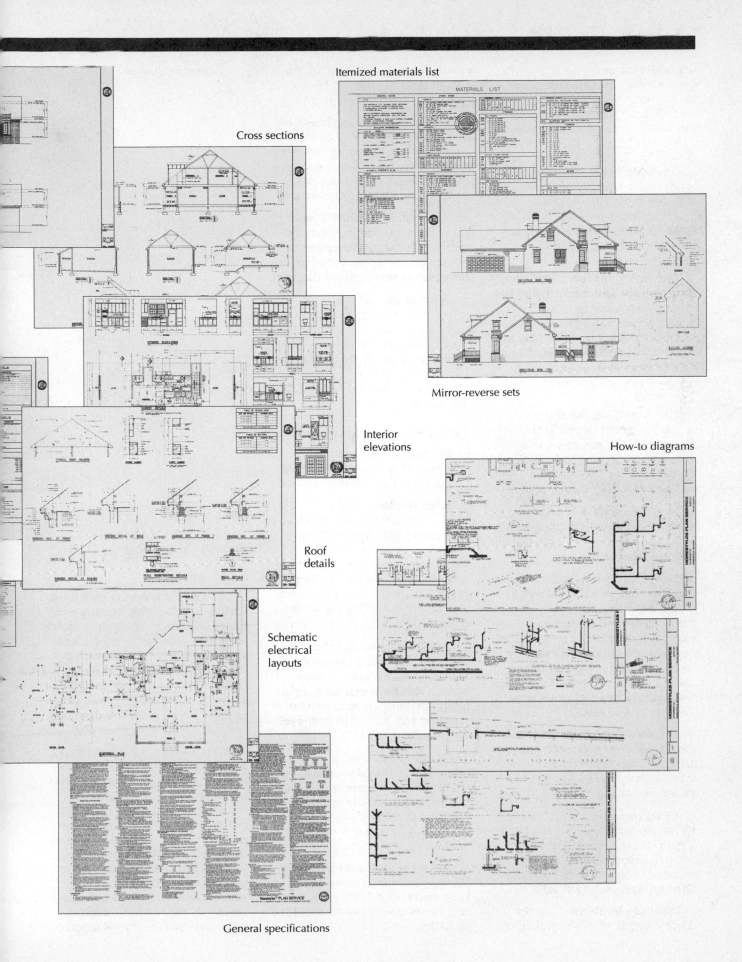

Itemized materials list

MATERIALS LIST

Cross sections

Mirror-reverse sets

Interior
elevations

How-to diagrams

Roof
details

Schematic
electrical
layouts

General specifications

Before You Order

Once you've chosen the one or two house plans that work best for you, you're ready to order blueprints. Before filling in the form on the facing page, note the information that follows.

How Many Blueprints Will You Need?

A single set of blueprints will allow you to study a home design in detail. You'll need more for obtaining bids and permits, as well as some to use as reference at the building site. If you'll be modifying your home plan, order a reproducible set (see page 2).

Figure you'll need at least one set each for yourself, your builder, the building department, and your lender. In addition, some subcontractors—foundation, plumber, electrician, and HVAC—may also need at least partial sets. If they do, ask them to return the sets when they're finished. The chart below can help you calculate how many sets you're likely to need.

Blueprint Checklist

____ Owner's set(s)

____ Builder usually requires at least three sets: one for legal documentation, one for inspections, and a minimum of one set for subcontractors.

____ Building department requires at least one set. Check with your local department before ordering.

____ Lending institution usually needs one set for a conventional mortgage, three sets for FHA or VA loans.

____ TOTAL SETS NEEDED

Blueprint Prices

The cost of having an architect design a new custom home typically runs from 5 to 15 percent of the building cost, or from $5,000 to $15,000 for a $100,000 home. A single set of blueprints for the plans in this book ranges from $245 to $685, depending on the house's size. Working with these drawings, you can save enough on design fees to add a deck, a swimming pool or a luxurious kitchen.

Pricing is based on "total finished living space." Garages, porches, decks and unfinished basements are not included.

Building Costs

Building costs vary widely, depending on a number of factors, includ-

Price Code (Size)	1 Set	4 Sets	7 Sets	Reproducible Set
AAA (under 500 sq. ft.)	$245	$295	$330	$430
AA (500-999 sq. ft.)	$285	$335	$370	$470
A (1,000-1,499 sq. ft.)	$365	$415	$450	$550
B (1,500-1,999 sq. ft.)	$405	$455	$490	$590
C (2,000-2,499 sq. ft.)	$445	$495	$530	$630
D (2,500-2,999 sq. ft.)	$485	$535	$570	$670
E (3,000-3,499 sq. ft.)	$525	$575	$610	$710
F (3,500-3,999 sq. ft.)	$565	$615	$650	$750
G (4,000-4,499 sq. ft.)	$605	$655	$690	$790
H (4,500-4,999 sq. ft.)	$645	$695	$730	$830
I (5,000 & above)	$685	$735	$770	$870

ing local material and labor costs and the finishing materials you select.

Foundation Options & Exterior Construction

Depending on your site and climate, your home will be built with a slab, pier, pole, crawlspace or basement foundation. Exterior walls will be framed with either 2 by 4s or 2 by 6s, determined by structural and insulation standards in your area. Most contractors can easily adapt a home to meet the foundation and/or wall requirements for your area. Or ask for a conversion how-to diagram (see page 2).

Service & Blueprint Delivery

Service representatives are available to answer questions and assist you in placing your order. Every effort is made to process and ship orders within 48 hours.

Returns & Exchanges

Each set of blueprints is specially printed and shipped to you in response to your specific order; consequently, requests for refunds cannot be honored. However, if the prints you order cannot be used, you may exchange them for another plan from any Sunset home plan book. For an exchange, you must return all sets of plans within 30 days. A nonrefundable service charge will be assessed for all exchanges; for more information, call the toll-free number on the facing page. Note: Reproducible sets cannot be exchanged.

Compliance with Local Codes & Regulations

Because of climatic, geographic and political variations, building codes and regulations vary from one area to another. These plans are authorized for your use expressly conditioned on your obligation and agreement to comply strictly with all local building codes, ordinances, regulations and requirements, including permits and inspections at time of construction.

Architectural & Engineering Seals

With increased concern about energy costs and safety, many cities and states now require that an architect or engineer review and "seal" a blueprint prior to construction. To find out whether this is a requirement in your area, contact your local building department.

License Agreement, Copy Restrictions & Copyright

When you purchase your blueprints, you are granted the right to use those documents to construct a single unit. All the plans in this publication are protected under the Federal Copyright Act, Title XVII of the United States Code and Chapter 37 of the Code of Federal Regulations. Each designer retains title and ownership of the original documents. The blueprints licensed to you cannot be used by or resold to any other person, copied or reproduced by any means. The copying restrictions do not apply to reproducible blueprints. When you buy a reproducible set, you may modify and reproduce it for your own use.

Blueprint Order Form

Complete this order form in just three easy steps. Then mail in your order or, for faster service, call toll-free.

1. Blueprints & Accessories

BLUEPRINT CHART

Price Code	1 Set	4 Sets	7 Sets	Reproducible Set*
AAA	$245	$295	$330	$430
AA	$285	$335	$370	$470
A	$365	$415	$450	$550
B	$405	$455	$490	$590
C	$445	$495	$530	$630
D	$485	$535	$570	$670
E	$525	$575	$610	$710
F	$565	$615	$650	$750
G	$605	$655	$690	$790
H	$645	$695	$730	$830
I	$685	$735	$770	$870

A reproducible set is produced on erasable paper for the purpose of modification. It is only available for plans with prefixes A, AG, AGH, AH, AHP, APS, AX, B, BOD, BRF, C, CC, CDG, CPS, DCL, DD, DW, E, EOF, FB, G, GA, GL, GSA, H, HDS, HFL, HOM, IDG, J, JWA, K, KD, KLF, L, LRD, LS, M, NBV, NW, OH, PH, PI, RD, S, SDG, SG, SUL, SUN, THD, TS, U, UD, UDA, UDG, V, WH. Prices subject to change

Mirror-Reverse Sets: $50 surcharge. From the total number of sets you ordered above, choose the number you want to be reversed. *Note: All writing on mirror-reverse plans is backwards. Order at least one regular-reading set.*

Itemized Materials List: One set $50; each additional set $15. Details the quantity, type, and size of materials needed to build your home.

Description of Materials: Sold in a set of two for $50 (for use in obtaining FHA or VA financing).

Typical How-To Diagrams: One set $20; two sets $30; three sets $40; four sets $45. General guides on plumbing, wiring, and solar heating, plus information on how to convert from one foundation or exterior framing to another. *Note: These diagrams are not specific to any one plan.*

2. Sales Tax & Shipping

Determine your subtotal and add appropriate local state sales tax, plus shipping and handling (see chart below).

SHIPPING & HANDLING

	1–3 Sets	4–6 Sets	7 or More Sets	Reproducible Set
U.S. Regular (5–6 business days)	$17.50	$20.00	$22.50	$17.50
U.S. Express (2–3 business days)	$29.50	$32.50	$35.00	$29.50
Canada Regular (2–3 weeks)	$20.00	$22.50	$25.00	$20.00
Canada Express (5–6 business days)	$35.00	$40.00	$45.00	$35.00
Overseas/Airmail (7–10 businessdays)	$57.50	$67.50	$77.50	$57.50

3. Customer Information

Choose the method of payment you prefer. Include check, money order, or credit card information, complete name and address portion, and mail, fax, or call using the information at the right.

SS21

COMPLETE THIS FORM

Plan Number _____ **Price Code** _____

Foundation _____
(Review your plan carefully for foundation options—basement, pole, pier, crawlspace, or slab. Many plans offer several options; others offer only one.)

Number of Sets: $_____
- ☐ One Set   (See chart at left)
- ☐ Four Sets
- ☐ Seven Sets
- ☐ One Reproducible Set

Additional Sets _____ $_____
($40 each)

Mirror-Reverse Sets _____ $_____
($50 surcharge)

Itemized Materials List $_____
Only available for plans with prefixes AH, AHP, APS*, AX*, B*, BOD*, C, CAR, CC, CDG*, CPS, DD*, DW, E, G, GSA, H, HFL, HOM, I*, IDG, J, K, I, I MR*, LRD, NW*, P, PH, R, S, SG*, SUN, THD, U, UDA, UDG, VL, WH, YS.
*Not available on all plans. Please call before ordering.

Description of Materials $_____
Only for plans with prefixes AHP, C, DW, H, J, K, P, PH, SUL, VL, YS.

Typical How-To Diagrams $_____
- ☐ Plumbing   ☐ Wiring   ☐ Solar Heating   ☐ Foundation & Framing Conversion

SUBTOTAL $_____

SALES TAX Minnesota residents add 6.5% $_____

SHIPPING & HANDLING $_____

GRAND TOTAL $_____

☐ Check/money order enclosed (in U.S. funds) payable to HomeStyles
☐ VISA   ☐ MasterCard   ☐ AmEx   ☐ Discover

Credit Card # _____ **Exp. Date** _____

Signature _____

Name _____

Address _____

City _____ **State** ____ **Country** _____

Zip _____ **Daytime Phone** (_____) _____

☐ Please check if you are a contractor.

Mail form to: Sunset/HomeStyles
P.O. Box 75488
St. Paul, MN 55175-0488

Or fax to: (612) 602-5002

FOR FASTER SERVICE CALL 1-800-820-1283

SS21

ONE-STORY HOMES UNDER 1,800 SQUARE FEET

Comfortable L-Shaped Ranch

- From the covered entry to the beautiful and spacious family gathering areas, this comfortable ranch-style home puts many extras into a compact space.
- Straight off the central foyer, an inviting fireplace and a bright bay window highlight the living and dining area, while sliding glass doors open to a wide backyard terrace.
- The combination kitchen/family room features a large eating bar. The nearby mudroom offers a service entrance, laundry facilities, access to the garage and room for a half-bath.
- In the isolated sleeping wing, the master bedroom boasts a private bath and plenty of closet space. Two additional bedrooms share another full bath.

Plan K-276-R

Bedrooms: 3	**Baths:** 2+

Living Area:	
Main floor	1,245 sq. ft.
Total Living Area:	**1,245 sq. ft.**
Standard basement	1,245 sq. ft.
Garage	499 sq. ft.

Exterior Wall Framing:	2x4 or 2x6

Foundation Options:
Standard basement
Crawlspace
Slab
(All plans can be built with your choice of foundation and framing. A generic conversion diagram is available. See order form.)

BLUEPRINT PRICE CODE: **A**

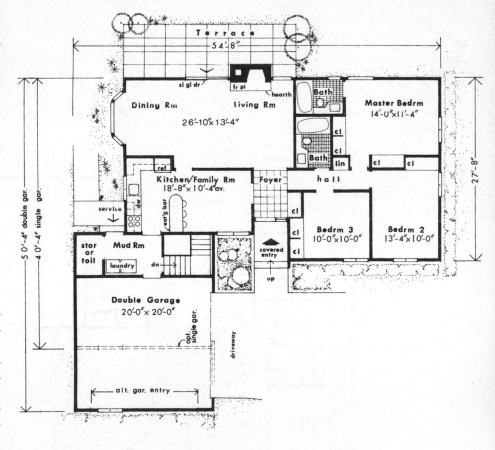

MAIN FLOOR

ORDER BLUEPRINTS ANYTIME!
CALL TOLL-FREE 1-800-820-1283

Plan K-276-R

PRICES AND DETAILS
ON PAGES 2-5

Photo courtesy of Larry Garnett & Associates, Inc.

Enchanting!

- This gracious French-style home is the picture of enchantment, with its striking Palladian window and its beautiful brick facade with lovely corner quoins.
- Beyond the leaded-glass front door, the open entry introduces the versatile living room. Guests will enjoy visiting for hours in front of the crackling fire!
- Visible over a half-wall, the formal dining room is worthy of any festive occasion. A wall of windows offers delightful views to a covered porch and your backyard's award-winning landscaping.

- The bayed morning room is the perfect spot for orange juice and waffles. If the weather permits, open the French door and dine alfresco on the porch!
- A handy snack bar highlights the gourmet kitchen. The sink is positioned for backyard views, to brighten those daily chores.
- The two-car garage is ideally located for easy unloading of groceries.
- Across the home, the master suite is a restful haven. Soak away your cares in the fabulous garden tub!
- Two secondary bedrooms, a nice hall bath and a central laundry room round out this enchanting plan.

Plan L-709-FA	
Bedrooms: 3	**Baths:** 2
Living Area:	
Main floor	1,707 sq. ft.
Total Living Area:	**1,707 sq. ft.**
Garage	572 sq. ft.
Exterior Wall Framing:	2x4
Foundation Options:	
Slab	
(All plans can be built with your choice of foundation and framing. A generic conversion diagram is available. See order form.)	
BLUEPRINT PRICE CODE:	B

**NOTE: The above photographed home may have been modified by the homeowner. Please refer to floor plan and/or drawn elevation shown for actual blueprint details.

TILE SHELF

W.I.C.

TILE

MASTER BATH

LINEN

PORCH

MORNING ROOM
10' X 10'

FRENCH DOOR

W.H.

2 CAR GARAGE
24'-0" X 21'-4"

D.W.

KITCHEN
12'-4" X 14'-0"

RFR.

MASTER BEDROOM
13'-8" X 16'-0"
11'-0" VAULTED CEILING

DINING
11'-4" X 13'-4"
10'-0" CEILING

PANTRY

36" HIGH WALL

50'-10"

D

W

UTILITY

HALL

HVAC

BATH 2

LINEN

ENTRY

LIVING ROOM
18' X 17'
9'-6" CEILING

SLOPE

F.P.

BEDROOM 2
11'-4" X 10'-4"

PLANT SHELF @ 8'-6"

SLOPE

PORCH

BEDROOM 3
11'-4" X 10'-8"
10'-0" CEILING

64'-0"

MAIN FLOOR

Photo by Anthony James Dugal

Single-Story with Sparkle

NOTE: The above photographed home may have been modified by the homeowner. Please refer to floor plan and/or drawn elevation shown for actual blueprint details.

- A lovely front porch with a cameo front door, decorative posts, bay windows and dormers give this country-style home extra sparkle.
- The Great Room is at the center of the floor plan, where it merges with the dining room and the screened porch. The Great Room features a 10-ft. tray ceiling, a fireplace, a built-in wet bar and a wall of windows to the patio.
- The eat-in kitchen has a half-wall that keeps it open to the Great Room and hallway. The dining room offers a half-wall facing the foyer and a bay window overlooking the front porch.
- The delectable master suite is isolated from the other bedrooms and includes a charming bay window, a 10-ft. tray ceiling and a luxurious private bath.
- The two smaller bedrooms are off the main foyer and separated by a full bath.
- A mudroom with a washer and dryer is accessible from the two-car garage.

Plan AX-91312

Bedrooms: 3	Baths: 2
Living Area:	
Main floor	1,595 sq. ft.
Total Living Area:	**1,595 sq. ft.**
Screened porch	178 sq. ft.
Basement	1,595 sq. ft.
Garage, storage and utility	508 sq. ft.
Exterior Wall Framing:	2x4

Foundation Options:
Daylight basement
Standard basement
Crawlspace
Slab
(All plans can be built with your choice of foundation and framing. A generic conversion diagram is available. See order form.)

BLUEPRINT PRICE CODE: B

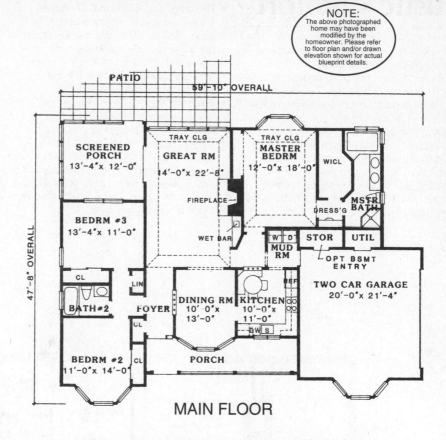

MAIN FLOOR

VIEW INTO GREAT ROOM

ORDER BLUEPRINTS ANYTIME!
CALL TOLL-FREE 1-800-820-1283

Plan AX-91312

PRICES AND DETAILS ON PAGES 2-5

Rustic Comfort

- Rustic charm highlights the exterior of this design, while the interior is filled with all the latest comforts.
- The wide, covered porch opens to a roomy entry, where two 7-ft.-high openings with decorative railings view into the dining room.
- Straight ahead lies the sunken living room, which features a 16-ft.-high vaulted ceiling with exposed beams. The fireplace is faced with floor-to-ceiling fieldstone, adding to the rustic look. A rear door opens to a large patio with luscious plant areas.

- The large and functional U-shaped kitchen features a china niche with glass shelves. Other bonuses include the adjacent sewing/hobby room, the oversized utility room and the storage area and built-in workbench in the side-entry garage.
- The secluded master suite hosts a sunken sleeping area with built-in bookshelves. One step up is a cozy sitting area that is defined by brick columns and a railed room divider. Double doors open to the deluxe bath, which offers a niche with glass shelves.
- Across the home, two more bedrooms share a second full bath.

Plan E-1607

Bedrooms: 3	Baths: 2
Living Area:	
Main floor	1,600 sq. ft.
Total Living Area:	**1,600 sq. ft.**
Standard basement	1,600 sq. ft.
Garage	484 sq. ft.
Storage	132 sq. ft.
Exterior Wall Framing:	2x6

Foundation Options:

Standard basement
Crawlspace
Slab
(All plans can be built with your choice of foundation and framing. A generic conversion diagram is available. See order form.)

BLUEPRINT PRICE CODE:	B

MAIN FLOOR

Designed for Livability

- With the removal of the master suite from the rest of the home, this design is ideal for the maturing family.
- Off the columned porch, the sidelighted front entry offers views through the bright living room to the backyard.
- An elegant column visually sets off the formal dining room from the adjacent living room.
- The kitchen offers a sunny morning room, a pantry and handy access to the laundry facilities and the garage.
- The sunny bay created by the morning room and the sitting area of the master suite adds interior and exterior excitement to this plan.
- The master bath boasts an exciting oval garden tub and a separate shower, as well as a spacious walk-in closet and a dressing area with a dual-sink vanity.
- All of the rooms mentioned above feature soaring 10-ft. ceilings.
- Across the home, three additional bedrooms share another full bath.

Plan DD-1696

Bedrooms: 4	Baths: 2
Living Area:	
Main floor	1,748 sq. ft.
Total Living Area:	**1,748 sq. ft.**
Standard basement	1,748 sq. ft.
Garage	393 sq. ft.
Exterior Wall Framing:	2x4

Foundation Options:

Standard basement

Crawlspace

Slab

(All plans can be built with your choice of foundation and framing. A generic conversion diagram is available. See order form.)

BLUEPRINT PRICE CODE:	B

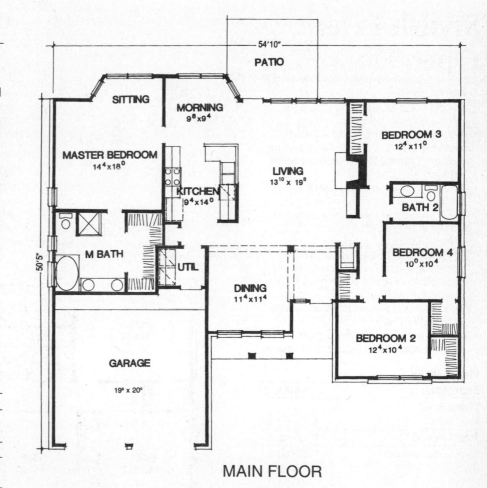

MAIN FLOOR

ORDER BLUEPRINTS ANYTIME!
CALL TOLL-FREE 1-800-820-1283

Plan DD-1696

PRICES AND DETAILS
ON PAGES 2-5

Stylish Exterior, Open Floor Plan

- With its simple yet stylish exterior, this modest-sized design is suitable for country or urban settings.
- A covered front porch and a gabled roof extension accent the facade while providing plenty of sheltered space for outdoor relaxation.
- Inside, the open floor plan puts available space to efficient use.
- The living room, which offers a warm fireplace, is expanded by a 10½-ft. cathedral ceiling. The addition of the kitchen and the bayed dining room creates an expansive gathering space.
- The master suite features a private bath and a large walk-in closet.
- Two more good-sized bedrooms share a second full bath.
- A utility area leads to the carport, which incorporates extra storage space.

Plan J-86155

Bedrooms: 3	Baths: 2
Living Area:	
Main floor	1,385 sq. ft.
Total Living Area:	**1,385 sq. ft.**
Standard basement	1,385 sq. ft.
Carport	380 sq. ft.
Storage	40 sq. ft.
Exterior Wall Framing:	2x4

Foundation Options:

Standard basement
Crawlspace
Slab

(All plans can be built with your choice of foundation and framing. A generic conversion diagram is available. See order form.)

BLUEPRINT PRICE CODE:	A

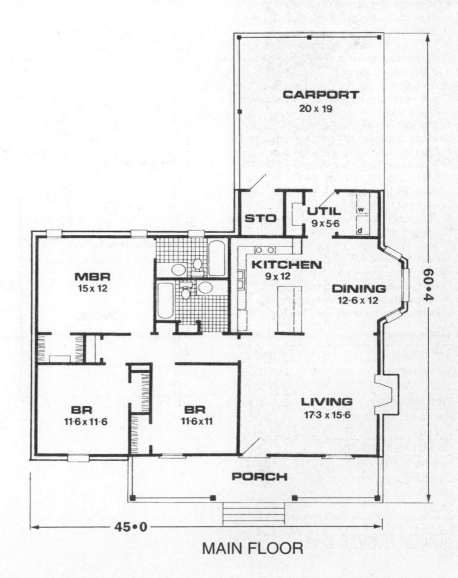

MAIN FLOOR

Porch Offers Three Entries

- Showy window treatments, stately columns and three sets of French doors give this Plantation-style home an inviting exterior.
- High 12-ft. ceilings in the living room, dining room and kitchen add volume to the economically-sized home.
- A corner fireplace and a view to the back porch are found in the living room. The porch is accessed from a door in the dining room.
- The adjoining kitchen features an angled snack bar that easily serves the dining room and the casual eating area.
- The secluded master suite offers a cathedral ceiling, a walk-in closet and a luxurious private bath with a spa tub and a separate shower.
- Across the home, two additional bedrooms share a second full bath.

Plan E-1602

Bedrooms: 3	Baths: 2
Living Area:	
Main floor	1,672 sq. ft.
Total Living Area:	**1,672 sq. ft.**
Standard basement	1,672 sq. ft.
Garage	484 sq. ft.
Exterior Wall Framing:	2x6

Foundation Options:

Standard basement
Crawlspace
Slab
(All plans can be built with your choice of foundation and framing. A generic conversion diagram is available. See order form.)

BLUEPRINT PRICE CODE: **B**

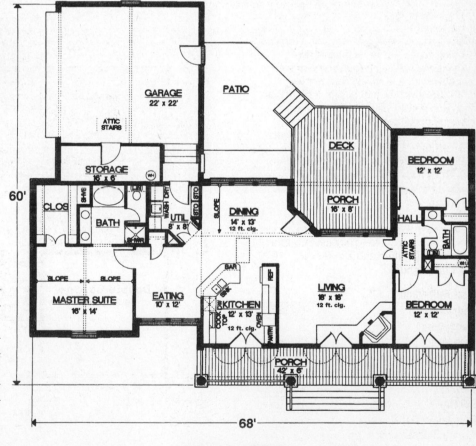

MAIN FLOOR

ORDER BLUEPRINTS ANYTIME!
CALL TOLL-FREE 1-800-820-1283

Plan E-1602

PRICES AND DETAILS
ON PAGES 2-5

Luxury in a Small Package

- The elegant exterior of this design sets the tone for the luxurious spaces within.
- The foyer opens to the centrally located living room, which features a 15-ft. cathedral ceiling, a handsome fireplace and access to a lovely rear terrace.
- The unusual kitchen design includes an angled snack bar that lies between the bayed breakfast den and the formal dining room. Sliding glass doors open to another terrace.
- The master suite is a dream come true, with its romantic fireplace, built-in desk and 9-ft.-high tray ceiling. The private bath includes a whirlpool tub and a dual-sink vanity.
- Another full bath serves the remaining two bedrooms, one of which boasts a cathedral ceiling and a beautiful arched window.

Plan AHP-9300

Bedrooms: 3	Baths: 2
Living Area:	
Main floor	1,513 sq. ft.
Total Living Area:	**1,513 sq. ft.**
Standard basement	1,360 sq. ft.
Garage	400 sq. ft.
Exterior Wall Framing:	2x4 or 2x6

Foundation Options:
Standard basement
Crawlspace
Slab
(All plans can be built with your choice of foundation and framing. A generic conversion diagram is available. See order form.)

BLUEPRINT PRICE CODE: B

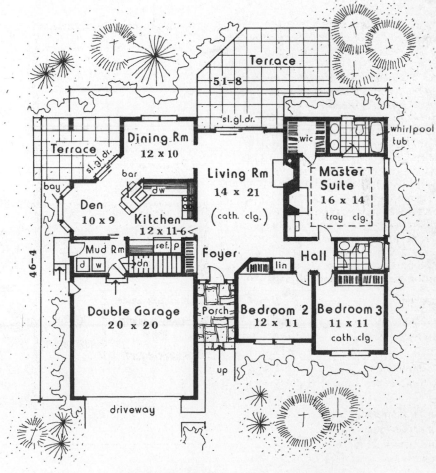

MAIN FLOOR

Rural Roots

- This nostalgic farmhouse reminds you of country life, bringing back memories or maybe just fond daydreams.
- Authentic Victorian details contribute to the comforting facade. Lovely fishscale shingles above the bay window and oval glass in the front door will command attention from visitors.
- Receive the long-awaited kinfolk on the delightful wraparound porch; you may want to sit a spell and catch up on family news!
- Then usher everyone into the family room, for memorable moments in front of the corner fireplace.

- When the feast is ready, eyes will sparkle as the turkey is presented in the bay-windowed dining room. A French door leads to the back porch for after-dinner chatting in the cool evening.
- The efficient kitchen handles meal preparation with ease. The "east" wall features a pantry and double ovens.
- The secluded master suite lets you unwind before a good night's rest. A fabulous bath and direct porch access make this suite really sweet!
- Two secondary bedrooms share a split bath. The bayed front bedroom boasts a 10-ft. ceiling and a walk-in closet.
- The blueprints include plans for a detached, two-car garage (not shown).

Plan L-1772	
Bedrooms: 3	**Baths:** 2
Living Area:	
Main floor	1,772 sq. ft.
Total Living Area:	**1,772 sq. ft.**
Detached garage	576 sq. ft.
Exterior Wall Framing:	2x4

Foundation Options:

Slab

(All plans can be built with your choice of foundation and framing. A generic conversion diagram is available. See order form.)

BLUEPRINT PRICE CODE:	B

MAIN FLOOR

ORDER BLUEPRINTS ANYTIME!
CALL TOLL-FREE 1-800-820-1283

Plan L-1772

PRICES AND DETAILS
ON PAGES 2-5

Simply Beautiful

- This four-bedroom design offers simplistic beauty, economical construction and ample space for both family life and formal entertaining—all on one floor.
- The charming cottage-style exterior gives way to a spacious interior. A 13-ft. vaulted, beamed ceiling soars above the huge living room, which features a

massive fireplace, built-in bookshelves and access to a backyard patio.

- The efficient galley-style kitchen flows between a sunny bayed eating area and the formal dining room.
- The deluxe master suite includes a dressing room, a large walk-in closet and a private bath.
- The three remaining bedrooms are larger than average and offer ample closet space.
- A nice-sized storage area and a deluxe utility room are accessible from the two-car garage.

Plan E-1702

Bedrooms: 4	Baths: 2
Living Area:	
Main floor	1,751 sq. ft.
Total Living Area:	**1,751 sq. ft.**
Garage	484 sq. ft.
Storage	105 sq. ft.
Exterior Wall Framing:	2x4

Foundation Options:

Crawlspace
Slab
(All plans can be built with your choice of foundation and framing. A generic conversion diagram is available. See order form.)

BLUEPRINT PRICE CODE: **B**

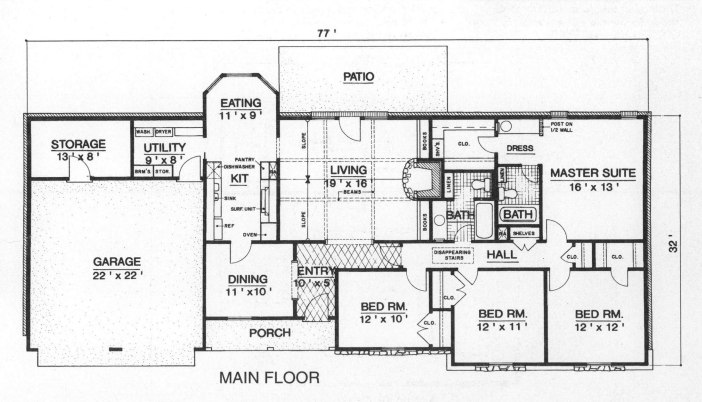

MAIN FLOOR

Angled Solar Design

- This passive-solar design with a six-sided core is angled to capture as much sunlight as possible.
- Finished in natural vertical cedar planks and stone veneer, this contemporary three-bedroom requires a minimum of maintenance.
- Double doors at the entry open into the spacious living and dining areas.

- The formal area features a 14-ft. domed ceiling with skylights, a freestanding fireplace and three sets of sliding glass doors. The central sliding doors lead to a glass-enclosed sun room.
- The bright eat-in kitchen merges with the den, where sliding glass doors lead to one of three backyard terraces.
- The master bedroom, in the quiet sleeping wing, boasts ample closets, a private terrace and a luxurious bath, complete with a whirlpool tub.
- The two secondary bedrooms share a convenient hall bath.

Plan K-534-L

Bedrooms: 3	**Baths:** 2

Living Area:

Main floor	1,647 sq. ft.
Total Living Area:	**1,647 sq. ft.**
Standard basement	1,505 sq. ft.
Garage	400 sq. ft.
Exterior Wall Framing:	2x4 or 2x6

Foundation Options:

Standard basement
Slab
(All plans can be built with your choice of foundation and framing. A generic conversion diagram is available. See order form.)

BLUEPRINT PRICE CODE:	**B**

VIEW INTO LIVING ROOM AND DINING ROOM

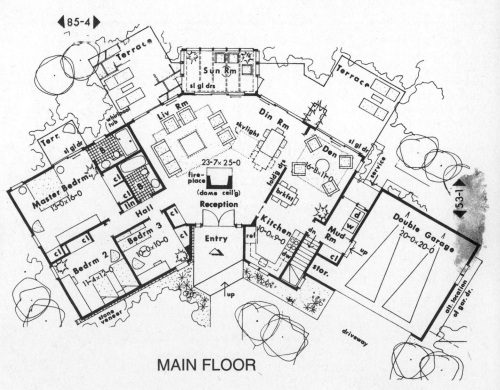

MAIN FLOOR

ORDER BLUEPRINTS ANYTIME!
CALL TOLL-FREE 1-800-820-1283

Plan K-534-L

PRICES AND DETAILS ON PAGES 2-5

Winning One-Story

- Affordability along with many amenities make this a winning one-story design.
- Wood shingles complement the gabled roofline, a column graces the covered front entry and a charming planter accents the paned-glass front windows.
- The interior gets off to a great start with a 13-ft. vaulted entry. A boxed wood beam spans the opening to the living room, which has a 13-ft. vaulted ceiling, a corner fireplace and sliding glass doors opening to a lovely patio.
- The dining room also enjoys a 13-ft. vaulted ceiling and sliding doors. The 13-ft. vaulted kitchen features a snack counter with an overhead plant shelf facing the dining room. A handy laundry area is concealed nearby.
- The sizable master suite boasts corner windows and a compartmentalized bath with a walk-in closet.
- The second bedroom has easy access to a hall bath. Double doors topped by a plant shelf open to the den or third bedroom.

Plan B-88003

Bedrooms: 2+	Baths: 2
Living Area:	
Main floor	1,159 sq. ft.
Total Living Area:	**1,159 sq. ft.**
Garage	425 sq. ft.
Exterior Wall Framing:	2x4

Foundation Options:

Slab

(All plans can be built with your choice of foundation and framing. A generic conversion diagram is available. See order form.)

BLUEPRINT PRICE CODE:	A

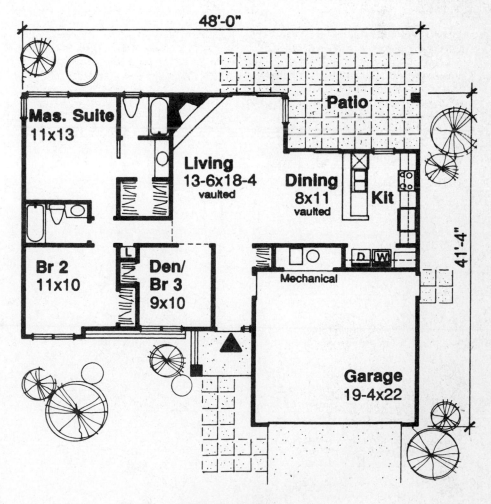

MAIN FLOOR

Dramatic Dining Room

- The highlight of this lovely one-story design is its dramatic dining room, which boasts a 14-ft. ceiling and a soaring window wall.
- The airy foyer ushers guests through an arched opening and into the vaulted Great Room, which is warmed by an inviting fireplace. This room will easily host both formal receptions and casual evenings of conversation.
- The gourmet kitchen features a handy pantry, a versatile serving bar and a pass-through to the Great Room.
- The bright breakfast area offers a laundry closet and outdoor access.
- Two secondary bedrooms share a compartmentalized bath.
- Across the home, the removed master suite boasts a tray ceiling, overhead plant shelves and an adjoining vaulted sitting room. An exciting garden tub is found in the luxurious master bath.

Plan FB-5008-ALLE

Bedrooms: 3	Baths: 2
Living Area:	
Main floor	1,715 sq. ft.
Total Living Area:	**1,715 sq. ft.**
Daylight basement	1,715 sq. ft.
Garage	400 sq. ft.
Exterior Wall Framing:	2x4

Foundation Options:

Daylight basement
Crawlspace
Slab

(All plans can be built with your choice of foundation and framing. A generic conversion diagram is available. See order form.)

BLUEPRINT PRICE CODE:	**B**

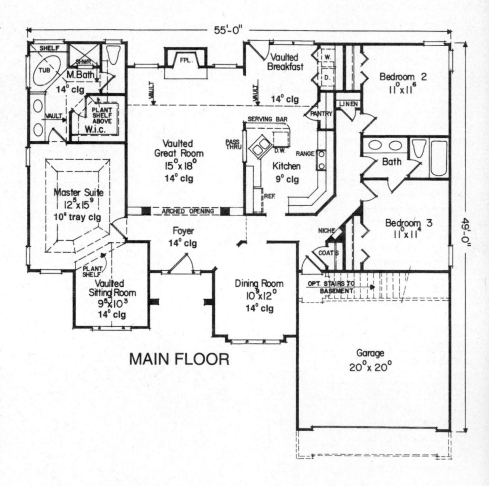

MAIN FLOOR

ORDER BLUEPRINTS ANYTIME!
CALL TOLL-FREE 1-800-820-1283

Plan FB-5008-ALLE

PRICES AND DETAILS
ON PAGES 2-5

Perfect Repose

- This perfectly planned home is well suited to serve as the haven your family retreats to for repose and relaxation.
- Out front, a covered porch includes just the right amount of space for your favorite two rockers and a side table.
- Inside, the foyer flows right into the Great Room, which will serve as home base for family gatherings. A fireplace flanked by a media center turns this room into a home theater.
- Nearby, sunlight pours into the versatile dining room. Along one wall, a beautiful built-in cabinet holds linens, china and other fine collectibles.
- Afternoon treats take on a fun twist at the kitchen's snack bar. For easy serving, the snack bar extends to a peninsula counter.
- A 10-ft., 8-in. tray ceiling and a cheery bay window in the master suite turn this space into a stylish oasis. A dressing area with a vanity table for morning preening leads to the master bath, where a skylight and a 15-ft. vaulted ceiling brighten the room.

REAR VIEW

Plan AX-95347

Bedrooms: 3	Baths: 2½
Living Area:	
Main floor	1,709 sq. ft.
Total Living Area:	**1,709 sq. ft.**
Standard basement	1,709 sq. ft.
Garage and storage	448 sq. ft.
Exterior Wall Framing:	2x4

Foundation Options:

Standard basement
Crawlspace
Slab
(All plans can be built with your choice of foundation and framing. A generic conversion diagram is available. See order form.)

BLUEPRINT PRICE CODE: B

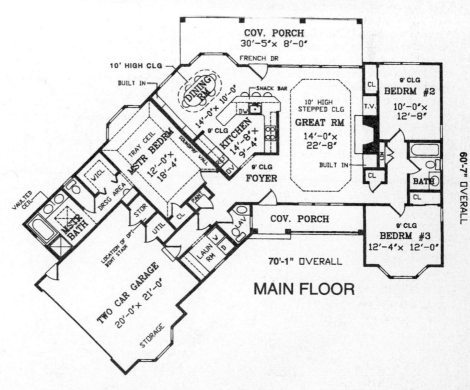

MAIN FLOOR

Tried and True

- Time-tested traditional touches abound in this familiar country-style home.
- The main attraction is the living room, which anchors the home and hosts a tremendous fireplace flanked by built-in bookshelves. Access to a quaint little porch is just a step away.
- An intriguingly shaped dining room borders the sunny kitchen, where you'll find a cozy pantry and plenty of space to whip up a culinary masterpiece!
- When you long for a good night's sleep, you'll appreciate the master suite, which offers a quiet sitting area for your night-owl spouse. The master bath is impeccably adorned, flaunting a stunning corner tub, a separate shower, two walk-in closets and a sink for each of you.
- The kids get their space, too: a pair of bedrooms with ample closet space, and a full bath.

Plan RD-1418

Bedrooms: 3	**Baths: 2**
Living Area:	
Main floor	1,418 sq. ft.
Total Living Area:	**1,418 sq. ft.**
Garage and storage	464 sq. ft.
Exterior Wall Framing:	2x4

Foundation Options:

Crawlspace
Slab
(All plans can be built with your choice of foundation and framing. A generic conversion diagram is available. See order form.)

BLUEPRINT PRICE CODE: **A**

MAIN FLOOR

ORDER BLUEPRINTS ANYTIME!
CALL TOLL-FREE 1-800-820-1283

Plan RD-1418

PRICES AND DETAILS
ON PAGES 2-5

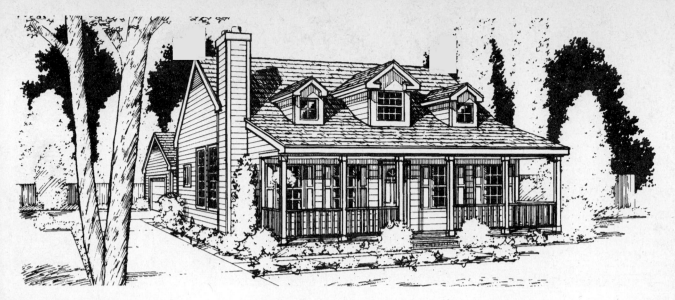

Real Charm

- A trio of attractive dormers and an inviting porch that signals instant friendliness make this one-story home a real country charmer.
- The porch is the perfect venue for swapping stories with the neighbors over a pitcher of something cool. Or send the kids to Grandma's, string up a hammock and lose yourself in a good book on a warm spring day.
- Enter the huge living/dining room area and you'll find another great setting for entertaining. Snuggle up around the

fireplace and revel in the cozy mood it creates. A 16-ft. vaulted ceiling adds a nice sense of openness.
- The master bedroom's 12-ft.-high cathedral ceiling gives it a touch of drama. A walk-in closet, a private bath with a whirlpool tub and access to a lovely secluded terrace makes it pleasantly functional.
- Two additional bedrooms offer space enough for a growing family; both are just steps from a full-sized bath. If needed, convert one to a den or office.
- Plans for a detached two-car garage are included with the blueprints.

Plan AHP-9620	
Bedrooms: 2+	**Baths: 2**
Living Area:	
Main floor	1,410 sq. ft.
Total Living Area:	**1,410 sq. ft.**
Standard basement	1,410 sq. ft.
Detached 2-car garage	576 sq. ft.
Exterior Wall Framing:	2x4 or 2x6
Foundation Options:	
Standard basement	
Crawlspace	
Slab	

(All plans can be built with your choice of foundation and framing. A generic conversion diagram is available. See order form.)

BLUEPRINT PRICE CODE:	A

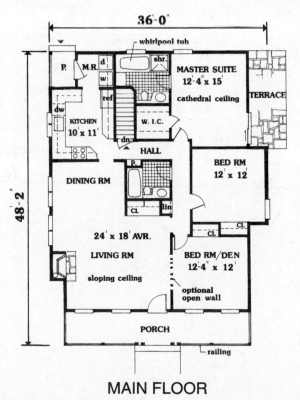

MAIN FLOOR

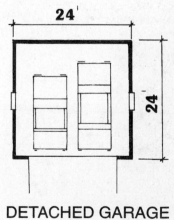

DETACHED GARAGE

Rustic Ranch

- This ranch-style home offers a warm facade featuring a railed front porch and stone accents.
- Inside, the inviting living room includes an eye-catching fireplace, patio access and a sloped, beamed ceiling.
- The dining room adjoins the efficient U-shaped kitchen, which includes a pantry and a broom closet.
- The master suite offers a large walk-in closet and a roomy master bath.
- At the other end of the home, two secondary bedrooms with abundant closet space share another full bath.

Plan E-1410

Bedrooms: 3	Baths: 2
Living Area:	
Main floor	1,418 sq. ft.
Total Living Area:	**1,418 sq. ft.**
Garage	484 sq. ft.
Storage	38 sq. ft.
Exterior Wall Framing:	2x4

Foundation Options:

Crawlspace

Slab

(All plans can be built with your choice of foundation and framing. A generic conversion diagram is available. See order form.)

BLUEPRINT PRICE CODE:	A

MAIN FLOOR

Plan E-1410

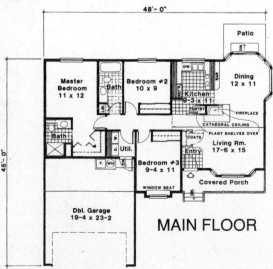

MAIN FLOOR

Even Flow

- A rustic exterior and a relaxed interior define this warm ranch-style home.
- The living room flows into the bayed dining room, which opens to a patio. Both rooms are enhanced by 14-ft. vaulted ceilings and a central fireplace.
- The functional kitchen includes a snack bar to the dining room, a pantry and plenty of cabinet space.
- The master bedroom boasts a mirrored dressing area, a private bath and abundant closet space.
- The third bedroom includes a cozy window seat.

Plan NW-521

Bedrooms: 3	Baths: 2
Living Area:	
Main floor	1,187 sq. ft.
Total Living Area:	**1,187 sq. ft.**
Garage	448 sq. ft.
Exterior Wall Framing:	2x6

Foundation Options:

Crawlspace

(All plans can be built with your choice of foundation and framing. A generic conversion diagram is available. See order form.)

BLUEPRINT PRICE CODE:	A

ORDER BLUEPRINTS ANYTIME!
CALL TOLL-FREE 1-800-820-1283

Plan NW-521

PRICES AND DETAILS
ON PAGES 2-5

Good Looks, Great Views

- Wood shutters, glamorous half-round windows and durable brick give this home its good looks.
- Entry drama is created with the use of high ceilings in the foyer, dining room and Great Room. The dining room is set off by elegant columned openings; your formal meals can be kept warm and out of sight in the handy serving station around the corner.

- Over the kitchen's snack counter, the TV center and fireplace in the Great Room create an attractive wall that complements the sliding French door tandem to the rear.
- Half-round windows accentuate the radiant bays protruding from the breakfast room and master suite, expanding the home's outdoor views.
- A private entrance accesses the master bedroom and its whirlpool bath.
- Wider doorways and an alternate garage plan with a ramp instead of a storage area make this home adaptable to wheelchair use.

Plan AX-95367

Bedrooms: 3	**Baths:** 2

Living Area:

Main floor	1,595 sq. ft.
Total Living Area:	**1,595 sq. ft.**
Standard basement	1,595 sq. ft.
Garage and storage	548 sq. ft.
Exterior Wall Framing:	2x4

Foundation Options:

Standard basement
Crawlspace
Slab
(All plans can be built with your choice of foundation and framing. A generic conversion diagram is available. See order form.)

BLUEPRINT PRICE CODE:	B

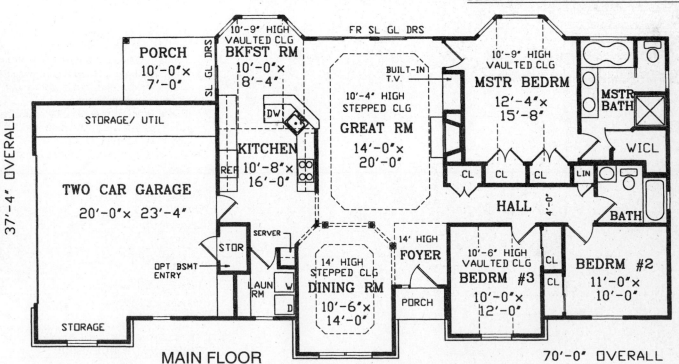

MAIN FLOOR

Quality Details

- A sparkling stucco finish, an eye-catching roofline and elegant window treatments hint at the quality features found inside this exquisite home.
- The entry opens to the living room, which is topped by a 10-ft. ceiling.
- The living room flows into a nice-sized dining area. A covered side porch expands the entertaining area.
- An eating bar and pantry are featured in the U-shaped kitchen. The nearby hallway to the garage neatly stores a washer, a dryer and a laundry sink.
- The master suite offers a romantic sitting area and a large walk-in closet. The master bath hosts an exciting oval tub.

Plan E-1435

Bedrooms: 3	Baths: 2
Living Area:	
Main floor	1,442 sq. ft.
Total Living Area:	**1,442 sq. ft.**
Garage and storage	516 sq. ft.
Exterior Wall Framing:	2x4
Foundation Options:	

Crawlspace
Slab
(All plans can be built with your choice of foundation and framing. A generic conversion diagram is available. See order form.)

BLUEPRINT PRICE CODE:	A

MAIN FLOOR

Plan E-1435

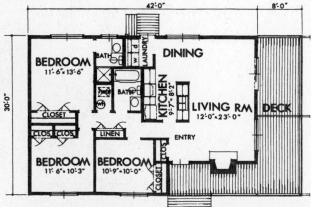

MAIN FLOOR

Easy Living

- This home is designed for easy, economical construction and active indoor/outdoor living.
- The galley-style kitchen and the sunny dining area are kept open to the living room, forming one huge Great Room that accesses a large deck.
- The secluded master bedroom offers a private bath, while the remaining bedrooms share a hall bath.
- Plan H-921-1A has a standard crawlspace foundation and an optional solar-heating system. Plan H-921-2A has a Plen-Wood system, which utilizes the sealed crawlspace as a chamber for distributing heated or cooled air.

Plans H-921-1A & -2A

Bedrooms: 3	Baths: 2
Living Area:	
Main floor	1,164 sq. ft.
Total Living Area:	**1,164 sq. ft.**
Exterior Wall Framing:	2x6
Foundation Options:	**Plan #**
Crawlspace	H-921-1A
Plen-Wood crawlspace	H-921-2A

(All plans can be built with your choice of foundation and framing. A generic conversion diagram is available. See order form.)

BLUEPRINT PRICE CODE:	A

ORDER BLUEPRINTS ANYTIME!
CALL TOLL-FREE 1-800-820-1283

Plans H-921-1A & -2A

PRICES AND DETAILS
ON PAGES 2-5

Affordable Charm

- An inviting columned porch introduces this affordable home.
- Inside, soaring ceilings and attention to detail highlight the efficient floor plan.
- The foyer leads to an eat-in kitchen, which includes a handy built-in pantry. A great 10-ft. ceiling enhances this sunny space.
- A convenient serving counter connects the kitchen to the open dining room. A beautiful bay window is topped by a half-round transom.
- The adjacent living room features an energy-efficient fireplace and French-door access to an inviting rear deck.
- A dramatic 14-ft. vaulted ceiling soars above the living and dining rooms.
- The spacious master bedroom boasts a striking 11-ft. vaulted ceiling, a large walk-in closet and private access to the hall bath.
- Two additional bedrooms and a linen closet round out the floor plan.

Plan B-93015

Bedrooms: 3	Baths: 1
Living Area:	
Main floor	1,227 sq. ft.
Total Living Area:	**1,227 sq. ft.**
Standard basement	1,217 sq. ft.
Garage	385 sq. ft.
Exterior Wall Framing:	2x6

Foundation Options:

Standard basement

(All plans can be built with your choice of foundation and framing. A generic conversion diagram is available. See order form.)

BLUEPRINT PRICE CODE:	**A**

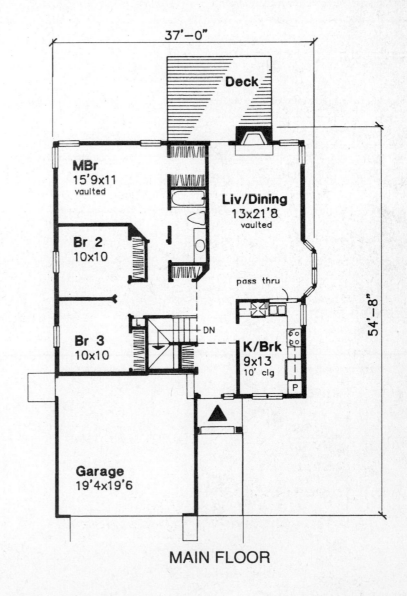

MAIN FLOOR

Affordable Comfort

- Compact and cozy, this attractive home gives you comfort and livability at an affordable price.
- The railed front porch is a nice touch; guests will certainly feel welcome when they come over to see you.
- Inside the front entry, the grand living room is immediately visible. A handsome fireplace sets a happy tone, while sliding glass doors give way to pleasant backyard landscaping.
- At the front of the home, a boxed-out corner window brightens the U-shaped kitchen. The open dining area is perfect for any meal, from a snack to a feast.
- Sleeping areas flank the living room, with each bedroom enjoying a measure of privacy. The quiet master suite boasts a walk-in closet and a personal bath. A corner window arrangement makes a nice spot to relax with a good book.
- Mirror-image secondary bedrooms share a nice-sized hall bath.
- Laundry facilities are located in the two-car garage, just off the foyer.

Plan L-1022

Bedrooms: 3	Baths: 2
Living Area:	
Main floor	1,078 sq. ft.
Total Living Area:	**1,078 sq. ft.**
Garage and utility	431 sq. ft.
Exterior Wall Framing:	2x4

Foundation Options:
Slab
(All plans can be built with your choice of foundation and framing. A generic conversion diagram is available. See order form.)

BLUEPRINT PRICE CODE:	A

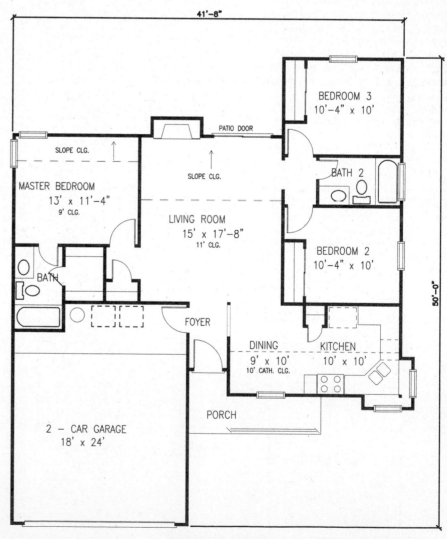

MAIN FLOOR

ORDER BLUEPRINTS ANYTIME!
CALL TOLL-FREE 1-800-820-1283

Plan L-1022

PRICES AND DETAILS
ON PAGES 2-5

Fine Dining

- This fine stucco home showcases a huge round-top window arrangement, which augments the central dining room with its 14½-ft. ceiling.
- A cute covered porch opens to the bright foyer, where a 13-ft.-high ceiling extends past a decorative column to the airy Great Room.
- The sunny dining room merges with the Great Room, which features a warm

fireplace, a kitchen pass-through and a French door to the backyard.
- The kitchen boasts a pantry closet, a nice serving bar and an angled sink. The vaulted breakfast nook with an optional bay hosts casual meals.
- The secluded master suite has a tray ceiling and a vaulted bath with a dual-sink vanity, a large garden tub and a separate shower. Across the home, two secondary bedrooms share another full bath.

Plan FB-5351-GENE	
Bedrooms: 3	**Baths:** 2
Living Area:	
Main floor	1,670 sq. ft.
Total Living Area:	**1,670 sq. ft.**
Daylight basement	1,670 sq. ft.
Garage	400 sq. ft.
Exterior Wall Framing:	2x4

Foundation Options:
Daylight basement
Crawlspace
(All plans can be built with your choice of foundation and framing. A generic conversion diagram is available. See order form.)

BLUEPRINT PRICE CODE:	B

MAIN FLOOR

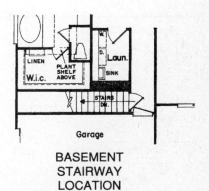

BASEMENT
STAIRWAY
LOCATION

Make It Yours!

- This home's attractive exterior and well-planned, amenity-packed interior, make it the perfect plan for today's family.
- Inside, the foyer leads directly into the centrally located living room. Whether you're holding a family powwow or you just want to relax with the paper, this room provides a comfortable setting. After a walk through a January snowstorm, your chilled toes will be warmed by the soothing fireplace.
- The see-through fireplace also warms the dining room. Imagine the soothing effects a crackling fire will bring to

meals. During the summer, open the doors to the backyard and enjoy the lazy sounds of a weekend afternoon.
- The efficient kitchen nearby will bring the dreams of even the most gourmet chef to life. A walk-in pantry stores sundries, while a serving counter eases the strain of meal cleanup.
- With a walk-in closet and a private bath, the master suite gives the adults of the house extra special treatment.
- Volume ceilings throughout the home add appeal. The den boasts a 12-ft., 8-in. vaulted ceiling, while the kitchen, dining room, living room and master bedroom all include 9-ft. ceilings.

Plan G-24701

Bedrooms: 2+	Baths: 2
Living Area:	
Main floor	1,625 sq. ft.
Total Living Area:	**1,625 sq. ft.**
Standard basement	1,625 sq. ft.
Garage	455 sq. ft.
Exterior Wall Framing:	2x4

Foundation Options:

Standard basement
Crawlspace
Slab
(All plans can be built with your choice of foundation and framing. A generic conversion diagram is available. See order form.)

BLUEPRINT PRICE CODE: B

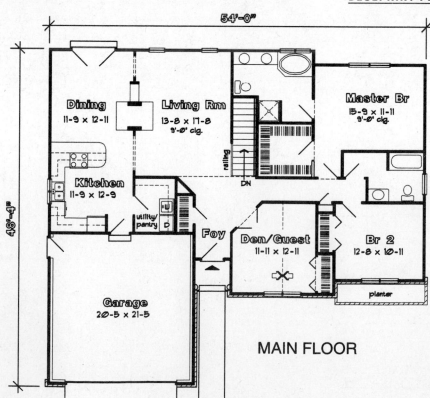

MAIN FLOOR

Plan G-24701

ORDER BLUEPRINTS ANYTIME!
CALL TOLL-FREE 1-800-820-1283

PRICES AND DETAILS
ON PAGES 2-5

Sunny
Breakfast Porch

- The charm of yesteryear's front porch is brought into contemporary focus with this design's unique sun porch/breakfast room. What a glorious spot to greet each new day!
- This stylish home offers other dramatic spaces, including a large vaulted living and dining room combination. From the entryway, you can view the massive corner fireplace, the rear deck through sliding glass doors and the railed stairway to the basement.
- The master bedroom is also vaulted and boasts its own deck access. Double walk-in closets and a private bath with a plant shelf and a garden tub are other extras you'll come to appreciate.
- A nearby secondary bedroom would make a great nursery or child's room for young families. Singles and empty nesters might turn this space into a cozy den for casual relaxing.
- Sunny weather begs you to step out to the rear deck and fire up the barbecue.

Plan B-86136

Bedrooms: 1+	Baths: 2
Living Area:	
Main floor	1,421 sq. ft.
Total Living Area:	**1,421 sq. ft.**
Standard basement	1,421 sq. ft.
Garage	400 sq. ft.
Exterior Wall Framing:	2x4

Foundation Options:

Standard basement

(All plans can be built with your choice of foundation and framing. A generic conversion diagram is available. See order form.)

BLUEPRINT PRICE CODE: A

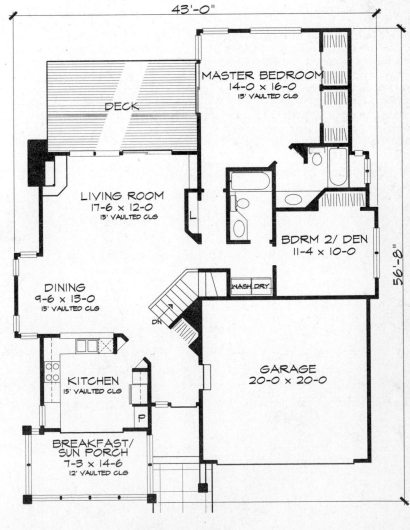

MAIN FLOOR

Inviting Porch

- A columned porch with double doors invites you into this ranch-style home.
- Inside, the living room boasts an exposed-beam ceiling and a massive fireplace with a wide stone hearth, a wood box and built-in bookshelves. A patio offers more entertaining space.
- The dining room and the efficient kitchen combine for easy meal service, with a serving bar separating the two.
- The main hallway leads to the sleeping wing, which offers a large master bedroom with a walk-in closet and a private bath.

Plan E-1304

Bedrooms: 3	Baths: 2
Living Area:	
Main floor	1,395 sq. ft.
Total Living Area:	**1,395 sq. ft.**
Garage and storage	481 sq. ft.
Exterior Wall Framing:	2x4
Foundation Options:	
Crawlspace, slab	

(All plans can be built with your choice of foundation and framing. A generic conversion diagram is available. See order form.)

BLUEPRINT PRICE CODE:	A

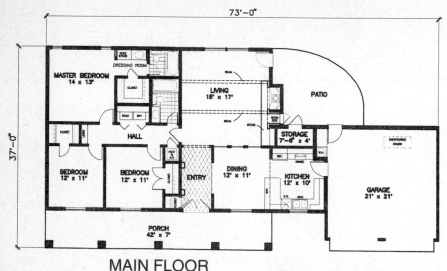

MAIN FLOOR

Plan E-1304

Friendly Charm

- An inviting front porch welcomes you to this friendly one-story home.
- The porch opens to a spacious central living room with a warm fireplace.
- The bay window of the dining room allows a view of the backyard.
- The nice-sized kitchen also has a windowed sink and easy access to the laundry room and carport.
- The master bedroom features a boxed-out window, two walk-in closets and a private bath.

Plan J-8692

Bedrooms: 3	Baths: 2
Living Area:	
Main floor	1,633 sq. ft.
Total Living Area:	**1,633 sq. ft.**
Standard basement	1,633 sq. ft.
Carport	380 sq. ft.
Exterior Wall Framing:	2x4
Foundation Options:	
Standard basement	
Crawlspace	
Slab	

(All plans can be built with your choice of foundation and framing. A generic conversion diagram is available. See order form.)

BLUEPRINT PRICE CODE:	B

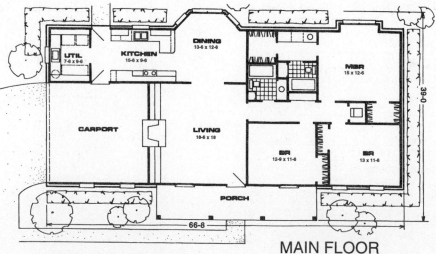

MAIN FLOOR

A Looker in Any Neighborhood

- This stylish, one-story home is sure to turn heads in any neighborhood.
- The bright, volume entry offers a spectacular view of the Great Room, the formal dining area and the backyard, which is seen through windows that flank the fireplace. This large, versatile area is crowned by a 10-ft. ceiling.
- The formal living room at the front of the home also has a 10-ft. ceiling and could be converted to a third bedroom.
- A covered deck fits nicely outside the kitchen and the breakfast area. The kitchen features a pantry, a lazy Susan and a corner sink with windows.
- A nice-sized laundry room with a coat and broom closet serves as a mudroom entry from the garage.
- The sleeping wing includes two bedrooms and two baths. The master suite boasts an indented, walk-in closet and a skylighted private bath with dual sinks and a whirlpool tub separated from the shower by a glass panel.

Plan DBI-2196

Bedrooms: 2+	Baths: 2
Living Area:	
Main floor	1,561 sq. ft.
Total Living Area:	**1,561 sq. ft.**
Standard basement	1,561 sq. ft.
Garage	446 sq. ft.
Exterior Wall Framing:	2x4
Foundation Options:	

Standard basement
(All plans can be built with your choice of foundation and framing. A generic conversion diagram is available. See order form.)

BLUEPRINT PRICE CODE:	B

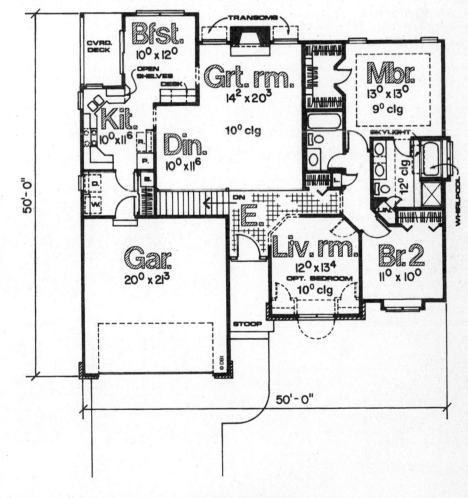

MAIN FLOOR

Distinctive Inside and Out

- A decorative columned entry, shuttered windows and a facade of stucco and stone offer a distinct look to this economical one-story home.
- The focal point of the interior is the huge, central family room. The room is enhanced by a dramatic corner fireplace, a 15-ft.-high vaulted ceiling and a neat serving bar that extends from the kitchen and includes a wet bar.
- A decorative plant shelf adorns the entrance to the adjoining breakfast room, which features a lovely bay window. The kitchen offers a pantry and a pass-through to the family room.
- The formal dining room is easy to reach from both the kitchen and the family room, and is set off with columned arches and a raised ceiling.
- The secluded master suite boasts a vaulted private bath with dual sinks, an oval garden tub, a separate toilet room and a large walk-in closet.
- Two more bedrooms share a second bath at the other end of the home.

Plan FB-5001-SAVA

Bedrooms: 3	Baths: 2
Living Area:	
Main floor	1,429 sq. ft.
Total Living Area:	**1,429 sq. ft.**
Daylight basement	1,429 sq. ft.
Garage and storage	436 sq. ft.
Exterior Wall Framing:	2x4

Foundation Options:
Daylight basement
Crawlspace
Slab
(All plans can be built with your choice of foundation and framing. A generic conversion diagram is available. See order form.)

BLUEPRINT PRICE CODE: A

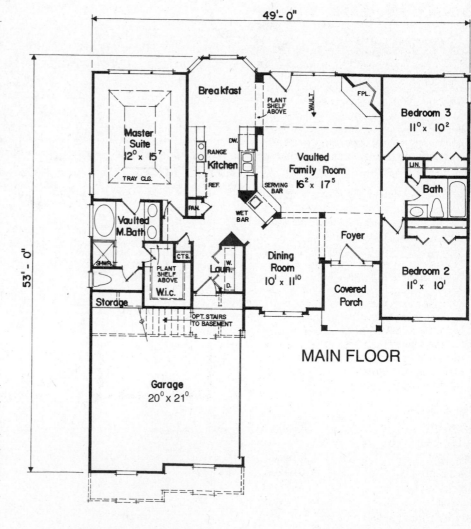

MAIN FLOOR

ORDER BLUEPRINTS ANYTIME!
CALL TOLL-FREE 1-800-820-1283

Plan FB-5001-SAVA

PRICES AND DETAILS
ON PAGES 2-5

Stately and Compact

- This dignified home offers a stately exterior and an exciting interior—all in a compact, affordable size.
- A cozy covered porch with columns and decorative latticework gives you a charming place to greet guests. Or mix a pitcher of lemonade and make a day of watching the neighborhood activities.
- The enormous living room features a grand corner fireplace, a 15½-ft. ceiling and access to a beautiful back porch.
- Efficient and attractive, the kitchen and dining room guarantee a harmonious mealtime. A handy serving bar is just the spot for a quick breakfast or for casual socializing over a cup of coffee.
- At the end of the day, soak your cares away in the master suite's glorious tub. Dual sinks, a cute corner vanity and a big walk-in closet add to the appeal.
- On the other side of the home are two nice-sized bedrooms and a full bath.
- Plenty of extra storage is provided just off the garage.

Plan E-1423

Bedrooms: 3	Baths: 2
Living Area:	
Main floor	1,408 sq. ft.
Total Living Area:	**1,408 sq. ft.**
Garage	462 sq. ft.
Storage	70 sq. ft.
Exterior Wall Framing:	2x6

Foundation Options:

Crawlspace

Slab

(All plans can be built with your choice of foundation and framing. A generic conversion diagram is available. See order form.)

BLUEPRINT PRICE CODE: **A**

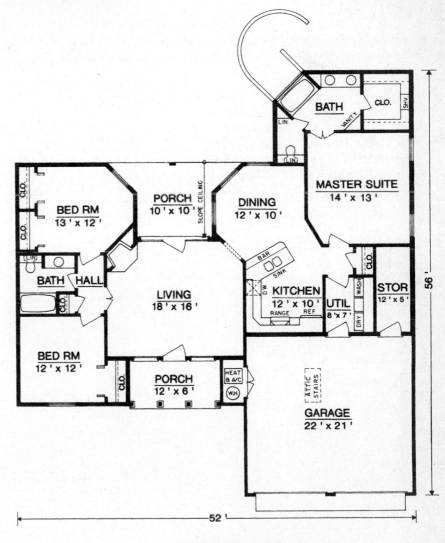

MAIN FLOOR

Dare to Dream

- It's time to imagine the possibilities and then turn your dreams into reality! This stunning one-story home is a fine place to start.
- Its solid yet elegant facade packs a wallop of curb appeal and shelters a floor plan that complements your pacesetting lifestyle.
- The central living room is sure to be the prime gathering spot for family and friends alike. A handsome fireplace spreads a warm glow over the room.
- Featuring access to a backyard patio, the dining room looks just as good with your best silver as it does with a delivered pizza.
- A breakfast bar joins the galley-style kitchen to the dining room. Let the kids pull up a stool to get their morning fix of toaster treats and chocolate milk!
- When you need some time to yourself, retreat to the master bedroom, which exemplifies modern living. A beautiful bath calms you with its zesty tub and separate shower. Two walk-in closets deliver an extra measure of privacy.
- Two additional bedrooms let the kids claim a place of their own; a full bath sits conveniently between each one.

Plan KD-1311

Bedrooms: 3	Baths: 2
Living Area:	
Main floor	1,311 sq. ft.
Total Living Area:	**1,311 sq. ft.**
Garage and storage	449 sq. ft.
Exterior Wall Framing:	2x4

Foundation Options:

Slab

(All plans can be built with your choice of foundation and framing. A generic conversion diagram is available. See order form.)

BLUEPRINT PRICE CODE:	A

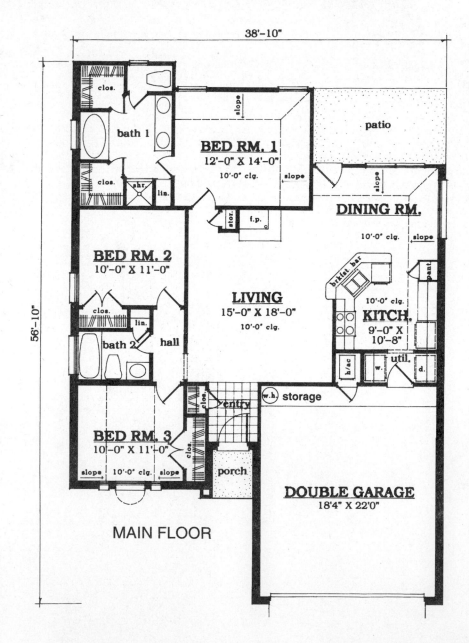

MAIN FLOOR

ORDER BLUEPRINTS ANYTIME!
CALL TOLL-FREE 1-800-820-1283

Plan KD-1311

PRICES AND DETAILS
ON PAGES 2-5

Off to a Great Start!

- This beautiful one-story's charming looks, efficient floor plan and elegant amenities make it a great starter home.
- Half-round windows, decorative corner quoins and a covered front porch add character to the distinctive exterior.
- Past the double-door entry, the foyer flows into the vaulted living room, which boasts a handsome fireplace and a ceiling that slopes to nearly 14 feet.

- The adjoining formal dining room is brightened by French doors to a covered patio. A convenient pass-through provides service from the kitchen, which enjoys a 10-ft. vaulted ceiling and a sunny breakfast nook with patio access.
- The luxurious master suite features a double walk-in closet. The roomy master bath includes a garden tub, a separate shower and a dual-sink vanity.
- Another full bath, a hallway linen closet and a laundry are convenient to the remaining rooms. The den or third bedroom offers a 10-ft. ceiling.

Plan B-93009

Bedrooms: 2+	**Baths:** 2
Living Area:	
Main floor	1,431 sq. ft.
Total Living Area:	**1,431 sq. ft.**
Standard basement	1,431 sq. ft.
Garage	380 sq. ft.
Exterior Wall Framing:	2x6

Foundation Options:

Standard basement

(All plans can be built with your choice of foundation and framing. A generic conversion diagram is available. See order form.)

BLUEPRINT PRICE CODE:	**A**

51'-4"

43'-8"

Patio

Brkfst
vaulted

Br 2
10x11-8

M Suite
14x11-8
coffered ceiling

Kit
10x19

Dining

Den/
Br 3
10x10'6

Living Rm
13'6x17
vaulted

Garage
19-4x19-8

MAIN FLOOR

Leisure Living

- This handsome ranch-style home features a floor plan that is great for family living and entertaining.
- The spacious formal areas flow together for a dramatic impact. The living room is enhanced by a fireplace and a sloped ceiling. A patio door in the dining room extends activities to the outdoors.
- A good-sized utility room includes a large storage room and disappearing stairs to even more storage space.
- Three bedrooms and two baths occupy the sleeping wing. The master suite features a large walk-in closet and a private bath.

Plan E-1308

Bedrooms: 3	Baths: 2
Living Area:	
Main floor	1,375 sq. ft.
Total Living Area:	**1,375 sq. ft.**
Carport	430 sq. ft.
Storage	95 sq. ft.
Exterior Wall Framing:	2x4
Foundation Options:	
Crawlspace	
Slab	

(All plans can be built with your choice of foundation and framing. A generic conversion diagram is available. See order form.)

BLUEPRINT PRICE CODE:	A

Plan E-1308 — MAIN FLOOR

All in One!

- This plan puts today's most luxurious design features into one package.
- The front porch and gabled roofline give the facade a homey appeal.
- Inside, a skylight and a pair of French doors framing the fireplace brighten the spacious living room. An 11-ft. ceiling extends into the formal dining room.
- The open kitchen offers lots of counter space, a washer and dryer and a sunny dinette that opens to a backyard terrace.
- The master suite features a bath with a whirlpool tub and a separate shower.

Plan HFL-1680-FL

Bedrooms: 3	Baths: 2
Living Area:	
Main floor	1,367 sq. ft.
Total Living Area:	**1,367 sq. ft.**
Standard basement	1,367 sq. ft.
Garage	431 sq. ft.
Exterior Wall Framing:	2x6
Foundation Options:	
Standard basement	

(All plans can be built with your choice of foundation and framing. A generic conversion diagram is available. See order form.)

BLUEPRINT PRICE CODE:	A

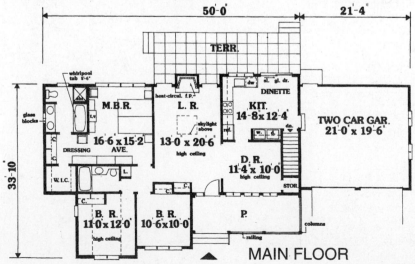

MAIN FLOOR

Plan HFL-1680-FL

ORDER BLUEPRINTS ANYTIME! CALL TOLL-FREE 1-800-820-1283

PRICES AND DETAILS ON PAGES 2-5

Elegance with Economy

- This handsome design offers the rich look of brick and an open floor plan with multipurpose living areas that cut down on wasted space.
- A sidelighted entry opens to the central Great Room. A cathedral ceiling and windows on either side of an inviting fireplace add volume to this family activity area.
- Between the adjoining breakfast room and the formal dining room is a see-through wet bar. The breakfast room also features a bay window with sliding glass doors to the backyard, a built-in work desk, a pantry and a snack bar.
- The fully equipped kitchen has a lovely window box above the sink and easy access to both eating areas.
- The sleeping wing's master bedroom has a private bath with a plant shelf, a skylighted dressing area, a whirlpool tub and a large walk-in closet. Two secondary bedrooms share a convenient hall bath.

Plan DBI-1767

Bedrooms: 3	Baths: 2
Living Area:	
Main floor	1,604 sq. ft.
Total Living Area:	**1,604 sq. ft.**
Standard basement	1,604 sq. ft.
Garage	466 sq. ft.
Exterior Wall Framing:	2x4

Foundation Options:

Standard basement

(All plans can be built with your choice of foundation and framing. A generic conversion diagram is available. See order form.)

BLUEPRINT PRICE CODE: B

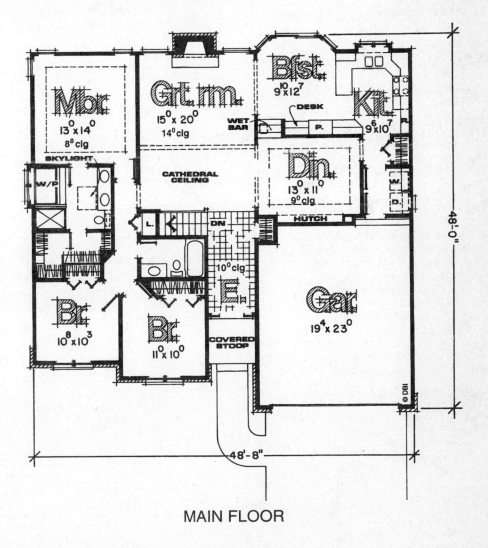

MAIN FLOOR

ORDER BLUEPRINTS ANYTIME!
CALL TOLL-FREE 1-800-820-1283

Plan DBI-1767

PRICES AND DETAILS
ON PAGES 2-5

Enticing Interior

- Filled with elegant features, this modern country home's exciting floor plan is as impressive as it is innovative.
- Past the inviting columned porch, the entrance gallery flows into the spacious living room/dining room area.
- Boasting a 14-ft.-high sloped ceiling, the living room is enhanced by a semi-circular window bay and includes a handsome fireplace. The adjoining dining room offers sliding glass doors to a backyard terrace.
- The skylighted kitchen features an eating bar that serves the sunny bayed dinette. A convenient half-bath and a laundry/mudroom are nearby.
- Brightened by a bay window, the luxurious master bedroom shows off his-and-hers walk-in closets. The master bath showcases a whirlpool garden tub under a glass sunroof.
- Two additional bedrooms share a skylighted hallway bath.

Plan K-685-DA

Bedrooms: 3	Baths: 2½
Living Area:	
Main floor	1,760 sq. ft.
Total Living Area:	**1,760 sq. ft.**
Standard basement	1,700 sq. ft.
Garage	482 sq. ft.
Exterior Wall Framing:	2x4 or 2x6

Foundation Options:

Standard basement

Slab

(All plans can be built with your choice of foundation and framing. A generic conversion diagram is available. See order form.)

BLUEPRINT PRICE CODE:	B

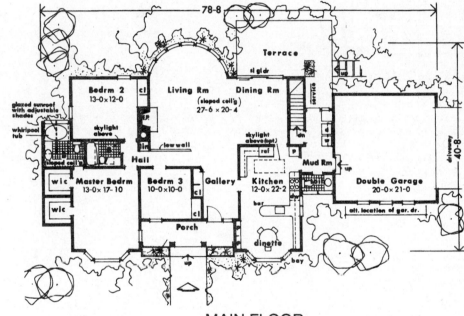

MAIN FLOOR

VIEW INTO LIVING AND DINING ROOMS

It's All in the Details!

- It's the mouthwatering details that give this home its distinctively country character. Its facade is a marvel; the graceful columns, railings, dormer windows and high transoms accentuate the inviting porch.
- Brightened by radiant windows, the large living room hosts a warming fireplace. Two high dormers admit additional natural light.

- Straight back, a bay window punctuated by French doors livens the dining area. A snack bar links it to the kitchen, which you'll find adaptable to both casual and formal meals.
- A sizable terrace overlooking the backyard is the perfect arena for lazy summer picnics and frolicsome Sunday afternoons.
- The sprawling master bedroom is blessed with a pair of windows in the sleeping chamber that wake you with morning light. A private bath offers a zesty whirlpool tub and a separate shower for busy weekday mornings.

Plan AHP-9615

Bedrooms: 3	Baths: 2
Living Area:	
Main floor	1,331 sq. ft.
Total Living Area:	**1,331 sq. ft.**
Standard basement	1,377 sq. ft.
Garage	459 sq. ft.
Exterior Wall Framing:	2x4 or 2x6

Foundation Options:
Standard basement
Crawlspace
Slab
(All plans can be built with your choice of foundation and framing. A generic conversion diagram is available. See order form.)

BLUEPRINT PRICE CODE: A

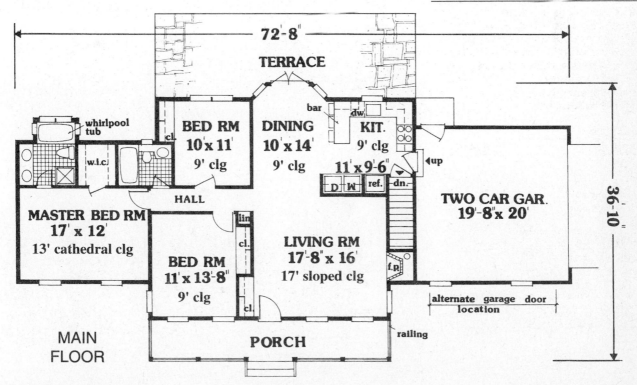

MAIN FLOOR

Sunny Disposition

- A lovely bay window and an entry door with oval glass illustrate this home's sunny disposition. Its design makes the most of modest space, while paying strict attention to your comfort.
- The foyer allows access to the garage and introduces visitors to the family room, which serves as the entertainment center of the home. A high, 9-ft. ceiling with sloped edges, a corner fireplace and French doors to the outside create an open, relaxed feeling.
- Nearby, the bayed dining room hosts formal occasions with ease. Imagine sunny brunches with the family, or intimate candlelight dinners with your favorite person!
- The U-shaped kitchen boasts a unique cathedral ceiling, plenty of counter space and a pantry closet.
- Sleeping quarters are positioned across the home for privacy. The master suite gives preferential treatment with a 10-ft. ceiling in the bedroom and a convenient bath with tons of closet space, a built-in desk and a garden tub.
- Two secondary bedrooms share a second full bath.

Plan L-1270

Bedrooms: 3	Baths: 2
Living Area:	
Main floor	1,270 sq. ft.
Total Living Area:	**1,270 sq. ft.**
Garage	452 sq. ft.
Exterior Wall Framing:	2x4

Foundation Options:

Slab

(All plans can be built with your choice of foundation and framing. A generic conversion diagram is available. See order form.)

BLUEPRINT PRICE CODE:	A

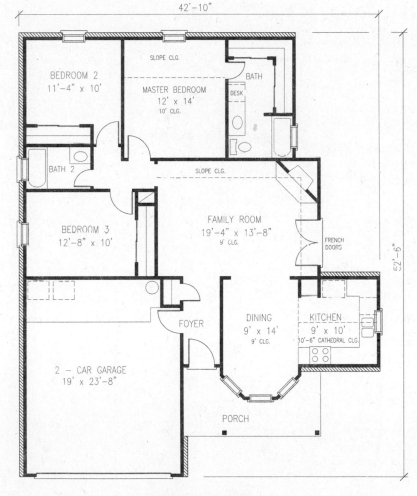

MAIN FLOOR

ORDER BLUEPRINTS ANYTIME!
CALL TOLL-FREE 1-800-820-1283

Plan L-1270

PRICES AND DETAILS
ON PAGES 2-5

Raised One-Story

- This clever plan raises the one-story ranch design to new heights.
- An open floor plan punctuated with high ceilings maximizes the home's square footage.
- The open living spaces consist of a vaulted living room with a fireplace, a dining room with a bay window and an efficient galley-style kitchen with a two-sided serving bar.
- A pantry closet, a laundry room and a nifty storage area are close to the kitchen, just off the garage entrance.
- Not to be overlooked, the outstanding master suite is beautifully finished with a tray ceiling and a vaulted bath with a garden tub, a separate shower, a dual-sink vanity and a walk-in closet.
- Two more bedrooms, one of which has a vaulted ceiling, share a hall bath.

Plan FB-5052-LENO

Bedrooms: 3	Baths: 2
Living Area:	
Main floor	1,346 sq. ft.
Total Living Area:	**1,346 sq. ft.**
Daylight Basement	1,346 sq. ft.
Garage	390 sq. ft.
Exterior Wall Framing:	2x4

Foundation Options:

Daylight basement
Crawlspace
Slab

(All plans can be built with your choice of foundation and framing. A generic conversion diagram is available. See order form.)

BLUEPRINT PRICE CODE:	A

MAIN FLOOR

Sunny and Cost-Efficient

- This home's big bright windows and economical square footage allow you to keep costs down without sacrificing aesthetics.
- The entry is brightened by clerestory windows, while the 14-ft. vaulted living room features floor-to-ceiling windows and is the perfect spot for hosting afternoon tea.
- The 9-ft. dining room has sliding glass doors opening to a backyard deck.

Invite the neighbors over for barbecue ribs on a warm summer day. The neat U-shaped kitchen includes a space-saving laundry closet and a pantry.

- The 11-ft.-high vaulted master bedroom offers a wonderful view of the backyard. The private master bath makes mornings run a little smoother.
- Two secondary bedrooms and another full bath round out the main floor.
- The full basement can be finished to provide more living space. Wouldn't a home office or a playroom be nice?
- This home's many windows and modest size make it a great choice for a vacation home.

Plan B-90066	
Bedrooms: 3	Baths: 2
Living Area:	
Main floor	1,135 sq. ft.
Total Living Area:	**1,135 sq. ft.**
Standard basement	1,135 sq. ft.
Garage	288 sq. ft.
Exterior Wall Framing:	2x4
Foundation Options:	

Standard basement
(All plans can be built with your choice of foundation and framing. A generic conversion diagram is available. See order form.)

BLUEPRINT PRICE CODE:	A

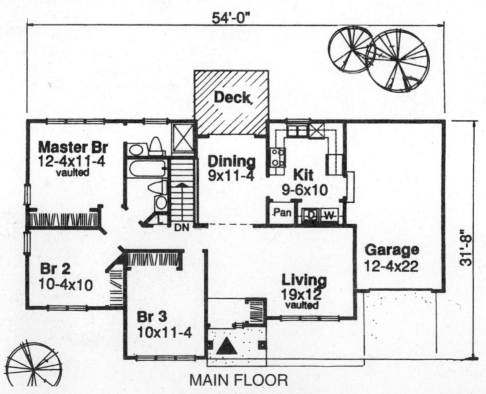

MAIN FLOOR

ORDER BLUEPRINTS ANYTIME!
CALL TOLL-FREE 1-800-820-1283

Plan B-90066

PRICES AND DETAILS
ON PAGES 2-5

Skylighted Country Kitchen

- This country ranch-style home combines rustic wood posts and shutters with stylish curved glass.
- The tiled foyer unfolds to the dramatic, flowing formal areas. The living room and the bayed dining room each offer a 9-ft. stepped ceiling and a view of one of the two covered porches.
- The skylighted country kitchen shares the family room's warm fireplace. The kitchen's central island cooktop and snack bar make serving a breeze!
- In addition to the fireplace, the family room also boasts an 11-ft. vaulted ceiling and gliding French doors to the adjacent porch.
- The bedroom wing houses three bedrooms and two full baths. The master bedroom shows off a relaxing sitting bay and a 9-ft., 9-in. tray ceiling. The skylighted master bath flaunts a whirlpool tub and a dual-sink vanity.
- Each of the secondary bedrooms has a 10-ft., 9-in. ceiling area above its lovely arched window.

Plan AX-92321

Bedrooms: 3	Baths: 2
Living Area:	
Main floor	1,735 sq. ft.
Total Living Area:	**1,735 sq. ft.**
Standard basement	1,735 sq. ft.
Garage, storage and utility	505 sq. ft.
Exterior Wall Framing:	2x4

Foundation Options:

Standard basement

Crawlspace

Slab

(All plans can be built with your choice of foundation and framing. A generic conversion diagram is available. See order form.)

BLUEPRINT PRICE CODE: B

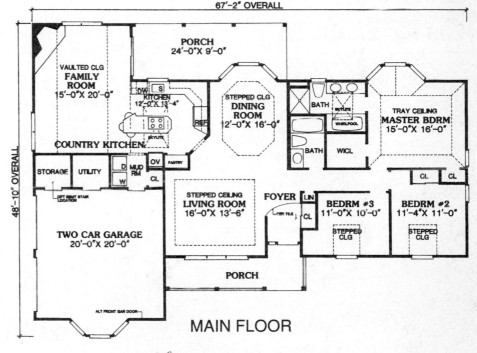

MAIN FLOOR

REAR VIEW

A Real Charmer

- This charming design is exceptionally livable. Maximum use of space allows for four bedrooms within its modest square footage.
- The living room and dining area flow together to create a large, open expanse suitable for entertaining on any scale. A formal holiday dinner with all the trimmings is as at home here as your raucous Super Bowl bash.
- The U-shaped kitchen surrounds the family chef, making dinner a joy to cook and serve. There's plenty of cabinet space, and a big pantry closet holds all your food essentials, plus some hidden goodies!
- The master suite boasts features you'd only expect to find in a larger home. The walk-in closet is tucked into a corner off the roomy private bath.
- Three secondary bedrooms share another bath. A door closes off the sleeping wing from the rest of the home.
- A wide backyard patio is a great place for stargazing on summer nights.
- Outdoor storage holds yard equipment.

Plan E-1211

Bedrooms: 4	Baths: 2
Living Area:	
Main floor	1,235 sq. ft.
Total Living Area:	**1,235 sq. ft.**
Carport	274 sq. ft.
Storage	51 sq. ft.
Exterior Wall Framing:	**2x6**

Foundation Options:

Crawlspace

Slab

(All plans can be built with your choice of foundation and framing. A generic conversion diagram is available. See order form.)

BLUEPRINT PRICE CODE:	**A**

Floor Plan

44'

42'

PATIO

STORAGE

CARPORT
20' x 12'

DISAPPEARING STAIRS

BED ROOM
12' x 10'

CLO.
CLO.

BED ROOM
10' x 10'

HEAT & A/C
CLO
CLO.

MASTER
BED RM.
12' x 11'

HALL

BED ROOM
10' x 10'

BATH

CLO

LINEN

LINEN

BATH

DRY   WASH

W.H.   PANTRY

KITCHEN
12' x 10'
REF

RANGE

DW   SINK

DINING
12' x 8'

LIVING
18' x 13'

MAIN FLOOR

ORDER BLUEPRINTS ANYTIME!
CALL TOLL-FREE 1-800-820-1283

Plan E-1211

PRICES AND DETAILS
ON PAGES 2-5

Touch of Class

- Fabulous windows and a striking roofline add a touch of class to this home's cozy demeanor.
- The floor plan, which neatly places living areas on one side of the home and sleeping areas on the other, is well designed to maximize space.
- The entry leads to the formal dining room and the adjacent Great Room, which features a corner fireplace and access to a backyard patio.
- A bayed breakfast nook flows from the Great Room and is a charming spot for morning tea and casual meals.
- The island kitchen provides a unique octagonal workspace and serves as Grand Central to the open living areas. An angled counter creates definition between these areas, while allowing friendly banter to fly fast.
- Tucked away for privacy, the master suite offers a lush bath complete with a garden tub, a separate shower, a dual-sink vanity and a walk-in closet.
- Two secondary bedrooms share another full bath; each enjoys a walk-in closet.

Plan DD-1736-1

Bedrooms: 3	Baths: 2
Living Area:	
Main floor	1,761 sq. ft.
Total Living Area:	**1,761 sq. ft.**
Standard basement	1,761 sq. ft.
Garage and storage	384 sq. ft.
Exterior Wall Framing:	2x4

Foundation Options:

Standard basement
Crawlspace
Slab
(All plans can be built with your choice of foundation and framing. A generic conversion diagram is available. See order form.)

BLUEPRINT PRICE CODE:	**B**

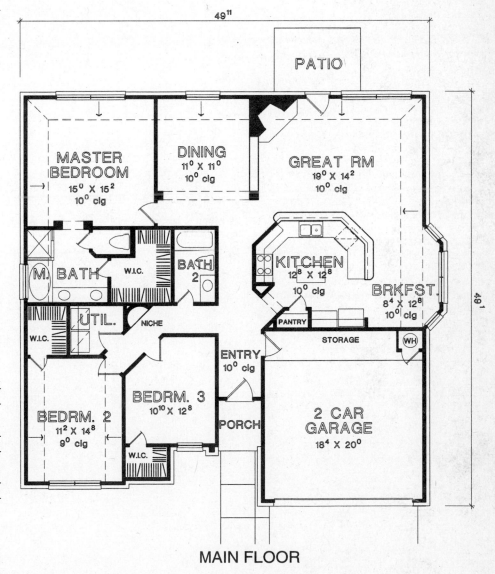

MAIN FLOOR

ORDER BLUEPRINTS ANYTIME!
CALL TOLL-FREE 1-800-820-1283

Plan DD-1736-1

*PRICES AND DETAILS
ON PAGES 2-5*

Breathtaking Open Space

- Soaring ceilings and an open floor plan add breathtaking volume to this charming country-style home.
- The inviting covered-porch entrance opens into the spacious living room, which boasts a spectacular 17-ft.-high cathedral ceiling. Two overhead dormers fill the area with natural light, while a fireplace adds warmth.
- Also under the cathedral ceiling, the kitchen and bayed breakfast room share an eating bar. Skylights brighten the convenient laundry room and the computer room, which provides access to a covered rear porch.
- The secluded master bedroom offers private access to another covered porch. The skylighted master bath has a walk-in closet and a 10-ft. sloped ceiling above a whirlpool tub.
- Optional upper-floor areas provide future expansion space for the needs of a growing family.

Plan J-9302

Bedrooms: 3+	Baths: 2
Living Area:	
Main floor	1,745 sq. ft.
Total Living Area:	**1,745 sq. ft.**
Upper floor (future area)	500 sq. ft.
Future area above garage	241 sq. ft.
Standard basement	1,745 sq. ft.
Garage and storage	559 sq. ft.
Exterior Wall Framing:	2x4

Foundation Options:

Standard basement
Crawlspace
Slab

(All plans can be built with your choice of foundation and framing. A generic conversion diagram is available. See order form.)

BLUEPRINT PRICE CODE:	**B**

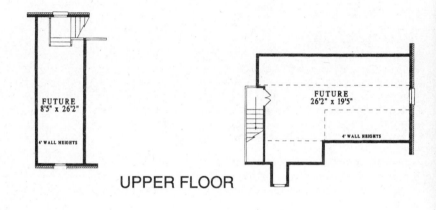

UPPER FLOOR

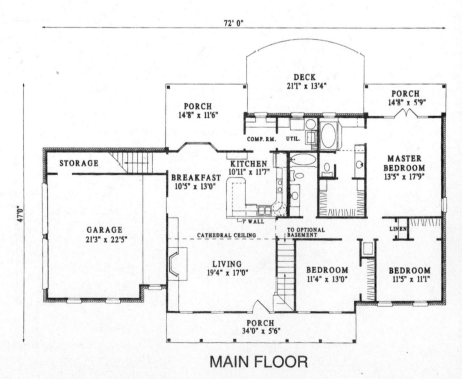

MAIN FLOOR

ORDER BLUEPRINTS ANYTIME!
CALL TOLL-FREE 1-800-820-1283

Plan J-9302

PRICES AND DETAILS
ON PAGES 2-5

Warm Welcome

- Warm, wood siding and unique window treatments welcome family and friends to this appealing home!
- Step from the foyer to the open activity areas. Here, a corner fireplace and a lovely bow window imbue the living room with simple charm.
- Nearby, the dining room's wall of French doors overlooks a sprawling rear deck. The scent of summer blooms will distinguish summer parties that extend to the outdoors.
- The neat kitchen reserves a corner for casual eating and boasts another French door to the rear deck. The large laundry room nearby includes an outside service entrance.
- For a measure of privacy, this efficient design clusters the sleeping quarters in their own wing.
- The master bath contributes a walk-in closet, a whirlpool tub and dual sinks to your comfort. A vaulted, 10-ft. ceiling tops the bedroom.
- Two other bedrooms share a hall bath.

Plan HFL-1910-JO

Bedrooms: 3	Baths: 2
Living Area:	
Main floor	1,387 sq. ft.
Total Living Area:	**1,387 sq. ft.**
Standard basement	1,387 sq. ft.
Garage and storage	493 sq. ft.
Exterior Wall Framing:	2x6

Foundation Options:

Standard basement
Slab
(All plans can be built with your choice of foundation and framing. A generic conversion diagram is available. See order form.)

BLUEPRINT PRICE CODE: A

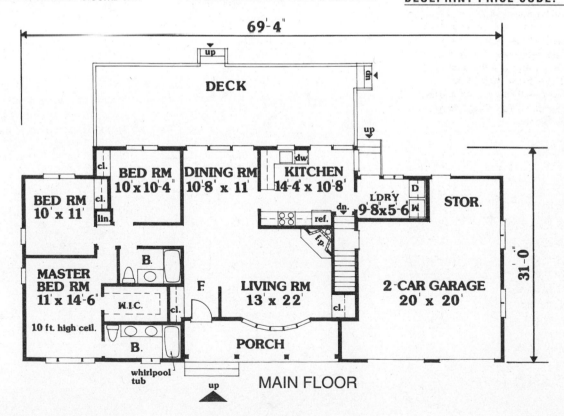

MAIN FLOOR

Cozy Brick One-Story

- A covered front porch accented by an oval window gives this cozy brick home a special look.
- The 9-ft.-high entry overlooks a huge living and dining area with a 10-ft., 8-in. ceiling. Tall windows brighten the entire area, and French doors open to a backyard patio. A tiled fireplace is flanked by built-in bookcases and a neat TV niche.
- A functional serving bar extends from the kitchen, which has a 9-ft. ceiling. A sunny breakfast nook looks out to the front yard. A convenient hanging rod is offered in the windowed utility room, which opens directly to the garage.
- Secluded to the rear of the home, the master bedroom boasts a 9-ft. stepped ceiling, two generous closets and private access to the patio. The deluxe master bath flaunts a romantic whirlpool tub, a separate shower, a dual-sink vanity and a tall linen closet.
- Two additional bedrooms are located on the opposite side of the home. A second full bath is close by.

Plan SDG-50103

Bedrooms: 3	Baths: 2
Living Area:	
Main floor	1,372 sq. ft.
Total Living Area:	**1,372 sq. ft.**
Garage and storage	496 sq. ft.
Exterior Wall Framing:	2x4

Foundation Options:

Slab

(All plans can be built with your choice of foundation and framing. A generic conversion diagram is available. See order form.)

BLUEPRINT PRICE CODE: A

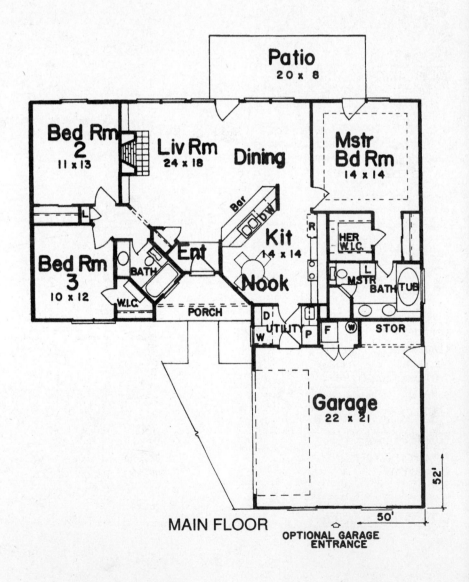

MAIN FLOOR

OPTIONAL GARAGE ENTRANCE

ORDER BLUEPRINTS ANYTIME! CALL TOLL-FREE 1-800-820-1283

Plan SDG-50103

PRICES AND DETAILS ON PAGES 2-5

Cozy, Rustic Country Home

- This cozy, rustic home offers a modern, open interior that efficiently maximizes the square footage.
- The large living room features a 13-ft. sloped ceiling accented by rustic beams and an eye-catching corner fireplace.
- The living room flows into the adjoining dining room and the efficient U-shaped kitchen for a spacious, open feel.
- The master and secondary bedrooms are separated by the activity areas. The master suite includes a private bath and a separate dressing area with a dual-sink vanity.
- The secondary bedrooms share another full bath.

Plan E-1109

Bedrooms: 3	Baths: 2
Living Area:	
Main floor	1,191 sq. ft.
Total Living Area:	**1,191 sq. ft.**
Garage	462 sq. ft.
Storage	55 sq. ft.
Utility	55 sq. ft.
Exterior Wall Framing:	2x6

Foundation Options:

Crawlspace
Slab
(All plans can be built with your choice of foundation and framing. A generic conversion diagram is available. See order form.)

BLUEPRINT PRICE CODE: A

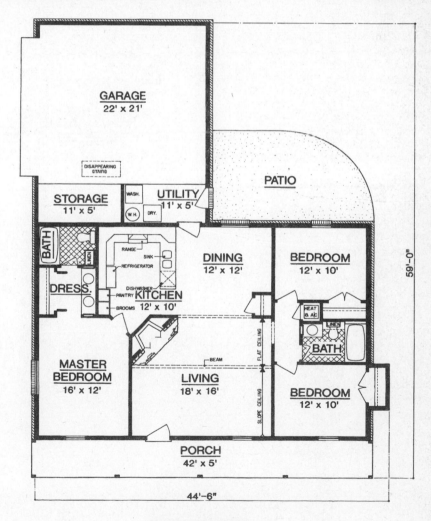

MAIN FLOOR

Build It Yourself

- Everything you need for a leisure or retirement retreat is neatly packaged in this affordable, easy-to-build design.
- The basic rectangular shape features a unique wraparound deck, entirely covered by a projecting roofline.
- A central fireplace and a vaulted ceiling that rises to 10 ft. visually enhance the cozy living and dining rooms.
- The efficient kitchen offers convenient service to the adjoining dining room. In the crawlspace version, the kitchen also includes a snack bar.
- Two main-floor bedrooms share a large full bath.
- The daylight-basement option is suitable for building on a sloping lot and consists of an extra bedroom, a general-purpose area and a garage.

Plans H-833-7 & -7A

Bedrooms: 2+	Baths: 1
Living Area:	
Main floor	952 sq. ft.
Daylight basement	676 sq. ft.
Total Living Area:	**952/1,628 sq. ft.**
Tuck-under garage	276 sq. ft.
Exterior Wall Framing:	2x6
Foundation Options:	**Plan #**
Daylight basement	H-833-7
Crawlspace	H-833-7A

(All plans can be built with your choice of foundation and framing. A generic conversion diagram is available. See order form.)

BLUEPRINT PRICE CODE:	**AA/B**

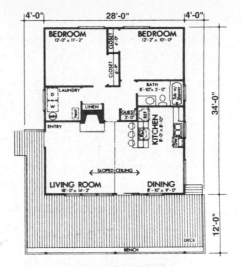

MAIN FLOOR
Crawlspace version

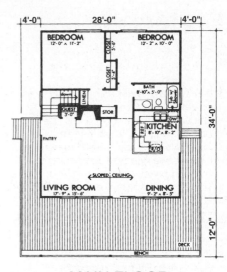

MAIN FLOOR
Basement version

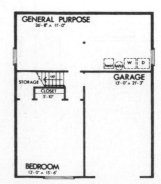

DAYLIGHT BASEMENT

ORDER BLUEPRINTS ANYTIME!
CALL TOLL-FREE 1-800-820-1283

Plans H-833-7 & -7A

PRICES AND DETAILS
ON PAGES 2-5

Planned to Perfection

- This attractive and stylish home offers an interior design that is planned to perfection.
- The covered entry and vaulted foyer create an impressive welcome.
- The vaulted Great Room features a corner fireplace, a wet bar and lots of windows. The adjoining dining room offers a bay window and access to a covered patio.
- The gourmet kitchen includes an island cooktop, a garden window above the sink and a built-in desk. The attached nook is surrounded by windows that overlook a delightful planter.
- The master suite boasts a tray ceiling that rises to 9½ ft. and a peaceful reading area that accesses a private patio. The superb master bath features a garden tub and a separate shower.
- Two secondary bedrooms share a compartmentalized bath.

Plan S-4789

Bedrooms: 3	Baths: 2
Living Area:	
Main floor	1,665 sq. ft.
Total Living Area:	**1,665 sq. ft.**
Standard basement	1,665 sq. ft.
Garage	400 sq. ft.
Exterior Wall Framing:	2x6

Foundation Options:

Standard basement
Crawlspace
Slab

(All plans can be built with your choice of foundation and framing. A generic conversion diagram is available. See order form.)

BLUEPRINT PRICE CODE: B

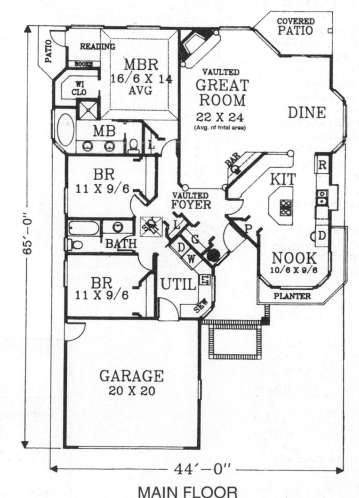

MAIN FLOOR

BASEMENT STAIRWAY LOCATION

Fresh Air

- With its nostalgic look and country style, this lovely home brings a breath of fresh air into any neighborhood.
- Past the inviting wraparound porch, the foyer is brightened by an arched transom window above the front door.
- The adjoining formal dining room is defined by decorative columns and features a 9-ft., 4-in. stepped ceiling.
- The bright and airy kitchen includes a pantry, a windowed sink and a sunny breakfast area with porch access.
- Enhanced by an 11-ft stepped ceiling, the spacious Great Room is warmed by a fireplace flanked by sliding glass doors to a covered back porch.
- The lush master bedroom boasts an 11-ft. tray ceiling and a bayed sitting area. The master bath showcases a circular spa tub with a glass-block wall.
- The two remaining bedrooms are serviced by a second bath and a nearby laundry room. The protruding bedroom has a 12-ft. vaulted ceiling.
- Additional living space can be made available by finishing the upper floor.

Plan AX-93308

Bedrooms: 3+	Baths: 2
Living Area:	
Main floor	1,793 sq. ft.
Total Living Area:	**1,793 sq. ft.**
Standard basement	1,793 sq. ft.
Unfinished upper floor	779 sq. ft.
Garage and utility	471 sq. ft.
Exterior Wall Framing:	2x4

Foundation Options:

Standard basement
Crawlspace
Slab

(All plans can be built with your choice of foundation and framing. A generic conversion diagram is available. See order form.)

BLUEPRINT PRICE CODE: B

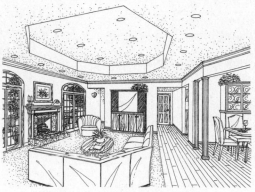

VIEW INTO GREAT ROOM

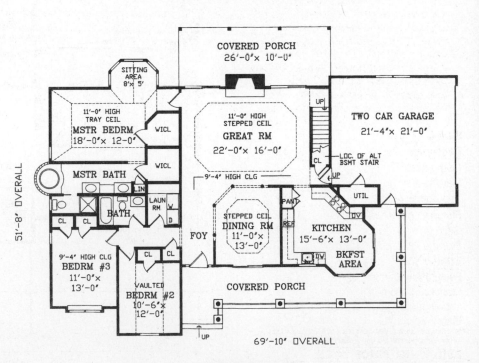

MAIN FLOOR

***ORDER BLUEPRINTS ANYTIME!*
*CALL TOLL-FREE 1-800-820-1283***

Plan AX-93308

***PRICES AND DETAILS
ON PAGES 2-5***

Free-Flowing Floor Plan

- A fluid floor plan with open indoor/outdoor living spaces characterizes this exciting luxury home.
- The stylish columned porch opens to a spacious living room and dining room expanse that overlooks the outdoor spaces. The breathtaking view also includes a dramatic corner fireplace.
- The dining area opens to a bright kitchen with an angled eating bar. The overall spaciousness of the living areas is increased with high 12-ft. ceilings.
- A sunny, informal eating area adjoins the kitchen, and an angled set of doors opens to a convenient main-floor laundry room near the garage entrance.
- The vaulted master bedroom has a walk-in closet and a sumptuous bath with an oval tub.
- A separate wing houses two additional bedrooms and another full bath.
- Attic space is accessible from stairs in the garage and in the bedroom wing.

REAR VIEW

Plan E-1710

Bedrooms: 3	Baths: 2
Living Area:	
Main floor	1,792 sq. ft.
Total Living Area:	**1,792 sq. ft.**
Standard basement	1,792 sq. ft.
Garage	484 sq. ft.
Storage	96 sq. ft.
Exterior Wall Framing:	2x6

Foundation Options:

Standard basement
Crawlspace
Slab

(All plans can be built with your choice of foundation and framing. A generic conversion diagram is available. See order form.)

BLUEPRINT PRICE CODE: B

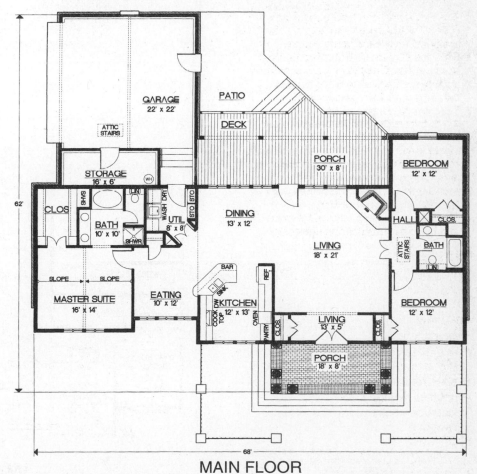

MAIN FLOOR

Authentic Charm

- Intricate fretwork, turned spindles and copper-topped bays lend authentic charm to this one-story home.
- Its unique shape and projecting gables make it aesthetically adaptable to nearly any lot orientation or size.
- The wraparound veranda ends at an angled entry and foyer; functional niches to the left and right provide display space for art or memorabilia.
- Handsome columns set off the central living room, with its corner fireplace and radiant window wall.
- A boxed-out bay and an attractive built-in hutch add interest and dimension to the formal dining room.
- Bifold doors close off the galley-style kitchen, where a snack bar and breakfast nook offer casual dining options. French doors entice you to dine outdoors on the porch.
- This same porch winds along to the master suite and its roomy garden bath. Two more bedrooms share a second full bath in the same wing.

Plan L-755-VA

Bedrooms: 3	Baths: 2
Living Area:	
Main floor	1,753 sq. ft.
Total Living Area:	**1,753 sq. ft.**
Exterior Wall Framing:	2x4

Foundation Options:

Slab

(All plans can be built with your choice of foundation and framing. A generic conversion diagram is available. See order form.)

BLUEPRINT PRICE CODE:	B

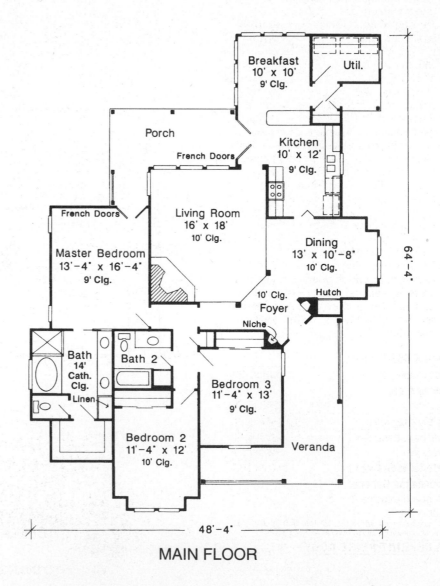

MAIN FLOOR

ORDER BLUEPRINTS ANYTIME!
CALL TOLL-FREE 1-800-820-1283

Plan L-755-VA

PRICES AND DETAILS
ON PAGES 2-5

High-Profile Contemporary

- This design does away with wasted space, putting the emphasis on quality rather than on size.
- The angled floor plan minimizes hall space and creates smooth traffic flow while adding architectural appeal. The roof framing is square, however, to allow for economical construction.
- The spectacular living and dining rooms share a 16-ft. cathedral ceiling and a fireplace. Both rooms have lots of glass overlooking an angled rear terrace.
- The dining room includes a glass-filled alcove and sliding patio doors topped by transom windows. Tall windows frame the living room fireplace and trace the slope of the ceiling.
- A pass-through joins the dining room to the combination kitchen and family room, which features a snack bar and a clerestory window.
- The sleeping wing provides a super master suite, which boasts a skylighted dressing area and a luxurious bath. The optional den, or third bedroom, shares a second full bath with another bedroom that offers a 14-ft. sloped ceiling.

Plan K-688-D

Bedrooms: 2+	Baths: 2½
Living Area:	
Main floor	1,340 sq. ft.
Total Living Area:	**1,340 sq. ft.**
Standard basement	1,235 sq. ft.
Garage	484 sq. ft.
Exterior Wall Framing:	2x4 or 2x6

Foundation Options:
Standard basement
Slab
(All plans can be built with your choice of foundation and framing. A generic conversion diagram is available. See order form.)

BLUEPRINT PRICE CODE: A

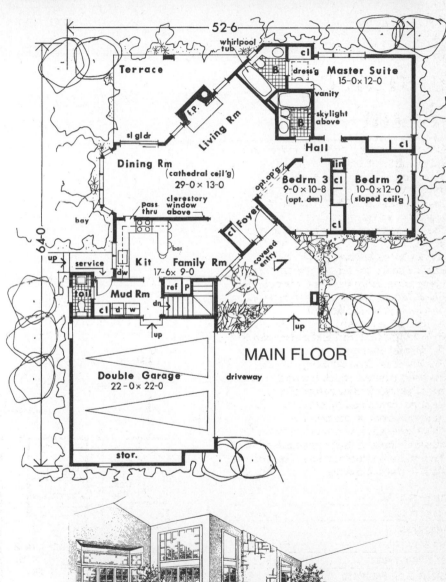

MAIN FLOOR

VIEW INTO DINING ROOM AND LIVING ROOM

Tradition Updated

- The nostalgic exterior of this home gives way to dramatic cathedral ceilings and illuminating skylights inside.
- The covered front porch welcomes guests into the stone-tiled foyer, which flows into the living spaces.
- The living and dining rooms merge, forming a spacious, front-oriented entertaining area.

- A large three-sided fireplace situated between the living room and the family room may be enjoyed in both areas.
- The skylighted family room is also brightened by sliding glass doors that access a rear patio.
- The sunny island kitchen offers a nice breakfast nook and easy access to the laundry room and the garage.
- The master suite boasts a walk-in closet and a skylighted bath with a dual-sink vanity, a soaking tub and a separate shower. Two additional bedrooms share another full bath.

Plan AX-90303-A

Bedrooms: 3	Baths: 2
Living Area:	
Main floor	1,615 sq. ft.
Total Living Area:	**1,615 sq. ft.**
Basement	1,615 sq. ft.
Garage	412 sq. ft.
Exterior Wall Framing:	2x4

Foundation Options:
Daylight basement
Standard basement
Crawlspace
Slab
(All plans can be built with your choice of foundation and framing. A generic conversion diagram is available. See order form.)

BLUEPRINT PRICE CODE: B

72'-4" OVERALL

32'-4" OVERALL

PATIO

SL GL DR

SKYLITE

CL W D

LAUN RM

UTIL RM

CATH CEIL
BRKFST RM
8'-6" x 11'-4"

DW S

CATH CEIL
KITCHEN
9'-6" x 13'-4"

SKYLITE

REF

CATH CEIL
FAMILY RM
15'-0" x 13'-4"

SKYLITE

MSTR BATH

BATH #2

WICL

MSTR BEDRM
15'-0" x 13'-4"

CL CL

FIREPLACE

CATH CEIL
DINING RM
10'-2" x 12'-4"

CATH CEIL
LIVING RM
12'-6" x 13'-4"

TWO CAR GARAGE
20'-0" x 20'-0"

LIN

CL

FOYER

BEDRM #3
10'-0" x 9'-8"

BEDRM #2
11'-4" x 11'-0"

PORCH

UP

MAIN FLOOR

Plan AX-90303-A

Covered Porch Invites Visitors

- This nice home welcomes visitors with its covered front porch and its wide-open living areas.
- Detailed columns, railings and shutters decorate the front porch that guides guests to the central entry.
- Just off the entry, the bright living room merges with the dining room. The side wall is lined with glass, including a glass door that opens to the yard.
- The angled kitchen features a serving counter facing the dining room. A handy laundry closet and access to a storage area and the garage are nearby.
- An angled hall leads to the bedroom wing. The master suite offers a private bath, a walk-in closet and a dressing area with a vanity. Two additional bedrooms and another full bath are located down the hall.

Plan E-1217

Bedrooms: 3	Baths: 2
Living Area:	
Main floor	1,266 sq. ft.
Total Living Area:	**1,266 sq. ft.**
Garage and storage	550 sq. ft.
Exterior Wall Framing:	2x6

Foundation Options:

Crawlspace

Slab

(All plans can be built with your choice of foundation and framing. A generic conversion diagram is available. See order form.)

BLUEPRINT PRICE CODE: A

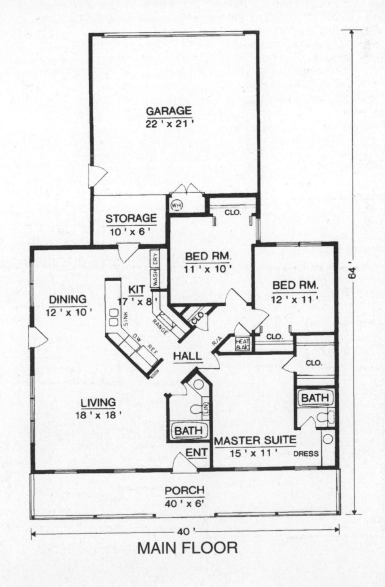

MAIN FLOOR

Adorable and Affordable

- This charming one-story home has much to offer, despite its modest size and economical bent.
- The lovely full-width porch has old-fashioned detailing, such as the round columns, decorative railings and ornamental molding.
- An open floor plan maximizes the home's square footage. The front door opens to the living room, where a railing creates a hallway effect while using very little space.
- Straight ahead, the dining room adjoins the island kitchen, while offering a compact laundry closet and sliding glass doors to a large rear patio.
- Focusing on quality, the home also offers features such as a 10-ft. tray ceiling in the living room and a 9-ft. stepped ceiling in the dining room.
- The three bedrooms are well proportioned. The master bedroom includes a private bathroom, while the two smaller bedrooms share another full bath. Note that the fixtures are arranged to reduce plumbing runs.

Plan AX-91316

Bedrooms: 3	Baths: 2
Living Area:	
Main floor	1,097 sq. ft.
Total Living Area:	**1,097 sq. ft.**
Basement	1,097 sq. ft.
Garage	461 sq. ft.
Exterior Wall Framing:	2x4

Foundation Options:
Daylight basement
Standard basement
Slab
(All plans can be built with your choice of foundation and framing. A generic conversion diagram is available. See order form.)

BLUEPRINT PRICE CODE: A

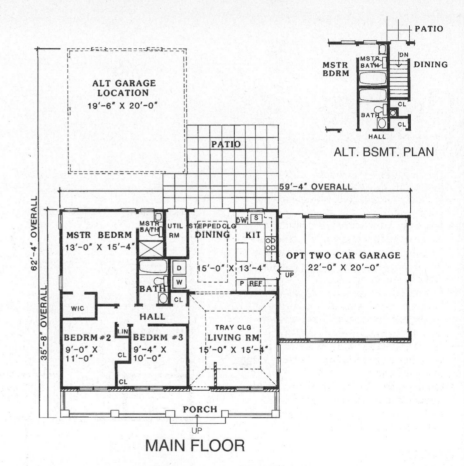

MAIN FLOOR

ALT. BSMT. PLAN

VIEW INTO LIVING ROOM AND DINING ROOM

ORDER BLUEPRINTS ANYTIME!
CALL TOLL-FREE 1-800-820-1283

Plan AX-91316

PRICES AND DETAILS
ON PAGES 2-5

Charming Traditional

- The attractive facade of this traditional home features decorative fretwork and louvers in the gables, plus eye-catching window and door treatments.
- The entry area features a commanding view of the living room, which boasts a 12½-ft. ceiling and a corner fireplace. A rear porch and patio are visible through French doors.
- The bayed dining room shares an eating bar with the U-shaped kitchen. The nearby utility room includes a pantry and laundry facilities.
- The quiet master suite includes a big walk-in closet and a private bath with a dual-sink vanity.
- On the other side of the home, double doors close off the two secondary bedrooms from the living areas. A full bath services this wing.

Plan E-1428

Bedrooms: 3	Baths: 2
Living Area:	
Main floor	1,415 sq. ft.
Total Living Area:	**1,415 sq. ft.**
Garage	484 sq. ft.
Storage	60 sq. ft.
Exterior Wall Framing:	2x6

Foundation Options:

Crawlspace
Slab
(All plans can be built with your choice of foundation and framing. A generic conversion diagram is available. See order form.)

BLUEPRINT PRICE CODE: **A**

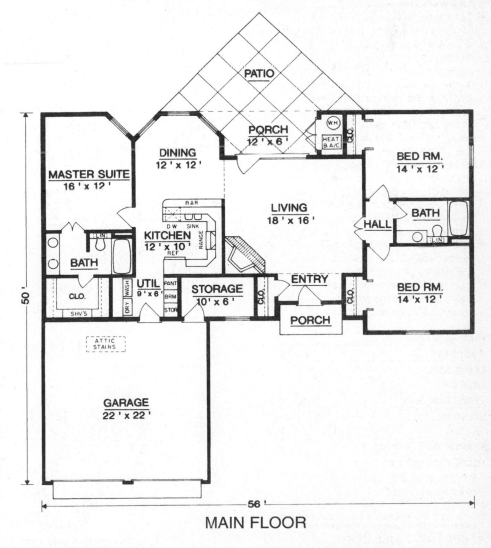

MAIN FLOOR

Rustic, Relaxed Living

- The screened porch of this rustic home offers a cool place to dine on warm summer days. The covered front porch provides an inviting welcome and a place for pure relaxation.
- With its warm fireplace and surrounding windows, the home's spacious living room is ideal for unwinding indoors. The living room unfolds to a nice-sized dining area that overlooks a backyard patio and opens to the screened porch.
- The U-shaped kitchen is centrally located and features a nice windowed sink. A handy pantry and a laundry room adjoin to the right.
- Three large bedrooms make up the home's sleeping wing. The master bedroom boasts a roomy private bath with a step-up spa tub, a separate shower and two walk-in closets.
- The secondary bedrooms share a compartmentalized hall bath.

Plan C-8650

Bedrooms: 3	**Baths: 2**

Living Area:

Main floor	1,773 sq. ft.
Total Living Area:	**1,773 sq. ft.**
Daylight basement	1,773 sq. ft.
Garage	441 sq. ft.

Exterior Wall Framing: 2x4

Foundation Options:

Daylight basement
Crawlspace
Slab

(All plans can be built with your choice of foundation and framing. A generic conversion diagram is available. See order form.)

BLUEPRINT PRICE CODE: B

MAIN FLOOR

Plan C-8650

Inviting Windows

- This comfortable home presents an impressive facade, with its large and inviting front window arrangement.
- A step down from the front entry, the Great Room boasts a 12-ft. vaulted ceiling with a barrel-vaulted area that outlines the half-round front window. The striking angled fireplace can be enjoyed from the adjoining dining area.
- The galley-style kitchen hosts a half-round cutout above the sink and a breakfast area that accesses a backyard deck and patio. The kitchen, breakfast area and dining area also are enhanced by 12-ft. vaulted ceilings.
- The master bedroom features a boxed-out window, a walk-in closet and a ceiling that vaults to 12 feet. The private bath includes a garden tub, a separate shower and a private toilet compartment.
- Another full bath serves the two remaining bedrooms, one of which has sliding glass doors to the deck and would make an ideal den.

Plan B-902

Bedrooms: 2+	Baths: 2
Living Area:	
Main floor	1,368 sq. ft.
Total Living Area:	**1,368 sq. ft.**
Standard basement	1,368 sq. ft.
Garage	412 sq. ft.
Exterior Wall Framing:	2x4
Foundation Options:	

Standard basement
(All plans can be built with your choice of foundation and framing. A generic conversion diagram is available. See order form.)

BLUEPRINT PRICE CODE: **A**

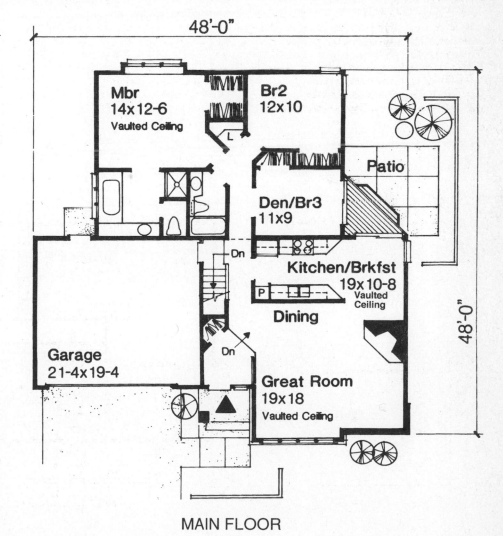

MAIN FLOOR

Design Fits Narrow Lot

- This compact, cozy and dignified plan makes great use of a small lot, while also offering an exciting interior design.
- In from the covered front porch, the living room features a warm fireplace and a 13-ft., 6-in. cathedral ceiling.
- The bay-windowed dining room joins the living room to provide a spacious area for entertaining.
- The galley-style kitchen has easy access to a large pantry closet, the utility room and the carport.
- The master suite includes a deluxe bath and a roomy walk-in closet.
- Two secondary bedrooms share another bath off the hallway.
- A lockable storage area is located off the rear patio.

Plan J-86161

Bedrooms: 3	Baths: 2
Living Area:	
Main floor	1,626 sq. ft.
Total Living Area:	**1,626 sq. ft.**
Standard basement	1,626 sq. ft.
Carport	410 sq. ft.
Storage	104 sq. ft.
Exterior Wall Framing:	2x4

Foundation Options:

Standard basement
Crawlspace
Slab
(All plans can be built with your choice of foundation and framing. A generic conversion diagram is available. See order form.)

BLUEPRINT PRICE CODE:	B

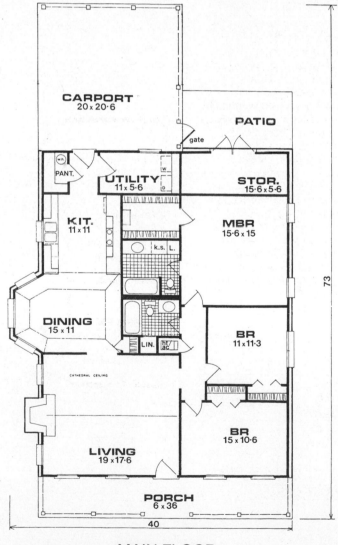

MAIN FLOOR

ORDER BLUEPRINTS ANYTIME!
CALL TOLL-FREE 1-800-820-1283

Plan J-86161

PRICES AND DETAILS
ON PAGES 2-5

Wide Angles
Add Style

- The comfortably-sized living areas of this gorgeous home are stylishly enhanced by wide, interesting angles.
- Past the covered front porch, the sidelighted front door brightens the living room just ahead.
- The spacious living room is warmed by a dramatic corner fireplace and opens to an angled, covered back porch.
- A stunning bayed dining room merges with the kitchen and its functional angled snack bar. Laundry facilities and access to the garage are nearby.
- The master suite is removed from the secondary bedrooms and features double doors to a deluxe private bath with an angled spa tub, a dual-sink vanity and a large walk-in closet.
- Another full bath serves the two additional bedrooms at the opposite end of the home.

Plan E-1426

Bedrooms: 3	Baths: 2
Living Area:	
Main floor	1,420 sq. ft.
Total Living Area:	**1,420 sq. ft.**
Garage and storage	540 sq. ft.
Exterior Wall Framing:	2x6

Foundation Options:

Crawlspace

Slab

(All plans can be built with your choice of foundation and framing. A generic conversion diagram is available. See order form.)

BLUEPRINT PRICE CODE: A

MAIN FLOOR

Suspended Sun Room

- This narrow-lot design is a perfect combination of economical structure and luxurious features.
- The living and dining rooms flow together to create a great space for parties or family gatherings. A 16-ft. sloped ceiling and clerestory windows add drama and brightness. A fabulous deck expands the entertaining area.
- An exciting sun room provides the advantages of passive-solar heating.
- The sunny, efficient kitchen is open to the dining room.
- A full bath serves the two isolated main-floor bedrooms.
- The optional daylight basement includes an additional bedroom and bath as well as a tuck-under garage and storage space.

Plans H-951-1A & -1B

Bedrooms: 2+	Baths: 1-2
Living Area:	
Main floor	1,075 sq. ft.
Sun room	100 sq. ft.
Daylight basement	662 sq. ft.
Total Living Area:	**1,175/1,837 sq. ft.**
Tuck-under garage	311 sq. ft.
Exterior Wall Framing:	2x6
Foundation Options:	**Plan #**
Daylight basement	H-951-1B
Crawlspace	H-951-1A

(All plans can be built with your choice of foundation and framing. A generic conversion diagram is available. See order form.)

BLUEPRINT PRICE CODE:	**A/B**

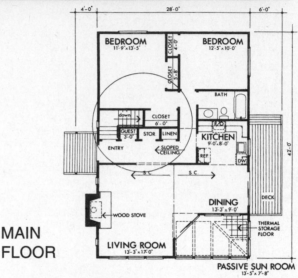

MAIN FLOOR

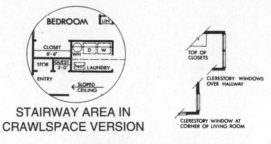

STAIRWAY AREA IN CRAWLSPACE VERSION

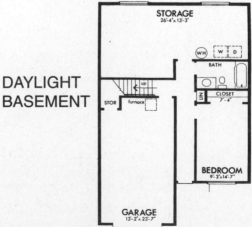

DAYLIGHT BASEMENT

Plans H-951-1A & -1B

PRICES AND DETAILS ON PAGES 2-5

Exciting Great Room Featured

- A brick and wood exterior accented by multiple gables and ornate windows gives this smart-looking one-story home lots of curb appeal.
- The amenity-filled interior is just as exciting. The 17-ft. vaulted foyer leads immediately into the spacious Great Room that also features a 17-ft.-high vaulted ceiling and a handsome fireplace flanked by windows.
- The adjoining dining room flows nicely into the breakfast area and the kitchen. The impressive kitchen offers an angled serving bar and a convenient pantry, while the sunny breakfast area has a French door to the backyard.
- The master suite boasts a 10-ft. tray ceiling and a walk-in closet with a plant shelf. The vaulted master bath features a garden tub and a dual-sink vanity.
- The two remaining bedrooms are serviced by another full bath.

Plan FB-1359

Bedrooms: 3	Baths: 2
Living Area:	
Main floor	1,359 sq. ft.
Total Living Area:	**1,359 sq. ft.**
Garage	407 sq. ft.
Exterior Wall Framing:	2x4

Foundation Options:

Crawlspace
Slab
(All plans can be built with your choice of foundation and framing. A generic conversion diagram is available. See order form.)

BLUEPRINT PRICE CODE: **A**

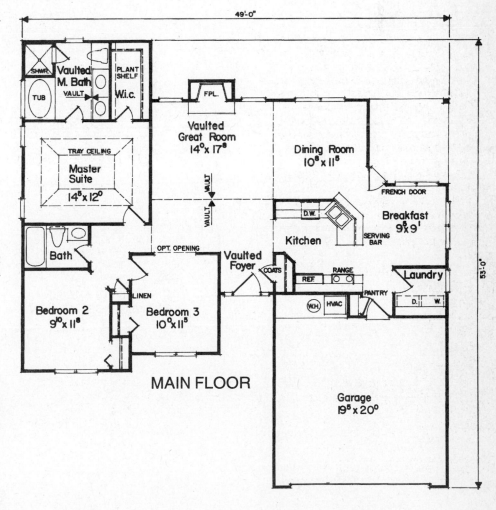

MAIN FLOOR

High-Styled One-Story

- Striking gables, columns and arches give this one-story home high style.
- The vaulted foyer is brightened by a half-round window that echoes the lines of the entryway.
- To the left, columns and an angled wall of windows outline the formal dining room. To the right, the vaulted living room features a picture window that is topped by an artistic transom.
- The living room flows into the vaulted family room, where sliding glass doors open to a backyard deck.
- The roomy kitchen boasts ample counter and closet space, a built-in desk and a center work island. The adjoining breakfast room features a semi-circular bank of windows.
- The secluded master suite offers a vaulted ceiling, abundant closet space and a private bath.
- Two additional bedrooms on the opposite side of the home share a second full bath.

Plan B-91025

Bedrooms: 3	Baths: 2
Living Area:	
Main floor	1,700 sq. ft.
Total Living Area:	**1,700 sq. ft.**
Standard basement	1,700 sq. ft.
Garage	384 sq. ft.
Exterior Wall Framing:	2x4

Foundation Options:

Standard basement

(All plans can be built with your choice of foundation and framing. A generic conversion diagram is available. See order form.)

BLUEPRINT PRICE CODE: **B**

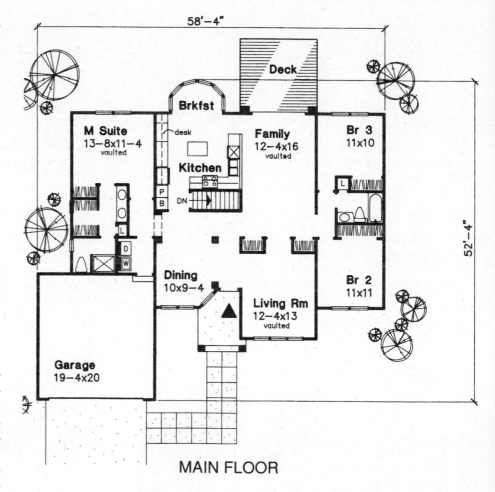

MAIN FLOOR

ORDER BLUEPRINTS ANYTIME!
CALL TOLL-FREE 1-800-820-1283

Plan B-91025

PRICES AND DETAILS
ON PAGES 2-5

Open Invitation

- Classic shutters, distinctive columns and a covered country porch invite you to explore this fine family home.
- Inside, oversized windows allow sunlight to flood the dining area. A handy snack bar fronts the kitchen and serves the adjoining Great Room, providing the perfect space for Super Bowl hors d'oeuvres.
- The Great Room, with its soaring 12½-ft. vaulted ceiling and generous floor space, allows for an abundance of furniture and ample space to mingle. Built-in shelves flank the cozy fireplace.
- A sprawling rear patio embraces the back of the home, and brick steps lead to the backyard. Whether you're barbecuing with friends or worshipping the sun, this haven is sure to please.
- The owner's bedroom enjoys a walk-in closet and a gracious master bath. At the opposite corner of the home, two additional bedrooms with ample closet space share a full bath. The front bedroom features a 10-ft. ceiling.

Plan J-9426

Bedrooms: 3+	Baths: 2
Living Area:	
Main floor	1,689 sq. ft.
Total Living Area:	**1,689 sq. ft.**
Standard basement	1,689 sq. ft.
Garage and storage	467 sq. ft.
Exterior Wall Framing:	2x4

Foundation Options:
Standard basement
Crawlspace
Slab
(All plans can be built with your choice of foundation and framing. A generic conversion diagram is available. See order form.)

BLUEPRINT PRICE CODE:	B

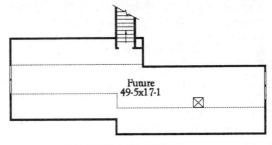

UPPER FLOOR

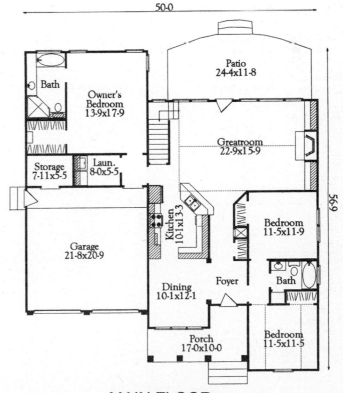

MAIN FLOOR

Victorian Form

- This beautiful home flaunts true-to-form Victorian styling in a modest one-story.
- A delightful, covered front porch and a stunning, sidelighted entry give way to the welcoming foyer.
- The foyer flows into the Great Room, which is topped by a 10-ft. ceiling.
- A turreted breakfast room overlooks the front porch beneath a 16-ft. ceiling!
- The master suite is graced by a window seat and crowned by a 10-ft. stepped ceiling.
- Unless otherwise specified, all rooms have 9-ft. ceilings.

Plan AX-94319

Bedrooms: 3	Baths: 2
Living Area:	
Main floor	1,466 sq. ft.
Total Living Area:	**1,466 sq. ft.**
Standard basement	1,498 sq. ft.
Garage, storage and utility	483 sq. ft.
Exterior Wall Framing:	2x4

Foundation Options:
Standard basement
Crawlspace
Slab
(All plans can be built with your choice of foundation and framing. A generic conversion diagram is available. See order form.)

BLUEPRINT PRICE CODE:	A

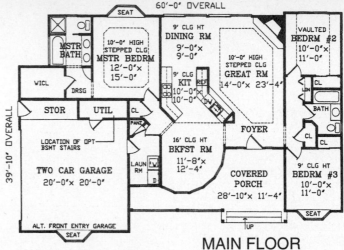

Plan AX-94319

MAIN FLOOR

Ritzy Rambler

- This inviting one-story home is full of fancy touches not usually associated with such an economical floor plan!
- A quaint, covered porch adorns the entry, which leads first to two secondary bedrooms and the well-placed laundry facilities between them.
- At the back of the home, the family room faces a warm fireplace.
- With a versatile center island, the adjoining kitchen and breakfast nook promise easy food preparation. Sliding glass doors lead to a backyard patio.
- Occupying a secluded corner, the master bedroom boasts a roomy walk-in closet and a private bath.

Plan NW-531

Bedrooms: 3	Baths: 2
Living Area:	
Main floor	1,214 sq. ft.
Total Living Area:	**1,214 sq. ft.**
Garage	380 sq. ft.
Exterior Wall Framing:	2x6

Foundation Options:
Crawlspace
(All plans can be built with your choice of foundation and framing. A generic conversion diagram is available. See order form.)

BLUEPRINT PRICE CODE:	A

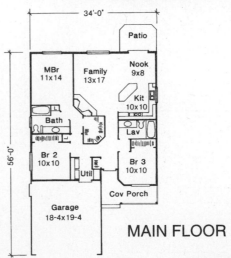

MAIN FLOOR

Plan NW-531

ORDER BLUEPRINTS ANYTIME!
CALL TOLL-FREE 1-800-820-1283

PRICES AND DETAILS
ON PAGES 2-5

First-Home Features

- The first-time home buyer will be delighted with the features included in this 1,040-sq.-ft. ranch design.
- The entry opens into the good-sized living room, which is brightened by corner windows. A handy serving counter that extends from the kitchen makes serving snacks or drinks an easy option when entertaining.
- The L-shaped kitchen provides enough room for a dining area. Sliding glass doors usher in the sun while providing access to the large deck in the backyard. The deck is the perfect spot for a warm-weather barbecue!
- The master bedroom offers two closets, one of which is a walk-in, as well as a personal dressing area with its own vanity and a private entrance to the main bath.
- A secondary bedroom makes a great nursery or guest room. Singles or empty nesters might prefer to use this space for a home office, a casual den or an exercise room.

Plan UDG-90015

Bedrooms: 2	**Baths: 1**

Living Area:

Main floor	1,040 sq. ft.
Total Living Area:	**1,040 sq. ft.**
Standard basement	1,040 sq. ft.
Garage	400 sq. ft.
Exterior Wall Framing:	**2x4**

Foundation Options:

Standard basement
(All plans can be built with your choice of foundation and framing. A generic conversion diagram is available. See order form.)

BLUEPRINT PRICE CODE:	**A**

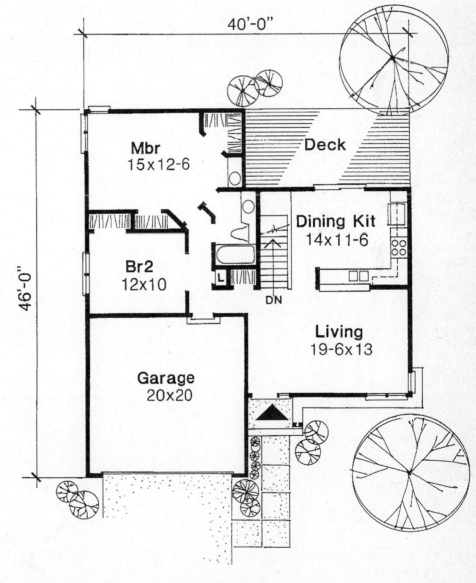

MAIN FLOOR

Stately but Affordable

- Stately columns set off transom windows and support an inviting porch in this well-planned design.
- French doors give classic charm to the central Great Room, which boasts a large fireplace.
- The formal dining room features access to a covered rear porch.

- The unique kitchen arrangement offers a bright, bayed breakfast nook. The peninsula counter allows the cook to view the outdoors while preparing meals or cleaning up.
- A perfect master suite is positioned for peace and quiet. It boasts backyard views, a walk-in closet and a private bath with a garden tub, a separate shower and a dual-sink vanity.
- The two remaining bedrooms feature porch views and walk-in closets, and share a compartmentalized bath.

Plan V-1595

Bedrooms: 3	Baths: 2
Living Area:	
Main floor	1,595 sq. ft.
Total Living Area:	**1,595 sq. ft.**
Garage	473 sq. ft.
Exterior Wall Framing:	2x6

Foundation Options:

Crawlspace
(All plans can be built with your choice of foundation and framing. A generic conversion diagram is available. See order form.)

BLUEPRINT PRICE CODE:	B

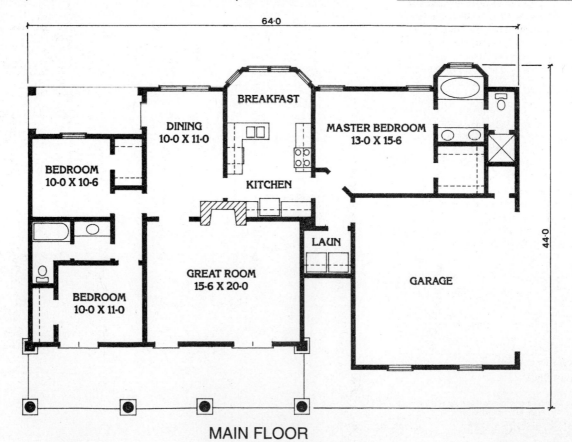

MAIN FLOOR

Plan V-1595

Compact Splendor

- Splendid details abound throughout this compact—and affordable!—home.
- Stunning arched windows greet and welcome impressed visitors. The durable brick exterior will stand the test of both time and the elements.
- Inside, the massive Great Room serves as the home's focal point. Family and friends will love to gather around the central fireplace to visit, play games or relax after a long day. The kitchen's breakfast bar is a great place for kids to enjoy after-school treats.
- The U-shaped kitchen allows the family cook plenty of room to maneuver. Meals in the bayed dining room will be a bit easier with the serving counter.
- You will enjoy countless summer afternoons on the secluded covered patio at the rear of the home.
- Adults can retreat from the patio to the master suite. Large walk-in closets flank the refreshing tub, while a dual-sink vanity with a sit-down makeup area eases morning stress.
- Walk-in closets are unusual additions to the two secondary bedrooms.

Plan KD-1398

Bedrooms: 3	Baths: 2
Living Area:	
Main floor	1,398 sq. ft.
Total Living Area:	**1,398 sq. ft.**
Garage and storage	465 sq. ft.
Exterior Wall Framing:	2x4

Foundation Options:

Slab

(All plans can be built with your choice of foundation and framing. A generic conversion diagram is available. See order form.)

BLUEPRINT PRICE CODE: A

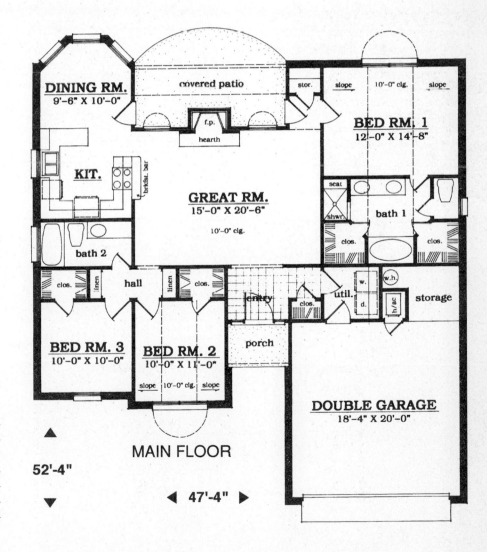

MAIN FLOOR

52'-4"

47'-4"

Captivating Showpiece

- This design is sure to be the showpiece of the neighborhood, with its captivating blend of traditional and contemporary features.
- The angled front porch creates an eye-catching look. Inside, the foyer, the dining room and the Great Room are expanded by 9-ft., 4-in. tray ceilings and separated by columns.
- The dining room features a spectacular arched window, while the spacious Great Room hosts a fireplace framed by windows overlooking the rear terrace.
- The glass-filled breakfast room is given added impact by a 9-ft., 4-in. tray ceiling. The adjoining kitchen offers an expansive island counter with an eating bar and a cooktop.
- A wonderful TV room or home office views out to the front porch.
- The master suite is highlighted by a 9-ft., 10-in. tray ceiling and a sunny sitting area with a large picture window topped by an arched transom.

Plan AX-92322

Bedrooms: 3+	Baths: 2
Living Area:	
Main floor	1,699 sq. ft.
Total Living Area:	**1,699 sq. ft.**
Standard basement	1,740 sq. ft.
Garage	480 sq. ft.
Exterior Wall Framing:	2x4

Foundation Options:
Standard basement
Crawlspace
Slab
(All plans can be built with your choice of foundation and framing. A generic conversion diagram is available. See order form.)

BLUEPRINT PRICE CODE: B

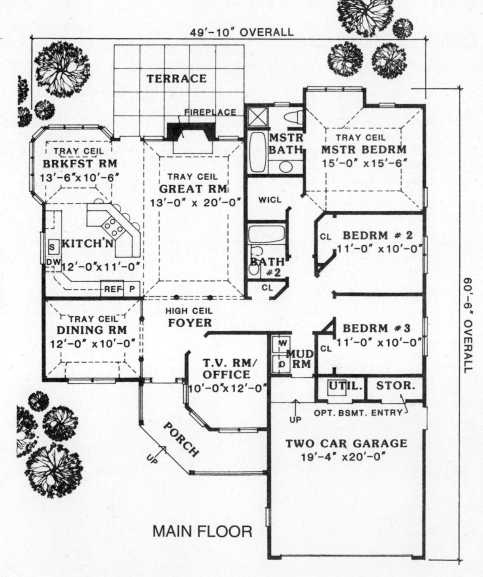

MAIN FLOOR

Plan AX-92322

ORDER BLUEPRINTS ANYTIME!
CALL TOLL-FREE 1-800-820-1283

PRICES AND DETAILS
ON PAGES 2-5

Country Charm, Cottage Look

- An interesting combination of stone and stucco gives a charming cottage look to this attactive country home.
- Off the inviting sidelighted entry, the formal dining room is defined by striking columns.
- The dining room expands into the living room, which boasts a fireplace and built-in shelves. A French door provides access to a cute backyard patio.
- The galley-style kitchen unfolds to a sunny morning room.
- All of the living areas are expanded by 10-ft. ceilings.
- The master bedroom features a 10-ft. ceiling and a nice bayed sitting area. The luxurious master bath boasts an exciting garden tub and a glass-block shower, as well as a big walk-in closet and a dressing area with two sinks.
- Across the home, two additional bedrooms with walk-in closets and private dressing areas share a tidy compartmentalized bath.

Plan DD-1790

Bedrooms: 3	Baths: 2½
Living Area:	
Main floor	1,790 sq. ft.
Total Living Area:	**1,790 sq. ft.**
Standard basement	1,790 sq. ft.
Garage	438 sq. ft.
Exterior Wall Framing:	2x4

Foundation Options:

Standard basement

Crawlspace

Slab

(All plans can be built with your choice of foundation and framing. A generic conversion diagram is available. See order form.)

BLUEPRINT PRICE CODE: B

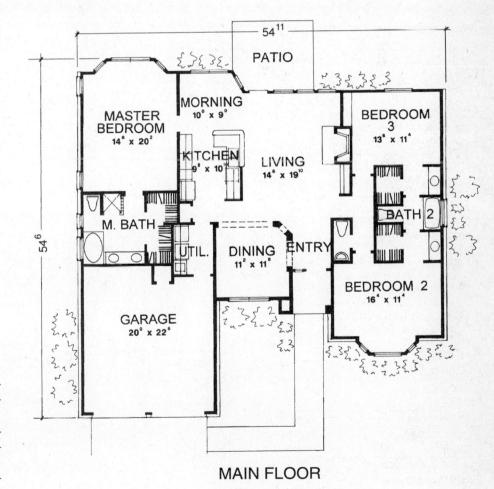

MAIN FLOOR

Gracious Demeanor

- Elegant windows and a covered porch adorn the facade of this country-style home, giving it a gracious demeanor.
- Directly ahead of the ornate foyer, the skylighted living room boasts a cozy fireplace flanked by shelves and cabinets. An impressive 12-ft., 5-in. vaulted ceiling rises overhead, while oversized windows provide great backyard views.
- The adjoining dining room is topped by an elaborate 10-ft. vaulted ceiling and offers a door to a skylighted porch. The porch unfolds to a large patio and accesses the huge garage.
- Behind double doors, the master bedroom presents a 12-ft., 5-in. vaulted ceiling. The master bath flaunts a garden tub and a private toilet.
- At the front of the home, two good-sized bedrooms share a full bath near the laundry room. The den or study may be used as an extra bedroom.

Plan J-9421

Bedrooms: 3+	Baths: 2
Living Area:	
Main floor	1,792 sq. ft.
Total Living Area:	**1,792 sq. ft.**
Standard basement	1,792 sq. ft.
Garage and storage	597 sq. ft.
Exterior Wall Framing:	2x4

Foundation Options:

Standard basement
Crawlspace
Slab
(All plans can be built with your choice of foundation and framing. A generic conversion diagram is available. See order form.)

BLUEPRINT PRICE CODE:	B

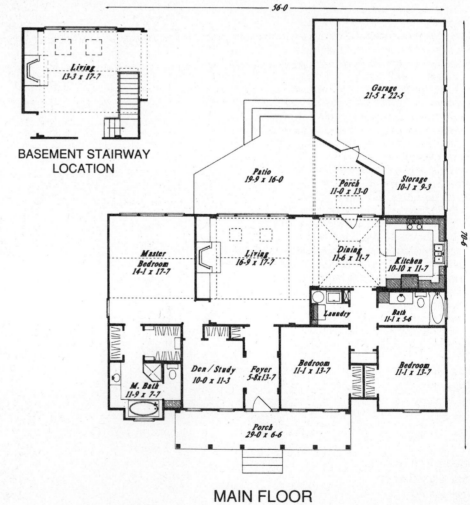

BASEMENT STAIRWAY LOCATION

MAIN FLOOR

French Charm

- The exterior of this charming French home displays great details, including attractive keystones, neat quoins and huge arched window arrangements.
- Inside the home, a high plant ledge adorns the tiled foyer, which boasts a dramatic 13-ft. ceiling.
- To the left, the elegant formal dining room extends to the huge living room, which boasts a warm fireplace and neat built-in bookshelves above functional cabinets. A striking 10-ft. ceiling soars above both rooms.
- A convenient serving bar links the gourmet kitchen to the sunny bayed breakfast nook. The adjacent utility room includes a handy pantry closet.
- Across the home, a tiled foyer features access to a covered porch and the luxurious master suite. The master suite boasts a sloped 10-ft. ceiling, a window seat and a lush private bath, which is highlighted by a marble tub set into a boxed-out window.
- Two more bedrooms share a hall bath. One bedroom features a sloped 10-ft. ceiling and a nice built-in desk.

Plan RD-1714

Bedrooms: 3	Baths: 2
Living Area:	
Main floor	1,714 sq. ft.
Total Living Area:	**1,714 sq. ft.**
Garage and storage	470 sq. ft.
Exterior Wall Framing:	2x4

Foundation Options:

Crawlspace
Slab

(All plans can be built with your choice of foundation and framing. A generic conversion diagram is available. See order form.)

BLUEPRINT PRICE CODE:	B

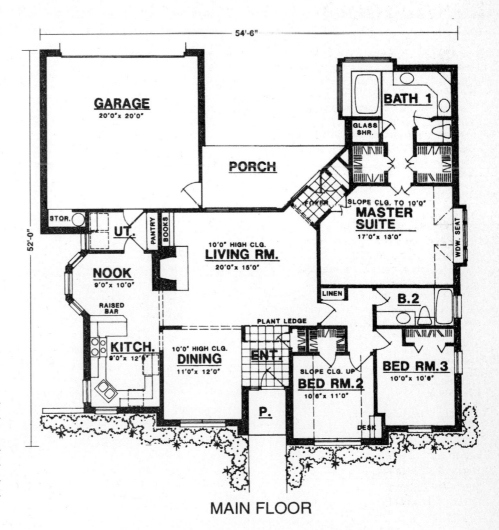

MAIN FLOOR

ORDER BLUEPRINTS ANYTIME!
CALL TOLL-FREE 1-800-820-1283

Plan RD-1714

PRICES AND DETAILS
ON PAGES 2-5

Compact Yet Comfortable

- This efficient and economical design offers a stylish exterior and an interior that provides for comfortable living.
- Smooth, clean lines and a recessed entry characterize the pleasant exterior.
- The combined living and dining area is huge for a home of this size, and the corner fireplace is a real eye-catcher. A French door leads out to the back patio,

a great spot for hosting a summer barbecue with a few good friends.
- The efficient U-shaped kitchen is open to the dining room and includes a floor-to-ceiling pantry as well as abundant cabinet space. A window over the sink brightens daily chores.
- The charming master suite boasts a private bath and a large walk-in closet.
- Two other nice-sized bedrooms share another full bath.
- A small side porch accesses the dining room as well as a large utility and storage area.

Plan E-1214

Bedrooms: 3	Baths: 2

Living Area:

Main floor	1,200 sq. ft.
Total Living Area:	**1,200 sq. ft.**
Utility and storage	100 sq. ft.
Exterior Wall Framing:	2x6

Foundation Options:

Crawlspace
Slab

(All plans can be built with your choice of foundation and framing. A generic conversion diagram is available. See order form.)

BLUEPRINT PRICE CODE:	**A**

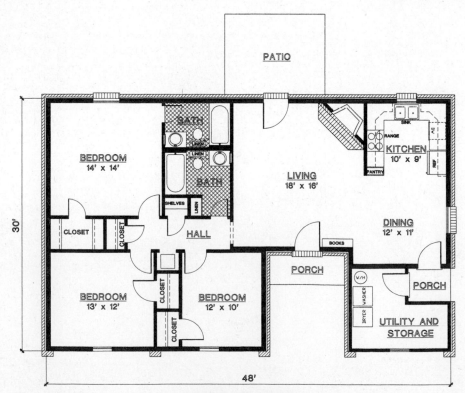

MAIN FLOOR

Plan E-1214

Universal Appeal

- As they observe its elegant window treatments and timeless brick exterior, passersby and guests will marvel at this appealing home.
- The central Great Room will be a surefire hit with young and old alike. For adult gatherings, there is plenty of room to mingle and converse. And what child wouldn't love to sneak an hors d'oeuvre from the breakfast bar and set up camp in front of the crackling fireplace?
- School lunches may be prepared more efficiently on the kitchen's island. Keep your snacks and sandwich bags in the handy pantry!
- If the outdoors calls to you on spring mornings, skip the bayed dining area and enjoy your tea and toast on the shaded backyard patio.
- Privacy and pampering are foremost in the master bedroom, with patio access a quick step away. In the master bath, an eye-pleasing plant shelf overlooks dual walk-in closets and twin vanities with knee space for the woman of the house.

Plan KD-1549

Bedrooms: 3	Baths: 2
Living Area:	
Main floor	1,549 sq. ft.
Total Living Area:	**1,549 sq. ft.**
Garage and storage	472 sq. ft.
Exterior Wall Framing:	2x4

Foundation Options:

Slab

(All plans can be built with your choice of foundation and framing. A generic conversion diagram is available. See order form.)

BLUEPRINT PRICE CODE:	**B**

◄ 49'-4" ►

DINING RM.
12'-4" X 12'-6"
8' clg.

covered patio

clos.

slope   10'-0" clg.   slope

BED RM. 1
12'-8" X 15'-8"

f.p.

hearth

island

pant.

KITCH.
8'-0" X 12'-4"

brkfst. bar

GREAT RM.
16'-4" X 19'-0"

10'-0" clg.

7' ceiling w/plant shelf above

seat.

shwr

bath 1
10'-0" clg.

clos.

clos.

bath 2

53'-8"

clos.   linen   **hall**   clos.

entry
10'-0" clg.   clos.

w.

d.

util.

w.h.

h/ac

storage

BED RM. 3
10'-0" X 11'-0"
8' clg.

BED RM. 2
11'-0" X 11'-0"

porch

slope   10'-0" clg.   slope

DOUBLE GARAGE
18'-4" X 20'-0"

MAIN FLOOR

Affordable Pleasures

- This compact home comes with an affordable price tag and plenty of amenities usually found only in much larger, and more costly, homes.
- An elegant porch with stately columns framing an oversized Palladian window will impress guests and passersby.
- Inside, the foyer looks into the living room at the rear of the home. A corner fireplace adds a comforting glow to all gatherings, while a counter provides a handy place to serve snacks.
- The walk-through kitchen is located between the dining room and the casual morning room. A cheery bay embraces the morning room; a beautiful French door opens to a backyard patio.
- An incredible master bath with a dual-sink vanity, two walk-in closets and a separate tub and shower highlights the master suite nearby.
- All of the rooms mentioned above have 10-ft. ceilings.
- Across the home, two spacious bedrooms with ample closet space share a full hall bath.

Plan DD-1382

Bedrooms: 3	Baths: 2
Living Area:	
Main floor	1,388 sq. ft.
Total Living Area:	**1,388 sq. ft.**
Garage	449 sq. ft.
Exterior Wall Framing:	2x4

Foundation Options:

Crawlspace
Slab

(All plans can be built with your choice of foundation and framing. A generic conversion diagram is available. See order form.)

BLUEPRINT PRICE CODE:	A

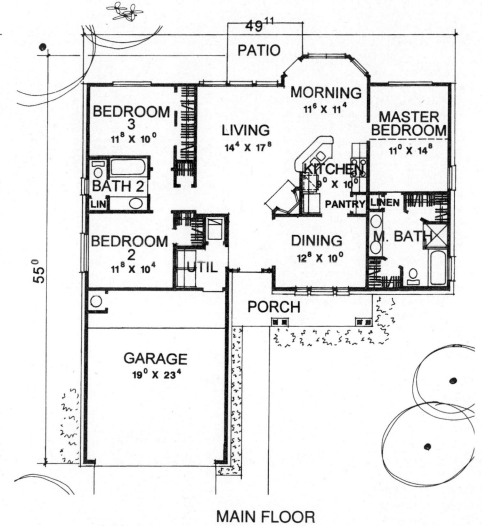

MAIN FLOOR

WOOD EXTERIOR
REAR VIEW

Panoramic Views

- This home lets you take maximum advantage of a particularly scenic or woodsy lot. Its octagonal design directs the focus of decking and window views outward in all directions.
- A fireplace warms the spacious living and dining area, where two sets of sliding glass doors offer deck access.
- The well-planned kitchen is adjacent to the laundry room, to minimize the time spent on chores.
- Bedrooms gain added character from the home's unusual angles. The master bedroom is secluded and boasts a private bath with a spacious shower.
- The basement option gives you a fourth bedroom with a nearby bath—perfect for an aging parent or a boomerang child! A cozy downstairs den lets you work or study in privacy.
- Plans can be ordered for either a wood or a stucco exterior.

STUCCO EXTERIOR
REAR VIEW

Plans H-942-1, -1A, -2 & -2A

Bedrooms: 3+	Baths: 2-3
Living Area:	
Main floor	1,564 sq. ft.
Daylight basement	1,170 sq. ft.
Total Living Area:	**1,564/2,734 sq. ft.**
Tuck-under garage	394 sq. ft.
Exterior Wall Framing:	2x6
Foundation Options:	**Plan #**
Daylight basement (wood)	H-942-1
Daylight basement (stucco)	H-942-2
Crawlspace (wood)	H-942-1A
Crawlspace (stucco)	H-942-2A

(All plans can be built with your choice of foundation and framing. A generic conversion diagram is available. See order form.)

BLUEPRINT PRICE CODE:	**B/D**

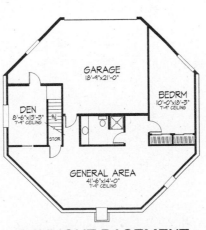

DAYLIGHT BASEMENT

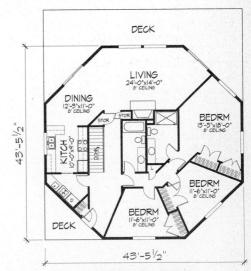

MAIN FLOOR

Mighty Cozy, Mighty Brick!

- Cozier confines can't be found! This one-story brick design's warmth and practicality will be mighty appealing to any prospective home owner.

- From the foyer, step down into the enormous living room—a natural magnet for all your family gatherings. Its impressive fireplace is flanked by a handy media center, while a convenient serving bar connects it to the kitchen. A plant shelf above the bar adds the charm of lush greenery.

- The U-shaped kitchen serves both the breakfast nook and the formal dining area, which steps out to the back patio via an attractive French door.

- A huge walk-in closet is one of the many highlights in the stylish master bedroom. A luxurious, and private, bath and access to the patio add to its excitement.

- Two additional bedrooms allow enough space for a growing family; the foremost bedroom would convert easily into a quiet study if need be.

Plan L-509-TRAD

Bedrooms: 2+	Baths: 2
Living Area:	
Main floor	1,529 sq. ft.
Total Living Area:	**1,529 sq. ft.**
Garage	452 sq. ft.
Exterior Wall Framing:	2x4

Foundation Options:
Slab
(All plans can be built with your choice of foundation and framing. A generic conversion diagram is available. See order form.)

BLUEPRINT PRICE CODE: B

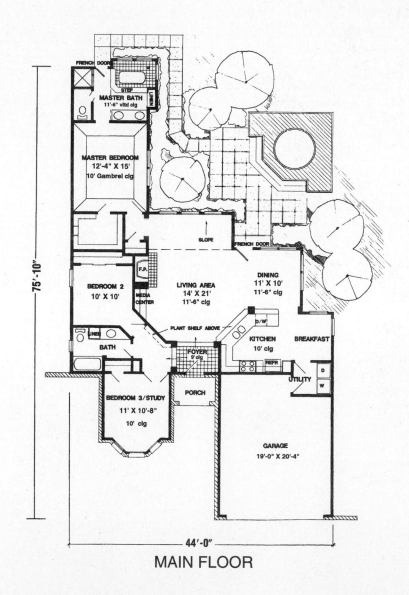

MAIN FLOOR

ORDER BLUEPRINTS ANYTIME!
CALL TOLL-FREE 1-800-820-1283

Plan L-509-TRAD

PRICES AND DETAILS
ON PAGES 2-5

Charming Simplicity

- This home boasts a covered front porch and a simple floor plan, each enhancing the home's charming appeal.
- In the living room, the cozy fireplace offers warmth and drama. Built-in bookcases are featured on either side.
- The adjoining dining room flows into the bright island kitchen and opens to the backyard. Laundry facilities and a carport entrance are nearby.
- The secluded master bedroom offers a sloped ceiling, a corner window, a walk-in closet, a dressing area and a separate bath.
- Two nice-sized bedrooms share a full bath at the opposite end of the home.

Plan J-8670

Bedrooms: 3	Baths: 2
Living Area:	
Main floor	1,522 sq. ft.
Total Living Area:	**1,522 sq. ft.**
Standard basement	1,522 sq. ft.
Carport and storage	436 sq. ft.
Exterior Wall Framing:	2x4

Foundation Options:

Standard basement
Crawlspace
Slab
(All plans can be built with your choice of foundation and framing. A generic conversion diagram is available. See order form.)

BLUEPRINT PRICE CODE: B

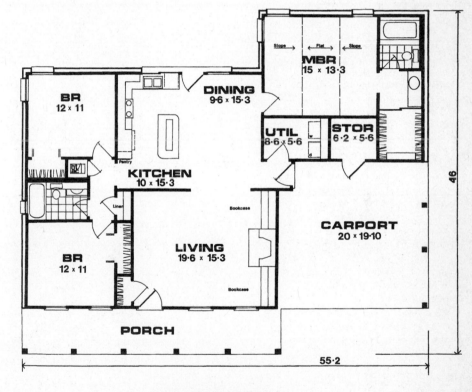

MAIN FLOOR

Easy Living

- This cozy one-story design makes the most of its square footage by neatly incorporating features usually found only in much larger homes.
- Off the covered porch is a spacious living room with a dramatic corner fireplace, a ceiling that slopes to 13 ft., 6 in. and a long view to the backyard patio.
- The living room unfolds to a lovely dining room with a patio door.
- The adjoining kitchen features a snack bar for convenient serving and quick meals. The efficient, U-shaped kitchen also offers a pantry and a broom closet, plus a nearby utility/storage room.
- The gorgeous master suite is positioned for privacy. The bright bedroom has a ceiling that slopes to 11 ft. and a large front window arrangement. The master bath features dual sinks.
- The secondary bedrooms are located at the opposite end of the home and share a convenient hall bath.

Plan E-1311

Bedrooms: 3	Baths: 2
Living Area:	
Main floor	1,380 sq. ft.
Total Living Area:	**1,380 sq. ft.**
Garage	440 sq. ft.
Utility and storage	84 sq. ft.
Exterior Wall Framing:	2x6

Foundation Options:

Crawlspace
Slab
(All plans can be built with your choice of foundation and framing. A generic conversion diagram is available. See order form.)

BLUEPRINT PRICE CODE: A

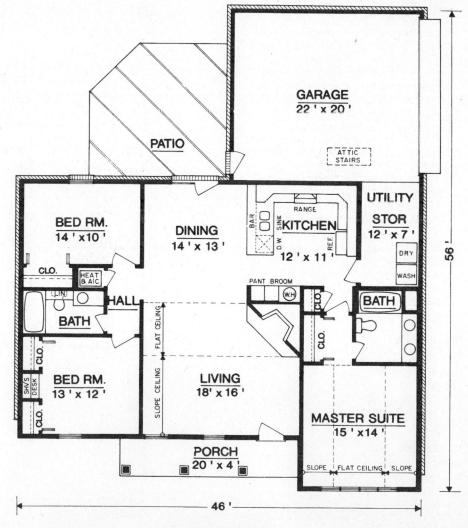

MAIN FLOOR

Plan E-1311

 ORDER BLUEPRINTS ANYTIME!
CALL TOLL-FREE 1-800-820-1283

PRICES AND DETAILS
ON PAGES 2-5

Cathedral of the Sun

- Multiple cathedral ceilings and bay windows turn the interior of this design into a bright, airy retreat.
- The entry porch is illuminated by a skylight. The double-door foyer boasts a cathedral ceiling and another skylight.
- The sunken living room also features a cathedral ceiling, and a bay window overlooks the front of your lot.
- One wall of the formal dining room is a large bay window, and there's another cathedral ceiling overhead.
- The open family room, breakfast room and kitchen offer plenty of space for casual family living. The family room includes a corner fireplace. The bayed breakfast area boasts a cathedral ceiling and Fench doors to the backyard. An angled snack counter connects the breakfast room to the U-shaped kitchen.
- The master bedroom has a bay window that faces the backyard, as well as a walk-in closet and a nice private bath.

Plan AX-98924

Bedrooms: 3	Baths: 2
Living Area:	
Main floor	1,585 sq. ft.
Total Living Area:	**1,585 sq. ft.**
Standard basement	1,633 sq. ft.
Garage	430 sq. ft.
Exterior Wall Framing:	2x4

Foundation Options:

Standard basement

Slab

(All plans can be built with your choice of foundation and framing. A generic conversion diagram is available. See order form.)

BLUEPRINT PRICE CODE: B

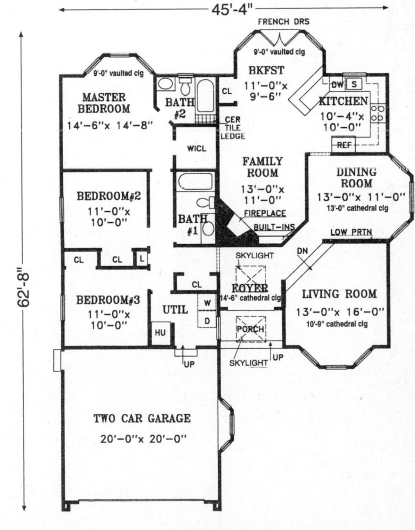

MAIN FLOOR

At One with the Sun

- An open floor plan and large windows on every side of this design allow you to take full advantage of the sun.
- The 12-ft. vaulted, pass-through kitchen opens to a cheerful 12-ft. vaulted sun porch that's the perfect spot to start your day. A serving counter makes the kitchen available to the adjoining formal dining area.
- The dining and living rooms flow together nicely, and are enhanced by 12-ft. vaulted ceilings and views of the large rear deck. A corner fireplace radiates warmth to the living area.
- The master bedroom has twin walk-in closets and a private bath. A 13-ft. vaulted ceiling adds a spacious feel; sliding glass doors open to the deck.
- Another full bath services a nearby secondary bedroom that may be used as a cozy den or home office.
- The full basement offers more potential living space. A guest suite, a family room or a hobby and craft area would nicely round out the floor plan.

Plan B-91012

Bedrooms: 1+	Baths: 2
Living Area:	
Main floor	1,421 sq. ft.
Total Living Area:	**1,421 sq. ft.**
Standard basement	1,421 sq. ft.
Garage	400 sq. ft.
Exterior Wall Framing:	2x4

Foundation Options:

Standard basement

(All plans can be built with your choice of foundation and framing. A generic conversion diagram is available. See order form.)

BLUEPRINT PRICE CODE: A

REAR VIEW

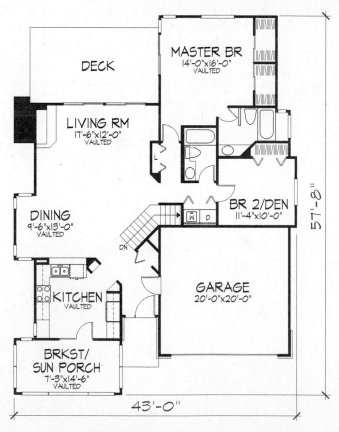

MAIN FLOOR

ORDER BLUEPRINTS ANYTIME!
CALL TOLL-FREE 1-800-820-1283

Plan B-91012

PRICES AND DETAILS
ON PAGES 2-5

Sun-Splashed One-Story

- This unique angled design offers spectacular backyard views, a delightful sun room and two enticing terraces.
- The reception hall opens to the huge combination living and dining area, which is enhanced by a 13½-ft.-high ceiling. A stone fireplace and walls of glass add to the expansive look and the inviting atmosphere.

- The adjoining family room, kitchen and nook are just as appealing. The family room features a built-in entertainment center and sliding glass doors that access the energy-saving sun room. The comfortable kitchen has a handy snack counter facing the sunny dinette.
- The sleeping wing offers three bedrooms and two baths. The master suite boasts a 13½-ft. sloped ceiling, a private terrace, a large walk-in closet and a personal bath with a whirlpool tub. The two remaining bedrooms are just steps away from another full bath.

Plan AHP-9330

Bedrooms: 3	Baths: 2
Living Area:	
Main floor	1,626 sq. ft.
Sun room	146 sq. ft.
Total Living Area:	**1,772 sq. ft.**
Standard basement	1,542 sq. ft.
Garage	427 sq. ft.
Exterior Wall Framing:	2x4 or 2x6

Foundation Options:
Standard basement
Crawlspace
Slab
(All plans can be built with your choice of foundation and framing. A generic conversion diagram is available. See order form.)

BLUEPRINT PRICE CODE.	**B**

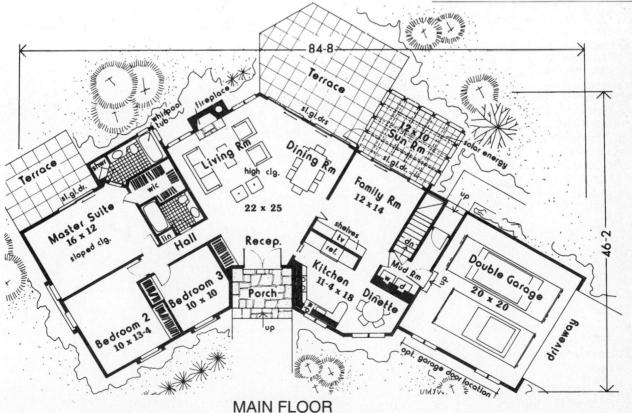

MAIN FLOOR

Smashing Master Suite!

- Corniced gables accented with arched louvers and striking columns take this one-story design beyond the ordinary.
- The vaulted ceiling in the foyer rises to join the family room's 19-ft. vaulted ceiling. A central fireplace is framed by a window and a French door.
- The master suite is smashing, with a 10-ft. ceiling and private access to the backyard. The 13-ft.-high vaulted sitting area offers an optional fireplace.

Plan FB-1671

Bedrooms: 3	Baths: 2
Living Area:	
Main floor	1,671 sq. ft.
Total Living Area:	**1,671 sq. ft.**
Daylight basement	1,671 sq. ft.
Garage	240 sq. ft.
Exterior Wall Framing:	2x4

Foundation Options:

Daylight basement

Crawlspace

(All plans can be built with your choice of foundation and framing. A generic conversion diagram is available. See order form.)

BLUEPRINT PRICE CODE:	B

MAIN FLOOR

Plan FB-1671

Traditional Heritage

- A distinctive roofline and a cozy porch reflect this home's traditional heritage.
- Enhanced by a cathedral ceiling, the living room is warmed by a fireplace and offers a French door to a patio.
- The dining area shares porch access with the stylish gourmet kitchen.
- The master suite features a lavish bath with a garden spa tub.

Plan J-86142

Bedrooms: 3	Baths: 2
Living Area:	
Main floor	1,536 sq. ft.
Total Living Area:	**1,536 sq. ft.**
Standard basement	1,536 sq. ft.
Carport and storage	520 sq. ft.
Exterior Wall Framing:	2x4

Foundation Options:

Standard basement

Crawlspace

Slab

(All plans can be built with your choice of foundation and framing. A generic conversion diagram is available. See order form.)

BLUEPRINT PRICE CODE:	B

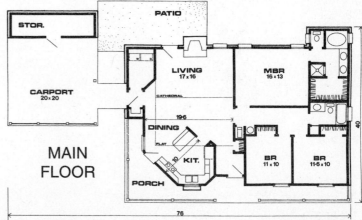

MAIN FLOOR

Plan J-86142

ORDER BLUEPRINTS ANYTIME! CALL TOLL-FREE 1-800-820-1283

PRICES AND DETAILS ON PAGES 2-5

Compact Home
Big on Style

- While compact in size, this stylish one-story presents a open, flowing floor plan with little wasted space.
- Staggered rooflines, elaborate brick accents and beautiful arched windows smarten the exterior.
- The interior offers a large central living room with a 10-ft. ceiling and a warming fireplace flanked by sparkling windows. A comfortable back patio is the perfect spot to relax on a warm spring day.
- The spacious breakfast area merges with the living room and the walk-through kitchen. The formal dining room is located at the opposite end of the kitchen.
- Separated from the other two bedrooms, the master suite is both private and spacious. It offers its own garden bath with twin sinks and walk-in closets, plus a separate tub and shower.

Plan DD-1296

Bedrooms: 3	Baths: 2
Living Area:	
Main floor	1,364 sq. ft.
Total Living Area:	**1,364 sq. ft.**
Standard basement	1,364 sq. ft.
Garage and storage	443 sq. ft.
Exterior Wall Framing:	2x4

Foundation Options:

Standard basement
Crawlspace
Slab

(All plans can be built with your choice of foundation and framing. A generic conversion diagram is available. See order form.)

BLUEPRINT PRICE CODE:	A

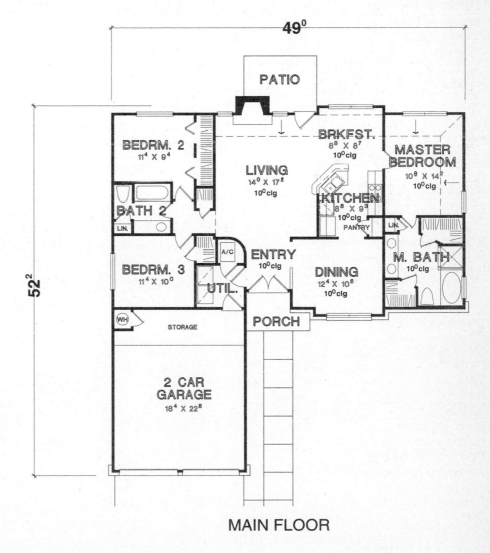

MAIN FLOOR

ELEVATION A

Exciting Exteriors

- Two exciting elevations are available with this striking stucco design. (Both are included with blueprint purchase.)
- With its modest width, this home is perfect for a narrow lot.
- The stately, covered front entry and elegant window treatments conceal a huge formal living and dining area that is topped by a stunning vaulted ceiling.
- A corner fireplace or media center highlights the adjoining family room, which also offers plenty of built-in shelving. Sliding glass doors open to a lovely covered patio with an optional summer kitchen.
- Wide, open spaces enhance the eat-in country kitchen, which overlooks the family room and features a long serving counter and a handy pantry. A tidy laundry closet and access to the two-car garage are nearby.
- Separated from two roomy secondary bedrooms, the master bedroom is a quiet retreat. It offers patio access and an oversized private bath with a huge walk-in closet, a luxurious corner tub and a dual-sink vanity with knee space.

ELEVATION B

Plan HDS-99-140

Bedrooms: 3	Baths: 2
Living Area:	
Main floor	1,550 sq. ft.
Total Living Area:	**1,550 sq. ft.**
Garage and storage	475 sq. ft.
Exterior Wall Framing:	
2x4 or 8-in. concrete block	
Foundation Options:	
Slab	

(All plans can be built with your choice of foundation and framing. A generic conversion diagram is available. See order form.)

BLUEPRINT PRICE CODE: B

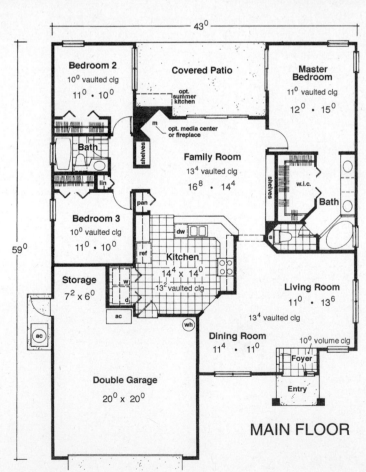

MAIN FLOOR

ORDER BLUEPRINTS ANYTIME!
CALL TOLL-FREE 1-800-820-1283

Plan HDS-99-140

PRICES AND DETAILS
ON PAGES 2-5

Attractive Details

- This appealing design offers dramatic 12-ft. ceilings in the foyer, the living room, the dining room and the kitchen.
- Half-round windows add excitement to the sunken living room. Half-round windows are also found above the kitchen sink and above the sliding patio doors in the dining room.
- The generous kitchen is handily situated between the family room and the dining room for easy food service and efficient

traffic flow. It features a large pantry closet and an eating bar that extends into the family room, where a fireplace invites you to gather with friends and loved ones on chilly evenings.
- Railings around the living room, and plant ledges off the foyer and hallway add decorative touches.
- Secluded to the rear of the home, the master suite has a dressing area with a vanity and a walk-in closet; it adjoins the private master bath.
- Two secondary bedrooms share their own full bath.
- A large rear patio is accessed via the dining room or the family room.

Plan U-87-101

Bedrooms: 3	Baths: 2
Living Area:	
Main floor without basement	1,546 sq. ft.
Main floor with basement	1,588 sq. ft.
Total Living Area:	**1,546/1,588 sq. ft.**
Standard basement	1,588 sq. ft.
Garage	564 sq. ft.
Exterior Wall Framing:	2x6

Foundation Options:

Standard basement
Crawlspace
Slab
(All plans can be built with your choice of foundation and framing. A generic conversion diagram is available. See order form.)

BLUEPRINT PRICE CODE: **B**

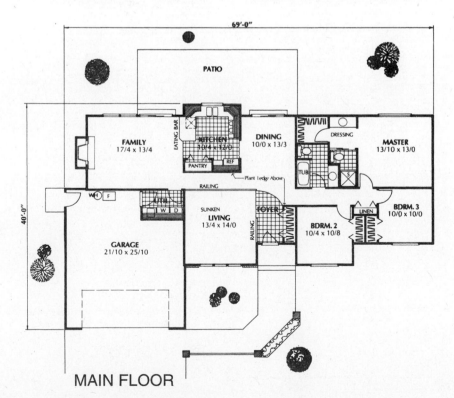

MAIN FLOOR

BASEMENT STAIRWAY LOCATION

Easy, Open Floor Plan

- This attractive home flaunts a mixture of vertical and horizontal wood siding, and the wide-open floor plan permits easy traffic flow.
- A large, central living room merges with a dining area at the back of the home. The skylighted living room features a 10-ft. ceiling, a handsome fireplace and a patio door to a covered side porch.
- The roomy U-shaped kitchen includes a pantry and a convenient eating bar. Nearby, a utility room offers garage access and extra freezer space.
- The isolated master suite boasts a sunny sitting area and a large walk-in closet. The private master bath has two sets of double doors and offers an exciting oval tub, a separate toilet room and his-and-hers sinks in a long, angled vanity.
- Two more bedrooms and another full bath are at the other end of the home.

Plan E-1430

Bedrooms: 3	Baths: 2
Living Area:	
Main floor	1,430 sq. ft.
Total Living Area:	**1,430 sq. ft.**
Garage and storage	465 sq. ft.
Exterior Wall Framing:	2x4

Foundation Options:

Crawlspace

Slab

(All plans can be built with your choice of foundation and framing. A generic conversion diagram is available. See order form.)

BLUEPRINT PRICE CODE:	**A**

MAIN FLOOR

ORDER BLUEPRINTS ANYTIME!
CALL TOLL-FREE 1-800-820-1283

Plan E-1430

PRICES AND DETAILS
ON PAGES 2-5

Welcome Home

- An inviting covered porch welcomes you home to this country-kissed ranch.
- Inside, a 16-ft. cathedral ceiling soars over the expansive living room, which boasts a fireplace flanked by windows.
- Bathed in sunlight from more windows, the dining room flaunts an elegant French door that opens to a delightful backyard porch.
- The gourmet kitchen features a planning desk, a pantry and a unique, angled bar—a great place to settle for an afternoon snack. Garage access is conveniently nearby.

- Smartly secluded in one corner of the home is the lovely and spacious master bedroom, crowned by a 10-ft. tray ceiling. Other amenities include huge his-and-hers walk-in closets and a private bath with a garden tub and a dual-sink vanity.
- A neat laundry closet near the master bedroom is handy for last-minute loads.
- Two secondary bedrooms round out this wonderful design. The front-facing bedroom is complemented by a 10-ft. vaulted ceiling, while the rear bedroom offers a sunny window seat. A full bath accented by a stylish round window is shared by both rooms.

Plan J-91085	
Bedrooms: 3	**Baths:** 2
Living Area:	
Main floor	1,643 sq. ft.
Total Living Area:	**1,643 sq. ft.**
Standard basement	1,643 sq. ft.
Garage and storage	480 sq. ft.
Exterior Wall Framing:	2x4
Foundation Options:	
Standard basement	
Crawlspace	
Slab	

(All plans can be built with your choice of foundation and framing. A generic conversion diagram is available. See order form.)

BLUEPRINT PRICE CODE:	B

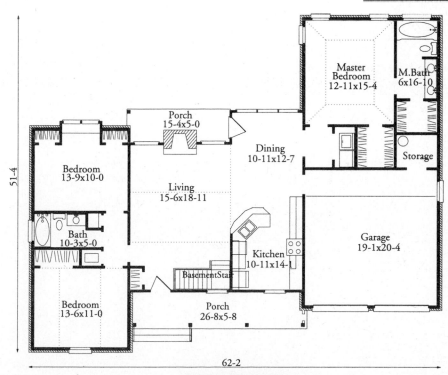

MAIN FLOOR

This Is It!

- This comfortable design is just the plan you're looking for. The affordable design includes all the features—both inside and out—today's family needs.
- The first days of spring will feel even better when you settle into a rocker on the porch and watch the kids play a game of Kick the Can in the front yard.
- Inside, the dining room awaits formal dinners. Built-in cabinets hold the fine china you pull out to celebrate a job promotion or a good report card.
- In the kitchen, a snack bar is the perfect place to feed the kids a snack. The sunshine that pours into the morning room will rouse the spirits of even the sleepiest family member.
- Friends and family will show up at your home to celebrate the Fourth of July on your fun-packed deck.
- In the busy living room, plenty of room is available to dance to your favorite music or gather the clan together to watch the newest release on video.
- When you need a break, retreat to the master suite, where you can savor the peace and quiet in the sitting area.

Plan DD-1716

Bedrooms: 3	Baths: 2
Living Area:	
Main floor	1,738 sq. ft.
Total Living Area:	**1,738 sq. ft.**
Standard basement	1,466 sq. ft.
Garage	425 sq. ft.
Exterior Wall Framing:	2x4

Foundation Options:

Standard basement

Crawlspace

Slab

(All plans can be built with your choice of foundation and framing. A generic conversion diagram is available. See order form.)

BLUEPRINT PRICE CODE: B

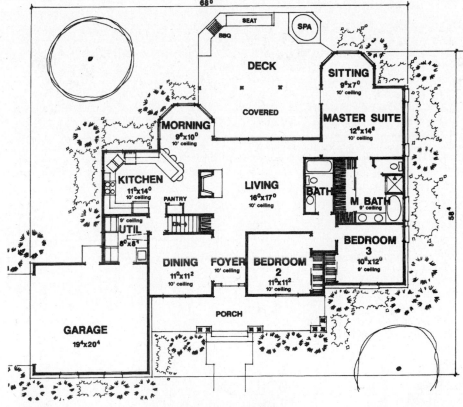

MAIN FLOOR

ORDER BLUEPRINTS ANYTIME!
CALL TOLL-FREE 1-800-820-1283

Plan DD-1716

PRICES AND DETAILS
ON PAGES 2-5

Mediterranean Delight

- Perfect for sunny climes, this delightful stucco home offers luxurious living spaces within a narrow-lot design.
- A clerestory window above the front door spotlights the plant shelves that frame the Great Room.
- The spectacular Great Room features a 12-ft. vaulted ceiling, a striking fireplace and access to a secluded patio.
- Efficiently designed, the cozy kitchen includes a sunny breakfast room, an angled serving bar and close proximity to the two-car garage.
- Isolated at the rear of the home, the master suite offers a 9½-ft. vaulted ceiling, a large walk-in closet and a lavish bath with a soothing garden tub.
- The den adjacent to the master suite could also serve as a guest or additional bedroom.
- The front-facing bedroom boasts a charming boxed-out window and easy access to a full bath.

Plan B-90502

Bedrooms: 2+	Baths: 2
Living Area:	
Main floor	1,200 sq. ft.
Total Living Area:	**1,200 sq. ft.**
Garage	387 sq. ft.
Exterior Wall Framing:	2x4

Foundation Options:

Slab

(All plans can be built with your choice of foundation and framing. A generic conversion diagram is available. See order form.)

BLUEPRINT PRICE CODE: A

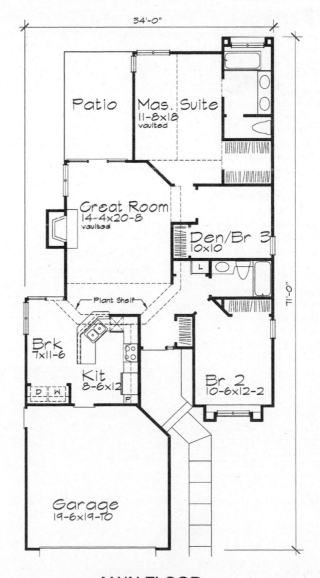

MAIN FLOOR

Roomy, Open Floor Plan

- An interesting mixture of exterior finish materials, including diagonal and vertical cedar siding, wood shingles and brick veneer, adds definition to this appealing one-story home.
- The interior packs a lot of punch as well, featuring an open floor plan accented by several skylights.
- Just off the foyer, the living and dining rooms flow together beneath a stunning 16-ft.-high cathedral ceiling. Skylights and expansive picture windows brighten the area, which is warmed by

an optional three-way fireplace that is shared with the family room.
- The skylighted family room also has a 16-ft. cathedral ceiling, as well as a wall of glass overlooking the backyard. Another option is a built-in entertainment center or shelving unit .
- The sunny kitchen features a 16-ft. ceiling topped with a skylight. A convenient island separates the kitchen from the breakfast room, which boasts a 15-ft. ceiling. The nearby laundry room includes extra closet space.
- The impressive master suite showcases a large sleeping area, two closets and a skylighted bath with a cathedral ceiling.
- The two remaining bedrooms share a second full bath.

Plan AX-98603	
Bedrooms: 3	**Baths:** 2
Living Area:	
Main floor	1,615 sq. ft.
Total Living Area:	**1,615 sq. ft.**
Standard basement	1,615 sq. ft.
Garage	400 sq. ft.
Exterior Wall Framing:	2x4

Foundation Options:

Standard basement

Crawlspace

Slab

(All plans can be built with your choice of foundation and framing. A generic conversion diagram is available. See order form.)

BLUEPRINT PRICE CODE: B

Floor Plan

BASEMENT STAIRWAY LOCATION

- BKFST. AREA
- W. / D.
- CL.
- DN / DN
- GAR.

72'-4''

32'-4''

MAIN FLOOR

- CL. / W. D. / LAUNDRY RM.
- UTIL.
- BKFST. AREA 8x11⁴
- DW / S. / KITCHEN 9x13⁴
- KIT. ISLAND
- SKYLITE
- REF.
- SL.GL.DR.
- FAMILY RM. CATH'DL. CLG. 15x13⁴
- OPT. BUILT-IN
- SKYLITE
- CATH'DL. CLG.
- SKYLITE
- MSTR. BTH.
- BTH. #2
- W.I.CL.
- MSTR. BDRM. 15x13⁴
- CL. / CL.
- OPT. FIREPLACE
- TWO CAR GARAGE 20x20⁰
- CATH'DL. CLG.
- SKYLITE
- DINING RM. 10x12⁴
- SKYLITE
- LIVING RM. 12x13⁴
- RAIL
- FOY
- LIN
- CL.
- CL.
- BDRM. #3 10x10⁰
- BDRM. #2 11x11⁰

ORDER BLUEPRINTS ANYTIME! CALL TOLL-FREE 1-800-820-1283

Plan AX-98603

PRICES AND DETAILS ON PAGES 2-5

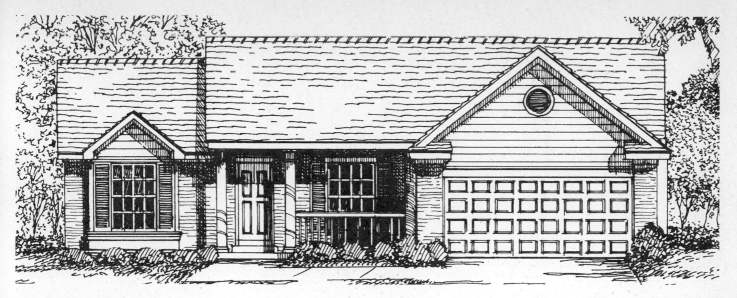

Wish You Were Here?

- This home's inviting front porch and welcoming interior is enough to make anyone wish for the sweet life within.
- With an air of mystery, the foyer allows guests a glimpse of the elegant dining room over a half-wall to the right.
- Ahead, the open living room leaves no room for guessing; its prominent fireplace practically begs you to pull up a chair and relax in the warmth.
- A serving bar brings a casual tone to your gatherings, and joins the living room to the kitchen. Here, you'll find vast counter space and an adjoining breakfast nook that should slow you down on those busy weekday mornings!
- Corner windows spruce up the master bedroom, which provides a pleasant oasis when the cares of your world press in. Past two roomy closets, a private bath awaits to spoil you, complete with a whirlpool tub, a separate shower and a dual-sink vanity.

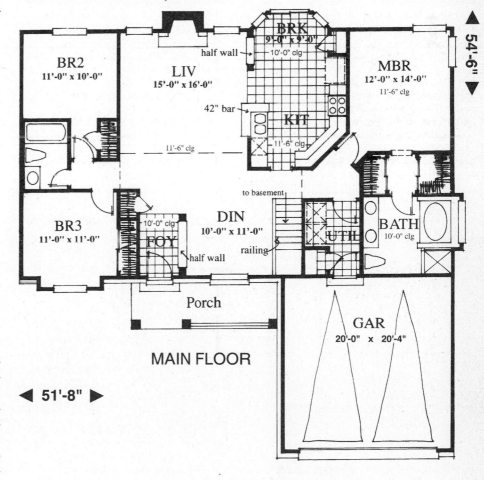

MAIN FLOOR

◄ 51'-8" ►

54'-6"

Plan BRF-1502

Bedrooms: 3	Baths: 2
Living Area:	
Main floor	1,502 sq. ft.
Total Living Area:	**1,502 sq. ft.**
Daylight basement	1,502 sq. ft.
Garage	413 sq. ft.
Exterior Wall Framing:	2x4

Foundation Options:

Daylight basement

(All plans can be built with your choice of foundation and framing. A generic conversion diagram is available. See order form.)

BLUEPRINT PRICE CODE:	B

Extraordinary Split-Level

- This design boasts a striking arched window in an inviting facade that introduces an extraordinary split-level floor plan.
- The recessed entry opens into the expansive living room, with its fabulous windows, handsome fireplace flanked by built-in shelves and breathtaking 12-ft. vaulted ceiling.
- The dining room, which features a 14-ft. vaulted ceiling, expands the open living area and lends an air of spaciousness to the entire main floor.
- The kitchen is a gourmet's dream, offering a wraparound counter, a double sink and a pass-through to the dining room. A 12-ft. vaulted ceiling is shared with the sunny breakfast room, which shows off a built-in desk and sliding-door access to a backyard deck.
- The sizable master suite, a second bedroom and a shared bath are several steps up from the main level, creating a sense of privacy.
- The third bedroom makes a great den, playroom, office or guest room.

Plan B-87112

Bedrooms: 2+	Baths: 2
Living Area:	
Main floor	1,452 sq. ft.
Total Living Area:	**1,452 sq. ft.**
Standard basement	1,452 sq. ft.
Garage	448 sq. ft.
Exterior Wall Framing:	2x4

Foundation Options:

Standard basement
(All plans can be built with your choice of foundation and framing. A generic conversion diagram is available. See order form.)

BLUEPRINT PRICE CODE: A

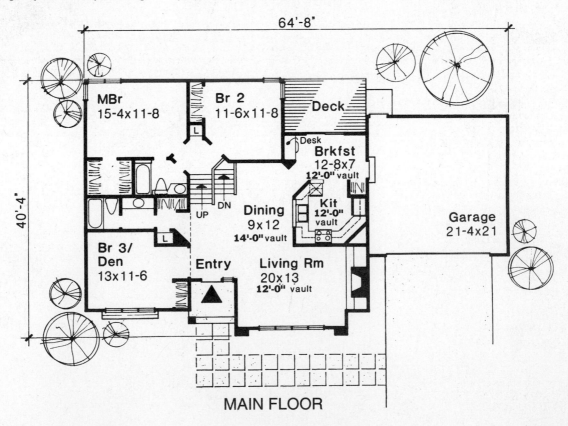

MAIN FLOOR

ORDER BLUEPRINTS ANYTIME! *CALL TOLL-FREE 1-800-820-1283*   Plan B-87112   *PRICES AND DETAILS ON PAGES 2-5*

Distinctive and Elegant

- A distinctive look is captured in the exterior of this elegant one-story. Half-round transoms grace the three glass doors that open to the columned, covered front porch.
- The spacious living room at the center of the homer commands attention, with its 15-ft. ceiling and inviting fireplace. A glass door flanked by windows opens to a skylighted porch, which is also accessible from the secondary bedroom at the back of the home.
- The unique dining room overlooks the two backyard porches and boasts an elegant octagonal design, shaped by columns and cased openings.
- A 14-ft. sloped, skylighted ceiling adds drama to the gourmet kitchen, which also showcases an angled cooktop bar and a windowed sink. Laundry facilities and storage space are nearby.
- The luxurious master suite is secluded at the rear of the home, with private access to the porch. The sumptuous master bath features an oval spa tub, a separate shower, dual vanities and a huge walk-in closet.

Plan E-1628

Bedrooms: 3	Baths: 2
Living Area:	
Main floor	1,655 sq. ft.
Total Living Area:	**1,655 sq. ft.**
Garage and storage	549 sq. ft.
Exterior Wall Framing:	2x6

Foundation Options:

Crawlspace
Slab
(All plans can be built with your choice of foundation and framing. A generic conversion diagram is available. See order form.)

BLUEPRINT PRICE CODE: B

MAIN FLOOR

Classic Country-Style

- The classic covered front porch with decorative railings and columns make this home reminiscent of an early 20th-century farmhouse.
- Dormers give the home the appearance of a two-story, even though it is designed for single-level living.
- The huge living room features a ceiling that slopes up to 13 feet. A corner fireplace radiates warmth to both the living room and the dining room.
- The dining room overlooks a backyard patio and shares a versatile serving bar with the open kitchen. A large utility room is just steps away.
- The master bedroom boasts a roomy bath with a dual-sink vanity. The two smaller bedrooms at the other end of the home share a full bath.

Plan E-1412

Bedrooms: 3	Baths: 2
Living Area:	
Main floor	1,484 sq. ft.
Total Living Area:	**1,484 sq. ft.**
Garage	440 sq. ft.
Exterior Wall Framing:	2x6

Foundation Options:

Crawlspace

Slab

(All plans can be built with your choice of foundation and framing. A generic conversion diagram is available. See order form.)

BLUEPRINT PRICE CODE: A

MAIN FLOOR

A Perfect Fit

- This country-style home will fit anywhere. Its charming character and narrow width make it ideal for those who value vintage styling along with plenty of yard space.
- The quaint covered front porch opens into the living room, which boasts a 12-ft., 8-in. cathedral ceiling and an inviting fireplace.
- The adjacent bay-windowed dining area features a 9-ft.-high vaulted ceiling and easy access to the efficient, galley-style kitchen.
- Off the kitchen, a handy laundry/utility room is convenient to the back entrance. The carport can accommodate two cars and includes a lockable storage area.
- The master bedroom suite offers a roomy walk-in closet, a private bath and sliding glass doors to a rear patio.
- Another full bath is centrally located for easy service to the rest of the home. Two more nice-sized bedrooms complete the plan.

Plan J-86119

Bedrooms: 3	Baths: 2
Living Area:	
Main floor	1,346 sq. ft.
Total Living Area:	**1,346 sq. ft.**
Standard basement	1,346 sq. ft.
Carport	400 sq. ft.
Exterior Wall Framing:	2x4

Foundation Options:

Standard basement

Crawlspace

Slab

(All plans can be built with your choice of foundation and framing. A generic conversion diagram is available. See order form.)

BLUEPRINT PRICE CODE:	A

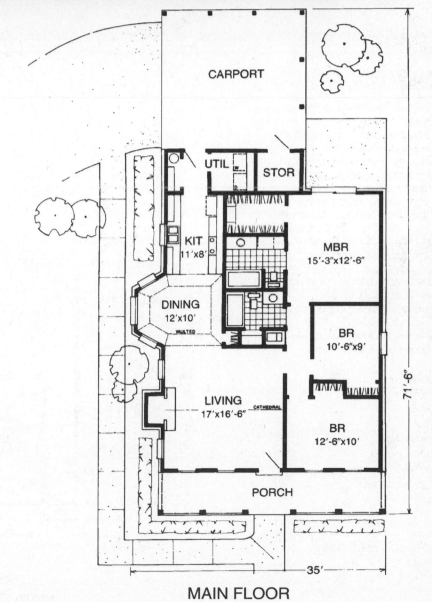

MAIN FLOOR

ORDER BLUEPRINTS ANYTIME!
CALL TOLL-FREE 1-800-820-1283

Plan J-86119

Sleek One-Story

- Steep, sleek rooflines and a trio of French doors with half-round transoms give this one-story a look of distinction.
- The covered front porch opens to the spacious living room, where a central fireplace cleverly incorporates a wet bar, bookshelves and a coat closet.
- Behind the fireplace, the adjoining dining room offers views to the backyard through an arched window arrangement. The two rooms are expanded by 11-ft. ceilings and a covered back porch.
- A snack bar connects the dining room to the U-shaped kitchen, which offers a pantry closet and large windows over the sink. Laundry facilities are nearby.
- The secluded master suite features a large walk-in closet and a private bath. Across the home, the secondary bedrooms each have a walk-in closet and share another full bath.

Plan E-1427

Bedrooms: 3	Baths: 2
Living Area:	
Main floor	1,444 sq. ft.
Total Living Area:	**1,444 sq. ft.**
Garage and storage	540 sq. ft.
Exterior Wall Framing:	2x4

Foundation Options:

Crawlspace

Slab

(All plans can be built with your choice of foundation and framing. A generic conversion diagram is available. See order form.)

BLUEPRINT PRICE CODE: A

MAIN FLOOR

ORDER BLUEPRINTS ANYTIME!
CALL TOLL-FREE 1-800-820-1283

Plan E-1427

PRICES AND DETAILS
ON PAGES 2-5

ONE-STORY HOMES
OVER 1,800 SQUARE FEET

Quite a Cottage

- This cottage's inviting wraparound veranda is topped by an eye-catching metal roof that will draw admiring gazes from neighbors out for a stroll.
- Inside, the raised foyer ushers guests into your home in style. Straight ahead, built-in bookshelves line one wall in the living room, creating a look reminiscent of an old-fashioned library. A neat pass-through to the wet bar in the kitchen saves trips back and forth when you entertain friends.
- The family chef will love the gourmet kitchen, where an island cooktop frees counter space for other projects. For morning coffee and casual meals, the breakfast nook sets a cheery, relaxed tone. When appearances count, move out to the formal dining room.
- Across the home, the master suite serves as an oasis of peace and quiet. First thing in the morning, step out to the veranda to watch the rising sun soak up the mist. When you want a little extra special treatment, sink into the oversized garden tub for a long bath.
- The foremost bedroom boasts a large walk-in closet and built-in bookshelves for the student of the house.

Plan L-893-VSA

Bedrooms: 3	Baths: 2
Living Area:	
Main floor	1,891 sq. ft.
Total Living Area:	**1,891 sq. ft.**
Exterior Wall Framing:	2x4

Foundation Options:

Slab
(All plans can be built with your choice of foundation and framing. A generic conversion diagram is available. See order form.)

BLUEPRINT PRICE CODE: B

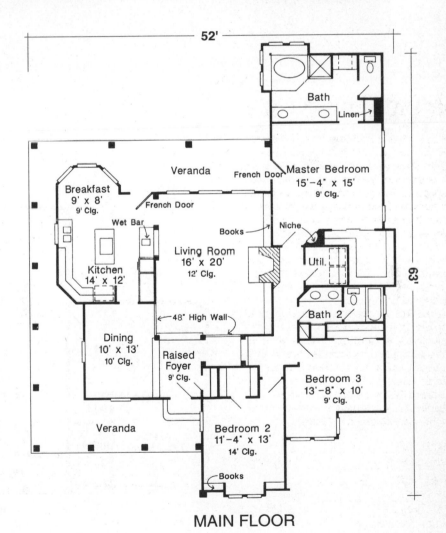

MAIN FLOOR

Wonderful Ranch-Style

- This wonderful ranch-style home offers an L-shaped porch with ornate post detail, an interesting roofline and a classic cupola atop the garage.
- The open floor plan is ultra-modern, beginning with the huge living and dining area. The living room is highlighted by a raised ceiling with rustic beams. The dining room, one step up, is outlined by a railing.

- The super U-shaped kitchen has tons of counter and storage space, including an island cabinet, a desk, a pantry closet and two lazy Susans. The adjoining eating area offers views to the patio and access to the side porch.
- An oversized utility room, a sewing room and a game room are extra features, as are the two storage areas at the rear of the garage.
- The big master suite hosts plenty of closet space, plus a deluxe bath behind double doors. The two smaller bedrooms, each with double closets, share a compartmentalized bath.

Plan E-2502

Bedrooms: 3+	Baths: 2½
Living Area:	
Main floor	2,522 sq. ft.
Total Living Area:	**2,522 sq. ft.**
Garage	484 sq. ft.
Storage	90 sq. ft.
Exterior Wall Framing:	2x6

Foundation Options:
Crawlspace
Slab
(All plans can be built with your choice of foundation and framing. A generic conversion diagram is available. See order form.)

BLUEPRINT PRICE CODE:	D

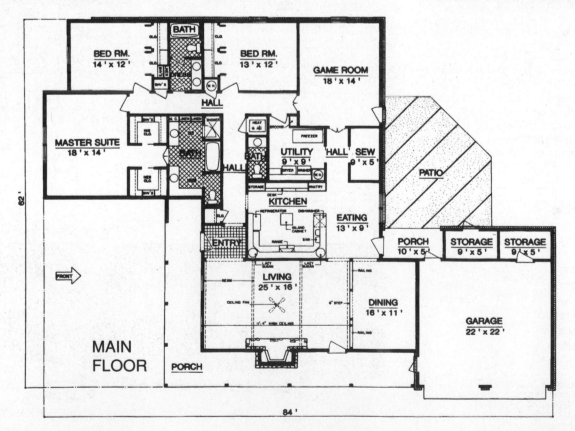

MAIN FLOOR

Plan E-2502

ORDER BLUEPRINTS ANYTIME!
CALL TOLL-FREE 1-800-820-1283

PRICES AND DETAILS
ON PAGES 2-5

Photo by Mark Englund/HomeStyles

Angled Interior

- This plan gives new dimension to one-story living. The exterior has graceful arched windows and a sweeping roofline. The interior is marked by unusual angles and stately columns.
- The living areas are clustered around a large lanai, or covered porch. French doors provide lanai access from the family room, the living room and the master bedroom.
- The central living room also offers arched windows and shares a two-sided fireplace with the family room.
- The island kitchen and the bayed morning room are open to the family room, which features a wet bar next to the striking fireplace.
- The master bedroom features an irresistible bath with a spa tub, a separate shower, dual vanities and two walk-in closets. Two more good-sized bedrooms share another full bath.
- A 12-ft. cathedral ceiling enhances the third bedroom. Standard 8-ft. ceilings are found in the second bedroom and the hall bath. All other rooms boast terrific 10-ft. ceilings.

Plan DD-2802

Bedrooms: 3+	Baths: 2½
Living Area:	
Main floor	2,899 sq. ft.
Total Living Area:	**2,899 sq. ft.**
Standard basement	2,899 sq. ft.
Garage	568 sq. ft.
Exterior Wall Framing:	2x4

Foundation Options:

Standard basement

Crawlspace

Slab

(All plans can be built with your choice of foundation and framing. A generic conversion diagram is available. See order form.)

BLUEPRINT PRICE CODE: D

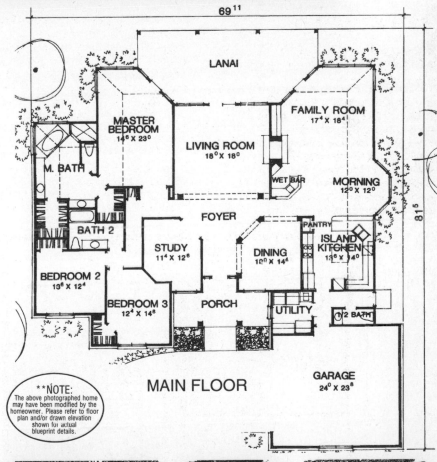

MAIN FLOOR

**NOTE: The above photographed home may have been modified by the homeowner. Please refer to floor plan and/or drawn elevation shown for actual blueprint details.

REAR VIEW

ORDER BLUEPRINTS ANYTIME!
CALL TOLL-FREE 1-800-820-1283

Plan DD-2802

PRICES AND DETAILS
ON PAGES 2-5

103

Sweet Tooth

- Sparkling paned windows and a sweet, many-leveled roofline make this a delectable home for those with taste.
- Guests will smile as they enter the raised foyer, which flows gracefully into the formal entertaining spaces.
- Conversation is easy around the cozy fireplace in the living room, and lively in the adjoining dining room. Open the French doors to the outside and add a touch of starry ambience to your meal.
- The expansive island kitchen features a windowed sink, plenty of counter space and a lovely octagonal morning room surrounded by windows.
- A window seat highlights the airy living room. A wet bar, with a plant shelf above it, keeps occasions festive.
- Three secondary bedrooms are tucked into a private sleeping area at the front of the home; two share a full bath, while another accesses a hall bath.
- Dominating the right wing of the home, the luscious master suite dishes up a variety of treats, including a sitting area with a gazebo ceiling, a massive walk-in closet and a skylighted bath with a luxurious spa tub.

Plan L-2885

Bedrooms: 4	Baths: 3
Living Area:	
Main floor	2,885 sq. ft.
Total Living Area:	**2,885 sq. ft.**
Exterior Wall Framing:	2x4

Foundation Options:

Slab

(All plans can be built with your choice of foundation and framing. A generic conversion diagram is available. See order form.)

BLUEPRINT PRICE CODE:	D

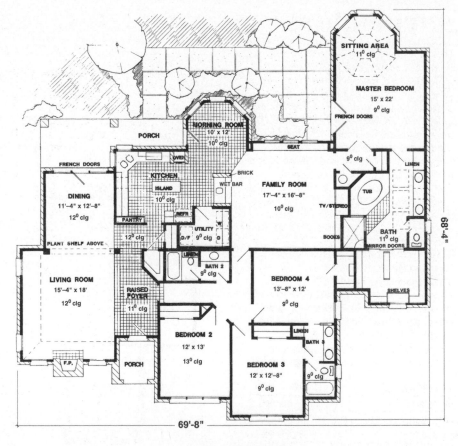

MAIN FLOOR

Intriguing Combination

- This intriguing home is finished with a combination of wood siding and brick, giving it a warm, rustic look.
- Geared for formal entertaining as well as family living, the home offers distinct activity zones. A built-in china hutch and a fireplace add style and function to the formal spaces at the front of the home. Both the living and dining rooms are set off by decorative columns.
- The large-scale family room features a 13-ft. ceiling, a fireplace and a built-in entertainment center. The skylighted sun room and the breakfast area include sloped ceilings and French doors opening to the patio. Typical ceiling heights elsewhere are 9 feet.
- The master suite has a 14-ft. sloped ceiling, private access to the patio and its own fireplace. The adjoining bath offers abundant storage space and a garden tub with glass-block walls.
- Three additional bedrooms and two baths are on the other side of the home.

Plan E-3102

Bedrooms: 4	**Baths:** 3
Living Area:	
Main floor	3,158 sq. ft.
Total Living Area:	**3,158 sq. ft.**
Garage	559 sq. ft.
Storage	64 sq. ft.
Exterior Wall Framing:	2x6

Foundation Options:

Crawlspace

Slab

(All plans can be built with your choice of foundation and framing. A generic conversion diagram is available. See order form.)

BLUEPRINT PRICE CODE: E

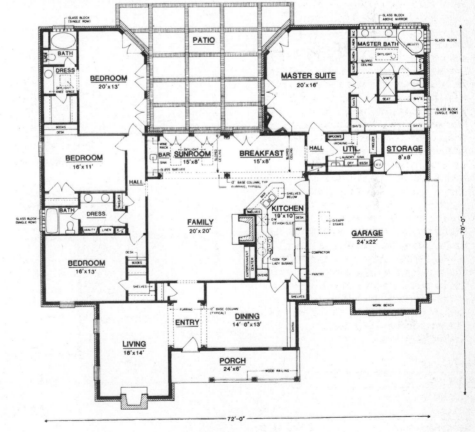

MAIN FLOOR

ORDER BLUEPRINTS ANYTIME!
CALL TOLL-FREE 1-800-820-1283

Plan E-3102

PRICES AND DETAILS
ON PAGES 2-5

Sprawling One-Story

- Stately yet comfortable, this sprawling brick design offers everything that you could desire in a home!
- An impressive vestibule with a raised floor ushers guests into the foyer and living room.
- The vast living room features a fireplace and a hardwood floor; it enters the dining room through a lovely archway.
- Two more brick arches mark the entrance to the family room, which

sports a media center, a fireplace and French doors leading to a rear porch.
- Adjacent to the family room, the gracious breakfast nook basks in sunlight. The galley-style kitchen boasts a snack counter and substantial pantry.
- A hallway behind the kitchen provides garage access and leads to a private guest room and a full bath.
- Across the home, the master suite creates a nest of comfort. Its perks include a romantic fireplace and an opulent bath with a Jacuzzi tub, a separate shower and a dual-sink vanity.
- Two additional bedrooms and another full bath round out this wing.

Plan L-751-HB

Bedrooms: 4	**Baths:** 3
Living Area:	
Main floor	2,749 sq. ft.
Total Living Area:	**2,749 sq. ft.**
Garage	464 sq. ft.
Exterior Wall Framing:	2x4

Foundation Options:

Slab
(All plans can be built with your choice of foundation and framing. A generic conversion diagram is available. See order form.)

BLUEPRINT PRICE CODE: D

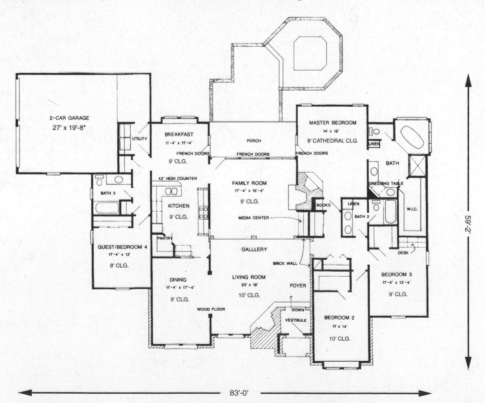

MAIN FLOOR

Plan L-751-HB

Photo by Mark Englund/HomeStyles

Alluring Arches

- Massive columns, high, dramatic arches and expansive glass attract passersby to this alluring one-story home.

- Inside, coffered ceilings are found in the living and dining rooms and the foyer. A bank of windows in the living room provides a great view of the covered patio, creating a bright, open effect that is carried throughout the home.

- The informal, family activity areas are oriented to the back of the home as well. Spectacular window walls in the breakfast room and family room offer tremendous views. The family room's inviting corner fireplace is positioned to be enjoyed from the breakfast area and the spacious island kitchen.

- Separated from the secondary bedrooms, the superb master suite is entered through double doors and features a sitting room and a garden bath. Another full bath is across the hall from the den, which would also make a great guest room or nursery.

Plan HDS-99-179

Bedrooms: 3+	Baths: 3
Living Area:	
Main floor	2,660 sq. ft.
Total Living Area:	**2,660 sq. ft.**
Garage	527 sq. ft.
Exterior Wall Framing:	2x4

Foundation Options:

Slab

(All plans can be built with your choice of foundation and framing. A generic conversion diagram is available. See order form.)

BLUEPRINT PRICE CODE: D

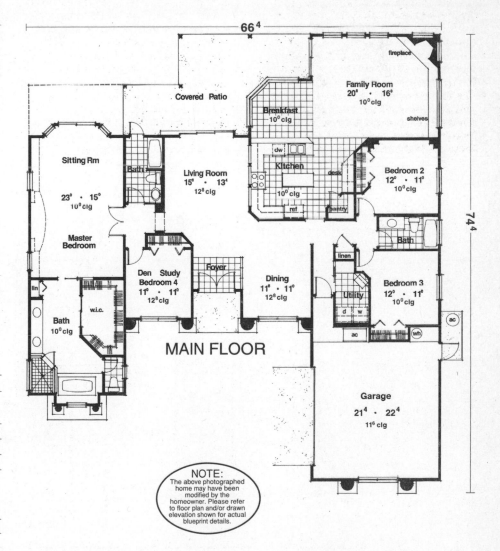

MAIN FLOOR

NOTE:
The above photographed home may have been modified by the homeowner. Please refer to floor plan and/or drawn elevation shown for actual blueprint details.

ORDER BLUEPRINTS ANYTIME!
CALL TOLL-FREE 1-800-820-1283

Plan HDS-99-179

PRICES AND DETAILS
ON PAGES 2-5

107

Vaulted Ceilings Expand Interior

- A dignified exterior and a gracious, spacious interior combine to make this an outstanding plan for today's families.
- A step down from the vaulted entry, the living room offers a 12-ft.-high vaulted ceiling brightened by an arch-top boxed window and a nice fireplace.
- The vaulted dining room ceiling rises to more than 15 ft., and sliding glass doors open to a unique central atrium.
- The island kitchen shares a snack bar with the bayed nook and provides easy service to the dining room.
- The spacious family room boasts a sloped ceiling that peaks at 18 ft. and a woodstove that warms the entire area.
- The master suite is first-class all the way, with a spacious sleeping room and an opulent bath, which features a walk-in closet, a sunken garden tub, a separate shower and a skylighted dressing area with a dual-sink vanity.
- Two secondary bedrooms have window seats and share another full bath.

Plans P-7697-4A & -4D

Bedrooms: 3	Baths: 2
Living Area:	
Main floor (crawlspace version)	2,003 sq. ft.
Main floor (basement version)	2,030 sq. ft.
Total Living Area:	**2,003/2,030 sq. ft.**
Daylight basement	2,015 sq. ft.
Garage	647 sq. ft.
Exterior Wall Framing:	**2x6**
Foundation Options:	**Plan #**
Daylight basement	P-7697-4D
Crawlspace	P-7697-4A

(All plans can be built with your choice of foundation and framing. A generic conversion diagram is available. See order form.)

BLUEPRINT PRICE CODE:	**C**

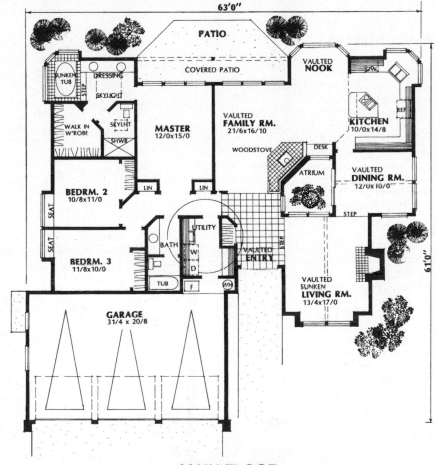

MAIN FLOOR

BASEMENT STAIRWAY LOCATION

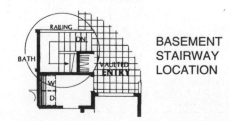
ORDER BLUEPRINTS ANYTIME!
CALL TOLL-FREE 1-800-820-1283

Plans P-7697-4A & -4D

PRICES AND DETAILS ON PAGES 2-5

Friendly Farmhouse

- Reminiscent of a turn-of-the-century farmhouse, this warm, friendly home is characterized by an authentic front porch with fine post-and-rail detailing.
- The open entry provides a sweeping view of the dining room and the adjoining living room. Three columns function as an elegant divider between the two rooms. The living room features a 12-ft.-high sloped ceiling with exposed beams, an inviting fireplace, built-in bookshelves and windows overlooking the rear patio.
- A nice-sized eating area opens to the airy kitchen, which offers a snack bar, a pantry and a lazy Susan. Double doors conceal a utility room with extra storage space.
- Another set of double doors opens to the bedroom wing, where all three bedrooms have walk-in closets. The master bedroom has a private bath with a dual-sink vanity. The secondary bedrooms share another full bath.

Plan E-1813

Bedrooms: 3	Baths: 2
Living Area:	
Main floor	1,892 sq. ft.
Total Living Area:	**1,892 sq. ft.**
Carport	440 sq. ft.
Storage	120 sq. ft.
Exterior Wall Framing:	2x6

Foundation Options:

Crawlspace
Slab
(All plans can be built with your choice of foundation and framing. A generic conversion diagram is available. See order form.)

BLUEPRINT PRICE CODE:	B

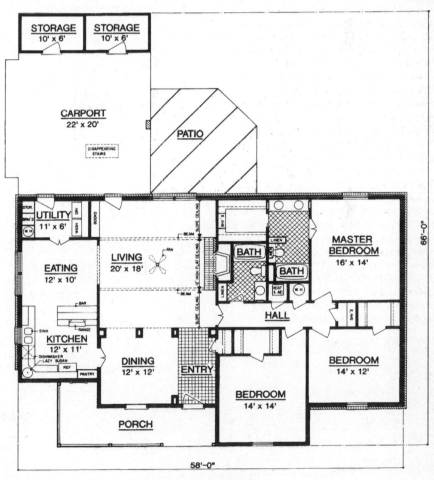

MAIN FLOOR

ORDER BLUEPRINTS ANYTIME!
CALL TOLL-FREE 1-800-820-1283

Plan E-1813

PRICES AND DETAILS
ON PAGES 2-5

109

Easy-Living Atmosphere

- Clean lines and a functional, well-designed floor plan create a relaxed, easy-living atmosphere for this sprawling ranch-style home.
- An inviting front porch with attractive columns and planter boxes opens to an airy entry, which flows into the living room and the family room.
- The huge central family room features a 14-ft. vaulted, exposed-beam ceiling and a handsome fireplace with a built-in wood box. A nice desk and plenty of bookshelves give the room a distinguished feel. A French door opens to a versatile covered rear porch.
- The large gourmet kitchen is highlighted by an arched brick pass-through to the family room. Double doors open to the intimate formal dining room, which hosts a built-in china hutch. The sunny informal eating area features lovely porch views on either side.
- The isolated sleeping wing includes four bedrooms. The enormous master bedroom has a giant walk-in closet and a private bath. A compartmentalized bath with two vanities serves the remaining bedrooms.

Plan E-2700

Bedrooms: 4	Baths: 2½

Living Area:

Main floor	2,719 sq. ft.
Total Living Area:	**2,719 sq. ft.**
Garage	533 sq. ft.
Storage	50 sq. ft.
Exterior Wall Framing:	2x6

Foundation Options:

Crawlspace
Slab
(All plans can be built with your choice of foundation and framing. A generic conversion diagram is available. See order form.)

BLUEPRINT PRICE CODE: **D**

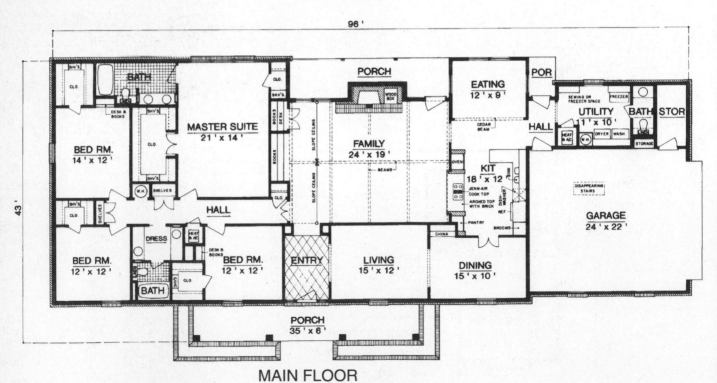

MAIN FLOOR

ORDER BLUEPRINTS ANYTIME!
CALL TOLL-FREE 1-800-820-1283

Plan E-2700

PRICES AND DETAILS
ON PAGES 2-5

Indoor/Outdoor Delights

- A curved porch in the front and a garden sun room in the back make this home an indoor/outdoor delight.
- Inside, a roomy kitchen is open to a five-sided, glassed-in dining room that views out to the porch.
- The living room features a fireplace nestled into a radiant glass wall that adjoins the gloriously sunny garden room—the perfect spot for morning tea!

- Wrapped in windows, the garden room accesses the backyard as well as a large storage area in the unobtrusive, side-entry garage.
- The master suite is no less luxurious, featuring a sumptuous master bath with a garden spa tub, a corner shower and a walk-in closet.
- Each of the two remaining bedrooms has a boxed-out window and a walk-in closet. A full bath with a corner shower and a dual-sink vanity is close by.
- A stairway leads to a bonus room and attic, which provide more potential living space.

Plan DD-1852

Bedrooms: 3	Baths: 2
Living Area:	
Main floor	1,680 sq. ft.
Garden room	240 sq. ft.
Total Living Area:	**1,920 sq. ft.**
Bonus room	316 sq. ft.
Attic	309 sq. ft.
Standard basement	1,680 sq. ft.
Garage and storage	570 sq. ft.
Exterior Wall Framing:	2x4

Foundation Options:

Standard basement
Crawlspace
Slab

(All plans can be built with your choice of foundation and framing. A generic conversion diagram is available. See order form.)

BLUEPRINT PRICE CODE: B

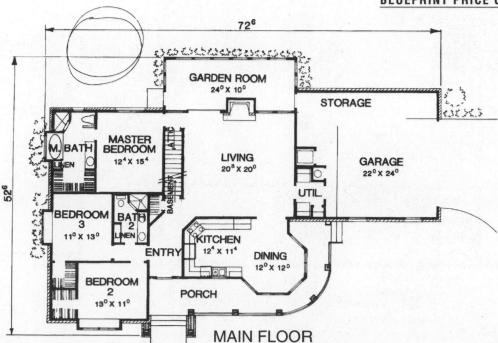

MAIN FLOOR

Plan DD-1852

Classic Styling

- This handsome one-story traditional would look great in town or in the country. The shuttered and paned windows, narrow lap siding and brick accents make it a classic.
- The sprawling design begins with the spacious, central living room, featuring a beamed ceiling that slopes up to 14 feet. A window wall overlooks the covered backyard porch, and an

inviting fireplace includes an extra-wide hearth and built-in bookshelves.
- The galley-style kitchen features a snack bar to the sunny eating area and a raised-panel door to the dining room.
- The isolated master suite is a quiet haven offering a large walk-in closet, a dressing room and a spacious bath.
- Three more bedrooms, two with walk-in closets, and a compartmentalized bath are located at the opposite side of the home.

Plan E-2206	
Bedrooms: 4	**Baths:** 2
Living Area:	
Main floor	2,200 sq. ft.
Total Living Area:	**2,200 sq. ft.**
Standard basement	2,200 sq. ft.
Garage and storage	624 sq. ft.
Exterior Wall Framing:	2x6

Foundation Options:

Standard basement
Crawlspace
Slab
(All plans can be built with your choice of foundation and framing. A generic conversion diagram is available. See order form.)

BLUEPRINT PRICE CODE: C

MAIN FLOOR

ORDER BLUEPRINTS ANYTIME!
CALL TOLL-FREE 1-800-820-1283

Plan E-2206

PRICES AND DETAILS
ON PAGES 2-5

Morning Room
with a View

- This modern-looking ranch is stylishly decorated with a pair of arched-window dormers, handsome brick trim and a covered front porch.
- Inside, the dining room is set off by columns, as it merges with the entry.
- The main living areas are oriented to the rear, where a huge central family room offers a patio view and a fireplace that may also be enjoyed from the bayed morning room and adjoining kitchen.
- The walk-through kitchen features a pantry, a snack bar to the family room and easy service to the formal dining room across the hall.
- The secluded master suite boasts a wide window seat and a private bath with a walk-in closet, a corner garden tub and a separate shower.
- Across the home, the three secondary bedrooms share another full bath. The fourth bedroom may double as a study.
- High 10-ft. ceilings are found throughout the home, except in the secondary bedrooms.

Plan DD-1962-1

Bedrooms: 3+	Baths: 2
Living Area:	
Main floor	1,962 sq. ft.
Total Living Area:	**1,962 sq. ft.**
Standard basement	1,962 sq. ft.
Garage	386 sq. ft.
Exterior Wall Framing:	2x4

Foundation Options:

Standard basement
Crawlspace
Slab
(All plans can be built with your choice of foundation and framing. A generic conversion diagram is available. See order form.)

BLUEPRINT PRICE CODE:	B

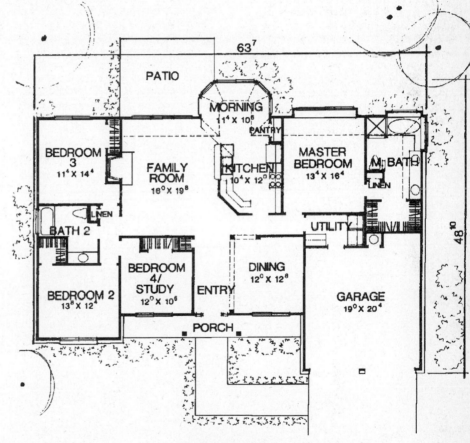

MAIN FLOOR

ORDER BLUEPRINTS ANYTIME!
CALL TOLL-FREE 1-800-820-1283

Plan DD-1962-1

PRICES AND DETAILS
ON PAGES 2-5

113

Elegant Effects

- Repeating arches accent the covered entry of this elegant one-story home.
- The volume entry opens to the formal spaces. The dining room features an 11-ft. ceiling and a built-in hutch. The living room shows off a dramatic boxed window topped with high glass.
- The gourmet kitchen unfolds to a gazebo dinette and a spacious family room with a fireplace and flanking bookshelves. A handy snack bar is incorporated into the kitchen's central island cooktop.

- A nice-sized laundry room sits near the entrance to the garage and offers room for an extra freezer.
- The sleeping wing consists of three bedrooms, two baths and a versatile den that could serve as a fourth bedroom. With the addition of double doors, bedroom no. 3 easily converts to a sitting area for the master suite.
- The luxurious master bath offers a huge walk-in closet and his-and-hers vanities. An exciting oval whirlpool tub is set into a bay window.
- A full basement offers expansion possibilities when the time arrives.

Plan DBI-2206	
Bedrooms: 3+	**Baths: 2½**
Living Area:	
Main floor	2,498 sq. ft.
Total Living Area:	**2,498 sq. ft.**
Standard basement	2,498 sq. ft.
Garage	710 sq. ft.
Exterior Wall Framing:	2x4
Foundation Options:	
Standard basement	

(All plans can be built with your choice of foundation and framing. A generic conversion diagram is available. See order form.)

BLUEPRINT PRICE CODE: C

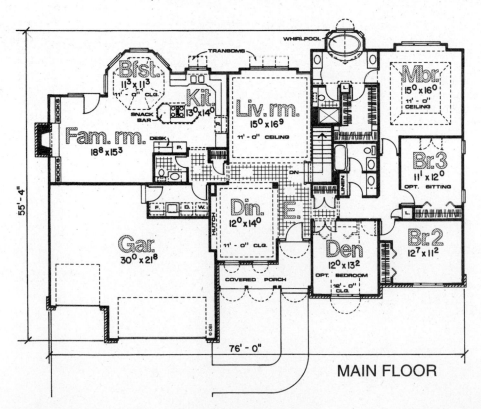

MAIN FLOOR

ORDER BLUEPRINTS ANYTIME!
CALL TOLL-FREE 1-800-820-1283

Plan DBI-2206

PRICES AND DETAILS
ON PAGES 2-5

Features Fit for a King

- Elegant exterior detailing in stucco banding reflects interior features that are fit for a king.
- The dramatic entry court features a raised roof and a Palladian window. The central living spaces offer vaulted ceilings and expansive windows.
- The front-facing den accesses the living room and the master suite and could serve equally well as a fourth bedroom.
- The glassed-in breakfast room overlooks the rear patio and opens to a spacious kitchen and a cozy family room. A wet bar is centrally located.
- A sunny sitting area, a handy juice bar and a luxurious bath are featured in the private master suite.
- Two additional bedrooms, a second full bath and a main-floor laundry room are found at the opposite end of the home, near the angled three-car garage.

Plan B-91017

Bedrooms: 3-4	Baths: 2½
Living Area:	
Main floor	3,381 sq. ft.
Total Living Area:	**3,381 sq. ft.**
Garage	726 sq. ft.
Exterior Wall Framing:	2x6

Foundation Options:

Slab

(All plans can be built with your choice of foundation and framing. A generic conversion diagram is available. See order form.)

BLUEPRINT PRICE CODE: E

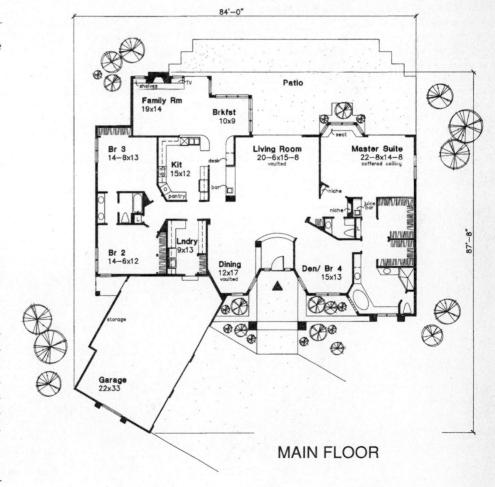

MAIN FLOOR

Sophisticated One-Story

- Beautiful windows accentuated by elegant keystones highlight the exterior of this sophisticated one-story design.
- An open floor plan is the hallmark of the interior, beginning with the foyer that provides instant views of the study as well as the dining and living rooms.
- The spacious living room boasts a fireplace with built-in bookshelves and a rear window wall that stretches into the morning room.
- The sunny morning room has a snack bar to the kitchen. The island kitchen includes a walk-in pantry, a built-in desk and easy access to the utility room and the convenient half-bath.
- The master suite features private access to a nice covered patio, plus an enormous walk-in closet and a posh bath with a spa tub and glass-block shower.
- A hall bath serves the two secondary bedrooms. These three rooms, plus the utility area, have standard 8-ft. ceilings. Other ceilings are 10 ft. high.

Plan DD-2455

Bedrooms: 3+	Baths: 2½
Living Area:	
Main floor	2,457 sq. ft.
Total Living Area:	**2,457 sq. ft.**
Standard basement	2,457 sq. ft.
Garage	585 sq. ft.
Exterior Wall Framing:	2x4

Foundation Options:
Standard basement
Crawlspace
Slab
(All plans can be built with your choice of foundation and framing. A generic conversion diagram is available. See order form.)

BLUEPRINT PRICE CODE:	C

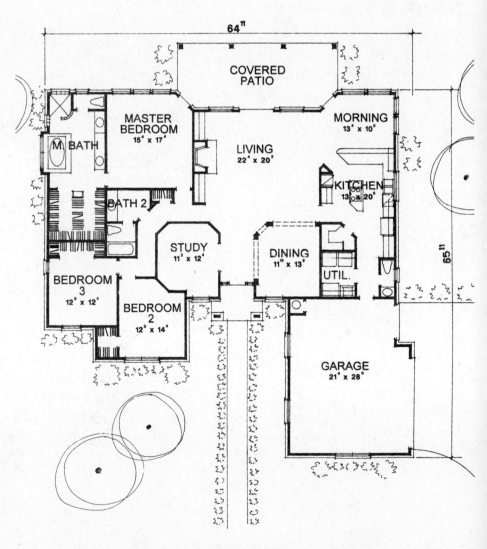

MAIN FLOOR

ORDER BLUEPRINTS ANYTIME!
CALL TOLL-FREE 1-800-820-1283

Plan DD-2455

PRICES AND DETAILS
ON PAGES 2-5

Beautifully Balanced

- The beautifully balanced facade of this warm one-story wraps around a central courtyard. Inside, exciting window treatments and high ceilings brighten and expand the spaces.
- The elegant entrance leads to an impressive foyer, which is enhanced by a 17-ft.-high ceiling and a Palladian dormer window. The adjoining dining room boasts a 10-ft.-high tray ceiling.
- A step down from the foyer, the living room is defined by a railing, a 10-ft. tray ceiling and a fireplace flanked by windows. Another fireplace, this one with an extended hearth for extra seating, can be found in the adjoining family room. The family room also has French doors to the backyard.
- The efficient U-shaped kitchen is paired with a spectacular breakfast room that features a 10½-ft.-high domed ceiling and a neat built-in brick barbecue!
- The huge master suite boasts a 10-ft. tray ceiling, a walk-in closet and a clever compartmentalized bath with a dressing area and a spa tub.
- Three additional bedrooms, one of which would make an ideal office, share a hall bath.

Plan AX-93302	
Bedrooms: 3+	**Baths: 2½**
Living Area:	
Main floor	2,553 sq. ft.
Total Living Area:	**2,553 sq. ft.**
Standard basement	2,424 sq. ft.
Garage	438 sq. ft.
Exterior Wall Framing:	2x4
Foundation Options:	

Standard basement
Slab
(All plans can be built with your choice of foundation and framing. A generic conversion diagram is available. See order form.)

BLUEPRINT PRICE CODE:	D

MAIN FLOOR

- 77'-8" OVERALL
- 53'-0" OVERALL
- FRENCH DRS.
- FIREPLACE
- LIVING RM 19'-4"x15'-0" TRAY CEIL
- BATH #2
- CL
- BEDRM #4 13'-0"x11'-0"
- FAMILY RM 14'-0"x19'-0"
- FIREPLACE
- BKFST 9'-2"x11'-2" DOMED CEIL
- S BW
- KITCHEN 10'-6"x13'-2"
- REF
- LAUN/MUD RM
- DN
- VAULTED CEIL
- DN
- HALL
- LIN
- BEDRM #3 13'-0"x11'-0"
- OFFICE/ BEDRM #2 10'-0"x 12'-0"
- WICL
- DINING RM 14'-0"x12'-0" TRAY CEIL
- FOYER
- CL
- LAV D W CL DN PANT
- DN
- PORCH
- CL CL
- UTIL W/O BSMT
- DRSG LIN CL
- TWO CAR GARAGE 21'-4"x20'-0"
- COURTYARD
- MSTR BATH
- MASTER BEDRM 13'-0"x19'-2" TRAY CEIL
- ALT GAR DR LOCAT →

Fantastic Family Living Space

- Luxury begins at the front door with this exciting one-story traditional home.
- The eye-catching front entry opens to an impressive vaulted foyer. Double doors open to an unusual living room that can be used as a den, a home office or an extra bedroom.
- The formal dining room is crowned by a tray ceiling and has easy access to the combination kitchen, breakfast room

and family room. This fantastic family living space is punctuated by floor-to-ceiling windows, a fireplace and views to the backyard deck.
- Double doors open to the vaulted master suite, which features French doors leading to the deck for romantic moonlight strolls. There's also a luxurious bath with a corner spa tub, as well as a large walk-in closet.
- Two more bedrooms and another full bath are isolated at the other side of the home. This sprawling design is further enhanced by 9-ft. ceilings throughout, unless otherwise indicated.

Plan APS-1812	
Bedrooms: 3+	**Baths: 2**
Living Area:	
Main floor	1,886 sq. ft.
Total Living Area:	**1,886 sq. ft.**
Garage	400 sq. ft.
Exterior Wall Framing:	2x4

Foundation Options:

Slab
(All plans can be built with your choice of foundation and framing. A generic conversion diagram is available. See order form.)

BLUEPRINT PRICE CODE: **B**

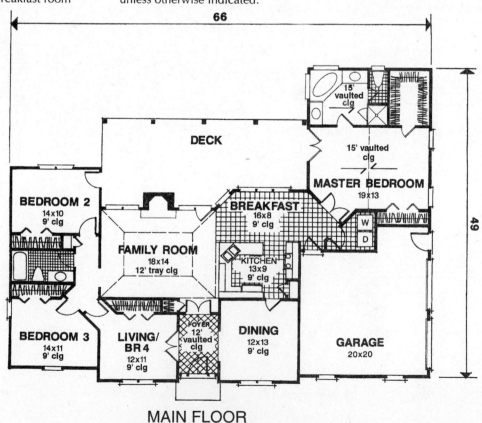

MAIN FLOOR

ORDER BLUEPRINTS ANYTIME!
CALL TOLL-FREE 1-800-820-1283

Plan APS-1812

PRICES AND DETAILS
ON PAGES 2-5

Exciting One-Story

- This exciting one-story home is dramatized by arched windows and a columned entry.
- The 10-ft.-high entry opens to a formal dining room and a spacious Great Room. The dining room features a 12-ft. ceiling and an arched window. The Great Room boasts a stunning two-way fireplace on an angled wall.
- A bay-windowed hearth area with a built-in entertainment center sits on the other side of the fireplace and opens to the breakfast nook and the kitchen.
- The gourmet kitchen caters to the serious cook, with a corner sink, a pantry and a snack bar. The nook has sliding glass doors to the backyard.
- Two secondary bedrooms share a skylighted bath at one end of the home. The addition of French doors to one bedroom turns it into an optional den.
- The master suite at the opposite end of the home has a private, skylighted bath with a whirlpool tub.

Plan DBI-1748

Bedrooms: 3	Baths: 2
Living Area:	
Main floor	1,911 sq. ft.
Total Living Area:	**1,911 sq. ft.**
Standard basement	1,911 sq. ft.
Garage	481 sq. ft.
Exterior Wall Framing:	2x4

Foundation Options:

Standard basement

(All plans can be built with your choice of foundation and framing. A generic conversion diagram is available. See order form.)

BLUEPRINT PRICE CODE: B

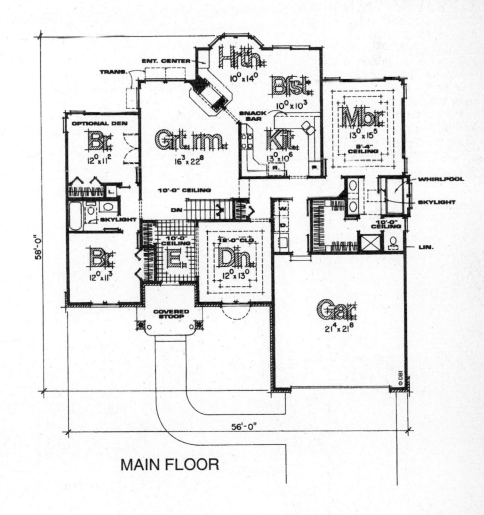

MAIN FLOOR

Quality and Elegance

- Quality brick construction, a sweeping roofline and ornate windows highlight the exterior of this elegant design.
- Inside, the spacious foyer is flanked by the study and the formal dining room, both of which boast 10-ft.-high ceilings.
- The huge living room features a sloped ceiling, a corner fireplace and a wet bar. French doors open to a partially covered patio.
- The kitchen and morning room make a delightful combination, presided over by a 10-ft. sloped ceiling. The kitchen offers a sunny corner sink, a walk-in pantry and a serving bar. The bayed morning room includes a built-in desk and a hutch.
- The private master suite has a 10-ft. sloped ceiling, French doors opening to the patio, a deluxe walk-in closet and an opulent bath with a spa tub and a glass-block shower.
- The two remaining bedrooms, each with a walk-in closet, have standard 8-ft. ceilings.

Plan DD-2572

Bedrooms: 3+	Baths: 2½
Living Area:	
Main floor	2,572 sq. ft.
Total Living Area:	**2,572 sq. ft.**
Standard basement	2,572 sq. ft.
Garage	619 sq. ft.
Exterior Wall Framing:	2x4

Foundation Options:
Standard basement
Crawlspace
Slab
(All plans can be built with your choice of foundation and framing.
A generic conversion diagram is available. See order form.)

BLUEPRINT PRICE CODE:	D

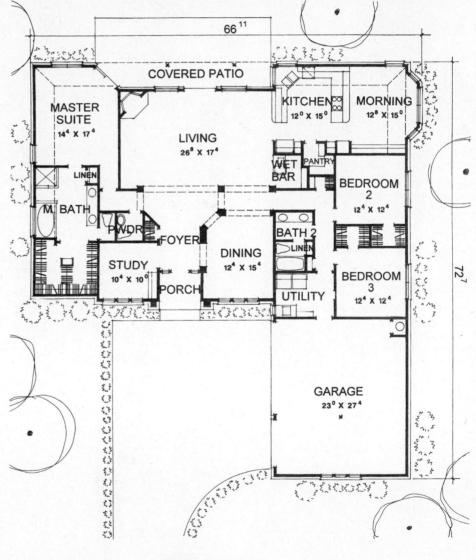

MAIN FLOOR

ORDER BLUEPRINTS ANYTIME!
CALL TOLL-FREE 1-800-820-1283

Plan DD-2572

*PRICES AND DETAILS
ON PAGES 2-5*

Adaptable to Many Lots

- This home's unique design makes it adaptable to almost any lot.
- The interior offers an open floor plan with many exciting amenities, including an arched ceiling at the entry.
- The focal point of the home is the huge central Great Room, which features a 12-ft. ceiling, a dramatic corner fireplace and access to a covered deck.
- The arresting design of the formal dining room, coupled with a beautifully

elegant 8-ft., 8-in. ceiling and easy access to the kitchen makes holiday entertaining a treat.
- The roomy kitchen features a work island with a snack bar, as well as a walk-in pantry, a built-in work desk and a sunny bayed breakfast area.
- The master suite is entered through gorgeous double doors. Inside, a tiered, 10-ft. ceiling soars overhead and a door leads out to the covered deck. The romantic master bath has a garden whirlpool tub, a separate shower and a big walk-in closet.
- Two secondary bedrooms boast plenty of closet space, and share a full bath.

Plan DBI-1689	
Bedrooms: 3	**Baths:** 2½
Living Area:	
Main floor	2,133 sq. ft.
Total Living Area:	**2,133 sq. ft.**
Standard basement	2,133 sq. ft.
Garage and storage	656 sq. ft.
Exterior Wall Framing:	2x4
Foundation Options:	

Standard basement
(All plans can be built with your choice of foundation and framing. A generic conversion diagram is available. See order form.)

BLUEPRINT PRICE CODE:	C

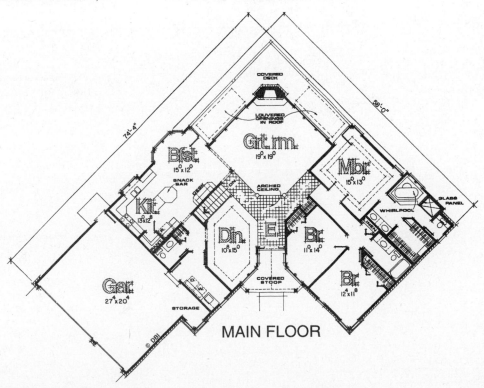

MAIN FLOOR

ORDER BLUEPRINTS ANYTIME!
CALL TOLL-FREE 1-800-820-1283

Plan DBI-1689

PRICES AND DETAILS
ON PAGES 2-5

121

Living Room Overlooks Deck

- This stylish, updated home offers an open floor plan that revolves around a spacious living room; an inviting deck is visible through a spectacular rear window wall. A fireplace flanked by bookshelves adds more drama to this attention center.
- An island kitchen, a morning room with a bow window and a family room combine for convenient family dining or entertaining.
- The formal dining room is also handy for meal serving.
- The sleeping wing includes three bedrooms, two baths and an elegant master suite. Adjoining window seats, a gambrel ceiling and a private bath with dual closets and vanities are highlights of the master suite.
- The entire home is expanded by soaring 10-ft. ceilings.

Plan DD-2755

Bedrooms: 4	**Baths:** 3

Living Area:

Main floor	2,868 sq. ft.
Total Living Area:	**2,868 sq. ft.**
Standard basement	2,800 sq. ft.
Garage	496 sq. ft.
Exterior Wall Framing:	2x4

Foundation Options:

Standard basement
Crawlspace
Slab

(All plans can be built with your choice of foundation and framing. A generic conversion diagram is available. See order form.)

BLUEPRINT PRICE CODE:	**D**

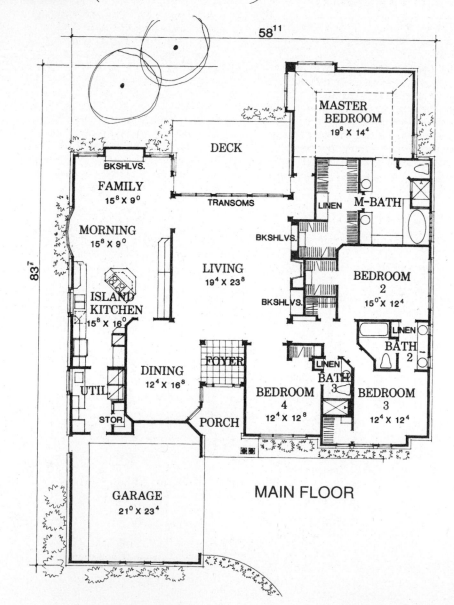

MAIN FLOOR

ORDER BLUEPRINTS ANYTIME!
CALL TOLL-FREE 1-800-820-1283

Plan DD-2755

PRICES AND DETAILS
ON PAGES 2-5

French Flair

- A varied roofline, corner quoins and half-round transoms give this French country home elegance and charm.
- The formal living areas at the front of the home combine to create an impressive sunny space fit for entertaining guests or simply enjoying family time; a see-through fireplace opens to the large island kitchen and bayed breakfast room, opposite.
- Visible from the sun room and kitchen area, the expansive rear patio offers a perfect spot for a hot tub.

- The foyer isolates the bedrooms; a gallery and luxury bath buffer the master suite and private sun room, which can be accessed from both areas. The master bath offers a garden tub, a dual-sink vanity, a corner shower and two walk-in closets.
- Two large secondary bedrooms, which share another full bath, fill out the rest of the sleeping wing.
- An attached two-car garage lies a peaceful distance from the main living areas and can be entered and exited from the nearby utility room, for easy access in inclement weather.

Plan DW-2198	
Bedrooms: 3	**Baths: 2**
Living Area:	
Main floor	2.198 sq. ft.
Total Living Area:	**2,198 sq. ft.**
Standard basement	2,198 sq. ft.
Garage	451 sq. ft.
Exterior Wall Framing:	2x4

Foundation Options:

Standard basement
Crawlspace
Slab
(All plans can be built with your choice of foundation and framing. A generic conversion diagram is available. See order form.)

BLUEPRINT PRICE CODE: **C**

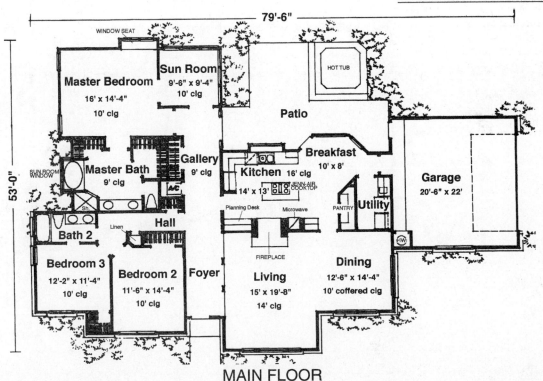

MAIN FLOOR

ORDER BLUEPRINTS ANYTIME!
CALL TOLL-FREE 1-800-820-1283

Plan DW-2198

PRICES AND DETAILS
ON PAGES 2-5

123

Town-and-Country Classic

- A railed front porch, a charming cupola and stylish shutters add town and country flair to this classic one-story.
- The welcoming entry flows into the vaulted family room, which boasts a 14-ft. vaulted ceiling with exposed beams, a handsome fireplace and a French door to a backyard patio.

- The living room and the formal dining room are separated by a half-wall with decorative wooden spindles. The adjoining kitchen features wraparound counter space. The eating nook has a laundry closet and garage access.
- The master bedroom enjoys a private bath with a separate dressing and a roomy walk-in closet.
- Two additional bedrooms are serviced by a compartmentalized hallway bath.
- The two car garage includes a separate storage area at the back.

Plan E-1815

Bedrooms: 3	**Baths:** 2

Living Area:

Main floor	1,898 sq. ft.
Total Living Area:	**1,898 sq. ft.**
Garage and storage	513 sq. ft.
Exterior Wall Framing:	2x4

Foundation Options:

Crawlspace
Slab
(All plans can be built with your choice of foundation and framing. A generic conversion diagram is available. See order form.)

BLUEPRINT PRICE CODE:	B

MAIN FLOOR

ORDER BLUEPRINTS ANYTIME!
CALL TOLL-FREE 1-800-820-1283

Plan E-1815

PRICES AND DETAILS
ON PAGES 2-5

One-Floor Gracious Living

- An impressive roofscape, stately brick with soldier coursing and an impressive columned entry grace the exterior of this exciting single-story home.
- The entry opens to the the free-flowing interior, where the formal areas merge near the den, or guest room.
- The living room offers a window wall to a wide backyard deck, and the dining room is convenient to the kitchen.

- The octagonal island kitchen area offers a sunny breakfast nook with a large corner pantry.
- The spacious family room adjoins the kitchen and features a handsome fireplace and deck access. Laundry facilities and garage access are nearby.
- The lavish master suite with a fireplace and a state-of-the-art bath is privately situated in the left wing.
- Three secondary bedrooms have abundant closet space and share two baths on the right side of the home.
- The entire home features expansive 9-ft. ceilings.

Plan DD-3076

Bedrooms: 4+	Baths: 3
Living Area:	
Main floor	3,076 sq. ft.
Total Living Area:	**3,076 sq. ft.**
Standard basement	3,076 sq. ft.
Garage	648 sq. ft.
Exterior Wall Framing:	2x4

Foundation Options:
Standard basement
Crawlspace
Slab
(All plans can be built with your choice of foundation and framing. A generic conversion diagram is available. See order form.)

BLUEPRINT PRICE CODE: E

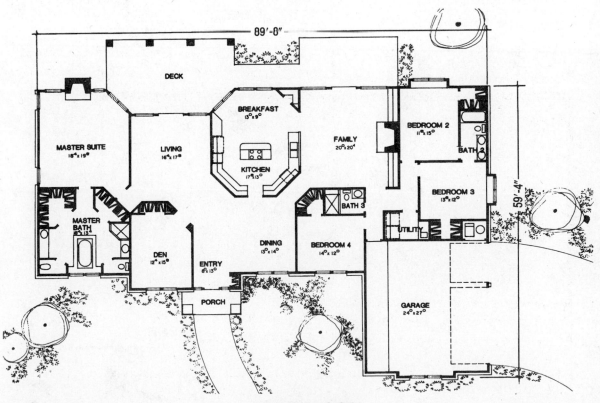

MAIN FLOOR

ORDER BLUEPRINTS ANYTIME!
CALL TOLL-FREE 1-800-820-1283

Plan DD-3076

PRICES AND DETAILS
ON PAGES 2-5

125

Impressive Columns

- Impressive columns and striking stucco give this home a distinguished look.
- Inside, a 14-ft. ceiling extends above the foyer, the formal living and dining rooms and the inviting family room.
- The stunning raised dining room is set off by decorative wood columns that support a wraparound overhead plant shelf. A two-way fireplace is shared with the family room, which also features built-in shelves and arched windows that overlook a large deck.
- The study includes built-in bookshelves and a ceiling that vaults to 13½ feet.
- The kitchen has an angled counter bar and a corner pantry while the breakfast nook provides deck access. Both rooms are enhanced by 10-ft. ceilings.
- The large master suite shows off a bayed sitting area and a roomy, private bath. Ceilings heights here are 10 ft. in the sleeping area and 9 ft. in the bath.
- Two secondary bedrooms with 12-ft. vaulted ceilings share a nice hall bath.

Plan DW-2342

Bedrooms: 3+	Baths: 2
Living Area:	
Main floor	2,342 sq. ft.
Total Living Area:	**2,342 sq. ft.**
Standard basement	2,342 sq. ft.
Garage	460 sq. ft.
Exterior Wall Framing:	2x4

Foundation Options:

Standard basement

Crawlspace

Slab

(All plans can be built with your choice of foundation and framing. A generic conversion diagram is available. See order form.)

BLUEPRINT PRICE CODE: C

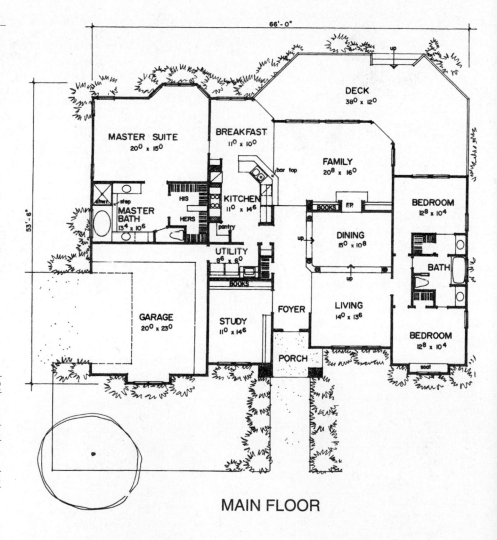

MAIN FLOOR

ORDER BLUEPRINTS ANYTIME!
CALL TOLL-FREE 1-800-820-1283

Plan DW-2342

PRICES AND DETAILS
ON PAGES 2-5

Lap of Luxury

- A high, sweeping roofline with dormers, half-round window details and a rich-looking arched entry with support columns give a formal, estate look to this luxurious one-story home.
- The cathedral-ceilinged entry leads guests between the island kitchen and library to the grand living room.
- With 10-ft. ceilings, a fireplace and glass-wall views to a rear terrace, the living and dining rooms can easily accommodate large, formal gatherings or day-to-day family life.
- French doors unfold to the terrace, which provides a nice spot to relax with a novel or to entertain the family's budding florist.
- The master suite features a fireplace with shelving, plus a lavish bath and an enormous walk-in closet. French doors open to the terrace. A bayed sitting room adds an extra measure of charm, allowing you to recharge your batteries while basking in sunny splendor!
- The three secondary bedrooms offer abundant closet space and share two more baths.

Plan DD-3512-A

Bedrooms: 4+	Baths: 3½
Living Area:	
Main floor	3,512 sq. ft.
Total Living Area:	**3,512 sq. ft.**
Standard basement	3,512 sq. ft.
Garage	810 sq. ft.
Exterior Wall Framing:	2x6

Foundation Options:

Standard basement

Crawlspace

Slab

(All plans can be built with your choice of foundation and framing. A generic conversion diagram is available. See order form.)

BLUEPRINT PRICE CODE:	F

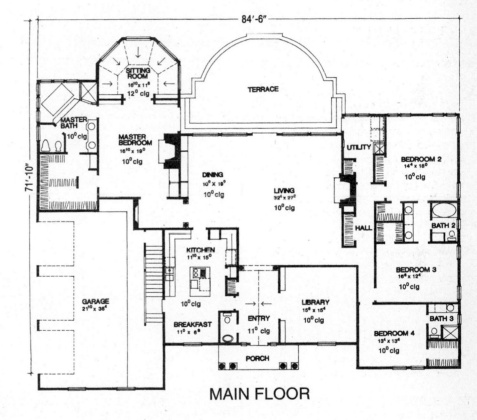

MAIN FLOOR

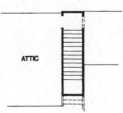

ORDER BLUEPRINTS ANYTIME!
CALL TOLL-FREE 1-800-820-1283

Plan DD-3512-A

PRICES AND DETAILS
ON PAGES 2-5

127

High Drama

- Enormous arched windows, decorative corner quoins and a high, sweeping roofline give this dazzling brick home its dramatic appeal.
- The formal living spaces flank the foyer, each with a vaulted ceiling and attractive windows. The living room also boasts a handsome fireplace.
- The U-shaped kitchen easily serves the dining room and the sunny breakfast nook, which offers French doors to a large backyard lanai.

- Two more sets of French doors brighten the family room, which is further expanded by a 10-ft. sloped ceiling. A unique fireplace with a built-in log bin is adjacent to a handy set of shelves.
- Secluded in its own wing, the luxurious master bedroom has private access to the lanai. The master bath showcases a spa tub, a separate shower, a dual-sink vanity with knee space and his-and-hers walk-in closets.
- Three additional bedrooms occupy a second sleeping wing and share a convenient hallway bath.

Plan DW-2403

Bedrooms: 4	Baths: 2½
Living Area:	
Main floor	2,403 sq. ft.
Total Living Area:	**2,403 sq. ft.**
Standard basement	2,403 sq. ft.
Garage	380 sq. ft.
Exterior Wall Framing:	2x4

Foundation Options:

Standard basement
Crawlspace
Slab

(All plans can be built with your choice of foundation and framing. A generic conversion diagram is available. See order form.)

BLUEPRINT PRICE CODE: **C**

MAIN FLOOR

Plan DW-2403

Garden Home with a View

- This clever design proves that privacy doesn't have to be compromised even in high-density urban neighborhoods. From within, views are oriented to a beautiful, lush entry courtyard and a covered rear porch.
- The exterior appearance is sheltered, but warm and welcoming.
- The innovative interior design centers on a unique kitchen, which directs traffic away from the working areas while still serving the entire home.
- The sunken family room features a 14-ft. vaulted ceiling and a warm fireplace.
- The master suite is highlighted by a sumptuous master bath with an oversized shower and a whirlpool tub, plus a large walk-in closet.
- The formal living room is designed and placed in such a way that it can become a third bedroom, a den, or an office or study room, depending on family needs and lifestyles.

Plan E-1824

Bedrooms: 2+	Baths: 2
Living Area:	
Main floor	1,891 sq. ft.
Total Living Area:	**1,891 sq. ft.**
Garage	506 sq. ft.
Storage	60 sq. ft.
Exterior Wall Framing:	2x4

Foundation Options:

Crawlspace

Slab

(All plans can be built with your choice of foundation and framing. A generic conversion diagram is available. See order form.)

BLUEPRINT PRICE CODE: B

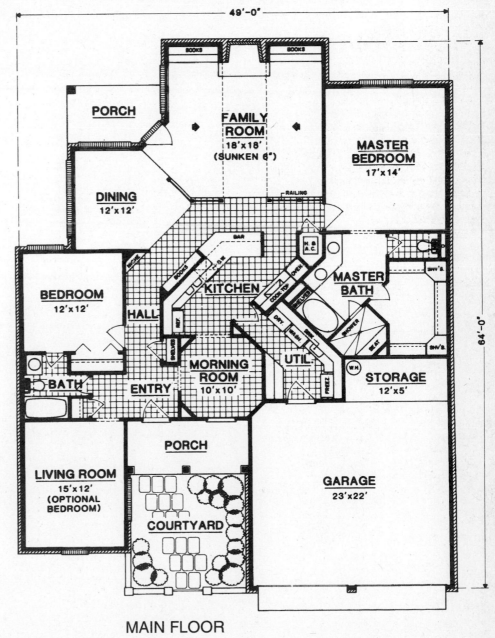

MAIN FLOOR

ORDER BLUEPRINTS ANYTIME!
CALL TOLL-FREE 1-800-820-1283

Plan E-1824

PRICES AND DETAILS
ON PAGES 2-5

129

Captivating Facade

- This home attracts the eye with stately columns, half-round transoms and a sidelighted entry.
- A tall, barrel-vaulted foyer flows between the radiant formal areas at the front of the home.
- The barrel vault opens from the foyer to an overwhelming 14½-ft. vaulted family room, where a striking fireplace and a media center are captivating features.
- The central kitchen offers a dramatic 14½-ft. vaulted ceiling and a snack bar to the breakfast nook and family room. The nook's bay window overlooks a covered backyard patio.
- Formal occasions are hosted in the dining room, which boasts its own bay window and a 10½-ft. vaulted ceiling.
- The secluded master bedroom opens to the patio and flaunts an 11-ft. vaulted ceiling. A large walk-in closet and a posh bath with a step-up garden tub and a separate shower are also featured. On the other side of the home are three additional vaulted bedrooms and two more full baths.

Plan HDS-90-807

Bedrooms: 4	Baths: 3
Living Area:	
Main floor	2,171 sq. ft.
Total Living Area:	**2,171 sq. ft.**
Garage	405 sq. ft.

Exterior Wall Framing:
2x4 and 8-in. concrete block

Foundation Options:
Slab
(All plans can be built with your choice of foundation and framing. A generic conversion diagram is available. See order form.)

BLUEPRINT PRICE CODE:	C

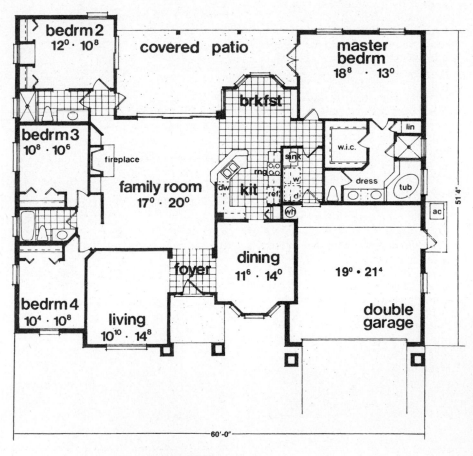

MAIN FLOOR

ORDER BLUEPRINTS ANYTIME!
CALL TOLL-FREE 1-800-820-1283

Plan HDS-90-807

PRICES AND DETAILS
ON PAGES 2-5

Wonderful Windows

- This one-story's striking stucco and stone facade is enhanced by great gables and wonderful windows.
- A beautiful bay augments the living room/den, which can be closed off.
- A wall of windows lets sunbeams brighten the exquisite formal dining room, which is defined by decorative columns and a high 14-ft. ceiling.
- The spacious family room offers a handsome fireplace flanked by glass.
- The kitchen boasts a large pantry, a corner sink and two convenient serving bars. A 13-ft. vaulted ceiling presides over the adjoining breakfast room.
- A lovely window seat highlights one of the two secondary bedrooms, which are serviced by a full bath with a 13-ft., 10-in. vaulted ceiling.
- The magnificent master suite features a symmetrical tray ceiling that sets off an attractive round-top window. The elegant master bath offers a 15-ft.-high vaulted ceiling, a garden tub and dual vanities, one with knee space.
- Ceilings not specified are 9 ft. high.

Plan FB-5009-CHAD

Bedrooms: 3	Baths: 2
Living Area:	
Main floor	2,115 sq. ft.
Total Living Area:	**2,115 sq. ft.**
Daylight basement	2,115 sq. ft.
Garage and storage	535 sq. ft.
Exterior Wall Framing:	2x4

Foundation Options:
Daylight basement
Slab
(All plans can be built with your choice of foundation and framing. A generic conversion diagram is available. See order form.)

BLUEPRINT PRICE CODE: C

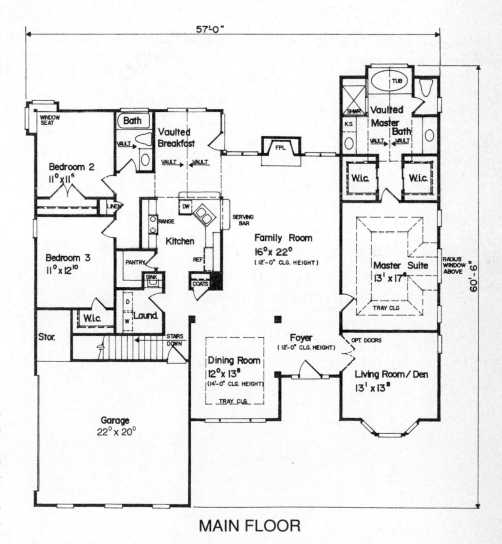

MAIN FLOOR

ORDER BLUEPRINTS ANYTIME!
CALL TOLL-FREE 1-800-820-1283

Plan FB-5009-CHAD

PRICES AND DETAILS
ON PAGES 2-5

131

Interior Angles Add Excitement

- Interior angles add a touch of excitement to this one-story home.
- A pleasantly charming exterior combines wood and stone to give the plan a solid, comfortable look for any neighborhood.
- Formal living and dining rooms flank the entry, which leads into the large family room, featuring a fireplace, a 19-ft. high vaulted ceiling and built-in bookshelves. A covered porch and a sunny patio are just steps away.
- The adjoining eating area with a built-in china cabinet angles off the roomy kitchen. Note the pantry and the convenient utility room.
- The master bedroom suite is both spacious and private, and includes a dressing room, a large walk-in closet and a secluded bath.
- The three secondary bedrooms are also zoned for privacy, and share a compartmentalized bath.

Plan E-1904	
Bedrooms: 4	**Baths:** 2½
Living Area:	
Main floor	1,997 sq. ft.
Total Living Area:	**1,997 sq. ft.**
Garage	484 sq. ft.
Storage	104 sq. ft.
Exterior Wall Framing:	2x4

Foundation Options:
Crawlspace
Slab
(All plans can be built with your choice of foundation and framing. A generic conversion diagram is available. See order form.)

BLUEPRINT PRICE CODE:	**B**

70'-0"

48'-0"

BEDROOM 12'-6" x 12'

PATIO 12'-6" x 12'

MASTER BEDROOM 14' x 14'

CLOSET

DRESSING

BEDROOM 12' x 11'

PORCH 12'-6" x 12'

EATING 11' x 10'

CHINA

CLOSET

STORAGE 13' x 8'

DRESSING

FAMILY 18'-6"x15'

KITCHEN 14' x 12'

DW

REF

PTRY

DISAPPEARING STAIRS

GARAGE 22' x 22'

BEAMS

BEDROOM 12' x 11'

LIVING 12'-6" x 12'

ENTRY

DINING 12'-6" x 12'

OVEN

BRM

UTIL 8'x6'

W

D

PORCH

MAIN FLOOR

Master Suite
Fit for a King

- This sprawling one-story features an extraordinary master suite that stretches from the front of the home to the back.
- Eye-catching windows and columns introduce the foyer, which flows back to the Grand Room. French doors open to the covered veranda, which offers a fabulous summer kitchen.
- The kitchen and bayed morning room are nestled between the Grand Room and a warm Gathering Room. A striking fireplace, an entertainment center and an ale bar are found here. This exciting core of living spaces also offers dramatic views of the outdoors.
- The isolated master suite features a stunning two-sided fireplace and an octagonal lounge area with veranda access. His-and-hers closets, separate dressing areas and a garden tub are other amenities. Across the home, three additional bedroom suites have private access to one of two more full baths.
- The private dining room at the front of the home has a 13-ft. coffered ceiling and a niche for a china cabinet.
- An oversized laundry room is located across from the kitchen and near the entrance to the three-car garage.

Plan EOF-60

Bedrooms: 4	Baths: 3
Living Area:	
Main floor	3,002 sq. ft.
Total Living Area:	**3,002 sq. ft.**
Garage	660 sq. ft.
Exterior Wall Framing:	2x6
Foundation Options:	
Slab	

(All plans can be built with your choice of foundation and framing. A generic conversion diagram is available. See order form.)

BLUEPRINT PRICE CODE:	E

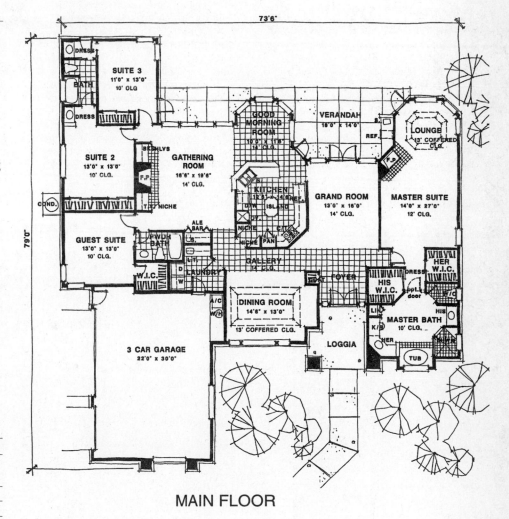

MAIN FLOOR

Ever-Popular Floor Plan

- Open living spaces that are well integrated with outdoor areas give this plan its popularity.
- The covered porch ushers guests into a roomy entry that separates the formal entertaining areas.
- Double doors open to the huge family room, which boasts a 13-ft. vaulted ceiling accented by rustic beams, a raised-hearth fireplace and built-in

bookshelves. Glass doors lead to a covered porch and an adjoining patio, creating a perfect poolside setting.
- A bayed eating area is open to the family room, separated only by a decorative half-wall, and features a large china hutch and great views. The adjacent kitchen has an angled sink for easy service to the family room and the eating area. The utility room and the garage are close by.
- The master suite is secluded to the rear of the home, with a private bath and access to the patio. The two remaining bedrooms share a dual-access bath.

Plan E-2000	
Bedrooms: 3	**Baths:** 2
Living Area:	
Main floor	2,009 sq. ft.
Total Living Area:	**2,009 sq. ft.**
Garage and storage	550 sq. ft.
Exterior Wall Framing:	2x4

Foundation Options:
Crawlspace
Slab
(All plans can be built with your choice of foundation and framing. A generic conversion diagram is available. See order form.)

BLUEPRINT PRICE CODE:	C

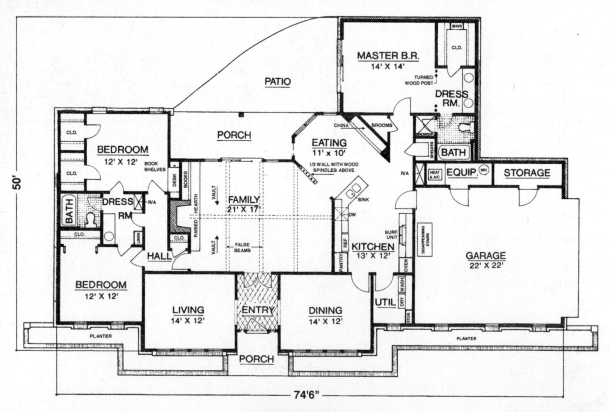

MAIN FLOOR

ORDER BLUEPRINTS ANYTIME!
CALL TOLL-FREE 1-800-820-1283

Plan E-2000

PRICES AND DETAILS
ON PAGES 2-5

Distinguished Living

- Beautiful arches, sweeping rooflines and a dramatic entry court distinguish this one-story from all the rest.
- Elegant columns outline the main foyer. To the right, the dining room has a 13-ft. coffered ceiling and an ale bar with a wine rack.
- The centrally located Grand Room can be viewed from the foyer and gallery. French doors and flanking windows allow a view of the veranda as well.
- A large island kitchen and sunny morning room merge with the casual Gathering Room. The combination offers a big fireplace, a TV niche, bookshelves and a handy snack bar.
- The extraordinary master suite flaunts a 12-ft. ceiling, an exciting three-sided fireplace and a TV niche shared with the private bayed lounge. A luxurious bath, a private library and access to the veranda are also featured.
- The two smaller bedroom suites have private baths and generous closets.

Plan EOF-62

Bedrooms: 3	Baths: 3½
Living Area:	
Main floor	3,090 sq. ft.
Total Living Area:	**3,090 sq. ft.**
Garage	660 sq. ft.
Exterior Wall Framing:	2x6

Foundation Options:

Slab
(All plans can be built with your choice of foundation and framing.
A generic conversion diagram is available. See order form.)

BLUEPRINT PRICE CODE: E

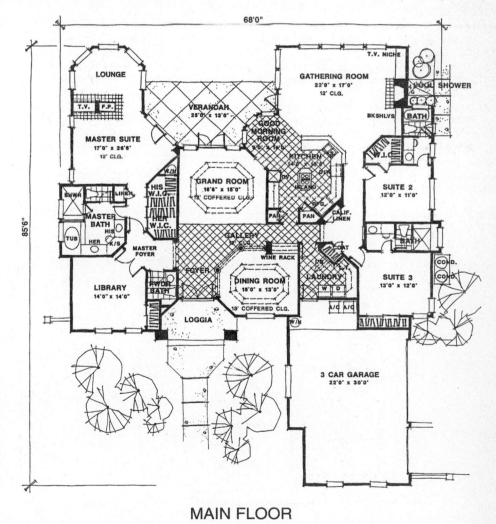

MAIN FLOOR

ORDER BLUEPRINTS ANYTIME!
CALL TOLL-FREE 1-800-820-1283

Plan EOF-62

PRICES AND DETAILS
ON PAGES 2-5

135

Stunning Style

- The stunning detailing of this stucco home includes a stately roofline and an arched window above the entry door.
- The open floor plan begins at the foyer, where a column is all that separates the dining room from the living room. A 13½-ft. ceiling creates a dramatic effect in the living room.
- A sunny breakfast room and a great kitchen with a huge serving bar adjoin a 14½-ft.-high vaulted family room.
- The master suite has an 11-ft. tray ceiling in the sleeping area and a luxurious bath with a spa tub, a separate shower and a walk-in closet.

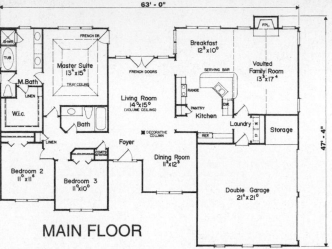

MAIN FLOOR

Plan FB-1802

Plan FB-1802

Bedrooms: 3	Baths: 2
Living Area:	
Main floor	1,802 sq. ft.
Total Living Area:	**1,802 sq. ft.**
Garage and storage	492 sq. ft.
Exterior Wall Framing:	2x4

Foundation Options:

Crawlspace, slab

(All plans can be built with your choice of foundation and framing. A generic conversion diagram is available. See order form.)

BLUEPRINT PRICE CODE:	B

Elegant Facade

- Eye-catching windows and columns add elegance to this ranch-style home.
- The columns of the front porch repeat inside, defining the gallery. The central section soars to 20 ft., 4 in., basking in sunlight from a windowed dormer. The Great Room features a fireplace.
- The gourmet kitchen offers a handy snack bar, while the breakfast room expands to a columned rear porch.
- Ceilings are at least 9½ ft. high throughout the home.

Plan AX-4315

Bedrooms: 3	Baths: 2
Living Area:	
Main floor	2,018 sq. ft.
Total Living Area:	**2,018 sq. ft.**
Basement	2,018 sq. ft.
Garage/storage/utility	474 sq. ft.
Exterior Wall Framing:	2x4

Foundation Options:

Daylight basement, standard basement, crawlspace, slab

(All plans can be built with your choice of foundation and framing. A generic conversion diagram is available. See order form.)

BLUEPRINT PRICE CODE:	C

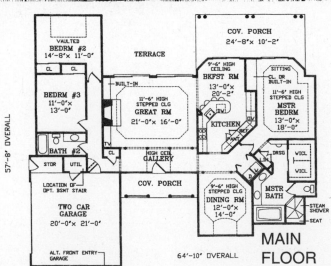

MAIN FLOOR

Plan AX-4315

ORDER BLUEPRINTS ANYTIME!
CALL TOLL-FREE 1-800-820-1283

PRICES AND DETAILS
ON PAGES 2-5

Classic Ranch

- This classic ranch design offers four bedrooms plus plenty of other space for living and entertaining.
- Double doors usher guests into the entry, which leads into the inviting family room. Here, a 17-ft. cathedral ceiling is supported by exposed beams. A fire crackles in the fireplace, and sliding glass doors lead out to a covered rear porch.
- The adjoining kitchen and sunny, raised eating area are sure to be the scene of some memorable family times. The

kitchen opens at the front end to the quiet dining room, which unfolds into the formal living room.
- The sumptuous master suite envelops you in luxury. The bedroom boasts a sun-drenched sitting area with double doors to the back porch. The dressing area has an adjoining walk-in closet. A sunken tub in the private bath waits to soothe your cares away.
- Three roomy secondary bedrooms share a full bath. Two of the rooms feature walk-in closets; the other has a built-in desk with bookshelves.
- The garage boasts a big storage closet.

Plan E-2602	
Bedrooms: 4	**Baths:** 2½
Living Area:	
Main floor	2,597 sq. ft.
Total Living Area:	**2,597 sq. ft.**
Garage	462 sq. ft.
Storage	64 sq. ft.
Exterior Wall Framing:	2x4

Foundation Options:

Crawlspace
Slab
(All plans can be built with your choice of foundation and framing. A generic conversion diagram is available. See order form.)

BLUEPRINT PRICE CODE:	D

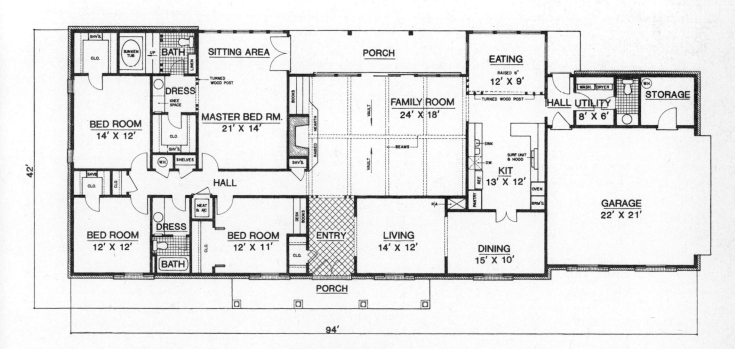

MAIN FLOOR

Bright Design

- Sweeping rooflines, arched transom windows and a stucco exterior give this exciting design a special flair.
- Inside the high, dramatic entry, guests are greeted with a stunning view of the living room, which is expanded by a 12-ft. volume ceiling. This formal expanse is augmented by an oversized bay that looks out onto a covered patio and possible pool area.
- To the left of the foyer is the formal dining room, accented by columns and a 14-ft. receding tray ceiling.
- The island kitchen overlooks a sunny breakfast nook and a large family room, each with 12-ft.-high ceilings. A handy pass-through transports food to the patio, which offers a summer kitchen.
- The master wing includes a large bedroom with a 10-ft.-high coffered ceiling, a sitting area with patio access, a massive walk-in closet and a sun-drenched garden bath.
- The private den/study could also serve as an extra bedroom.
- Two to three more bedrooms share two full baths. The front bedrooms boast 12-ft. ceilings and the rear bedroom is accented by a 10-ft. ceiling.

Plan HDS-90-814

Bedrooms: 3+	Baths: 3½
Living Area:	
Main floor	3,743 sq. ft.
Total Living Area:	**3,743 sq. ft.**
Garage	725 sq. ft.

Exterior Wall Framing:
2x4 and 8-in. concrete block

Foundation Options:
Slab
(All plans can be built with your choice of foundation and framing. A generic conversion diagram is available. See order form.)

BLUEPRINT PRICE CODE: F

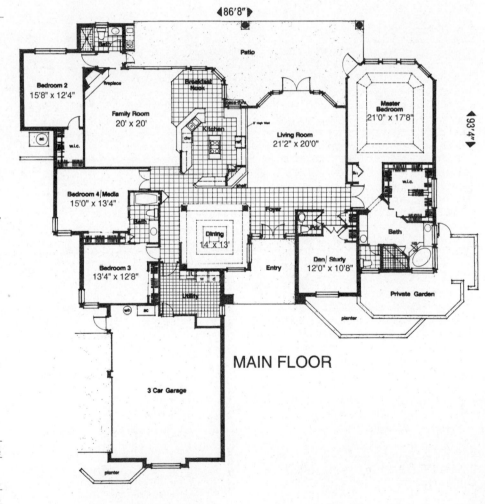

MAIN FLOOR

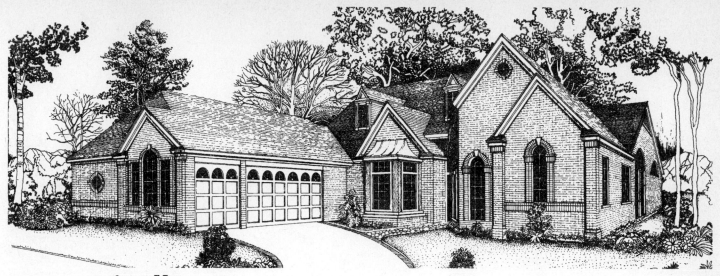

Dramatically Different

- Dramatic angles distinguish this stunning home, allowing it to take full advantage of surrounding views.
- The impressive entry welcomes guests to the formal areas of the home. The delightful bayed dining room leads to the spacious living room with its soaring cathedral ceiling and French doors to a covered rear porch. An inviting fireplace is centered between built-in shelves on one wall.
- The exceptional dual island kitchen provides a unique and functional cooking experience. A cathedral ceiling tops the sun-filled breakfast area.
- An angled family room adjoins the kitchen and features a coffered ceiling, a dramatic fireplace set in a windowed bay and access to the rear porch.
- The angled master suite, two secondary bedrooms, a full bath, a powder room and a study occupy the main sleeping wing. The master suite has his-and-hers walk in closets, a luxurious private bath and porch access.
- A guest bedroom and another bath are located near the kitchen and could be used as an in-law suite.

Plan KLF-9229

Bedrooms: 4	Baths: 3½
Living Area:	
Main floor	3,195 sq. ft.
Total Living Area:	**3,195 sq. ft.**
Garage	650 sq. ft.
Exterior Wall Framing:	2x4

Foundation Options:

Slab
(All plans can be built with your choice of foundation and framing. A generic conversion diagram is available. See order form.))

BLUEPRINT PRICE CODE: E

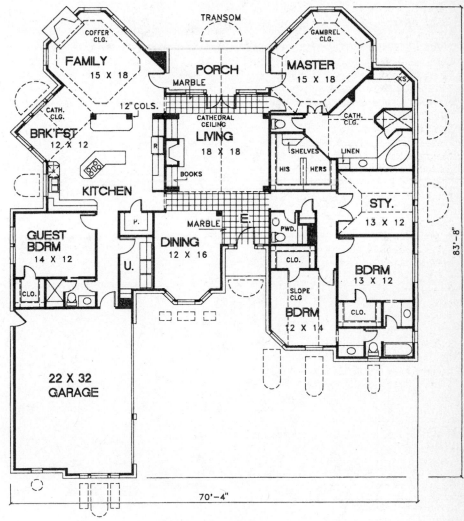

MAIN FLOOR

ORDER BLUEPRINTS ANYTIME!
CALL TOLL-FREE 1-800-820-1283

Plan KLF-9229

PRICES AND DETAILS
ON PAGES 2-5

139

In a Class by Itself

- The endless number and variety of exquisite features ensures that every possible urge is met, and puts this wonderful home in a class by itself!
- The raised foyer steps into the remarkable family room, complete with a fireplace, book cabinets and French doors to the back porch.

- Interesting areas abound, including a media center designed to make movie nights as thrilling as the local multiplex.
- A raised dining room with its own china hutch sits next to a gorgeous fireplaced living room to provide the perfect places for entertaining. Lots of windows help to coax in the sun.
- The master suite leaves nothing out, with a wet bar, a two-way fireplace, a sitting room, a stunning private bath and three different accesses to the outdoors via French doors.

Plan L-062-EME

Bedrooms: 4+	**Baths:** 3½
Living Area:	
Main floor	4,958 sq. ft.
Total Living Area:	**4,958 sq. ft.**
Optional loft	1072 sq. ft.
Optional maid's quarters	608 sq. ft.
Garage and storage	866 sq. ft.
Exterior Wall Framing:	2x4

Foundation Options:

Slab
(All plans can be built with your choice of foundation and framing. A generic conversion diagram is available. See order form.)

BLUEPRINT PRICE CODE: H

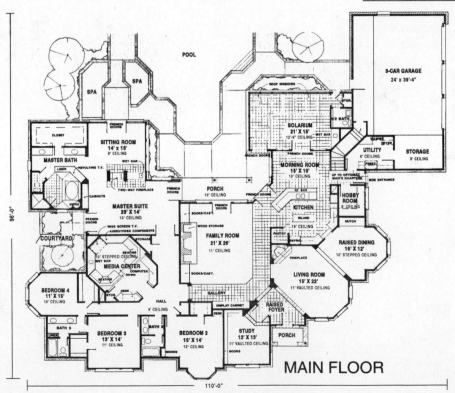

MAIN FLOOR

Patio Living

- A well-executed floor plan sets this impeccable design apart from the ordinary. Rooms of various shapes are arranged to maintain openness and to take advantage of a wonderful patio.
- The granite-paved foyer is open to the large living room, which provides a terrific view of the covered patio.
- The octagonal dining room and den or study flank the foyer and also face the living room.
- The uniquely shaped family room, with a fireplace centered between a wall of

built-ins, has a dynamic view of the outdoors and is open to the kitchen.
- The spacious kitchen has an island range, a pantry and an octagonal nook.
- All of the living areas are enhanced by 11-ft.-high volume ceilings.
- Two nicely placed bedrooms allow for privacy. They have 9-ft., 4-in. ceilings and share a full bath, which is also accessible from the patio.
- The master suite is a wing in itself. The bedroom boasts a fireplace, walls of glass and a 9-ft., 8-in. ceiling. The posh bath includes a whirlpool tub, a corner shower and separate dressing areas.

Plan HDS-99-137	
Bedrooms: 3	**Baths:** 2½
Living Area:	
Main floor	2,656 sq. ft.
Total Living Area:	**2,656 sq. ft.**
Garage	503 sq. ft.

Exterior Wall Framing:
2x4 and 8-in. concrete block

Foundation Options:
Slab
(All plans can be built with your choice of foundation and framing. A generic conversion diagram is available. See order form.)

BLUEPRINT PRICE CODE:	D

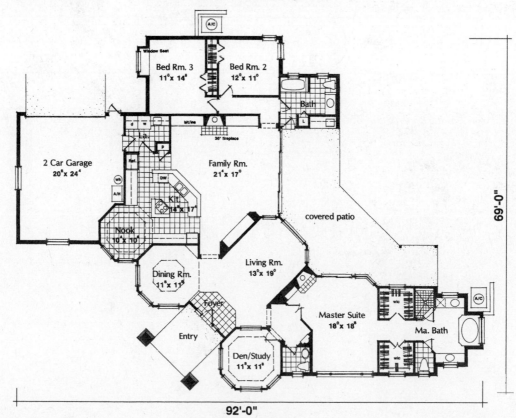

MAIN FLOOR

ORDER BLUEPRINTS ANYTIME!
CALL TOLL-FREE 1-800-820-1283

Plan HDS-99-137

PRICES AND DETAILS
ON PAGES 2-5

141

Room to Boast

- You'll have plenty to boast about if you choose to make this brick-clad French charmer your home!
- Serving as the hub of the home, the centralized living room flaunts cheery windows, a high ceiling and a stunning fireplace that spreads its flickering warmth as far as the kitchen.
- Here, corner windows brighten the sink, and service to both the formal and informal meal areas is a simple matter of a step or two.
- Like fresh air with your Wheaties? French doors open from the breakfast nook to a lovely covered porch.
- The master bedroom is breathtaking in its simplicity. Private access to a covered porch will have you thinking romantic thoughts when midnight rolls around, and the sprawling bath allows for two people to prepare for bedtime without bumping elbows.
- The two remaining bedrooms each have their own walk-in closet, plus a shared bath between them.
- Placing the laundry facilities near the kids' bedrooms is a stroke of genius that you'll come to appreciate when the weekend arrives!

Plan L-1943

Bedrooms: 3	Baths: 2
Living Area:	
Main floor	1,943 sq. ft.
Total Living Area:	**1,943 sq. ft.**
Detached 2-car garage	506 sq. ft.
Exterior Wall Framing:	2x4

Foundation Options:

Slab

(All plans can be built with your choice of foundation and framing. A generic conversion diagram is available. See order form.)

BLUEPRINT PRICE CODE: B

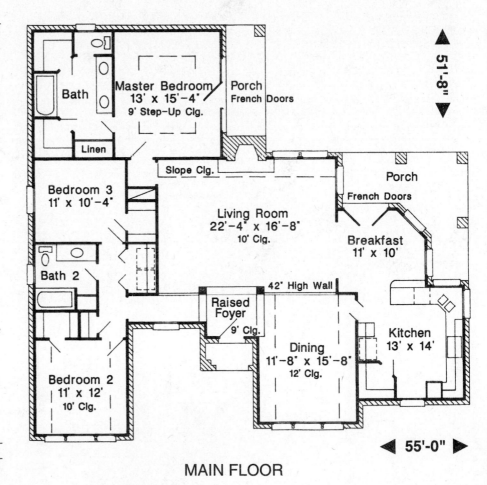

MAIN FLOOR

ORDER BLUEPRINTS ANYTIME!
CALL TOLL-FREE 1-800-820-1283

Plan L-1943

PRICES AND DETAILS
ON PAGES 2-5

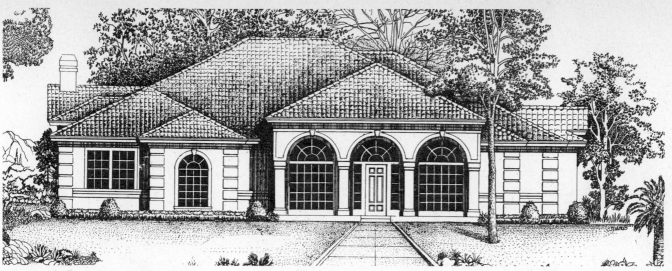

Regal Residence

- Dramatic half-round transom windows accented by beautiful arches and columns showcase this regal residence.
- Inside, high ceilings and several transoms add light and spaciousness.
- Guests are entertained in the formal dining and living rooms off the foyer. Informal gatherings are reserved for the family room, which boasts a cathedral ceiling and a fireplace flanked by windows with quarter-round transoms.

- The kitchen has an island range, a corner pantry and an angled snack bar that overlooks a sunny breakfast area.
- A gallery hallway off the family room leads to three of the home's bedrooms, each of which has a walk-in closet and easy access to a bathroom.
- The secluded master suite features a vaulted sleeping area with a sweeping window wall and porch access. The private bath showcases a cathedral ceiling, a garden tub and a unique dual-sink vanity with knee space.

Plan KLF-9312

Bedrooms: 4	Baths: 3

Living Area:

Main floor	3,119 sq. ft.
Total Living Area:	**3,119 sq. ft.**
Garage	456 sq. ft.
Exterior Wall Framing:	2x4

Foundation Options:

Slab

(All plans can be built with your choice of foundation and framing. A generic conversion diagram is available. See order form.)

BLUEPRINT PRICE CODE: E

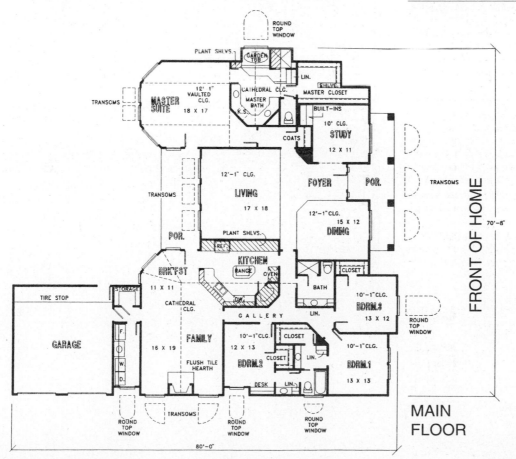

MAIN FLOOR

ORDER BLUEPRINTS ANYTIME!
CALL TOLL-FREE 1-800-820-1283

Plan KLF-9312

PRICES AND DETAILS
ON PAGES 2-5

143

LEFT VIEW

Mediterranean Splendor

- This splendid Mediterranean design has sunny living spaces both inside and out.
- Handsome double doors open to a huge covered porch/loggia. French doors beyond escort you into the tiled foyer. Windows along the left wall overlook a dramatic courtyard/arbor.
- Stately columns and overhead plant shelves accent the living and dining rooms, which are designed to view the courtyard. The living room features a built-in media center and a fireplace.
- The kitchen boasts a pantry, a Jenn-Air range, a serving counter and a sunny breakfast nook. A wet bar serves both the indoor and outdoor entertainment areas.
- The gorgeous master bedroom, crowned by a 9-ft. ceiling, shares a rotating entertainment cabinet and a see-through fireplace with the luxurious master bath. The bath includes a sunken bathing area and a huge walk-in closet.
- A second bedroom features a peaceful window seat, a walk-in closet and private bath access. The third bedroom also has a walk-in closet.
- For added spaciousness, all ceilings are 10 ft. high unless otherwise specified.

Plan L-2176-MC

Bedrooms: 3	Baths: 2
Living Area:	
Main floor	2,176 sq. ft.
Total Living Area:	**2,176 sq. ft.**
Garage	549 sq. ft.
Exterior Wall Framing:	2x4

Foundation Options:

Slab

(All plans can be built with your choice of foundation and framing. A generic conversion diagram is available. See order form.)

BLUEPRINT PRICE CODE:	C

FRONT VIEW

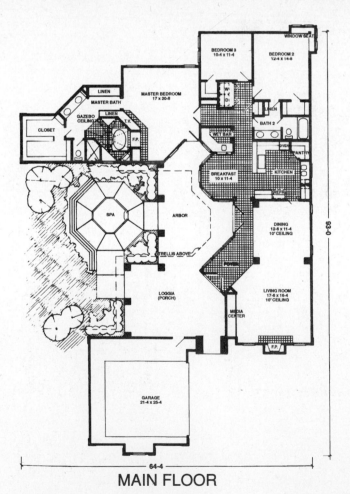

MAIN FLOOR

ORDER BLUEPRINTS ANYTIME!
CALL TOLL-FREE 1-800-820-1283

Plan L-2176-MC

*PRICES AND DETAILS
ON PAGES 2-5*

Classic Country-Style

- At the center of this rustic country-style home is an enormous living room with a flat beamed ceiling and a massive stone fireplace. A sunny patio and a covered rear porch are just steps away.
- The adjoining eating area and kitchen provide plenty of room for casual dining and meal preparation. The eating area is visually enhanced by a 14-ft. sloped ceiling with false beams. The kitchen includes a snack bar, a pantry closet and a built-in spice cabinet.
- The formal dining room gets plenty of pizzazz from a stone-faced wall and an arched planter facing the living room.
- The secluded master suite has it all, including a private bath, a separate dressing area and a large walk-in closet with built-in shelves.
- The two remaining bedrooms have big closets and easy access to a full bath.

Plan E-1808	
Bedrooms: 3	**Baths:** 2
Living Area:	
Main floor	1,800 sq. ft.
Total Living Area:	**1,800 sq. ft.**
Garage	605 sq. ft.
Exterior Wall Framing:	2x4
Foundation Options:	
Crawlspace	
Slab	

(All plans can be built with your choice of foundation and framing. A generic conversion diagram is available. See order form.)

BLUEPRINT PRICE CODE:	**B**

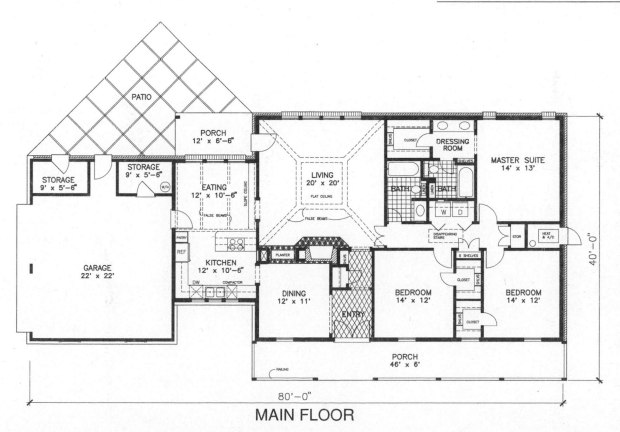

MAIN FLOOR

ORDER BLUEPRINTS ANYTIME!
CALL TOLL-FREE 1-800-820-1283

Plan E-1808

PRICES AND DETAILS
ON PAGES 2-5

145

Parlez-vous français?

- This elegant one-story lets you parlay your love of French styling into a home that meets all of your needs.
- Just inside the front entry, a raised, sidelighted foyer directs guests into the living and dining rooms.
- A fireplace transforms the living room into a welcoming parlor, where good conversation may be enjoyed.
- For casual family times or for watching the big game on TV, the large family

room fills the bill. An L-shaped window seat adds a nice touch.
- The open kitchen allows you to serve snacks or hors d'oeuvres on its versatile wraparound bar.
- The bay-windowed morning room will host breakfasts and everyday meals in style. Backyard views will relax you before or after a hard day at work.
- The secluded master bedroom is enhanced by a nice bayed sitting area. The private bath contains two walk-in closets, a garden tub and a shower.
- Across the home, two bedrooms share a bath, while the fourth bedroom offers direct access to a hall bath.

Plan L-2602-C	
Bedrooms: 4	**Baths:** 3
Living Area:	
Main floor	2,602 sq. ft.
Total Living Area:	**2,602 sq. ft.**
Exterior Wall Framing:	2x4
Foundation Options:	
Slab	

(All plans can be built with your choice of foundation and framing. A generic conversion diagram is available. See order form.)

BLUEPRINT PRICE CODE:	D

MAIN FLOOR

(Plans for a detached two-car garage included with blueprints.)

ORDER BLUEPRINTS ANYTIME!
CALL TOLL-FREE 1-800-820-1283

Plan L-2602-C

PRICES AND DETAILS
ON PAGES 2-5

Modern Charmer

- This attractive plan combines country-style charm with a modern floor plan.
- The central foyer ushers guests past a study and on into the huge living room, which is highlighted by an 11-ft. ceiling, a corner fireplace and access to a big, covered backyard porch.
- An angled snack bar joins the living room to the bayed nook and the efficient kitchen. The formal dining room is easily reached from the kitchen and the foyer. A utility room and a half-bath are just off the garage entrance.
- The master suite, isolated for privacy, boasts a magnificent bath with a garden tub, a separate shower, double vanities and two walk-in closets.
- Two more bedrooms are located on the opposite side of the home and are separated by a hall bath.
- Ceilings in all rooms are at least 9 ft. high for added spaciousness.

REAR VIEW

Plan VL-2069

Bedrooms: 3	**Baths:** 2½

Living Area:	
Main floor	2,069 sq. ft.
Total Living Area:	**2,069 sq. ft.**
Garage	460 sq. ft.
Exterior Wall Framing:	2x4

Foundation Options:

Crawlspace
Slab

(All plans can be built with your choice of foundation and framing. A generic conversion diagram is available. See order form.)

BLUEPRINT PRICE CODE:	C

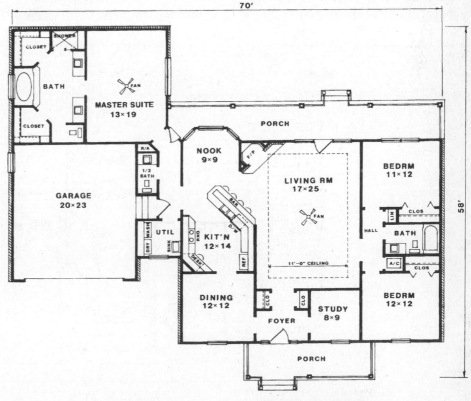

MAIN FLOOR

ORDER BLUEPRINTS ANYTIME!
CALL TOLL-FREE 1-800-820-1283

Plan VL-2069

PRICES AND DETAILS
ON PAGES 2-5

147

Picture-Perfect!

- With graceful arches, columns and railings, the wonderful front porch makes this home the picture of country charm. Decorative chimneys, shutters and quaint dormers add more style.
- Inside, the foyer shows off sidelights and a fantail transom. The foyer is flanked by the dining room and a bedroom, both of which boast porch views and arched transoms. All three areas are expanded by 10-ft. ceilings.
- The living room also flaunts a 10-ft. ceiling, plus a fireplace and French doors that open to a skylighted porch. The remaining rooms offer 9-ft. ceilings.
- The L-shaped kitchen has an island cooktop and a sunny breakfast nook.
- A Palladian window arrangement brightens the sitting alcove in the master suite. Other highlights include porch access and a fantastic bath with a garden tub and a separate shower.
- The upper floor is perfect for future expansion space.

Plan J-9401

Bedrooms: 3+	Baths: 2½
Living Area:	
Main floor	2,089 sq. ft.
Total Living Area:	**2,089 sq. ft.**
Upper floor (unfinished)	878 sq. ft.
Standard basement	2,089 sq. ft.
Garage and storage	530 sq. ft.
Exterior Wall Framing:	2x4

Foundation Options:

Standard basement
Crawlspace
Slab
(All plans can be built with your choice of foundation and framing. A generic conversion diagram is available. See order form.)

BLUEPRINT PRICE CODE: C

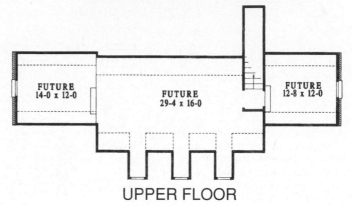

UPPER FLOOR

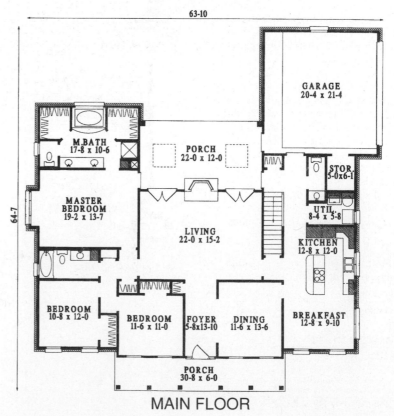

MAIN FLOOR

ORDER BLUEPRINTS ANYTIME! CALL TOLL-FREE 1-800-820-1283

Plan J-9401

PRICES AND DETAILS ON PAGES 2-5

Spectacular Design

- The spectacular brick facade of this home conceals a stylish floor plan. Endless transoms crown the windows that wrap around the rear of the home, flooding the interior with natural light.
- The foyer opens to a huge Grand Room with a 14-ft. ceiling. French doors access a delightful covered porch.
- A three-sided fireplace warms the three casual rooms, which share a high 12-ft. ceiling. The Gathering Room is surrounded by tall windows; the Good Morning Room features porch access; and the island kitchen offers a double oven, a pantry and a snack bar.
- Guests will dine in style in the formal dining room, with its 13-ft. tray ceiling and trio of tall, arched windows.
- Curl up with a good book in the quiet library, which has an airy 10-ft. ceiling.
- A 12-ft. ceiling enhances the fantastic master suite, which is wrapped in windows. The superb master bath boasts a step-up garden tub, a separate shower, two vanities, a makeup table and a bidet.
- Two sleeping suites on the other side of the home have 10-ft. ceilings and share a unique bath with private vanities.

Plan EOF-8	
Bedrooms: 3+	**Baths:** 3½
Living Area:	
Main floor	3,392 sq. ft.
Total Living Area:	**3,392 sq. ft.**
Garage	871 sq. ft.
Exterior Wall Framing:	2x6
Foundation Options:	
Slab	

(All plans can be built with your choice of foundation and framing. A generic conversion diagram is available. See order form.)

BLUEPRINT PRICE CODE:	E

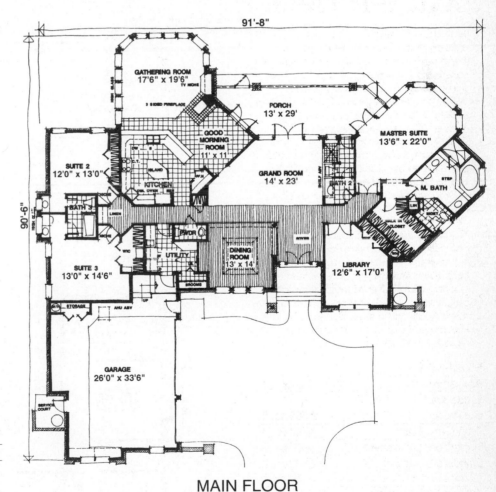

MAIN FLOOR

High Luxury in One Story

- Beautiful arched windows lend a luxurious feeling to the exterior of this one-story home.
- Soaring 12-ft. ceilings add volume to both the wide entry area and the central living room, which boasts a large fireplace and access to a covered porch and the patio beyond.
- Double doors separate the formal dining room from the corridor-style kitchen. Features of the kitchen include a pantry and an angled eating bar. The sunny, bayed eating area is perfect for casual family meals.
- The plush master suite has amazing amenities: a walk-in closet, a skylighted, angled whirlpool tub, a separate shower and private access to the laundry/utility room and the patio.
- Three good-sized bedrooms and a full bath are situated across the home.

Plan E-2302

Bedrooms: 4	Baths: 2

Living Area:	
Main floor	2,396 sq. ft.
Total Living Area:	**2,396 sq. ft.**
Standard basement	2,396 sq. ft.
Garage	484 sq. ft.
Exterior Wall Framing:	2x6

Foundation Options:

Standard basement

Crawlspace

Slab

(All plans can be built with your choice of foundation and framing. A generic conversion diagram is available. See order form.)

BLUEPRINT PRICE CODE: C

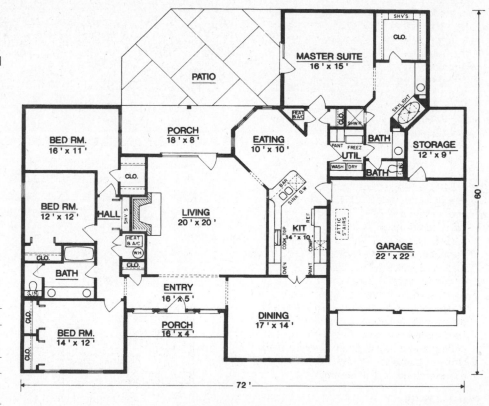

MAIN FLOOR

ORDER BLUEPRINTS ANYTIME!
CALL TOLL-FREE 1-800-820-1283

Plan E-2302

PRICES AND DETAILS
ON PAGES 2-5

Genteel Luxury

- This extraordinary home offers countless details and genteel luxury.
- In the foyer, an elegant marble floor and an 11-ft. ceiling define the sunny space.
- A fireplace serves as the focal point of the living room, which extends to the dining room to isolate formal affairs. The dining room features a bay window and a French door to a lush courtyard. Both rooms feature 11-ft. ceilings.
- A columned serving counter separates the kitchen from the breakfast nook and the family room. A convenient built-in desk to the right is a great place to jot down a grocery list.
- A 14-ft. ceiling soars over the versatile family room, where a corner fireplace and a French door to the backyard are great additions.
- A 10-ft. stepped ceiling, a romantic fireplace, a quiet desk and access to the backyard make the master bedroom an inviting retreat. A luxurious raised tub and a sit-down shower highlight the master bath, which also includes a neat dressing table between two sinks.
- Two more bedrooms, one with an 11-ft. ceiling and a bay window, share a bath.
- Unless otherwise mentioned, each room includes a 9-ft. ceiling.

Plan L-483-HB

Bedrooms: 3	Baths: 2
Living Area:	
Main floor	2,481 sq. ft.
Total Living Area:	**2,481 sq. ft.**
Garage	706 sq. ft.
Exterior Wall Framing:	2x4

Foundation Options:

Slab
(All plans can be built with your choice of foundation and framing. A generic conversion diagram is available. See order form.)

BLUEPRINT PRICE CODE: C

VIEW INTO KITCHEN

REAR VIEW

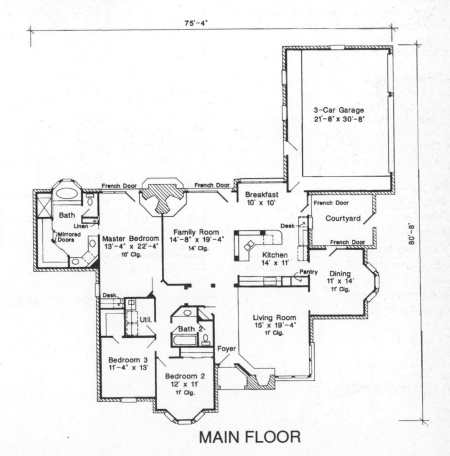

MAIN FLOOR

ORDER BLUEPRINTS ANYTIME!
CALL TOLL-FREE 1-800-820-1283

Plan L-483-HB

PRICES AND DETAILS
ON PAGES 2-5

151

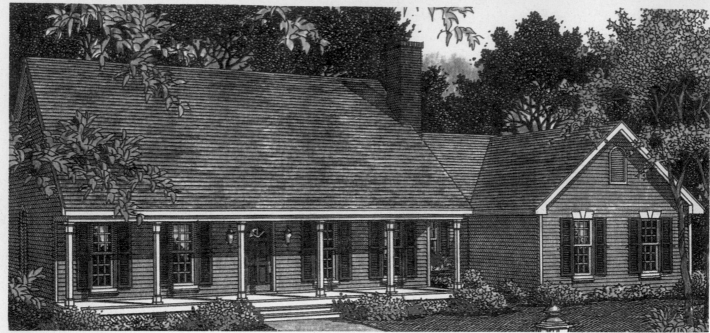

Versatile
Sun Room

- This cozy country-style home offers an inviting front porch and an interior just as welcoming.
- The spacious living room features a warming fireplace and windows that overlook the porch.
- The living room opens to a dining area, where French doors access a covered porch and a sunny patio.
- The island kitchen has a sink view, plenty of counter space, and a handy pass-through to the adjoining sun room. The bright sun room is large enough to serve as a formal dining room, a family room or a hobby room.
- The private master suite is secluded to the rear. A garden spa tub, dual walk-in closets and separate dressing areas are nice features found in the master bath.

Plan J-90014

Bedrooms: 3	Baths: 2½
Living Area:	
Main floor	2,190 sq. ft.
Total Living Area:	**2,190 sq. ft.**
Standard basement	2,190 sq. ft.
Garage	465 sq. ft.
Storage	34 sq. ft.
Exterior Wall Framing:	2x6

Foundation Options:

Standard basement

Crawlspace

Slab

(All plans can be built with your choice of foundation and framing. A generic conversion diagram is available. See order form.)

BLUEPRINT PRICE CODE:	C

MAIN FLOOR

ORDER BLUEPRINTS ANYTIME!
CALL TOLL-FREE 1-800-820-1283

Plan J-90014

PRICES AND DETAILS
ON PAGES 2-5

Family Home, Formal Accents

- Captivating roof angles and European detailing highlight the exterior of this graceful home.
- The generous foyer is flanked by the spacious living and dining rooms; both with tall, ornate windows.
- Beyond the foyer lies an expansive family room, highlighted by a dramatic fireplace and sliding glass doors that open to a sunny patio.
- The kitchen makes use of an L-shaped counter and a central island to maximaze efficiency. The adjacent breakfast room offers casual dining. A nearby utility room features a washer and dryer and a door to the backyard.
- The large master suite boasts two closets and a private bath with a dual-sink vanity and a step-up tub.
- Across the hall, two additional bedrooms share a second full bath.

Plan C-8103	
Bedrooms: 3	**Baths:** 2
Living Area:	
Main floor	1,940 sq. ft.
Total Living Area:	**1,940 sq. ft.**
Daylight basement	1,870 sq. ft.
Garage	400 sq. ft.
Exterior Wall Framing:	2x4

Foundation Options:

Daylight basement
Crawlspace
Slab
(All plans can be built with your choice of foundation and framing. A generic conversion diagram is available. See order form.)

BLUEPRINT PRICE CODE: B

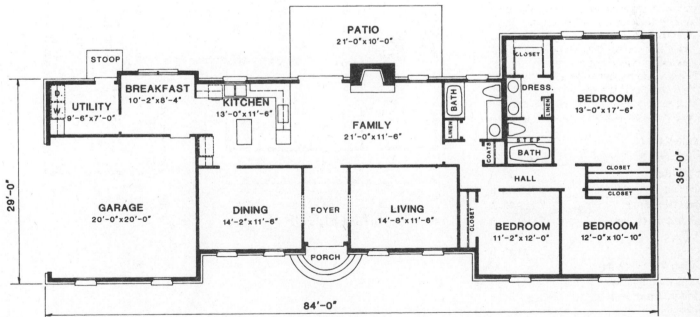

MAIN FLOOR

ORDER BLUEPRINTS ANYTIME!
CALL TOLL-FREE 1-800-820-1283

Plan C-8103

PRICES AND DETAILS
ON PAGES 2-5

153

Exciting Angles and Amenities

- The interior of this elegant stucco design oozes in luxury, with an exciting assortment of angles and glass.
- Beyond the 14-ft.-high foyer and gallery is a huge parlour with an angled stand-behind ale bar and an adjoining patio accessed through two sets of glass doors.
- The diamond-shaped kitchen offers a sit-down island, a spacious walk-in pantry and a pass-through window to a summer kitchen.
- Opposite the kitchen is an octagonal morning room surrounded in glass and a spacious, angled gathering room with a fireplace and a TV niche.
- The luxurious master suite features a glassed lounge area and a spectacular two-sided fireplace, and is separated from the three secondary bedroom suites. The stunning master bath boasts a central linen island and an assortment of amenities designed for two.
- The library could serve as a fifth bedroom or guest room; the bath across the hall could serve as a pool bath.
- An alternate brick elevation is included

Plan EOF-59

Bedrooms: 4+	Baths: 4
Living Area:	
Main floor	4,021 sq. ft.
Total Living Area:	**4,021 sq. ft.**
Garage	737 sq. ft.
Exterior Wall Framing:	2x6

Foundation Options:

Slab

(All plans can be built with your choice of foundation and framing. A generic conversion diagram is available. See order form.)

BLUEPRINT PRICE CODE: G

MAIN FLOOR

ORDER BLUEPRINTS ANYTIME!
CALL TOLL-FREE 1-800-820-1283

Plan EOF-59

PRICES AND DETAILS
ON PAGES 2-5

Wonderful Detailing

- The wonderfully detailed front porch, with its graceful arches, columns and railings, gives this home a character all its own. Dormer windows and arched transoms further accentuate the porch.
- The floor plan features a central living room with a 10-ft.-high ceiling and a fireplace framed by French doors. These doors open to a covered porch or a sun room, and a sheltered deck beyond.
- Just off the living room, the island kitchen and breakfast area provide a spacious place for family or guests. The nearby formal dining room has arched transom windows and a 10-ft. ceiling, as does the bedroom off the foyer. All of the remaining rooms have 9-ft. ceilings.
- The unusual master suite includes a window alcove, access to the porch and a fantastic bath with a garden tub.
- A huge utility room, a storage area off the garage and a 1,000-sq.-ft. attic space are other bonuses of this design.

Plan J-90019

Bedrooms: 3	Baths: 2½
Living Area:	
Main floor	2,410 sq. ft.
Total Living Area:	**2,410 sq. ft.**
Standard basement	2,410 sq. ft.
Garage	512 sq. ft.
Storage	86 sq. ft.
Exterior Wall Framing:	2x6

Foundation Options:

Standard basement
Crawlspace
Slab
(All plans can be built with your choice of foundation and framing. A generic conversion diagram is available. See order form.)

BLUEPRINT PRICE CODE:	C

64' 4"

71' 6"

GARAGE
20' 4" X 23' 4"

DECK
20' 0" X 14' 0"

STORAGE
12' 8" X 5' 8"

PORCH OR SUNROOM
21' 6" X 12' 2"

UTILITY

MASTER BEDROOM
11' 8" X 16' 8"

LIVING
21' 9" X 17' 2"

KITCHEN

BEDROOM
11' 0" X 12' 0"

BEDROOM
11' 0" X 13' 6"

FOYER

DINING
11' 0" X 16' 4"

BREAKFAST
12' 9" X 11' 6"

PORCH
29' 8" X 6' 2"

MAIN FLOOR

ORDER BLUEPRINTS ANYTIME!
CALL TOLL-FREE 1-800-820-1283

Plan J-90019

PRICES AND DETAILS
ON PAGES 2-5

155

A Real Original

- This home's round window, elegant entry and transom windows create an eye-catching, original look.
- Inside, high ceilings and tremendous views let the eyes wander. The foyer provides an exciting look at the expansive deck and the inviting spa through the living room's tall windows. The windows frame a handsome fireplace, while a 10-ft. ceiling adds volume and interest.
- To the right of the foyer is a cozy den or home office with its own fireplace, 10-ft. ceiling and dramatic windows.
- The spacious kitchen/breakfast area features an oversized snack bar island and opens to a large screen porch. Within easy reach are the laundry room and the entrance to the garage.
- The bright formal dining room overlooks the deck and boasts a ceiling that vaults up to 10 feet.
- The secluded master suite looks out to the deck as well, with access through a patio door. The private bath features a dynamite corner spa tub, a separate shower and a large walk-in closet.
- A second bedroom and bath complete the main floor.

Plan B-90065

Bedrooms: 2+	Baths: 2
Living Area:	
Main floor	1,889 sq. ft.
Total Living Area:	**1,889 sq. ft.**
Standard basement	1,889 sq. ft.
Garage	406 sq. ft.
Exterior Wall Framing:	2x6

Foundation Options:

Standard basement

(All plans can be built with your choice of foundation and framing. A generic conversion diagram is available. See order form.)

BLUEPRINT PRICE CODE: B

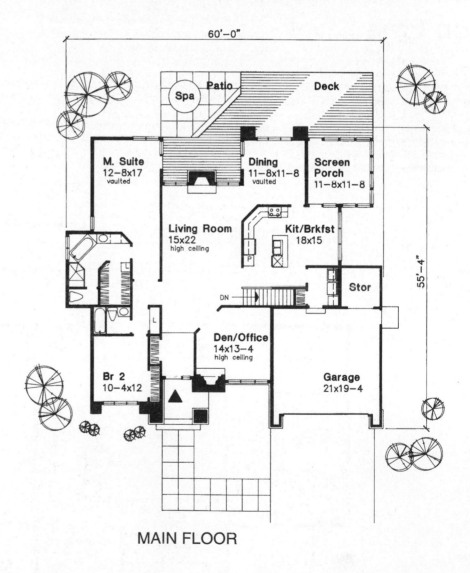

MAIN FLOOR

ORDER BLUEPRINTS ANYTIME!
CALL TOLL-FREE 1-800-820-1283

Plan B-90065

PRICES AND DETAILS
ON PAGES 2-5

Photo by Mark Englund/HomeStyles

Luxurious Living on One Level

- The elegant exterior of this spacious one-story presents a classic air of quality and distinction.
- Three French doors brighten the inviting entry, which flows into the spacious living room. Boasting a 13-ft. ceiling, the living room enjoys a fireplace with a wide hearth and adjoining built-in bookshelves. A wall of glass, including

a French door, provides views of the sheltered backyard porch.
- A stylish angled counter joins the spacious kitchen to the sunny bay-windowed eating nook.
- Secluded for privacy, the master suite features a nice dressing area, a large walk-in closet and private backyard access. A convenient laundry/utility room is adjacent to the master bath.
- At the opposite end of the home, double doors lead to three more bedrooms, a compartmentalized bath and lots of closet space.

Plan E-2208

Bedrooms: 4	Baths: 2
Living Area:	
Main floor	2,252 sq. ft.
Total Living Area:	**2,252 sq. ft.**
Standard basement	2,252 sq. ft.
Garage and storage	592 sq. ft.
Exterior Wall Framing:	2x6

Foundation Options:

Standard basement
Crawlspace
Slab
(All plans can be built with your choice of foundation and framing. A generic conversion diagram is available. See order form.)

BLUEPRINT PRICE CODE: C

**NOTE: The above photographed home may have been modified by the homeowner. Please refer to floor plan and/or drawn elevation shown for actual blueprint details.

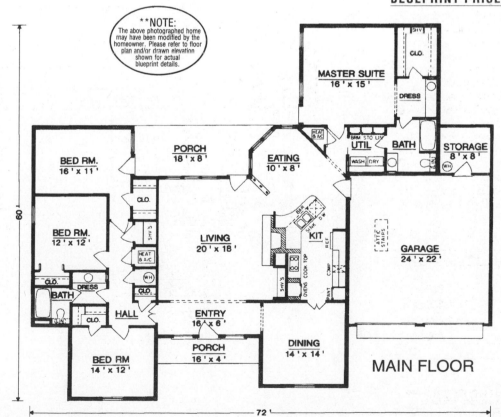

MAIN FLOOR

ORDER BLUEPRINTS ANYTIME!
CALL TOLL-FREE 1-800-820-1283

Plan E-2208

PRICES AND DETAILS
ON PAGES 2-5

157

Photo by Mark Englund/HomeStyles

A Real Charmer

- A tranquil railed porch makes this country one-story a real charmer.
- The main entry opens directly into the Great Room, which serves as the home's focal point. A 14-ft. cathedral ceiling soars above, while a fireplace and a built-in cabinet for games make the space a fun gathering spot.
- Beautiful French doors expand the Great Room to a peaceful covered porch at the rear of the home. Open the doors and let in the fresh summer air!
- A bayed breakfast nook unfolds from the kitchen, where the family cook will love the long island snack bar and the pantry. The carport is located nearby to save steps when you unload groceries.
- Across the home, the master bedroom features a walk-in closet with built-in shelves. A 10-ft. cathedral ceiling tops the master bath, which boasts a private toilet, a second walk-in closet and a separate tub and shower.
- A skylighted hall bath services the two secondary bedrooms.

Plan J-9508

Bedrooms: 3	Baths: 2½
Living Area:	
Main floor	1,875 sq. ft.
Total Living Area:	**1,875 sq. ft.**
Standard basement	1,875 sq. ft.
Carport	418 sq. ft.
Storage	114 sq. ft.
Exterior Wall Framing:	2x4

Foundation Options:
Standard basement
Crawlspace
Slab
(All plans can be built with your choice of foundation and framing. A generic conversion diagram is available. See order form.)

BLUEPRINT PRICE CODE: B

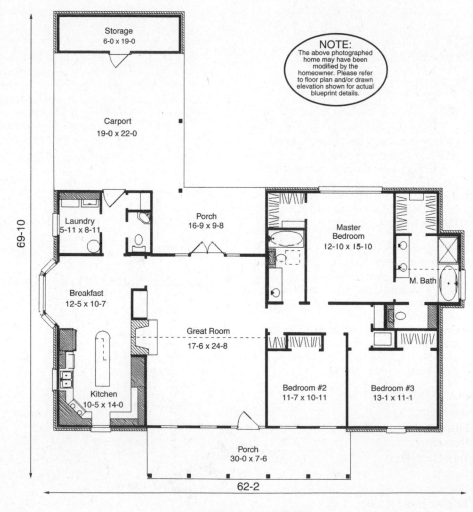

NOTE:
The above photographed home may have been modified by the homeowner. Please refer to floor plan and/or drawn elevation shown for actual blueprint details.

Storage
6-0 x 19-0

Carport
19-0 x 22-0

Laundry
5-11 x 8-11

Porch
16-9 x 9-8

Master Bedroom
12-10 x 15-10

M. Bath

Breakfast
12-5 x 10-7

Great Room
17-6 x 24-8

Kitchen
10-5 x 14-0

Bedroom #2
11-7 x 10-11

Bedroom #3
13-1 x 11-1

Porch
30-0 x 7-6

69-10

62-2

MAIN FLOOR

Elegance Inside and Out

- The raised front porch of this home is finely detailed with wood columns, railings, moldings, and French doors with half-round transoms.
- The living room, dining room and entry have 12-ft.-high ceilings. Skylights illuminate the living room, which offers a fireplace and access to a roomy deck.
- The efficient kitchen permits easy service to both the dining room and the casual eating area.
- The master suite features a raised tray ceiling and an enormous skylighted bath with a walk-in closet, dual vanities and a large quarter-circle spa tub surrounded by a mirror wall.
- On the left, two secondary bedrooms are insulated from the more active areas of the home by an efficient hallway, and also share another full bath.

Plan E-1909

Bedrooms: 3	Baths: 2
Living Area:	
Main floor	1,936 sq. ft.
Total Living Area:	**1,936 sq. ft.**
Garage	484 sq. ft.
Storage	132 sq. ft.
Exterior Wall Framing:	2x6

Foundation Options:

Crawlspace
Slab
(All plans can be built with your choice of foundation and framing. A generic conversion diagram is available. See order form.)

BLUEPRINT PRICE CODE: **B**

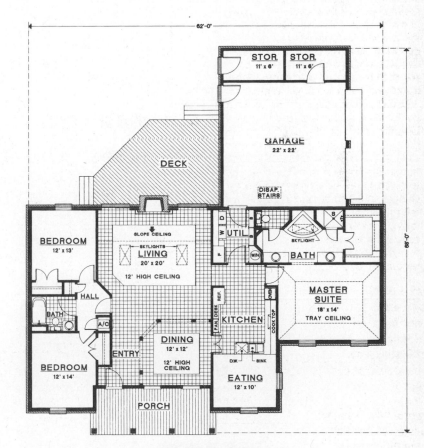

MAIN FLOOR

ORDER BLUEPRINTS ANYTIME!
CALL TOLL-FREE 1-800-820-1283

Plan E-1909

PRICES AND DETAILS
ON PAGES 2-5

159

Photo by Mark Englund/HomeStyles

French Garden Design

- A creative, angular design gives this traditional French garden home an exciting, open and airy floor plan.
- Guests enter through a covered, columned porch that opens into the large, angled living and dining rooms.
- High 12-ft. ceilings highlight the living and dining area, which also features corner windows, a wet bar, a cozy fireplace and access to a huge covered backyard porch.
- The angled walk-through kitchen, also with a 12-ft.-high ceiling, offers plenty of work space and an adjoining informal eating nook that faces a delightful private courtyard. The nearby utility area has extra freezer space, a walk-in pantry and garage access.
- The home's bedrooms are housed in two separate wings. One wing boasts a luxurious master suite, which features a large walk-in closet, an angled tub and a separate shower.
- Two large bedrooms in the other wing share a hall bath. Each bedroom has a walk-in closet.

Plan E-2004

Bedrooms: 3	Baths: 2
Living Area:	
Main floor	2,023 sq. ft.
Total Living Area:	**2,023 sq. ft.**
Garage	484 sq. ft.
Storage	87 sq. ft.
Exterior Wall Framing:	2x6

Foundation Options:

Crawlspace

Slab

(All plans can be built with your choice of foundation and framing. A generic conversion diagram is available. See order form.)

BLUEPRINT PRICE CODE: C

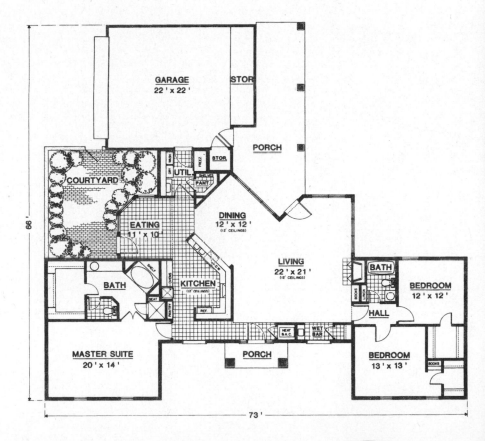

MAIN FLOOR

**NOTE: The above photographed home may be modified by the homeowner. Please refer to floor plan and/or drawn elevation shown for actual blueprint details.

ORDER BLUEPRINTS ANYTIME! *CALL TOLL-FREE 1-800-820-1283*

Plan E-2004

PRICES AND DETAILS ON PAGES 2-5

Symmetry and Style

- This appealing one-story home boasts a striking facade with symmetrical rooflines, stately columns and gently curved transoms.
- The formal living spaces have a classic split design, perfect for quiet times and conversation.
- The unique layout of the bedroom wing gives each bedroom easy access to a

full bath. The rear bedroom also enjoys pool and patio proximity.
- The huge family room opens up to the patio with 12-ft. pocket sliding doors, and boasts a handsome fireplace flanked by built-in shelves, perfect for your media equipment.
- The master suite just off the kitchen and nook is private, yet easily accessible. One unique feature is its bed wall with high glass above. The master bath offers a huge walk-in closet, a relaxing corner tub, a step-down shower, dual sinks and a private toilet.

Plan HDS-99-147	
Bedrooms: 4	**Baths:** 3
Living Area:	
Main floor	2,089 sq. ft.
Total Living Area:	**2,089 sq. ft.**
Garage	415 sq. ft.
Exterior Wall Framing:	2x4

Foundation Options:

Slab
(All plans can be built with your choice of foundation and framing. A generic conversion diagram is available. See order form.)

BLUEPRINT PRICE CODE: C

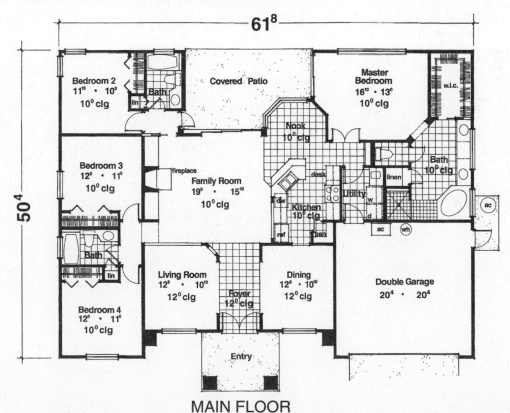

MAIN FLOOR

ORDER BLUEPRINTS ANYTIME!
CALL TOLL-FREE 1-800-820-1283

Plan HDS-99-147

PRICES AND DETAILS
ON PAGES 2-5

161

Never Better!

- Safe and secure within the walls of this bold, brick design, you'll appreciate the comfort and fun it provides and soon realize that life has never been better.
- Corner quoins, soldier coursing and an arched window and entryway present a distinctive, meticulous image to visitors or passersby.
- Step into the foyer and view the splendors of the interior spaces.
- You've dreamt about master bedrooms like this one! Past its entry you'll find an incredibly spacious sleeping area, a huge walk-in closet and French doors to the backyard. A beautiful octagonal

sitting area with a gazebo ceiling leads to a peaceful, skylighted bath with a wonderfully soothing garden tub.
- The two additional bedrooms boast walk-in closets and share a large bath.
- The family room provides a great gathering place for big social events. It offers a pass-through to the kitchen's wet bar and a fireplace to keep you warm and happy.
- Designed to serve several areas at once, the island kitchen will see plenty of action. It's positioned smartly between the formal dining room and a breakfast nook with a comfy corner window seat.
- Unless otherwise noted, each room features a 9-ft. ceiling.

Plan L-2314-FTC	
Bedrooms: 3	**Baths:** 2
Living Area:	
Main floor	2,314 sq. ft.
Total Living Area:	**2,314 sq. ft.**
Exterior Wall Framing:	2x4
Foundation Options:	
Slab	

(All plans can be built with your choice of foundation and framing. A generic conversion diagram is available. See order form.)

BLUEPRINT PRICE CODE:	C

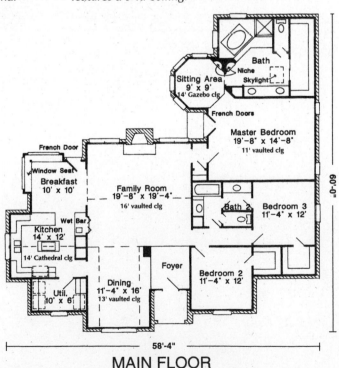

MAIN FLOOR

Plan L-2314-FTC

Peace of Mind

- Peace and privacy were the inspiration for this tranquil home.
- Past the inviting columned entry, the bright foyer flows into the spacious 13½-ft.-high vaulted living room, which includes a wet bar.
- The gourmet kitchen enjoys a 14-ft. vaulted ceiling and includes an angled snack counter and a large pantry. Sliding glass doors in the adjoining breakfast nook lead to a covered patio with a functional summer kitchen.
- The adjacent family room boasts a 15-ft. vaulted ceiling and a handsome window-flanked fireplace.
- The master suite offers an 11½-ft. vaulted ceiling, a windowed sitting area and patio access. His-and-hers walk-in closets flank the entrance to the plush master bath, which is highlighted by a garden tub overlooking a privacy yard.
- Three more bedrooms have vaulted ceilings that are at least 11½ ft. high. With a nearby full bath and back door entrance, the rear bedroom could be made into a great guest or in-law suite.

Plan HDS-99-157

Bedrooms: 4	Baths: 3

Living Area:

Main floor	2,224 sq. ft.
Total Living Area:	**2,224 sq. ft.**
Garage	507 sq. ft.

Exterior Wall Framing:
2x4 and concrete block

Foundation Options:
Slab
(All plans can be built with your choice of foundation and framing. A generic conversion diagram is available. See order form.)

BLUEPRINT PRICE CODE:	C

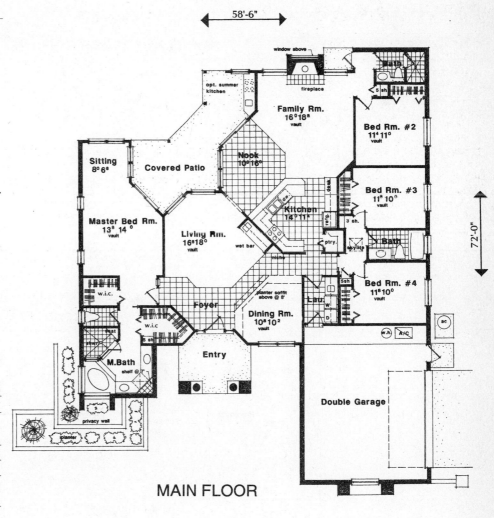

MAIN FLOOR

Formal Yet Fun

- Upright and elegant in front and filled with French doors at the back, this one-level home has an air of composure as well as excitement.
- A gazebo ceiling over the breakfast nook brings height and stature to the kitchen area.
- This home's accommodating game room, centralized wet bar, skylighted rear porch and courtyard space that's perfect for a hot tub, make it a terrific place to entertain in any season.

- A secluded fourth bedroom with a nearby full bath is just the thing for the independent teenager or the private overnight guest.
- The living room's 14-ft. ceilings and high fireplace chimney give the room volume and imbue the whole home with a soaring grace.
- A porch off the utility room, a tiled front foyer, a spacious kitchen and large closets throughout contribute to the home's frank practicality.
- Plans for a detached, two-car garage are included with the blueprints.

Plan L-2516-C

Bedrooms: 4	**Baths:** 3

Living Area:	
Main floor	2,516 sq. ft.

Total Living Area:	**2,516 sq. ft.**
Exterior Wall Framing:	2x4

Foundation Options:

Slab
(All plans can be built with your choice of foundation and framing. A generic conversion diagram is available. See order form.)

BLUEPRINT PRICE CODE:	D

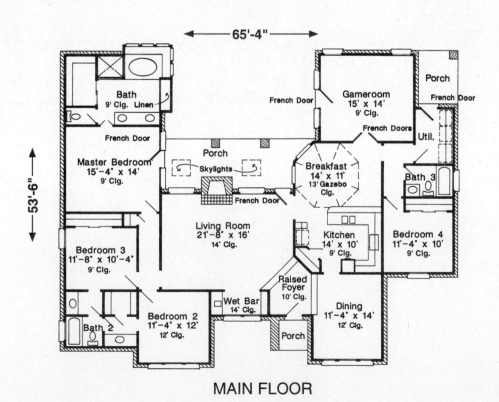

MAIN FLOOR

ORDER BLUEPRINTS ANYTIME!
CALL TOLL-FREE 1-800-820-1283

Plan L-2516-C

PRICES AND DETAILS
ON PAGES 2-5

Super Features!

- Super indoor/outdoor living features are the main ingredients of this sprawling one-story home.
- Beyond the columned entry, the foyer features a 16-ft.-high ceiling and is brightened by a fantail transom. The dining room and the living room enjoy ceilings that vault to nearly 11 feet.
- The family room, with a 15-ft. vaulted ceiling, sits at the center of the floor plan and extends to the outdoor living spaces. A handsome fireplace flanked by built-in shelves adds excitement.
- The adjoining kitchen shares the family room's vaulted ceiling and offers a cooktop island, a large pantry and a breakfast nook that opens to the patio.
- The master suite is intended to offer the ultimate in comfort. A double-door entry, a 10-ft. tray ceiling and private patio access are featured in the bedroom. The master bath shares a see-through fireplace with the bedroom.
- Three secondary bedrooms share two full baths at the other end of the home.

Plan HDS-99-164

Bedrooms: 4	Baths: 3

Living Area:

Main floor	2,962 sq. ft.
Total Living Area:	**2,962 sq. ft.**
Garage	567 sq. ft.

Exterior Wall Framing:
2x4 and 8-in. concrete block

Foundation Options:

Slab
(All plans can be built with your choice of foundation and framing. A generic conversion diagram is available. See order form.)

BLUEPRINT PRICE CODE: D

MAIN FLOOR

ORDER BLUEPRINTS ANYTIME!
CALL TOLL-FREE 1-800-820-1283

Plan HDS-99-164

PRICES AND DETAILS
ON PAGES 2-5

165

Three to One

- This stunning brick-clad home harbors three cozy bedrooms in its spacious one-story design.
- A masterpiece of comfort, the master bedroom unfolds, beckoning you to sweet relaxation after tiresome days. Double doors introduce the sanctuary of the bath, where you'll find a zesty shower and a soothing tub. On warm nights, slip through the French doors and enjoy the night sky's starry dance.
- When the evening calls for fun, stage your gathering in the family room. Here, window seats provide comfort for larger crowds, and a cheery fireplace adds to the spirit of the night.
- Do you prefer a more sophisticated setting? The living room easily fills the bill, with its welcoming angles and handsome fireplace.
- The dining room is a marvel, too. There's plenty of room for in-laws and grandkids, and dazzling French doors to a back porch add elegant intrigue.
- Not surprisingly, the kitchen is placed to serve as the hub of the home. Its walk-through configuration smoothly handles large traffic levels while maintaining a decidedly casual appeal.

Plan L-62-FAB

Bedrooms: 3	**Baths:** 2

Living Area:	
Main floor	2,060 sq. ft.
Total Living Area:	**2,060 sq. ft.**
Garage	527 sq. ft.
Exterior Wall Framing:	2x4

Foundation Options:

Slab

(All plans can be built with your choice of foundation and framing. A generic conversion diagram is available. See order form.)

BLUEPRINT PRICE CODE:	C

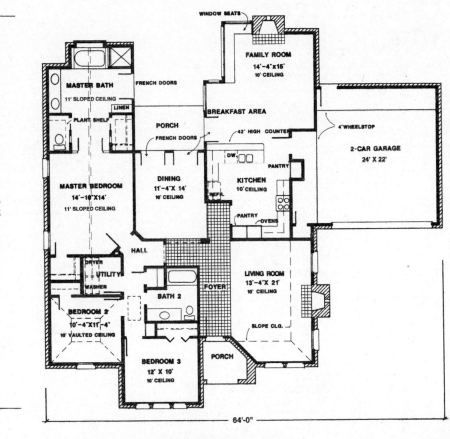

MAIN FLOOR

Plan L-62-FAB

PRICES AND DETAILS
ON PAGES 2-5

Ornate French Provincial

- The brick and stucco exterior of this elegant French Provincial home is adorned with quoins and keystones.
- The interior is designed for maximum openness and livability. High 12-ft. ceilings are found throughout the main living areas, including the foyer.
- At the center of the floor plan, the huge family room is framed by a ceramic tile floor that continues into the morning room and the airy kitchen. Bookshelves

flank a dramatic tile-faced fireplace and two sets of doors open to a back porch.
- Past a spectacular carousel atrium with a center planter and bright sky windows is an exciting game room with a refreshing wet bar.
- The formal spaces include a raised dining room and a living room that could also serve as a private sitting room for the master suite.
- The removed master suite overlooks a courtyard and side porch, and includes a private skylighted bath.
- The secondary bedrooms form a wing of their own. The third bedroom could also be used as a library.

Plan E-2704

Bedrooms: 3+	Baths: 2

Living Area:

Main floor	2,791 sq. ft.
Total Living Area:	**2,791 sq. ft.**
Garage	682 sq. ft.
Exterior Wall Framing:	2x4

Foundation Options:

Crawlspace
Slab
(All plans can be built with your choice of foundation and framing. A generic conversion diagram is available. See order form.)

BLUEPRINT PRICE CODE:	C

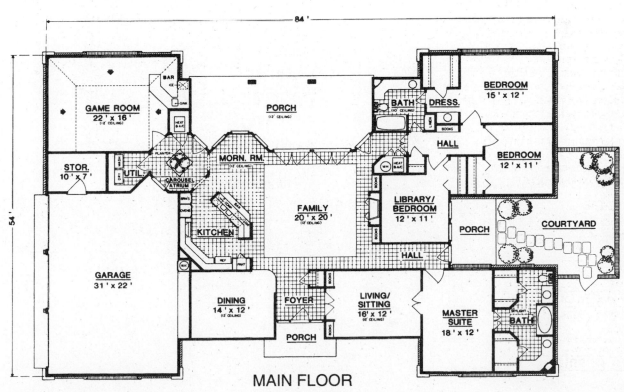

MAIN FLOOR

ORDER BLUEPRINTS ANYTIME!
CALL TOLL-FREE 1-800-820-1283

Plan E-2704

PRICES AND DETAILS
ON PAGES 2-5

167

Sought-After Elegance

- Decorative corner quoins, copper accents and gorgeous windows take the brick and stucco facade of this home to the height of elegance.
- Luxurious appointments continue inside, with a sidelighted 11-ft.-high foyer leading to the formal living and dining rooms. The living room boasts a 14-ft. vaulted ceiling, while the dining room has an 11-ft. ceiling.
- Smoothly accessed from the dining room, the flow-through kitchen offers a serving counter to the breakfast nook. Bright windows light the two areas, which share an 11-ft. vaulted ceiling.

- Adjacent to the nook, the luxurious family room sports a handsome fireplace and access to a sprawling backyard deck. A fancy fan hangs from the soaring 14-ft. vaulted ceiling.
- Just off the family room, two roomy secondary bedrooms share a nice compartmentalized bath.
- The sumptuous master bedroom flaunts its own deck access, a quaint morning porch for quiet cups of coffee and a large walk-in closet.
- The master bath is highlighted by a plant shelf, a garden tub and a separate shower. An 11-ft. ceiling crowns the master bedroom and bath.
- Unless otherwise noted, all rooms have 9-ft. ceilings.
- A bonus room above the garage offers expansion possibilities.

Plan APS-2018

Bedrooms: 3+	Baths: 2½
Living Area:	
Main floor	2,088 sq. ft.
Total Living Area:	**2,088 sq. ft.**
Bonus room (unfinished)	282 sq. ft.
Daylight basement	2,088 sq. ft.
Garage	460 sq. ft.
Storage	35 sq. ft.
Exterior Wall Framing:	2x4

Foundation Options:

Daylight basement
(All plans can be built with your choice of foundation and framing. A generic conversion diagram is available. See order form.)

BLUEPRINT PRICE CODE: C

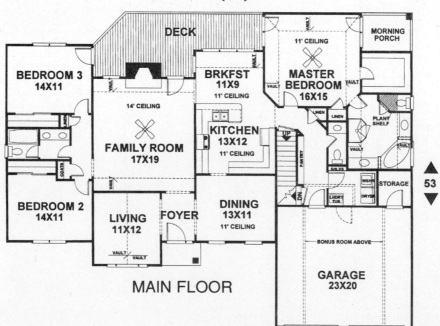

MAIN FLOOR

ORDER BLUEPRINTS ANYTIME!
CALL TOLL-FREE 1-800-820-1283

Plan APS-2018

PRICES AND DETAILS
ON PAGES 2-5

Mediterranean Spice Is Nice!

- An exotic stucco facade, an inviting courtyard, gorgeous windows and a stunning backyard lanai flavor this marvelous Mediterranean-style home.
- Past the courtyard, the covered entry leads through French doors to a grand Great Room, which features a soaring 13-ft. ceiling. Three sets of French doors open onto the lanai.
- Lazy summer breezes will sweep through the four stately columns gracing the lanai, which can be reached from the breakfast nook and the master bedroom, as well as the Great Room.
- The well-appointed kitchen is enhanced by a convenient built-in desk, a center island and a 10-ft. ceiling.
- Cheery windows brighten the adjoining breakfast nook.
- On the other side of the home, the sumptuous master suite boasts two overhead plant shelves, two entrances to the lanai and two large walk-in closets. The full bath features a platform tub and a dual-sink vanity.
- Around the corner, a full bath is shared by two bedrooms; one of these may be used as a den, if desired.

Plan B-92002

Bedrooms: 2+	Baths: 2
Living Area:	
Main floor	1,859 sq. ft.
Total Living Area:	**1,859 sq. ft.**
Garage	390 sq. ft.
Exterior Wall Framing:	2x6

Foundation Options:

Slab
(All plans can be built with your choice of foundation and framing. A generic conversion diagram is available. See order form.)

BLUEPRINT PRICE CODE:	B

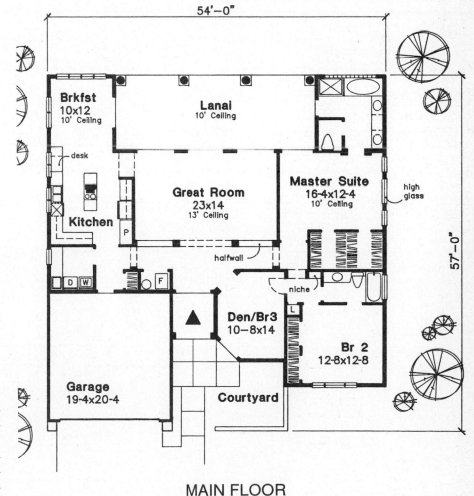

MAIN FLOOR

ORDER BLUEPRINTS ANYTIME!
CALL TOLL-FREE 1-800-820-1283

Plan B-92002

PRICES AND DETAILS
ON PAGES 2-5
169

Neo-Traditional

- Bright, open spaces are the hallmarks of this upbeat neo-traditional design.
- A covered porch adorns the front entry, which is framed by a copper-topped bay window on one side and an arched window on the other.
- The raised foyer provides a sweeping view of the dining room and the living room. A dramatic arched opening with columns leads from the living room to the two secondary bedrooms. Bookshelves topped by plant shelves further accentuate the archway.
- The fourth bedroom or study, which is accessible from the bedroom hall, includes a 10-ft. coffered ceiling, a bay window and a walk-in closet bordered by bookshelves. Optional doors provide direct access from the living room.
- A spacious kitchen, a gazebo-like breakfast area and an inviting family room are the home's centerpiece. High ceilings expand the entire area.
- French doors open into the isolated master suite, which features sloped ceilings in the sleeping area and in the bath. French doors, topped with a half-round window and framed by columns, open to the spectacular master bath.

Plan BOD-25-7B

Bedrooms: 3+	Baths: 2½
Living Area:	
Main floor	2,561 sq. ft.
Total Living Area:	**2,561 sq. ft.**
Garage	457 sq. ft.
Exterior Wall Framing:	2x4

Foundation Options:

Crawlspace

Slab

(All plans can be built with your choice of foundation and framing. A generic conversion diagram is available. See order form.)

BLUEPRINT PRICE CODE:	D

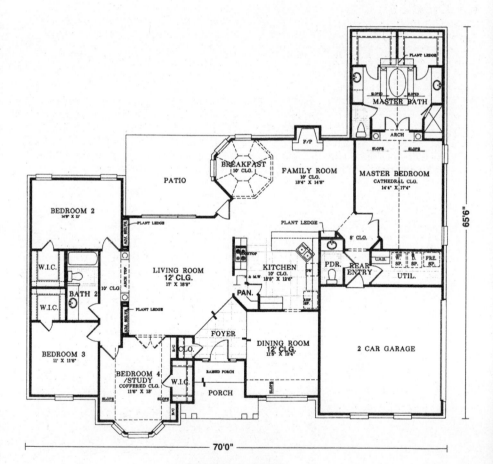

MAIN FLOOR

Plan BOD-25-7B

PRICES AND DETAILS
ON PAGES 2-5

Exclusive Elegance

- A stunning array of elegant windows frames the columned, two-story-high entry of this exclusive home.
- Inside, bold columns define the foyer and the dining room, which is brightened by a wall of gracefully arched windows.
- The formal living room has a matching wall of windows, plus a two-way fireplace that is shared with the family room. Sliding doors in the family room access a covered patio with a wet bar and an outdoor grill.
- The island kitchen gives way to a bright breakfast nook with patio access.
- The private master suite is absolutely superb, featuring a two-way fireplace that can be enjoyed from the sleeping area and from the lavish step-up spa tub. The sleeping area accesses the covered patio, while the bathing area is embraced by a sun-filled solarium.
- A bayed study, two bedrooms and two baths are on the left side of the home.
- The home features 16-ft. sloped ceilings throughout, with the exception of the two secondary bedrooms.

Plan HDS-90-801	
Bedrooms: 3+	**Baths:** 3
Living Area:	
Main floor	2,987 sq. ft.
Total Living Area:	**2,987 sq. ft.**
Garage	528 sq. ft.
Exterior Wall Framing:	2x4 and block
Foundation Options:	
Slab	

(All plans can be built with your choice of foundation and framing. A generic conversion diagram is available. See order form.)

BLUEPRINT PRICE CODE: D

MAIN FLOOR

ORDER BLUEPRINTS ANYTIME!
CALL TOLL-FREE 1-800-820-1283

Plan HDS-90-801

PRICES AND DETAILS
ON PAGES 2-5

171

Quiet Relaxation

- This elegant brick one-story home features a stunning master bedroom with a sunny morning porch for quiet relaxation. The bedroom's 11-ft. vaulted ceiling extends into the master bath, which boasts a corner garden tub and an attractive plant shelf.
- A few steps away, the open kitchen shares its 11-ft. ceiling and handy snack bar with the bright breakfast nook.
- A handsome fireplace warms the spacious family room, which is enhanced by a soaring 14-ft. ceiling. A striking French door provides access to a roomy deck that may also be reached from the master bedroom.
- The formal living areas flank the sidelighted foyer. The living room shows off a 14-ft. cathedral ceiling.
- Three secondary bedrooms with 9-ft. ceilings have easy access to a split bath. The center bedroom features a built-in desk with shelves above. Two of the bedrooms have walk-in closets.
- A convenient half-bath and a good-sized laundry room are located near the two-car garage, which offers additional storage space and excellent lighting from three bright windows.

Plan APS-2117	
Bedrooms: 4	**Baths:** 2½
Living Area:	
Main floor	2,187 sq. ft.
Total Living Area:	**2,187 sq. ft.**
Garage	460 sq. ft.
Exterior Wall Framing:	2x4
Foundation Options:	

Crawlspace
(All plans can be built with your choice of foundation and framing. A generic conversion diagram is available. See order form.)

BLUEPRINT PRICE CODE:	C

MAIN FLOOR

ORDER BLUEPRINTS ANYTIME!
CALL TOLL-FREE 1-800-820-1283

Plan APS-2117

PRICES AND DETAILS
ON PAGES 2-5

Classic Styling

- Classic styling transcends the exterior and interior of this sprawling one-story.
- Outside, sweeping rooflines, arched windows and brick planters combine for an elegant curb appeal.
- The angled entry opens to a tiled foyer, which overlooks the spacious central living room. A handsome fireplace and a string of windows lend light and volume to this high-profile area.

- Unfolding to the right, the kitchen and dining room flow together, making the space seem even larger. A snack counter, bar sink and corner pantry are attractive kitchen efficiencies.
- The master suite is drenched in luxury with a romantic fireplace, a private porch and a grand Jacuzzi bath with lush surrounding plant shelves.
- Two good-sized secondary bedrooms share another full bath.
- Extra storage is offered in the garage.

Plan L-824-EMB

Bedrooms: 3	Baths: 2

Living Area:

Main floor	1,826 sq. ft.
Total Living Area:	**1,826 sq. ft.**
Garage and storage	534 sq. ft.
Exterior Wall Framing:	2x4

Foundation Options:

Slab

(All plans can be built with your choice of foundation and framing. A generic conversion diagram is available. See order form.)

BLUEPRINT PRICE CODE: B

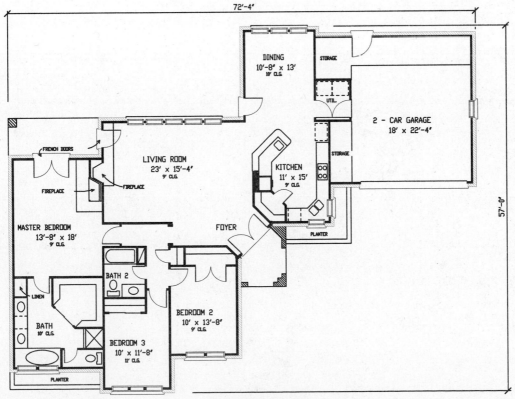

MAIN FLOOR

ORDER BLUEPRINTS ANYTIME!
CALL TOLL-FREE 1-800-820-1283

Plan L-824-EMB

PRICES AND DETAILS
ON PAGES 2-5

173

Design Excellence

- This stunning one-story home features dramatic detailing and an exceptionally functional floor plan.
- The brick exterior and exciting window treatments beautifully hint at the spectacular interior design.
- High ceilings, a host of built-ins and angled window walls are just some of the highlights.
- The family room showcases a curved wall of windows and a three-way fireplace that can be enjoyed from the adjoining kitchen and breakfast room.
- The octagonal breakfast room offers access to a lovely porch and a handy half-bath. The large island kitchen boasts a snack bar and a unique butler's pantry that connects with the dining room. The sunken living room includes a second fireplace and a window wall.
- The master suite sports a coffered ceiling, a private sitting area and a luxurious bath with a gambrel ceiling.
- Each of the four possible bedrooms has private access to a bath.

Plan KLF-922

Bedrooms: 3+	Baths: 3½
Living Area:	
Main floor	3,450 sq. ft.
Total Living Area:	**3,450 sq. ft.**
Garage	698 sq. ft.
Exterior Wall Framing:	2x4

Foundation Options:
Slab
(All plans can be built with your choice of foundation and framing. A generic conversion diagram is available. See order form.)

BLUEPRINT PRICE CODE:	E

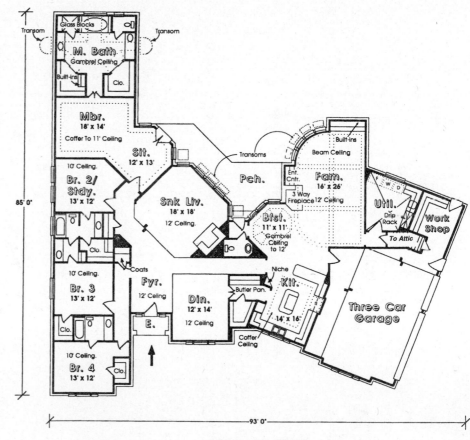

MAIN FLOOR

ORDER BLUEPRINTS ANYTIME!
CALL TOLL-FREE 1-800-820-1283

Plan KLF-922

PRICES AND DETAILS
ON PAGES 2-5

While Away an Afternoon

- The pretty porch that stretches along the front of this traditional home provides plenty of room for sitting and whiling away an afternoon. Try a porch swing on one end and a cluster of comfortable wicker furniture on the other.
- Inside, handsome columns introduce the living room and the dining room, on either side of the foyer. A 10-ft. tray ceiling lends a touch of elegance to the living room, while the open relationship to the dining room consolidates formal affairs in one impressive space.
- At the rear, the Great Room, the breakfast nook and the kitchen flow into one another, creating an easygoing, casual spot for family fun. In the Great Room, a neat media wall holds the TV, the VCR and the stereo. An angled fireplace adds a bit of rustic charm to the setting.
- Tucked away for privacy, the master bedroom provides a pleasant retreat. A stepped ceiling crowns the room, while a bay window serves as a sitting area.

VIEW INTO GREAT ROOM

Plan AX-5374	
Bedrooms: 3	**Baths:** 2
Living Area:	
Main floor	1,902 sq. ft.
Total Living Area:	**1,902 sq. ft.**
Standard basement	1,925 sq. ft.
Garage and storage	552 sq. ft.
Exterior Wall Framing:	2x4

Foundation Options:
Standard basement
Crawlspace
Slab
(All plans can be built with your choice of foundation and framing. A generic conversion diagram is available. See order form.)

BLUEPRINT PRICE CODE:	**B**

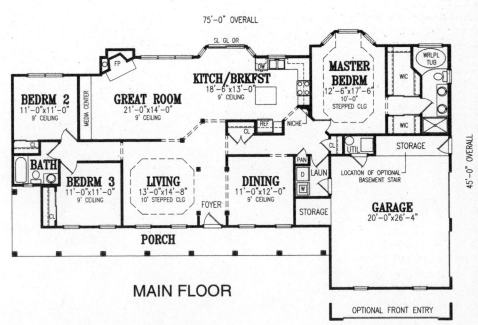

MAIN FLOOR

ORDER BLUEPRINTS ANYTIME!
CALL TOLL-FREE 1-800-820-1283

Plan AX-5374

PRICES AND DETAILS
ON PAGES 2-5

175

One-Story for Today's Living

- This trendsetting design, with its enormous master suite, integrated family room and kitchen area and energy-efficient construction, is perfect for today's lifestyles.
- The huge master suite is brightened by 9-ft.-high corner windows and enhanced by an elegant master bath with a sizable walk-in closet and a garden tub.
- The family room features sliding glass doors to the covered lanai, high accent windows that frame the fireplace, a built-in entertainment center and direct access to the kitchen.
- The island kitchen, which adjoins a sunny breakfast area with sliding glass doors to the lanai, is integrated with the informal family room to maximize family living space.
- Ten-ft.-high ceilings throughout the entire floor plan give it an open, airy feel. The home's energy efficiency is boosted by 2x6 exterior wall framing.

Plan B-92028

Bedrooms: 2+	Baths: 2
Living Area:	
Main floor	2,228 sq. ft.
Total Living Area:	**2,228 sq. ft.**
Garage	607 sq. ft.
Exterior Wall Framing:	2x6

Foundation Options:

Slab

(All plans can be built with your choice of foundation and framing. A generic conversion diagram is available. See order form.)

BLUEPRINT PRICE CODE: C

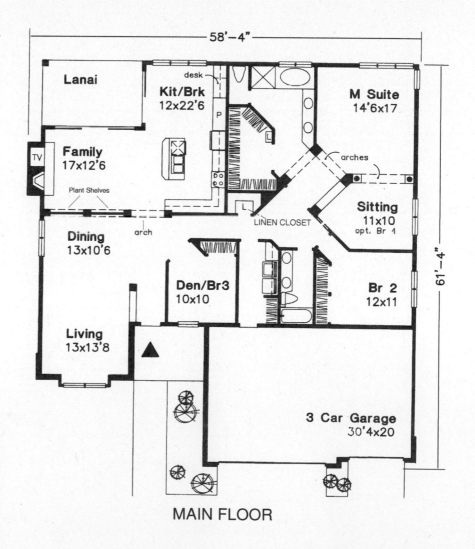

MAIN FLOOR

ORDER BLUEPRINTS ANYTIME!
CALL TOLL-FREE 1-800-820-1283

Plan B-92028

PRICES AND DETAILS
ON PAGES 2-5

Stately Ranch

- This stately ranch, with its brick exterior, Palladian windows and quoin accents, is a vision of elegance.
- Inside, guests will be greeted by a dramatic living room with a 10-ft. tray ceiling, a fireplace, built-in bookcases and a unique window wall with French doors leading to an expansive deck.
- The formal dining room has mitered corners and a 10-ft. tray ceiling as well.
- Under a 14-ft. vaulted ceiling, the gourmet kitchen and the sunny breakfast room share a dramatic view of the deck through a Palladian window.

A half-bath and a laundry room are conveniently nearby.

- The inviting family room is highlighted by a 10-ft. tray ceiling, a second fireplace and deck access.
- The sumptuous master suite features his-and-hers walk-in closets, French doors leading to the deck and a 10-ft. tray ceiling. The 14-ft.-high vaulted master bath includes a garden tub, a separate shower and twin vanities.
- The adjoining bedroom would be ideal as a sitting room or a nursery.
- The second bedroom boasts a 14-ft. vaulted ceiling, while the third and fourth bedrooms have 9-ft. ceilings.

Plan APS-2410	
Bedrooms: 4	**Baths:** 2½-3½
Living Area:	
Main floor	2,559 sq. ft.
Total Living Area:	**2,559 sq. ft.**
Standard basement	2,559 sq. ft.
Garage	456 sq. ft.
Exterior Wall Framing:	2x4
Foundation Options:	
Standard basement	
Crawlspace	
Slab	

(All plans can be built with your choice of foundation and framing. A generic conversion diagram is available. See order form.)

BLUEPRINT PRICE CODE:	D

DECK

FAMILY ROOM 18 x 14
TRAY CEILING

BREAKFAST 13 x 9
VAULT

KITCHEN 13 x 12

STORAGE

W D

DINING 12 x 14
TRAY CEILING

GARAGE 19 X 24

LIVING ROOM 14 x 19
TRAY CEILING

BEDROOM 2 12 x 13⁶
VAULT

MASTER BEDROOM 20 x 13
TRAY CEILING

VAULT

69

BEDROOM 4 12 x 11

5 x 14

BEDROOM 3 12 x 15⁶

70

MAIN FLOOR

OPTIONAL EXTRA BATH

ORDER BLUEPRINTS ANYTIME!
CALL TOLL-FREE 1-800-820-1283

Plan APS-2410

PRICES AND DETAILS
ON PAGES 2-5
177

Sprawling Brick Beauty

- Exquisite exterior details hint at the many exciting features you'll find inside this sprawling brick beauty.
- The raised foyer boasts a neat display niche above the coat closet to spark interest for your guests.
- Attractive formal spaces unfold from the foyer and share a lofty 11-ft. ceiling.

The fireplace to the left is creatively nestled between built-in book cabinets. French doors whisk you to a lavish backyard covered porch.
- The kitchen and breakfast area flow together near the garage and laundry room for maximum mobility.
- Three bedrooms and two convenient dual-sink baths make up the sleeping wing. Entered through elegant double doors, the master suite offers the owners of the home a private library, garden bath and outdoor access.

Plan L-998-FA	
Bedrooms: 3	Baths: 2
Living Area:	
Main floor	1,996 sq. ft.
Total Living Area:	**1,996 sq. ft.**
Garage	449 sq. ft.
Exterior Wall Framing:	2x4

Foundation Options:

Slab
(All plans can be built with your choice of foundation and framing. A generic conversion diagram is available. See order form.)

BLUEPRINT PRICE CODE: B

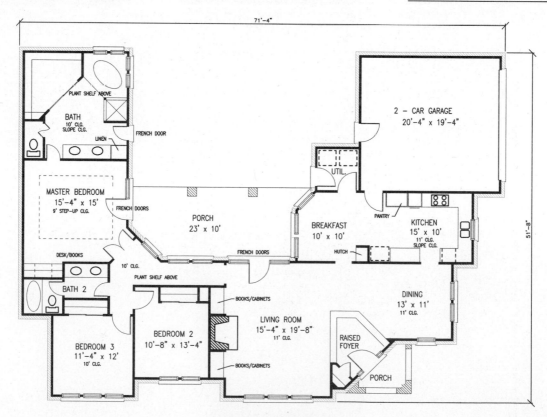

MAIN FLOOR

Plan L-998-FA

Grand Style

- This grandly appointed home flaunts a veritable feast of stylish amenities!
- The gem in the home's crown is a magnificent screened lanai that overlooks the backyard. At its center is an exciting pool and spa combo that delivers hours of splashy fun.
- A built-in barbecue grill can serve up a mouthwatering menu of Pacific salmon, succulent steaks or hearty chicken— you name it. For speedy refreshment, a

handy pass-through accesses a wet bar that faces the island kitchen.
- Three sets of sliding glass doors reveal the home's mammoth living and dining rooms, which merge to provide the ultimate space for raucous parties!
- In quiet moments, the family room will calm you with its fireplace.
- A fireplace also graces the master suite, which boasts access to a lovely garden. The stunning bath hosts a luxurious garden tub and a spectacular shower edged by a curved glass-block wall.

Plan B-93025	
Bedrooms: 4+	Baths: 4½
Living Area:	
Main floor	4,783 sq. ft.
Total Living Area:	4,783 sq. ft.
Garage	720 sq. ft.
Exterior Wall Framing:	8-in. concrete block

Foundation Options:

Slab
(All plans can be built with your choice of foundation and framing. A generic conversion diagram is available. See order form.)

BLUEPRINT PRICE CODE: **H**

Floor Plan

113'-8"

97'-2"

Screened Lanai
10' Clg

Glass Block

Cook out

Guest Br
16x14'4
10' Clg

Pool w/ Spa

M Bath
18x16
13' Vaulted Clg

Glass Block

Br 2
14x14'8
10' Clg

Family Rm
21x26
15' Clg

Pass-thru

Wet bar

Sitting
12x17
10' Vaulted Clg

Wet bar

See-thru Fireplace

High Glass

Entertainment Center

Garden

Wet bar

Living/Dining Room
36x17
18' High Clg

Buffet

Master Br
18'4x18
13' Vaulted Clg

Br 3
14x14'8
10' Clg

Kitchen
12' Clg

Shelves

Glass Block

Wine

P Desk

Brkfst
12x13
12'-8" Clg

Library
13'4x12
12'-8" Vaulted Clg

Garden

MAIN FLOOR

Garage
23x31'4

ORDER BLUEPRINTS ANYTIME!
CALL TOLL-FREE 1-800-820-1283

Plan B-93025

PRICES AND DETAILS
ON PAGES 2-5

179

Lovely Cottage

- Past its quaint exterior, this lovely cottage home's bright and airy floor plan is bursting with features.
- The inviting covered front porch opens into a high-ceilinged sidelighted foyer. The adjacent formal dining room is defined by striking columns.
- The efficient, galley-style kitchen includes a pass-through to the Great Room. The adjoining breakfast area offers a French door to a backyard deck. Laundry facilities and garage access are conveniently nearby.
- Highlighted by a beautiful arched dormer window, the vaulted Great Room boasts a 17-ft.-high vaulted ceiling. A handsome fireplace and built-in shelves add character to the room. Sliding glass doors open to the deck.
- The deluxe master bedroom is enhanced by a 14-ft. cathedral ceiling and features his-and-hers walk-in closets. The master bath showcases a garden spa tub, a separate shower and dual vanities.
- Two additional bedrooms on the opposite side of the home enjoy private access to a shared full bath.

Plan C-9405

Bedrooms: 3	Baths: 2½
Living Area:	
Main floor	1,845 sq. ft.
Total Living Area:	**1,845 sq. ft.**
Garage	484 sq. ft.
Exterior Wall Framing:	2x4

Foundation Options:

Crawlspace

Slab

(All plans can be built with your choice of foundation and framing. A generic conversion diagram is available. See order form.)

BLUEPRINT PRICE CODE: **B**

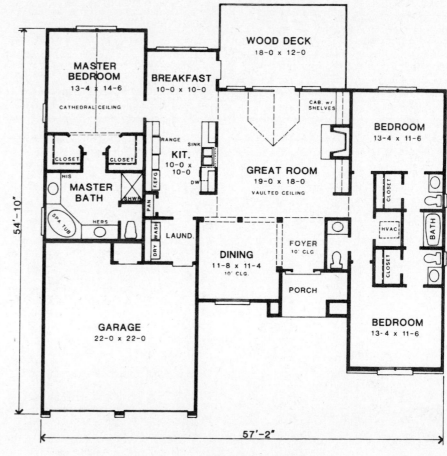

MAIN FLOOR

ORDER BLUEPRINTS ANYTIME!
CALL TOLL-FREE 1-800-820-1283

Plan C-9405

PRICES AND DETAILS
ON PAGES 2-5

Visible Value

- With just a glance, this Southern-style home's value is readily apparent.
- Its eclectic brick, stucco and siding facade displays a range of features, including regal columns, keystones, quoins and dormer windows.
- Inside, a uniquely angled foyer empties into the formal living areas. Business matters may be attended to in the study.
- A small vestibule provides a fitting introduction to the opulent master bedroom, which boasts private access to a backyard patio.

- The master bath is equally rich, with its whirlpool tub, sit-down shower and twin sinks. The walk-in closet is divided into his-and-hers areas, and features a nifty fold-down ironing board!
- Sure to be a magnet for the young ones, the family room is accented by a cozy fireplace and opens to the walk-through kitchen and breakfast nook. The angled serving counter in the kitchen makes a great spot to line up the eats!
- Three secondary bedrooms cluster about a full bath. If you wish, the largest of them could become an exciting game or hobby room.

Plan BOD-28-3A

Bedrooms: 3+	Baths: 2½

Living Area:	
Main floor	2,846 sq. ft.
Total Living Area:	**2,846 sq. ft.**
Garage	458 sq. ft.
Exterior Wall Framing:	2x4

Foundation Options:

Crawlspace
Slab
(All plans can be built with your choice of foundation and framing. A generic conversion diagram is available. See order form.)

BLUEPRINT PRICE CODE: D

84'-6"

65'-6"

GARAGE
20-4x20-4

BRKFST
11-0x10-0
10 FT CLG

PATIO

D
W

PAN

MASTER
BEDROOM
13-4x17-0
10 FT CLG

MSTR
BATH
10 FT CLG

LEDGE

SEAT

FAMILY
16-0x15-4
10 FT CLG

FP

KITCH
12-6x13-4
10 FT CLG

LIVING
15-4x18-0
12 FT CLG

HIS

HERS

PWDR

BED 4/
GAME RM
14-8x13-0

BATH
2

LIN

ARCH

ARCH

ARCH

ARCH

FOYER
12 FT CLG

STUDY
12-8x10-4

BEDRM 3
14-4x13-0

BEDRM 2
12-8x12-4

DINING
11-8x13-4
12 FT CLG

PORCH

ARCH

SEAT

MAIN FLOOR

ORDER BLUEPRINTS ANYTIME!
CALL TOLL-FREE 1-800-820-1283

Plan BOD-28-3A

PRICES AND DETAILS
ON PAGES 2-5

181

Nicely Done!

- An inviting window-covered exterior, coupled with an interior designed to give a sunny, open feel, will have you saying, "Nicely done!"
- Two eye-catching dormers, front-facing gables and two stately columns on the covered porch add a balanced sense of high style.
- The gallery, with its 13-ft. ceiling, presents guests with a dramatic entrance, and offers a gorgeous view into the huge Great Room through three elegantly inviting openings.

- The island kitchen will lure any gourmet. Nestled between the formal dining room and the breakfast room, it stands ready for all types of meals. Just steps away, the mudroom lets you keep an eye on the laundry while you cook.
- The lovely master bedroom greets you with an abundance of charms: an enormous walk-in closet, a private bath with a dual-sink vanity and a garden tub, plus convenient access to the large covered patio in back.
- That patio, you'll find, is the stuff of dreams—allowing you to enjoy outdoor meals come rain or shine!

Plan DD-2228	
Bedrooms: 3	**Baths:** 2
Living Area:	
Main floor	2,228 sq. ft.
Total Living Area:	**2,228 sq. ft.**
Standard basement	2,228 sq. ft.
Garage	431 sq. ft.
Exterior Wall Framing:	2x4

Foundation Options:
Standard basement
Crawlspace
Slab
(All plans can be built with your choice of foundation and framing. A generic conversion diagram is available. See order form.)

BLUEPRINT PRICE CODE:	C

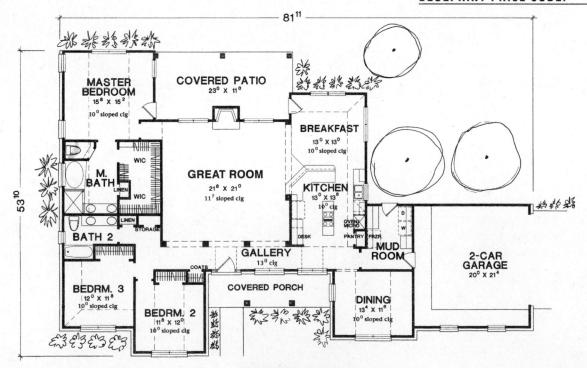

MAIN FLOOR

ORDER BLUEPRINTS ANYTIME!
CALL TOLL-FREE 1-800-820-1283

Plan DD-2228

PRICES AND DETAILS
ON PAGES 2-5

Healthy Appetite

- There's plenty of opportunity for fun and food in this home, which boasts a big backyard porch that's tailor-made for your active lifestyle!
- From the sheltered front entry, the foyer forks to introduce the living areas. To the left, a dramatic glass-block wall nicely defines the formal dining room.
- The centerpiece of the home is the angled family room, where a prominent

fireplace promises countless evenings of warmth and togetherness. Banks of windows deliver great views to the porch and beyond.
- If you like to greet nature face-to-face each morning, you'll love the master bedroom's private porch access. The master bath is equally well appointed, and includes a garden tub, a corner shower and a sink for each of you.
- Hectic meals are a thing of the past in the wide-open kitchen. Here, an island cooktop and lots of counter space work to your advantage. A cute nook with a corner window seat has porch access.

Plan DW-1830	
Bedrooms: 3	Baths: 2
Living Area:	
Main floor	1,830 sq. ft.
Total Living Area:	**1,830 sq. ft.**
Standard basement	1,830 sq. ft.
Garage	490 sq. ft.
Exterior Wall Framing:	2x4

Foundation Options:
Standard basement
Crawlspace
Slab
(All plans can be built with your choice of foundation and framing. A generic conversion diagram is available. See order form.)

BLUEPRINT PRICE CODE:	B

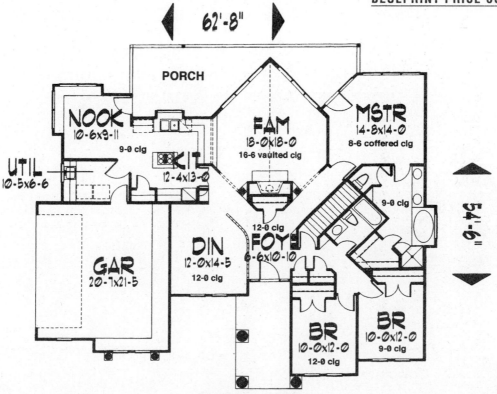

MAIN FLOOR

ORDER BLUEPRINTS ANYTIME!
CALL TOLL-FREE 1-800-820-1283

Plan DW-1830

PRICES AND DETAILS
ON PAGES 2-5

183

Sprawling One-Story

- A high hip roof, a stone-accented facade and alluring arched windows adorn this sprawling one-story.
- The recessed entry opens to the foyer, where regal columns introduce the elegant formal dining room.
- The spacious living room ahead is highlighted by a bright wall of windows and sliding glass doors that overlook the covered lanai.
- The island kitchen includes a handy pass-through window to the lanai and a snack counter that serves the family room and the breakfast room.

- The family room warms the entire area with a handsome fireplace and opens to a cozy covered patio.
- A French door from the sunny breakfast nook accesses the lanai.
- The secluded master bedroom also features a great view of the lanai, and includes a dressing room, an enormous walk-in closet and a private bath with French-door lanai access.
- The quiet study off the foyer could also serve as a guest bedroom.
- Two additional bedrooms share a hall bath with a dual-sink vanity. Laundry facilities are just steps away. The cozy corner bedroom has an 8-ft. ceiling. Airy 10-ft. ceilings are found throughout the rest of this delightfully comfortable home.

Plan DD-2241-1

Bedrooms: 3+	Baths: 2
Living Area:	
Main floor	2,256 sq. ft.
Total Living Area:	**2,256 sq. ft.**
Standard basement	2,256 sq. ft.
Garage	469 sq. ft.
Exterior Wall Framing:	2x4

Foundation Options:
Standard basement
Crawlspace
Slab
(All plans can be built with your choice of foundation and framing. A generic conversion diagram is available. See order form.)

BLUEPRINT PRICE CODE: C

Plan DD-2241-1

ORDER BLUEPRINTS ANYTIME!
CALL TOLL-FREE 1-800-820-1283

PRICES AND DETAILS
ON PAGES 2-5

High Interest!

- Angles, high ceilings and an excellent use of space add interest and volume to the living areas of this efficient four-bedroom home.
- Beyond the beautiful stucco facade, the spacious central living room extends a warm welcome with its handsome fireplace; a French door whisks you outside to the covered back porch.
- The kitchen and breakfast room's unique designs ensure easy access and mobility for the family.
- A giant-sized walk-in closet, a separate dressing room and an adjoining bath pamper you in the secluded master suite. The bath conveniently opens to the utility room, which houses the washer and dryer and an extra freezer.
- Three more bedrooms share another bath at the opposite end of the home.
- To the rear of the garage, a handy storage room and a built-in workbench help to organize your lawn and maintenance equipment.

Plan E-1828

Bedrooms: 4	Baths: 2
Living Area:	
Main floor	1,828 sq. ft.
Total Living Area:	**1,828 sq. ft.**
Standard basement	1,828 sq. ft.
Garage	605 sq. ft.
Storage	120 sq. ft.
Exterior Wall Framing:	2x6

Foundation Options:

Standard basement

Crawlspace

Slab

(All plans can be built with your choice of foundation and framing. A generic conversion diagram is available. See order form.)

BLUEPRINT PRICE CODE: B

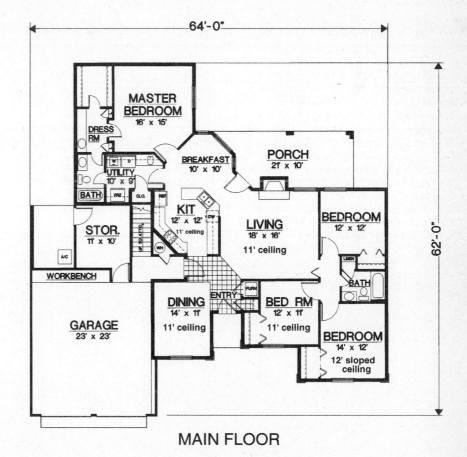

MAIN FLOOR

ORDER BLUEPRINTS ANYTIME!
CALL TOLL-FREE 1-800-820-1283

Plan E-1828

PRICES AND DETAILS
ON PAGES 2-5

185

Light and Bright

- This outstanding home features a light, inviting facade with arched windows, unique transoms and twin dormers.
- The sheltered front porch opens to an airy entry, which is flanked by a quiet study and the formal dining room. Straight ahead, the living room offers backyard views through three windows.
- The well-designed island kitchen is brightened by fluorescent lighting and enhanced by a nice corner window and a step-in pantry. The adjoining morning room features a lovely window seat, a built-in hutch and a snack bar.
- An inviting fireplace with a tile hearth is the focal point of the cozy family room. French doors open to a large deck.
- Walk-in closets are featured in each of the three bedrooms. The master suite includes deck access and a private bath with a garden tub, a separate shower and a dual-sink vanity.
- In the second bedroom, the ceiling slopes up to 11½ ft., accenting the elegant front window. The third bedroom has a standard 8-ft. ceiling.
- Unless otherwise specified, all rooms have high 10-ft. ceilings.

Plan DD-2372

Bedrooms: 3+	Baths: 2½
Living Area:	
Main floor	2,376 sq. ft.
Total Living Area:	**2,376 sq. ft.**
Standard basement	2,376 sq. ft.
Garage	473 sq. ft.
Exterior Wall Framing:	2x4

Foundation Options:

Standard basement

Crawlspace

Slab

(All plans can be built with your choice of foundation and framing. A generic conversion diagram is available. See order form.)

BLUEPRINT PRICE CODE: C

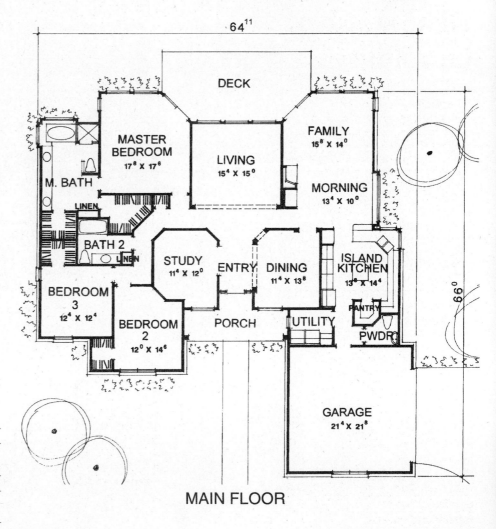

MAIN FLOOR

ORDER BLUEPRINTS ANYTIME!
CALL TOLL-FREE 1-800-820-1283

Plan DD-2372

*PRICES AND DETAILS
ON PAGES 2-5*

Distinguished Durability

- Sturdy tapered columns with brick pedestals give this unique home a feeling of durability and security.
- Off the foyer, the spacious living room is brightened by the incoming light of the double dormers above. The high 14-ft. ceiling and the glass-framed fireplace add further ambience. An atrium door opens to the wraparound porch.
- Decorative wood columns and an 11-ft. ceiling enhance the dining room.
- The neat kitchen shares serving counters with the breakfast nook and the living room, for easy service to both locations. A central cooktop island and a built-in desk are other conveniences.
- The main bath has twin sinks and is easily accessible from the secondary bedrooms and the living areas.
- An oval garden tub, an isolated toilet and dual sinks are featured in the master bath. The master suite also boasts a 13-ft. vaulted ceiling, a huge walk-in closet and a private porch.

Plan DW-1883

Bedrooms: 3	Baths: 2
Living Area:	
Main floor	1,883 sq. ft.
Total Living Area:	**1,883 sq. ft.**
Standard basement	1,883 sq. ft.
Exterior Wall Framing:	2x4

Foundation Options:

Standard basement

Crawlspace

Slab

(All plans can be built with your choice of foundation and framing. A generic conversion diagram is available. See order form.)

BLUEPRINT PRICE CODE:	B

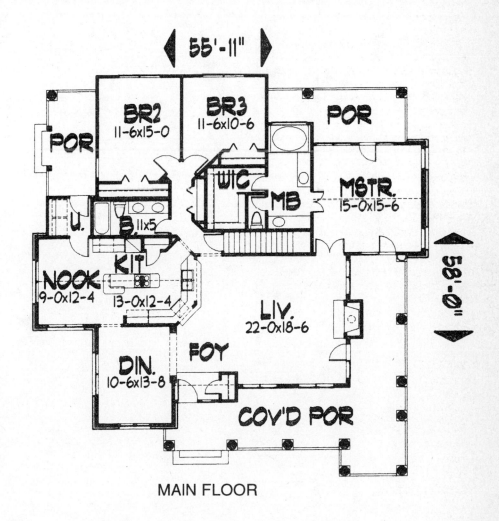

MAIN FLOOR

ORDER BLUEPRINTS ANYTIME!
CALL TOLL-FREE 1-800-820-1283

Plan DW-1883

PRICES AND DETAILS
ON PAGES 2-5

187

Superbly Done!

- A tile roof and extravagant glass are a just a prelude to the many amenities found in this superb home.
- The raised 13-ft. foyer offers a gorgeous view through French doors to a lanai and a potential pool area beyond.
- The grand living room has a curved wall of glass, plus a 22-ft. sloped ceiling with exposed rafters under a metal deck roof.
- High 12-ft. vaulted ceilings enhance both the nearby den and the sitting room in the posh master suite.
- The master suite offers a three-way fireplace and a raised exercise room with a 9½-ft. ceiling and a private deck. An 11-ft. ceiling tops the sleeping area and the bath, which boasts a whirlpool tub and a sit-down shower, each defined by a glass-block wall.
- The formal dining room is enhanced by tall glass and a 14½-ft. vaulted ceiling.
- High 14-ft. ceilings augment the bright morning room, the island kitchen and the family room, where a fireplace, a TV niche and deck access are featured.
- A nice ale bar has a pass-through for easy service to the pool area. A summer kitchen on the deck hosts barbecues.
- Three secondary bedrooms and two full baths complete this wing of the home.

Plan EOF-70

Bedrooms: 4+	Baths: 3½
Living Area:	
Main floor	5,013 sq. ft.
Total Living Area:	**5,013 sq. ft.**
Garage and shop	902 sq. ft.
Exterior Wall Framing:	8-in. concrete block

Foundation Options:

Slab

(All plans can be built with your choice of foundation and framing. A generic conversion diagram is available. See order form.)

BLUEPRINT PRICE CODE: I

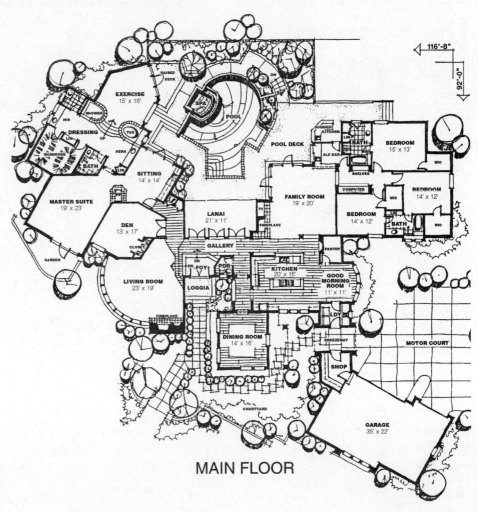

MAIN FLOOR

188   *ORDER BLUEPRINTS ANYTIME!*
CALL TOLL-FREE 1-800-820-1283   Plan EOF-70   *PRICES AND DETAILS*
ON PAGES 2-5

Double Take

- Family entertainment is a priority in one corner of this stunning home, where you'll find a joined family room and media room.

- If you care for lively conversation, settle into a comfortable furniture ensemble in the family room. If the evening calls for homespun cinema, treat yourselves to a big-screen flick in the media room. Even your in-laws' home movies will look great!

- Under a blistering sky, a dip in the backyard spa will cool and refresh you. It's nestled into a partially covered deck so you can run for shelter and still enjoy a steamy summer storm.

- Inside, the island kitchen lends itself easily to formal entertainment and everyday routines.

- Escape to the master suite for a little pampering. You can slip out to the deck on cool spring mornings or curl up with a crossword puzzle by the bay window. The master bath offers two walk-in closets and a dual-sink vanity.

Plan DD-2665

Bedrooms: 3+	Baths: 2½
Living Area:	
Main floor	2,666 sq. ft.
Total Living Area:	**2,666 sq. ft.**
Standard basement	2,666 sq. ft.
Garage	411 sq. ft.
Exterior Wall Framing:	2x4

Foundation Options:

Standard basement
Crawlspace
Slab

(All plans can be built with your choice of foundation and framing. A generic conversion diagram is available. See order form.)

BLUEPRINT PRICE CODE:	D

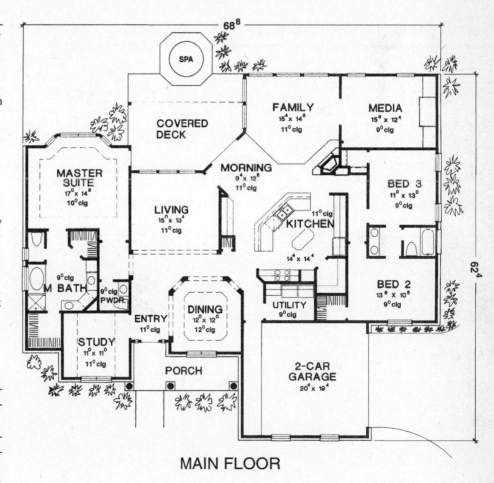

MAIN FLOOR

Deluxe Suite!

- Decorative corner quoins, arched windows and a sleek hip roofline give this charming home a European look.
- The inviting foyer extends its 12-ft. ceiling into the formal spaces. The airy living room is brightened by high half- and quarter-round windows.
- The adjoining formal dining room is set off with elegant columned openings and high plant shelves.
- The island kitchen features a pantry and a sunny breakfast bay. A pass-through over the sink serves the family room.
- Boasting a 17-ft. vaulted ceiling and a glass-flanked fireplace, the family room also enjoys backyard access.
- The deluxe master suite includes a private sitting room. Both the bedroom and the sitting room have an 11-ft. tray ceiling and a view of a romantic two-sided fireplace. The master bath boasts a 13½-ft. vaulted ceiling, a garden tub, a three-sided mirror and a dual-sink vanity with knee space.
- A second bath is shared by the two remaining bedrooms.
- Unless otherwise noted, all rooms have 9-ft. ceilings.

Plan FB-5154-GEOR

Bedrooms: 3	Baths: 2½
Living Area:	
Main floor	2,236 sq. ft.
Total Living Area:	**2,236 sq. ft.**
Daylight basement	2,236 sq. ft.
Garage	483 sq. ft.
Exterior Wall Framing:	2x4

Foundation Options:

Daylight basement

Crawlspace

(All plans can be built with your choice of foundation and framing. A generic conversion diagram is available. See order form.)

BLUEPRINT PRICE CODE: C

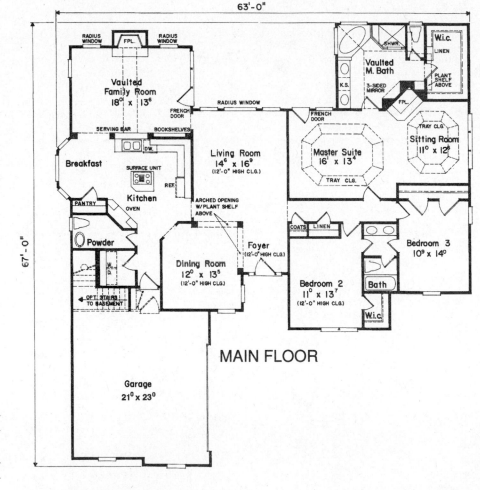

MAIN FLOOR

ORDER BLUEPRINTS ANYTIME!
CALL TOLL-FREE 1-800-820-1283

Plan FB-5154-GEOR

PRICES AND DETAILS
ON PAGES 2-5

All Good Things

- This stone-sturdy home pleases the eye with a rustic, country facade and a multitude of interior luxuries.
- Designed with your loved ones in mind, the family room, island kitchen and bayed breakfast nook flow into each other for a feeling of togetherness. From the nook, a huge backyard deck is quickly accessible.

- For formal gatherings, the living and dining rooms serve effortlessly.
- The master suite epitomizes comfort, with its private deck and adjoining office space. Opulence is apparent in the master bath, which features a spa tub and two walk-in closets.
- A stunning guest suite delivers a private deck and a kitchen area. With its full bath, it's the perfect spot for relatives who are enjoying their golden years.

Plan DD-3152	
Bedrooms: 3+	**Baths:** 3½
Living Area:	
Main floor	3,152 sq. ft.
Total Living Area:	**3,152 sq. ft.**
Standard basement	3,152 sq. ft.
Garage	610 sq. ft.
Exterior Wall Framing:	2x4
Foundation Options:	
Standard basement	
Crawlspace	
Slab	

(All plans can be built with your choice of foundation and framing. A generic conversion diagram is available. See order form.)

BLUEPRINT PRICE CODE: E

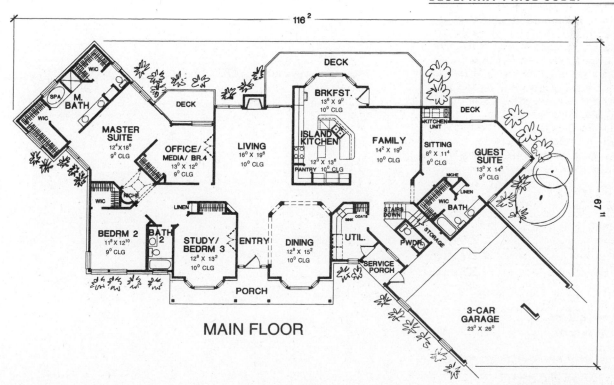

MAIN FLOOR

ORDER BLUEPRINTS ANYTIME!
CALL TOLL-FREE 1-800-820-1283

Plan DD-3152

PRICES AND DETAILS
ON PAGES 2-5

191

Outdoor Surprises!

- A private entry courtyard topped by an intricate trellis draws attention to this beautiful brick home.
- The drama continues inside, where you'll find high ceilings, sprawling openness and breathtaking views of the many outdoor living spaces.
- The central hearth room is a great spot to welcome your guests and keep them entertained with its dazzling fireplace and media center combination.
- Appetizers and refreshments can be served at the long snack bar extending from the triangular kitchen.
- Plenty of space for formal mingling is offered in the spacious living and dining room expanse beyond. The screened porch, adjoining patio and panoramic views will inspire hours of conversation.
- Ideal for the empty nester, this home includes two private bedroom suites. The master suite boasts his-and-hers closets, vanities and toilets.
- The studio at the front of the home could also serve as an extra bedroom or home office.

Plan EOF-86-B

Bedrooms: 2+	Baths: 2½
Living Area:	
Main floor	1,830 sq. ft.
Total Living Area:	**1,830 sq. ft.**
Screened porch	134 sq. ft.
Garage	433 sq. ft.
Exterior Wall Framing:	2x4

Foundation Options:

Slab
(All plans can be built with your choice of foundation and framing. A generic conversion diagram is available. See order form.)

BLUEPRINT PRICE CODE: B

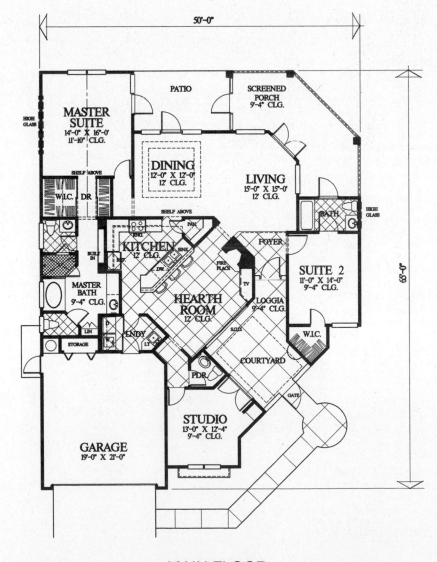

MAIN FLOOR

ORDER BLUEPRINTS ANYTIME!
CALL TOLL-FREE 1-800-820-1283

Plan EOF-86-B

PRICES AND DETAILS
ON PAGES 2-5

Cozy Covered Porches

- Twin dormers give this raised one-story design the appearance of a two-story. Two covered porches and a deck supplement the main living areas with plenty of outdoor entertaining space.
- The large central living room features a dramatic fireplace, a 12-ft. ceiling with a skylight and access to both porch areas.
- Double doors open to a bayed eating area, which overlooks the adjoining deck and includes a sloped ceiling that rises to 12 ft. in the kitchen. An angled snack bar and a pantry are also featured.
- The elegant master suite is tucked to one side of the home and also overlooks the backyard and deck. Laundry facilities and garage access are nearby.
- Across the home, two additional bedrooms share another full bath.

Plan E-1826

Bedrooms: 3	Baths: 2

Living Area:

Main floor	1,800 sq. ft.
Total Living Area:	**1,800 sq. ft.**
Garage	550 sq. ft.
Storage	84 sq. ft.
Exterior Wall Framing:	**2x6**

Foundation Options:

Crawlspace
Slab
(All plans can be built with your choice of foundation and framing. A generic conversion diagram is available. See order form.)

BLUEPRINT PRICE CODE: B

MAIN FLOOR

ORDER BLUEPRINTS ANYTIME!
CALL TOLL-FREE 1-800-820-1283

Plan E-1826

PRICES AND DETAILS
ON PAGES 2-5

193

Spacious Country-Style

- This distinctive country-style home is highlighted by a wide front porch and multi-paned windows with shutters.
- Inside, the dining room is off the foyer and open to the living room, but is defined by elegant columns and beams above.
- The central living room boasts a 12-ft. cathedral ceiling, a fireplace and French doors to the rear patio.
- The delightful kitchen/nook area is spacious and well planned for both work and play.
- A handy utility room and a half-bath are on either side of a short hallway leading to the carport, which includes a large storage area.
- The master suite offers his-and-hers walk-in closets and an incredible bath that incorporates a plant shelf above the raised spa tub.
- The two remaining bedrooms share a hall bath that is compartmentalized to allow more than one user at a time.

Plan J-86140

Bedrooms: 3	Baths: 2½
Living Area:	
Main floor	2,177 sq. ft.
Total Living Area:	**2,177 sq. ft.**
Standard basement	2,177 sq. ft.
Carport	440 sq. ft.
Storage	120 sq. ft.
Exterior Wall Framing:	2x4

Foundation Options:

Standard basement

Crawlspace

Slab

(All plans can be built with your choice of foundation and framing. A generic conversion diagram is available. See order form.)

BLUEPRINT PRICE CODE: C

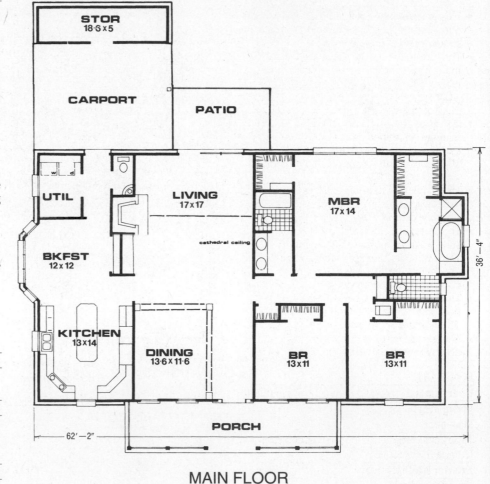

MAIN FLOOR

ORDER BLUEPRINTS ANYTIME!
CALL TOLL-FREE 1-800-820-1283

Plan J-86140

PRICES AND DETAILS
ON PAGES 2-5

Masterful
Master Suite

- This gorgeous home features front and rear covered porches and a master suite so luxurious it deserves its own wing.
- The expansive entry welcomes visitors into a spacious, skylighted living room, which boasts a handsome fireplace. The adjacent formal dining room overlooks the front porch.
- Designed for efficiency, the kitchen features an angled snack bar, a bayed eating area and views of the porch. An all-purpose utility room is conveniently located off the kitchen.
- The kitchen, eating area, living room and dining room are all heightened by 12-ft. ceilings.
- The sumptuous and secluded master suite features a tub and a separate shower, a double-sink vanity, a walk-in closet with built-in shelves and a compartmentalized toilet.
- The two secondary bedrooms share a hall bath at the other end of the home. The rear bedroom offers porch access.
- The garage features built-in storage and access to unfinished attic space.

Plan E-1811

Bedrooms: 3	Baths: 2
Living Area:	
Main floor	1,800 sq. ft.
Total Living Area:	**1,800 sq. ft.**
Garage and storage	634 sq. ft.
Exterior Wall Framing:	2x6

Foundation Options:

Crawlspace
Slab
(All plans can be built with your choice of foundation and framing. A generic conversion diagram is available. See order form.)

BLUEPRINT PRICE CODE:	B

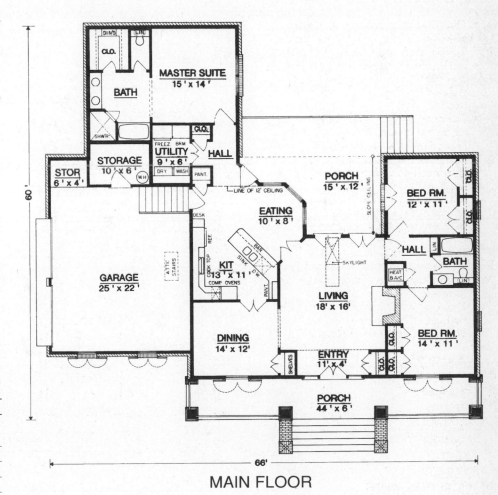

MAIN FLOOR

ORDER BLUEPRINTS ANYTIME!
CALL TOLL-FREE 1-800-820-1283

Plan E-1811

PRICES AND DETAILS
ON PAGES 2-5

195

Bright Outlook

- Brighten your perspective in this cozy, country-style home! Passersby will gaze admiringly at its glorious paned windows, accented by keystones and shutters; those within will enjoy viewing the great outdoors!
- A unique gallery introduces the magnificent Great Room, which showcases a fireplace flanked by two archtop windows. A sloped, 11-ft., 7-in. ceiling completes the picture of spaciousness.
- Flowing from the Great Room, the dining room offers access to a covered

patio overlooking the backyard, and also shares an angled snack counter with the island kitchen.
- A cooktop island, a gigantic walk-in pantry and a built-in desk distinguish the spacious kitchen. A windowed sink adds interest to those daily chores!
- Across the home , the master suite provides an ideal retreat. Its perks include a huge walk-in closet, a whirlpool tub, a separate shower, a private toilet and a dual-sink vanity. A huge archtop window and private access to the patio create romance.
- Two secondary bedrooms share another full bath.

Plan DD-1982	
Bedrooms: 3	**Baths:** 2
Living Area:	
Main floor	1,993 sq. ft.
Total Living Area:	**1,993 sq. ft.**
Standard basement	1,993 sq. ft.
Garage and storage	538 sq. ft.
Exterior Wall Framing:	2x4
Foundation Options:	
Standard basement	
Crawlspace	
Slab	

(All plans can be built with your choice of foundation and framing. A generic conversion diagram is available. See order form.)

BLUEPRINT PRICE CODE:	B

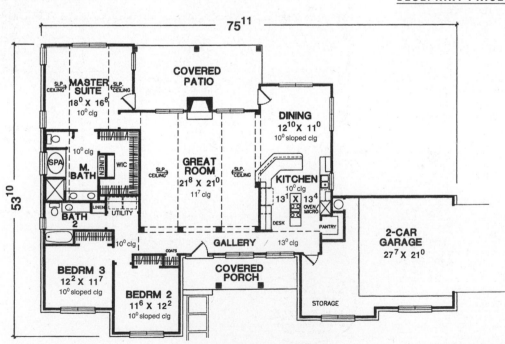

MAIN FLOOR

ORDER BLUEPRINTS ANYTIME!
CALL TOLL-FREE 1-800-820-1283

Plan DD-1982

PRICES AND DETAILS
ON PAGES 2-5

Photo by Mark Englund/HomeStyles

Elaborate Entry

- This home's important-looking covered entry greets guests with heavy, banded support columns, sunburst transom windows and dual sidelights.
- Once inside the home, the 15-ft.-high foyer is flanked by the formal living and dining rooms, which have 10½-ft. vaulted ceilings. Straight ahead and beyond five decorative columns lies the spacious family room.
- Surrounded by 8-ft.-high walls, the family room features a 13-ft. vaulted ceiling, a fireplace and sliding doors to a covered patio. A neat plant shelf above the fireplace adds style.
- The bright and airy kitchen has a 13-ft. ceiling and serves the family room and the breakfast area, which is enhanced by a corner window and a French door.
- The master suite enjoys a 13-ft. vaulted ceiling and features French-door patio access, a large walk-in closet and a private bath with a corner platform tub and a separate shower.
- Across the home, three secondary bedrooms share a hall bath, which boasts private access to the patio.

Plan HDS-90-806

Bedrooms: 4	Baths: 2

Living Area:

Main floor	2,056 sq. ft.
Total Living Area:	**2,056 sq. ft.**
Garage	452 sq. ft.

Exterior Wall Framing:

2x4 or 8-in. concrete block

Foundation Options:

Slab

(All plans can be built with your choice of foundation and framing. A generic conversion diagram is available. See order form.)

BLUEPRINT PRICE CODE: C

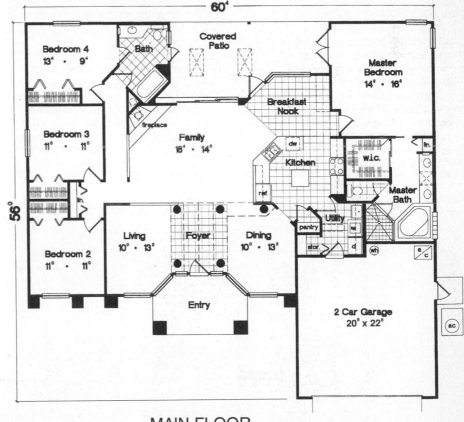

MAIN FLOOR

NOTE: The above photographed home may have been modified by the homeowner. Please refer to floor plan and/or drawn elevation shown for actual blueprint details.

ORDER BLUEPRINTS ANYTIME!
CALL TOLL-FREE 1-800-820-1283

Plan HDS-90-806

PRICES AND DETAILS
ON PAGES 2-5

197

Updated Tudor

- Updated Tudor styling gives this home an extra-appealing exterior. Inside, the bright and open living spaces are embellished with a host of wonderfully contemporary details.

- An inviting brick arch frames the front door, which opens directly into the living room. Here, a 14-ft. sloped ceiling, a fireplace and a view to the covered rear porch provide an impressive welcome.

- The octagonal dining area is absolutely stunning—the perfect complement for the skylighted kitchen, which boasts an angled cooktop/snack bar and a 12-ft. sloped ceiling. Double doors in the kitchen lead to a roomy utility area and the cleverly disguised side-entry garage.

- No details were left out in the sumptuous master suite, which features access to a private porch with a 14-ft. sloped ceiling and skylights. The luxurious bath offers a platform tub, a sit-down shower, his-and-hers vanities and lots of storage and closet space.

- Two more bedrooms are situated at the opposite side of the home and share a hall bath. One bedroom features a window seat, while the other has direct access to the central covered porch.

Plan E-1912

Bedrooms: 3	Baths: 2
Living Area:	
Main floor	1,946 sq. ft.
Total Living Area:	**1,946 sq. ft.**
Garage and storage	562 sq. ft.
Exterior Wall Framing:	2x6

Foundation Options:

Crawlspace

Slab

(All plans can be built with your choice of foundation and framing. A generic conversion diagram is available. See order form.)

BLUEPRINT PRICE CODE: C

MAIN FLOOR

ORDER BLUEPRINTS ANYTIME!
CALL TOLL-FREE 1-800-820-1283

Plan E-1912

PRICES AND DETAILS ON PAGES 2-5

Photo by Mark Englund/HomeStyles

Full of Surprises

- While dignified and reserved on the outside, this plan presents intriguing angles, vaulted ceilings and surprising spaces throughout the interior.
- The elegant, vaulted living room flows from the expansive foyer and includes a striking fireplace and a beautiful bay.
- The spacious island kitchen offers wide corner windows above the sink and easy service to both the vaulted dining room and the skylighted nook.
- The adjoining vaulted family room features a warm corner woodstove and sliding doors to the backyard patio.
- The superb master suite includes a vaulted sleeping area and an exquisite private bath with a skylighted dressing area, a large walk-in closet, a step-up spa tub and a separate shower.
- Three secondary bedrooms are located near another full bath and a large laundry room with garage access.

Plans P-7711-3A & -3D

Bedrooms: 4	**Baths:** 2

Living Area:

Main floor (crawlspace version)	2,510 sq. ft.
Main floor (basement version)	2,580 sq. ft.
Total Living Area:	**2,510/2,580 sq. ft.**
Daylight basement	2,635 sq. ft.
Garage	806 sq. ft.
Exterior Wall Framing:	**2x6**
Foundation Options:	**Plan #**
Daylight basement	P-7711-3D
Crawlspace	P-7711-3A

(All plans can be built with your choice of foundation and framing. A generic conversion diagram is available. See order form.)

BLUEPRINT PRICE CODE:	**D**

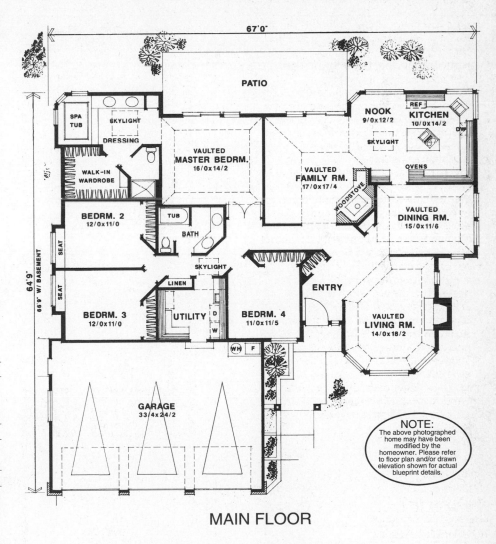

MAIN FLOOR

NOTE:
The above photographed home may have been modified by the homeowner. Please refer to floor plan and/or drawn elevation shown for actual blueprint details.

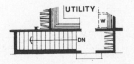

BASEMENT STAIRWAY LOCATION

ORDER BLUEPRINTS ANYTIME!
CALL TOLL-FREE 1-800-820-1283

Plans P-7711-3A & -3D

PRICES AND DETAILS
ON PAGES 2-5

199

Updated Creole

- This Louisiana-style raised cottage features a tin roof, shuttered windows and three pairs of French doors, all of which add to the comfort and nostalgic appeal of this Creole classic.
- The French doors enter from the cool and relaxing front porch to the formal living areas and a front bedroom.
- The central living room, which features a 12-ft. ceiling, merges with the dining room and the kitchen's eating area. A fireplace warms the whole space while more French doors access a porch.
- The efficient kitchen offers a 12-ft. flat ceiling, an angled snack bar and a bayed nook with a 12-ft. sloped ceiling.
- A secluded master suite showcases a private bath, fit for the most demanding tastes. Across the home, the secondary bedrooms include abundant closet space and share a full bath.
- This full-featured, energy-efficient design also includes a large utility room and extra storage space in the garage.

Plan E-1823

Bedrooms: 3	Baths: 2
Living Area:	
Main floor	1,800 sq. ft.
Total Living Area:	**1,800 sq. ft.**
Garage	550 sq. ft.
Exterior Wall Framing:	2x6

Foundation Options:

Crawlspace

Slab

(All plans can be built with your choice of foundation and framing. A generic conversion diagram is available. See order form.)

BLUEPRINT PRICE CODE:	**B**

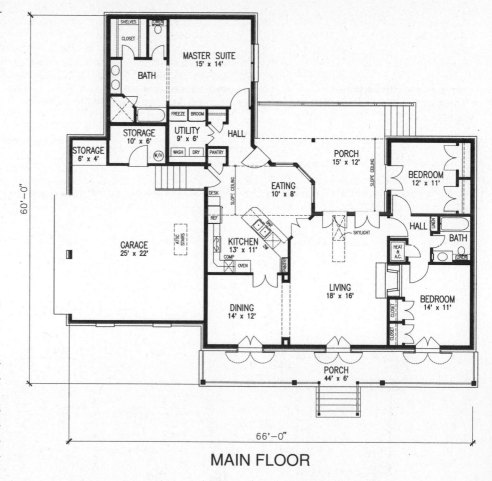

MAIN FLOOR

ORDER BLUEPRINTS ANYTIME! CALL TOLL-FREE 1-800-820-1283   Plan E-1823   **PRICES AND DETAILS ON PAGES 2-5**

Photo by Mark Englund/HomeStyles

Extraordinary Estate Living

- Extraordinary estate living is at its best in this palatial beauty.
- The double-doored entry opens to a large central living room that overlooks a covered patio with a vaulted ceiling. High 14-ft. ceilings are found in the living room, in the formal dining room and in the den or study, which may serve as a fourth bedroom.
- The gourmet chef will enjoy the spacious kitchen, which flaunts a

cooktop island, a walk-in pantry and a peninsula snack counter shared with the breakfast room and family room.
- This trio of informal living spaces also shares a panorama of glass and a corner fireplace centered between TV and media niches.
- Isolated at the opposite end of the home is the spacious master suite, which offers private patio access. Dual walk-in closets define the entrance to the adjoining master bath, complete with a garden Jacuzzi, a designer shower and separate dressing areas.
- The hall bath also opens to the outdoors for use as a pool bath.

Plan HDS-99-177

Bedrooms: 3+	**Baths:** 3

Living Area:	
Main floor	2,597 sq. ft.
Total Living Area:	**2,597 sq. ft.**
Garage	785 sq. ft.

Exterior Wall Framing:	2x4

Foundation Options:

Slab

(All plans can be built with your choice of foundation and framing. A generic conversion diagram is available. See order form.)

BLUEPRINT PRICE CODE:	**D**

NOTE:
The above photographed home may have been modified by the homeowner. Please refer to floor plan and/or drawn elevation shown for actual blueprint details.

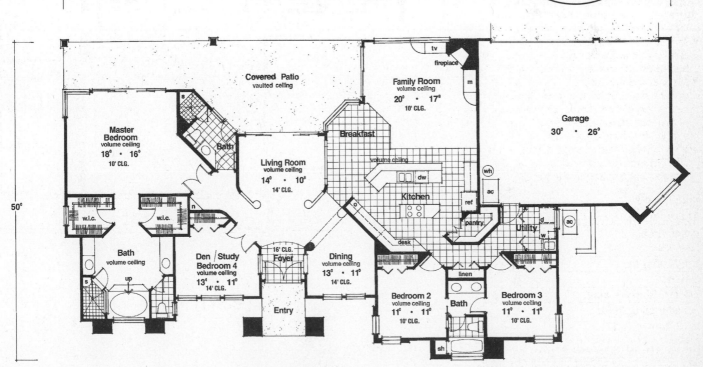

MAIN FLOOR

ORDER BLUEPRINTS ANYTIME!
CALL TOLL-FREE 1-800-820-1283

Plan HDS-99-177

PRICES AND DETAILS
ON PAGES 2-5

201

Photo by Mark Englund/hd/HomeStyles

Strength of Character

- The solid, permanent feel of brick and the intelligent, efficient floor plan of this stately one-story home give it an obvious strength of character.
- Guests are welcomed inside by an attractive raised foyer, from which virtually any room can be reached with just a few steps.
- With a high ceiling, a built-in bookcase, a gorgeous fireplace and French doors that lead to the backyard, the centrally located living room is well equipped to serve as a hub of activity.
- Smartly designed and positioned, the galley-style kitchen easily serves the cozy breakfast nook and the formal dining room.
- The beautiful master bedroom provides a nice blend of elegance and seclusion, and features a striking stepped ceiling, a large walk-in closet, a private bath and its own access to the backyard.
- Two additional bedrooms feature walk-in closets and share a full-sized bath.

Plan L-851-A

Bedrooms: 3	Baths: 2

Living Area:

Main floor	1,849 sq. ft.
Total Living Area:	**1,849 sq. ft.**
Garage	437 sq. ft.
Exterior Wall Framing:	2x4

Foundation Options:

Slab

(All plans can be built with your choice of foundation and framing. A generic conversion diagram is available. See order form.)

BLUEPRINT PRICE CODE: B

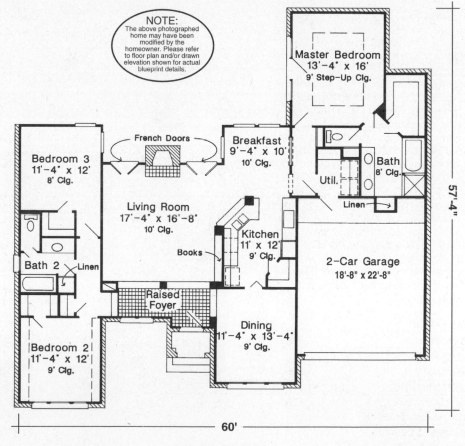

NOTE:
The above photographed home may have been modified by the homeowner. Please refer to floor plan and/or drawn elevation shown for actual blueprint details.

MAIN FLOOR

ORDER BLUEPRINTS ANYTIME!
CALL TOLL-FREE 1-800-820-1283

Plan L-851-A

PRICES AND DETAILS
ON PAGES 2-5

Showy One-Story

- Dramatic windows embellish the exterior of this showy one-story home.
- Inside, the entry provides a sweeping view of the living room, where sliding glass doors open to the backyard patio and flank a dramatic fireplace.
- Skylights accent the living room's 12-ft. sloped ceiling, while arched openings define the formal dining room.
- Double doors lead from the dining room to the kitchen and informal eating area. The kitchen features a built-in work desk and a pantry. An oversized utility room adjoins the kitchen and accesses the two-car garage.
- A 10-ft. tray ceiling adorns the master suite. The private bath is accented with a skylight above the fabulous fan-shaped marble tub. His-and-hers vanities, a separate shower and a huge walk-in closet are also featured.
- Two more bedrooms and a full bath are located at the other end of the home.
- The front-facing bedroom boasts a 12-ft. sloped ceiling.

Plan E-1830

Bedrooms: 3	Baths: 2
Living Area:	
Main floor	1,868 sq. ft.
Total Living Area:	**1,868 sq. ft.**
Garage and storage	616 sq. ft.
Exterior Wall Framing:	2x6

Foundation Options:

Crawlspace

Slab

(All plans can be built with your choice of foundation and framing. A generic conversion diagram is available. See order form.)

BLUEPRINT PRICE CODE: B

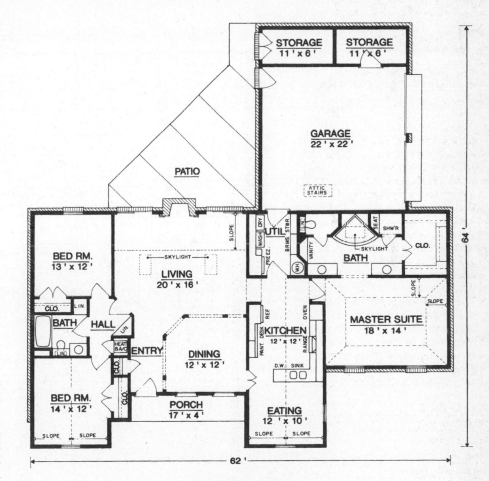

MAIN FLOOR

Attainable Luxury

- This traditional ranch home offers a large, central living room with a 12-ft. ceiling, a corner fireplace and an adjoining patio.
- The U-shaped kitchen easily services both the formal dining room and the bayed eating area.
- The luxurious master suite features a large bath with separate vanities and dressing areas.
- Two secondary bedrooms share a second full bath.
- A covered carport boasts a decorative brick wall and attic space above. Two additional storage areas provide plenty of room for gardening supplies and sports equipment.

Plan E-1812

Bedrooms: 3	Baths: 2
Living Area:	
Main floor	1,860 sq. ft.
Total Living Area:	**1,860 sq. ft.**
Carport	484 sq. ft.
Storage	132 sq. ft.
Exterior Wall Framing:	2x6

Foundation Options:

Crawlspace
Slab

(All plans can be built with your choice of foundation and framing. A generic conversion diagram is available. See order form.)

BLUEPRINT PRICE CODE: B

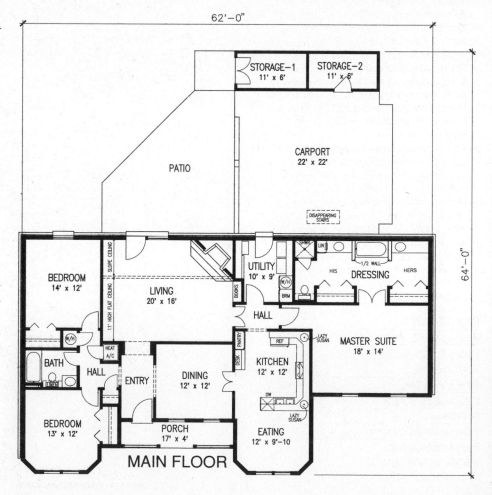

MAIN FLOOR

ORDER BLUEPRINTS ANYTIME! ***CALL TOLL-FREE 1-800-820-1283*** Plan E-1812 **PRICES AND DETAILS ON PAGES 2-5**

Classic Ranch

- With decorative brick quoins, a columned porch and stylish dormers, the exterior of this classic one-story provides an interesting blend of Early American and European design.
- Just off the foyer, the bay-windowed formal dining room is enhanced by an 11-ft., 6-in.-high stepped ceiling.
- The spacious Great Room, separated from the dining room by a columned arch, features a stepped ceiling, a built-in media center and a striking fireplace. Lovely French doors lead to a big backyard patio.
- The breakfast room, which shares an eating bar with the kitchen, boasts a ceiling that slopes to 12 feet. French doors access a covered rear porch.
- The master bedroom has a 10-ft. tray ceiling, a sunny bay window and a roomy walk-in closet. The master bath features a whirlpool tub in a bayed nook and a separate shower.
- The front-facing bedroom is enhanced by a 10-ft.-high vaulted area over an arched transom window.

Plan AX-93304

Bedrooms: 3	Baths: 2
Living Area:	
Main floor	1,860 sq. ft.
Total Living Area:	**1,860 sq. ft.**
Standard basement	1,860 sq. ft.
Garage	434 sq. ft.
Exterior Wall Framing:	2x4

Foundation Options:

Standard basement
Crawlspace
Slab

(All plans can be built with your choice of foundation and framing. A generic conversion diagram is available. See order form.)

BLUEPRINT PRICE CODE: B

VIEW INTO GREAT ROOM

MAIN FLOOR

ORDER BLUEPRINTS ANYTIME!
CALL TOLL-FREE 1-800-820-1283

Plan AX-93304

PRICES AND DETAILS
ON PAGES 2-5

205

Photo courtesy of Breland & Farmer Designers, Inc.

Luxurious Master Suite

- The inviting facade of this gorgeous one-story design boasts a sheltered porch, symmetrical architecture and elegant window treatments.
- Inside, beautiful arched openings frame the living room, which features a 12-ft. ceiling, a dramatic fireplace and a wet bar that is open to the deluxe kitchen.
- The roomy kitchen is highlighted by an island cooktop, a built-in desk and a snack bar that faces the bayed eating area and the covered back porch.
- Isolated to the rear of the home, the master suite is a romantic retreat, offering an intimate sitting area and a luxurious bath. Entered through elegant double doors, the private bath showcases a skylighted corner tub, a separate shower, his-and-hers vanities, and a huge walk-in closet.
- The two remaining bedrooms have walk-in closets and share a hall bath.
- Unless otherwise specified, the home has 9-ft. ceilings throughout.

Plan E-2106

Bedrooms: 3	Baths: 2
Living Area:	
Main floor	2,177 sq. ft.
Total Living Area:	**2,177 sq. ft.**
Standard basement	2,177 sq. ft.
Garage and storage	570 sq. ft.
Exterior Wall Framing:	2x4

Foundation Options:

Standard basement

Crawlspace

Slab

(All plans can be built with your choice of foundation and framing. A generic conversion diagram is available. See order form.)

BLUEPRINT PRICE CODE: C

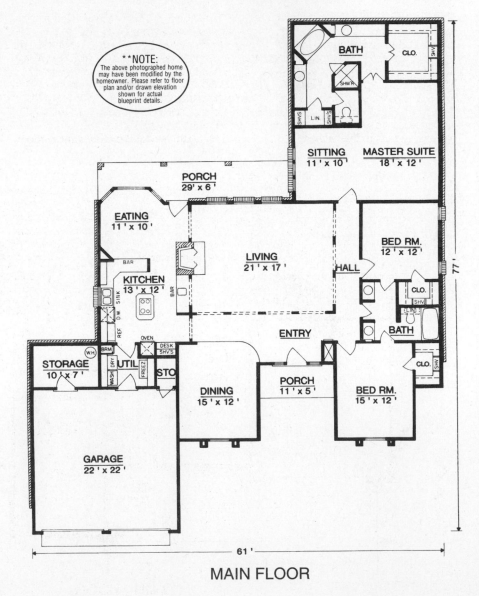

NOTE: The above photographed home may have been modified by the homeowner. Please refer to floor plan and/or drawn elevation shown for actual blueprint details.

MAIN FLOOR

ORDER BLUEPRINTS ANYTIME!
CALL TOLL-FREE 1-800-820-1283

Plan E-2106

PRICES AND DETAILS ON PAGES 2-5

Outstanding One-Story

- This sharp one-story home has an outstanding floor plan, attractively enhanced by a stately brick facade.
- A vestibule introduces the foyer, which flows between the formal living spaces at the front of the home.
- The large living room features a 14-ft., 8-in. sloped ceiling and dramatic, high windows. The spacious dining room has easy access to the kitchen.

- The expansive family room is the focal point of the home, with a 16-ft. beamed cathedral ceiling, a slate-hearth fireplace and sliding glass doors to a backyard terrace.
- The adjoining kitchen has a snack bar and a sunny dinette framed by a curved window wall that overlooks the terrace.
- Included in the sleeping wing is a luxurious master suite with a private bath. A skylighted dressing room and a big walk-in closet are also featured.
- The two secondary bedrooms share a hall bath that has a dual-sink vanity. A half-bath is near the mud/laundry room.

Plan K-278-M	
Bedrooms: 3	**Baths:** 2½
Living Area:	
Main floor	1,803 sq. ft.
Total Living Area:	**1,803 sq. ft.**
Standard basement	1,778 sq. ft.
Garage and storage	586 sq. ft.
Exterior Wall Framing:	2x4 or 2x6
Foundation Options:	
Standard basement	
Slab	

(All plans can be built with your choice of foundation and framing. A generic conversion diagram is available. See order form.)

BLUEPRINT PRICE CODE: B

MAIN FLOOR

(Floor plan labels:) Terrace 79-4 · service · dinette 9-0x10-0 · opt. screen or pt'n. · sl gl dr · fireplace · vanity · dress'g · skylight above · laundry · wash rm · Mud Rm · stor · dn to bsmt · Kitchen 10-0x12-0 · Family Rm (cathedral ceil'g) 16-8x18-0 · Bath · wic · Master Suite 13-4x16-2 · Double Garage 20-0x23-2 · ref · Bath · cl · lin · screen · hall · Dining Rm 11-0x13-4 · Foyer · Living Rm (sloped ceil'g) 13-0x20-3 · Bedrm 3 10-0x11-0 · Bedrm 2 11-0x13-4 · cl · vest · cl · covered entry · driveway · up · up · brick veneer · 43-4

ORDER BLUEPRINTS ANYTIME!
CALL TOLL-FREE 1-800-820-1283

Plan K-278-M

PRICES AND DETAILS
ON PAGES 2-5

207

Impressive Master Suite

- This attractive one-story home features an impressive master suite located apart from the secondary bedrooms.
- A lovely front porch opens to the entry, which flows to the formal dining room, the rear-oriented living room and the secondary bedroom wing.
- The living room boasts a large corner fireplace, a ceiling that slopes to 11 ft. and access to a backyard patio.
- A U-shaped kitchen services the dining room and its own eating area. It also boasts a built-in desk, a handy pantry closet and access to the nearby laundry room and carport.
- The wide master bedroom hosts a lavish master bath with a spa tub, a separate shower and his-and-hers dressing areas.
- Across the home, the two secondary bedrooms share another full bath.

Plan E-1818

Bedrooms: 3	Baths: 2
Living Area:	
Main floor	1,868 sq. ft.
Total Living Area:	**1,868 sq. ft.**
Carport	484 sq. ft.
Storage	132 sq. ft.
Exterior Wall Framing:	2x6

Foundation Options:

Crawlspace

Slab

(All plans can be built with your choice of foundation and framing. A generic conversion diagram is available. See order form.)

BLUEPRINT PRICE CODE: B

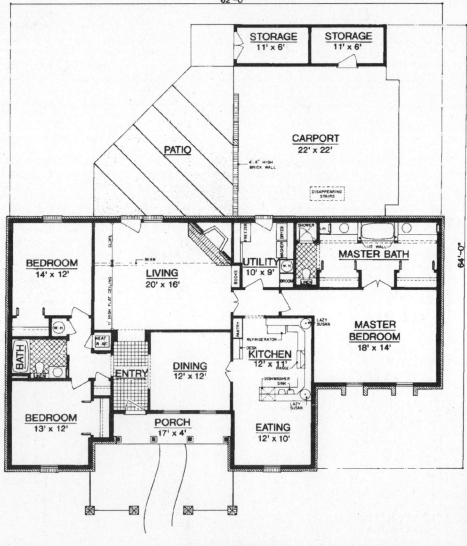

MAIN FLOOR

Spectacular One-Story!

- The angled, covered entry of this spectacular one-story home opens into its thoroughly up-to-date interior.
- Past the inviting foyer, the spacious dining area shares a soaring 13-ft. ceiling with the adjoining Great Room.
- Brightened by sliding glass doors to a covered backyard patio, the Great Room also includes an extensive built-in media center.
- The gourmet kitchen has a 13-ft. ceiling and serves a sunny bay-windowed breakfast area over an angled counter. A convenient laundry/utility area with garage access is nearby.
- Enhanced by a 10-ft. ceiling and windows on three sides, the master bedroom has an air of elegance. The lavish master bath boasts a spa tub, a separate shower, a dual-sink vanity and a roomy walk-in closet.
- Two additional bedrooms are expanded by 11-ft. ceilings and share a full bath.
- Featuring an enormous front window and a walk-in closet, the study would make a fantastic fourth bedroom.

Plan HDS-99-143

Bedrooms: 3+	Baths: 2
Living Area:	
Main floor	1,865 sq. ft.
Total Living Area:	**1,865 sq. ft.**
Garage	377 sq. ft.
Exterior Wall Framing:	2x4

Foundation Options:

Slab
(All plans can be built with your choice of foundation and framing. A generic conversion diagram is available. See order form.)

BLUEPRINT PRICE CODE:	B

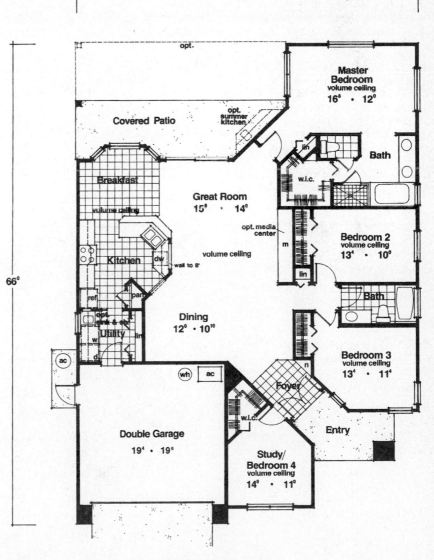

MAIN FLOOR

ORDER BLUEPRINTS ANYTIME!
CALL TOLL-FREE 1-800-820-1283

Plan HDS-99-143

PRICES AND DETAILS
ON PAGES 2-5

209

Open Invitation

- The wide front porch of this friendly country farmhouse presents an open invitation to all who visit.
- Highlighted by a round-topped transom, the home's entrance opens directly into the spacious living room, which features a warm fireplace flanked by windows.
- The adjoining dining area is enhanced by a lovely bay window and is easily serviced by the updated kitchen's angled snack bar.
- A bright sun room off the kitchen provides a great space for informal meals or relaxation. Access to a covered backyard porch is nearby.
- The good-sized master bedroom is secluded from the other sleeping areas. The lavish master bath includes a garden tub, a separate shower, a dual-sink vanity and a walk-in closet.
- Two more bedrooms share a second full bath. A laundry/utility room is nearby.
- An additional 1,007 sq. ft. of living space can be made available by finishing the upper floor.
- All ceilings are 9 ft. high for added spaciousness.

Plan J-91078

Bedrooms: 3	Baths: 2
Living Area:	
Main floor	1,846 sq. ft.
Total Living Area:	**1,846 sq. ft.**
Future upper floor	1,007 sq. ft.
Standard basement	1,846 sq. ft.
Garage	484 sq. ft.
Exterior Wall Framing:	2x6

Foundation Options:

Standard basement
Crawlspace
Slab
(All plans can be built with your choice of foundation and framing. A generic conversion diagram is available. See order form.)

BLUEPRINT PRICE CODE: B

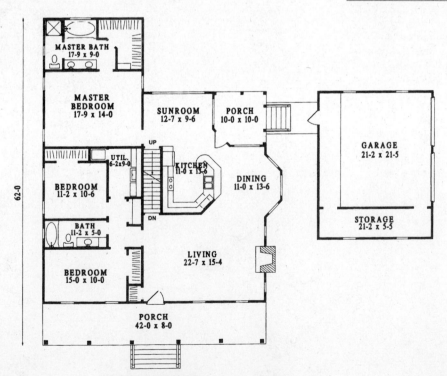

MAIN FLOOR

Ultra-Modern Mediterranean

- Soaring ceilings, a luxurious master suite and a clean stucco exterior with stylish arched windows give this nouveau-Mediterranean home its unique appeal.
- The magnificent living room and the elegant dining room combine to form one large, open area. The dining room has a tall, arched window and a 12-ft. coffered ceiling. The living room boasts a flat ceiling that is over 12 ft. high, a convenient wet bar and sliding glass doors to the covered patio.
- The informal family room is warmed by a fireplace and shares a soaring 12-ft. flat ceiling with the sunny breakfast area and the large, modern kitchen.
- The kitchen is easily accessible from the family area and the formal dining room, and features an eating bar and a spacious pantry.
- The luxurious master suite offers patio access and is enhanced by an elegant 11-ft., 6-in. tray ceiling and his-and-hers walk-in closets. The huge master bath features a dual-sink vanity, a large tiled shower and a whirlpool tub.

Plan HDS-99-158

Bedrooms: 4	Baths: 3
Living Area:.	
Main floor	2,352 sq. ft.
Total Living Area:	**2,352 sq. ft.**
Garage	440 sq. ft.

Exterior Wall Framing:
8-in. concrete block and 2x4

Foundation Options:

Slab
(All plans can be built with your choice of foundation and framing. A generic conversion diagram is available. See order form.)

BLUEPRINT PRICE CODE: C

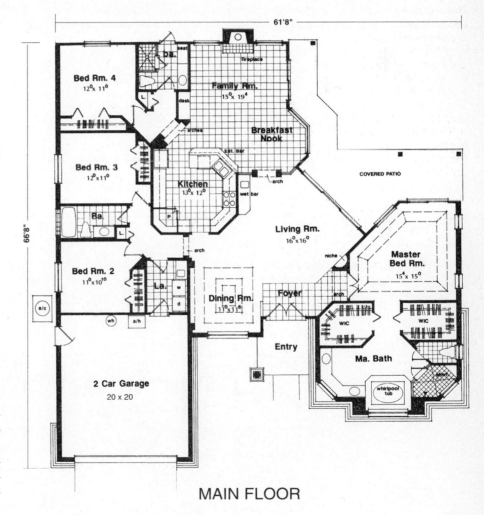

MAIN FLOOR

ORDER BLUEPRINTS ANYTIME!
CALL TOLL-FREE 1-800-820-1283

Plan HDS-99-158

PRICES AND DETAILS
ON PAGES 2-5

Upscale Charm

- Country charm and the very latest in conveniences mark this upscale home. To add extra appeal, all of the living areas are housed on one floor, yet may be expanded to the upper floor later.
- Set off from the foyer, the dining room is embraced by elegant columns. Arched windows in the dining room and in the bedroom across the hall echo the delicate detailing of the covered front porch.
- Straight ahead, the family room flaunts a wall of French doors overlooking a covered back porch and a large deck.
- A curved island snack bar smoothly connects the gourmet kitchen to the sunny breakfast area, which features a dramatic 13-ft. vaulted ceiling brightened by skylights. All other rooms have 9-ft. ceilings. A nearby computer room and a laundry/utility room with a recycling center are other amenities.
- The master bedroom's private bath includes a dual-sink vanity and a floor-to-ceiling storage unit with a built-in chest of drawers. Other extras include a step-up spa tub and a separate shower.

Plan J-92100

Bedrooms: 3+	Baths: 2
Living Area:	
Main floor	1,877 sq. ft.
Total Living Area:	**1,877 sq. ft.**
Upper floor (future areas)	1,500 sq. ft.
Standard basement	1,877 sq. ft.
Garage and storage	551 sq. ft.
Exterior Wall Framing:	2x4

Foundation Options:

Standard basement

Crawlspace

Slab

(All plans can be built with your choice of foundation and framing. A generic conversion diagram is available. See order form.)

BLUEPRINT PRICE CODE: B

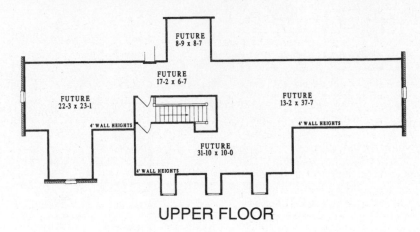

UPPER FLOOR

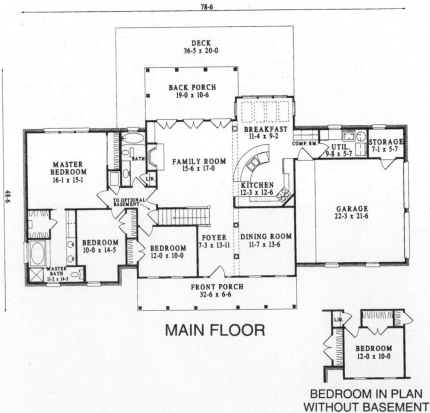

MAIN FLOOR

BEDROOM IN PLAN
WITHOUT BASEMENT

ORDER BLUEPRINTS ANYTIME!
CALL TOLL-FREE 1-800-820-1283

Plan J-92100

PRICES AND DETAILS
ON PAGES 2-5

Splashy Design

- This French design features a charming bathhouse that would be the perfect complement to a splashy pool.
- Beyond the home's brick entry, the 10-ft.-high foyer unfolds to the dining room, which boasts a 12-ft. ceiling. French doors introduce a study, which boasts a nice fireplace, an 11-ft. ceiling and built-in shelves.
- A posh gallery embraces the family room, where a second fireplace flanked by a media center adds a warm glow. A 12-ft. ceiling further increases appeal.
- The sunny breakfast room opens to a peaceful covered porch through a French door, and the efficient kitchen features a convenient snack bar.
- Eye-catching hardwood floors enhance all of the rooms mentioned above.
- Two bedrooms share a bath that offers a private vanity for each room.
- Across the home, an 11-ft. tray ceiling rises above the master bedroom. The lush bath is highlighted by a garden tub.
- The main-floor ceiling heights not mentioned above are all 9 feet.
- A vast bonus area above the garage includes a full bath.

Plan L-2908-FC

Bedrooms: 3+	Baths: 3½-4½
Living Area:	
Main floor	2,908 sq. ft.
Bonus area	479 sq. ft.
Bathhouse	131 sq. ft.
Total Living Area:	**3,518 sq. ft.**
Garage	748 sq. ft.
Exterior Wall Framing:	2x4

Foundation Options:

Slab

(All plans can be built with your choice of foundation and framing. A generic conversion diagram is available. See order form.)

BLUEPRINT PRICE CODE: F

REAR VIEW

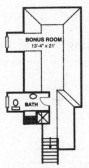

BONUS AREA

BATHHOUSE

MAIN FLOOR

ORDER BLUEPRINTS ANYTIME!
CALL TOLL-FREE 1-800-820-1283

Plan L-2908-FC

PRICES AND DETAILS
ON PAGES 2-5

213

Classic Arches

- A stucco facade and exterior arches lend a classic flavor to this elegant home.
- The coffered foyer is entered through double doors and flanked by the formal areas. Flooded by sunlight from clerestory windows, this area is expanded by a 14-ft. ceiling.
- The focal point of the home is the open family room, which showcases a handsome fireplace surrounded by built-ins and offers access to the back patio through sliding glass doors.
- The adjacent kitchen provides an island work area, a planning desk and a peninsular bar that serves the family room and the bayed breakfast nook. These three areas share a 12-ft. ceiling.
- Secluded in the corner of the home is the spectacular master suite, highlighted by a three-way fireplace and a wet bar that separates the bedroom and the sitting area. The luxurious bath includes a garden tub, a separate shower and a dual-sink vanity with knee space.
- Three additional bedrooms and two full baths complete this exciting design.
- Unless otherwise specified, all rooms have 10-ft.-high ceilings.

Plan HDS-99-189

Bedrooms: 4	Baths: 3
Living Area:	
Main floor	2,726 sq. ft.
Total Living Area:	**2,726 sq. ft.**
Garage	506 sq. ft.
Exterior Wall Framing:	2x4

Foundation Options:

Slab

(All plans can be built with your choice of foundation and framing. A generic conversion diagram is available. See order form.)

BLUEPRINT PRICE CODE: D

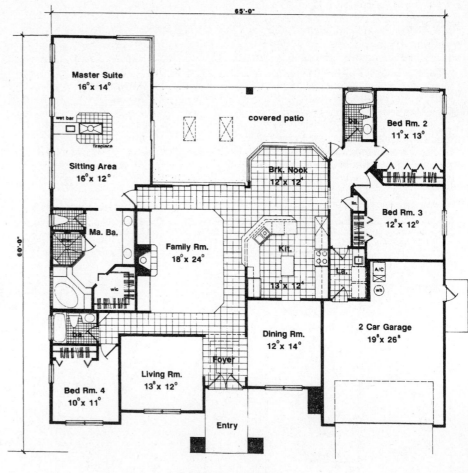

MAIN FLOOR

ORDER BLUEPRINTS ANYTIME!
CALL TOLL-FREE 1-800-820-1283

Plan HDS-99-189

PRICES AND DETAILS
ON PAGES 2-5

Memories in the Making

- You will enjoy years of memories in this peaceful country home.
- A tranquil covered porch opens into the foyer, where regal columns introduce the formal dining room. Soaring 10-ft. ceilings enhance the foyer, dining room, kitchen and breakfast nook.
- Past two closets, a 15-ft., 4-in. cathedral ceiling adds glamour to the living room. A grand fireplace flanked by French doors under beautiful quarter-round transoms will wow your guests! The

French doors open to an inviting porch that is great for afternoon get-togethers.
- The sunny breakfast bay merges with the gourmet kitchen, which includes a large pantry and an island snack bar. Bi-fold doors above the sink create a handy pass-through to the living room.
- A neat computer room nearby allows the kids to do their homework under a parent's watchful eye.
- Across the home, a stylish 10-ft. tray ceiling crowns the master suite. The skylighted master bath features a refreshing whirlpool tub.
- A hall bath services two additional bedrooms. The larger bedroom is expanded by a 10-ft. vaulted ceiling.

Plan J-9294	
Bedrooms: 3	**Baths:** 2
Living Area:	
Main floor	2,018 sq. ft.
Total Living Area:	**2,018 sq. ft.**
Standard basement	2,018 sq. ft.
Garage and storage	556 sq. ft.
Exterior Wall Framing:	2x4

Foundation Options:
Standard basement
Crawlspace
Slab
(All plans can be built with your choice of foundation and framing. A generic conversion diagram is available. See order form.)

BLUEPRINT PRICE CODE:	C

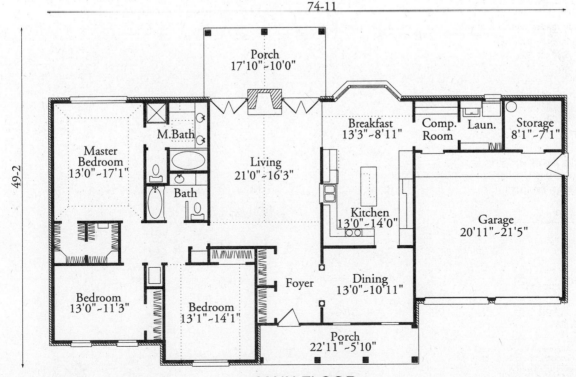

MAIN FLOOR

ORDER BLUEPRINTS ANYTIME!
CALL TOLL-FREE 1-800-820-1283

Plan J-9294

**PRICES AND DETAILS
ON PAGES 2-5**

215

Arched Entry

- A beautiful arched entry introduces this grand Mediterranean home.
- Elegant double doors open into a tiled foyer, which is flanked by the home's formal living and dining rooms. Both rooms boast 12-ft. ceilings, and the dining room offers a tray ceiling.
- In the huge family room, sliding glass doors open to a covered patio. A fireplace flanked by built-in cabinets sets the stage for fun evenings at home.
- An 8-ft. wall separates the family room from the kitchen, which shares an

angled serving counter with the sunny bayed breakfast nook. A built-in desk nearby is a great spot to pay the bills.
- The secluded master suite includes a sprawling overhead plant shelf and sliding glass doors to the patio. A dramatic arch introduces the private bath, which includes a huge tub, a separate shower and a dual-sink vanity.
- Across the home, two more bedrooms share a hall bath. A quiet rear bedroom is serviced by another full bath. Each room boasts a neat plant shelf.
- Unless otherwise noted, a 10-ft. ceiling enhances every room in the home.

Plan HDS-99-233	
Bedrooms: 4	**Baths:** 3
Living Area:	
Main floor	2,140 sq. ft.
Total Living Area:	**2,140 sq. ft.**
Garage	430 sq. ft.
Exterior Wall Framing:	8-in. concrete block

Foundation Options:

Slab

(All plans can be built with your choice of foundation and framing. A generic conversion diagram is available. See order form.)

BLUEPRINT PRICE CODE: C

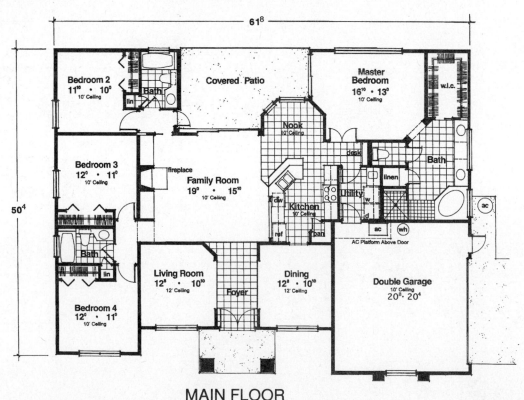

MAIN FLOOR

ORDER BLUEPRINTS ANYTIME!
CALL TOLL-FREE 1-800-820-1283

Plan HDS-99-233

PRICES AND DETAILS
ON PAGES 2-5

Tasteful Charm

- Columned covered porches lend warmth and charm to the front and rear of this tasteful traditional home.
- Sidelight and transom glass brightens the entry foyer, which shares a 10-ft. ceiling with the elegant dining room.
- The dining room provides a quiet spot for formal meals, while a Palladian window arrangement adds light and flair.
- The spacious living room offers a warm fireplace and an adjacent TV cabinet. The dramatic ceiling vaults to a height of 11 ft., 8 inches. French doors give way to the skylighted rear porch, which is finished with lovely brick pavers.

Two brick steps descend to the adjoining patio, which is also beautifully paved with brick.
- The gourmet kitchen offers a built-in oven/microwave cabinet, a separate cooktop and an island snack bar with a sink. Its 10-ft. ceiling extends into the sunny breakfast nook.
- The oversized laundry room includes a handy half-bath, a wall-to-wall storage cabinet, a hanging rod, a large sink and nearby porch access.
- The secluded master bedroom boasts a 12-ft. vaulted ceiling and a large walk-in closet. In the private master bath, a glass-block divider separates the whirlpool tub from the shower stall.

Plan J-9414	
Bedrooms: 3	**Baths: 2½**
Living Area:	
Main floor	1,974 sq. ft.
Total Living Area:	**1,974 sq. ft.**
Standard basement	1,974 sq. ft.
Garage and storage	518 sq. ft.
Exterior Wall Framing:	2x4

Foundation Options:
Standard basement
Crawlspace
Slab
(All plans can be built with your choice of foundation and framing. A generic conversion diagram is available. See order form.)

BLUEPRINT PRICE CODE:	B

BASEMENT
STAIRWAY
LOCATION

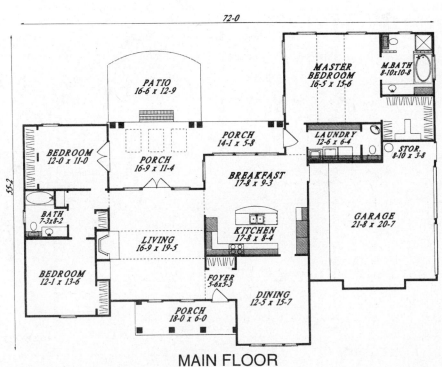

MAIN FLOOR

ORDER BLUEPRINTS ANYTIME!
CALL TOLL-FREE 1-800-820-1283

Plan J-9414

PRICES AND DETAILS
ON PAGES 2-5

217

Prominent Portico

- A prominent portico accented by dramatic windows and a Spanish tile roof draws attention to this home. Grand double doors open into a foyer with an airy 14-ft. ceiling.
- Straight ahead, an elegant curved gallery frames the living room, which opens to a skylighted patio. Arched openings along one wall add high style.
- The quiet den and the formal dining room feature striking 12-ft. ceilings.
- The island kitchen boasts a big pantry and a neat pass-through to the patio, which offers a summer kitchen with a bar sink. A powder room is nearby.
- A 14-ft. vaulted ceiling, plus a fireplace set into a media wall make the family room a fun indoor gathering place.
- Two secondary bedrooms share a split bath with a dual-sink vanity.
- Across the home, a three-way fireplace and an entertainment center separate the master bedroom from its bayed sitting room. An exercise area, a wet bar and a posh bath are other pleasures!
- Unless otherwise mentioned, every room features a 10-ft. ceiling.

Plan HDS-99-242

Bedrooms: 3+	Baths: 3½
Living Area:	
Main floor	3,556 sq. ft.
Total Living Area:	**3,556 sq. ft.**
Garage	809 sq. ft.
Exterior Wall Framing:	8-in. concrete block

Foundation Options:

Slab

(All plans can be built with your choice of foundation and framing. A generic conversion diagram is available. See order form.)

BLUEPRINT PRICE CODE:	F

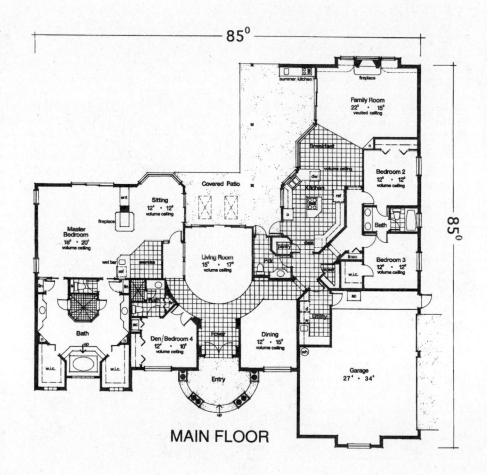

MAIN FLOOR

ORDER BLUEPRINTS ANYTIME!
CALL TOLL-FREE 1-800-820-1283

Plan HDS-99-242

PRICES AND DETAILS
ON PAGES 2-5

Ultimate French Comfort

- Delightful interior touches coupled with a striking French facade make this home the ultimate in one-story comfort.
- In the sidelighted entry, an attractive overhead plant ledge captures the eye.
- The entry opens to the formal dining and living rooms—both of which boast 10-ft. ceilings.
- In the living room, a handy wet bar and a media center flank a handsome fireplace. Large windows frame wide backyard views. Around the corner, French doors open to a back porch.
- Adjacent to the dining room, the kitchen offers a speedy serving bar. A bayed nook lights up with morning sun.
- Double doors open to the master bedroom, with its cute window seat and TV shelf. A 10-ft. ceiling tops it off.
- Two walk-in closets with glamorous mirror doors flank the walkway to the master bath, which offers an exotic garden tub and a separate shower.
- One of the two roomy secondary bedrooms offers a walk-in closet, a built-in desk and a gorgeous window.

Plan RD-1895

Bedrooms: 3	Baths: 2
Living Area:	
Main floor	1,895 sq. ft.
Total Living Area:	**1,895 sq. ft.**
Garage and storage	485 sq. ft.
Exterior Wall Framing:	2x4

Foundation Options:

Crawlspace
Slab
(All plans can be built with your choice of foundation and framing. A generic conversion diagram is available. See order form.)

BLUEPRINT PRICE CODE:	B

MAIN FLOOR

ORDER BLUEPRINTS ANYTIME!
CALL TOLL-FREE 1-800-820-1283

Plan RD-1895

PRICES AND DETAILS
ON PAGES 2-5

219

Large-Scale Strategy

- If your family is growing or already large, this plan is sure to please you!
- The oversized living spaces are open and comfortable—and oriented toward a backyard covered patio.
- The exterior also has a surplus of attractions, including a durable textured finish, a concrete tile roof, a stately column and elegant windows.
- The foyer and the formal areas are enhanced with high 12-ft. ceilings and set off with beautiful arched openings.
- An 8-ft.-high wall nicely separates the informal spaces, which are strategically geared for family interaction.
- The kitchen's island is ideal for serving appetizers. The family room supplies the entertainment with its enticing fireplace and media center duo.
- An 11-ft. tray ceiling, patio access and his-and-hers walk-in closets add to the appeal of the quiet master bedroom. The posh private bath features a gorgeous garden tub.
- Where not otherwise noted, all rooms are expanded by 10-ft. ceilings.

Plan HDS-99-256

Bedrooms: 4	Baths: 3
Living Area:	
Main floor	2,131 sq. ft.
Total Living Area:	**2,131 sq. ft.**
Garage	595 sq. ft.
Exterior Wall Framing:	8-in. concrete block

Foundation Options:

Slab

(All plans can be built with your choice of foundation and framing. A generic conversion diagram is available. See order form.)

BLUEPRINT PRICE CODE: C

MAIN FLOOR

ORDER BLUEPRINTS ANYTIME!
CALL TOLL-FREE 1-800-820-1283

Plan HDS-99-256

**PRICES AND DETAILS
ON PAGES 2-5**

Delightful
Great Room

- An expansive Great Room with a 10-ft. vaulted ceiling, a warm corner fireplace and an angled wet bar highlights this tastefully appointed home.
- On the exterior, decorative plants thrive in the lush wraparound planter that leads to the sheltered entry. The foyer is brightened by a sidelight and a skylight.
- To the left, the kitchen offers an island cooktop with lots room for food preparation and serving. The bayed breakfast nook is enhanced by bright windows and a 12½-ft. vaulted ceiling.
- Formal dining is hosted in the space adjoining the Great Room. Graced by a lovely bay window, the room also offers French doors to a covered patio.
- In the sleeping wing of the home, the master bedroom features a sitting area and a walk-in closet. The private master bath boasts a relaxing Jacuzzi tub.
- Two secondary bedrooms share a full bath nearby. Laundry facilities are also convenient.

Plan S-52394

Bedrooms: 3	Baths: 2
Living Area:	
Main floor	1,841 sq. ft.
Total Living Area:	**1,841 sq. ft.**
Standard basement	1,789 sq. ft.
Garage	432 sq. ft.
Exterior Wall Framing:	2x6

Foundation Options:
Standard basement
Crawlspace
Slab
(All plans can be built with your choice of foundation and framing. A generic conversion diagram is available. See order form.)

BLUEPRINT PRICE CODE: B

Floor Plan

46'

65'

COVERED PATIO

SIT

MBR
19/6 X 14
INC. SITTING AREA

WI CLO

VAULTED
GREAT ROOM
23 X 23/6
INC DIN RM

DIN RM
10 X 13/6
AVERAGE

M BATH

TUB

BR
12/4 X 11

KIT

DW
R
DESK

PAN

GUEST

FOYER

LIN
D W

UTIL

BATH

BR
10/4 X 11

VAULTED
NOOK
10 X 13

COVERED
ENTRY

SEW

GARAGE
22 X 19/8

OPTIONAL 3RD
CAR GARAGE

MAIN FLOOR

ORDER BLUEPRINTS ANYTIME!
CALL TOLL-FREE 1-800-820-1283

Plan S-52394

***PRICES AND DETAILS
ON PAGES 2-5***

221

Terrific Arched Transoms

- This terrific home greets guests with its wide arched transom windows and French doors that open to the foyer.
- Beyond the bright foyer, the expansive Great Room features a dynamic fireplace and sliding glass doors to a covered backyard patio.
- The walk-through kitchen easily services the adjoining breakfast area and the formal dining room. A pantry closet, laundry facilities and garage access are all nearby.
- The superb master bedroom boasts an enormous walk-in closet and an ideal bath with a step-up spa tub, a dual-sink vanity and a huge private shower.
- The alternate master bedroom offers a fireplace, a wet bar and a sitting room.
- The quiet den or study could be used to accomodate overnight guests.
- On the opposite end of the home, a pocket door introduces two secondary bedrooms, another full bath and private patio access.

Plan HDS-99-130

Bedrooms: 3+	Baths: 2
Living Area:	
Main floor	2,125 sq. ft.
Total Living Area:	**2,125 sq. ft.**
Garage	559 sq. ft.

Exterior Wall Framing:
2x4 and 8-in. concrete block

Foundation Options:
Slab
(All plans can be built with your choice of foundation and framing. A generic conversion diagram is available. See order form.)

BLUEPRINT PRICE CODE: C

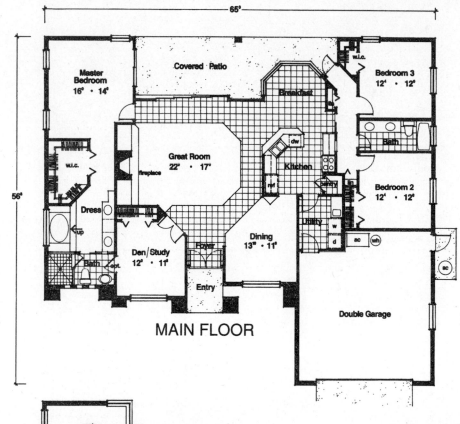

MAIN FLOOR

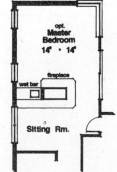

ALTERNATE
MASTER BEDROOM

Suite Trio

- This gorgeous home's symmetrical facade conceals a sleeping wing with three separate suites—giving luxurious privacy to all family members!
- The bayed master bedroom boasts a high 11-ft. ceiling, a walk-in closet, a whirlpool bath and two linen closets.
- The exterior of the home features an elegant combination of brick and stucco, accented by half-round transoms, keystones and shutters.
- In from the gracious, columned front porch, the sidelighted foyer shows off an 11-ft. ceiling as it welcomes guests. A lovely staircase ascends to future expansion space on the upper floor.

- The bright and spacious Great Room is warmed by a fireplace, making it a great spot for entertaining or relaxing.
- A curved serving bar highlights the open kitchen, where a china hutch, stacked ovens and a handy pantry line the right wall.
- Casual meals will be delightful in the adjacent breakfast nook; French doors expand the charming experience to a columned porch and a brick patio.
- Facing the door to the two-car garage, a computer desk offers a special area to work on the budget or write letters.
- A powder room and cheery laundry facilities round out the floor plan.
- Where not otherwise specified, ceilings are 9 ft. high for added spaciousness.

Plan J-9307	
Bedrooms: 3+	**Baths:** 3½
Living Area:	
Main floor	2,497 sq. ft.
Total Living Area:	**2,497 sq. ft.**
Future upper floor	966 sq. ft.
Standard basement	2,497 sq. ft.
Garage and storage	587 sq. ft.
Exterior Wall Framing:	2x4

Foundation Options:
Standard basement
Crawlspace
Slab
(All plans can be built with your choice of foundation and framing. A generic conversion diagram is available. See order form.)

BLUEPRINT PRICE CODE:	C

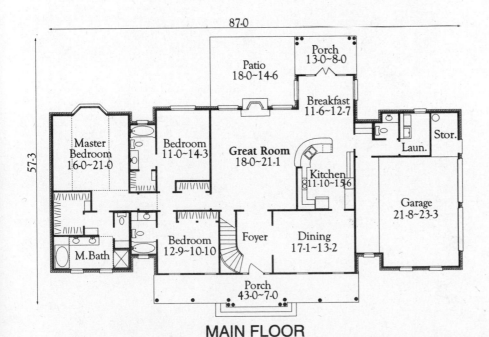

MAIN FLOOR

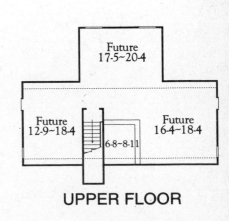

UPPER FLOOR

ORDER BLUEPRINTS ANYTIME!
CALL TOLL-FREE 1-800-820-1283

Plan J-9307

PRICES AND DETAILS
ON PAGES 2-5

Tall and Proud

- This stately home's proud exterior gives way to a luxurious and impressive interior.
- The step-down parlour is the home's centerpiece, and boasts a 13-ft.-high ceiling and a full-wall fireplace and entertainment center.
- The master suite features a step-down sitting room and a corner fireplace. The opulent master bath has a linen island, a morning kitchen and a bidet.
- The library offers private access to the main hall bath.
- Graceful arches and a high, coffered ceiling adorn the formal dining room.
- The spacious kitchen includes a cooktop island, a walk-in pantry, a menu desk, a vegetable sink and a bright good morning room.
- Each of the three secondary suites has a large closet and direct access to a bath.
- The huge Gathering Room boasts wraparound glass and another fireplace and entertainment wall.

Plan EOF-58

Bedrooms: 4+	Baths: 4
Living Area:	
Main floor	4,021 sq. ft.
Total Living Area:	**4,021 sq. ft.**
Garage	879 sq. ft.
Exterior Wall Framing:	2x4

Foundation Options:

Slab

(All plans can be built with your choice of foundation and framing. A generic conversion diagram is available. See order form.)

BLUEPRINT PRICE CODE:	**G**

MAIN FLOOR

ORDER BLUEPRINTS ANYTIME!
CALL TOLL-FREE 1-800-820-1283

Plan EOF-58

PRICES AND DETAILS
ON PAGES 2-5

Sunny Delight

- The unmistakable Mediterranean flavor of this one-story home evokes pleasing, restful images of easygoing days. Inside, 10-ft. ceilings and the minimal use of hallways and walls foster the home's cool, open feel.
- On either side of the foyer, the living room and the dining room each reserve a quiet, elegant space for special events. Built-in niches offer a great way to display artwork and photos.

- Casual affairs have a place of their own in the family room. Here, built-in shelving flanks the fireplace, providing ideal spots for media equipment.
- The walls that set off the kitchen stop two feet below the ceiling, creating great shelves to display greenery.
- Adjacent to the kitchen, sunny sliding glass doors in the breakfast nook let you enjoy morning coffee inside or out.
- As an extra bonus, the master suite also includes pretty sliding glass doors that open to the backyard.

Plan HDS-99-286

Bedrooms: 3	**Baths:** 2

Living Area:

Main floor	1,833 sq. ft.
Total Living Area:	**1,833 sq. ft.**
Garage	392 sq. ft.
Exterior Wall Framing:	2x4

Foundation Options:

Slab
(All plans can be built with your choice of foundation and framing. A generic conversion diagram is available. See order form.)

BLUEPRINT PRICE CODE:	**B**

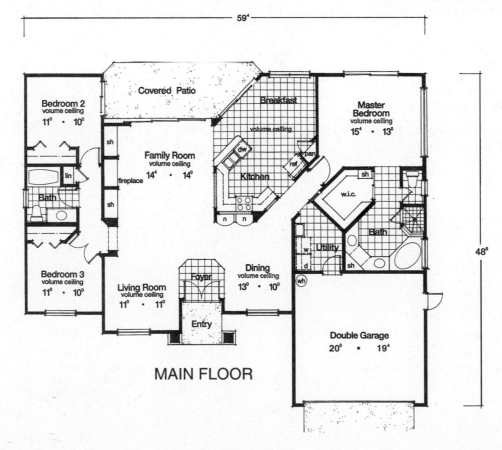

MAIN FLOOR

ORDER BLUEPRINTS ANYTIME!
CALL TOLL-FREE 1-800-820-1283

Plan HDS-99-286

PRICES AND DETAILS
ON PAGES 2-5

225

Hip and Happening

- A striking hip roof tops this vibrant home's attractive facade. Front and rear porches add to its magnetic personality.
- The Great Room anchors the home and serves as the prime gathering spot. Bright windows at the back overlook a rear porch and the yard beyond.
- The galley-style kitchen is perfectly situated for easy service to the Great Room and the dining area.
- You make the call when it comes to the multipurpose room's use. It may serve as a formal dining room, a hobby room or a bedroom as your family grows.
- Boasting private porch access through French doors, the master bedroom also has a beautiful bath that includes a garden tub and a sit-down shower.
- The secluded guest room may become a retreat for older relatives, if desired. A private entry to a handicapped-accessible bath and nearby laundry facilities make it the perfect hideaway.

Plan J-9524

Bedrooms: 3+	Baths: 3
Living Area:	
Main floor	2,035 sq. ft.
Total Living Area:	**2,035 sq. ft.**
Standard basement	2,035 sq. ft.
Garage	716 sq. ft.
Exterior Wall Framing:	2x4

Foundation Options:

Standard basement
Crawlspace
Slab

(All plans can be built with your choice of foundation and framing. A generic conversion diagram is available. See order form.)

BLUEPRINT PRICE CODE: C

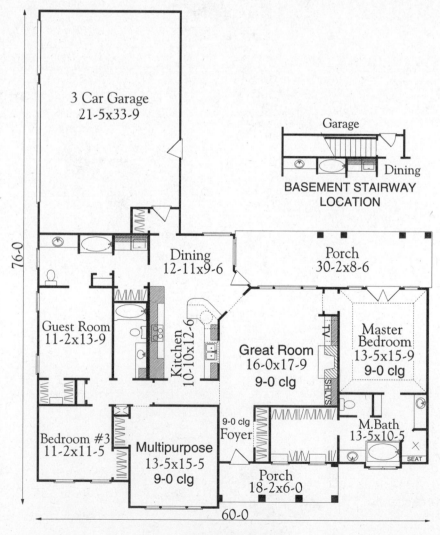

MAIN FLOOR

ORDER BLUEPRINTS ANYTIME!
CALL TOLL-FREE 1-800-820-1283

Plan J-9524

PRICES AND DETAILS
ON PAGES 2-5

Small in Size, Big in Comfort

- Space-efficient and cost-effective, this stylish, feature-filled home is designed with comfort in mind.
- An angled entrance off the inviting covered porch opens to the 17-ft.-high foyer, which is brightened by a half-round clerestory window.
- The dramatic 17-ft. vaulted ceiling extends into the adjoining formal living areas. The living room features a stone fireplace, while the dining room is highlighted by an overhead plant shelf.
- A bay window brings great outdoor views into the eat-in kitchen, which serves the family room over a long snack bar.
- An atrium door in the family room offers access to a backyard deck. A half-bath, a pantry and a laundry room with garage access are within easy reach.
- Upstairs, the bay-windowed master suite is entered through elegant double doors and boasts a 12-ft. vaulted ceiling, a big walk-in closet and a private bath with twin sinks.
- Two additional bedrooms and a second full bath complete the upper floor.

Plan B-93004

Bedrooms: 3	Baths: 2½
Living Area:	
Upper floor	799 sq. ft.
Main floor	932 sq. ft.
Total Living Area:	**1,731 sq. ft.**
Standard basement	932 sq. ft.
Garage	420 sq. ft.
Exterior Wall Framing:	2x6

Foundation Options:

Standard basement
(All plans can be built with your choice of foundation and framing. A generic conversion diagram is available. See order form.)

BLUEPRINT PRICE CODE: B

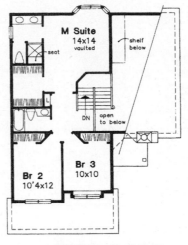

UPPER FLOOR

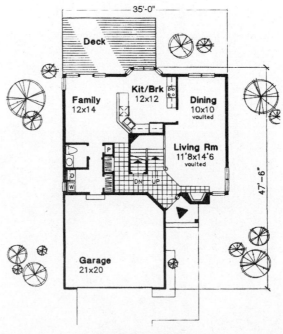

MAIN FLOOR

ORDER BLUEPRINTS ANYTIME!
CALL TOLL-FREE 1-800-820-1283

Plan B-93004

PRICES AND DETAILS
ON PAGES 2-5

227

Scenic Site?

- A wraparound deck and multiple windows offering panoramic views make this the perfect vacation home for your lakeside, mountain or ocean lot.
- The large living room features floor-to-ceiling windows and is topped by an airy 20½-ft. vaulted ceiling. A rustic stone fireplace warms this space on chilly evenings.
- Sliding glass doors in the living room access the deck, which beckons you to step outside and soak up the view.
- A good-sized kitchen surrounds the family chef. A breakfast bar divides the kitchen from the living room.
- The main-floor bedroom has easy access to a full bath.
- Upstairs, a balcony overlooks the living room. Two secondary bedrooms with 12-ft. vaulted ceilings share a full bath.
- The furnace and water heater are located in the crawlspace or the basement, depending on which plan you choose.

Plans H-876-1 & -1A

Bedrooms: 3	Baths: 2
Living Area:	
Upper floor	592 sq. ft.
Main floor	960 sq. ft.
Total Living Area:	**1,552 sq. ft.**
Standard basement	960 sq. ft.
Garage	262 sq. ft.
Carport	232 sq. ft.
Exterior Wall Framing:	**2x4**
Foundation Options:	**Plan #**
Standard basement	H-876-1
Crawlspace	H-876-1A

(All plans can be built with your choice of foundation and framing. A generic conversion diagram is available. See order form.)

BLUEPRINT PRICE CODE:	**B**

UPPER FLOOR

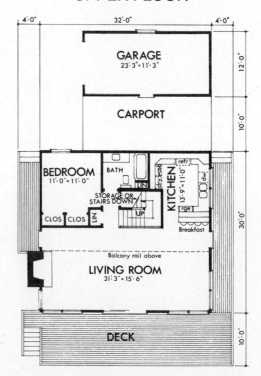

MAIN FLOOR

ORDER BLUEPRINTS ANYTIME! ***CALL TOLL-FREE 1-800-820-1283***

Plans H-876-1 & -1A

PRICES AND DETAILS ON PAGES 2-5

Life of Leisure

- In this appealing country home, you're free to kick back and pursue a life of leisure and comfort. Indoor and outdoor relaxation is tops on the list!
- A railed front porch reminiscent of simpler times wraps around the side of the home. Picture your little ones scampering down its length, intent on catching the family puppy.
- Inside, pocket doors can separate the joined living and family rooms, creating a cozy ambience in each.
- Sliding glass doors open from the casual dining area to a fabulous backyard deck that is perfect for a family picnic!
- Parents will appreciate the openness of the walk-through kitchen, which gives them plenty of room to serve meals while ruling the roost. A built-in desk aids in scheduling each day's events. Nearby laundry facilities and close proximity to the garage are pluses, too.
- Upstairs, a balcony hall leads to the sleeping chambers. In the master suite you'll find radiant windows and a private bath that includes two vanities.

Plan GL-1966

Bedrooms: 4	Baths: 2½
Living Area:	
Upper floor	934 sq. ft.
Main floor	1,032 sq. ft.
Total Living Area:	**1,966 sq. ft.**
Standard basement	1,032 sq. ft.
Garage	532 sq. ft.
Exterior Wall Framing:	2x6

Foundation Options:

Standard basement

(All plans can be built with your choice of foundation and framing. A generic conversion diagram is available. See order form.)

BLUEPRINT PRICE CODE: B

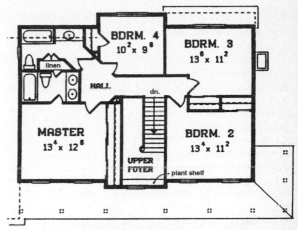

UPPER FLOOR

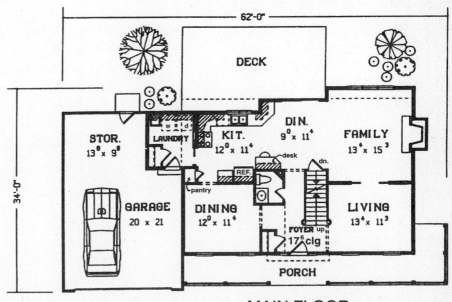

MAIN FLOOR

ORDER BLUEPRINTS ANYTIME!
CALL TOLL-FREE 1-800-820-1283

Plan GL-1966

PRICES AND DETAILS
ON PAGES 2-5

229

Clean, Stylish Lines

- The sweeping roofline and arched windows give this home plenty of "presence" despite its modest size.
- Besides being stylish, the plan is also sturdy and energy-efficient, making it a great place to begin your family.
- The sheltered entry leads visitors into an effective foyer which opens to the combined living and dining area. These two spaces flow together to create a

huge space for entertaining. A 15½-ft, vaulted ceiling tops the living room.
- The roomy kitchen includes abundant cabinet and counter space.
- A large main-floor bedroom adjoins a full bath and includes a large walk-in closet. This would make a great guest or in-law suite.
- Upstairs, the master bedroom is highlighted by a 12-ft. cathedral ceiling and a beautiful private bath.
- A versatile loft overlooks the living room below, and provides room for children to play or for adults to use it as a library, sewing room or study.

Plans H-1448-1 & -1A	
Bedrooms: 3	**Baths: 2**
Living Area:	
Upper floor	487 sq. ft.
Main floor	1,278 sq. ft.
Total Living Area:	**1,765 sq. ft.**
Standard basement	1,278 sq. ft.
Garage	409 sq. ft.
Exterior Wall Framing:	**2x6**
Foundation Options:	**Plan #**
Standard basement	H-1448-1
Crawlspace	H-1448-1A

(All plans can be built with your choice of foundation and framing. A generic conversion diagram is available. See order form.)

BLUEPRINT PRICE CODE:	**B**

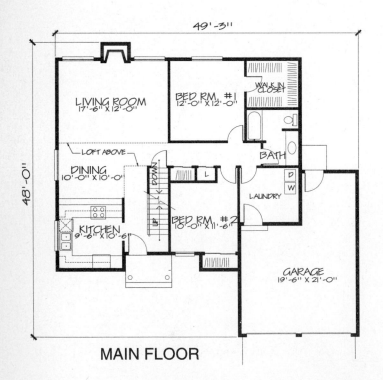

MAIN FLOOR

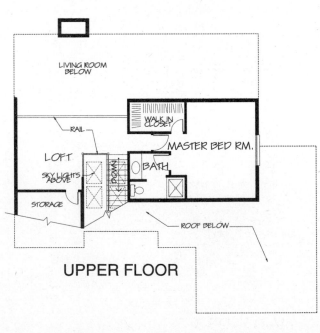

UPPER FLOOR

ORDER BLUEPRINTS ANYTIME!
CALL TOLL-FREE 1-800-820-1283

Plans H-1448-1 & -1A

PRICES AND DETAILS
ON PAGES 2-5

Soup's On!

- The floor plan of this two-story home places unprecedented focus on the kitchen, the busiest room in just about any home. The open design features a corner fireplace that conjures up images of yesterday's cozy country kitchens.
- Out front, double columns and an arch with a stylish keystone usher guests inside, where a 17-ft. ceiling in the foyer gives a grand first impression.
- A half-wall defines the adjacent living room, where, over the years, good friends will visit, birthdays will pass and holidays will be celebrated. The formal dining room awaits those times when you want an extra-special meal.

- Nearby, the huge kitchen and breakfast nook include space to accommodate the entire family comfortably. As Mom and Dad whip up a quick dinner, the kids can read or color beside the warm fireplace. Sunlight floods in through a cheery bay with access to a patio.
- In the master suite, an 8-ft. tray ceiling lends style to this important refuge. First thing in the morning and late at night, the master bath hits just the right nerve. A dual-sink vanity, a built-in seat and a platform tub treat you well, while a large walk-in closet will satisfy even the biggest clothes fanatic.
- Upstairs, the kids will love their bath's dual-sink vanity, which allows each of them to have his or her own space.

Plan B-93031	
Bedrooms: 3	**Baths:** 2½
Living Area:	
Upper floor	503 sq. ft.
Main floor	1,499 sq. ft.
Total Living Area:	**2,002 sq. ft.**
Standard basement	1,499 sq. ft.
Garage	413 sq. ft.
Exterior Wall Framing:	2x6

Foundation Options:

Standard basement
(All plans can be built with your choice of foundation and framing. A generic conversion diagram is available. See order form.)

BLUEPRINT PRICE CODE:	C

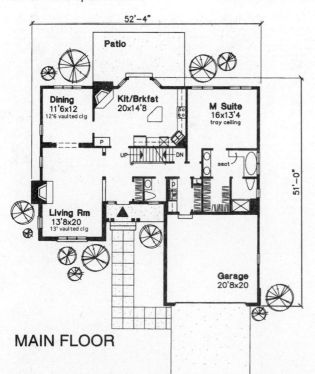

MAIN FLOOR

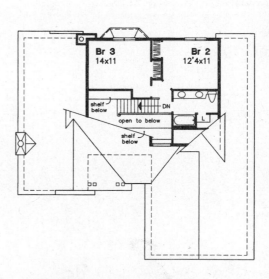

UPPER FLOOR

ORDER BLUEPRINTS ANYTIME!
CALL TOLL-FREE 1-800-820-1283

Plan B-93031

PRICES AND DETAILS
ON PAGES 2-5

231

Scenic Hideaway

- The perfect complement to any scenic hideaway spot, this A-frame is as affordable as it is adorable.
- A large deck embraces the front of the chalet, providing ample space for outdoor dining and recreation. Inside, vaulted ceilings and high windows lend a feeling of spaciousness.
- The living room is dramatically expanded by a 17-ft.-high vaulted ceiling and soaring windows facing the deck. This room also boasts a woodstove with a masonry hearth.
- The galley kitchen is well organized and includes a stacked washer/dryer unit and easy outdoor access. Nearby is a skylighted full bath.
- The romantic bedroom/loft overlooks the living room and features a 16-ft. ceiling. Windows at both ends of the room provide stunning views.
- On both floors, areas with limited headroom are utilized effectively for storage.

Plan H-968-1A	
Bedrooms: 1	**Baths:** 1
Living Area:	
Upper floor	144 sq. ft.
Main floor	391 sq. ft.
Total Living Area:	**535 sq. ft.**
Exterior Wall Framing:	2x6

Foundation Options:

Crawlspace
(All plans can be built with your choice of foundation and framing. A generic conversion diagram is available. See order form.)

BLUEPRINT PRICE CODE:	**AA**

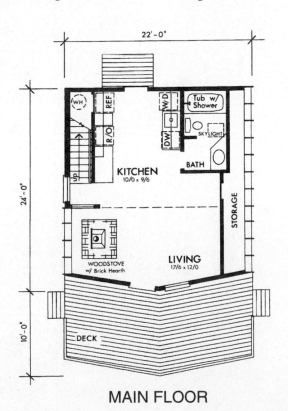

MAIN FLOOR

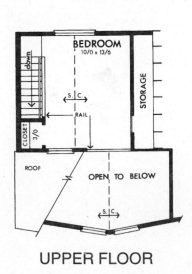

UPPER FLOOR

Tastefully Appointed

- Cheery dormer windows and a wide, columned front porch greet guests to this tastefully appointed home.
- Inside, the inviting living room boasts a 17-ft. vaulted ceiling and a neat TV nook for casual entertainment.
- A classy, three-sided fireplace warms both the living room and the adjoining formal dining room. Sliding glass doors open onto a nice deck, which is bordered on two sides by a large patio.
- The contemporary island kitchen offers a nifty nook for quick snacks or relaxed breakfasts. A sliding glass door leads to the patio, and a built-in desk is perfect for recording favorite recipes.
- The master bedroom shows off a large walk-in closet and a private bath with a whirlpool tub and a dual-sink vanity.
- Upstairs, eye-catching stepped plant shelves and an impressive loft space overlook the living room below.
- Two secondary bedrooms—one with a walk-in closet—share a full bath.

Plan B-93017

Bedrooms: 3+	Baths: 2½
Living Area:	
Upper floor	672 sq. ft.
Main floor	1,327 sq. ft.
Total Living Area:	**1,999 sq. ft.**
Standard basement	1,327 sq. ft.
Garage	400 sq. ft.
Exterior Wall Framing:	2x4

Foundation Options:

Standard basement

(All plans can be built with your choice of foundation and framing. A generic conversion diagram is available. See order form.)

BLUEPRINT PRICE CODE:	B

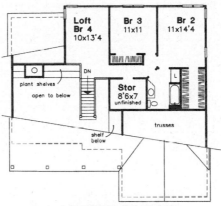

UPPER FLOOR

MAIN FLOOR

ORDER BLUEPRINTS ANYTIME!
CALL TOLL-FREE 1-800-820-1283

Plan B-93017

PRICES AND DETAILS
ON PAGES 2-5

233

Woodsy Forest Chalet

- There'll be plenty of sleeping room for family and guests with this five-bedroom forest chalet.
- Three separate decks bring the indoors out. Your grill can be stationed within easy reach, just outside the kitchen door. Two more balcony decks off upstairs bedrooms provide quiet retreats for early morning birdwatching or late night stargazing.

- The guest bedroom above the garage could double as a trophy room, card room, or private den.
- Abundant storage areas in the attic space under the eaves provide room for everything from winter clothes to fishing gear.
- Meanwhile, the wide 2-car garage frees up even more space for daily living. The one-car family keeps a boat high and dry in here!
- Bathrooms upstairs and down, plus a washer/dryer station central to the main floor keep housework and cleanup close at hand.

Plans H-804-2 & -2A	
Bedrooms: 5	**Baths:** 2
Living Area:	
Upper floor	767 sq. ft.
Main floor	952 sq. ft.
Total Living Area:	**1,719 sq. ft.**
Standard basement	952 sq. ft.
Garage	500 sq. ft.
Storage	sq. ft.
Exterior Wall Framing:	2x4
Foundation Options:	**Plan #**
Standard basement	H-804-2
Crawlspace	H-804-2A

(All plans can be built with your choice of foundation and framing. A generic conversion diagram is available. See order form.)

BLUEPRINT PRICE CODE:	B

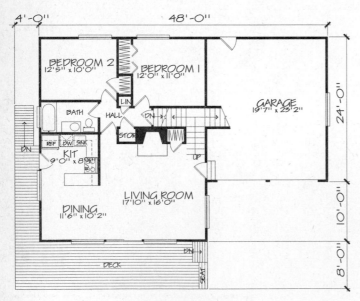

MAIN FLOOR

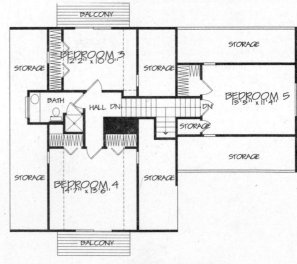

UPPER FLOOR

ORDER BLUEPRINTS ANYTIME!
CALL TOLL-FREE 1-800-820-1283

Plans H-804-2 & -2A

**PRICES AND DETAILS
ON PAGES 2-5**

Essential Peace

- This home's nostalgic porch and charming interior wrap you up in peace and comfort.
- On a warm summer night, you can rig up a hammock on the porch and enjoy a cold drink while watching fireflies, the air around you so quiet you can hear the ice in your drink settling.
- Inside, a wide passageway joins the formal living room to the strikingly angled kitchen and dining room. An island greatly simplifies your food preparation efforts. Sliding glass doors let you deliver that potato salad to hungry picnickers in the backyard!
- A design option included with the blueprints for this home substitutes one main-floor bedroom for a greatly expanded master bedroom with an amenity-laden bath.
- Upstairs, two secondary bedrooms are placed at each end of a balcony hall for privacy. Dormer windows grace each room, and a third dormer between them houses an optional third bath.
- All rooms have 9-ft. ceilings.

Plan AX-94341

Bedrooms: 4+	Baths: 1½-3
Living Area:	
Upper floor	597 sq. ft.
Main floor	1,040 sq. ft.
Total Living Area:	**1,637 sq. ft.**
Standard basement	1,040 sq. ft.
Exterior Wall Framing:	2x4

Foundation Options:

Standard basement
Crawlspace
Slab

(All plans can be built with your choice of foundation and framing. A generic conversion diagram is available. See order form.)

BLUEPRINT PRICE CODE: B

VIEW INTO KITCHEN
AND DINING ROOM

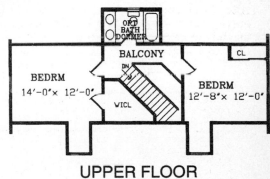

UPPER FLOOR

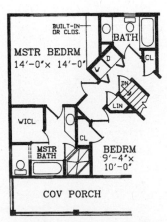

ALTERNATE MAIN FLOOR

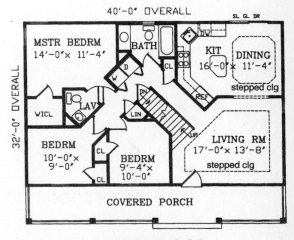

MAIN FLOOR

ORDER BLUEPRINTS ANYTIME!
CALL TOLL-FREE 1-800-820-1283

Plan AX-94341

PRICES AND DETAILS
ON PAGES 2-5

235

Graceful Facade

- Elegant half-round transoms spruce up the wood-shuttered facade of this charming traditional two-story.
- The wide front porch opens to a two-story foyer that flows between the formal dining room and a two-story-high library or guest room. Sliding French doors close off the library from the Great Room.
- Perfect for entertaining, the spacious Great Room shows off a handsome fireplace and a TV center. Beautiful French doors on either side extend the room to a large backyard deck.
- The adjoining dinette has its own view of the backyard through a stunning semi-circular glass wall, which sheds light on the nice-sized attached kitchen.
- A pantry and a laundry room are neatly housed near the two-car garage. The adjacent full bath could be downsized to a half-bath with storage space.
- The master suite and its private whirlpool bath are isolated from the three upper-floor bedrooms and features a 14-ft.-high cathedral ceiling.
- Unless otherwise specified, all main-floor ceilings are 9 ft. high.

Plan AHP-9490

Bedrooms: 4+	Baths: 2½-3
Living Area:	
Upper floor	722 sq. ft.
Main floor	1,497 sq. ft.
Total Living Area:	**2,219 sq. ft.**
Standard basement	1,165 sq. ft.
Garage	420 sq. ft.
Exterior Wall Framing:	2x4 or 2x6

Foundation Options:
Standard basement
Crawlspace
Slab
(All plans can be built with your choice of foundation and framing. A generic conversion diagram is available. See order form.)

BLUEPRINT PRICE CODE: C

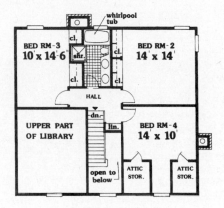

UPPER FLOOR

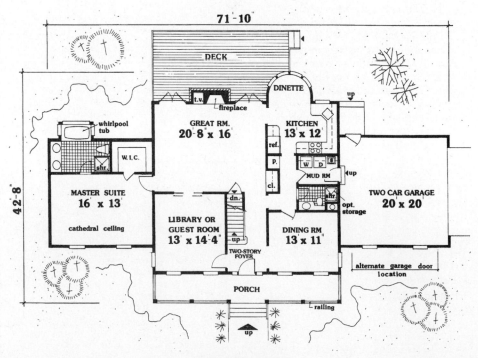

MAIN FLOOR

ORDER BLUEPRINTS ANYTIME!
CALL TOLL-FREE 1-800-820-1283

Plan AHP-9490

PRICES AND DETAILS
ON PAGES 2-5

REAR VIEW

The Sunshine of Your Life!

- A huge sun room and an abundance of windows in this fascinating home will bring the sunshine into your life!

- The huge living room's sparkling sun roof gathers solar heat, which is stored in the tile floor and the two-story-high masonry wall behind the woodstove. The cozy woodstove creates a glowing charm that's sure to light up all your family events.

- Efficiently designed, the galley-style kitchen makes meal preparation a breeze. Nearby access to a spacious deck lets you cool off after dining.

- Two nice-sized bedrooms and a full bath complete the main floor.

- Occupying the entire upper floor is the beautiful master suite, which features a big walk-in closet and a private bath. A balcony overlooking the living room lets you check in on the kids below.

Plans H-947-1A & -1B

Bedrooms: 3+	Baths: 2-3
Living Area:	
Upper floor	516 sq. ft.
Main floor	1,162 sq. ft.
Daylight basement	966 sq. ft.
Total Living Area:	**1,678/2,644 sq. ft.**
Garage	279 sq. ft.
Exterior Wall Framing:	2x6
Foundation Options:	**Plan #**
Daylight basement	H-947-1B
Crawlspace	H-947-1A

(All plans can be built with your choice of foundation and framing. A generic conversion diagram is available. See order form.)

BLUEPRINT PRICE CODE:	**B/D**

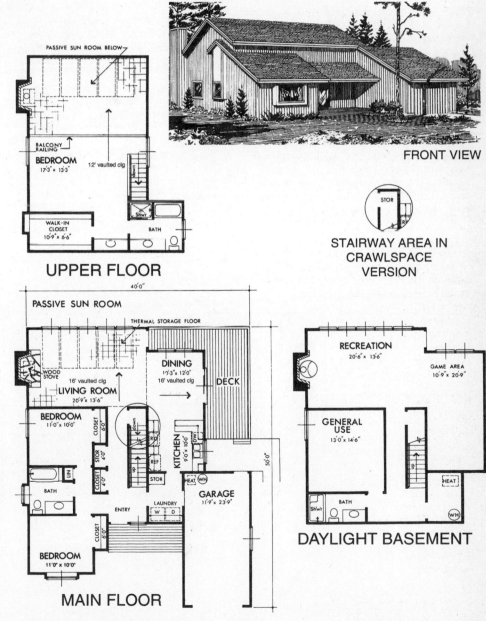

FRONT VIEW

STAIRWAY AREA IN CRAWLSPACE VERSION

UPPER FLOOR

MAIN FLOOR

DAYLIGHT BASEMENT

The Best of Both Worlds

- Looking for a home with the feel of the country without sacrificing up-to-date conveniences? This design offers you the best of both worlds!
- Virtually barrier-free, the open floor plan provides plenty of room to roam. A formal living and dining room flank the foyer, but they connect easily to the big casual space at the back of the home.
- The family room, kitchen and informal eating area form a continuous expanse

that's the perfect spot for fun family times or laid-back entertaining. A big angled work island in the kitchen acts as a serving bar, and a fireplace casts a warm glow on winter nights.
- On the upper floor, the master suite offers a large bedroom, a walk-in closet and a private bath that's a necessity on busy mornings when you're in a rush to get to work.
- Two secondary bedrooms are on opposite sides of a balcony hallway with views to the foyer below. The bedrooms share a full bath.
- A full basement offers you a complete range of expansion possibilities.

Plan GL-1950	
Bedrooms: 3	**Baths:** 2½
Living Area:	
Upper floor	912 sq. ft.
Main floor	1,038 sq. ft.
Total Living Area:	**1,950 sq. ft.**
Standard basement	1,038 sq. ft.
Garage	484 sq. ft.
Exterior Wall Framing:	2x6
Foundation Options:	

Standard basement
(All plans can be built with your choice of foundation and framing. A generic conversion diagram is available. See order form.)

BLUEPRINT PRICE CODE:	B

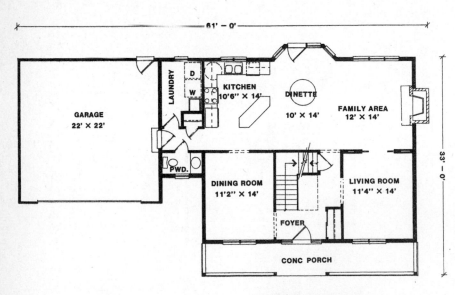

MAIN FLOOR

UPPER FLOOR

ORDER BLUEPRINTS ANYTIME!
CALL TOLL-FREE 1-800-820-1283

Plan GL-1950

PRICES AND DETAILS
ON PAGES 2-5

Delightful Choices

- Its simple structure makes this four-bedroom, two-story home the perfect choice for the economical family. This versatile plan is available with a siding or brick exterior finish.
- Comfortably sized formal spaces, open informal areas and lots of windows make the floor plan light and bright. An optional bay window in the living room and fireplace in the family room can add further ambience.
- The breakfast nook's delightful boxed bay provides a sunny site for casual dining. The adjoining kitchen has a windowed sink and easy access to the garage and to the formal dining room.
- All four bedrooms are housed on the upper floor. The master bedroom has a private bath, while the secondary bedrooms share another.

Plan CH-110-A

Bedrooms: 4	**Baths:** 2½
Living Area:	
Upper floor	860 sq. ft.
Main floor	846 sq. ft.
Total Living Area:	**1,706 sq. ft.**
Basement	834 sq. ft.
Garage	380 sq. ft.
Exterior Wall Framing:	2x4

Foundation Options:

Daylight basement

Standard basement

Crawlspace

(All plans can be built with your choice of foundation and framing. A generic conversion diagram is available. See order form.)

BLUEPRINT PRICE CODE: B

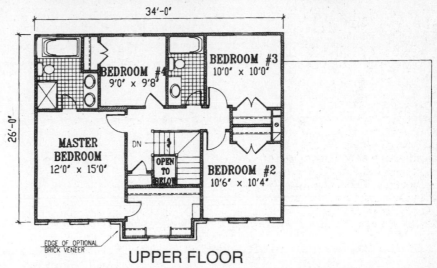

UPPER FLOOR

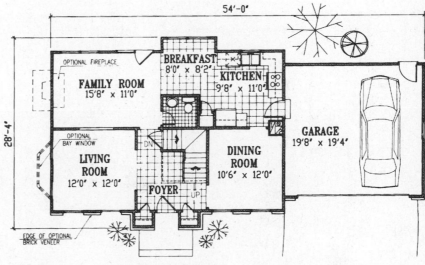

MAIN FLOOR

ORDER BLUEPRINTS ANYTIME!
CALL TOLL-FREE 1-800-820-1283

Plan CH-110-A

PRICES AND DETAILS
ON PAGES 2-5

239

Nobility Defined

- This Mediterranean-style home is the very definition of nobility, with its regal rooflines, arched entry and gorgeous window treatments.
- Double doors grace the foyer, which unfolds to the formal living and dining rooms. Sliding glass doors lead from the living room to a fabulous covered patio in the back.
- A gourmet's delight, the island kitchen provides every modern amenity, including a cute niche and an adjoining nook for the cheeriest of breakfasts!

- Nothing stands in your way if you wish to relax in the family room. A corner fireplace with a rustic hearth warms your loved ones' spirits, while sliding glass doors allow guests to relax on the patio. Perhaps a drink as the sun sets?
- The isolated master suite is just the ticket for frazzled nerves! In addition to private sliding-glass-door access to the patio, it also flaunts a classy bath to die for! Here, a splashy whirlpool tub waits, tucked into a fabulous curved glass-block wall. Each morning, the separate shower will refresh you.
- Two secondary bedrooms on the upper floor give the kids a generous helping of privacy and enough room for both recreation and study.

Plan HDS-99-253	
Bedrooms: 3	**Baths:** 2½
Living Area:	
Upper floor	480 sq. ft.
Main floor	1,482 sq. ft.
Total Living Area:	**1,962 sq. ft.**
Garage	397 sq. ft.
Exterior Wall Framing:	2x4
Foundation Options:	
Slab	

(All plans can be built with your choice of foundation and framing. A generic conversion diagram is available. See order form.)

BLUEPRINT PRICE CODE: B

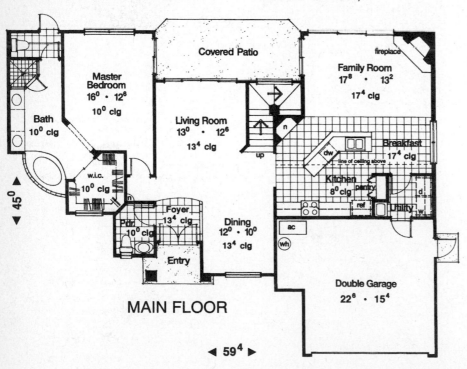

MAIN FLOOR

◄ 59⁴ ►

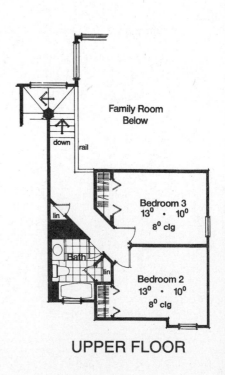

UPPER FLOOR

ORDER BLUEPRINTS ANYTIME!
CALL TOLL-FREE 1-800-820-1283

Plan HDS-99-253

PRICES AND DETAILS
ON PAGES 2-5

Photo by Mark Englund/HomeStyles

NOTE:
The above photographed home may have been modified by the homeowner. Please refer to floor plan and/or drawn elevation shown for actual blueprint details.

Distinctive Family Design

- This beautiful, time-tested traditional design packs many features into a highly livable floor plan.
- To the left of the foyer, the 16½-ft. vaulted living room flows into the dining room, providing a huge space for both formal entertaining and family gatherings.
- The big kitchen includes a handy work island and a sunny dinette, which opens to the backyard. A half-bath, laundry facilities and garage access are nearby.
- The large family room adjoins the casual dinette area and boasts a handsome fireplace.
- Upstairs, the master bedroom features two large closets and a private bath. Three additional bedrooms share another full bath. A central balcony overlooks the foyer below.

Plan A-2109-DS

Bedrooms: 4	Baths: 2½
Living Area:	
Upper floor	942 sq. ft.
Main floor	1,148 sq. ft.
Total Living Area:	**2,090 sq. ft.**
Standard basement	1,148 sq. ft.
Garage	484 sq. ft.
Exterior Wall Framing:	2x4

Foundation Options:

Standard basement

(All plans can be built with your choice of foundation and framing. A generic conversion diagram is available. See order form.)

BLUEPRINT PRICE CODE:	C

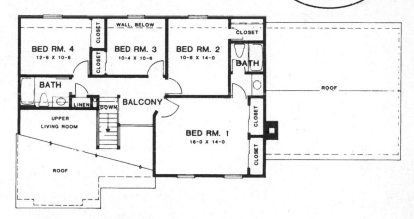

UPPER FLOOR

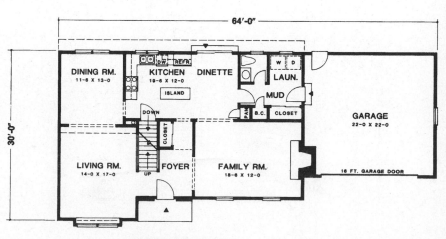

MAIN FLOOR

***ORDER BLUEPRINTS ANYTIME!*
*CALL TOLL-FREE 1-800-820-1283***

Plan A-2109-DS

*PRICES AND DETAILS
ON PAGES 2-5*

241

Photo by Bob Hallinen

Soaring Design

- Dramatic windows soar to the peak of this prowed chalet, offering unlimited views of outdoor scenery.
- The spacious living room flaunts a fabulous fireplace, a soaring 26-ft. vaulted ceiling, a striking window wall and sliding glass doors to a wonderful wraparound deck.
- An oversized window brightens a dining area on the left side of the living room. The sunny, L-shaped kitchen is spacious and easily accessible.
- The secluded main-floor bedroom has convenient access to a full bath, a linen

closet, a good-sized laundry room and the rear entrance.
- A central, open-railed staircase leads to the upper floor, which contains two more bedrooms and a full bath.
- A skylighted balcony is the high point of this design, offering a railed overlook into the living room below and sweeping outdoor vistas through the wall of windows.
- The optional daylight basement provides another fireplace in a versatile recreation room. The extra-long, tuck-under garage includes plenty of room for hobbies, while the service room offers additional storage space.

Plans H-930-1 & -1A	
Bedrooms: 3	**Baths:** 2
Living Area:	
Upper floor	710 sq. ft.
Main floor	1,210 sq. ft.
Daylight basement	605 sq. ft.
Total Living Area:	**1,920/2,525 sq. ft.**
Tuck-under garage/shop	605 sq. ft.
Exterior Wall Framing:	2x6
Foundation Options:	**Plan #**
Daylight basement	H-930-1
Crawlspace	H-930-1A

(All plans can be built with your choice of foundation and framing. A generic conversion diagram is available. See order form.)

BLUEPRINT PRICE CODE:	**B/D**

DAYLIGHT BASEMENT

STAIRWAY AREA IN
CRAWLSPACE VERSION

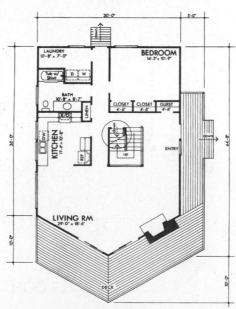

MAIN FLOOR

UPPER FLOOR

NOTE:
The above photographed home may have been modified by the homeowner. Please refer to floor plan and/or drawn elevation shown for actual blueprint details.

ORDER BLUEPRINTS ANYTIME!
CALL TOLL-FREE 1-800-820-1283

Plans H-930-1 & -1A

PRICES AND DETAILS
ON PAGES 2-5

Photo courtesy of Breland & Farmer Designers, Inc.

Stylish and Compact

- This country-style home has a classic exterior and a space-saving and compact interior.
- A quaint covered porch extends along the front of the home. The oval-glassed front door opens to the entry, which leads to the spacious living room with a handsome fireplace, windows at either end and access to a big screened porch.
- The formal dining room flows from the living room and is easily served by the convenient U-shaped kitchen.
- A nice-sized laundry room and a full bath are nearby. The two-car garage offers a super storage area.
- The deluxe master suite features a huge walk-in closet. A separate dressing area leads to an adjoining, dual-access bath.
- The upper floor offers two more bedrooms and another full bath. Each bedroom has generous closet space and independent access to attic space.

Plan E-1626

Bedrooms: 3	Baths: 2
Living Area:	
Upper floor	464 sq. ft.
Main floor	1,136 sq. ft.
Total Living Area:	**1,600 sq. ft.**
Garage	462 sq. ft.
Exterior Wall Framing:	2x6

Foundation Options:

Crawlspace
Slab
(All plans can be built with your choice of foundation and framing. A generic conversion diagram is available. See order form.)

BLUEPRINT PRICE CODE:	B

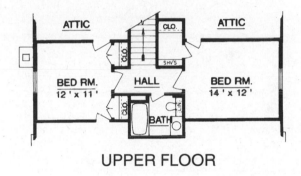

UPPER FLOOR

**NOTE:
The above photographed home may have been modified by the homeowner. Please refer to floor plan and/or drawn elevation shown for actual blueprint details.

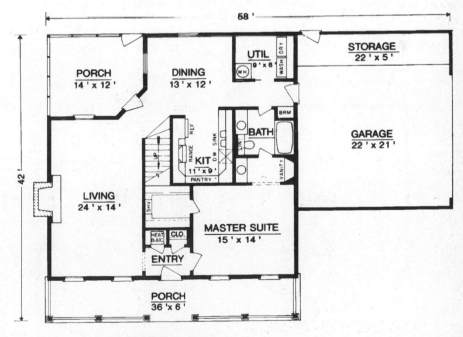

MAIN FLOOR

ORDER BLUEPRINTS ANYTIME!
CALL TOLL-FREE 1-800-820-1283

Plan E-1626

PRICES AND DETAILS
ON PAGES 2-5

243

Front Porch Invites Visitors

- This neat and well-proportioned design exudes warmth and charm.
- The roomy foyer connects the formal dining room and living room for special occasions, and the living and family rooms join together to create abundant space for large gatherings.
- The large kitchen, dinette and family room flow from one to the other for great casual family living.
- Upstairs, the roomy master suite is complemented by a master bath available in two configurations. The unique library is brightened by a beautiful arched window.

Plan GL-2161

Bedrooms: 3	Baths: 2½
Living Area:	
Upper floor	991 sq. ft.
Main floor	1,170 sq. ft.
Total Living Area	**2,161 sq. ft.**
Standard basement	1,170 sq. ft.
Garage	462 sq. ft.
Exterior Wall Framing	2x6

Foundation Options:

Standard basement

(All plans can be built with your choice of foundation and framing. A generic conversion diagram is available. See order form.)

BLUEPRINT PRICE CODE	**C**

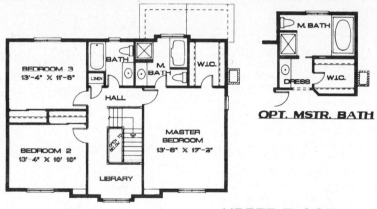

UPPER FLOOR

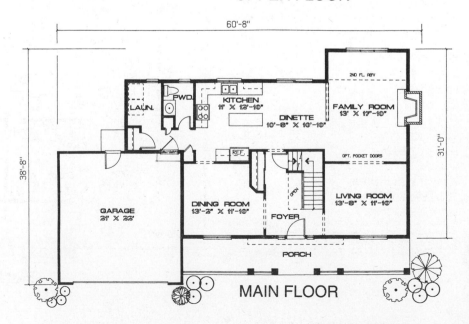

MAIN FLOOR

ORDER BLUEPRINTS ANYTIME!
CALL TOLL-FREE 1-800-820-1283

Plan GL-2161

PRICES AND DETAILS
ON PAGES 2-5

Today's Tradition

- This two-story country home combines traditional standards with the exciting new designs of today.
- Visitors are welcomed by the wraparound porch and the symmetrical bay windows of the living and dining rooms.
- The front half of the main floor lends itself to entertaining as the angled entry creates a flow between the formal areas.
- French doors lead from the living room to the spacious family room, which boasts a beamed ceiling, a warm fireplace and porch access.
- The super kitchen features an island cooktop with a snack bar. A nice-sized laundry room is nearby.
- The spacious upper level hosts a master suite with two walk-in closets and a large bath with a dual-sink vanity, a tub and a separate shower. Three more bedrooms share another full bath.

Plan AGH-2143

Bedrooms: 4	Baths: 2½
Living Area:	
Upper floor	1,047 sq. ft.
Main floor	1,096 sq. ft.
Total Living Area:	**2,143 sq. ft.**
Daylight basement	1,096 sq. ft.
Garage	852 sq. ft.
Exterior Wall Framing:	2x6

Foundation Options:

Daylight basement

(All plans can be built with your choice of foundation and framing. A generic conversion diagram is available. See order form.)

BLUEPRINT PRICE CODE:	C

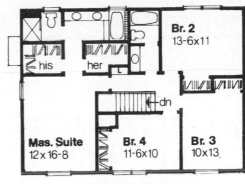

UPPER FLOOR

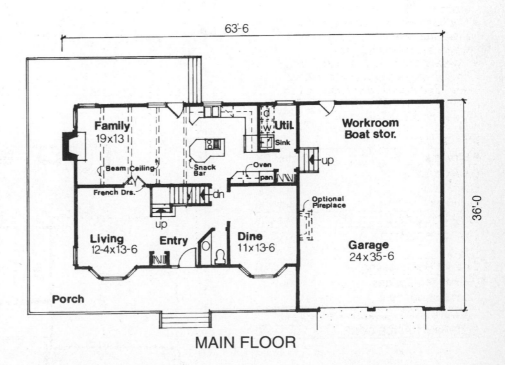

MAIN FLOOR

ORDER BLUEPRINTS ANYTIME!
CALL TOLL-FREE 1-800-820-1283

Plan AGH-2143

PRICES AND DETAILS
ON PAGES 2-5

245

Panoramic Prow View

- This glass-filled prow gable design is almost as spectacular as the panoramic view from inside.
- French doors open from the front deck to the dining room. A stunning window wall illuminates the adjoining living room, which flaunts a 20-ft.-high cathedral ceiling.

- The open, corner kitchen is perfectly angled to service the dining room and the family room, while offering views of the front and rear decks.
- A handy utility/laundry room opens to the rear deck. Two bedrooms share a full bath, to complete the main floor.
- A dramatic, open-railed stairway leads up to the secluded master bedroom, which boasts a dressing room and a private bath with a dual-sink vanity and a separate tub and shower.

Plan NW-196	
Bedrooms: 3	**Baths:** 2
Living Area:	
Upper floor	394 sq. ft.
Main floor	1,317 sq. ft.
Total Living Area:	**1,711 sq. ft.**
Exterior Wall Framing:	2x6
Foundation Options:	
Crawlspace	

(All plans can be built with your choice of foundation and framing. A generic conversion diagram is available. See order form.)

BLUEPRINT PRICE CODE:	**B**

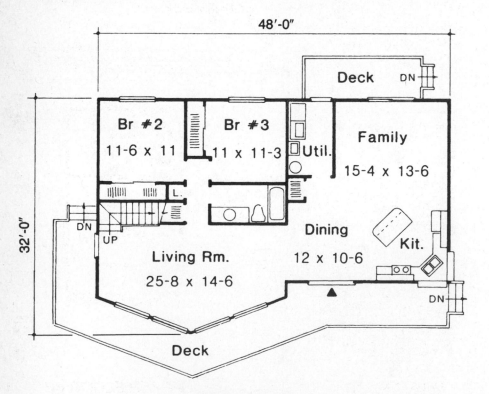

MAIN FLOOR

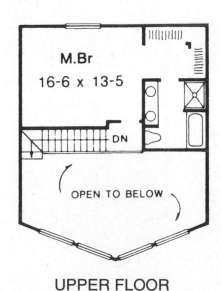

UPPER FLOOR

ORDER BLUEPRINTS ANYTIME!
CALL TOLL-FREE 1-800-820-1283

Plan NW-196

PRICES AND DETAILS
ON PAGES 2-5

A Chalet for Today

- With its wraparound deck and soaring windows, this chalet-style home is ideal for recreational living and scenic sites.
- The living and dining rooms are combined to take advantage of the dramatic 23-ft. cathedral ceiling, the rugged stone fireplace and the view through the spectacular windows.
- A quaint balcony above adds to the warm country feeling of the living area, which extends to the expansive deck.

- The open kitchen features a bright corner sink and a nifty breakfast bar that adjoins the living area.
- The handy main-floor laundry area is close to two bedrooms and a full bath.
- A 17-ft. sloped ceiling crowns the quiet study, which is a feature rarely found in a home of this size and style.
- The master suite and a storage area encompass the upper floor. A 13-ft., 8-in. cathedral ceiling, a whirlpool bath and sweeping views from the balcony give this space an elegant feel.
- The basement option includes a tuck-under garage, additional storage space and a separate utility area.

Plan AHP-9340

Bedrooms: 3+	**Baths:** 2

Living Area:	
Upper floor	332 sq. ft.
Main floor	974 sq. ft.
Total Living Area:	**1,306 sq. ft.**
Basement	624 sq. ft.
Tuck-under garage	350 sq. ft.
Exterior Wall Framing:	2x4 or 2x6

Foundation Options:
Standard basement
Daylight basement
Crawlspace
Slab
(All plans can be built with your choice of foundation and framing. A generic conversion diagram is available. See order form.)

BLUEPRINT PRICE CODE:	**A**

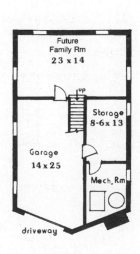

BASEMENT

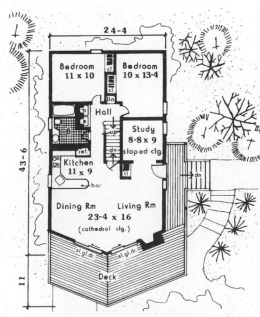

MAIN FLOOR

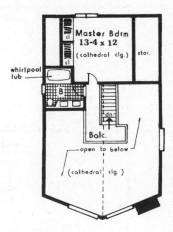

UPPER FLOOR

Unexpected Amenities

- Surprising interior amenities are found within the casual exterior of this good-looking design.
- A dramatic fireplace warms the comfortable formal areas. The living and dining rooms share a 20-ft. cathedral ceiling and high windows that flank the fireplace. Sliding glass doors access the outdoors.

- The efficient walk-through kitchen provides plenty of counter space, in addition to a windowed sink and a pass-through to the living areas.
- A large bedroom, a full bath and an oversized utility room complete the main floor. The utility room offers space for a washer and dryer, plus a sink and an extra freezer.
- Upstairs, the spacious and secluded master suite boasts a walk-in closet, a private bath and lots of storage space. A railed loft area overlooks the living and dining rooms.

Plan I-1249-A	
Bedrooms: 2	**Baths:** 2
Living Area:	
Upper floor	297 sq. ft.
Main floor	952 sq. ft.
Total Living Area:	**1,249 sq. ft.**
Standard basement	952 sq. ft.
Exterior Wall Framing:	2x6
Foundation Options:	
Standard basement	
Crawlspace	

(All plans can be built with your choice of foundation and framing. A generic conversion diagram is available. See order form.)

BLUEPRINT PRICE CODE: **A**

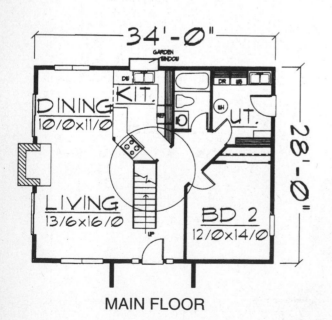

MAIN FLOOR

BASEMENT STAIRWAY LOCATION

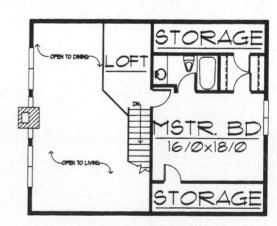

UPPER FLOOR

Poised and Pure

- This pure country-style home stands poised with plenty of eye-catching features to grab your attention.
- Relaxation is the rule on the railed veranda in front; on starry summer nights it's the perfect place to cuddle up with your loved ones.
- From the raised foyer you can step down to the living room or dining room. The living room features a cozy boxed-out window and a pleasant fireplace to cheer up the large space.
- The dining room also contains a boxed-out window, and is just a step from the island kitchen, which helps to make serving and cleaning up meals fast and easy.
- Sunshine pours into the corner breakfast nook via two walls of windows. Sit down and enjoy the great views or step outside via a handy French door.
- French doors are also a key feature in the beautiful master suite—they invite you to a private patio. Other highlights include a huge bath and an equally spacious walk-in closet.
- Two more bedrooms complete the main floor. A large game room upstairs converts easily to a fourth bedroom.

Plan L-284-VB

Bedrooms: 3+	Baths: 3
Living Area:	
Upper floor	445 sq. ft.
Main floor	1,837 sq. ft.
Total Living Area:	**2,282 sq. ft.**
Exterior Wall Framing:	2x4

Foundation Options:

Slab

(All plans can be built with your choice of foundation and framing. A generic conversion diagram is available. See order form.)

BLUEPRINT PRICE CODE: C

UPPER FLOOR

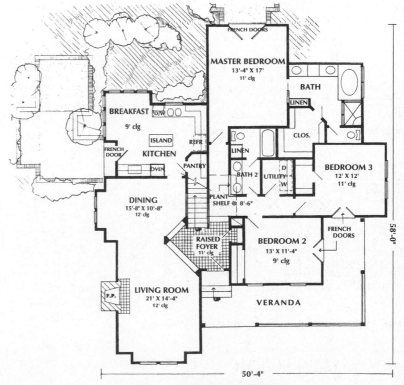

MAIN FLOOR

ORDER BLUEPRINTS ANYTIME!
CALL TOLL-FREE 1-800-820-1283

Plan L-284-VB

PRICES AND DETAILS
ON PAGES 2-5

249

Instant Impact

- Bold rooflines, interesting angles and unusual window treatments give this stylish home lots of impact.
- Inside, high ceilings and an open floor plan maximize the home's square footage. At only 28 ft. wide, the home also is ideal for a narrow lot.
- A covered deck leads to the main entry, which features a sidelighted door, angled glass walls and a view of the striking open staircase.
- The Great Room is stunning, with its 16-ft. vaulted ceiling, energy-efficient woodstove and access to a large deck.
- A flat ceiling distinguishes the dining area, which shares an angled snack bar/cooktop with the step-saving kitchen. A laundry/mudroom is nearby.
- Upstairs, the master suite offers a sloped 13-ft. ceiling and a clerestory window. A walk-through closet leads to the private bath, which is enhanced by a skylighted, sloped ceiling.
- Another full bath and plenty of storage serve the other bedrooms, one of which has a sloped ceiling and a dual closet.

Plans H-1427-3A & -3B

Bedrooms: 3	Baths: 2½
Living Area:	
Upper floor	880 sq. ft.
Main floor	810 sq. ft.
Total Living Area:	**1,690 sq. ft.**
Daylight basement	810 sq. ft.
Garage	409 sq. ft.
Exterior Wall Framing:	2x4
Foundation Options:	**Plan #**
Daylight basement	H-1427-3B
Crawlspace	H-1427-3A

(All plans can be built with your choice of foundation and framing. A generic conversion diagram is available. See order form.)

BLUEPRINT PRICE CODE:	B

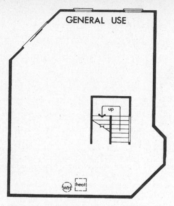

DAYLIGHT BASEMENT

UPPER FLOOR

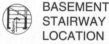

BASEMENT STAIRWAY LOCATION

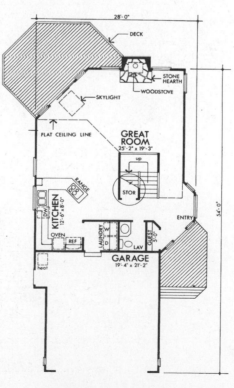

MAIN FLOOR

Plans H-1427-3A & -3B

PRICES AND DETAILS ON PAGES 2-5

Compact Three-Bedroom

- Both openness and privacy are possible in this economical three-bedroom home design.
- The bright living room boasts a 17-ft. vaulted ceiling, a warming fireplace and a corner window. A high clerestory window lets in additional natural light.
- The modern, U-shaped kitchen features a handy corner pantry and a versatile snack bar.
- The adjacent open dining area provides access to a backyard deck through sliding glass doors.
- A lovely corner window brightens the secluded master bedroom, which also includes a roomy walk-in closet and private access to a compartmentalized hall bath.
- Upstairs, two good-sized bedrooms share a second split bath.

Plan B-101-8501

Bedrooms: 3	Baths: 2
Living Area:	
Upper floor	400 sq. ft.
Main floor	846 sq. ft.
Total Living Area:	**1,246 sq. ft.**
Garage	400 sq. ft.
Standard basement	846 sq. ft.
Exterior Wall Framing:	2x4

Foundation Options:

Standard basement
(All plans can be built with your choice of foundation and framing. A generic conversion diagram is available. See order form.)

BLUEPRINT PRICE CODE:	A

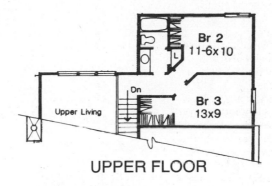

UPPER FLOOR

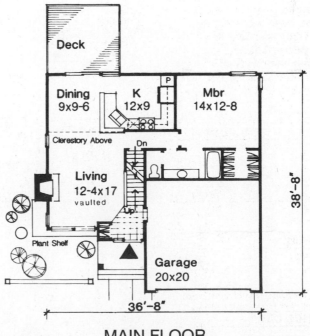

MAIN FLOOR

ORDER BLUEPRINTS ANYTIME!
CALL TOLL-FREE 1-800-820-1283

Plan B-101-8501

PRICES AND DETAILS
ON PAGES 2-5

251

Decked-Out Chalet

- This gorgeous chalet is partially surrounded by a large and roomy deck that is great for indoor/outdoor living.
- The living and dining area shows off a fireplace with a raised hearth, plus large windows to take in the outdoor views. The area is further expanded by a 17½-ft.-high vaulted ceiling in the dining room and sliding glass doors that lead to the deck.
- The kitchen offers a breakfast bar that separates it from the dining area. A convenient laundry room is nearby.
- The main-floor master bedroom is just steps away from a linen closet and a hall bath. Two upstairs bedrooms share a second full bath.
- The highlight of the upper floor is a balcony room with a 12½-ft.-high vaulted ceiling, exposed beams and tall windows. A decorative railing provides an overlook into the dining area below.

Plans H-919-1 & -1A

Bedrooms: 3	Baths: 2
Living Area:	
Upper floor	869 sq. ft.
Main floor	1,064 sq. ft.
Daylight basement	475 sq. ft.
Total Living Area:	**1,933/2,408 sq. ft.**
Tuck-under garage	501 sq. ft.
Exterior Wall Framing:	2x6
Foundation Options:	**Plan #**
Daylight basement	H-919-1
Crawlspace	H-919-1A

(All plans can be built with your choice of foundation and framing. A generic conversion diagram is available. See order form.)

BLUEPRINT PRICE CODE:	**B/C**

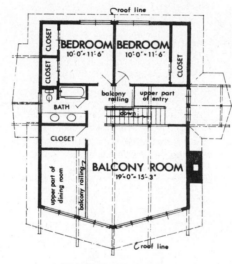

UPPER FLOOR

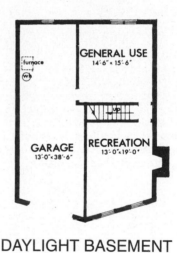

DAYLIGHT BASEMENT

MAIN FLOOR

Affordable Victorian

- This compact Victorian design incorporates four bedrooms and three full baths into an attractive, affordable home that's only 30 ft. wide.
- Just in from the covered front porch, family members and guests will gather in the spacious parlor to relax in front of the soothing fireplace. A beautiful bay window adds cheer and elegance to the formal dining room nearby.

- The galley-style kitchen offers efficient service to the breakfast nook. A laundry closet and a pantry are nearby.
- The main-floor bedroom makes a great office or guest bedroom, with a convenient full bath nearby.
- Upstairs, the master suite features an adjoining sitting room with a 14-ft. cathedral ceiling. The luxurious master bath includes a dual-sink vanity and a whirlpool tub with a shower. Two more bedrooms share another bath.
- An attached two-car garage off the kitchen is available upon request.

Plan C-8347-A

Bedrooms: 3+	Baths: 3
Living Area:	
Upper floor	783 sq. ft.
Main floor	954 sq. ft.
Total Living Area:	**1,737 sq. ft.**
Exterior Wall Framing:	2x4

Foundation Options:

Crawlspace
Slab
(All plans can be built with your choice of foundation and framing. A generic conversion diagram is available. See order form.)

BLUEPRINT PRICE CODE:	B

MAIN FLOOR

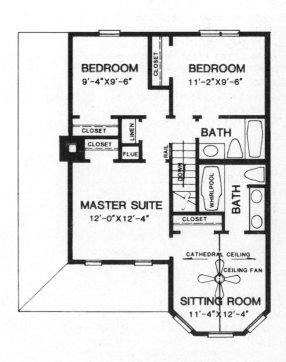

UPPER FLOOR

ORDER BLUEPRINTS ANYTIME!
CALL TOLL-FREE 1-800-820-1283
Plan C-8347-A
PRICES AND DETAILS
ON PAGES 2-5
253

Attractive and Cozy Cottage

- This cozy country cottage is attractive, economical and easy to build.
- A striking front door with oval glass and sidelights opens directly into the huge living room, which is warmed by a nice fireplace. French doors provide access to the expansive covered front porch.
- The dining room is brightened by a boxed-out area with lots of glass.
- The efficient kitchen includes a snack bar, a windowed sink and a lazy Susan.
- The quiet main-floor master bedroom offers porch access through French doors. The master bath boasts a garden tub, a separate shower, two vanities and a walk-in closet.
- A powder room and a convenient laundry room round out the main floor.
- Upstairs, two bedrooms share another full bath. Hall closets provide additional storage space.
- A storage area for outdoor equipment is offered in the secluded carport.

Plan J-86131

Bedrooms: 3	Baths: 2½
Living Area:	
Upper floor	500 sq. ft.
Main floor	1,369 sq. ft.
Total Living Area:	**1,869 sq. ft.**
Standard basement	1,369 sq. ft.
Carport and storage	540 sq. ft.
Exterior Wall Framing:	2x4

Foundation Options:

Standard basement

Crawlspace

Slab

(All plans can be built with your choice of foundation and framing. A generic conversion diagram is available. See order form.)

BLUEPRINT PRICE CODE: B

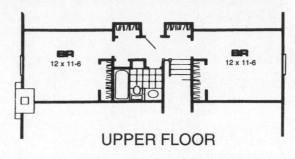

UPPER FLOOR

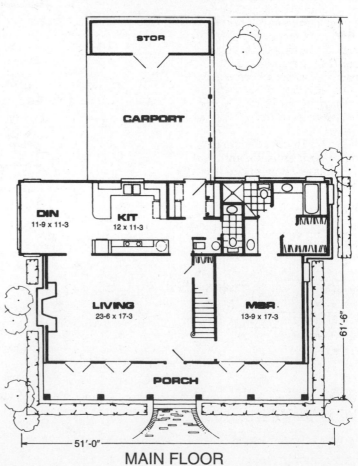

MAIN FLOOR

ORDER BLUEPRINTS ANYTIME!
CALL TOLL-FREE 1-800-820-1283

Plan J-86131

PRICES AND DETAILS
ON PAGES 2-5

Lofty Cottage Retreat

- This generous cottage home offers wide-open living areas and a delightful balcony space.
- Off the recessed entry, the living room merges into the dining room for a spacious effect. A woodstove or fireplace adds an inviting ambience.
- The adjacent kitchen has a convenient raised service counter over the sink area and handy access to both the laundry closet and the back porch.
- The master suite offers a huge walk-in closet, a bayed sitting alcove and private access to the main bath, which features a soaking tub and a sit-down angled vanity.
- Upstairs, a large balcony bedroom overlooks the living areas below. This lofty space boasts a built-in desk and a bath with a shower.

Plan E-1002

Bedrooms: 1+	Baths: 2
Living Area:	
Upper floor	267 sq. ft.
Main floor	814 sq. ft.
Total Living Area:	**1,081 sq. ft.**
Standard basement	814 sq. ft.
Exterior Wall Framing:	2x4

Foundation Options:

Standard basement

Crawlspace

Slab

(All plans can be built with your choice of foundation and framing. A generic conversion diagram is available. See order form.)

BLUEPRINT PRICE CODE:　　　**A**

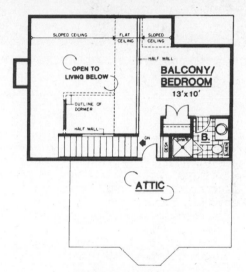

UPPER FLOOR

MAIN FLOOR

ORDER BLUEPRINTS ANYTIME!
CALL TOLL-FREE 1-800-820-1283

Plan E-1002

PRICES AND DETAILS
ON PAGES 2-5

255

Eye-Catching Chalet

- Steep rooflines, dramatic windows and wide cornices give this chalet a distinctive alpine appearance.
- The large living and dining area offers a striking 20-ft.-high vaulted ceiling and a breathtaking view of the outdoors through a soaring wall of windows. Sliding glass doors access an inviting wood deck.

- The efficient U-shaped kitchen shares an eating bar with the dining area.
- Two main-floor bedrooms share a hall bath, and laundry facilities are nearby.
- The upper floor hosts a master bedroom with a 12-ft. vaulted ceiling, plenty of storage space and easy access to a full bath with a shower.
- The pièce de résistance is a balcony with a 12-ft. vaulted ceiling, offering sweeping outdoor views as well as an overlook into the living/dining area below. Additional storage areas flank the balcony.

Plans H-886-3 & -3A	
Bedrooms: 3	**Baths: 2**
Living Area:	
Upper floor	486 sq. ft.
Main floor	994 sq. ft.
Total Living Area:	**1,480 sq. ft.**
Daylight basement	715 sq. ft.
Tuck-under garage	279 sq. ft.
Exterior Wall Framing:	**2x6**
Foundation Options:	**Plan #**
Daylight basement	H-886-3
Crawlspace	H-886-3A

(All plans can be built with your choice of foundation and framing. A generic conversion diagram is available. See order form.)

BLUEPRINT PRICE CODE:	**A**

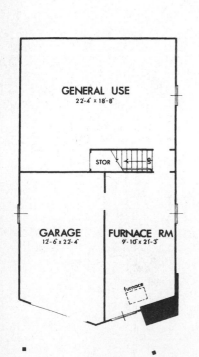

DAYLIGHT BASEMENT

GENERAL USE
22'-4" x 18'-8"

STOR

GARAGE
12'-6" x 22'-4"

FURNACE RM
9'-10" x 21'-3"

furnace

MAIN FLOOR

23' - 8"

4' - 0"

BEDROOM
8'-10" x 11'-0"

BEDROOM
10'-0" x 13'-0"

CLOSET
5'-0"

W D

BATH

LIN

CLOSET
4'-0"

CLOSET
4'-0"

down

up

DW Ref

KITCHEN
7'-1" x 8'-3"

R/O

DINING LIVING
22'-7" x 22'-10"

44' - 0"

10' - 0"

UPPER FLOOR

STORAGE

BEDROOM
12'-11" x 13'-10"

STORAGE

Shower

LIN

CLOSET
7'-9"

down

BATH

STORAGE

BALCONY
12'-10" x 9'-7"

STORAGE

Handrail

ORDER BLUEPRINTS ANYTIME!
CALL TOLL-FREE 1-800-820-1283

Plans H-886-3 & -3A

PRICES AND DETAILS ON PAGES 2-5

Spacious and Open

- A brilliant wall of windows invites guests into the two-story-high foyer of this striking traditional home.
- At the center of this open floor plan, the sunken family room boasts a 21-ft. vaulted ceiling and a striking fireplace with flanking windows.
- The cozy dinette merges with the family room and the island kitchen, creating a spacious, open atmosphere. A pantry closet, a laundry room, a half-bath and garage access are all nearby.
- The formal living and dining rooms are found at the front of the home. The living room boasts a 10½-ft. cathedral ceiling and a lovely window arrangement.
- The main-floor master bedroom has a 10-ft., 10-in. tray ceiling, a walk-in closet and a lush bath designed for two.
- Upstairs, two bedrooms share another full bath and a balcony landing that overlooks the family room and foyer.

Plan A-2207-DS

Bedrooms: 3	Baths: 2½
Living Area:	
Upper floor	518 sq. ft.
Main floor	1,389 sq. ft.
Total Living Area:	**1,907 sq. ft.**
Standard basement	1,389 sq. ft.
Garage	484 sq. ft.
Exterior Wall Framing:	2x6

Foundation Options:

Standard basement

(All plans can be built with your choice of foundation and framing. A generic conversion diagram is available. See order form.)

BLUEPRINT PRICE CODE:	B

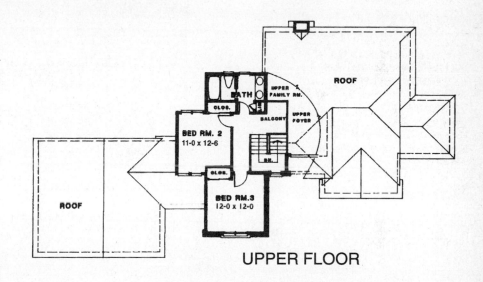

UPPER FLOOR

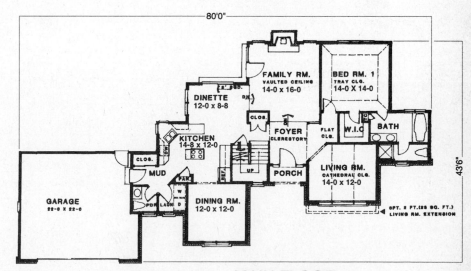

MAIN FLOOR

ORDER BLUEPRINTS ANYTIME!
CALL TOLL-FREE 1-800-820-1283

Plan A-2207-DS

PRICES AND DETAILS
ON PAGES 2-5

257

Relax on the Front Porch

- With its wraparound covered porch, this quaint two-story home makes summer evenings a breeze.
- Inside, a beautiful open stairway welcomes guests into the vaulted foyer, which connects the formal areas. The front-facing living and dining rooms have views of the covered front porch.
- French doors open from the living room to the family room, where a fireplace and corner windows warm and brighten this spacious activity area.
- The breakfast nook, set off by a half-wall, hosts a handy work desk and opens to the back porch.
- The country kitchen offers an oversized island, a pantry closet and illuminating windows flanking the corner sink.
- The upper-floor master suite boasts two walk-in closets and a private bath with a tub and a separate shower. Two more bedrooms, another full bath and a laundry room are also included.

Plan AGH-1997

Bedrooms: 3	Baths: 2½
Living Area:	
Upper floor	933 sq. ft.
Main floor	1,064 sq. ft.
Total Living Area:	**1,997 sq. ft.**
Standard basement	1,064 sq. ft.
Garage	662 sq. ft.
Exterior Wall Framing:	2x6

Foundation Options:

Standard basement

(All plans can be built with your choice of foundation and framing. A generic conversion diagram is available. See order form.)

BLUEPRINT PRICE CODE: **B**

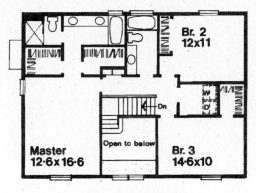

UPPER FLOOR

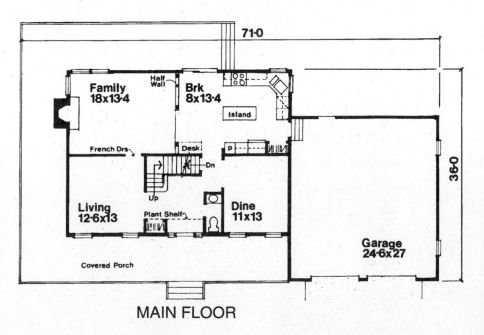

MAIN FLOOR

Colonial for Today

- Designed for a growing family, this handsome traditional home offers four bedrooms plus a den and three complete baths. The Colonial exterior is updated by a covered front entry porch with a fanlight window above.
- The dramatic tiled foyer is two stories high and provides direct access to all of the home's living areas. The spacious living room has an inviting brick fireplace and sliding pocket doors to the adjoining dining room.
- Overlooking the backyard, the huge combination kitchen/family room is the

home's hidden charm. The kitchen features a peninsula breakfast bar with seating for six.
- The family room includes a window wall with sliding glass doors that open to an enticing terrace. A built-in entertainment center and bookshelves line another wall.
- The adjacent mudroom houses a pantry closet and the washer/dryer. A full bath and a big den complete the main floor.
- The upper floor is highlighted by a beautiful balcony that overlooks the foyer below. The luxurious master suite boasts a skylighted dressing area and two closets, including an oversized walk-in closet. The private master bath offers a whirlpool tub and a dual-sink vanity.

Plan AHP-7050	
Bedrooms: 4+	**Baths:** 3
Living Area:	
Upper floor	998 sq. ft.
Main floor	1,153 sq. ft.
Total Living Area:	**2,151 sq. ft.**
Standard basement	1,067 sq. ft.
Garage and storage	439 sq. ft.
Exterior Wall Framing:	2x6
Foundation Options:	
Standard basement	
Crawlspace	
Slab	

(All plans can be built with your choice of foundation and framing. A generic conversion diagram is available. See order form.)

BLUEPRINT PRICE CODE:	C

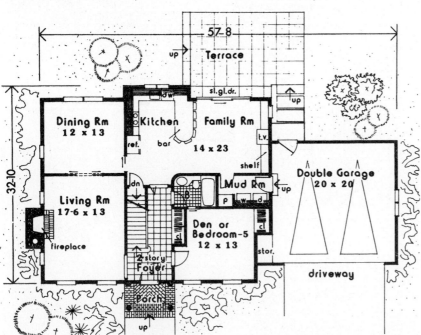

MAIN FLOOR

UPPER FLOOR

ORDER BLUEPRINTS ANYTIME!
CALL TOLL-FREE 1-800-820-1283

Plan AHP-7050

PRICES AND DETAILS
ON PAGES 2-5

259

Striking Design

- Tall windows and a rustic stone chimney give this home its striking look.
- Inside, a raised foyer leads to the living room, which has a 16-ft. vaulted ceiling.
- The adjoining dining room offers access to an inviting deck.
- A convenient pass-through lies between the dining room and the open kitchen and nook.
- A skylighted staircase leads upstairs to the master suite, with its private bath and large walk-in closet.
- A second bedroom shares another full bath with a loft or third bedroom.

Plan B-224-8512

Bedrooms: 2+	Baths: 2½
Living Area:	
Upper floor	691 sq. ft.
Main floor	668 sq. ft.
Total Living Area:	**1,359 sq. ft.**
Standard basement	668 sq. ft.
Garage	458 sq. ft.
Exterior Wall Framing:	2x4
Foundation Options:	
Standard basement	

(All plans can be built with your choice of foundation and framing. A generic conversion diagram is available. See order form.)

BLUEPRINT PRICE CODE:	**A**

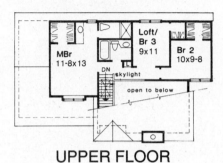

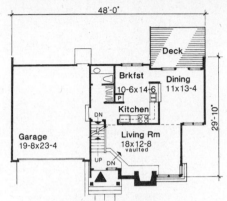

MAIN FLOOR

UPPER FLOOR

Plan B-224-8512

Swiss Chalet

- Three decks, lots of views and Swiss styling make this three-bedroom chalet the perfect design for that special site.
- A stone-faced fireplace is the focal point of the central living area, which includes sliding glass doors to a deck.
- The main-floor bedroom is located conveniently close to a full bath.
- Upstairs, each of the two bedrooms has a sloped ceiling, accessible attic storage space and a private deck.
- The optional daylight basement provides opportunity for expansion.

Plans H-755-5E & -6E

Bedrooms: 3	Baths: 2
Living Area:	
Upper floor	454 sq. ft.
Main floor	896 sq. ft.
Daylight basement	896 sq. ft.
Total Living Area:	**1,350/2,246 sq. ft.**
Exterior Wall Framing:	2x4
Foundation Options:	**Plan #**
Daylight basement	H-755-6E
Crawlspace	H-755-5E

(All plans can be built with your choice of foundation and framing. A generic conversion diagram is available. See order form.)

BLUEPRINT PRICE CODE:	**A/C**

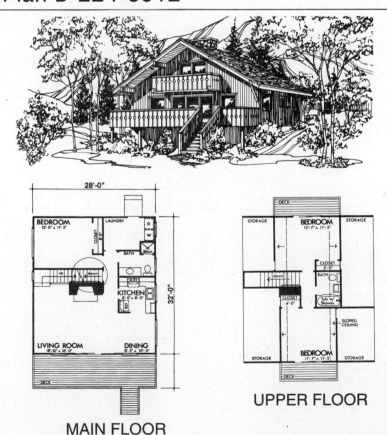

MAIN FLOOR

UPPER FLOOR

ORDER BLUEPRINTS ANYTIME!
CALL TOLL-FREE 1-800-820-1283

Plans H-755-5E & -6E

PRICES AND DETAILS
ON PAGES 2-5

A Distinguished Solution

- Trying to solve the problem of which home is just right for your special lot? We offer this distinguished solution.
- Sidelights and a big transom window flood the foyer with sunshine. To the right, a bay window adds spaciousness to the formal dining room.
- A boxed-out window brightens the living room. The adjoining family room, which is warmed by a fireplace, easily handles the overflow crowd when you entertain on a grand scale.
- The bayed casual dinette features sliding glass doors to the backyard.
- A mudroom with a large coat closet adjoins the roomy laundry facilities and a convenient half-bath.
- The upper-floor master bedroom is topped by an elegant tray ceiling. A big walk-in closet and private access to a full bath make this a nice retreat for the home owners.
- Two more bedrooms border a balcony hallway that overlooks the open foyer.

Plan A-2238-DS

Bedrooms: 3	Baths: 1½
Living Area:	
Upper floor	724 sq. ft.
Main floor	1,048 sq. ft.
Total Living Area:	**1,772 sq. ft.**
Standard basement	1,048 sq. ft.
Garage	484 sq. ft.
Exterior Wall Framing:	2x6

Foundation Options:

Standard basement

(All plans can be built with your choice of foundation and framing. A generic conversion diagram is available. See order form.)

BLUEPRINT PRICE CODE:	B

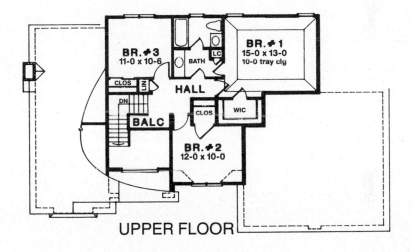

UPPER FLOOR

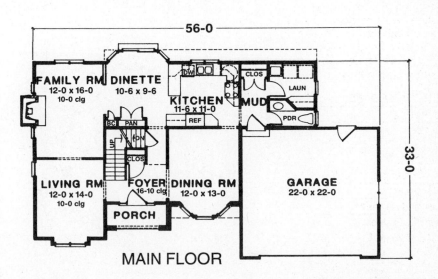

MAIN FLOOR

ORDER BLUEPRINTS ANYTIME!
CALL TOLL-FREE 1-800-820-1283

Plan A-2238-DS

PRICES AND DETAILS
ON PAGES 2-5

261

What a View!

- The oversized, arch-topped window arrangement that fronts this home provides glorious panoramic views.
- The high vaulted ceiling over the entry merges into the second floor and living room ceilings, creating a marvelous sense of space.
- A handsome, wood-burning fireplace warms the living room, which is one step up from the center hall.
- Casual times are reserved for the family room, which adjoins the pass-through kitchen and the bayed breakfast room. The family room and kitchen share a serving counter, and sliding glass doors from the breakfast room lead outside.
- The secluded main-floor master suite features a dramatic, angled entry and a private, skylighted bath with a raised whirlpool tub and a vaulted ceiling.
- The balcony hallway on the second floor looks out on the living room. The hall connects two secondary bedrooms and a full bath. The blueprints include an alternate plan with four bedrooms.

Plan AX-89320

Bedrooms: 3	Baths: 2½
Living Area:	
Upper floor	486 sq. ft.
Main floor	1,582 sq. ft.
Total Living Area:	**2,068 sq. ft.**
Standard basement	1,582 sq. ft.
Garage	436 sq. ft.
Exterior Wall Framing:	2x4

Foundation Options:

Standard basement

Slab

(All plans can be built with your choice of foundation and framing. A generic conversion diagram is available. See order form.)

BLUEPRINT PRICE CODE: C

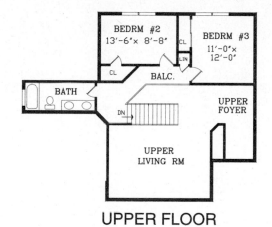

UPPER FLOOR

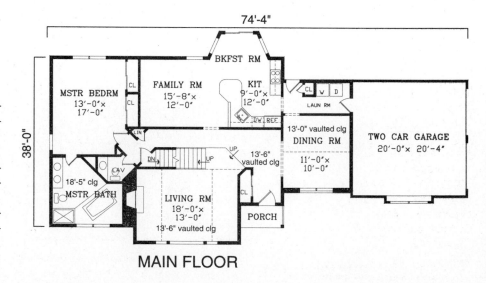

MAIN FLOOR

ORDER BLUEPRINTS ANYTIME! *CALL TOLL-FREE 1-800-820-1283*   Plan AX-89320   *PRICES AND DETAILS ON PAGES 2-5*

Eye-Catching Colonial

- Elegant bay windows embellish the rich brick exterior of this distinguished Colonial-style home.
- Inside, the entry is flanked by the formal living areas. The living room is warmed by a fireplace and separated from the family room by a decorative wood partition.
- The family room's ceiling slopes to nearly 17 feet, while French doors open to a backyard terrace.
- The adjoining peninsula kitchen features a 15-ft. sloped ceiling, a tidy pantry closet and a circular dinette surrounded by windows.
- The secluded master bedroom has an 11-ft.-high cathedral ceiling, a large walk-in closet and French doors to a private terrace. The master bath features a whirlpool tub and a separate shower.
- Three more bedrooms are found upstairs. Unless otherwise noted, all rooms have 8-ft. ceilings.

Plan AHP-9121

Bedrooms: 4	Baths: 2½
Living Area:	
Upper floor	557 sq. ft.
Main floor	1,183 sq. ft.
Total Living Area:	**1,740 sq. ft.**
Standard basement	1,183 sq. ft.
Garage and storage	440 sq. ft.
Exterior Wall Framing:	2x4 or 2x6

Foundation Options:
Standard basement
Crawlspace
Slab
(All plans can be built with your choice of foundation and framing. A generic conversion diagram is available. See order form.)

BLUEPRINT PRICE CODE: B

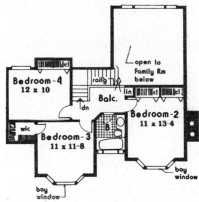

UPPER FLOOR

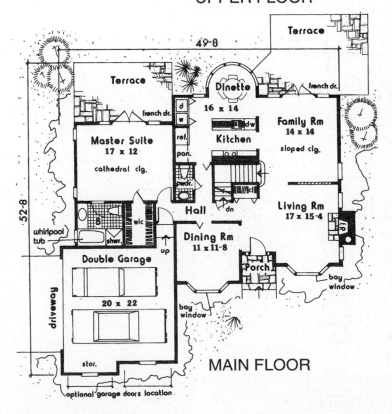

MAIN FLOOR

ORDER BLUEPRINTS ANYTIME!
CALL TOLL-FREE 1-800-820-1283

Plan AHP-9121

PRICES AND DETAILS
ON PAGES 2-5

263

Big, Bright Country Kitchen

- Decorative dormers, shuttered windows and a large covered front porch give this charming two-story home a pleasant country flavor.
- Inside, the central Great Room is warmed by a handsome fireplace. The adjoining dining room offers sliding glass doors to a backyard deck.
- The enormous country kitchen features a sunny bay-windowed eating area and a convenient island counter. The nearby laundry/utility area accesses the garage and the backyard.
- The main-floor master bedroom boasts a roomy walk-in closet and private access to a compartmentalized bath with an oversized linen closet.
- Upstairs, two bedrooms with window seats share a full bath. An easy-to-access storage area is above the garage. Another convenient storage area can be reached from the garage.

Plan C-8040

Bedrooms: 3	Baths: 2
Living Area:	
Upper floor	718 sq. ft.
Main floor	1,318 sq. ft.
Total Living Area:	**2,036 sq. ft.**
Daylight basement	1,221 sq. ft.
Garage	436 sq. ft.
Exterior Wall Framing:	2x4

Foundation Options:

Daylight basement
Crawlspace
Slab
(All plans can be built with your choice of foundation and framing. A generic conversion diagram is available. See order form.)

BLUEPRINT PRICE CODE:	C

UPPER FLOOR

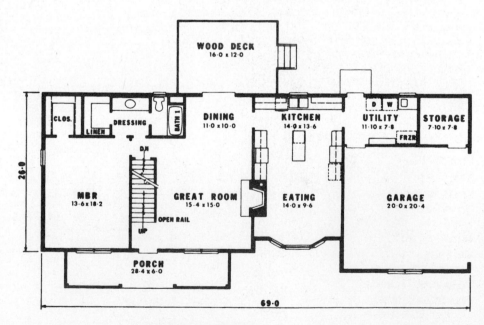

MAIN FLOOR

ORDER BLUEPRINTS ANYTIME!
CALL TOLL-FREE 1-800-820-1283

Plan C-8040

PRICES AND DETAILS
ON PAGES 2-5

Exemplary Colonial

- Inside this traditionally designed home is an exciting floor plan for today's lifestyles.
- The classic center-hall arrangement of this Colonial allows easy access to each of the living areas.
- Plenty of views are possible from the formal rooms at the front of the home, as well as from the informal areas at the rear.
- The spacious kitchen offers lots of counter space, a handy work island, a laundry closet and a sunny bayed breakfast nook.
- The adjoining family room shows off a fireplace and elegant double doors to the rear. An optional set of double doors opens to the living room.
- The beautiful master suite on the upper level boasts a 10-ft., 10-in. vaulted ceiling, two closets, dual sinks, a garden tub and a separate shower.

Plan CH-100-A

Bedrooms: 4	Baths: 2½
Living Area:	
Upper floor	923 sq. ft.
Main floor	965 sq. ft.
Total Living Area:	**1,888 sq. ft.**
Basement	952 sq. ft.
Garage	462 sq. ft.
Exterior Wall Framing:	2x4

Foundation Options:

Daylight basement
Standard basement
Crawlspace
(All plans can be built with your choice of foundation and framing. A generic conversion diagram is available. See order form.)

BLUEPRINT PRICE CODE: B

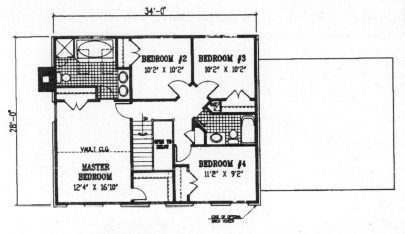

UPPER FLOOR

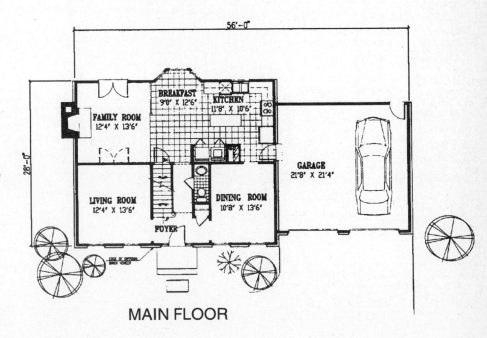

MAIN FLOOR

ORDER BLUEPRINTS ANYTIME!
CALL TOLL-FREE 1-800-820-1283

Plan CH-100-A

PRICES AND DETAILS
ON PAGES 2-5

265

Tradition Recreated

- Classic traditional styling is recreated in this home, with its covered porch, triple dormers and half-round windows.
- A central hall stems from the 17-ft.-high foyer and accesses each of the main living areas.
- A large formal space is created by the merging of the living room and the dining room. The living room boasts a fireplace and a view of the front porch.

- The kitchen features an island cooktop that frees up plenty of counter space. The sunny dining nook is wrapped by a circular glass wall. The family room has a built-in media center and access to the backyard terrace.
- A convenient main-floor mud room sits near the garage entrance.
- Upstairs, the master suite is topped by a 12½-ft. cathedral ceiling and includes a cozy window seat. The private bath flaunts a whirlpool tub, a separate shower and dual walk-in closets.
- Three secondary bedrooms and a full bath round out the upper floor.

Plan AHP-9393

Bedrooms: 4+	Baths: 3
Living Area:	
Upper floor	989 sq. ft.
Main floor	1,223 sq. ft.
Total Living Area:	**2,212 sq. ft.**
Standard basement	1,223 sq. ft.
Garage and storage	488 sq. ft.
Exterior Wall Framing:	2x4 or 2x6

Foundation Options:

Standard basement
Crawlspace
Slab

(All plans can be built with your choice of foundation and framing. A generic conversion diagram is available. See order form.)

BLUEPRINT PRICE CODE: C

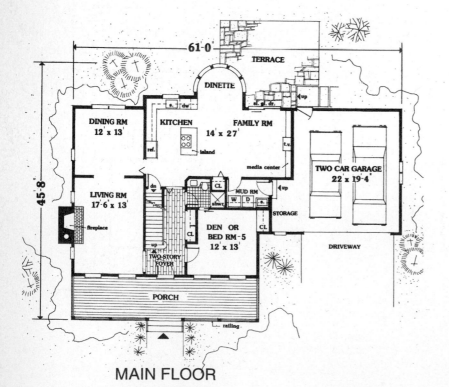

MAIN FLOOR

UPPER FLOOR

Modern Multi-Level

- This contemporary multi-tiered design has living areas on three levels, making it perfect for a sloping lot.
- Just off the entry is the living room, which is brightened by a triple window arrangement that lets in lots of sun. The presence of a casual family room in the daylight basement allows you to reserve the living room for formal occasions.
- Up a short flight of stairs, the kitchen and dining area overlook the living room. A boxed-out window nook adds space to the kitchen; the dining room features sliding glass doors to a rear patio that's sure to be a favorite spot.
- The master suite has two closets and a private bath with a separate dressing area. The suite also boasts its own access to the patio.
- Two more bedrooms and another full bath round out the main floor.
- The daylight basement contains a family room with a fireplace to take the chill off winter nights. A nearby bonus room may be used as a bedroom.
- There's plenty of storage space on the lowest level of the home.

Plan B-7825	
Bedrooms: 3+	**Baths:** 3
Living Area:	
Main floor	1,440 sq. ft.
Daylight basement	723 sq. ft.
Total Living Area:	**2,163 sq. ft.**
Tuck-under garage	483 sq. ft.
Storage	295 sq. ft.
Exterior Wall Framing:	2x6
Foundation Options:	

Daylight basement
(All plans can be built with your choice of foundation and framing. A generic conversion diagram is available. See order form.)

BLUEPRINT PRICE CODE:	C

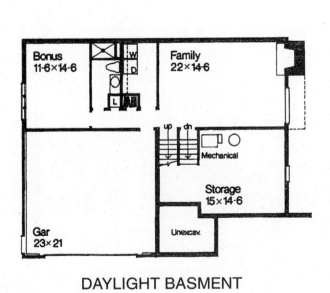

DAYLIGHT BASMENT

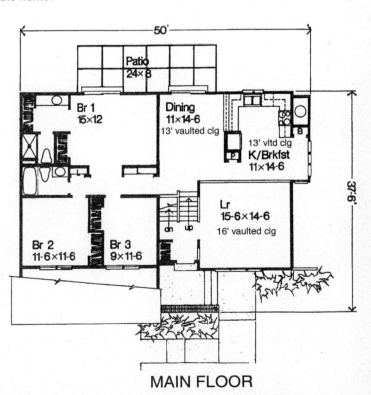

MAIN FLOOR

ORDER BLUEPRINTS ANYTIME!
CALL TOLL-FREE 1-800-820-1283

Plan B-7825

PRICES AND DETAILS
ON PAGES 2-5

267

CH-210-A

CH-210-B

Outstanding Options

- A functional floor plan and the option of two exteriors make this traditional home an outstanding choice.
- Guests will be impressed by the large, light-filled living room, with its classic columns and optional fireplace. The adjoining dining room offers an optional bay window.
- The adjacent kitchen offers an island work area and a sunny breakfast nook tucked into a large bay window.
- An open railing separates the nook from the skylighted family room, which boasts a 10½-ft. vaulted ceiling, a cozy fireplace and outdoor access through triple French doors.
- A utility room and a half-bath are located near the garage entrance.
- Upstairs, the master bedroom flaunts a 10-ft. vaulted ceiling, a huge walk-in closet and a private luxury bath with a whirlpool tub. Two additional bedrooms share another full bath.

Plans CH-210-A & -B

Bedrooms: 3	Baths: 2½
Living Area:	
Upper floor	823 sq. ft.
Main floor	1,079 sq. ft.
Total Living Area:	**1,902 sq. ft.**
Basement	978 sq. ft.
Garage	400 sq. ft.
Exterior Wall Framing:	2x4

Foundation Options:

Daylight basement

Standard basement

Crawlspace

(All plans can be built with your choice of foundation and framing. A generic conversion diagram is available. See order form.)

BLUEPRINT PRICE CODE:	B

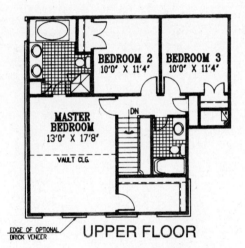

UPPER FLOOR

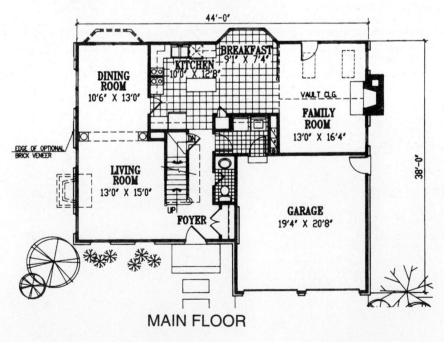

MAIN FLOOR

ORDER BLUEPRINTS ANYTIME!
CALL TOLL-FREE 1-800-820-1283

Plans CH-210-A & -B

PRICES AND DETAILS
ON PAGES 2-5

Comfort on a Narrow Lot

- With its narrow width of only 24 ft., this home is well suited for zero-lot developments or duplex construction.
- The covered entry opens to an efficient foyer that leads traffic into the living room or the family room. Also note the convenient powder room off the entry.
- The unique living room contains an impressive fireplace and a 16-ft. vaulted ceiling. The adjoining family room provides additional entertainment space, with sliding glass doors that lead to a corner patio.
- The kitchen is efficient and open, with a laundry area conveniently close.
- Upstairs, the master bedroom includes a generous-sized walk-in closet and a private bath. A railing offers views of the living room below.
- Two secondary bedrooms share a second full bath.

Plan H-1427-1A

Bedrooms: 3	Baths: 2½
Living Area:	
Upper floor	755 sq. ft.
Main floor	655 sq. ft.
Total Living Area:	**1,410 sq. ft.**
Garage	404 sq. ft.
Exterior Wall Framing:	2x4

Foundation Options:

Crawlspace
(All plans can be built with your choice of foundation and framing. A generic conversion diagram is available. See order form.)

BLUEPRINT PRICE CODE: A

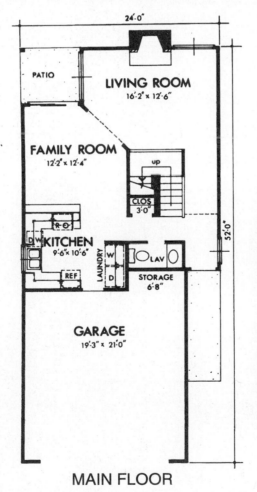

MAIN FLOOR

UPPER FLOOR

Easy Living

- The living is easy in this affordable home, which is perfect for a scenic lot.
- The main living areas look out over an inviting wraparound deck. The living room offers a 16-ft.-high sloped ceiling, a handsome fireplace and deck access.
- Two bedrooms near the main entrance feature 13-ft. sloped ceilings.
- The secluded upper-floor master suite boasts a 14-ft. vaulted ceiling, a walk-in closet, a full bath and a private deck.

Plans H-925-1 & -1A

Bedrooms: 3	Baths: 2
Living Area:	
Upper floor	288 sq. ft.
Main floor	951 sq. ft.
Total Living Area:	**1,239 sq. ft.**
Daylight basement	951 sq. ft.
Garage	266 sq. ft.
Exterior Wall Framing:	2x4
Foundation Options:	**Plan #**
Daylight basement	H-925-1
Crawlspace	H-925-1A

(All plans can be built with your choice of foundation and framing. A generic conversion diagram is available. See order form.)

BLUEPRINT PRICE CODE:	**A**

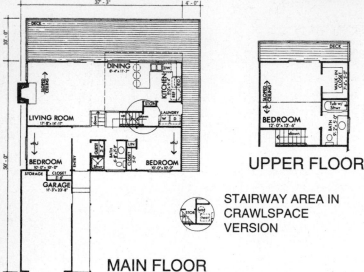

UPPER FLOOR

STAIRWAY AREA IN CRAWLSPACE VERSION

MAIN FLOOR

Plans H-925-1 & -1A

New Traditions

- A lovely front porch and an open floor plan give this new traditional its appeal.
- The foyer opens to a fabulous living room with a 16-ft. vaulted ceiling, a fireplace and an open staircase. Railings introduce the bayed breakfast area, while the galley-style kitchen leads to a covered back porch.
- The sizable master suite is enhanced by a 10-ft. raised ceiling, a cozy bay window and a compartmentalized bath. Another bedroom and bath are nearby.
- The upper floor hosts a large bedroom, a full bath and an optional bonus room.

Plan J-8636

Bedrooms: 3	Baths: 3
Living Area:	
Upper floor	270 sq. ft.
Main floor	1,253 sq. ft.
Bonus room	270 sq. ft.
Total Living Area:	**1,793 sq. ft.**
Standard basement	1,287 sq. ft.
Exterior Wall Framing:	2x4

Foundation Options:

Standard basement, crawlspace, slab

(All plans can be built with your choice of foundation and framing. A generic conversion diagram is available. See order form.)

BLUEPRINT PRICE CODE:	**B**

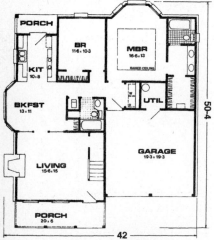

MAIN FLOOR

UPPER FLOOR

ORDER BLUEPRINTS ANYTIME!
CALL TOLL-FREE 1-800-820-1283

Plan J-8636

PRICES AND DETAILS
ON PAGES 2-5

Clean Lines, Quaint Feeling

- Clean lines complemented by a covered porch, an arched window and a half-round louver above the garage door give this design a quaint, homey feeling.
- The 17-ft. vaulted entry is brightened by a transom window and set off by an attention-getting plant ledge.
- The entry is open to the formal dining room, which features a boxed-out window. Straight ahead is the inviting Great Room with a large boxed-out window and a warm fireplace.
- A natural extension of the Great Room, the breakfast area has a built-in desk and sliders to the backyard. The kitchen includes a snack counter, a garden window above the sink and a pantry closet. A pass-through utility room lies between the kitchen and the garage.
- The upper floor hosts three bedrooms and two full baths, including a great master suite with a boxed ceiling, a walk-in closet and a private spa bath.

Plan DBI-2248

Bedrooms: 3	Baths: 2½
Living Area:	
Upper floor	759 sq. ft.
Main floor	891 sq. ft.
Total Living Area:	**1,650 sq. ft.**
Standard basement	891 sq. ft.
Garage	484 sq. ft.
Exterior Wall Framing:	2x4

Foundation Options:

Standard basement

(All plans can be built with your choice of foundation and framing. A generic conversion diagram is available. See order form.)

BLUEPRINT PRICE CODE:	B

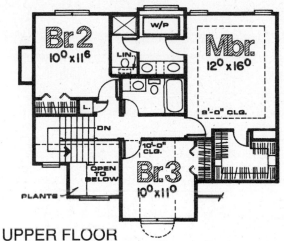

UPPER FLOOR

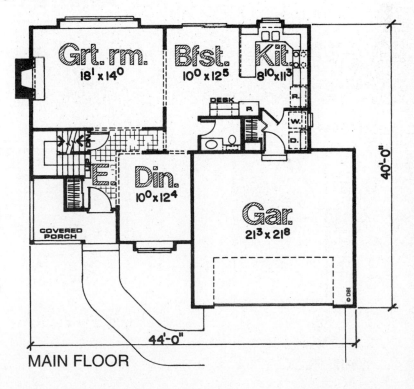

MAIN FLOOR

ORDER BLUEPRINTS ANYTIME!
CALL TOLL-FREE 1-800-820-1283

Plan DBI-2248

PRICES AND DETAILS
ON PAGES 2-5

271

Compact, Cozy, Inviting

- Full-width porches at the front and the rear of this home add plenty of space for outdoor living and entertaining.
- The huge, centrally located living room is the core of this three-bedroom home. The room features a corner fireplace, a 16-ft. sloped, open-beam ceiling and access to the back porch.
- The dining room combines with the kitchen to create an open, more spacious atmosphere. A long, central work island and a compact laundry closet are other space-saving features.
- The main-floor master suite offers a private bath with dual vanities and a large walk-in closet. Two additional bedrooms, a full bath and an intimate sitting area that overlooks the living room and entry are upstairs.
- A separate two-car garage is included with the blueprints.

Plan E-1421

Bedrooms: 3	Baths: 2
Living Area:	
Upper floor	561 sq. ft.
Main floor	924 sq. ft.
Total Living Area:	**1,485 sq. ft.**
Standard basement	924 sq. ft.
Exterior Wall Framing:	2x6

Foundation Options:

Standard basement
Crawlspace
Slab

(All plans can be built with your choice of foundation and framing. A generic conversion diagram is available. See order form.)

BLUEPRINT PRICE CODE: A

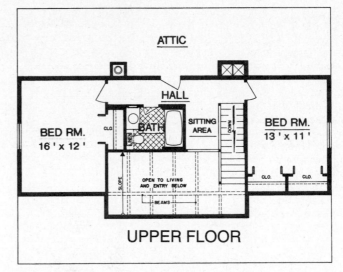

UPPER FLOOR

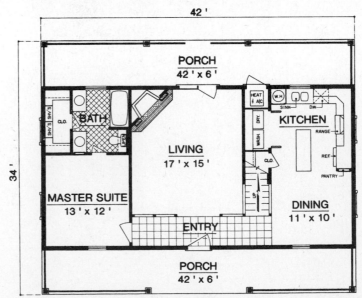

MAIN FLOOR

ORDER BLUEPRINTS ANYTIME!
CALL TOLL-FREE 1-800-820-1283

Plan E-1421

PRICES AND DETAILS ON PAGES 2-5

Stylish Two-Story

- This two-story design combines contemporary features with traditional elements, transforming it into a stylish place to call home.
- A smooth flow of traffic throughout the living areas is achieved by an open, yet compact, floor plan.
- Entertain family and friends in the spacious living room. Extend the invitation to include a tasty meal in the adjoining formal dining room.

- Designed to take advantage of the available space, the functional kitchen offers a windowed sink, ample cupboard and counter space and convenient access to both eating areas.
- Savor that first cup of coffee each morning over the daily *Times* in the sunny breakfast nook. It sports sliding glass doors to a backyard patio.
- Upstairs, the handsome master bedroom promises many nights of peaceful slumber. A private bath and a wide closet top the list of amenities.
- Two nice-sized secondary bedrooms also occupy the upper floor, rounding out the plan.

Plan GL-1382

Bedrooms: 3	Baths: 2½
Living Area:	
Upper floor	710 sq. ft.
Main floor	672 sq. ft.
Total Living Area:	**1,382 sq. ft.**
Standard basement	672 sq. ft.
Garage	420 sq. ft.
Exterior Wall Framing:	2x6

Foundation Options:

Standard basement
(All plans can be built with your choice of foundation and framing. A generic conversion diagram is available. See order form.)

BLUEPRINT PRICE CODE:	A

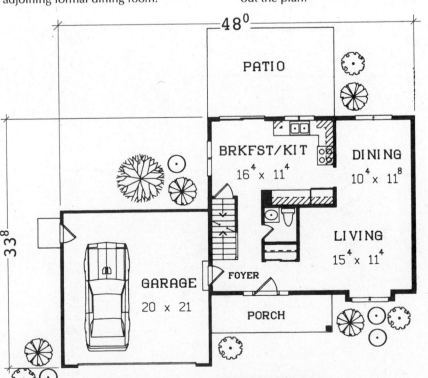

MAIN FLOOR

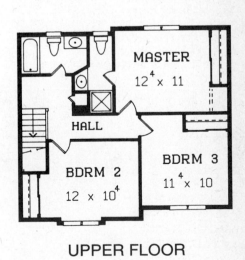

UPPER FLOOR

ORDER BLUEPRINTS ANYTIME!
CALL TOLL-FREE 1-800-820-1283

Plan GL-1382

***PRICES AND DETAILS
ON PAGES 2-5***

273

A Country Classic

- The exterior of this cozy country-style home boasts a charming combination of woodwork and stone.
- A graceful, arched entryway leads into the spacious living room with a 19-ft. vaulted ceiling, tall windows and a fireplace.
- The dining area has a lovely view of a patio and shares the living room's fireplace and vaulted ceiling.
- The impressive kitchen is brightened by a large window bank with skylights above, and offers ample counter space, a full pantry and easy access to the dining room.
- The master bedroom features a 14½-ft. vaulted ceiling, a walk-in closet, a linen closet, its own two-sink master bath and sliding-door access to the side patio.
- Two second-floor bedrooms share another full bath.

Plan B-87157

Bedrooms: 3	Baths: 2½
Living Area:	
Upper floor	452 sq. ft.
Main floor	1,099 sq. ft.
Total Living Area:	**1,551 sq. ft.**
Standard basement	1,099 sq. ft.
Garage	412 sq. ft.
Exterior Wall Framing:	2x4

Foundation Options:

Standard basement

(All plans can be built with your choice of foundation and framing. A generic conversion diagram is available. See order form.)

BLUEPRINT PRICE CODE:	**B**

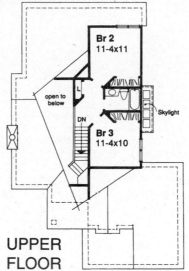

UPPER FLOOR

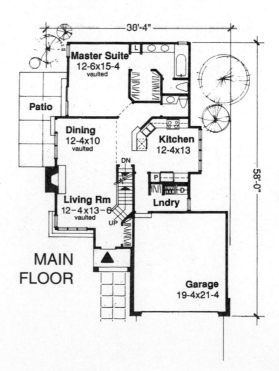

MAIN FLOOR

ORDER BLUEPRINTS ANYTIME! CALL TOLL-FREE 1-800-820-1283

Plan B-87157

PRICES AND DETAILS ON PAGES 2-5

Vacation Living

- An expansive deck across the back of the home sets a casual outdoor living theme for this compact plan.
- Two bedrooms flank the entry and share a roomy bath.
- The kitchen, the dining room and the 16½-ft. vaulted living room are several steps down from the entry level for a dramatic effect. The kitchen provides a handy snack counter and has easy access to the laundry room. The living room's handsome fireplace warms the

entire area. Sliding glass doors extend functions to the outdoors.
- Upstairs, a hideaway bedroom includes an 11½-ft. open-beam vaulted ceiling, a personal bath, a walk-in closet and a romantic private deck.
- The optional daylight basement (not shown) features a large recreation room with a fireplace and sliding glass doors to a patio underneath the rear deck.
- A fourth bedroom and a third bath are also included, in addition to large area that could be used for a hobby room or a children's play area.

Plans H-877-1 & -1A	
Bedrooms: 3+	**Baths:** 2-3
Living Area:	
Upper floor	320 sq. ft.
Main floor	1,200 sq. ft.
Daylight basement	1,200 sq. ft.
Total Living Area:	**1,520/2,720 sq. ft.**
Garage	155 sq. ft.
Exterior Wall Framing:	2x6
Foundation Options:	**Plan #**
Daylight basement	H-877-1
Crawlspace	H-877-1A

(All plans can be built with your choice of foundation and framing. A generic conversion diagram is available. See order form.)

BLUEPRINT PRICE CODE:	**B/D**

FRONT OF HOME

BASEMENT STAIRWAY LOCATION

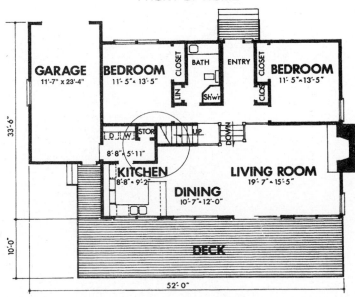

MAIN FLOOR

UPPER FLOOR

Cozy, Cost-Saving Retreat

- This cozy cabin is the perfect vacation retreat for that special mountain, lake or river location.
- The design is large enough to provide comfortable living quarters and small enough to fit a modest building budget.
- An 18½-ft. vaulted ceiling and expanses of glass add volume to the living and dining area. Double doors provide access to an inviting deck or patio.
- The U-shaped kitchen offers a bright sink and a convenient pass-through to the dining area.
- A quiet bedroom and a hall bath complete the main floor.
- The upper floor consists of a 9½-ft.-high vaulted loft that provides sweeping views of the living areas below and the scenery outside. The railed loft could serve as an extra sleeping area or a quiet haven for reading, relaxing and other activities.

Plan I-880-A

Bedrooms: 1+	Baths: 1
Living Area:	
Upper floor	308 sq. ft.
Main floor	572 sq. ft.
Total Living Area:	**880 sq. ft.**
Exterior Wall Framing:	2x6

Foundation Options:

Crawlspace

(All plans can be built with your choice of foundation and framing. A generic conversion diagram is available. See order form.)

BLUEPRINT PRICE CODE:	**AA**

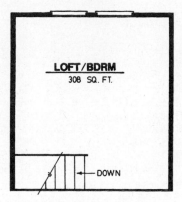

LOFT/BDRM
308 SQ. FT.

← DOWN

UPPER FLOOR

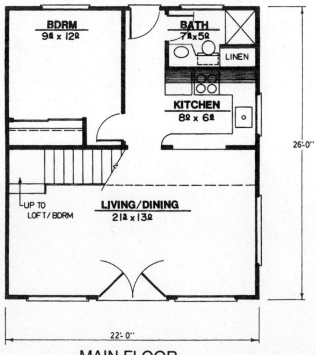

BDRM
9⁹ x 12⁹

BATH
7⁹ x 5⁹

LINEN

KITCHEN
8⁹ x 6⁹

UP TO LOFT/BDRM

LIVING/DINING
21⁹ x 13⁹

26'-0"

22'-0"

MAIN FLOOR

ORDER BLUEPRINTS ANYTIME!
CALL TOLL-FREE 1-800-820-1283

Plan I-880-A

PRICES AND DETAILS
ON PAGES 2-5

Starter Home Offers Options

- Country styling adds to the appeal of this two-story, ideal as a starter home.
- Beyond the wide front porch, the foyer flows to both the living room and the kitchen. Limited hall space maximizes the living area of the home.
- The large living room enjoys a view of the porch through a pair of shuttered windows. Sliding glass doors in the adjoining dining area offer a view of the backyard from either location.
- The open and efficient kitchen has easy access to the one-car garage and the main-floor laundry room. Closed off by a pocket door, the generous-sized laundry area has a convenient folding counter that can also serve as a work desk or planning center.
- Three bedrooms and two baths are located on the upper floor. An alternate one-bathroom version is included with the blueprints.
- An optional two-car garage adds four feet to the overall width of the home.

Plan GL-1430-P

Bedrooms: 3	Baths: 1½-2½
Living Area:	
Upper floor	720 sq. ft.
Main floor	710 sq. ft.
Total Living Area:	**1,430 sq. ft.**
Standard basement	710 sq. ft.
One-car garage	341 sq. ft.
Optional two-car garage	427 sq. ft.
Exterior Wall Framing:	2x4
Foundation Options:	

Standard basement
(All plans can be built with your choice of foundation and framing. A generic conversion diagram is available. See order form.)

| **BLUEPRINT PRICE CODE:** | **A** |

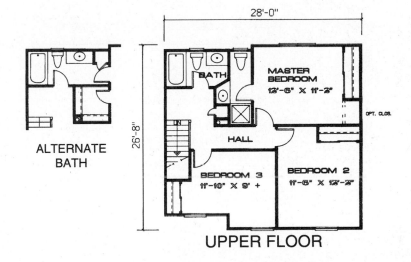

ALTERNATE BATH

UPPER FLOOR

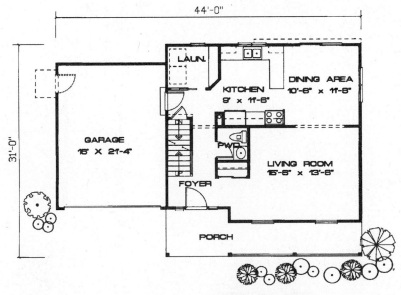

MAIN FLOOR

Casual, Cozy Retreat

- This cozy home is perfect as a weekend retreat, a summer home or a casual permanent residence.
- The living room, the kitchen and the dining area flow together, creating a huge space for relaxing or entertaining guests. A 23-ft.-high cathedral ceiling soars above a striking wall of glass that overlooks a nice front deck. Sliding glass doors access the deck.
- Two bedrooms and a full bath round out the main floor.
- The upstairs loft could serve as a private master bedroom or as a quiet study, den or studio. An open railing provides gorgeous views of both the living area below and the scenery beyond.
- Two outside storage areas offer plenty of space for tools and equipment.

Plan CPS-1095

Bedrooms: 2+	Baths: 1
Living Area:	
Upper floor	320 sq. ft.
Main floor	784 sq. ft.
Total Living Area:	**1,104 sq. ft.**
Standard basement	784 sq. ft.
Exterior Wall Framing:	2x6

Foundation Options:

Standard basement

(All plans can be built with your choice of foundation and framing. A generic conversion diagram is available. See order form.)

BLUEPRINT PRICE CODE: **A**

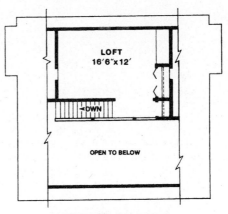

UPPER FLOOR

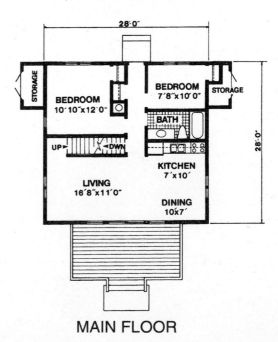

MAIN FLOOR

ORDER BLUEPRINTS ANYTIME!
CALL TOLL-FREE 1-800-820-1283

Plan CPS-1095

PRICES AND DETAILS
ON PAGES 2-5

A Deck for Each Room

- Exciting outdoor living is made possible by the many decks of this three-level contemporary design.
- The front entrance and garage are located at the daylight basement level, along with a dressing room, a full bath and laundry facilities.
- A lofty 16½-ft. vaulted ceiling tops the living room, highlighting the main floor. This expansive room includes a massive stone wall with a heat-circulating

fireplace; two sets of sliding glass doors step out to a sprawling front deck, the perfect spot for watching colorful summer sunsets.
- Designed to make efficient use of space, the U-shaped kitchen will please the chef in your family. When warmer weather permits, use the outdoor barbecue to add a little zest to your favorite meats.
- Upstairs, the exquisite master bedroom boasts a 13½-ft. vaulted ceiling, its own fireplace and a private viewing deck.
- The other upper-floor bedroom sports a 9½-ft. vaulted ceiling. Both secondary bedrooms access private decks.

Plan HFL-2176	
Bedrooms: 3	**Baths:** 3½
Living Area:	
Upper floor	712 sq. ft.
Main floor	1,001 sq. ft.
Daylight basement	463 sq. ft.
Total Living Area:	**2,176 sq. ft.**
Tuck-under garage/storage	448 sq. ft.
Exterior Wall Framing:	2x6
Foundation Options:	
Daylight basement	

(All plans can be built with your choice of foundation and framing. A generic conversion diagram is available. See order form.)

BLUEPRINT PRICE CODE:	C

DAYLIGHT

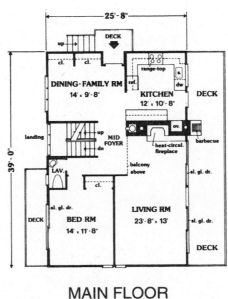

MAIN FLOOR

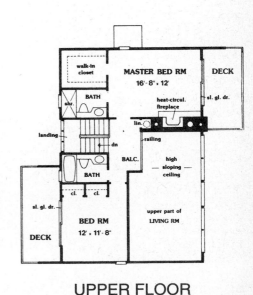

UPPER FLOOR

ORDER BLUEPRINTS ANYTIME!
CALL TOLL-FREE 1-800-820-1283

Plan HFL-2176

PRICES AND DETAILS
ON PAGES 2-5

279

Alluring
Two-Story

- This dramatic contemporary is adorned with staggered rooflines that overlap and outline large expanses of glass.
- Flanking the two-story-high foyer are the formal dining room and the sunken living room, which is expanded by an airy 16-ft. cathedral ceiling.
- The adjoining sunken family room boasts a fireplace and sliding glass doors to a backyard patio.
- A step up, the bright breakfast area enjoys an eating bar that extends from the efficient U-shaped kitchen. A half-bath and laundry facilities are convenient.
- The second level features a spacious master bedroom with a 12-ft. sloped ceiling, dual closets and a private bath. Two secondary bedrooms, another full bath and an optional expansion room above the garage are also included.

Plan AX-8596-A

Bedrooms: 3+	Baths: 2½
Living Area:	
Upper floor	738 sq. ft.
Main floor	1,160 sq. ft.
Bonus room	226 sq. ft.
Total Living Area:	**2,124 sq. ft.**
Standard basement	1,160 sq. ft.
Garage	465 sq. ft.
Exterior Wall Framing:	2x4

Foundation Options:

Standard basement

(All plans can be built with your choice of foundation and framing. A generic conversion diagram is available. See order form.)

BLUEPRINT PRICE CODE: C

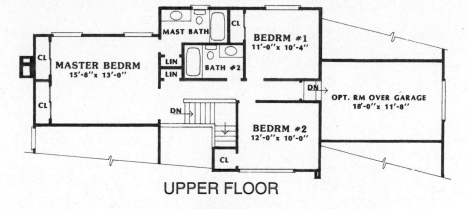

UPPER FLOOR

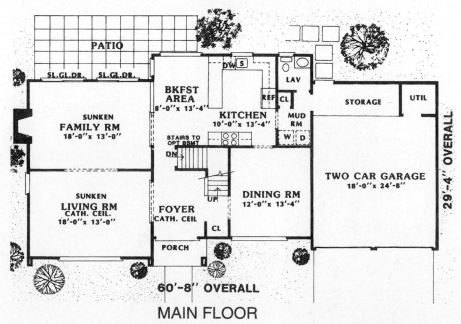

MAIN FLOOR

ORDER BLUEPRINTS ANYTIME!
CALL TOLL-FREE 1-800-820-1283

Plan AX-8596-A

PRICES AND DETAILS
ON PAGES 2-5

Exploding Views

- This spectacular two-story has it all!
- An exploding view from the two-story foyer is just a preview of the excitement that follows.
- Every major living space on the main floor has a view of the outdoors, whether it's looking over a pool area or the fifth tee.
- The expansive formal living and dining area is perfect for entertaining or candlelight dinners.

- The modern island kitchen overlooks the breakfast area and the family room, which boasts an exciting and functional media wall. Sliding glass doors open to the backyard.
- Luxurious double doors open to reveal the stunning master bedroom. Among its highlights are a private garden bath and a sparkling window wall. An optional second set of doors could access a nursery or a private study. Or, this room could be used as a conventional fourth bedroom.
- The home also offers your choice of elevation. Both elevations shown above are included in the working blueprints.

Plan HDS-99-145

Bedrooms: 3+	Baths: 2½
Living Area:	
Upper floor	982 sq. ft.
Main floor	982 sq. ft.
Total Living Area:	**1,964 sq. ft.**
Garage	646 sq. ft.
Exterior Wall Framing:	2x4

Foundation Options:

Slab
(All plans can be built with your choice of foundation and framing. A generic conversion diagram is available. See order form.)

BLUEPRINT PRICE CODE:	**B**

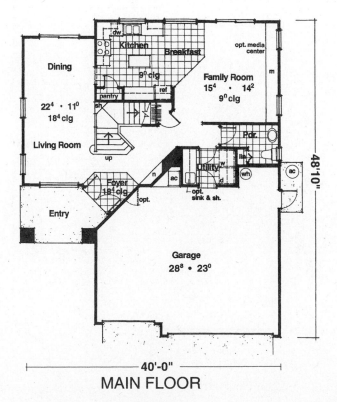

MAIN FLOOR

40'-0"

48'10"

UPPER FLOOR

ORDER BLUEPRINTS ANYTIME!
CALL TOLL-FREE 1-800-820-1283

Plan HDS-99-145

PRICES AND DETAILS
ON PAGES 2-5

281

Flexible Cottage

- This charming cottage is big enough to be a permanent home, yet small enough to fit on a narrow or lakeside lot.
- If you love to entertain, imagine the events you can host in the L-shaped living room! A two-sided fireplace serves as the focal point, while a corner window seat is great for conversation.
- Move the party into the glass-embraced dining room for a light meal or even a surprise birthday cake.
- A French door leads to a third party venue—your lovely backyard. Throw some horseshoes, fire up the barbecue or show off your prized fruit trees.
- Do you like to cook? Then you'll adore the open, U-shaped kitchen, complete with a pantry closet, double ovens and a brick cooktop.
- Was your nest recently emptied? You'll appreciate the main-floor master suite, with its vast sleeping area. The well-designed private bath opens to the backyard through a French door.
- Upstairs, children, boarders or guests are nicely accommodated by two bedrooms and a full bath.

Plan L-818-CSA

Bedrooms: 3	Baths: 2½
Living Area:	
Upper floor	486 sq. ft.
Main floor	1,330 sq. ft.
Total Living Area:	**1,816 sq. ft.**
Exterior Wall Framing:	2x4

Foundation Options:

Slab

(All plans can be built with your choice of foundation and framing. A generic conversion diagram is available. See order form.)

BLUEPRINT PRICE CODE:	**B**

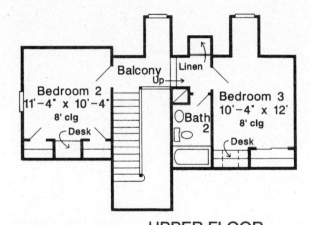

UPPER FLOOR

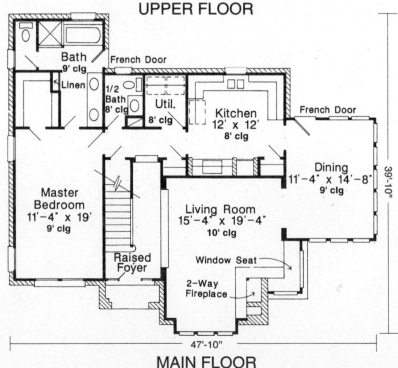

MAIN FLOOR

ORDER BLUEPRINTS ANYTIME!
CALL TOLL-FREE 1-800-820-1283

Plan L-818-CSA

PRICES AND DETAILS
ON PAGES 2-5

Cottage Basks in Brilliance

- The vaulted areas of this brilliant cottage bask in light that streams through its window walls and skylights.
- French doors are surrounded by dramatic glass to illuminate the 20-ft.-high entry as it flows into the formal areas.
- The soaring vaulted space of the living and dining rooms allows heat from the angled woodstove to spread into the loft area above.
- The U-shaped kitchen has a bright sink and abundant counter space. Laundry facilities are located by the back entry.
- Two corner bedrooms are separated by an oversized laundry room and are serviced by a full bath off the main hall.
- An outside stairway offers private access to the loft, which boasts a 10-ft.-high vaulted ceiling.

Plan NW-990-A

Bedrooms: 2+	Baths: 1
Living Area:	
Upper floor	330 sq. ft.
Main floor	1,008 sq. ft.
Total Living Area:	**1,338 sq. ft.**
Exterior Wall Framing:	2x6
Foundation Options:	

Crawlspace
(All plans can be built with your choice of foundation and framing. A generic conversion diagram is available. See order form.)

BLUEPRINT PRICE CODE:	**A**

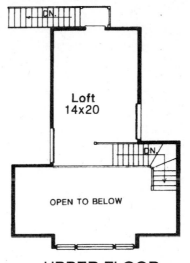

UPPER FLOOR

Loft 14x20

OPEN TO BELOW

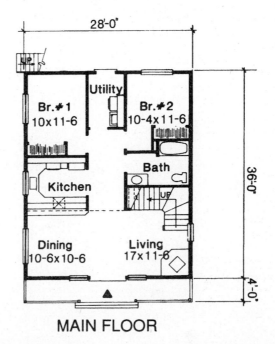

MAIN FLOOR

28'-0"

Br.#1 10x11-6

Utility

Br.#2 10-4x11-6

Bath

Kitchen

Dining 10-6x10-6

Living 17x11-6

36'-0"

4'-0"

ORDER BLUEPRINTS ANYTIME!
CALL TOLL-FREE 1-800-820-1283

Plan NW-990-A

PRICES AND DETAILS
ON PAGES 2-5

283

Style and Affordability

- This attractive family home offers affordability with style and openness.
- A brick planter accents the inviting covered porch. Inside, the sidelighted entry flows into the bright and spacious living room, with its 16½-ft. sloped ceiling and heat-circulating fireplace. Next to the fireplace, a wood bin is located beneath TV and stereo shelves.
- The sizable dining room opens to a backyard patio through French doors. The efficient U-shaped kitchen shares a serving counter with the dining room, for easy entertaining.
- On the upper floor, a railed balcony overlooks the entry and the living room.
- The bright master bedroom boasts a private bath, a walk-in closet and a handy linen closet.
- Two nice secondary bedrooms share a full bath with a large linen closet. A hallway closet provides additional storage space.

Plans H-3741-1 & -1A

Bedrooms: 3	Baths: 2½
Living Area:	
Upper floor	900 sq. ft.
Main floor	853 sq. ft.
Total Living Area:	**1,753 sq. ft.**
Standard basement	853 sq. ft.
Garage	520 sq. ft.
Exterior Wall Framing:	2x6
Foundation Options:	**Plan #**
Standard basement	H-3741-1
Crawlspace	H-3741-1A

(All plans can be built with your choice of foundation and framing. A generic conversion diagram is available. See order form.)

BLUEPRINT PRICE CODE: B

UPPER FLOOR

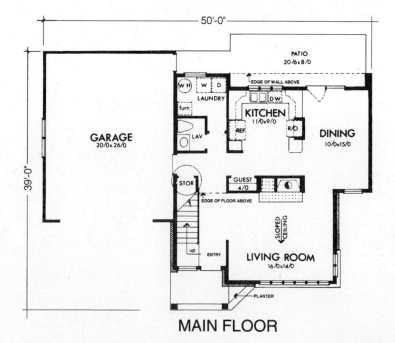

MAIN FLOOR

BASEMENT STAIRWAY LOCATION

ORDER BLUEPRINTS ANYTIME!
CALL TOLL-FREE 1-800-820-1283

Plans H-3741-1 & -1A

PRICES AND DETAILS
ON PAGES 2-5

Deluxe Cottage

- Plenty of luxuries are found in this cute cottage-style home.
- A 17-ft. vaulted ceiling, a massive fireplace, a corner window and a cozy library alcove highlight the living room.
- A window wall in the dining room provides views of the backyard and the deck, which are accessible through sliding glass doors in the bayed breakfast nook.
- The roomy country kitchen features a built-in desk, a pantry closet and a nearby powder room.
- Upstairs, the beautiful master suite offers such amenities as a 14-ft. vaulted ceiling, a corner window, a plant shelf and a private bath.
- Up one step are two more bedrooms, another full bath and a hall loft that overlooks the vaulted living room and the entryway.

Plan B-88002

Bedrooms: 3	Baths: 2½
Living Area:	
Upper floor	833 sq. ft.
Main floor	744 sq. ft.
Total Living Area:	**1,577 sq. ft.**
Standard basement	744 sq. ft.
Garage	528 sq. ft.
Exterior Wall Framing:	2x6

Foundation Options:

Standard basement

(All plans can be built with your choice of foundation and framing. A generic conversion diagram is available. See order form.)

BLUEPRINT PRICE CODE: B

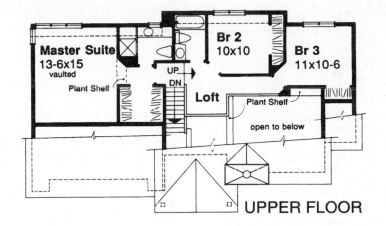

UPPER FLOOR

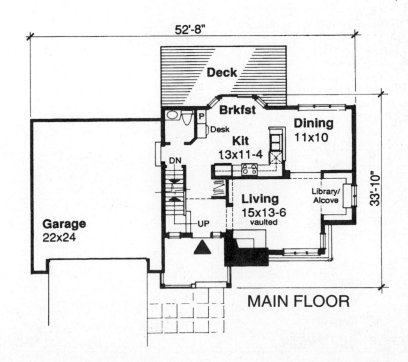

MAIN FLOOR

ORDER BLUEPRINTS ANYTIME!
CALL TOLL-FREE 1-800-820-1283

Plan B-88002

PRICES AND DETAILS
ON PAGES 2-5

285

Inviting Veranda

- This traditional farmhouse design is fronted by an inviting veranda where you'll love greeting guests and visiting with friends on sunny afternoons.
- Just off the 16½-ft. vaulted foyer is a huge sunken Great Room with a front-facing bay window and an inviting fireplace. A doorway offers access to the wood porch.
- The spacious kitchen is conveniently located between the formal dining room and the casual bayed dinette, which shares the kitchen's snack counter.
- A large main-floor laundry room and a half-bath are found near the garage entrance.
- Upstairs is a roomy master bedroom with an elegant bay window that adds space as well as architectural interest. A dual-sink dressing area adjoins a walk-in closet, and the skylighted private bath boasts a luxury tub. An optional master bath layout is included.
- Two more bedrooms share a full bath.

Plan GL-4161

Bedrooms: 3	Baths: 2½
Living Area:	
Upper floor	978 sq. ft.
Main floor	1,074 sq. ft.
Total Living Area:	**2,052 sq. ft.**
Standard basement	1,074 sq. ft.
Garage	484 sq. ft.
Exterior Wall Framing:	2x6

Foundation Options:

Standard basement

(All plans can be built with your choice of foundation and framing. A generic conversion diagram is available. See order form.)

BLUEPRINT PRICE CODE: C

OPTIONAL MASTER BATH

UPPER FLOOR

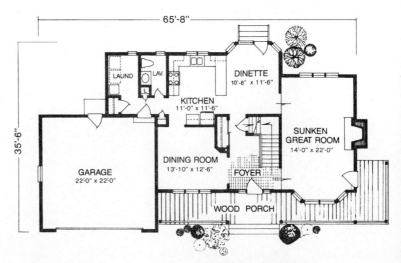

MAIN FLOOR

ORDER BLUEPRINTS ANYTIME!
CALL TOLL-FREE 1-800-820-1283

Plan GL-4161

PRICES AND DETAILS
ON PAGES 2-5

Super Chalet

- The charming Alpine detailing of the exterior and the open, flexible layout of the interior make this one of our most popular plans.
- In from the large front deck, the living room wraps around a central fireplace or woodstove, providing a warm and expansive multipurpose living space. Sliding glass doors open to the deck for outdoor entertaining.
- The adjoining dining room is easily serviced from the galley-style kitchen. A

convenient full bath serves a nearby bedroom and the remainder of the main floor.
- Two upper-floor bedrooms have 12-ft.-high sloped ceilings, extra closet space and access to another full bath. The larger bedroom offers sliding glass doors to a lofty deck.
- The blueprints recommend finishing the interior walls with solid lumber paneling for a rich, rustic look.
- In addition to a large general-use area and a shop, the optional daylight basement has space for a car or a boat.

Plans H-26-1 & -1A	
Bedrooms: 3	**Baths:** 2
Living Area:	
Upper floor	476 sq. ft.
Main floor	728 sq. ft.
Daylight basement	410 sq. ft.
Total Living Area:	**1,204/1,614 sq. ft.**
Tuck-under garage	318 sq. ft.
Exterior Wall Framing:	2x4
Foundation Options:	**Plan #**
Daylight basement	H-26-1
Crawlspace	H-26-1A

(All plans can be built with your choice of foundation and framing. A generic conversion diagram is available. See order form.)

BLUEPRINT PRICE CODE:	**A/B**

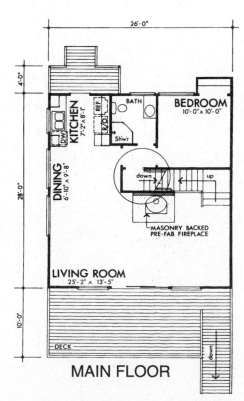

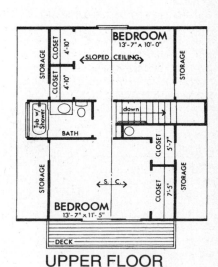

DAYLIGHT BASEMENT

STORAGE

STAIRWAY AREA IN CRAWLSPACE VERSION

MAIN FLOOR

UPPER FLOOR

ORDER BLUEPRINTS ANYTIME!
CALL TOLL-FREE 1-800-820-1283

Plans H-26-1 & -1A

PRICES AND DETAILS
ON PAGES 2-5

287

Familiar Face, Modern Place

- This affordable design puts a traditional face to an interior floor plan that's designed for the modern lifestyle.
- Formal living areas share the left side of the home; the living room offers an array of front windows that overlook the porch. The adjoining dining room may be accented by a bay window.
- At the center of the floor plan is an open, updated kitchen with a handy work island, a laundry closet and an adjoining breakfast bay.
- The large family room features a vaulted ceiling, a cozy fireplace and quick backyard access.
- The sleeping areas on the upper floor includes a vaulted master bedroom with a private garden bath and generous closet space. With the addition of double doors, the fourth bedroom also could serve as a cozy sitting room for the master bedroom.

Plan CH-230-A

Bedrooms: 3+	Baths: 2½
Living Area:	
Upper floor	971 sq. ft.
Main floor	1,207 sq. ft.
Total Living Area:	**2,178 sq. ft.**
Basement	1,207 sq. ft.
Garage	400 sq. ft.
Exterior Wall Framing:	2x4

Foundation Options:

Daylight basement

Standard basement

(All plans can be built with your choice of foundation and framing. A generic conversion diagram is available. See order form.)

BLUEPRINT PRICE CODE: C

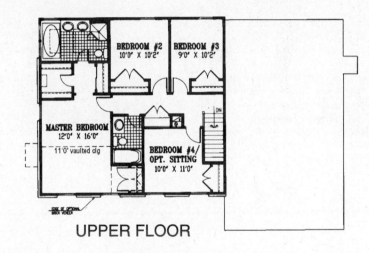

UPPER FLOOR

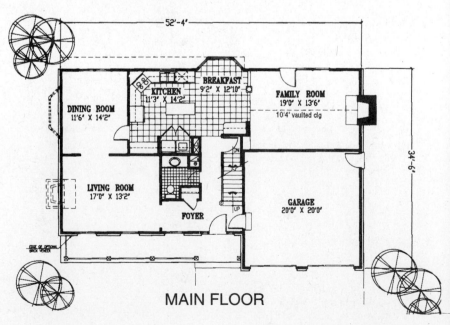

MAIN FLOOR

ORDER BLUEPRINTS ANYTIME!
CALL TOLL-FREE 1-800-820-1283

Plan CH-230-A

PRICES AND DETAILS
ON PAGES 2-5

Dreaming of the Countryside

- This home's brick facade, gentle angles and front-facing gables evoke images of the picturesque English countryside.
- Inside, the living and dining rooms flank the foyer, creating an open, inviting setting. When guests come by for dinner, they can move easily between cocktails and the main course.
- In the kitchen, an island workstation makes room for helpers. At the rear, an alcove is perfectly sized to serve as a breakfast nook. Without the optional garage, the alcove becomes a wraparound window seat.
- By the entrance to the nearby garage, a built-in wall of cabinets keeps boots, scarves and mittens neat and tidy.
- Across the home, a deluxe bath distinguishes the master suite as a place for a little pampering. Features here include an 11-ft. ceiling, a dual-sink vanity and a huge walk-in closet.
- Unless otherwise noted, all main-floor rooms include 9-ft. ceilings.
- Upstairs, students will love the built-in desks in both of the bedrooms.

Plan L-778-CSA

Bedrooms: 3	Baths: 2½
Living Area:	
Upper floor	525 sq. ft.
Main floor	1,319 sq. ft.
Total Living Area:	**1,844 sq. ft.**
Garage	451 sq. ft.
Exterior Wall Framing:	2x4
Foundation Options:	

Slab
(All plans can be built with your choice of foundation and framing. A generic conversion diagram is available. See order form.)

BLUEPRINT PRICE CODE:	B

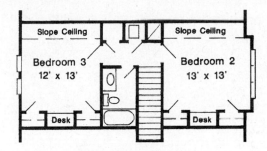

UPPER FLOOR

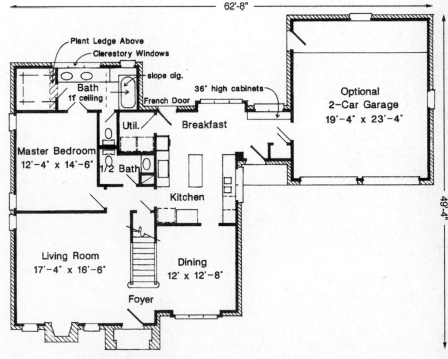

MAIN FLOOR

ORDER BLUEPRINTS ANYTIME!
CALL TOLL-FREE 1-800-820-1283

Plan L-778-CSA

PRICES AND DETAILS
ON PAGES 2-5

289

Visual Splendor

- The smooth transitions inside and eye-catching forms outside make this contemporary design an object of visual pleasure.
- From the covered porch, a grand two-story entry presents you with a multitude of options.
- The octagonal dining area on one side features a coffered ceiling, while the sunken living room flanking the other side boasts a 14½-ft. vaulted ceiling and a soaring fireplace.
- Form and function combine in the Great Room, where the sliding doors provide access to the back patio. The adjoining kitchen, with a built-in desk and a walk-in pantry, make this area a place where the family can relax and play in style.
- A beautiful, U-shaped staircase, open to both the Great Room and the living room, takes you to the balcony and upstairs bedrooms.
- Entrance to the master suite through double doors reveals the natural light pouring through the front window and skylight in the master bath.

Plan SUN-2515

Bedrooms: 3	Baths: 2½
Living Area:	
Upper floor	750 sq. ft.
Main floor	1,066 sq. ft.
Total Living Area:	**1,816 sq. ft.**
Garage	495 sq. ft.
Exterior Wall Framing:	2x6

Foundation Options:

Crawlspace

(All plans can be built with your choice of foundation and framing. A generic conversion diagram is available. See order form.)

BLUEPRINT PRICE CODE: B

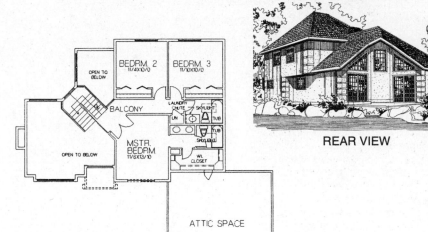

UPPER FLOOR

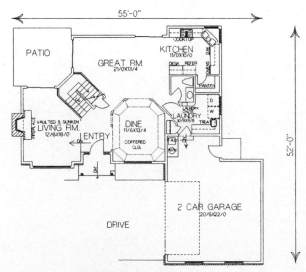

REAR VIEW

MAIN FLOOR

ORDER BLUEPRINTS ANYTIME!
CALL TOLL-FREE 1-800-820-1283

Plan SUN-2515

PRICES AND DETAILS
ON PAGES 2-5

Space-Saving Tri-Level

- This clever tri-level design offers an open, airy interior while taking up a minimum of land space.
- The Great Room features a spectacular 15-ft. vaulted and skylighted ceiling, an inviting woodstove and sliding glass doors to a full-width deck.
- The Great Room also incorporates a dining area, which is easily serviced from the efficient, space-saving kitchen.
- The main-floor bedroom boasts two closets. A compact laundry closet, a guest closet and a storage area line the hallway to the spacious main bath.
- The large loft offers infinite possibilities, such as extra sleeping quarters, a home office, an art studio or a recreation room. Clerestory windows and a sloped ceiling enhance the bright, airy feeling.
- The tuck-under garage saves on building costs and lets you make the most of your lot.

Plan H-963-2A

Bedrooms: 1+	Baths: 1
Living Area:	
Upper floor	432 sq. ft.
Main floor	728 sq. ft.
Total Living Area:	**1,160 sq. ft.**
Tuck-under garage	728 sq. ft.
Exterior Wall Framing:	2x4

Foundation Options:

Slab

(All plans can be built with your choice of foundation and framing. A generic conversion diagram is available. See order form.)

BLUEPRINT PRICE CODE:	A

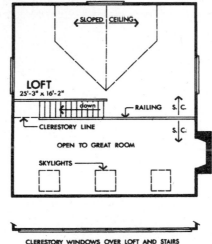

UPPER FLOOR

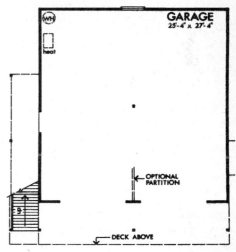

LOWER FLOOR

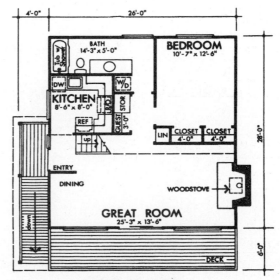

MAIN FLOOR

Cottage with Open Interior

- The exterior of this contemporary cottage features a delightful covered porch and a pair of matching dormers.
- The entry has a dramatic 13-ft. ceiling and flows into an expansive Great Room. The Great Room is also highlighted by a vaulted ceiling that rises to a height of 17 feet. Tall windows brighten both corners, while a fireplace serves as a handsome centerpiece.
- Sliding doors between the Great Room and the breakfast nook open to an angled deck.
- The sunny 16½-ft.-high vaulted nook provides a cozy setting for family dining with a view of the backyard.
- Ample cabinets and counter space are offered in the efficient kitchen, which also features a handy snack counter that extends into the nook.
- The main-floor master bedroom has a walk-in closet and easy access to the full bath beyond.
- The upper floor offers another bedroom, plus a full bath with space for a laundry closet. The loft could serve as an extra sleeping space.

Plan JWB-9307

Bedrooms: 2+	Baths: 2
Living Area:	
Upper floor	349 sq. ft.
Main floor	795 sq. ft.
Total Living Area:	**1,144 sq. ft.**
Standard basement	712 sq. ft.
Exterior Wall Framing:	2x4 or 2x6

Foundation Options:

Standard basement

(All plans can be built with your choice of foundation and framing. A generic conversion diagram is available. See order form.)

BLUEPRINT PRICE CODE: A

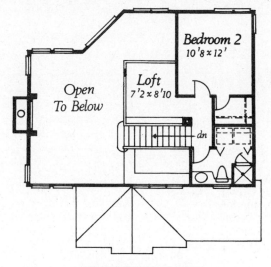

UPPER FLOOR

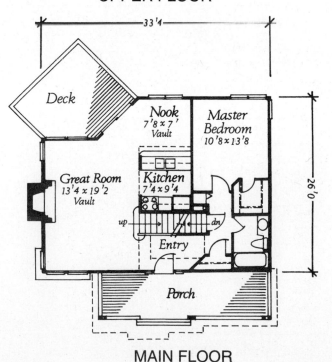

MAIN FLOOR

ORDER BLUEPRINTS ANYTIME!
CALL TOLL-FREE 1-800-820-1283

Plan JWB-9307

PRICES AND DETAILS
ON PAGES 2-5

Casual Sensibility

- You'll immediately sense the casual sensibility in this efficient and lovely two-story home.
- A covered porch protects visitors from the elements before they enter to the foyer, where they'll get a nice view of the attractive living and dining rooms.
- On cold days you can use the living room's grand fireplace to defrost your

chilly toes; when it warms up outside use the room's access to the backyard to step out and get some sun!
- The extra-large master suite boasts a ceiling that slopes up to 10-ft. and a private bath that you can use to escape your cares after a long day at work.
- Plant shelves above the dining room and living room area, as well as in the master suite, provide a warm touch of soft glamour.
- Two large bedrooms, a full bath and an option for another bedroom make up the upper floor.

Plan L-257-A	
Bedrooms: 3+	**Baths: 2½**
Living Area:	
Upper floor	453 sq. ft.
Main floor	804 sq. ft.
Optional fourth bedroom	163 sq. ft.
Total Living Area:	**1,420 sq. ft.**
Garage	407 sq. ft.
Exterior Wall Framing:	2x4
Foundation Options:	

Slab
(All plans can be built with your choice of foundation and framing. A generic conversion diagram is available. See order form.)

BLUEPRINT PRICE CODE:	**A**

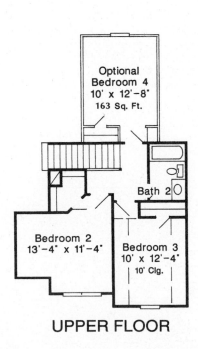

MAIN FLOOR

- 37'-6"
- 45'-2"

Master Bedroom
15' x 11'-4"
10' Clg.
Plant Shelf Above

Bath

Living Room
13' x 15'-4"
10' Clg.

Plant Shelf Above

Dining
9' x 9'
10' Clg.

Foyer

2-Car Garage
19' X 22'-4"

Kitchen
9' x 10'
10' Clg.

UPPER FLOOR

Optional
Bedroom 4
10' x 12'-8"
163 Sq. Ft.

Bath 2

Bedroom 2
13'-4" x 11'-4"

Bedroom 3
10' x 12'-4"
10' Clg.

ORDER BLUEPRINTS ANYTIME!
CALL TOLL-FREE 1-800-820-1283

Plan L-257-A

PRICES AND DETAILS
ON PAGES 2-5

293

Easy to Build

- The basic rectangular shape of this two-story home makes it economical to build. The well-zoned interior isolates all four bedrooms on the upper floor.
- Off the covered porch, the airy foyer reveals the open stairway and unfolds to each of the living areas.
- The formal rooms are positioned at the front of the home and overlook the porch. The large living room boasts a handsome fireplace and extends to a rear porch through sliding glass doors.
- The central family room hosts casual family activities and shows off a rustic wood-beam ceiling. This room also opens to the porch and integrates with the kitchen and the bright dinette for a big, open atmosphere.
- A half-bath, a laundry area and a handy service porch are located near the entrance from the garage.
- Two dual-sink bathrooms serve the bedrooms upstairs. The spacious master bedroom has a private bath and a big walk-in closet.

Plan HFL-1070-RQ

Bedrooms: 4	Baths: 2½

Living Area:

Upper floor	1,013 sq. ft.
Main floor	1,082 sq. ft.
Total Living Area:	**2,095 sq. ft.**
Standard basement	889 sq. ft.
Garage and storage	481 sq. ft.
Exterior Wall Framing:	**2x6**

Foundation Options:

Standard basement
Slab
(All plans can be built with your choice of foundation and framing. A generic conversion diagram is available. See order form.)

BLUEPRINT PRICE CODE:	**C**

VIEW INTO FAMILY ROOM, KITCHEN AND DINETTE

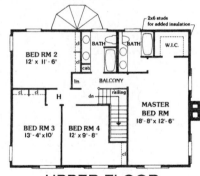

UPPER FLOOR

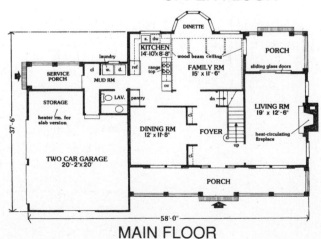

MAIN FLOOR

ORDER BLUEPRINTS ANYTIME!
CALL TOLL-FREE 1-800-820-1283

Plan HFL-1070-RQ

PRICES AND DETAILS
ON PAGES 2-5

Compact Design Flair

- This compact, but extremely livable, home features unique design flair in an efficient flow of space.
- The foyer opens into a big, central family room that boasts a handsome fireplace. A half-wall offers a view into the breakfast room, where a door accesses the backyard. A stone patio would be a nice addition.
- An angled counter bar separates the generous kitchen from the family room and the adjoining breakfast room.

- Formal living spaces are on the left side of the home. Both the living room and the dining room boast vaulted ceilings; an optional fireplace would add elegance to the living room. The rooms open to one another to give you the space for large-scale entertaining.
- Upstairs, the vaulted master suite features a dressing area with lots of wardrobe space, including a walk-in closet. The luxurious private bath has a splashy garden tub and a separate shower for hurried mornings.
- Two pleasantly sized secondary bedrooms complete the upper floor. Each one is just a few steps away from a nicely equipped hall bath.

Plan CH-611-A	
Bedrooms: 3	**Baths:** 2½
Living Area:	
Upper floor	771 sq. ft.
Main floor	1,008 sq. ft.
Total Living Area:	**1,779 sq. ft.**
Basement	901 sq. ft.
Garage	390 sq. ft.
Exterior Wall Framing:	2x4

Foundation Options:

Daylight basement

Standard basement

Crawlspace

(All plans can be built with your choice of foundation and framing. A generic conversion diagram is available. See order form.)

BLUEPRINT PRICE CODE:	**B**

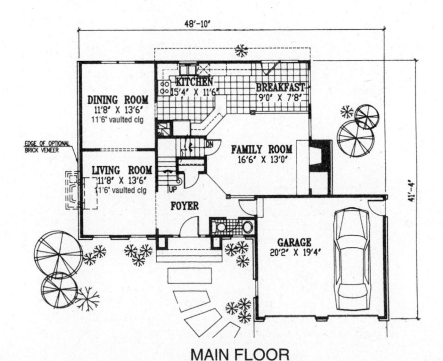

MAIN FLOOR

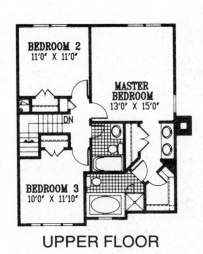

UPPER FLOOR

ORDER BLUEPRINTS ANYTIME!
CALL TOLL-FREE 1-800-820-1283

Plan CH-611-A

PRICES AND DETAILS
ON PAGES 2-5

295

Comfortable and Affordable

- This plan proves that comfort and affordability can go hand in hand.
- Unlike some elaborate modern homes, this traditional floor plan offers a smooth flow of traffic.
- The home's square shape and simple lines make it easy to build, but it's far from plain. Any of a range of customizing touches can be added to define it as your very own and give it distinction.

- A gabled roofline and a decorative front porch render a warm, appealing look. Inside, the floor plan is generous with little wasted space.
- The large living room features a grand fireplace and opens to the dining room, maximizing space. The dining room, in turn, flows into the kitchen and dinette. A pocket door leads to a mudroom, half-bath and laundry area, all of which are also accessible from the garage.
- Three bedrooms lie on the upper floor and share a full bath. The master bedroom has two closets and private access to the bath.

Plan GL-1473

Bedrooms: 3	**Baths: 1½**

Living Area:

Upper floor	676 sq. ft.
Main floor	797 sq. ft.
Total Living Area:	**1,473 sq. ft.**
Standard basement	797 sq. ft.
Garage	440 sq. ft.
Exterior Wall Framing:	2x6

Foundation Options:

Standard basement

(All plans can be built with your choice of foundation and framing. A generic conversion diagram is available. See order form.)

BLUEPRINT PRICE CODE:	**A**

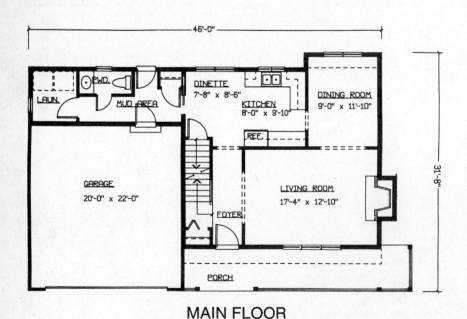

MAIN FLOOR

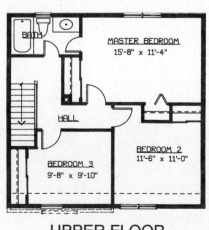

UPPER FLOOR

ORDER BLUEPRINTS ANYTIME!
CALL TOLL-FREE 1-800-820-1283

Plan GL-1473

PRICES AND DETAILS
ON PAGES 2-5

Plenty of Presence

- A stucco facade complemented by fieldstone, a dramatic roofline and handsome keystones accenting the window treatments gives this home plenty of presence.
- Inside, the two-story foyer boasts an open stairway with a balcony overlook. Straight ahead, the huge family room is expanded by a 16½-ft. vaulted ceiling, plus a tall window and a French door that frame the fireplace.
- The adjoining dining room flows into the kitchen and breakfast room, which feature an angled serving bar, a bright window wall and a French door that opens to a covered patio.
- The main-floor master suite is the pride of the floor plan, offering a 10-ft. tray ceiling. The deluxe master bath has a 14-ft. vaulted ceiling, a garden tub and a spacious walk-in closet.
- The upper floor offers two more bedrooms, a full bath and attic space.

Plan FB-1681

Bedrooms: 3	Baths: 2½
Living Area:	
Upper floor	449 sq. ft.
Main floor	1,232 sq. ft.
Total Living Area:	**1,681 sq. ft.**
Daylight basement	1,232 sq. ft.
Garage and storage	435 sq. ft.
Exterior Wall Framing:	2x4

Foundation Options:
Daylight basement
Crawlspace
(All plans can be built with your choice of foundation and framing. A generic conversion diagram is available. See order form.)

BLUEPRINT PRICE CODE:	B

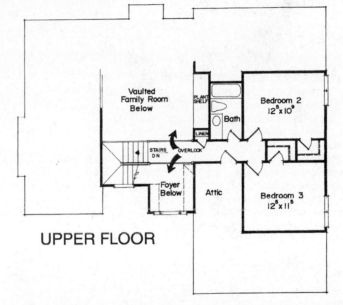

UPPER FLOOR

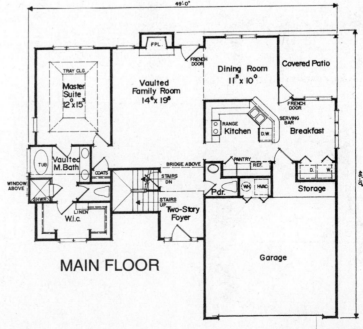

MAIN FLOOR

ORDER BLUEPRINTS ANYTIME!
CALL TOLL-FREE 1-800-820-1283

Plan FB-1681

PRICES AND DETAILS
ON PAGES 2-5

297

Full of Dreams

- The thrill of owning a first home is one of the greatest of a lifetime. In this perfect two-story, all of those years of dreams will play out to their fullest.
- Out front, a covered porch protects guests from the elements when they arrive for dinner or a night of cards.
- Inside, a lush plant shelf ushers them into the formal dining room, which is great for life's many special occasions.
- Located just steps away, the kitchen provides fast, efficient service to even the most elaborate of meals. A pretty garden window over the sink brings a ray of sunshine to chores. Nearby, the morning room comfortably hosts breakfast and casual lunches.
- In the living room at the rear of the home, folks will gather to watch the evening news or read the latest best-seller. A French door leads outside to a patio—a soothing backdrop to a lazy summer afternoon.
- Nearby, a private bath and a walk-in closet distinguish the master suite. A window seat calls you to sit and reflect.
- Upstairs, an open loft gives the kids a place of their own, while still within earshot of parents downstairs.

Plan L-705-A

Bedrooms: 3	Baths: 2½
Living Area:	
Upper floor	540 sq. ft.
Main floor	1,163 sq. ft.
Total Living Area:	**1,703 sq. ft.**
Garage	494 sq. ft.
Exterior Wall Framing:	2x4

Foundation Options:

Slab

(All plans can be built with your choice of foundation and framing. A generic conversion diagram is available. See order form.)

BLUEPRINT PRICE CODE:	**B**

UPPER FLOOR

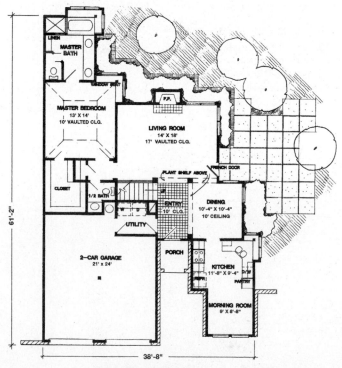

MAIN FLOOR

ORDER BLUEPRINTS ANYTIME!
CALL TOLL-FREE 1-800-820-1283

Plan L-705-A

**PRICES AND DETAILS
ON PAGES 2-5**

Unique Inside and Out

- This delightful design is as striking on the inside as it is on the outside.
- The focal point of the home is the huge Grand Room, which features a 23½-ft.-high vaulted ceiling, plant shelves and lots of glass, including a clerestory window. French doors flanking the fireplace lead to the covered porch and the two adjoining sun decks.
- The centrally located kitchen offers easy access from any room; a full bath, a laundry area and the garage entrance are nearby.
- The two main-floor master suites are another unique design element of the home. Each suite showcases a 13-ft. vaulted ceiling, a sunny window seat, a walk-in closet, a private bath and French doors that open to a sun deck.
- Upstairs, two guest suites under a 15-ft. vaulted peak overlook the Grand Room below.
- The multiple suites make this design a perfect shared vacation home.

Plan EOF-13

Bedrooms: 4	Baths: 3
Living Area:	
Upper floor	443 sq. ft.
Main floor	1,411 sq. ft.
Total Living Area:	**1,854 sq. ft.**
Garage	264 sq. ft.
Storage	50 sq. ft.
Exterior Wall Framing:	2x6

Foundation Options:

Crawlspace

(All plans can be built with your choice of foundation and framing. A generic conversion diagram is available. See order form.)

BLUEPRINT PRICE CODE:	B

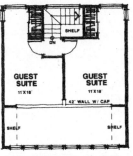

UPPER FLOOR

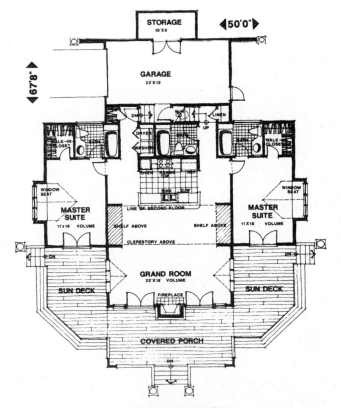

MAIN FLOOR

ORDER BLUEPRINTS ANYTIME!
CALL TOLL-FREE 1-800-820-1283

Plan EOF-13

PRICES AND DETAILS
ON PAGES 2-5

299

Space-Saving Floor Plan

- Easy, affordable living is the basis for this great town-and-country design.
- The welcoming porch and the graceful arched windows give the home its curb appeal. Inside, the floor plan provides large, highly livable spaces rather than several specialized rooms.
- The foyer opens to the living room, while an elegant column separates the foyer from the formal dining room, which features a bay window and an alcove that is perfect for a china hutch.
- The country kitchen enjoys a generous view to the rear of the home and is large enough to accommodate family and guests alike.
- A beautiful open staircase leads to the second floor, where three bedrooms and two baths offer plenty of comfort. The master bedroom flaunts a 10-ft. tray ceiling and a luxurious bath with a 10-ft. sloped ceiling and a corner shower.

Plan AX-92320

Bedrooms: 3	**Baths:** 2½

Living Area:	
Upper floor	706 sq. ft.
Main floor	830 sq. ft.
Total Living Area:	**1,536 sq. ft.**
Standard basement	754 sq. ft.
Garage	510 sq. ft.
Exterior Wall Framing:	2x6

Foundation Options:

Standard basement

Slab

(All plans can be built with your choice of foundation and framing. A generic conversion diagram is available. See order form.)

BLUEPRINT PRICE CODE:	**B**

REAR VIEW

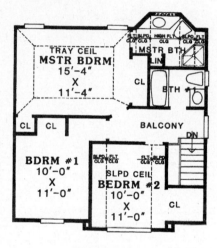

UPPER FLOOR

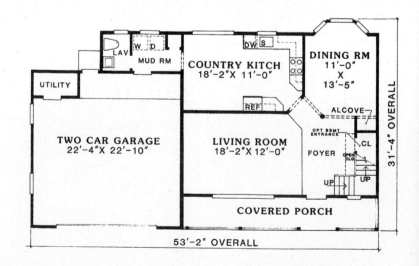

MAIN FLOOR

ORDER BLUEPRINTS ANYTIME!
CALL TOLL-FREE 1-800-820-1283

Plan AX-92320

PRICES AND DETAILS
ON PAGES 2-5

Sweet Communion

- With easy access to the front and rear porches, and a private exit from the master bedroom to the great outdoors, this heartwarming home encourages communion with nature.
- The wide foyer allows guests to freely enter the dining and living rooms.
- In the living room, a prominent fireplace charms the eye and a battery of windows admits light. French doors lead from the living room to a quaint library, complete with a window seat.

- Mornings were made for the breakfast room and kitchen combo. French doors lead from the breakfast room to the front and rear porches, because that first meal of the day tastes better when it's drenched with fresh air!
- If you're concerned about getting a good night's sleep, rest assured you'll enjoy sweet slumber in the master bedroom. French doors let you take in the night sky before turning in.
- The master bath pampers you with a gorgeous oval tub, a separate shower and a dual-sink vanity.
- Upstairs, a balcony hall ushers you past a bookshelf to one of two bedrooms. A full bath completes the scene.

Plan L-268-VSB	
Bedrooms: 3+	**Baths:** 2½
Living Area:	
Upper floor	613 sq. ft.
Main floor	1,653 sq. ft.
Total Living Area:	**2,266 sq. ft.**
Detached garage	521 sq. ft.
Exterior Wall Framing:	2x4
Foundation Options:	

Slab
(All plans can be built with your choice of foundation and framing. A generic conversion diagram is available. See order form.)

BLUEPRINT PRICE CODE: C

REAR VIEW

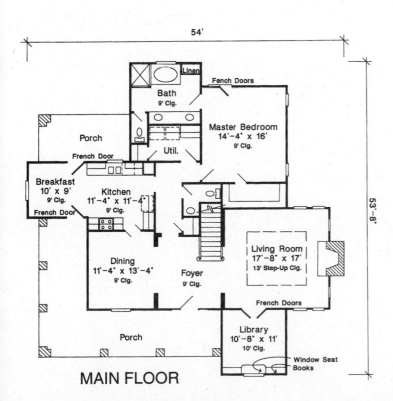

MAIN FLOOR

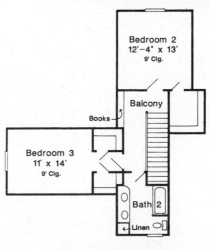

UPPER FLOOR

ORDER BLUEPRINTS ANYTIME!
CALL TOLL-FREE 1-800-820-1283

Plan L-268-VSB

*PRICES AND DETAILS
ON PAGES 2-5*

301

Dynamic Design

- This dynamic five-sided design is perfect for scenic sites. The front (or street) side of the home is shielded by a two-car garage, while the back of the home hosts a glass-filled living area surrounded by a spectacular deck.
- The unique shape of the home allows for an unusually open and spacious interior design.
- The living/dining room is further expanded by a 20-ft.-high vaulted ceiling. The centrally located fireplace provides a focal point while distributing heat efficiently.
- The space-saving galley-style kitchen is connected to the living/dining area by a snack bar.
- A large main-floor bedroom has two closets and easy access to a full bath.
- The upper floor is highlighted by a breathtaking balcony overlook. Also, two bedrooms share a nice-sized bath.
- The optional daylight basement includes a huge recreation room.

Plans H-855-1 & -1A

Bedrooms: 3	Baths: 2
Living Area:	
Upper floor	625 sq. ft.
Main floor	1,108 sq. ft.
Daylight basement	1,108 sq. ft.
Total Living Area:	**1,733/2,841 sq. ft.**
Garage	346 sq. ft.
Exterior Wall Framing:	2x6
Foundation Options:	**Plan #**
Daylight basement	H-855-1
Crawlspace	H-855-1A

(All plans can be built with your choice of foundation and framing. A generic conversion diagram is available. See order form.)

BLUEPRINT PRICE CODE:	**B/D**

UPPER FLOOR

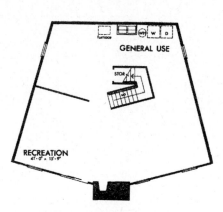

DAYLIGHT BASEMENT

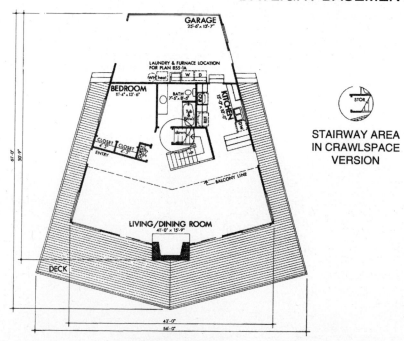

STAIRWAY AREA
IN CRAWLSPACE
VERSION

MAIN FLOOR

ORDER BLUEPRINTS ANYTIME!
CALL TOLL-FREE 1-800-820-1283

Plans H-855-1 & -1A

PRICES AND DETAILS
ON PAGES 2-5

Farmhouse for Today

- An inviting covered porch and decorative dormer windows lend traditional warmth and charm to this attractive design.
- The up-to-date interior includes ample space for entertaining as well as for daily family activities.
- The elegant foyer is flanked on one side by the formal, sunken living room and on the other by a sunken family room with a fireplace and an entertainment center. Each room features an 8½-ft. tray ceiling and views of the porch.
- The dining room flows from the living room to increase the entertaining space.
- The kitchen/nook/laundry area forms a large expanse for casual family living and domestic chores.
- Upstairs, the grand master suite includes a large closet and a private bath with a garden tub, a designer shower and a private deck.
- A second full bath serves the two secondary bedrooms.

Plan U-87-203

Bedrooms: 3	Baths: 2½
Living Area:	
Upper floor	857 sq. ft.
Main floor	1,064 sq. ft.
Total Living Area:	**1,921 sq. ft.**
Standard basement	1,064 sq. ft.
Garage	552 sq. ft.
Exterior Wall Framing:	2x4 or 2x6

Foundation Options:

Standard basement

Crawlspace

Slab

(All plans can be built with your choice of foundation and framing. A generic conversion diagram is available. See order form.)

BLUEPRINT PRICE CODE: B

UPPER FLOOR

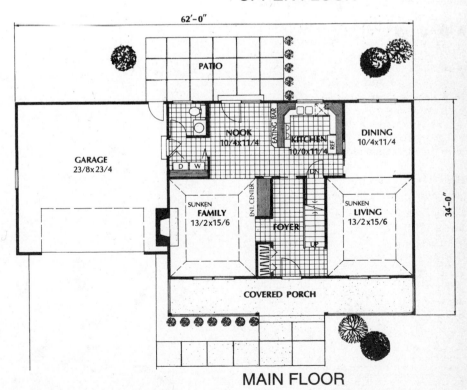

MAIN FLOOR

ORDER BLUEPRINTS ANYTIME!
CALL TOLL-FREE 1-800-820-1283

Plan U-87-203

PRICES AND DETAILS
ON PAGES 2-5

303

Peaceful Days

- This beautiful home's wraparound veranda and adjacent piazza recall the peaceful days of the past when friends spent restful afternoons mingling at pretty garden parties.
- Inside, a series of handsome columns create a dignified gallery that ushers guests into the living and dining rooms. When appearances count, serve dinner in the dining room. Afterwards, step out to the piazza for a breath of night air.
- Day-to-day, the kitchen and breakfast nook will bustle with activity. Perfect for family meals, the nook is also a great spot for a student to do homework under the watchful eye of a parent in the kitchen. Nearby access to the garage saves steps when unloading groceries.
- In the master suite, a number of perks provide special treatment for the home owners. Access to the veranda offers a romantic escape, while a Jacuzzi tub in the bath pampers a weary spirit.
- Upstairs, all three bedrooms include sizable walk-in closets. The front-facing bedroom also boasts a soaring vaulted ceiling and a separate vanity.
- A convenient laundry chute in the hall helps keep kids' bedrooms neat.

Plan L-215-VSB

Bedrooms: 4	Baths: 2½
Living Area:	
Upper floor	862 sq. ft.
Main floor	1,351 sq. ft.
Total Living Area:	**2,213 sq. ft.**
Garage	477 sq. ft.
Exterior Wall Framing:	2x4

Foundation Options:

Slab

(All plans can be built with your choice of foundation and framing. A generic conversion diagram is available. See order form.)

BLUEPRINT PRICE CODE:	C

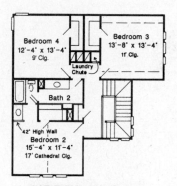

UPPER FLOOR

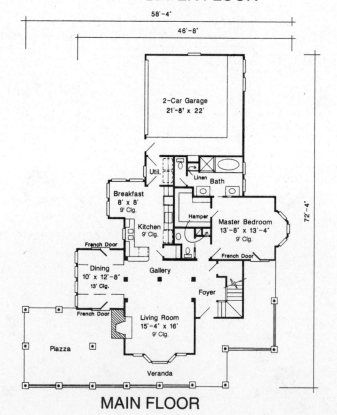

MAIN FLOOR

ORDER BLUEPRINTS ANYTIME!
CALL TOLL-FREE 1-800-820-1283

Plan L-215-VSB

PRICES AND DETAILS
ON PAGES 2-5

Simple Elegance

- This design's simple yet elegant exterior houses a roomy interior that is efficient in its use of space.
- The living room just off the foyer is brightened by a boxed-out window. An optional fireplace is a nice addition, giving the room a warm focal point.
- Formal as well as casual dining spaces are included in the plan. The kitchen serves both with equal ease.
- The generous family room overlooks the backyard and has a view into the dinette over a half-wall. The room's proximity to the kitchen means the family chef never misses a beat while preparing dinner.
- Dual closets are a highlight of the master suite. The private bath and a triple window arrangement that lets in plenty of light are other thoughtful touches you'll enjoy.
- Three secondary bedrooms boast lots of closet space and share another full bath.

Plan GL-1926

Bedrooms: 4	Baths: 2½
Living Area:	
Upper floor	972 sq. ft.
Main floor	954 sq. ft.
Total Living Area:	**1,926 sq. ft.**
Standard basement	954 sq. ft.
Garage	484 sq. ft.
Exterior Wall Framing:	2x6

Foundation Options:
Standard basement
(All plans can be built with your choice of foundation and framing. A generic conversion diagram is available. See order form.)

BLUEPRINT PRICE CODE: B

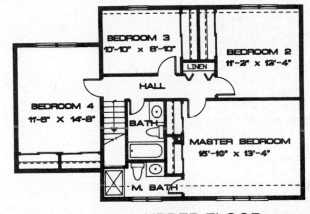

UPPER FLOOR

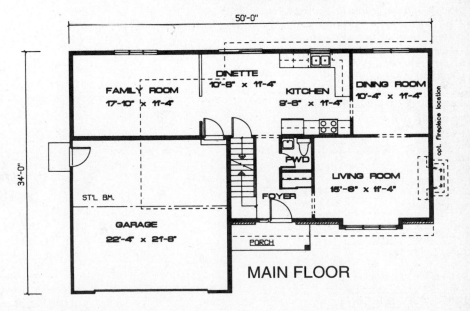

MAIN FLOOR

ORDER BLUEPRINTS ANYTIME!
CALL TOLL-FREE 1-800-820-1283

Plan GL-1926

PRICES AND DETAILS
ON PAGES 2-5

305

REAR VIEW

Comfortable, Rustic Styling

- A compact, space-efficient floor plan transforms this rustic-styled design into a comfortable place to call home. Its deck is perfect for a sloping, scenic lot.
- The living area spans the entire width of the home, and rises 14 ft. into the air, creating a sensational space for entertaining. A majestic fireplace at one end adds ambience to any occasion. Natural light pours in through sparkling windows, and sliding glass doors lead out to the huge viewing deck.
- A functional breakfast bar distinguishes the efficient kitchen from the living and dining area.
- Several steps lead up to a pair of bedrooms with 11½-ft.-high ceilings and a full bath, all on the entry level.
- Upstairs, another large bedroom with a 10½-ft. ceiling includes a compact bath and its own private deck.
- The basement houses laundry facilities and a large storage area.

UPPER FLOOR

FRONT VIEW

Plan H-25-C

Bedrooms: 3	Baths: 2
Living Area:	
Upper floor	222 sq. ft.
Main floor	936 sq. ft.
Total Living Area:	**1,158 sq. ft.**
Partial basement	365 sq. ft.
Garage	276 sq. ft.
Carport	230 sq. ft.
Exterior Wall Framing:	2x4

Foundation Options:

Partial basement

(All plans can be built with your choice of foundation and framing. A generic conversion diagram is available. See order form.)

BLUEPRINT PRICE CODE: **A**

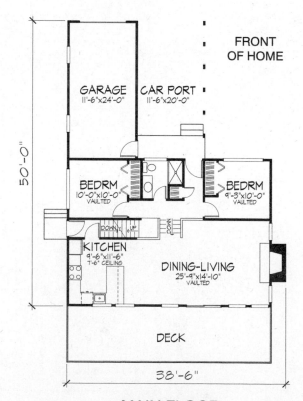

MAIN FLOOR

Plan H-25-C

PRICES AND DETAILS
ON PAGES 2-5

Distinctive Two-Story

- The playful and distinctive exterior of this two-story encloses a functional, contemporary interior.
- The living areas unfold from the skylighted foyer, which is open to the upper-floor balcony. The formal sunken living room features a soaring 17-ft. cathedral ceiling. The adjoining step-down family room offers a fireplace and sliding glass doors to a wonderful deck.
- A low partition allows a view of the family room's fireplace from the breakfast area and the island kitchen.
- A luxurious master suite with a 13-ft. cathedral ceiling and room for three additional bedrooms are found on the upper floor, in addition to a dramatic view of the foyer below.

Plan AX-8922-A

Bedrooms: 4	Baths: 2½
Living Area:	
Upper floor	1,080 sq. ft.
Main floor	1,213 sq. ft.
Total Living Area:	**2,293 sq. ft.**
Standard basement	1,138 sq. ft.
Garage	470 sq. ft.
Exterior Wall Framing:	2x4

Foundation Options:

Standard basement

Slab

(All plans can be built with your choice of foundation and framing. A generic conversion diagram is available. See order form.)

BLUEPRINT PRICE CODE: C

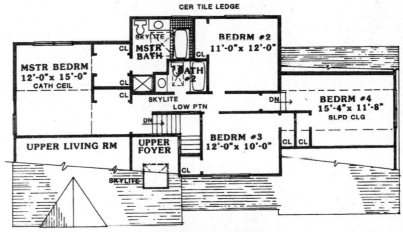

UPPER FLOOR

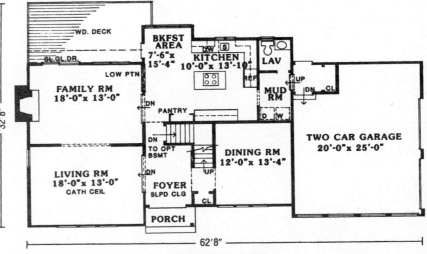

MAIN FLOOR

ORDER BLUEPRINTS ANYTIME!
CALL TOLL-FREE 1-800-820-1283

Plan AX-8922-A

PRICES AND DETAILS
ON PAGES 2-5

307

Convenient Contemporary

- In this plan, a thoroughly contemporary exterior wraps a design with so many convenient features, you'll wonder how you ever lived without them.
- The vaulted foyer leads into the vaulted Great Room, which features a warm woodstove and a built-in entertainment center. The two spaces are separated by a balcony bridge on the upper floor that creates a spacious, modern look with an immediate impression.

- The large, open kitchen includes plenty of working space. An island cooktop features a snack bar for casual meals. The adjoining dining room has sliding doors to a wraparound deck.
- Two secondary bedrooms each have an alcove designed to hold a study desk.
- Secluded upstairs, the master suite boasts a walk-in closet and a dressing area that leads to a skylighted bath, which is also accessible from the den.
- As an option, the vaulted area over the Great Room may be enclosed to create a fourth bedroom or a rec room.
- A long closet at the end of the hall provides the extra storage you need.

Plan S-72485	
Bedrooms: 3+	**Baths: 2**
Living Area:	
Upper floor	650 sq. ft.
Main floor	1,450 sq. ft.
Total Living Area:	**2,100 sq. ft.**
Standard basement	1,450 sq. ft.
Garage	502 sq. ft.
Exterior Wall Framing:	2x6
Foundation Options:	

Standard basement
Crawlspace
(All plans can be built with your choice of foundation and framing. A generic conversion diagram is available. See order form.)

BLUEPRINT PRICE CODE:	**C**

MAIN FLOOR

UPPER FLOOR

Plan S-72485

PRICES AND DETAILS ON PAGES 2-5

Solar Design that Shines

- A passive-solar sun room, an energy-efficient woodstove and a panorama of windows make this design really shine.
- The open living/dining room features a 16-ft.-high vaulted ceiling, glass-filled walls and access to the dramatic decking. A balcony above gives the huge living/dining area definition while offering spectacular views.
- The streamlined kitchen has a convenient serving bar that connects it to the living/dining area.
- The main-floor bedroom features dual closets and easy access to a full bath. The laundry room, located just off the garage, doubles as a mudroom and includes a handy coat closet.
- The balcony hallway upstairs is bathed in natural light. The two nice-sized bedrooms are separated by a second full bath.

Plans H-855-3A & -3B

Bedrooms: 3	Baths: 2-3
Living Area:	
Upper floor	586 sq. ft.
Main floor	1,192 sq. ft.
Sun room	132 sq. ft.
Daylight basement	1,192 sq. ft.
Total Living Area:	**1,910/3,102 sq. ft.**
Garage	520 sq. ft.
Exterior Wall Framing:	**2x6**
Foundation Options:	**Plan #**
Daylight basement	H-855-3B
Crawlspace	H-855-3A

(All plans can be built with your choice of foundation and framing. A generic conversion diagram is available. See order form.)

BLUEPRINT PRICE CODE: **B/E**

UPPER FLOOR

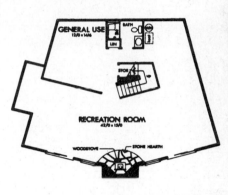

DAYLIGHT BASEMENT

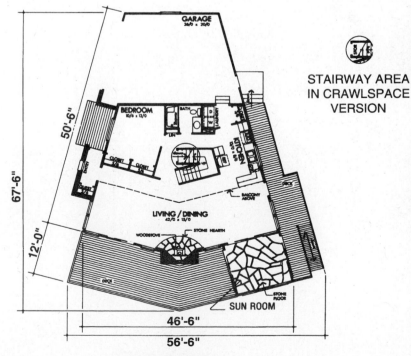

MAIN FLOOR

STAIRWAY AREA IN CRAWLSPACE VERSION

Family Farmhouse

- There's more to this house than its charming front porch, steeply pitched roof and dormer windows.
- A feeling of spaciousness is emphasized by the open floor plan, with the living room adjoining the kitchen and bayed breakfast area. A snack bar allows easy service to the living room.
- The back door leads from the carport to the utility room, which is convenient to the kitchen and half-bath.
- The secluded main-floor master bedroom offers a large walk-in closet and a private bathroom.
- Upstairs, two bedrooms share another full bath. One includes dormer windows and the other a window seat. A door at the top of the stairs provides access to attic space that could be turned into an extra bedroom.

Plan J-86133

Bedrooms: 3	Baths: 2½
Living Area:	
Upper floor	559 sq. ft.
Main floor	1,152 sq. ft.
Total Living Area:	**1,711 sq. ft.**
Standard basement	1,152 sq. ft.
Carport	387 sq. ft.
Storage	85 sq. ft.
Exterior Wall Framing:	2x4

Foundation Options:

Standard basement
Crawlspace
Slab

(All plans can be built with your choice of foundation and framing. A generic conversion diagram is available. See order form.)

BLUEPRINT PRICE CODE: B

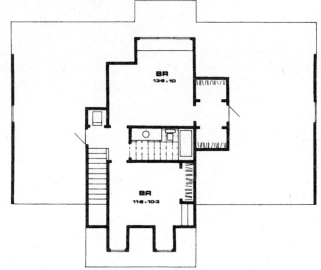

UPPER FLOOR

MAIN FLOOR

ORDER BLUEPRINTS ANYTIME!
CALL TOLL-FREE 1-800-820-1283

Plan J-86133

**PRICES AND DETAILS
ON PAGES 2-5**

Above and Beyond!

- The strong brick exterior, front-facing gables, eye-catching arched entryway and open, amenity-packed interior let you know that this two-story home has gone above and beyond the norm!
- At the foyer, you're met by the two stunning formal areas; the spacious living room boasts a two-way fireplace while the dining room's bay window adds elegance during dressy meals.
- Smartly situated between both eating areas, the corner kitchen is ready for any culinary mood, from hot dogs to filet mignon. The breakfast area's bay window adds sunshine to your morning.
- For large events, take advantage of the family room's expansiveness, as well as its fireplace, built-in media center and handy access to the backyard.
- An extra sense of openness results from the main floor's 9-ft. ceilings.
- The master suite anchors the upper floor; a cozy sitting area and an enormous private bath are highlights.

Plan L-295-NA

Bedrooms: 3	Baths: 2½
Living Area:	
Upper floor	1,066 sq. ft.
Main floor	1,208 sq. ft.
Total Living Area:	**2,274 sq. ft.**
Garage	568 sq. ft.
Exterior Wall Framing:	2x4

Foundation Options:
Slab
(All plans can be built with your choice of foundation and framing. A generic conversion diagram is available. See order form.)

BLUEPRINT PRICE CODE: C

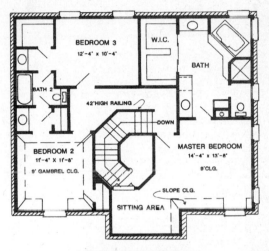

UPPER FLOOR

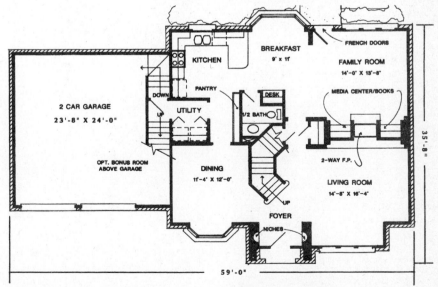

MAIN FLOOR

ORDER BLUEPRINTS ANYTIME!
CALL TOLL-FREE 1-800-820-1283

Plan L-295-NAB

PRICES AND DETAILS
ON PAGES 2-5

311

Economical and Convenient

REAR VIEW

- This home was designed to contain a relatively modest square footage without sacrificing the convenience afforded by an open, flowing floor plan.
- Down a short stairway from the entry, the main living area consists of a large living room with an airy vaulted ceiling and an inviting fireplace. The adjoining kitchen and dining area share a handy snack bar for quick meals.
- Sliding doors in the living room access the main-floor deck, which provides all the space you'll need to entertain in style during warm-weather months.
- Two secondary bedrooms and a full bath flank the entryway.
- Tucked away upstairs in complete privacy, the master suite is equipped with its own bath, a walk-in closet and a romantic private deck.
- The two decks make this home a perfect choice for a vacation retreat.

Plans H-925-2 & -2A

Bedrooms: 3	Baths: 2
Living Area:	
Upper floor	360 sq. ft.
Main floor	1,217 sq. ft.
Total Living Area:	**1,577 sq. ft.**
Daylight basement	1,217 sq. ft.
Garage and storage	309 sq. ft.
Exterior Wall Framing:	2x4
Foundation Options:	**Plan #**
Daylight basement	H-925-2
Crawlspace	H-925-2A

(All plans can be built with your choice of foundation and framing. A generic conversion diagram is available. See order form.)

BLUEPRINT PRICE CODE:	**B**

UPPER FLOOR

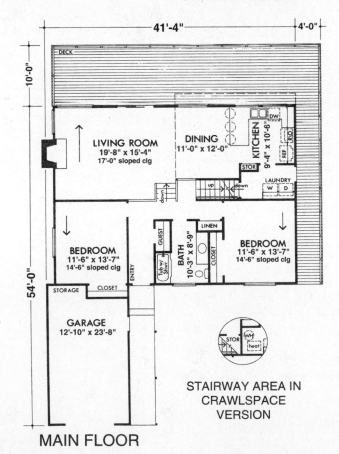

MAIN FLOOR

STAIRWAY AREA IN CRAWLSPACE VERSION

ORDER BLUEPRINTS ANYTIME!
CALL TOLL-FREE 1-800-820-1283

Plans H-925-2 & -2A

PRICES AND DETAILS ON PAGES 2-5

Light-Filled Interior

- A stylish contemporary exterior and an open, light-filled interior define this two-level home.
- The covered entry leads to a central gallery. The huge living room and dining room combine to generate a spacious ambience that is enhanced by a 15½-ft. cathedral ceiling and a warm fireplace with tall flanking windows.
- Oriented to the rear and overlooking a terrace and backyard landscaping are the informal spaces. The family room, the sunny semi-circular dinette and the modern kitchen share a snack bar.
- The main-floor master suite boasts a 13-ft. sloped ceiling, a private terrace, a dressing area and a personal bath with a whirlpool tub.
- Two to three extra bedrooms with 11-ft. ceilings share a skylighted bath on the upper floor.

Plan K-683-D

Bedrooms: 3+	Baths: 2½+
Living Area:	
Upper floor	491 sq. ft.
Main floor	1,475 sq. ft.
Total Living Area:	**1,966 sq. ft.**
Standard basement	1,425 sq. ft.
Garage and storage	487 sq. ft.
Exterior Wall Framing:	2x4 or 2x6

Foundation Options:

Standard basement
Slab
(All plans can be built with your choice of foundation and framing. A generic conversion diagram is available. See order form.)

BLUEPRINT PRICE CODE: **B**

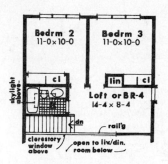

UPPER FLOOR

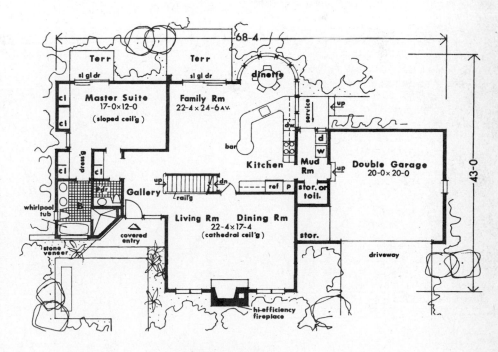

MAIN FLOOR

ORDER BLUEPRINTS ANYTIME!
CALL TOLL-FREE 1-800-820-1283

Plan K-683-D

PRICES AND DETAILS
ON PAGES 2-5

313

Quaint Country Design

- The simply elegant look of country is evident in this quaint two-story home.
- The front of the design is enveloped in a wraparound porch where you'll love greeting guests. Sit a spell and enjoy a refreshing glass of lemonade.
- The huge Great Room is the focal point of first-floor living. This wonderful expanse is brightened by multiple windows, and there's a fireplace to take the chill off of winter evenings.
- A nice-sized den that could serve as a home office, a guest room or an extra bedroom is directly off the foyer.
- The kitchen flows into a sunny bayed dinette with access to the backyard.
- On the upper floor, the master suite includes two closets, one of which is a walk-in, plus a skylighted private bath with a luxurious tiled tub.
- The two secondary bedrooms have easy access to another full bath.

Plan AX-89311

Bedrooms: 3+	Baths: 2½
Living Area:	
Upper floor	736 sq. ft.
Main floor	1,021 sq. ft.
Total Living Area:	**1,757 sq. ft.**
Standard basement	1,021 sq. ft.
Garage	440 sq. ft.
Exterior Wall Framing:	2x4

Foundation Options:

Standard basement

Slab

(All plans can be built with your choice of foundation and framing. A generic conversion diagram is available. See order form.)

BLUEPRINT PRICE CODE: B

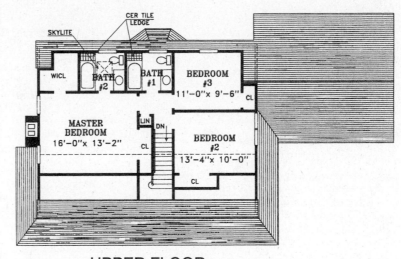

UPPER FLOOR

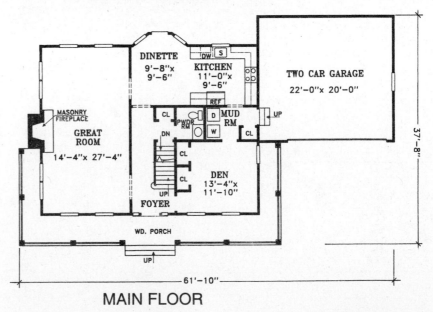

MAIN FLOOR

ORDER BLUEPRINTS ANYTIME!
CALL TOLL-FREE 1-800-820-1283

Plan AX-89311

PRICES AND DETAILS ON PAGES 2-5

Some Romantic Feeling

- Seemingly saved from some romantic era, this picturesque Victorian-style home will capture your heart.
- You can spend almost the entire day outside if you want; a great wraparound veranda in front and a covered porch in back are nice spots to while away a sunny day.
- Indoors, the family room offers an incredible amount of space, highlighted by a huge bay window and a heartwarming fireplace.
- Gourmets will appreciate the ambience of the formal dining room, while casual meals in the breakfast room are sparked by the bright bay window.
- Upstairs, the deluxe master suite handles you with care. A bayed sitting area, a skylighted private bath and an L-shaped walk-in closet ensure the peacefulness of this gorgeous retreat.
- Included in the blueprints is an optional attached garage off the utility room.

Plan L-2066

Bedrooms: 3	Baths: 2½
Living Area:	
Upper floor	1,069 sq. ft.
Main floor	997 sq. ft.
Total Living Area:	**2,066 sq. ft.**
Optional attached garage	506 sq. ft.
Exterior Wall Framing:	2x4

Foundation Options:

Slab

(All plans can be built with your choice of foundation and framing. A generic conversion diagram is available. See order form.)

BLUEPRINT PRICE CODE:	**C**

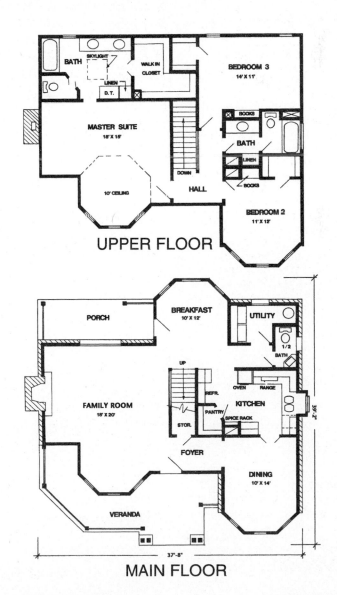

UPPER FLOOR

MAIN FLOOR

ORDER BLUEPRINTS ANYTIME!
CALL TOLL-FREE 1-800-820-1283

Plan L-2066

PRICES AND DETAILS
ON PAGES 2-5

REAR VIEW

FRONT VIEW

Flexible Design

- Designed for flexibility, this home can be built on a narrow or sloping lot, with either two bedrooms or three.
- The living room boasts a 16-ft.-high sloped ceiling and is warmed by a handsome woodstove. Sliding glass doors open to an inviting corner deck.
- The skylighted, passive-solar dining room is wrapped by windows and has a slate floor to capture and retain solar heat. A French door opens to the deck.
- The kitchen is open to the dining room but is separated from the living room by a 7½-ft.-high wall.
- The main-floor bedroom is located across the hall from a full bath with laundry facilities.
- In the plan's two-bedroom version, the upper-floor loft hosts a spacious master suite with a 12-ft. sloped ceiling, a huge walk-in closet and a private bath.
- In the plan's three-bedroom version, two bedrooms share the upper floor.

Plans H-946-1A, -1B, -2A & -2B

Bedrooms: 2+	Baths: 1-2
Living Area:	
Upper floor (3-bedroom plan)	290 sq. ft.
Upper floor (2-bedroom plan)	381 sq. ft.
Main floor	814 sq. ft.
Total Living Area:	**1,104/1,195 sq. ft.**
Daylight basement	814 sq. ft.
Garage	315 sq. ft.
Exterior Wall Framing:	2x6
Foundation Options:	Plan #
Daylight basement (2 bedrooms)	H-946-1B
Daylight basement (3 bedrooms)	H-946-2B
Crawlspace (2 bedrooms)	H-946-1A
Crawlspace (3 bedrooms)	H-946-2A

(All plans can be built with your choice of foundation and framing. A generic conversion diagram is available. See order form.)

BLUEPRINT PRICE CODE:	A

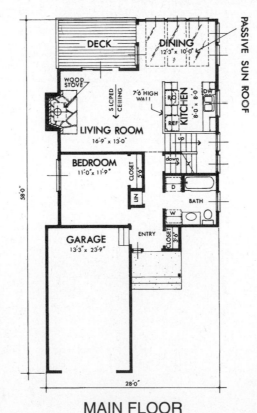

MAIN FLOOR

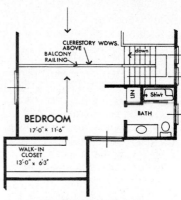

UPPER FLOOR
(TWO-BEDROOM PLAN)

UPPER FLOOR
(THREE-BEDROOM PLAN)

ORDER BLUEPRINTS ANYTIME! CALL TOLL-FREE 1-800-820-1283 Plans H-946-1A, -1B, -2A, -2B *PRICES AND DETAILS ON PAGES 2-5*

Country Living

- A covered porch, half-round transom windows and three dormers give this home its warm, nostalgic appeal. Shuttered windows and a louvered vent beautify the side-entry, two-car garage.

- Designed for the ultimate in country living, the floor plan starts off with a dynamic Great Room that flows to a bayed dining area. A nice fireplace adds warmth, while a French door provides access to a backyard covered porch. A powder room is just steps away.

- A 12-ft., 4-in. vaulted ceiling presides over the large country kitchen, which offers a bayed nook, an oversized breakfast bar and a convenient pass-through to the rear porch.

- The exquisite master suite boasts a tray ceiling, a bay window and an alcove for built-in shelves or extra closet space. Other amenities include a large walk-in closet and a compartmentalized bath.

- Upstairs, 9-ft. ceilings enhance two more bedrooms and a second full bath. Each bedroom boasts a cozy dormer window and two closets.

Plan AX-93311

Bedrooms: 3	Baths: 2½
Living Area:	
Upper floor	570 sq. ft.
Main floor	1,375 sq. ft.
Total Living Area:	**1,945 sq. ft.**
Standard basement	1,280 sq. ft.
Garage	450 sq. ft.
Exterior Wall Framing:	2x4

Foundation Options:

Standard basement

Crawlspace

Slab

(All plans can be built with your choice of foundation and framing. A generic conversion diagram is available. See order form.)

BLUEPRINT PRICE CODE: **B**

VIEW INTO GREAT ROOM

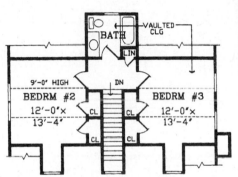

UPPER FLOOR

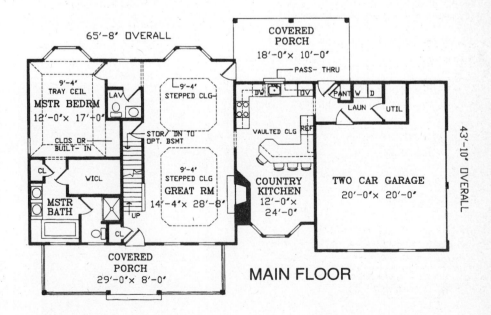

MAIN FLOOR

ORDER BLUEPRINTS ANYTIME!
CALL TOLL-FREE 1-800-820-1283

Plan AX-93311

PRICES AND DETAILS
ON PAGES 2-5

317

REAR VIEW

Bright Ideas!

- Four clerestory windows, a boxed-out window and wing walls sheltering the entry porch give this home definition.
- Inside, an open room arrangement coupled with vaulted ceilings, abundant windows and a sensational sun room make this home a definite bright spot.
- The living room features a 22-ft.-high vaulted ceiling, a warm woodstove and a glass-filled wall that offers views into the sun room. A patio door in the sun room opens to a large backyard deck.
- The adjoining dining room flows into the kitchen, which offers a versatile snack bar. A handy laundry room is just steps away, near the garage.
- Upstairs, the intimate bedroom suite includes a 14-ft.-high vaulted ceiling, a view to the living room, a walk-in closet and a private bath.
- The optional daylight basement boasts a spacious recreation room with a second woodstove, plus a fourth bedroom and a third bath. A shaded patio occupies the area under the deck.

FRONT VIEW

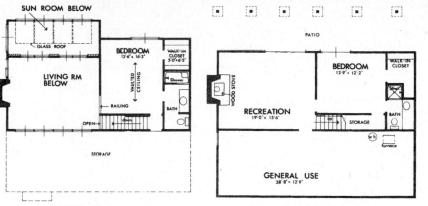

UPPER FLOOR   DAYLIGHT BASEMENT

Plans H-877-5A & -5B

Bedrooms: 3+	Baths: 2-3
Living Area:	
Upper floor	382 sq. ft.
Main floor	1,200 sq. ft.
Sun room	162 sq. ft.
Daylight basement	1,200 sq. ft.
Total Living Area:	**1,744/2,944 sq. ft.**
Garage	457 sq. ft.
Exterior Wall Framing:	2x6
Foundation Options:	**Plan #**
Daylight basement	H-877-5B
Crawlspace	H-877-5A

(All plans can be built with your choice of foundation and framing. A generic conversion diagram is available. See order form.)

BLUEPRINT PRICE CODE: **B/D**

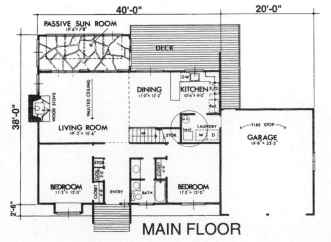

MAIN FLOOR

BASEMENT STAIRWAY LOCATION

ORDER BLUEPRINTS ANYTIME!
CALL TOLL-FREE 1-800-820-1283

Plans H-877-5A & -5B

PRICES AND DETAILS
ON PAGES 2-5

FRONT VIEW

REAR VIEW

More for Less

- Big in function but small in square footage, this passive-solar plan can be built as a single-family home or as part of a multiple-unit complex.
- The floor plan flows visually from its open foyer to its high-ceilinged Great Room, where a high-efficiency fireplace is flanked by glass. Sliding glass doors open to a brilliant south-facing sun room that overlooks a backyard terrace.
- The eat-in kitchen has a pass-through to a bright dining area that opens to a nice side terrace.
- The master bedroom boasts a pair of tall windows, a deluxe private bath and three roomy closets.
- A handy laundry closet and a half-bath are located at the center of the floor plan, near the garage.
- Upstairs, a skylighted bath serves two more bedrooms, one with a private, rear-facing balcony.

Plan K-507-S

Bedrooms: 3	Baths: 2½
Living Area:	
Upper floor	397 sq. ft.
Main floor	915 sq. ft.
Sun room	162 sq. ft.
Total Living Area:	**1,474 sq. ft.**
Standard basement	915 sq. ft.
Garage	400 sq. ft.
Exterior Wall Framing:	2x4 or 2x6

Foundation Options:

Standard basement

Slab

(All plans can be built with your choice of foundation and framing. A generic conversion diagram is available. See order form.)

BLUEPRINT PRICE CODE: A

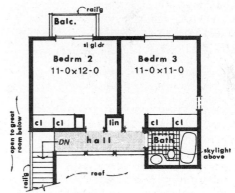

UPPER FLOOR

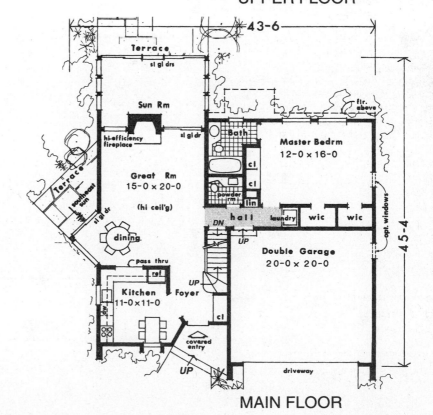

MAIN FLOOR

ORDER BLUEPRINTS ANYTIME!
CALL TOLL-FREE 1-800-820-1283

Plan K-507-S

PRICES AND DETAILS
ON PAGES 2-5

319

Trendsetting Country Kitchen

- An impressive columned porch, fanciful gable details and a trendsetting country kitchen give this home unique appeal.
- Warmed by a fireplace, the 11-ft., 8-in. vaulted living room overlooks the bright split foyer through a wooden rail.
- An elegant columned arch leads into the spacious kitchen, which includes a pantry, a serving bar and sliding glass doors to a backyard deck.
- The luxurious master suite is enhanced by a 10½-ft. vaulted ceiling and features a sunny boxed-out window, a roomy walk-in closet and a private bath.
- Two other bedrooms share a hallway linen closet and a second full bath.
- The basement bonus space can be used as an optional family room, a recreation area or extra bedroom.

Plan B-90012

Bedrooms: 3+	Baths: 2+
Living Area:	
Main floor	1,203 sq. ft.
Daylight basement (finished)	460 sq. ft.
Total Living Area:	**1,663 sq. ft.**
Daylight basement (unfinished)	436 sq. ft.
Tuck-under garage	509 sq. ft.
Exterior Wall Framing:	2x4

Foundation Options:

Daylight basement

(All plans can be built with your choice of foundation and framing. A generic conversion diagram is available. See order form.)

BLUEPRINT PRICE CODE:	B

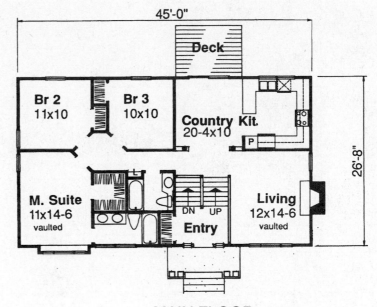

MAIN FLOOR

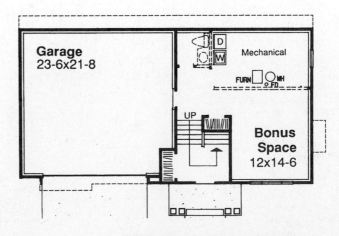

DAYLIGHT BASEMENT

 ORDER BLUEPRINTS ANYTIME! CALL TOLL-FREE 1-800-820-1283 Plan B-90012 *PRICES AND DETAILS ON PAGES 2-5*

Indoor/Outdoor Pleasure

- For a scenic lake or mountain lot, this spectacular design takes full advantage of the views.
- A three-sided wraparound deck makes indoor/outdoor living a pleasure.
- The sunken living room—with a 19-ft. cathedral ceiling, a skylight, a beautiful fireplace and glass galore—is the heart of the floor plan.
- Both the formal dining room and the kitchen overlook the living room and the surrounding deck beyond.
- The main-floor master bedroom has a 12-ft. cathedral ceiling and private access to the deck and hall bath.
- Upstairs, two more bedrooms share a skylighted bath and flank a dramatic balcony sitting area that views to the living room below.

Plan AX-98607

Bedrooms: 3	Baths: 2
Living Area:	
Upper floor	531 sq. ft.
Main floor	1,098 sq. ft.
Total Living Area:	**1,629 sq. ft.**
Standard basement	894 sq. ft.
Garage	327 sq. ft.
Exterior Wall Framing:	2x4

Foundation Options:

Standard basement

Slab

(All plans can be built with your choice of foundation and framing. A generic conversion diagram is available. See order form.)

BLUEPRINT PRICE CODE: **B**

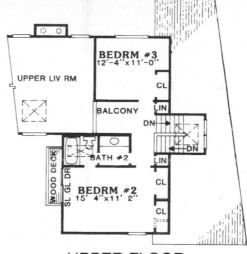

UPPER FLOOR

◀ 45'-0'' ▶

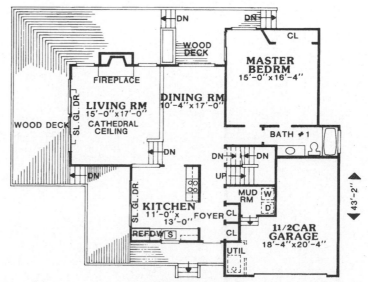

MAIN FLOOR

ORDER BLUEPRINTS ANYTIME!
CALL TOLL-FREE 1-800-820-1283

Plan AX-98607

PRICES AND DETAILS
ON PAGES 2-5

321

Spacious Economy

- This economical country cottage features wide, angled spaces and 9-ft., 4-in. ceilings in both the Great Room and the master bedroom for roomy appeal and year-round comfort.
- The Great Room boasts a cozy fireplace with a raised hearth and a built-in niche for a TV, making this room perfect for winter gatherings. On warm nights, a homey covered porch at the rear can be accessed through sliding glass doors.
- Amenities in the luxurious master bedroom include a large walk-in closet, a private whirlpool bath and a dual-sink vanity.
- The nicely appointed kitchen offers nearby laundry facilities and porch access. A serving bar allows for casual dining and relaxed conversation.
- The optional daylight basement includes a tuck-under, two-car garage.

Plan AX-94322

Bedrooms: 3	Baths: 2½
Living Area:	
Upper floor	545 sq. ft.
Main floor	1,134 sq. ft.
Total Living Area:	**1,679 sq. ft.**
Daylight basement	618 sq. ft.
Standard basement	1,134 sq. ft.
Tuck-under garage	516 sq. ft.
Exterior Wall Framing:	2x4

Foundation Options:
Daylight basement
Standard basement
Crawlspace
Slab
(All plans can be built with your choice of foundation and framing. A generic conversion diagram is available. See order form.)

BLUEPRINT PRICE CODE: B

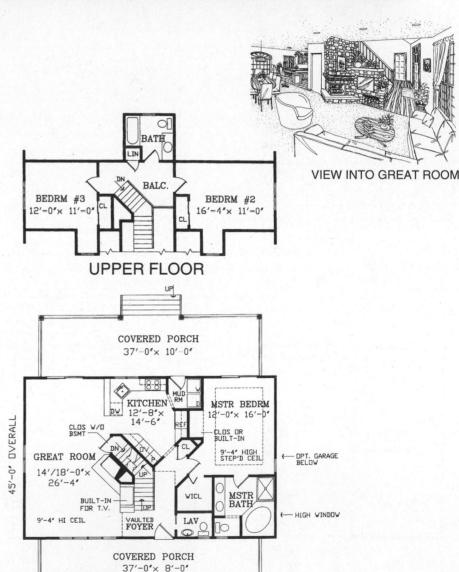

VIEW INTO GREAT ROOM

UPPER FLOOR

BATH
LIN
BEDRM #3 12'-0" x 11'-0"
DN
BALC.
CL
BEDRM #2 16'-4" x 11'-0"
CL

MAIN FLOOR

UP
COVERED PORCH 37'-0" x 10'-0"
45'-0" OVERALL
KITCHEN 12'-8" x 14'-6"
MUD RM
MSTR BEDRM 12'-0" x 16'-0"
CLOS W/O BSMT
REF
CLOS OR BUILT-IN
GREAT ROOM 14'/18'-0" x 26'-4"
DN
CL
9'-4" HIGH STEP'D CEIL
← OPT. GARAGE BELOW
BUILT-IN FOR T.V.
UP
WICL
MSTR BATH
← HIGH WINDOW
9'-4" HI CEIL
VAULTED FOYER
LAV
COVERED PORCH 37'-0" x 8'-0"
42'-0" OVERALL
UP

Romantic Retreat

- The romance and appeal of the Alpine chalet have remained constant over time. With more than 1,500 sq. ft. of living area, this chalet would make a great full-time home or vacation retreat.
- The L-shaped living room, dining room and kitchen flow together for casual living. This huge area is warmed by a

freestanding fireplace and surrounded by an ornate deck, which is accessed through sliding glass doors.
- The main-level bedroom, with its twin closets and adjacent bath, could serve as a nice master suite.
- Upstairs, two large bedrooms share another full bath. One bedroom features a walk-in closet, while the other boasts its own private deck.
- The daylight basement offers laundry facilities, plenty of storage space and an extra-long garage.

Plan H-858-2	
Bedrooms: 3	**Baths:** 2
Living Area:	
Upper floor	576 sq. ft.
Main floor	960 sq. ft.
Total Living Area:	**1,536 sq. ft.**
Daylight basement	530 sq. ft.
Tuck-under garage	430 sq. ft.
Exterior Wall Framing:	2x6

Foundation Options:

Daylight basement
(All plans can be built with your choice of foundation and framing. A generic conversion diagram is available. See order form.)

BLUEPRINT PRICE CODE:	B

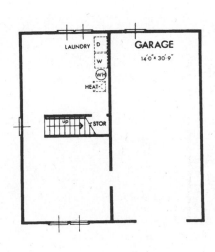

DAYLIGHT BASEMENT

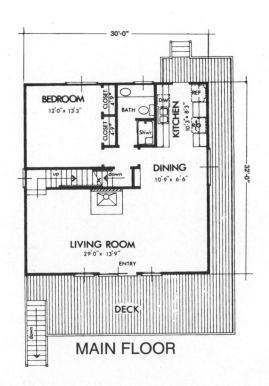

MAIN FLOOR

UPPER FLOOR

ORDER BLUEPRINTS ANYTIME!
CALL TOLL-FREE 1-800-820-1283

Plan H-858-2

PRICES AND DETAILS
ON PAGES 2-5

323

Sunny Comfort

- A covered wraparound porch and lovely arched windows give this home a comfortable country style.
- Inside, an elegant columned archway introduces the formal dining room.
- The huge Great Room features an 18-ft. vaulted ceiling, a dramatic wall of windows and two built-in wall units on either side of the fireplace.
- Ample counter space and a convenient work island allow maximum use of the roomy kitchen.
- The sunny breakfast nook opens to a porch through sliding glass doors.
- On the other side of the home, a dramatic bay window and a 10-ft. ceiling highlight the master bedroom. The enormous master bath features a luxurious whirlpool tub.
- Unless otherwise noted, all main-floor rooms have 9-ft. ceilings.
- Open stairs lead up to a balcony with a magnificent view of the Great Room. Two upstairs bedrooms, one with an 11-ft. vaulted ceiling, share a bath.

Plan AX-94317

Bedrooms: 3	Baths: 2½
Living Area:	
Upper floor	525 sq. ft.
Main floor	1,720 sq. ft.
Total Living Area:	**2,245 sq. ft.**
Standard basement	1,720 sq. ft.
Garage	502 sq. ft.
Storage/utility	51 sq. ft.
Exterior Wall Framing:	2x4

Foundation Options:

Standard basement
Crawlspace
Slab

(All plans can be built with your choice of foundation and framing. A generic conversion diagram is available. See order form.)

BLUEPRINT PRICE CODE: C

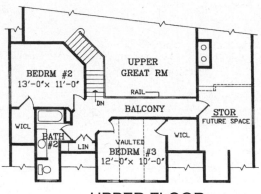

UPPER FLOOR

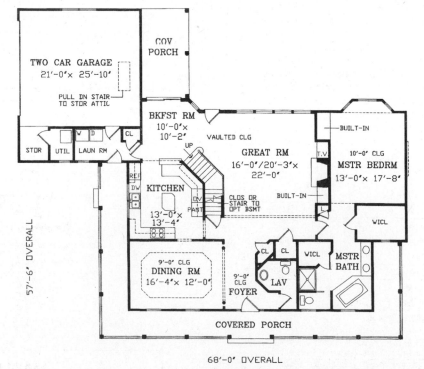

MAIN FLOOR

ORDER BLUEPRINTS ANYTIME!
CALL TOLL-FREE 1-800-820-1283

Plan AX-94317

PRICES AND DETAILS
ON PAGES 2-5

Fairy-Tale Feel

- Charming and whimsical, this comfy cottage jumps right out of the pages of your favorite fairy tale.
- Back in the real world, the home's inside spaces offer every modern convenience.
- Flowing from the foyer, the dining and living rooms are separated only by a lovely staircase. Imagine the parties you can host in this vast expanse! A nice fireplace adds ambience, while a French door opens onto a sunny patio.
- The open kitchen boasts an unusual layout; a central wet bar with a built-in wine rack facilitates the serving of refreshing beverages. Handy laundry facilities are nearby.
- The grocery shopper of the family will love the kitchen's proximity to the oversized two-car garage.
- The master suite is a relaxing haven. Its private bath and big walk-in closet make morning preparation easy.
- The children have their own space upstairs. A skylighted loft with bookshelves is a cozy spot to curl up with that favorite story. Walk-in closets and a shared, split bath give everyone a measure of comfort.

REAR VIEW

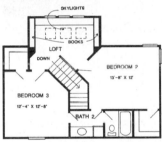

UPPER FLOOR

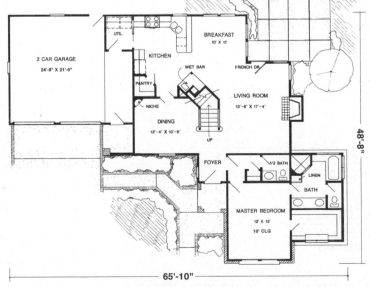

MAIN FLOOR

Plan L-867-HA

Bedrooms: 3	Baths: 2½
Living Area:	
Upper floor	603 sq. ft.
Main floor	1,262 sq. ft.
Total Living Area:	**1,865 sq. ft.**
Garage	478 sq. ft.
Exterior Wall Framing:	2x4

Foundation Options:

Slab

(All plans can be built with your choice of foundation and framing. A generic conversion diagram is available. See order form.)

BLUEPRINT PRICE CODE:	**B**

ORDER BLUEPRINTS ANYTIME!
CALL TOLL-FREE 1-800-820-1283

Plan L-867-HA

***PRICES AND DETAILS
ON PAGES 2-5***

Surrounded by Shade

- Comfort reigns in this delightful domicile, which boasts a shaded veranda that nearly surrounds the home. There's enough room for a porch hammock! When it rains during the family reunion, the festivities can be moved to this glorious covered area.
- Inside, a fireplace-blessed living room joins seamlessly with the welcoming foyer. Opposite, the big dining room will hold the largest dinner parties.

- Your whole family can participate in meal preparation, since the kitchen and connecting breakfast room flow into each other. A French door gives veranda access.
- In the master bedroom, an atrium door offers private passage to the veranda. The private bath includes a bubbly tub, a separate shower and a planter for your lush greenery.
- Upstairs, two more bedrooms flank a peaceful sitting area. A large split bath features a dual-sink vanity.
- All rooms in the home are topped by airy 9-ft. ceilings, for added spaciousness.

Plan L-88-VB

Bedrooms: 3	**Baths: 2½**

Living Area:

Upper floor	751 sq. ft.
Main floor	1,308 sq. ft.

Total Living Area:	**2,059 sq. ft.**
Detached two-car garage	505 sq. ft.

Exterior Wall Framing:	2x4

Foundation Options:

Slab
(All plans can be built with your choice of foundation and framing. A generic conversion diagram is available. See order form.)

BLUEPRINT PRICE CODE: C

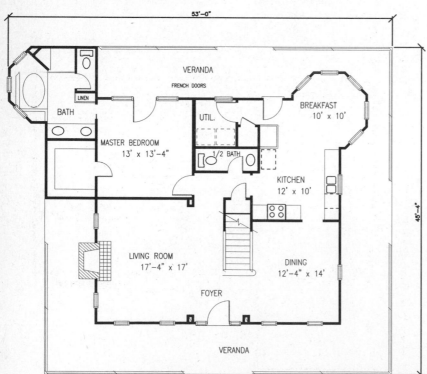

MAIN FLOOR

UPPER FLOOR

ORDER BLUEPRINTS ANYTIME!
CALL TOLL-FREE 1-800-820-1283

Plan L-88-VB

PRICES AND DETAILS ON PAGES 2-5

Appealing and Well Appointed

- A feature-filled interior and a warm, appealing exterior are the keynotes of this spacious two-story home.
- Beyond the charming front porch, the foyer is brightened by sidelights and an octagonal window. To the right, a cased opening leads into the open living room and dining room. Plenty of windows, including a beautiful boxed-out window, bathe the formal area in light.
- The casual area consists of an extra-large island kitchen, a sizable breakfast area and a spectacular family room with a corner fireplace and a skylighted cathedral ceiling that slopes from 11 ft. to 17 ft. high.
- The upper floor hosts a superb master suite, featuring a skylighted bath with an 11-ft. sloped ceiling, a platform spa tub and a separate shower.
- A balcony hall leads to two more bedrooms, a full bath and an optional bonus room that would make a great loft, study or extra bedroom.

Plan AX-8923-A

Bedrooms: 3+	Baths: 2½
Living Area:	
Upper floor	853 sq. ft.
Main floor	1,199 sq. ft.
Optional loft/bedroom	180 sq. ft.
Total Living Area:	**2,232 sq. ft.**
Standard basement	1,184 sq. ft.
Garage	420 sq. ft.
Exterior Wall Framing:	2x4

Foundation Options:

Standard basement

Slab

(All plans can be built with your choice of foundation and framing. A generic conversion diagram is available. See order form.)

BLUEPRINT PRICE CODE: C

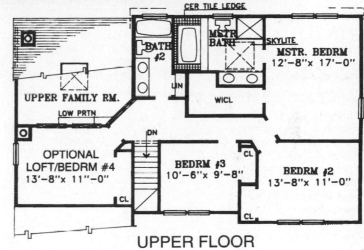

UPPER FLOOR

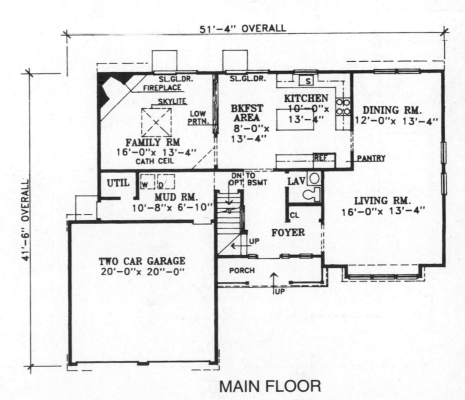

MAIN FLOOR

ORDER BLUEPRINTS ANYTIME!
CALL TOLL-FREE 1-800-820-1283

Plan AX-8923-A

PRICES AND DETAILS
ON PAGES 2-5

327

Photo by Miguel Weinstein

Open, Flowing Floor Plan

- Open, flowing rooms punctuated with wonderful windows enhance this spacious four-bedroom home.
- The two-story-high foyer is brightened by an arched window above. To the left lies the living room, which flows into the family room. An inviting fireplace and windows overlooking a rear terrace highlight the family room.
- The centrally located kitchen serves both the formal dining room and the dinette, with a view of the family room beyond. Sliding glass doors in the dinette open to a lovely terrace.
- Upstairs, the master suite features an arched window and a walk-in closet with a dressing area. The private master bath includes a dual-sink vanity, a skylighted whirlpool tub and a separate shower.
- The three remaining bedrooms share another skylighted bath.

Plan AHP-9020

Bedrooms: 4	Baths: 2½
Living Area:	
Upper floor	1,021 sq. ft.
Main floor	1,125 sq. ft.
Total Living Area:	**2,146 sq. ft.**
Standard basement	1,032 sq. ft.
Garage	480 sq. ft.
Exterior Wall Framing:	2x6

Foundation Options:

Standard basement
Crawlspace
Slab
(All plans can be built with your choice of foundation and framing. A generic conversion diagram is available. See order form.)

BLUEPRINT PRICE CODE: C

NOTE:
The above photographed home may have been modified by the homeowner. Please refer to floor plan and/or drawn elevation shown for actual blueprint details.

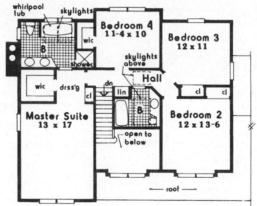

UPPER FLOOR

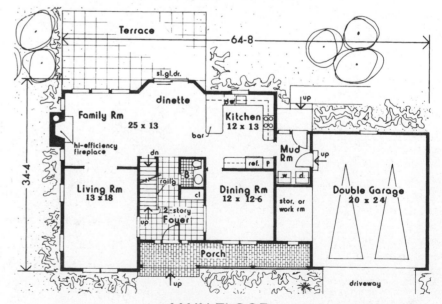

MAIN FLOOR

ORDER BLUEPRINTS ANYTIME! CALL TOLL-FREE 1-800-820-1283

Plan AHP-9020

PRICES AND DETAILS ON PAGES 2-5

Photo by Mark Englund/HomeStyles

Irresistible Master Suite

- This traditional three-bedroom home features a main-floor master suite that is hard to resist, with an inviting window seat and a delightful bath.
- The home is introduced by a covered front entry, topped by a dormer with a half-round window.
- Just off the front entry, the formal dining room is distinguished by a tray ceiling and a large picture window overlooking the front porch.
- Straight back, the Great Room features a 16-ft.-high vaulted ceiling with a window wall facing the backyard. The fireplace can be enjoyed from the adjoining kitchen and breakfast area.
- The gourmet kitchen includes a corner sink, an island cooktop and a walk-in pantry. A 12-ft. vaulted ceiling expands the breakfast nook, which features a built-in desk and backyard deck access.
- The spacious master suite offers a 14-ft. vaulted ceiling and a luxurious private bath with a walk-in closet, a garden tub, a separate shower and a dual-sink vanity with a sit-down makeup area.
- An open-railed stairway leads up to another full bath that serves two additional bedrooms.

Plan B-89061

Bedrooms: 3	Baths: 2½
Living Area:	
Upper floor	436 sq. ft.
Main floor	1,490 sq. ft.
Total Living Area:	**1,926 sq. ft.**
Standard basement	1,490 sq. ft.
Garage	400 sq. ft.
Exterior Wall Framing:	2x4

Foundation Options:

Standard basement
(All plans can be built with your choice of foundation and framing. A generic conversion diagram is available. See order form.)

BLUEPRINT PRICE CODE: B

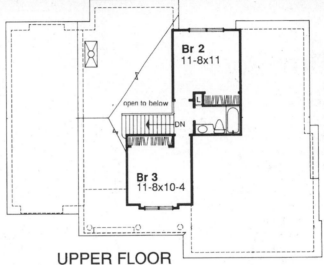

NOTE:
The above photographed home may have been modified by the homeowner. Please refer to floor plan and/or drawn elevation shown for actual blueprint details.

UPPER FLOOR

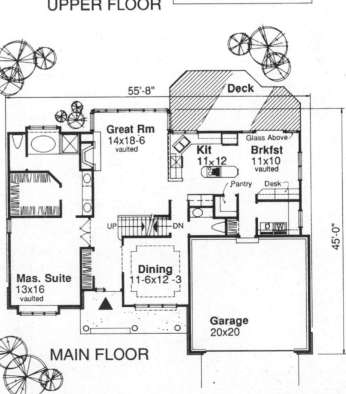

MAIN FLOOR

ORDER BLUEPRINTS ANYTIME!
CALL TOLL-FREE 1-800-820-1283

Plan B-89061

PRICES AND DETAILS
ON PAGES 2-5

329

Photo by Mark Englund/HomeStyles

Luxury and Livability

- Big on style, this modest-sized home features a quaint Colonial exterior and an open interior.
- The covered front porch leads to a two-story foyer that opens to the formal living and dining rooms. A coat closet, an attractive display niche and a powder room are centrally located, as is the stairway to the upper floor.
- The kitchen, breakfast nook and family room are designed so that each room has its own definition yet also functions as part of a whole. The angled sink separates the kitchen from the breakfast nook, which is outlined by a bay window. The large family room includes a fireplace.
- The upper floor has an exceptional master suite, featuring an 8½-ft. tray ceiling in the sleeping area and an 11-ft. vaulted ceiling in the spa bath.
- Two more bedrooms and a balcony hall add to this home's luxury and livability.

Plan FB-1600

Bedrooms: 3	Baths: 2½
Living Area:	
Upper floor	772 sq. ft.
Main floor	828 sq. ft.
Total Living Area:	**1,600 sq. ft.**
Daylight basement	828 sq. ft.
Garage	473 sq. ft.
Exterior Wall Framing:	2x4

Foundation Options:

Daylight basement
Crawlspace
Slab

(All plans can be built with your choice of foundation and framing. A generic conversion diagram is available. See order form.)

BLUEPRINT PRICE CODE:	B

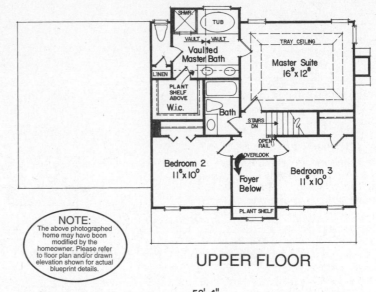

NOTE:
The above photographed home may have been modified by the homeowner. Please refer to floor plan and/or drawn elevation shown for actual blueprint details.

UPPER FLOOR

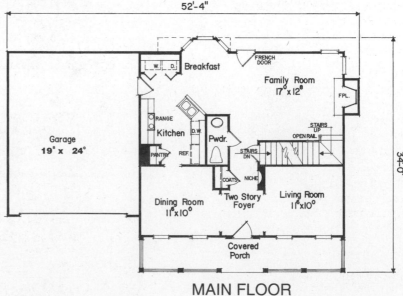

MAIN FLOOR

ORDER BLUEPRINTS ANYTIME!
CALL TOLL-FREE 1-800-820-1283

Plan FB-1600

PRICES AND DETAILS
ON PAGES 2-5

Classic Victorian

- This classic exterior is built around an interior that offers all the amenities desired by today's families.
- In from the covered front porch, the entry features a curved stairway and a glass-block wall to the dining room.
- A step down from the entry, the Great Room boasts a dramatic 24½-ft. cathedral ceiling and provides ample space for large family gatherings.
- The formal dining room is available for special occasions, while the 13-ft.-high breakfast nook serves everyday needs.
- The adjoining island kitchen offers plenty of counter space and opens to a handy utility room and a powder room.
- The deluxe main-floor master suite features a 14½-ft. cathedral ceiling and an opulent private bath with a garden spa tub and a separate shower.
- Upstairs, two secondary bedrooms share a full bath and a balcony overlooking the Great Room below.
- Plans for a two-car garage are available upon request.

Plan DW-2112

Bedrooms: 3	Baths: 2½
Living Area:	
Upper floor	514 sq. ft.
Main floor	1,598 sq. ft.
Total Living Area:	**2,112 sq. ft.**
Standard basement	1,598 sq. ft.
Exterior Wall Framing:	2x4

Foundation Options:
Standard basement
Crawlspace
Slab
(All plans can be built with your choice of foundation and framing. A generic conversion diagram is available. See order form.)

BLUEPRINT PRICE CODE: C

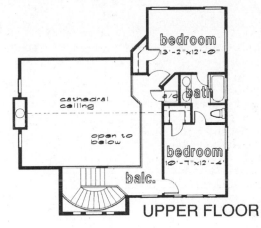

UPPER FLOOR

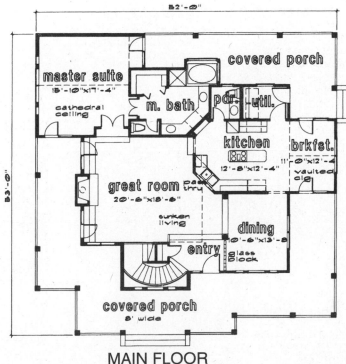

MAIN FLOOR

ORDER BLUEPRINTS ANYTIME!
CALL TOLL-FREE 1-800-820-1283

Plan DW-2112

PRICES AND DETAILS
ON PAGES 2-5

331

Unique and Dramatic

- This home's unique interior and dramatic exterior make it perfect for a sloping, scenic lot.
- The expansive and impressive Great Room, warmed by a woodstove, flows into the island kitchen, which is completely open in design.
- The passive-solar sun room collects and stores heat from the sun, while offering a good view of the surroundings. Its ceiling rises to a height of 16 feet.
- Upstairs, a glamorous, skylighted master suite features an 11-ft. vaulted ceiling, a private bath and a huge walk-in closet.
- A skylighted hall bath serves the bright second bedroom. Both bedrooms open to the vaulted sun room below.
- The daylight basement adds a sunny sitting room, a third bedroom and a large recreation room.

Plans P-536-2A & -2D

Bedrooms: 2+	Baths: 2½-3½
Living Area:	
Upper floor	642 sq. ft.
Main floor	863 sq. ft.
Daylight basement	863 sq. ft.
Total Living Area:	**1,505/2,368 sq. ft.**
Garage	445 sq. ft.
Exterior Wall Framing:	2x6
Foundation Options:	**Plan #**
Daylight basement	P-536-2D
Crawlspace	P-536-2A

(All plans can be built with your choice of foundation and framing. A generic conversion diagram is available. See order form.)

BLUEPRINT PRICE CODE:	B/C

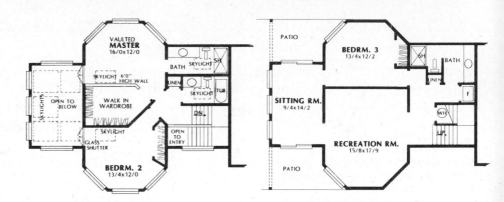

UPPER FLOOR   **DAYLIGHT BASEMENT**

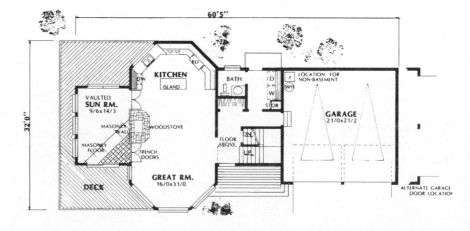

MAIN FLOOR

Country Kitchen

- A lovely front porch, dormers and shutters give this home a country-style exterior and complement its comfortable and informal interior.
- The roomy country kitchen connects with the sunny breakfast nook and the formal dining room.
- The central portion of the home consists of a large family room with a handsome fireplace and easy access to a backyard deck.
- The main-floor master suite, particularly impressive for a home of this size, features a majestic master bath with a corner garden tub, two walk-in closets and a dual-sink vanity with knee space.
- Upstairs, you will find two more good-sized bedrooms, a double bath and a large storage area.

Plan C-8645

Bedrooms: 3	Baths: 2½
Living Area:	
Upper floor	704 sq. ft.
Main floor	1,477 sq. ft.
Total Living Area:	**2,181 sq. ft.**
Daylight basement	1,400 sq. ft.
Garage and storage	561 sq. ft.
Exterior Wall Framing:	2x4

Foundation Options:

Daylight basement
Crawlspace
Slab

(All plans can be built with your choice of foundation and framing. A generic conversion diagram is available. See order form.)

BLUEPRINT PRICE CODE:	C

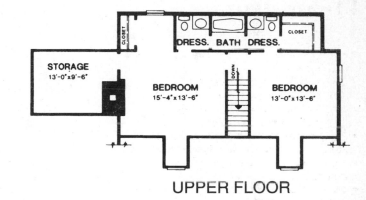

UPPER FLOOR

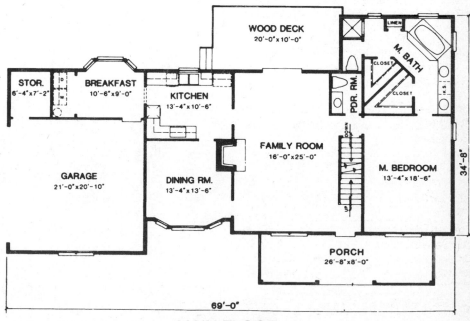

MAIN FLOOR

ORDER BLUEPRINTS ANYTIME!
CALL TOLL-FREE 1-800-820-1283

Plan C-8645

PRICES AND DETAILS
ON PAGES 2-5

333

Photo by Mark Englund

Fantastic Floor Plan!

- Featured on "Hometime," the popular PBS television program, this unique design combines a dynamic exterior with a fantastic floor plan.

- The barrel-vaulted entry leads into the vaulted foyer, which is outlined by elegant columns. To the left, the living room features a 13-ft. vaulted ceiling, a curved wall and corner windows. To the right, the formal dining room is enhanced by a tray ceiling.

- Overlooking a large backyard deck, the island kitchen includes a corner pantry and a built-in desk. The breakfast room shares a columned snack bar with the family room, which has a fireplace and a 17-ft., 8-in. vaulted ceiling.

- The master suite boasts a 15-ft. vaulted ceiling and private access to a romantic courtyard. The sunken master bath features an enticing spa tub and a separate shower, both encased by a curved glass-block wall.

- The two upstairs bedrooms have private access to a large full bath.

Plan B-88015

Bedrooms: 3	Baths: 2½
Living Area:	
Upper floor	534 sq. ft.
Main floor	1,689 sq. ft.
Total Living Area:	**2,223 sq. ft.**
Standard basement	1,689 sq. ft.
Garage	455 sq. ft.
Exterior Wall Framing:	2x4

Foundation Options:

Standard basement
(All plans can be built with your choice of foundation and framing. A generic conversion diagram is available. See order form.)

BLUEPRINT PRICE CODE: **C**

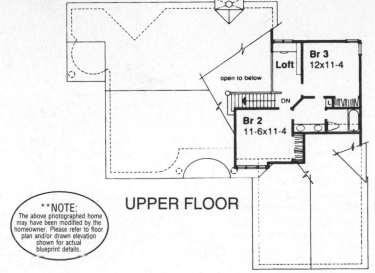

**NOTE: The above photographed home may have been modified by the homeowner. Please refer to floor plan and/or drawn elevation shown for actual blueprint details.

UPPER FLOOR

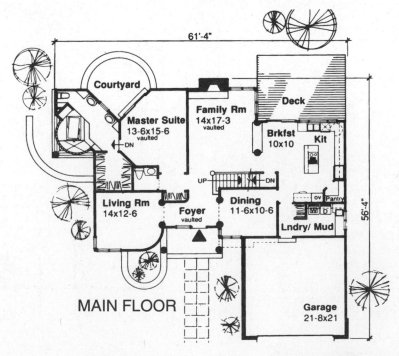

MAIN FLOOR

ORDER BLUEPRINTS ANYTIME!
CALL TOLL-FREE 1-800-820-1283

Plan B-88015

PRICES AND DETAILS
ON PAGES 2-5

Hillside Design Fits Contours

- The daylight-basement version of this popular plan is perfect for a scenic, sloping lot.
- A large, wraparound deck embraces the rear-oriented living areas, accessed through sliding glass doors.
- The spectacular living room boasts a corner fireplace and a 19-ft. vaulted ceiling with three clerestory windows.
- The secluded master suite upstairs offers a walk-in closet, a private bath and sliding doors to a sun deck.
- The daylight basement (not shown) includes a fourth bedroom with a private bath and a walk-in closet, as well as a recreation room with a fireplace and access to a rear patio.
- The standard basement (not shown) includes a recreation room with a fireplace and a room for hobbies or child's play.
- Both basements also have a large unfinished area below the main-floor bedrooms.

Plans H-877-4, -4A & -4B

Bedrooms: 3+	Baths: 2-3
Living Area:	
Upper floor	333 sq. ft.
Main floor	1,200 sq. ft.
Basement (finished area)	591 sq. ft.
Total Living Area:	**1,533/2,124 sq. ft.**
Basement (unfinished area)	493 sq. ft.
Garage	480 sq. ft.
Exterior Wall Framing:	2x6
Foundation Options:	**Plan #**
Daylight basement	H-877-4B
Standard basement	H-877-4
Crawlspace	H-877-4A

(All plans can be built with your choice of foundation and framing. A generic conversion diagram is available. See order form.)

BLUEPRINT PRICE CODE: B/C

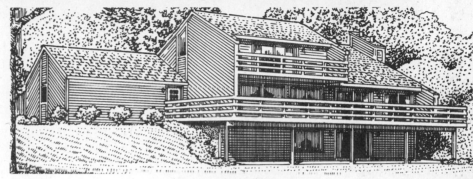

REAR VIEW

UPPER FLOOR

STAIRWAY AREA IN CRAWLSPACE VERSION

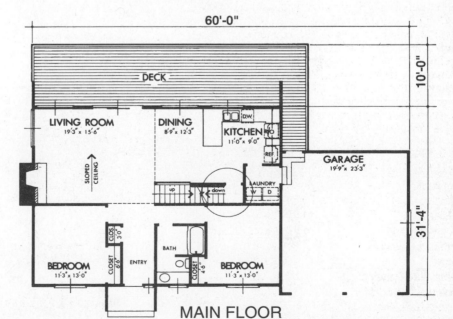

MAIN FLOOR

Casual Country Living

- With its covered wraparound porch, this gracious design is ideal for warm summer days or starry evenings.
- The spacious living room boasts a handsome brick-hearth fireplace and built-in book and gun storage. A French door accesses the backyard.
- The open kitchen design provides plenty of space for food storage and preparation with its pantry and oversized central island.
- Two mirror-imaged baths service the three bedrooms on the upper floor. Each secondary bedroom features a window seat and two closets. The master bedroom has a large walk-in closet and a private bath.
- A versatile hobby or sewing room is also included.
- An optional carport off the dining room is available upon request. Please specify when ordering.

Plan J-8895

Bedrooms: 3	Baths: 2½
Living Area:	
Upper floor	860 sq. ft.
Main floor	919 sq. ft.
Total Living Area:	**1,779 sq. ft.**
Standard basement	919 sq. ft.
Optional carport	462 sq. ft.
Exterior Wall Framing:	2x4

Foundation Options:
Standard basement
Crawlspace
Slab
(All plans can be built with your choice of foundation and framing. A generic conversion diagram is available. See order form.)

BLUEPRINT PRICE CODE: **B**

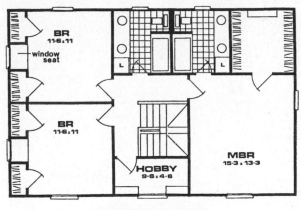

UPPER FLOOR

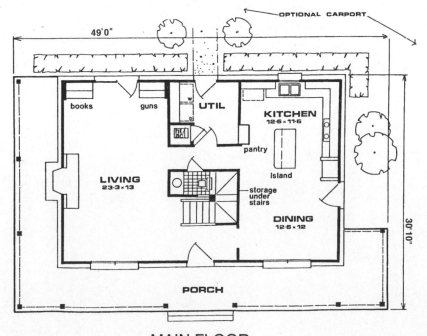

MAIN FLOOR

ORDER BLUEPRINTS ANYTIME!
CALL TOLL-FREE 1-800-820-1283

Plan J-8895

PRICES AND DETAILS
ON PAGES 2-5

Vacation Home with Views

- The octagonal shape and window-filled walls of this home create a powerful interior packed with panoramic views.
- Straight back from the angled entry, the Great Room is brightened by expansive windows and sliding glass doors to a huge wraparound deck. An impressive spiral staircase at the center of the floor plan lends even more character.
- The walk-through kitchen offers a handy pantry. A nice storage closet and a coat closet are located between the entry and the two-car garage.
- The main-floor bedroom is conveniently located near a full bath.
- The upper-floor master suite is a sanctuary, featuring lots of glass, a walk-in closet, a private bath and access to concealed storage rooms.
- The optional daylight basement offers an extra bedroom, a full bath, a laundry area and a large recreation room.

Plans H-964-1A & -1B

Bedrooms: 2+	Baths: 2-3
Living Area:	
Upper floor	346 sq. ft.
Main floor	1,067 sq. ft.
Daylight basement	1,045 sq. ft.
Total Living Area:	**1,413/2,458 sq. ft.**
Garage	512 sq. ft.
Storage (upper floor)	134 sq. ft.
Exterior Wall Framing:	**2x6**
Foundation Options:	**Plan #**
Daylight basement	H-964-1B
Crawlspace	H-964-1A

(All plans can be built with your choice of foundation and framing. A generic conversion diagram is available. See order form.)

BLUEPRINT PRICE CODE:	**A/C**

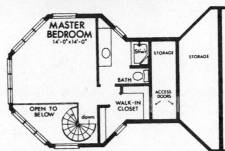

UPPER FLOOR

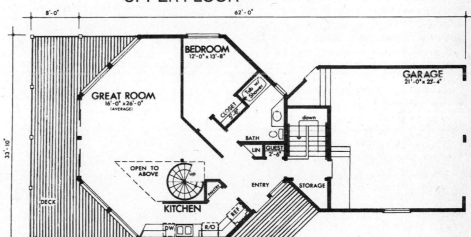

MAIN FLOOR

DAYLIGHT BASEMENT

ORDER BLUEPRINTS ANYTIME!
CALL TOLL-FREE 1-800-820-1283

Plans H-964-1A & -1B

**PRICES AND DETAILS
ON PAGES 2-5**

337

Down-Home Country Flavor!

- Open living areas, decorative dormers and a spacious wraparound porch give this charming home its country feel.
- The main entrance opens into an enormous living room, which boasts a handsome fireplace flanked by bright windows and built-in cabinets.
- The adjoining dining room is brightened by windows on three sides. A rear French door opens to the porch.
- The modern kitchen serves the dining room over an eating bar. A half-bath and a laundry/utility area with access to the garage and porch are nearby.
- The removed master bedroom includes a roomy walk-in closet and a private bath with a corner shower and a dual sink vanity with knee space.
- All main-floor rooms have 9-ft. ceilings.
- Two upper-floor bedrooms share a hallway bath, which is enhanced by one of three dormer windows.

Plan J-90013

Bedrooms: 3	Baths: 2½
Living Area:	
Upper floor	823 sq. ft.
Main floor	1,339 sq. ft.
Total Living Area:	**2,162 sq. ft.**
Standard basement	1,339 sq. ft.
Garage	413 sq. ft.
Storage	106 sq. ft.
Exterior Wall Framing:	2x4
Foundation Options:	
Standard basement	
Crawlspace	
Slab	

(All plans can be built with your choice of foundation and framing. A generic conversion diagram is available. See order form.)

BLUEPRINT PRICE CODE: C

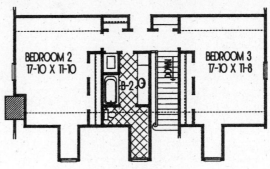

UPPER FLOOR

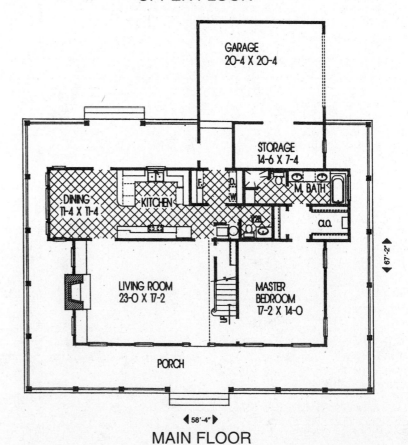

MAIN FLOOR

ORDER BLUEPRINTS ANYTIME!
CALL TOLL-FREE 1-800-820-1283

Plan J-90013

*PRICES AND DETAILS
ON PAGES 2-5*

Elevation A

Elevation B

Simply Elegant

- The clean, classic lines of this two-story design are simply elegant, regardless of which front elevation you choose.
- Inside, the efficient floor plan begins with a 16½-ft.-high vaulted foyer flanked by the formal living and dining rooms.
- The family room, nook and kitchen are combined at the rear of the home for integrated family living. The step-saving, U-shaped kitchen features an angled snack bar. The bayed nook overlooks the backyard, which is accessible through French doors in the family room.
- A laundry closet and a powder room are convenient to both the kitchen and the two-car garage.
- Upstairs, the roomy master suite includes a beautiful skylighted bath and a large walk-in closet.
- Two more good-sized bedrooms share a hall bath.
- Both of the elevations shown are included in the blueprints.

Plan S-22189

Bedrooms: 3	Baths: 2½
Living Area:	
Upper floor	774 sq. ft.
Main floor	963 sq. ft.
Total Living Area:	**1,737 sq. ft.**
Standard basement	963 sq. ft.
Garage	462 sq. ft.
Exterior Wall Framing:	2x6

Foundation Options:

Standard basement

Crawlspace

Slab

(All plans can be built with your choice of foundation and framing. A generic conversion diagram is available. See order form.)

BLUEPRINT PRICE CODE: **B**

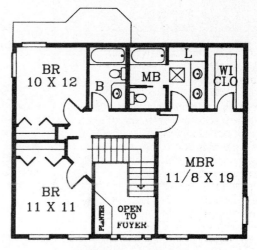

UPPER FLOOR

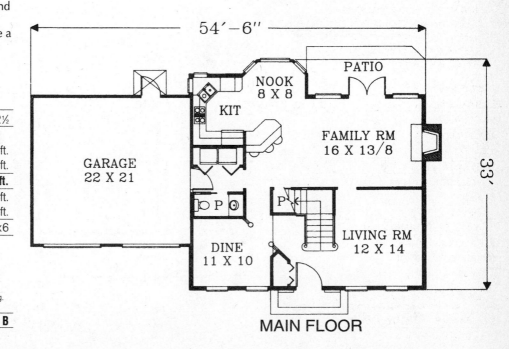

MAIN FLOOR

ORDER BLUEPRINTS ANYTIME!
CALL TOLL-FREE 1-800-820-1283

Plan S-22189

PRICES AND DETAILS
ON PAGES 2-5

339

Off to a Great Start!

- Perfectly sized for families starting out, this charming, feature-filled home is a great choice!
- The entry, which flows directly into the Great Room, is graced by overhead plant shelves and a high 10-ft. ceiling.
- The central Great Room boasts a handsome fireplace under a 14-ft. vaulted ceiling. The right side of the room has a 17-ft. flat ceiling and sliding French doors to a nice backyard patio.
- The dining room is easily served from the open kitchen, which includes a handy pass-through, a bayed breakfast area, a pantry and a laundry closet. The two-car garage is conveniently nearby.
- Upstairs, a railed balcony provides a dramatic view of the Great Room.
- The secluded master suite features a 10-ft., 5-in. vaulted ceiling, a roomy walk-in closet and a private bath.
- Two additional bedrooms and a hallway bath complete the upper floor.

Plan AG-1301-A

Bedrooms: 3	Baths: 2½
Living Area:	
Upper floor	652 sq. ft.
Main floor	673 sq. ft.
Total Living Area:	**1,325 sq. ft.**
Standard basement	620 sq. ft.
Garage	406 sq. ft.
Exterior Wall Framing:	2x4

Foundation Options:
Standard basement
Crawlspace
(All plans can be built with your choice of foundation and framing. A generic conversion diagram is available. See order form.)

BLUEPRINT PRICE CODE:	**A**

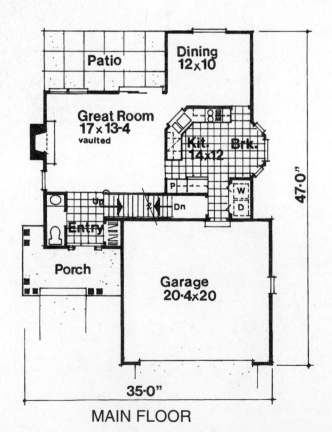

MAIN FLOOR

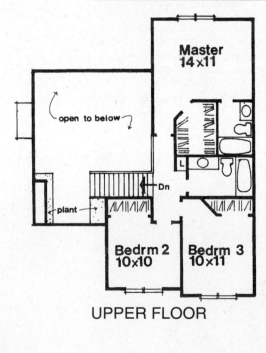

UPPER FLOOR

ORDER BLUEPRINTS ANYTIME!
CALL TOLL-FREE 1-800-820-1283

Plan AG-1301-A

*PRICES AND DETAILS
ON PAGES 2-5*

Deck and Spa!

- Designed for relaxation as well as for active indoor/outdoor living, this popular home offers a gigantic deck and an irresistible spa room.
- A covered porch welcomes guests into the entry hall, which flows past the central, open-railed stairway to the spectacular Great Room.
- Sliding glass doors on each side of the Great Room extend the living space to the huge V-shaped deck. The 22-ft. sloped ceiling and a woodstove add to the stunning effect.
- The master suite features a cozy window seat, a walk-in closet and private access to a full bath.
- The passive-solar spa room can be reached from the master suite as well as the backyard deck.
- The upper floor hosts two additional bedrooms, a full bath and a balcony hall that overlooks the Great Room.

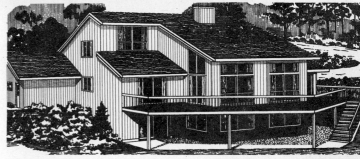

REAR VIEW

Plans H-952-1A & -1B

Bedrooms: 3+	Baths: 2-3
Living Area:	
Upper floor	470 sq. ft.
Main floor	1,207 sq. ft.
Passive spa room	102 sq. ft.
Daylight basement	1,105 sq. ft.
Total Living Area:	**1,779/2,884 sq. ft.**
Garage	496 sq. ft.
Exterior Wall Framing:	2x6
Foundation Options:	**Plan #**
Daylight basement	H-952-1B
Crawlspace	H-952-1A

(All plans can be built with your choice of foundation and framing. A generic conversion diagram is available. See order form.)

BLUEPRINT PRICE CODE: B/D

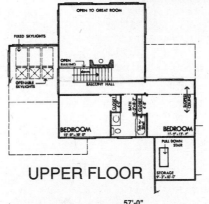

UPPER FLOOR

VIEW INTO PASSIVE SPA ROOM

MAIN FLOOR

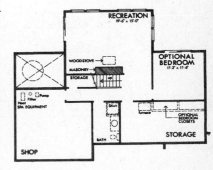

DAYLIGHT BASEMENT

ORDER BLUEPRINTS ANYTIME!
CALL TOLL-FREE 1-800-820-1283

Plans H-952-1A & -1B

PRICES AND DETAILS
ON PAGES 2-5

341

Updated Classic

- Light-filled and airy, this classic country-style home is filled with modern amenities.
- Brightened by high transom windows, the inviting two-story-high foyer flows into the spacious living room and the formal dining room.
- The efficient kitchen features a breakfast bar and a window over the sink. The adjoining dinette offers sliding glass doors to a backyard terrace. The nearby mudroom/laundry room has garage and backyard access.
- The friendly family room enjoys a view of the backyard through a row of three windows. The handsome fireplace is flanked by glass.
- Upstairs, the spectacular master bedroom boasts a 10-ft. cathedral ceiling and a roomy walk-in closet. The skylighted master bath showcases a whirlpool tub, a separate shower and a dual-sink vanity.
- Another skylighted bath services the three remaining bedrooms.

Plan AHP-9402

Bedrooms: 4	Baths: 2½
Living Area:	
Upper floor	1,041 sq. ft.
Main floor	1,129 sq. ft.
Total Living Area:	**2,170 sq. ft.**
Standard basement	1,129 sq. ft.
Garage and storage	630 sq. ft.
Exterior Wall Framing:	2x4 or 2x6

Foundation Options:

Standard basement

Crawlspace

Slab

(All plans can be built with your choice of foundation and framing. A generic conversion diagram is available. See order form.)

BLUEPRINT PRICE CODE: C

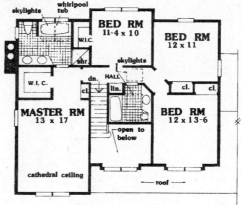

UPPER FLOOR

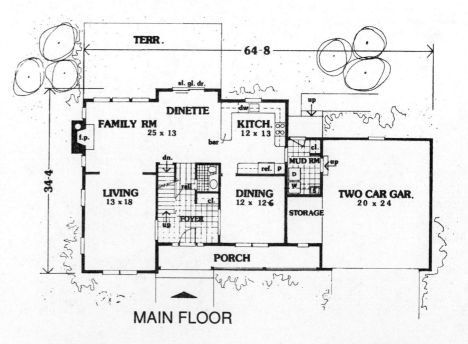

MAIN FLOOR

ORDER BLUEPRINTS ANYTIME!
CALL TOLL-FREE 1-800-820-1283

Plan AHP-9402

PRICES AND DETAILS
ON PAGES 2-5

A Hearty Hello

- Guests will appreciate the hearty welcome they receive as they approach the nostalgic wraparound porch of this classic two-story farmhouse.
- A dramatic vaulted foyer flows neatly into the spacious dining room, which boasts a distinctive built-in cabinet to house your heirloom china and other collectables.
- A crackling fire adds warmth to the vaulted Great Room, while sliding glass doors open to the expansive backyard deck, providing ample space for summer parties.
- An intriguing kitchen design, featuring a pie-shaped island with an eating bar and a bayed breakfast room, will delight the cooks in your family.
- The secluded master bedroom showcases an impressive master bath with dual walk-in closests, a whirlpool tub and a separate shower.
- A bridge over the first floor and a pair of bedrooms with a dual-access bath highlight the upstairs.

Plan AX-95365

Bedrooms: 3+	Baths: 2½
Living Area:	
Upper floor	591 sq. ft.
Main floor	1,662 sq. ft.
Total Living Area:	**2,253 sq. ft.**
Standard basement	1,662 sq. ft.
Exterior Wall Framing:	2x4

Foundation Options:

Standard basement

Crawlspace

Slab

(All plans can be built with your choice of foundation and framing. A generic conversion diagram is available. See order form.)

BLUEPRINT PRICE CODE:	C

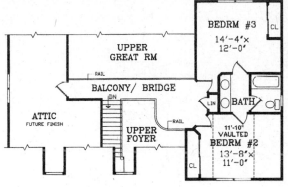

UPPER FLOOR

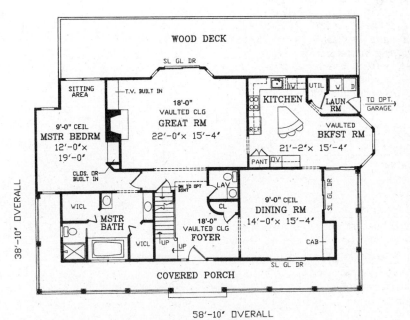

MAIN FLOOR

ORDER BLUEPRINTS ANYTIME!
CALL TOLL-FREE 1-800-820-1283

Plan AX-95365

PRICES AND DETAILS
ON PAGES 2-5

343

A Hint of Romance

- An ornate front porch and a decorative gable with fishscale shingles give this lovely home a romantic Victorian look.
- The central foyer flows to all areas of the home, including the convenient powder room to the left.
- Directly ahead, the airy kitchen features a functional eating bar and a sunny breakfast area with sliding glass doors to a backyard deck. Access to both the garage and a fully appointed laundry room is also a cinch.
- The formal dining room expands into the spacious bayed family room, where a handsome fireplace adds warmth and character to the room.
- Upstairs, the incredible master bedroom boasts a stunning bay window and an optional 15-ft. vaulted ceiling. His-and-hers closets and a private bath with a spa tub, a separate shower and twin vanities are also included.
- A second full bath and two more bedrooms complete the upper floor.

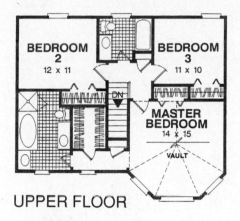

UPPER FLOOR

Plan APS-1514

Bedrooms: 3	Baths: 2½
Living Area:	
Upper floor	786 sq. ft.
Main floor	812 sq. ft.
Total Living Area:	**1,598 sq. ft.**
Garage and storage	560 sq. ft.
Exterior Wall Framing:	2x4

Foundation Options:

Crawlspace

Slab

(All plans can be built with your choice of foundation and framing. A generic conversion diagram is available. See order form.)

BLUEPRINT PRICE CODE: B

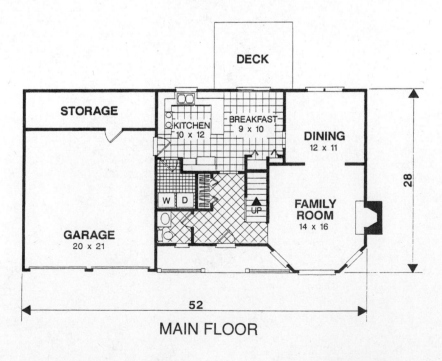

MAIN FLOOR

ORDER BLUEPRINTS ANYTIME!
CALL TOLL-FREE 1-800-820-1283

Plan APS-1514

PRICES AND DETAILS
ON PAGES 2-5

The Simple Life

- With a look that answers your call to get back to nature, this rustic home reminds you of a simpler life.
- Unfolding from the air-lock entry, the spacious living room is warmed by a beautiful woodstove and brightened by a pair of skylights. A 15-ft. vaulted ceiling soars overhead.
- The dining room is just steps away, and is easily serviced by the kitchen.
- French doors in the dining room offer access to the cheery sun room, a

wonderful spot to relax and enjoy the warm rays of the sun.
- A tidy pantry closet, a windowed sink and a central work island highlight the U-shaped kitchen.
- A versatile room near the entry could serve as a study or another bedroom.
- Step outside to the expansive deck for a summer barbecue with friends.
- An open staircase leads to the upper floor, where two bedrooms share a skylighted bath. The master bedroom features a trio of closets and a handy built-in desk.

Plans H-970-1 & -1A	
Bedrooms: 2+	**Baths:** 1½
Living Area:	
Upper floor	563 sq. ft.
Main floor	817 sq. ft.
Sun space	192 sq. ft.
Total Living Area:	**1,572 sq. ft.**
Standard basement	768 sq. ft.
Garage	288 sq. ft.
Exterior Wall Framing:	2x6
Foundation Options:	**Plan #**
Standard basement	H-970-1
Crawlspace	H-970-1A

(All plans can be built with your choice of foundation and framing. A generic conversion diagram is available. See order form.)

BLUEPRINT PRICE CODE: **B**

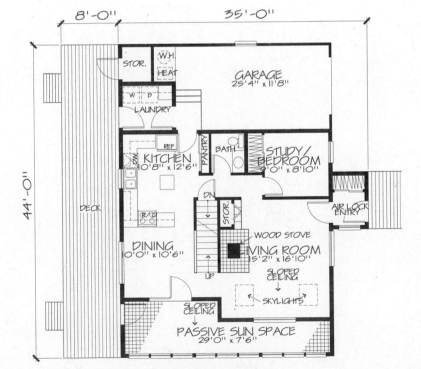

MAIN FLOOR

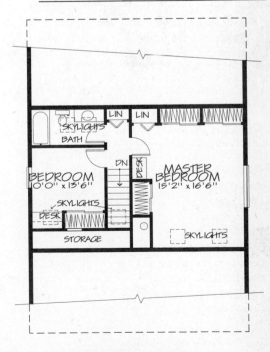

UPPER FLOOR

ORDER BLUEPRINTS ANYTIME!
CALL TOLL-FREE 1-800-820-1283

Plans H-970-1 & -1A

PRICES AND DETAILS
ON PAGES 2-5

345

Great Expectations

- If a growing family is in your future, give thought to this charming home, which offers a bonus space in its daylight basement that can be finished off as a rollicking family room.
- From the 12-ft., 8-in.-high split entry, stairs lead up to the formal gathering areas. In the living room, a fireplace teams up with a trio of windows to create stylish ambience. An 11-ft., 4-in. vaulted ceiling tops the room.
- Decorative columns nicely frame the dining room's entrance. Beyond, sliding glass doors introduce a backyard deck that practically begs you to enjoy summer with zest and spontaneity!
- Pair up with your favorite cook in the roomy kitchen and serve up a feast fit for royalty.
- The master suite resides at the end of the hall, and features a 10-ft., 8-in. vaulted ceiling over the sleeping chamber. A private bath livens you each morning with a splashy shower.

Plan B-90067

Bedrooms: 3+	Baths: 2
Living Area:	
Main floor	1,203 sq. ft.
Total Living Area:	**1,203 sq. ft.**
Daylight basement	510 sq. ft.
Tuck-under garage	560 sq. ft.
Exterior Wall Framing:	2x4

Foundation Options:
Daylight basement
(All plans can be built with your choice of foundation and framing. A generic conversion diagram is available. See order form.)

BLUEPRINT PRICE CODE: A

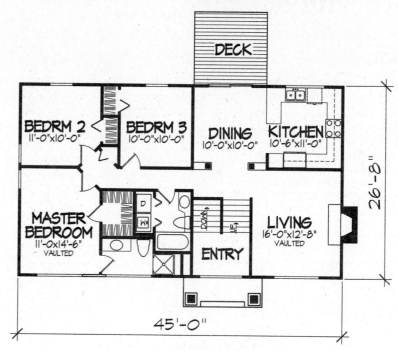

MAIN FLOOR

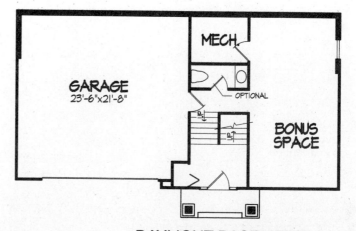

DAYLIGHT BASEMENT

ORDER BLUEPRINTS ANYTIME! *CALL TOLL-FREE 1-800-820-1283*   Plan B-90067   *PRICES AND DETAILS ON PAGES 2-5*

Masterful Suite

- The entire second floor of this home belongs to the luxurious master suite!
- Stairs to the left of the home lead to a deck, which introduces the sidelighted, 12-ft., 11-in.-high vaulted entry.
- Natural light drenches the living room, with its rustic fireplace and 17-ft., 5-in. vaulted ceiling. A bay window beautifies the adjoining dining room, which offers French-door access to a second deck.
- The gourmet kitchen boasts tremendous space. Its island hosts an informal breakfast bar and a vegetable sink.
- Down the skylighted hallway, two bedrooms share a skylighted bath. One bedroom flaunts private deck access, while the other has a cute window seat.
- Upstairs, the master bedroom enjoys a cozy fireplace under a 12½-ft. vaulted ceiling. To the right of the fireplace, a French door opens to a private deck. A bayed sitting room offers serenity beneath a 10-ft., 4-in. vaulted ceiling.
- The master bath boasts a skylighted garden tub and a separate shower.
- A wood-carving room with a garden window adjoins the master suite.

Plan LMB-9600

Bedrooms: 3	Baths: 2½
Living Area:	
Upper floor	763 sq. ft.
Main floor	1,338 sq. ft.
Daylight basement	68 sq. ft.
Total Living Area:	**2,169 sq. ft.**
Tuck-under garage and storage	780 sq. ft.
Exterior Wall Framing:	2x6

Foundation Options:

Daylight basement
(All plans can be built with your choice of foundation and framing. A generic conversion diagram is available. See order form.)

BLUEPRINT PRICE CODE: C

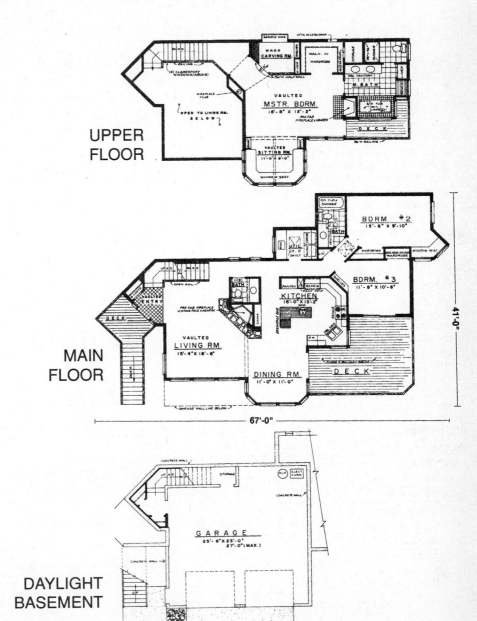

UPPER FLOOR

MAIN FLOOR

DAYLIGHT BASEMENT

67'-0"

41'-0"

Build Your Family Tree

- Classic styling enhances the traditional appeal of this two-story country home, creating a place the family will appreciate for generations to come.
- Stroll into the living area from the 17-ft.-high foyer and enjoy the company of your guests, then retire to the formal dining room for a delectable feast.
- A trio of skylights will illuminate the leisurely afternoon conversations with your children in the broad family room, which boasts a raised hearth fireplace.
- Share meal preparation duties with all the family members in the spacious island kitchen, which includes an informal dinnette.
- Rest assured you will sleep well in the master suite, featuring a 10-ft. cathedral ceiling, a generous walk-in closet and a whirlpool tub in the bath.
- Upstairs, three additional bedrooms, a full bath and a balcony overlooking the foyer complete the plan.

Plan GL-2140

Bedrooms: 4	Baths: 2½
Living Area:	
Upper floor	1,007 sq. ft.
Main floor	1,133 sq. ft.
Total Living Area:	**2,140 sq. ft.**
Standard basement	1,133 sq. ft.
Garage and storage	507 sq. ft.
Exterior Wall Framing:	2x6

Foundation Options:

Standard basement

(All plans can be built with your choice of foundation and framing. A generic conversion diagram is available. See order form.)

BLUEPRINT PRICE CODE:	C

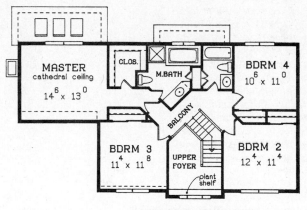

UPPER FLOOR

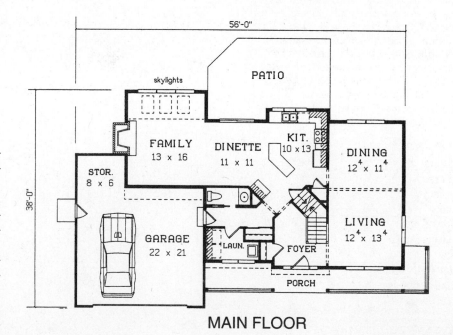

MAIN FLOOR

 ORDER BLUEPRINTS ANYTIME!
CALL TOLL-FREE 1-800-820-1283

Plan GL-2140

PRICES AND DETAILS
ON PAGES 2-5

Your Own Place

- This compact, affordable floor plan makes that dream of owning your own home a real possibility. Even better, the layout includes everything you need to lead a comfortable lifestyle.
- Out front, handsome columns usher guests up to the covered entry, which protects them from inclement weather.
- Inside, the good-sized living room includes plenty of room for entertaining friends on a Friday evening. Also, when the kids need a place to spread out and work on a project, they'll naturally turn to this versatile spot.
- When mealtime tops the agenda, the combined kitchen and dining area fits the bill. The open design of this space simplifies the task of meal cleanup, while nearby access to the garage saves steps when unloading groceries.
- For a change of scenery, how about enjoying dinner on the backyard patio? No doubt, barbecued chicken and fresh potato salad taste even better outdoors.
- Upstairs, a 9½-ft. vaulted ceiling lends a dash of style and elegance to the master suite, which also boasts private access to a hall bath.

Plan B-92007

Bedrooms: 3	Baths: 1½
Living Area:	
Upper floor	676 sq. ft.
Main floor	624 sq. ft.
Total Living Area:	**1,300 sq. ft.**
Standard basement	624 sq. ft.
Garage	225 sq. ft.
Exterior Wall Framing:	**2x6**

Foundation Options:

Standard basement

(All plans can be built with your choice of foundation and framing. A generic conversion diagram is available. See order form.)

BLUEPRINT PRICE CODE: A

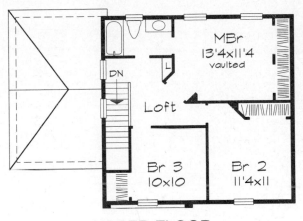

UPPER FLOOR

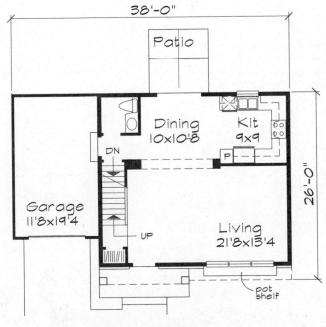

MAIN FLOOR

ORDER BLUEPRINTS ANYTIME!
CALL TOLL-FREE 1-800-820-1283

Plan B-92007

PRICES AND DETAILS
ON PAGES 2-5

349

Charming Chateau

- A two-story arched entry introduces this charming French chateau.
- To the left of the tiled foyer, the elegant formal dining room will impress friends when you entertain.
- In the kitchen, a handy island worktop and a step-in pantry take advantage of the unique space. The cheery breakfast nook is a great spot for family meals.
- A neat see-through fireplace and built-in bookshelves define the formal living

room and the casual family room. Lovely French doors open to a quiet covered porch in back.
- The secluded master suite on the main floor boasts two enormous walk-in closets and a lush private bath with an inviting marble tub, a separate shower and his-and-hers vanities.
- The kitchen and the nook have 9- and 8-ft. ceilings, respectively. All other main-floor rooms are enhanced by soaring 10-ft. ceilings.
- On the upper floor, two bedrooms share a unique bath. The front bedroom offers a 10-ft. ceiling. A bonus room can be adapted to fit your future needs.

Plan RD-2225	
Bedrooms: 3+	**Baths:** 2½
Living Area:	
Upper floor	547 sq. ft.
Main floor	1,678 sq. ft.
Total Living Area:	**2,225 sq. ft.**
Bonus room (unfinished)	136 sq. ft.
Garage and storage	519 sq. ft.
Exterior Wall Framing:	2x4
Foundation Options:	
Crawlspace	
Slab	

(All plans can be built with your choice of foundation and framing. A generic conversion diagram is available. See order form.)

BLUEPRINT PRICE CODE:	C

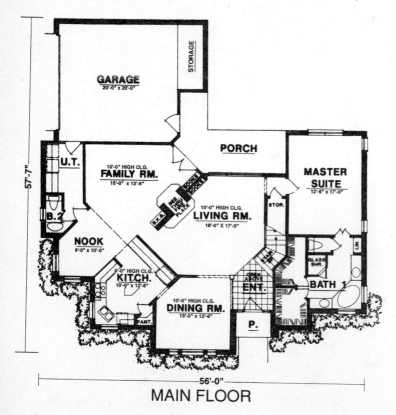

MAIN FLOOR

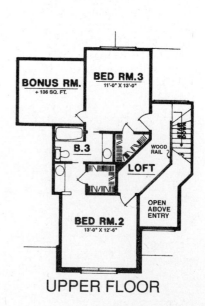

UPPER FLOOR

Two-Story Treasure

- Space-efficient and stylish, this distinctive two-story home is designed for cost-effective construction.
- Past the inviting columned front porch, the impressive raised foyer is enhanced by a two-story-high ceiling and a row of clerestory windows.
- The living room features a boxed-out window bay and adjoins the dining room to create a continuous formal entertaining space.
- The gourmet island kitchen offers an eating bar, a corner pantry and a bright bay-windowed breakfast area.
- A handsome, glass-flanked fireplace is the focal point of the family room. A French door opens to a backyard patio.
- Upstairs, a railed balcony overlooks the foyer below. The master bedroom, to the left, boasts an elegant 10-ft. tray ceiling and a roomy walk-in closet. The master bath flaunts a garden spa tub, a separate shower and a dual-sink vanity.
- A second full bath is shared by the three remaining bedrooms.

Plan B-92022

Bedrooms: 4	Baths: 2½
Living Area:	
Upper floor	964 sq. ft.
Main floor	959 sq. ft.
Total Living Area:	**1,923 sq. ft.**
Standard basement	959 sq. ft.
Garage	407 sq. ft.
Exterior Wall Framing:	2x6

Foundation Options:

Standard basement

(All plans can be built with your choice of foundation and framing. A generic conversion diagram is available. See order form.)

BLUEPRINT PRICE CODE:	**B**

UPPER FLOOR

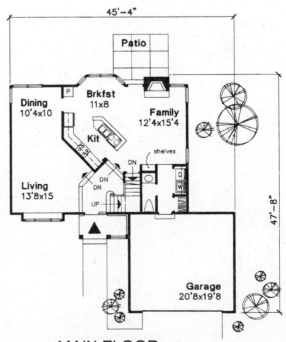

MAIN FLOOR

ORDER BLUEPRINTS ANYTIME!
CALL TOLL-FREE 1-800-820-1283

Plan B-92022

PRICES AND DETAILS
ON PAGES 2-5

351

Splendor on the Land

- Plantation touches adorn the facade of this breathtaking home, making it a splendid companion to your pastoral tract of land.
- The columned porch leads to an exquisite interior. A cozy two-way fireplace and a fun wet bar unite the formal living room and the more casual Great Room. The media shelf will spice up your weekends!
- Mornings are glorious in the cozy bayed dinette. Access to a backyard terrace is just a step away. The adjoining kitchen boasts an island cooktop and snack bar, plus a cheery windowed sink.
- Spoil yourself in the master suite, which offers a deluxe private bath that includes a whirlpool tub, a separate shower and a dual-sink vanity.
- Upstairs, a beautiful balcony introduces three more bedrooms and a full bath.

Plan AHP-9605

Bedrooms: 4	Baths: 2½
Living Area:	
Upper floor	698 sq. ft.
Main floor	1,512 sq. ft.
Total Living Area:	**2,210 sq. ft.**
Standard basement	1,512 sq. ft.
Garage and storage	484 sq. ft.
Exterior Wall Framing:	2x4 or 2x6

Foundation Options:

Standard basement

Crawlspace

Slab

(All plans can be built with your choice of foundation and framing. A generic conversion diagram is available. See order form.)

BLUEPRINT PRICE CODE: C

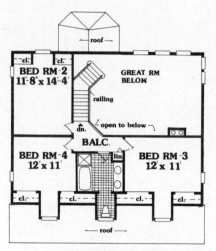

UPPER FLOOR

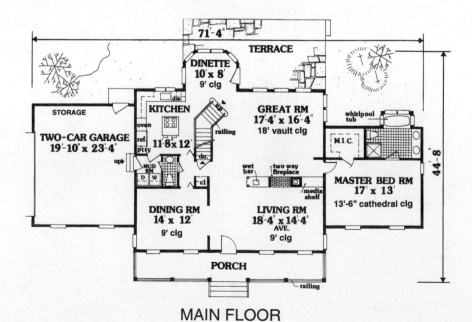

MAIN FLOOR

ORDER BLUEPRINTS ANYTIME!
CALL TOLL-FREE 1-800-820-1283

Plan AHP-9605

PRICES AND DETAILS
ON PAGES 2-5

Living on Four Levels

- Perfect for a narrow or side-sloping lot, this charming transitional home offers four levels of excitement.
- The entry, and the combined living and dining rooms share a 16-ft. vaulted ceiling on the home's main level.
- The adjacent kitchen includes a great snack bar and a pantry. An open railing in the adjoining bay-windowed breakfast nook overlooks the family room. The nook also provides a convenient built-in desk.

- The family room boasts a 17-ft. vaulted ceiling and a handsome fireplace as it sits one level below the dining room and nook. Sliding glass doors open to a backyard patio. A half-bath and access to the garage are nearby.
- Upstairs, a railed balcony bridge overlooks the family and living rooms.
- Two bedrooms with window seats are serviced by a full bath. The convenient upper-floor laundry room minimizes trips up and down the stairs.
- Double doors lead into the secluded master suite of the highest level. The master bath flaunts a soothing whirlpool tub, a separate shower and a roomy walk-in closet.

Plan AG-1902	
Bedrooms: 3	**Baths:** 2½
Living Area:	
Upper floor	860 sq. ft.
Main floor	1,070 sq. ft.
Total Living Area:	**1,930 sq. ft.**
Partial basement	800 sq. ft.
Garage	424 sq. ft.
Exterior Wall Framing:	2x4
Foundation Options:	

Partial basement
(All plans can be built with your choice of foundation and framing. A generic conversion diagram is available. See order form.)

BLUEPRINT PRICE CODE:	B

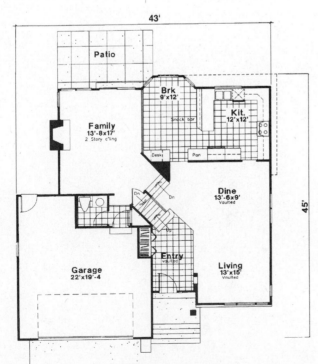

MAIN FLOOR

UPPER FLOOR

ORDER BLUEPRINTS ANYTIME!
CALL TOLL-FREE 1-800-820-1283

Plan AG-1902

PRICES AND DETAILS
ON PAGES 2-5

353

A Splash of Style

- Eye-catching keystones, arched window arrangements and a varied roofline give this home a refreshing splash of style.
- Inside, the 10-ft., 8-in.-high entry leads to the dining room and the Great Room. A 12-ft. sloped ceiling expands the Great Room, which features a brick fireplace that soars to the ceiling.
- A sunny bay brightens the cheery breakfast nook and the adjacent kitchen. A built-in desk, a pantry, an island workstation and a nearby powder room make the most of this busy area.
- A split staircase at the center of the plan leads to the upper-floor bedrooms.
- A 13-ft., 4-in. cathedral ceiling, a sunny bay and a plant ledge spice up the master bedroom. The private bath boasts a whirlpool tub under an 11-ft., 4-in. sloped ceiling. Two vanities and a separate shower are also included.
- The secondary bedrooms share a split hall bath. The front bedroom has a built-in bookcase and an 11-ft., 4-in. sloped ceiling; the left, rear bedroom has a 13-ft., 10-in. cathedral ceiling.

Plan CC-1990-M

Bedrooms: 4	Baths: 2½
Living Area:	
Upper floor	967 sq. ft.
Main floor	1,023 sq. ft.
Total Living Area:	**1,990 sq. ft.**
Standard basement	1,023 sq. ft.
Garage	685 sq. ft.
Exterior Wall Framing:	2x4

Foundation Options:

Standard basement

(All plans can be built with your choice of foundation and framing. A generic conversion diagram is available. See order form.)

BLUEPRINT PRICE CODE: B

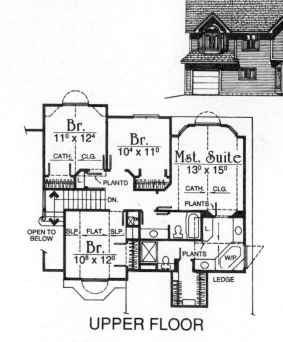

REAR VIEW

UPPER FLOOR

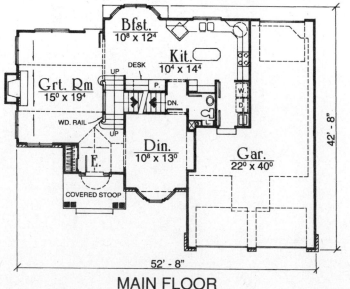

MAIN FLOOR

Bright and Airy Country Kitchen

- A smart, stylish exterior and a modest width make this attractive family home a great choice for a narrow lot.
- The sidelighted entry flows directly into the inviting two-story-high living room, which features a handsome fireplace.
- A columned arch leads into the bright and airy country kitchen. Expanded by a 10-ft. ceiling, the kitchen includes a central work island, a pantry and a bayed nook with access to an expansive backyard deck. A half-bath, a laundry room and a den or formal dining room with deck access are nearby.
- The master bedroom also opens to the deck and includes a private bath with a platform tub, a separate shower and a dual-sink vanity.
- Upstairs, a railed loft overlooks the living room. Two additional bedrooms share a second full bath.
- A skylighted bonus room above the garage can be used as desired.

Plan B-92032

Bedrooms: 3+	Baths: 3
Living Area:	
Upper floor	536 sq. ft.
Main floor	1,343 sq. ft.
Bonus room	221 sq. ft.
Total Living Area:	**2,100 sq. ft.**
Standard basement	1,343 sq. ft.
Garage	452 sq. ft.
Exterior Wall Framing:	2x6
Foundation Options:	
Standard basement	

(All plans can be built with your choice of foundation and framing. A generic conversion diagram is available. See order form.)

BLUEPRINT PRICE CODE:	C

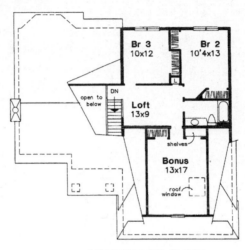

UPPER FLOOR

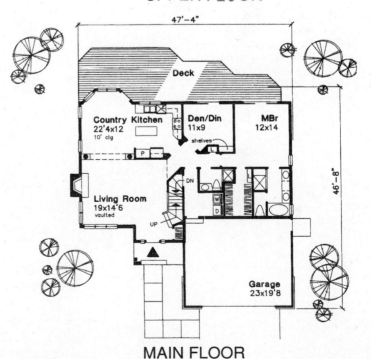

MAIN FLOOR

ORDER BLUEPRINTS ANYTIME!
CALL TOLL-FREE 1-800-820-1283

Plan B-92032

PRICES AND DETAILS
ON PAGES 2-5

355

An Easy Pace

- With its metal roof, latticework and louver shutters, this home breathes an air of easy Southern gentility. The wraparound porch offers up a spot to sit and enjoy the smell of the hydrangeas.
- Inside, the dining and living rooms flank the entry, providing a consolidated space for entertaining. If you prefer, the living room can be modified to serve as a bedroom, with a walk-in closet and private access to a hall bath.
- Everyday activities have a place of their own in the family room. Here, a built-in bookcase beside the fireplace artfully displays pretty framed photographs.
- A cheery wall of windows joins the family room to the eating area, where a china niche and a snack bar simplify meals. The walk-through kitchen is conveniently located near the garage.
- Across the home, the master suite awaits those days when you need some quiet time alone. In the bath, the garden tub provides luxurious treatment.
- Each of the bedrooms upstairs features a walk-in closet and a private bath.

Plan E-1913

Bedrooms: 3+	Baths: 4
Living Area:	
Upper floor	636 sq. ft.
Main floor	1,320 sq. ft.
Total Living Area:	**1,956 sq. ft.**
Standard basement	1,320 sq. ft.
Garage and storage	544 sq. ft.
Exterior Wall Framing:	2x6

Foundation Options:
Standard basement
Crawlspace
Slab

(All plans can be built with your choice of foundation and framing. A generic conversion diagram is available. See order form.)

BLUEPRINT PRICE CODE: B

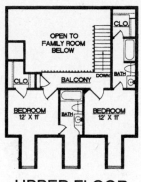

UPPER FLOOR

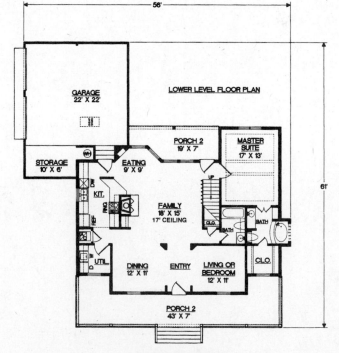

MAIN FLOOR

OPTIONAL BEDROOM

ORDER BLUEPRINTS ANYTIME!
CALL TOLL-FREE 1-800-820-1283

Plan E-1913

PRICES AND DETAILS ON PAGES 2-5

Contemporary Retreat

- Designed for lots with spectacular views, this exciting contemporary home would make the perfect lake or mountain retreat.
- The side entryway opens to a relaxed and open atmosphere, which prevails throughout the home.
- A beamed ceiling and a charming balcony overlook the vast living area. Its highlights include a soaring 21½-ft.

vaulted ceiling, a majestic fireplace and sliding glass doors and windows that permit both visual and actual access to the splendid wraparound deck.
- Open to the living area, the dining room and U-shaped kitchen enhance the spacious feel.
- One large bedroom and a full bath complete the main floor.
- Upstairs, the master bedroom has a 12-ft., 10-in. vaulted ceiling and a private bath; a 10-ft. ceiling tops the other bedroom.
- The daylight basement has room for a huge recreation area, if you choose.

Plans H-929-1 & -1A	
Bedrooms: 3	**Baths:** 3
Living Area:	
Upper floor	685 sq. ft.
Main floor	960 sq. ft.
Total Living Area:	**1,645 sq. ft.**
Daylight basement	960 sq. ft.
Garage	400 sq. ft.
Exterior Wall Framing:	2x6
Foundation Options:	**Plan #**
Daylight basement	H-929-1
Crawlspace	H-929-1A

(All plans can be built with your choice of foundation and framing. A generic conversion diagram is available. See order form.)

BLUEPRINT PRICE CODE: **B**

MAIN FLOOR

UPPER FLOOR

State-of-the-Art Floor Plan

- This design's state-of-the-art floor plan begins with a two-story-high foyer that introduces a stunning open staircase and a bright Great Room.
- The Great Room is expanded by a 17-ft. vaulted ceiling and a window wall with French doors that open to a rear deck.
- Short sections of half-walls separate the Great Room from the open kitchen and dining room. Natural light streams in through a greenhouse window above the sink and lots of glass facing the deck.
- The main-floor master suite has a 9-ft. coved ceiling and private access to an inviting hot tub on the deck. Walk-in closets frame the entrance to the luxurious bath, highlighted by a 10-ft. vaulted ceiling and an arched window above a raised spa tub.
- Upstairs, a balcony hall leads to two bedrooms and a continental bath, plus a den and a storage room.

Plan S-2100

Bedrooms: 3	Baths: 2½
Living Area:	
Upper floor	660 sq. ft.
Main floor	1,440 sq. ft.
Total Living Area:	**2,100 sq. ft.**
Standard basement	1,440 sq. ft.
Garage	552 sq. ft.
Exterior Wall Framing:	2x6

Foundation Options:

Standard basement
Crawlspace
Slab

(All plans can be built with your choice of foundation and framing. A generic conversion diagram is available. See order form.)

BLUEPRINT PRICE CODE:	**C**

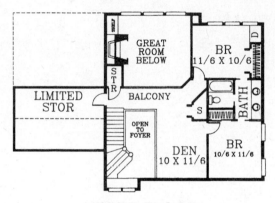

UPPER FLOOR

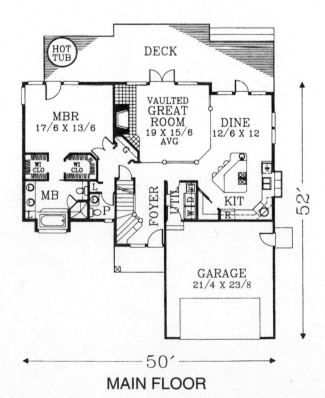

MAIN FLOOR

ORDER BLUEPRINTS ANYTIME!
CALL TOLL-FREE 1-800-820-1283

Plan S-2100

PRICES AND DETAILS ON PAGES 2-5

Traditional Family

- A cute columned porch adds character to this traditional family home.
- A walk-in closet and a half-bath in the two-story foyer accommodate guests.
- To the right, the formal living and dining rooms make entertaining your guests a snap.
- The open kitchen includes a space-saving island and a windowed sink. Sliding glass doors in the bright dinette extend dining to an enormous patio that is perfect for a barbecue.
- A striking 11-ft. cathedral ceiling soars over the family room, where a cozy fireplace adds warmth.
- An open staircase leads up to the magnificent master bedroom, which is embellished with a 9½-ft. tray ceiling and a private whirlpool bath.
- Three secondary bedrooms share a conveniently located full bath.

Plan GL-2223

Bedrooms: 4	Baths: 2½
Living Area:	
Upper floor	1,007 sq. ft.
Main floor	1,216 sq. ft.
Total Living Area:	**2,223 sq. ft.**
Standard basement	1,207 sq. ft.
Garage	484 sq. ft.
Exterior Wall Framing:	2x6

Foundation Options:

Standard basement

(All plans can be built with your choice of foundation and framing. A generic conversion diagram is available. See order form.)

BLUEPRINT PRICE CODE:	C

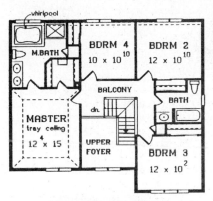

UPPER FLOOR

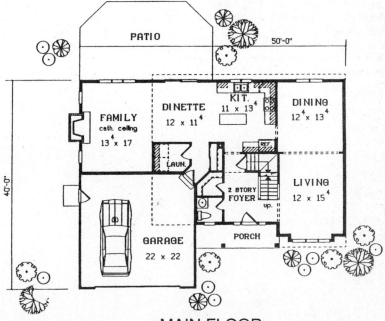

MAIN FLOOR

A Move Up

- Narrow lap siding and repeated round-top windows with divided panes give this traditional home a different look.
- The roomy interior offers space for the upwardly mobile family, with four to five bedrooms and large activity areas.
- The two-story foyer welcomes guests into a spacious formal area that combines the living and dining rooms. The rooms share a dramatic 13-ft. cathedral ceiling, while a handsome fireplace adds a peaceful glow.
- Behind double doors is a cozy study or fifth bedroom.
- A second fireplace and a media center make the family room a fun retreat. French doors open to a lovely terrace.
- Adjoining the family room is a well-designed kitchen with a bayed dinette.
- Double doors introduce the secluded master suite, which boasts a 12-ft. sloped ceiling and a quiet terrace. The private bath offers an invigorating whirlpool tub under a skylight.
- Three more bedrooms and another bath occupy the upper floor.

Plan AHP-9396

Bedrooms: 4+	Baths: 2½
Living Area:	
Upper floor	643 sq. ft.
Main floor	1,553 sq. ft.
Total Living Area:	**2,196 sq. ft.**
Standard basement	1,553 sq. ft.
Garage and storage	502 sq. ft.
Exterior Wall Framing:	2x4 or 2x6

Foundation Options:

Standard basement

Crawlspace

Slab

(All plans can be built with your choice of foundation and framing. A generic conversion diagram is available. See order form.)

BLUEPRINT PRICE CODE: C

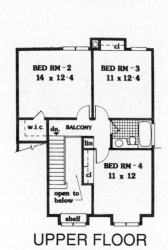

UPPER FLOOR

VIEW INTO LIVING AND DINING ROOMS

MAIN FLOOR

ORDER BLUEPRINTS ANYTIME!
CALL TOLL-FREE 1-800-820-1283

Plan AHP-9396

*PRICES AND DETAILS
ON PAGES 2-5*

TWO-STORY HOMES OVER 2,300 SQUARE FEET

Second-Floor Family Room

- This dramatic contemporary home offers a skylighted family room on the upper floor. A sloped ceiling and a railed overlook add further interest.
- Cathedral ceilings grace the foyer and the sunken living room, which features a fireplace flanked by windows and sliding glass doors.
- The den and the breakfast area also offer outdoor access.
- The main-floor master suite boasts an oversized walk-in closet, a cathedral ceiling and a skylighted bath, plus private access to the den.
- An upper-floor bridge overlooks the living room and the foyer, and leads through the family room to three secondary bedrooms and a full bath.
- The blueprints show an optional guest suite that can be built above the master suite and den.

Plan AX-989308

Bedrooms: 4+	Baths: 2½-3½
Living Area:	
Upper floor	923 sq. ft.
Main floor	1,890 sq. ft.
Optional guest suite	528 sq. ft.
Total Living Area:	**3,341 sq. ft.**
Standard basement	1,890 sq. ft.
Garage	600 sq. ft.
Exterior Wall Framing:	2x4

Foundation Options:

Standard basement

(All plans can be built with your choice of foundation and framing. A generic conversion diagram is available. See order form.)

BLUEPRINT PRICE CODE: E

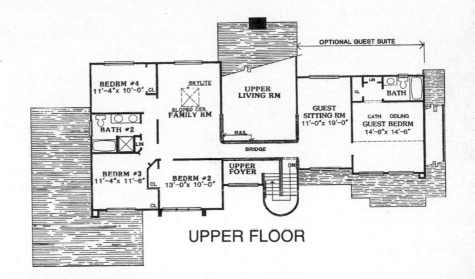

UPPER FLOOR

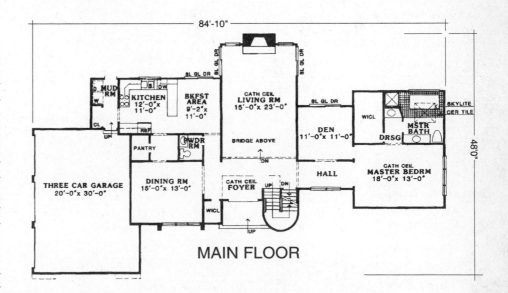

MAIN FLOOR

A Family Tradition

- This traditional design has clean, sharp styling, with family-sized areas for formal and casual gatherings.
- The sidelighted foyer is graced with a beautiful open staircase and a wide coat closet. Flanking the foyer are the spacious formal living areas.
- The everyday living areas include an island kitchen, a bayed dinette and a large family room with a fireplace.
- Just off the entrance from the garage, double doors open to the quiet study, which boasts built-in bookshelves.
- A powder room and a deluxe laundry room with cabinets are convenient to the active areas of the home.
- Upstairs, the master suite features a roomy split bath and a large walk-in closet. Three more bedrooms share another split bath.

Plan A-118-DS

Bedrooms: 4+	Baths: 2½
Living Area:	
Upper floor	1,344 sq. ft.
Main floor	1,556 sq. ft.
Total Living Area:	**2,900 sq. ft.**
Standard basement	1,556 sq. ft.
Garage	576 sq. ft.
Exterior Wall Framing:	2x4

Foundation Options:

Standard basement

(All plans can be built with your choice of foundation and framing. A generic conversion diagram is available. See order form.)

BLUEPRINT PRICE CODE: D

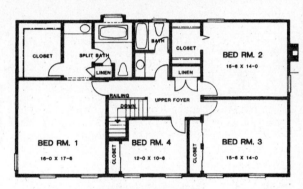

UPPER FLOOR

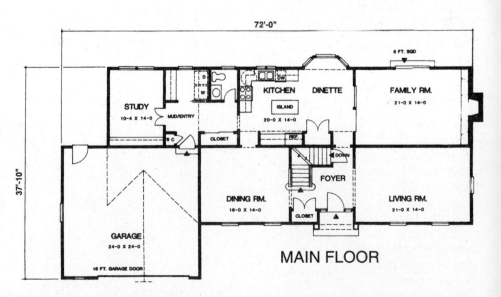

MAIN FLOOR

   ORDER BLUEPRINTS ANYTIME!
CALL TOLL-FREE 1-800-820-1283   Plan A-118-DS   **PRICES AND DETAILS**
ON PAGES 2-5

Play to Win

- You'll stack the deck of life in your favor by choosing this beautiful classy Colonial as your "home base."
- Your guests will feel secure as they stride up to the warmly lit entry and are ushered into the foyer and past arches into the living and dining rooms.
- An island cooktop in the kitchen helps you prepare culinary delights that would turn a master chef green with envy!
- After a delicious meal, you may choose to escort everyone to the family room, where a fireplace will spark invigorating conversation. Sliding glass doors open to a wide deck, if the weather allows.
- After the company has left, you may retire to the master bedroom, which boasts twin walk-in closets flanking the walk to your private bath.
- Three more bedrooms should handle all the kids or even overnight visitors.
- If you wish, a vast bonus room may be added. Imagine the possibilities here: a game or hobby room, a home office, even an artist's loft!

Plan B-95014

Bedrooms: 3+	Baths: 2½
Living Area:	
Upper floor	1,034 sq. ft.
Main floor	1,375 sq. ft.
Total Living Area:	**2,409 sq. ft.**
Bonus room (unfinished)	265 sq. ft.
Standard basement	1,375 sq. ft.
Garage and storage	534 sq. ft.
Exterior Wall Framing:	2x6
Foundation Options:	

Standard basement
(All plans can be built with your choice of foundation and framing. A generic conversion diagram is available. See order form.)

BLUEPRINT PRICE CODE:	C

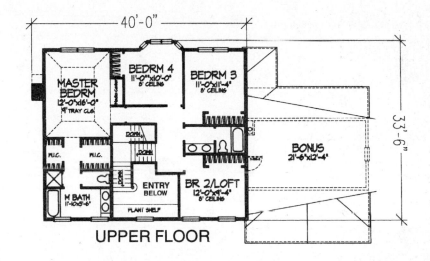

UPPER FLOOR

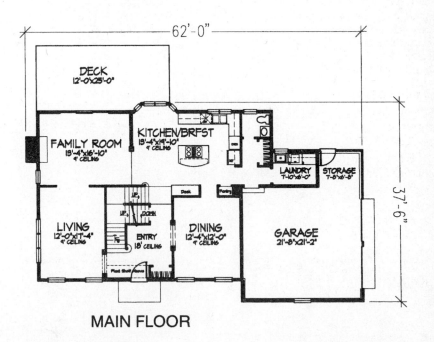

MAIN FLOOR

ORDER BLUEPRINTS ANYTIME!
CALL TOLL-FREE 1-800-820-1283

Plan B-95014

PRICES AND DETAILS
ON PAGES 2-5

363

Grand French

- A grand balcony overlooks the inviting front porch of this French-style home.
- The spectacular entry showcases two sweeping staircases. To the right, French doors introduce a study with private access to a quaint powder room.
- Beneath the stairs, a passage opens to the dramatic Great Room. Stunning windows illuminate the room, while a French door opens to a huge backyard patio with a brick planter. A handsome fireplace, an entertainment center and a cool wet bar make this room an excellent relaxation spot.
- Open to the Great Room, the spacious kitchen is joined to a cheery corner nook by a high breakfast bar. The neat

island cooktop makes meal preparation a treat, rather than a task.
- From the kitchen, the formal dining and living rooms are easily accessed.
- Occupying its own wing, the quiet master bedroom flaunts a bright sitting area with French-door patio access. Double doors lead to the master bath, where a whirlpool tub, a separate shower and dual vanities await.
- The entry's gently curved stairways lead past a fabulous landing to a bridge with French doors introducing the front balcony. Secondary bedrooms are located along the bridge, each with a walk-in closet and private bath access. The reading loft is a nice touch.
- A massive bonus room at the end of a deck is a great choice for a game room.

Plan SDG-41118	
Bedrooms: 4+	**Baths: 3½**
Living Area:	
Upper floor	1,162 sq. ft.
Main floor	2,608 sq. ft.
Bonus room	360 sq. ft.
Total Living Area:	**4,130 sq. ft.**
Garage	727 sq. ft.
Exterior Wall Framing:	2x4
Foundation Options:	

Slab
(All plans can be built with your choice of foundation and framing. A generic conversion diagram is available. See order form.)

| **BLUEPRINT PRICE CODE:** | **G** |

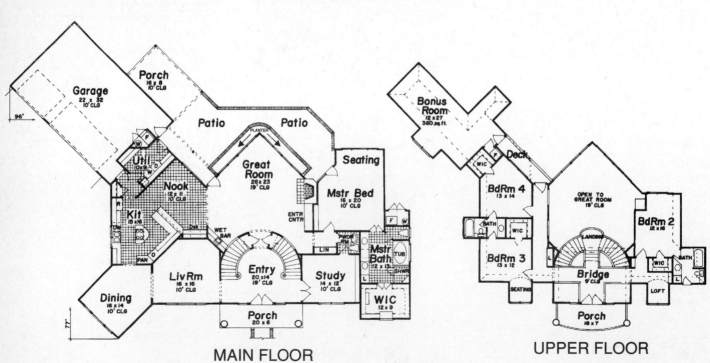

MAIN FLOOR

UPPER FLOOR

ORDER BLUEPRINTS ANYTIME!
CALL TOLL-FREE 1-800-820-1283
364

Plan SDG-41118

PRICES AND DETAILS
ON PAGES 2-5

Warm Country

- Three beautiful fireplaces exude wonderful warmth and ambience throughout this stately country home.
- A wide wraparound porch encloses the facade and frames the sidelighted entry. The 23-ft.-high foyer shows off a sweeping stairway as it flows into the formal dining room.
- On the opposite side of the foyer, a roomy study is accessed by French doors and features a handsome fireplace accented by built-in bookshelves.
- A gallery unfolds to the family room, where a French door opens to a porch.
- This porch can also be accessed from the master bedroom. The master bath boasts a large walk-in closet, a Jacuzzi tub and a separate shower.
- The kitchen has a long snack/serving bar that is also great for meal preparation. The adjacent nook sports a built-in breakfast booth and a French door to another porch.
- Along the 14-ft.-high balcony hall are three more bedrooms. One bedroom flaunts its own private bath; another has a built-in desk.
- Unless otherwise specified, all rooms are topped by 9-ft. ceilings.

Plan L-934-VSB

Bedrooms: 4+	Baths: 3½
Living Area:	
Upper floor	933 sq. ft.
Main floor	1,999 sq. ft.
Total Living Area:	**2,932 sq. ft.**
Garage	530 sq. ft.
Exterior Wall Framing:	2x4

Foundation Options:

Slab

(All plans can be built with your choice of foundation and framing. A generic conversion diagram is available. See order form.)

BLUEPRINT PRICE CODE:	D

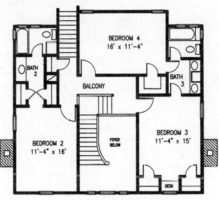

UPPER FLOOR

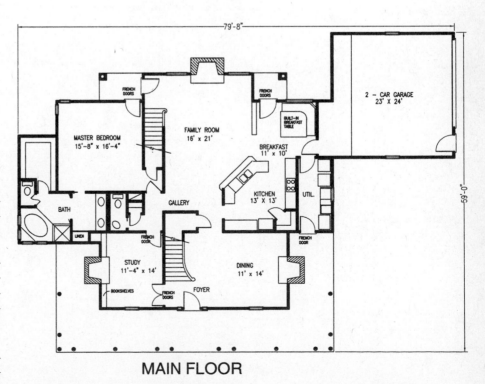

MAIN FLOOR

ORDER BLUEPRINTS ANYTIME!
CALL TOLL-FREE 1-800-820-1283

Plan L-934-VSB

PRICES AND DETAILS
ON PAGES 2-5

365

It's All Yours!

- When you want an executive home that boasts every imaginable feature, and conveys a successful image, this is it!
- Elegant front and rear porches embrace the main floor, which offers plenty of room for entertaining.
- The central living room flows from the foyer. Nearby, a cozy game room leads to an inviting pub with a cool wet bar.
- Let the kids play in the two-story family room and admire the crackling fire.
- The gourmet kitchen is situated to easily serve both the breakfast nook and the formal dining room.

- A combination library and study gives you a serene place to devour the latest best-seller or classic novel.
- Upstairs, every bedroom includes its own private bath!
- The master suite was designed with your wishes in mind. The sleeping chamber has a sitting area for times of reflection. Two big walk-in closets lead to the opulent bath, which is anchored by a corner Jacuzzi tub.
- Overnight guests may be housed in the fifth bedroom, above the main entry. Or, why not utilize the space above the garage as a private apartment for guests or workers?

Plan L-874-HD

Bedrooms: 5+		**Baths:** 5–6 full, 2 half
Living Area:		
Upper floor		2,055 sq. ft.
Main floor		2,817 sq. ft.
Total Living Area:		**4,872 sq. ft.**
Optional guest quarters		467 sq. ft.
Garage		768 sq. ft.
Exterior Wall Framing:		2x4
Foundation Options:		
Slab		

(All plans can be built with your choice of foundation and framing. A generic conversion diagram is available. See order form.)

BLUEPRINT PRICE CODE: H

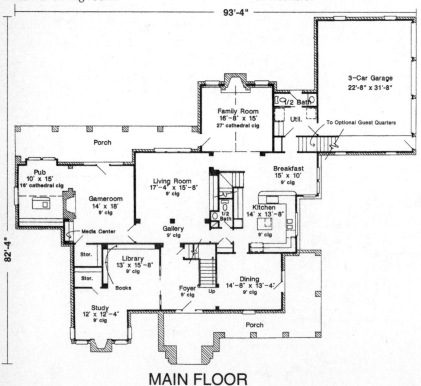

MAIN FLOOR

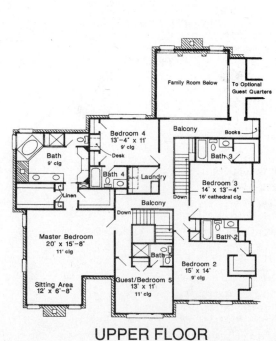

UPPER FLOOR

ORDER BLUEPRINTS ANYTIME! CALL TOLL-FREE 1-800-820-1283   Plan L-874-HD   **PRICES AND DETAILS ON PAGES 2-5**

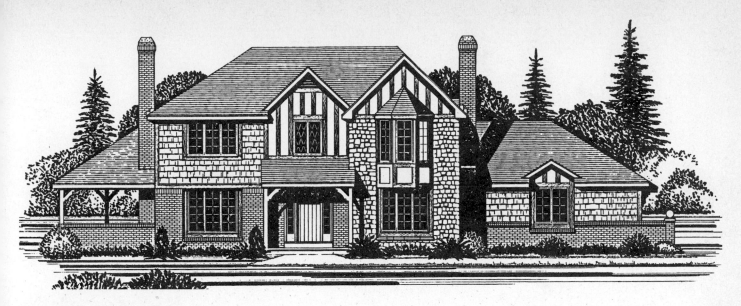

Space and Elegance

- This two-story combines elegant European exterior touches with a thoroughly modern American interior.
- The living and dining rooms are separately defined, yet can easily be used as one unit for entertaining during large holiday gatherings. The dining room offers side access to a charming covered porch.
- A huge country kitchen with a handy work island includes a tidy pantry closet and a cozy dinette, perfect for casual family meals. Step out to the backyard through sliding glass doors to enjoy a warm summer evening.
- Note the convenient utility and half-bath area in the garage entryway.
- Upstairs, the deluxe master suite invites you to relax in style. It includes a handsome bay window, a private bath and a large walk-in closet.
- Three good-sized secondary bedrooms share another full bath, completing the floor plan.

Plan A-2102-DS

Bedrooms: 4	Baths: 2½
Living Area:	
Upper floor	1,244 sq. ft.
Main floor	1,224 sq. ft.
Total Living Area:	**2,468 sq. ft.**
Standard basement	1,224 sq. ft.
Garage	484 sq. ft.
Exterior Wall Framing:	2x4

Foundation Options:

Standard basement

(All plans can be built with your choice of foundation and framing. A generic conversion diagram is available. See order form.)

BLUEPRINT PRICE CODE:	C

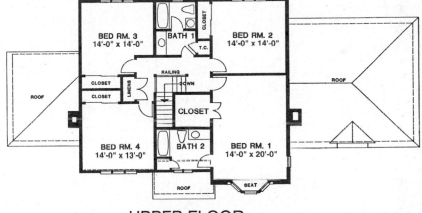

UPPER FLOOR

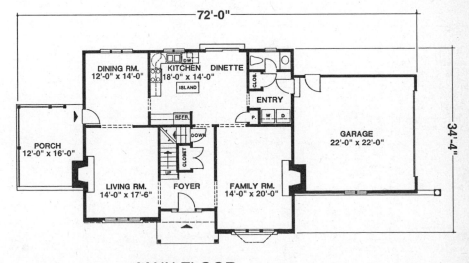

MAIN FLOOR

ORDER BLUEPRINTS ANYTIME!
CALL TOLL-FREE 1-800-820-1283

Plan A-2102-DS

PRICES AND DETAILS
ON PAGES 2-5

Soaring Gables

- Majestic arched windows and soaring gables adorn the exterior of this incredible brick home.
- Inside, the two-story entry provides breathtaking views into the open Great Room, which showcases a wet bar and a handsome fireplace flanked by picture windows and high arched transoms.
- Lovely columns define the sun-drenched dining room, which includes hutch space and a lovely bay window.
- The spacious kitchen features access to the upper floor, plus a columned island that serves the breakfast nook and adjoining hearth room.
- French doors open to the luxurious master suite. Amenities here include two huge walk-in closets and a glamorous whirlpool bath.
- A curved stairway climbs gracefully to the upper floor, which overlooks the entry below.
- Three bedrooms are housed on this level, one of which boasts a private balcony and bi-fold doors that look out over the breakfast nook.

Plan CC-3505-M

Bedrooms: 4+	Baths: 3½
Living Area:	
Upper floor	1,013 sq. ft.
Main floor	2,492 sq. ft.
Total Living Area:	**3,505 sq. ft.**
Standard basement	2,492 sq. ft.
Garage	769 sq. ft.
Exterior Wall Framing:	2x4

Foundation Options:

Standard basement
(All plans can be built with your choice of foundation and framing. A generic conversion diagram is available. See order form.)

BLUEPRINT PRICE CODE:	F

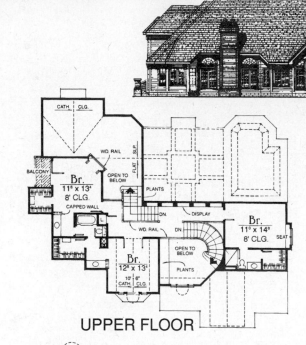

REAR VIEW

UPPER FLOOR

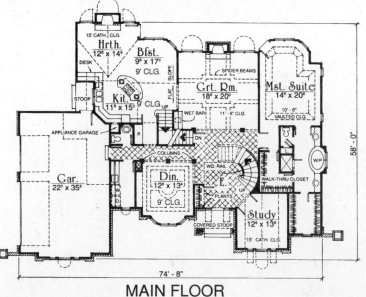

MAIN FLOOR

ORDER BLUEPRINTS ANYTIME! CALL TOLL-FREE 1-800-820-1283

Plan CC-3505-M

PRICES AND DETAILS ON PAGES 2-5

Noble
Camelot

- Noble and proud, and with plenty of pleasing personal touches, this distinctive modern-day castle will be your own private Camelot.
- Exterior charm is created by a bold brick facade, a beautiful wraparound planter and a sprinkling of keystones over the entry and several windows.
- Inside, guests will naturally be drawn to the inviting family room, which features a cozy fireplace, its very own library and access to the back porch.
- The island kitchen easily serves both the breakfast nook and the formal dining room, and is also just steps from the back porch.
- Secluded comfort is waiting in the outstanding master suite, which includes a large walk-in closet, a skylighted garden bath and access to the backyard via a pretty French door.
- Two additional bedrooms and a versatile game room make up the upper floor—the game room converts nicely to a fifth bedroom when necessary.

Plan L-2942-C

Bedrooms: 4+	Baths: 3½
Living Area:	
Upper floor	900 sq. ft.
Main floor	2,042 sq. ft.
Total Living Area:	**2,942 sq. ft.**
Exterior Wall Framing:	2x4

Foundation Options:
Slab
(All plans can be built with your choice of foundation and framing. A generic conversion diagram is available. See order form.)

BLUEPRINT PRICE CODE:	D

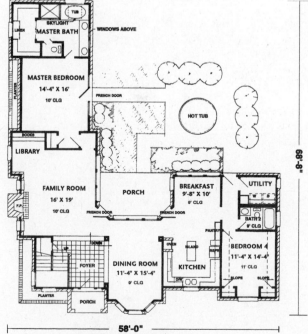

REAR VIEW

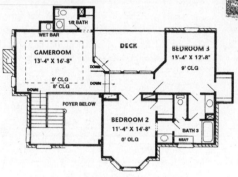

UPPER FLOOR

MAIN FLOOR

ORDER BLUEPRINTS ANYTIME!
CALL TOLL-FREE 1-800-820-1283

Plan L-2942-C

PRICES AND DETAILS
ON PAGES 2-5

369

Horizontal Distinction

- A metal roof with 4-ft. overhangs offers energy savings and distinction to this unique home. The use of concrete blocks creates a horizontal effect.
- Inside, the living room shows off a dynamic see-through fireplace shared with the family room on the opposite side. The living and dining rooms each have spectacular front window walls with decorative planters below.

- Casual areas combine at the rear of the home and overlook the expansive rear patio. The kitchen offers a convenient snack bar and a tidy pantry closet, while the breakfast nook features its own warm fireplace.
- Double doors introduce the main-floor master suite, which boasts his-and-hers walk-in closets, in addition to patio access. The lavish private bath is accented by a soothing whirlpool tub, a separate shower, dual sinks and a private toilet.
- Two good-sized bedrooms share a full bath upstairs.

Plan DW-2394	
Bedrooms: 3	**Baths: 2½**
Living Area:	
Upper floor	501 sq. ft.
Main floor	1,893 sq. ft.
Total Living Area:	**2,394 sq. ft.**
Standard basement	1,893 sq. ft.
Garage	390 sq. ft.
Exterior Wall Framing:	2x4
Foundation Options:	
Standard basement	
Crawlspace	
Slab	

(All plans can be built with your choice of foundation and framing. A generic conversion diagram is available. See order form.)

BLUEPRINT PRICE CODE:	C

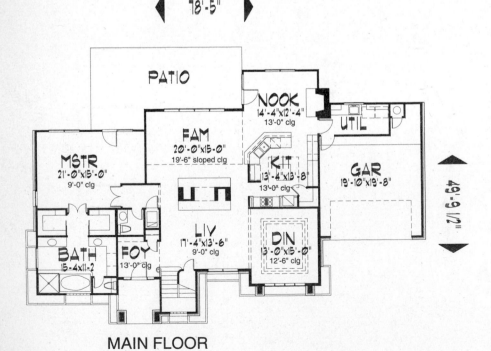

MAIN FLOOR

UPPER FLOOR

Great Family Living Areas

- The covered front porch and multi-windowed facade give this home its countrypolitan appeal and comfort.
- Inside, a wonderful kitchen, breakfast nook and family room combination makes a statement. The step-saving kitchen includes a large pantry closet, an oversized worktop island/snack bar and a built-in desk. The bay-windowed breakfast nook steps down to the vaulted family room.
- Options include a living room fireplace, and a bay window in the dining room.
- A half-bath is just off the foyer, as is a charming study.
- The upper floor features a spectacular master suite, offering a vaulted ceiling in the sleeping area, a dressing area with a walk-in closet, and a skylighted bath with a corner platform tub.
- Blueprints include details for finishing the exterior with brick or wood siding.

Plan CH-240-A

Bedrooms: 4+	Baths: 2½
Living Area:	
Upper floor	1,019 sq. ft.
Main floor	1,300 sq. ft.
Total Living Area:	**2,319 sq. ft.**
Basement	1,300 sq. ft.
Garage	384 sq. ft.
Exterior Wall Framing:	2x4

Foundation Options:

Daylight basement

Standard basement

Crawlspace

(All plans can be built with your choice of foundation and framing. A generic conversion diagram is available. See order form.)

BLUEPRINT PRICE CODE: C

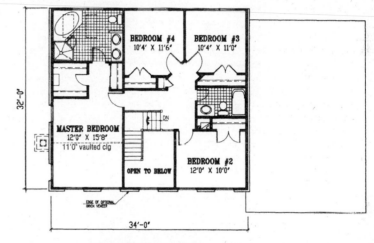

UPPER FLOOR

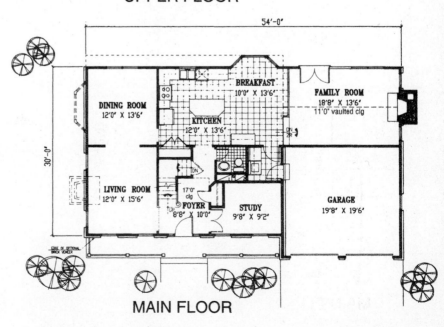

MAIN FLOOR

ORDER BLUEPRINTS ANYTIME!
CALL TOLL-FREE 1-800-820-1283

Plan CH-240-A

PRICES AND DETAILS
ON PAGES 2-5

371

Two-Story Palace

- Decorative brick borders, a columned porch and dramatic arched windows give a classy look to this magnificent two-story palace.
- The open, sidelighted entry is flanked by the formal dining and living rooms, both of which feature elegant paned-glass windows. A coat closet and a powder room are just steps away.
- The spacious family room is warmed by a fireplace and brightened by a beautiful arched window set into a high-ceilinged area.
- The well-planned kitchen, highlighted by an island worktop and a windowed sink, is centrally located to provide easy

service to both the dining room and the bayed morning room. The morning room offers access to a large, inviting backyard deck.
- A bright and heartwarming sun room also overlooks the deck, and is a perfect spot to read or just relax.
- A handy laundry/utility area is located at the entrance to the two-car garage.
- Windows surround the main-floor master suite, which boasts a luxurious bath with a garden tub, a separate shower and a dual-sink vanity. Three walk-in closets provide plenty of space for wardrobe storage.
- Ceilings in all main-floor rooms are 9 ft. high for added spaciousness.
- Upstairs, three good-sized bedrooms share a compartmentalized bath. A large and convenient attic area offers additional storage possibilities.

Plan DD-2689	
Bedrooms: 4	**Baths:** 2½
Living Area:	
Upper floor	755 sq. ft.
Main floor	1,934 sq. ft.
Total Living Area:	**2,689 sq. ft.**
Standard basement	1,934 sq. ft.
Garage	436 sq. ft.
Exterior Wall Framing:	2x4
Foundation Options:	

Standard basement
Crawlspace
Slab
(All plans can be built with your choice of foundation and framing. A generic conversion diagram is available. See order form.)

BLUEPRINT PRICE CODE:	D

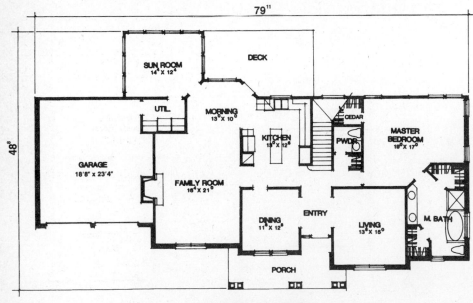

MAIN FLOOR

UPPER FLOOR

Arched Accents

- Elegant arches add drama to the covered porch of this lovely home.
- Interior arches flank the two-story-high foyer, offering eye-catching entrances to the formal dining and living rooms.
- A dramatic window-framed fireplace and a 17-ft. ceiling enhance the spacious family room. A columned archway leads into the island kitchen, which offers a convenient serving bar.
- The adjoining breakfast area features a pantry closet, open shelves and a French door to the backyard. A half-bath and a laundry room are close by.
- The ceilings in all main-floor rooms are 9 ft. high unless otherwise specified.
- Upstairs, a balcony overlooks the family room and the foyer. The master suite flaunts a 10-ft. tray ceiling, a beautiful window showpiece and a private bath with a 13-ft. vaulted ceiling and a garden tub. The bedroom may be extended to include a sitting area.
- Boasting its own dressing vanity, the rear-facing bedroom offers private access to a compartmentalized bath that also serves the two remaining bedrooms.

Plan FB-2368

Bedrooms: 4	Baths: 2½

Living Area:	
Upper floor	1,168 sq. ft.
Main floor	1,200 sq. ft.
Total Living Area:	**2,368 sq. ft.**
Daylight basement	1,200 sq. ft.
Garage	504 sq. ft.
Exterior Wall Framing:	2x4

Foundation Options:
Daylight basement
Slab
(All plans can be built with your choice of foundation and framing. A generic conversion diagram is available. See order form.)

BLUEPRINT PRICE CODE: C

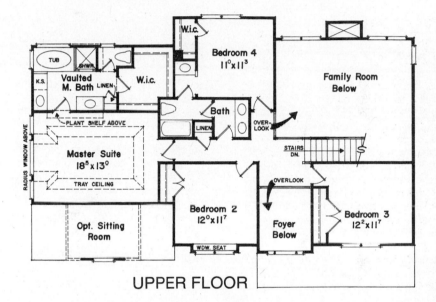

UPPER FLOOR

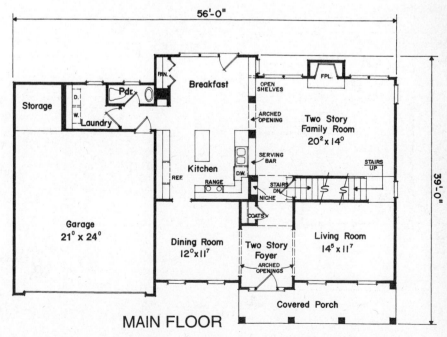

MAIN FLOOR

ORDER BLUEPRINTS ANYTIME!
CALL TOLL-FREE 1-800-820-1283

Plan FB-2368

PRICES AND DETAILS
ON PAGES 2-5

373

Estate Living

- This grand estate is as big and beautiful on the inside as it is on the outside.
- The formal dining room and parlor, each with a tall window, flank the entry's graceful curved staircase.
- The sunken family room is topped by a two-story-high ceiling and wrapped in floor-to-ceiling windows. A patio door opens to the covered porch, which features a nifty built-in barbecue.
- The island kitchen and the bright breakfast area also overlook the porch, with access through the deluxe utility room.

- The master suite has it all, including a romantic fireplace framed by bookshelves. The opulent bath offers a raised spa tub, a separate shower, his-and-hers walk-in closets and a dual-sink vanity. The neighboring bedroom, which also has a private bath, would make an ideal nursery.
- The upper floor hosts a balcony hall that provides a breathtaking view of the family room below. Each of the two bedrooms here has its own bath.
- The main floor is expanded by 10-ft. ceilings, while 9-ft. ceilings grace the upper floor.

Plan DD-4300-B	
Bedrooms: 4	**Baths: 4½**
Living Area:	
Upper floor	868 sq. ft.
Main floor	3,416 sq. ft.
Total Living Area:	**4,284 sq. ft.**
Standard basement	3,416 sq. ft.
Garage and storage	633 sq. ft.
Exterior Wall Framing:	2x4 or 2x6
Foundation Options:	
Standard basement	
Crawlspace	
Slab	

(All plans can be built with your choice of foundation and framing. A generic conversion diagram is available. See order form.)

BLUEPRINT PRICE CODE: G

MAIN FLOOR

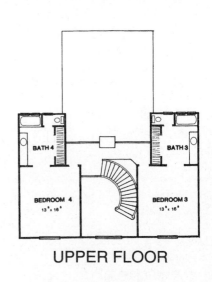

UPPER FLOOR

ORDER BLUEPRINTS ANYTIME!
CALL TOLL-FREE 1-800-820-1283

Plan DD-4300-B

PRICES AND DETAILS
ON PAGES 2-5

Four Fabulous Bedroom Suites

- Extravagant arches and windows complement this distinctive home.
- The spectacular two-story entry shows off an elegant curved stairway and dramatic columns that introduce the sunken living room. This spacious room boasts a 10-ft. ceiling, a beautiful bow window, a fireplace and a wonderful wet bar.
- Open railings allow a view into the formal dining room across the hall. A built-in hutch, a nearby serving center and a bow window accent this room.
- The family room is oriented to the back of the home, integrated with the kitchen and the breakfast room. A large snack bar and a fireplace are highlights here.
- French doors open to a quiet den near the master suite, which is also entered through double doors. The plush suite offers a private bath with an oval whirlpool tub, a toilet room, a huge walk-in closet and sliding glass doors to the covered back porch.
- Two stairways access the upper floor, which hosts three secondary bedrooms, each with a walk-in closet and a full private bath.

Plan DBI-2218

Bedrooms: 4+	Baths: 4½
Living Area:	
Upper floor	1,072 sq. ft.
Main floor	2,617 sq. ft.
Total Living Area:	**3,689 sq. ft.**
Standard basement	2,617 sq. ft.
Garage	1,035 sq. ft.
Exterior Wall Framing:	2x4

Foundation Options:

Standard basement

(All plans can be built with your choice of foundation and framing. A generic conversion diagram is available. See order form.)

BLUEPRINT PRICE CODE:	F

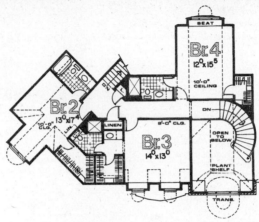

UPPER FLOOR

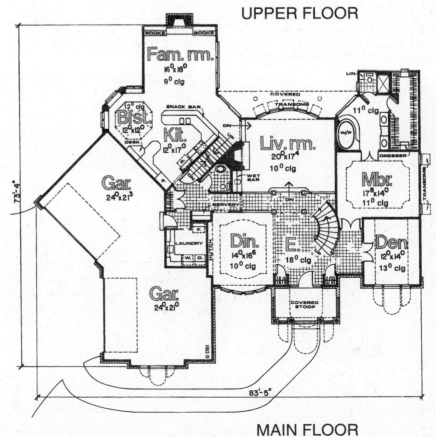

MAIN FLOOR

ORDER BLUEPRINTS ANYTIME!
CALL TOLL-FREE 1-800-820-1283

Plan DBI-2218

PRICES AND DETAILS
ON PAGES 2-5

375

Fantastic Front Entry

- A fantastic arched window presides over the 18-ft.-high entry of this two-story, giving guests a bright welcome.
- The spacious living room is separated from the dining room by a pair of boxed columns with built-in shelves.
- The kitchen offers a walk-in pantry, a serving bar and a sunny breakfast room with a French door to the backyard.
- A boxed column accents the entry to the 18-ft. vaulted family room, which boasts a dramatic window bank and an inviting fireplace.
- The main-floor den is easily converted into an extra bedroom or guest room.
- The master suite has a 10-ft. tray ceiling, a huge walk-in closet and decorative plant shelves. The 15½-ft. vaulted bath features an oval tub and two vanities, one with knee space.
- Three additional bedrooms share another full bath near the second stairway to the main floor.

Plan FB-2680

Bedrooms: 4+	Baths: 3
Living Area:	
Upper floor	1,256 sq. ft.
Main floor	1,424 sq. ft.
Total Living Area:	**2,680 sq. ft.**
Daylight basement	1,424 sq. ft.
Garage	496 sq. ft.
Exterior Wall Framing:	2x4

Foundation Options:
Daylight basement
(All plans can be built with your choice of foundation and framing. A generic conversion diagram is available. See order form.)

BLUEPRINT PRICE CODE: D

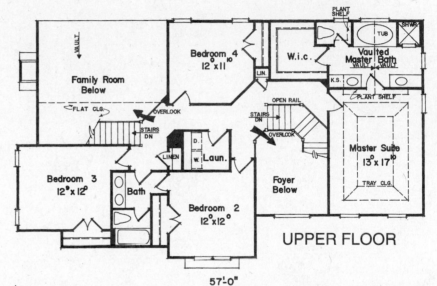

UPPER FLOOR

57'-0"

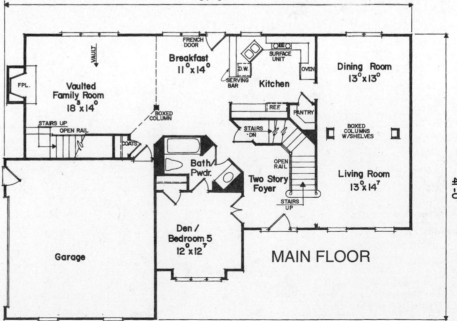

MAIN FLOOR

41'-0"

ORDER BLUEPRINTS ANYTIME!
CALL TOLL-FREE 1-800-820-1283

Plan FB-2680

PRICES AND DETAILS ON PAGES 2-5

Elegant Arches

- Gracious arched windows and an entry portico create rhythm and style for this home's brick-clad exterior.
- An elegant curved staircase lends interest to the raised, two-story foyer.
- Two steps down to the left of the foyer lies the living room, with its dramatic 14-ft. cathedral ceiling. Lovely columns define the adjoining dining room. A cozy fireplace warms the entire area.
- The island kitchen overlooks the bayed breakfast room and offers a handy pass-through to the adjoining family room.
- The two-story-high family room boasts a second fireplace and a wall of windows topped by large transoms.
- The quiet master bedroom features a bay window and an 11-ft. sloped ceiling. The master bath shows off a garden tub and a separate shower.
- A sizable deck is accessible from both the breakfast room and the master suite.
- Three more bedrooms and two baths share the upper floor. A balcony bridge overlooks the foyer and family room.

Plan DD-3639

Bedrooms: 4+	Baths: 3½
Living Area:	
Upper floor	868 sq. ft.
Main floor	2,771 sq. ft.
Total Living Area:	**3,639 sq. ft.**
Standard basement	2,771 sq. ft.
Garage	790 sq. ft.
Exterior Wall Framing:	2x6

Foundation Options:
Standard basement
Crawlspace
Slab
(All plans can be built with your choice of foundation and framing. A generic conversion diagram is available. See order form.)

BLUEPRINT PRICE CODE: F

UPPER FLOOR

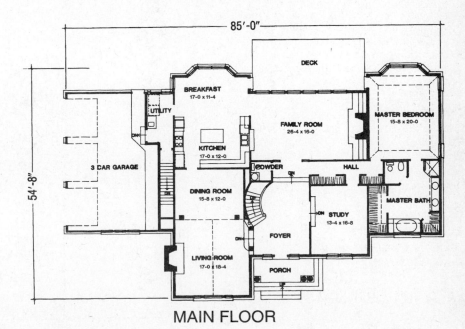

MAIN FLOOR

ORDER BLUEPRINTS ANYTIME!
CALL TOLL-FREE 1-800-820-1283

Plan DD-3639

PRICES AND DETAILS
ON PAGES 2-5

377

Stately and Roomy

- The exquisite exterior of this two-story home opens to a very roomy interior.
- The magnificent two-story-high foyer shows off a curved, open-railed stairway to the upper floor and opens to a study on the right and the formal living areas on the left.
- The spacious living room flows into a formal dining room that overlooks the outdoors through a lovely bay window.
- A large work island and snack counter sit at the center of the open kitchen and breakfast room. An oversized pantry closet, a powder room and a laundry room are all close at hand.
- Adjoining the breakfast room is the large sunken family room, featuring a 12-ft.-high vaulted ceiling, a cozy fireplace and outdoor access.
- The upper floor includes a stunning master bedroom with an 11-ft. vaulted ceiling and a luxurious private bath.
- Three additional bedrooms share a second full bath.

Plan CH-280-A

Bedrooms: 4+	Baths: 2½
Living Area:	
Upper floor	1,262 sq. ft.
Main floor	1,797 sq. ft.
Total Living Area:	**3,059 sq. ft.**
Basement	1,797 sq. ft.
Garage	462 sq. ft.
Exterior Wall Framing:	2x4

Foundation Options:

Daylight basement

Standard basement

Crawlspace

(All plans can be built with your choice of foundation and framing. A generic conversion diagram is available. See order form.)

BLUEPRINT PRICE CODE: E

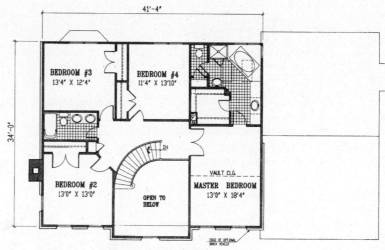

UPPER FLOOR

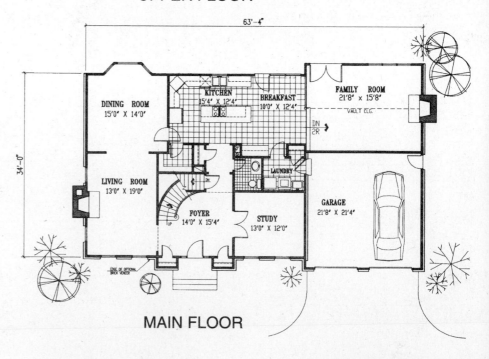

MAIN FLOOR

ORDER BLUEPRINTS ANYTIME! CALL TOLL-FREE 1-800-820-1283

Plan CH-280-A

PRICES AND DETAILS ON PAGES 2-5

Farmhouse with Victorian Flair

- A wraparound porch, detailed trim and fishscale shingles lend a Victorian flair to this charming farmhouse design.
- The gracious foyer, featuring two decorative niches, is flanked by the living room and the formal dining room.
- Built-in bookshelves frame a gorgeous fireplace in the expansive family room. Step out to the back deck to enjoy a warm summer evening.
- The walk-through kitchen is perfectly placed to access both the formal dining room and the bayed breakfast nook.
- All main-floor rooms have 9-ft. ceilings for added spaciousness.
- Upstairs, the master bedroom flaunts a stunning private bath with a pleasing garden tub, a separate shower, a planter and dual sinks.
- Two huge secondary bedrooms share a full bath, completing the floor plan.

Plan C-8865-S

Bedrooms: 3	Baths: 2½
Living Area:	
Upper floor	1,196 sq. ft.
Main floor	1,366 sq. ft.
Total Living Area:	**2,562 sq. ft.**
Basement	1,250 sq. ft.
Garage	455 sq. ft.
Exterior Wall Framing:	2x4

Foundation Options:

Daylight basement

Standard basement

Crawlspace

(All plans can be built with your choice of foundation and framing. A generic conversion diagram is available. See order form.)

BLUEPRINT PRICE CODE:	D

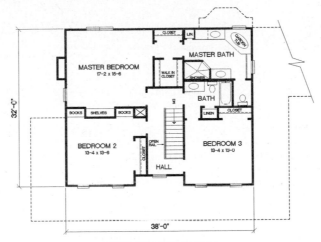

UPPER FLOOR

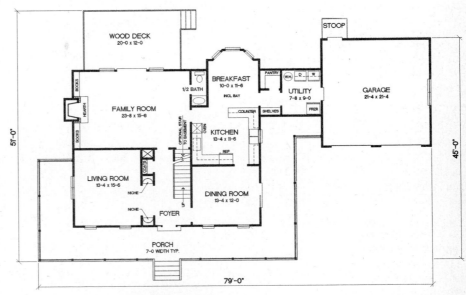

MAIN FLOOR

ORDER BLUEPRINTS ANYTIME!
CALL TOLL-FREE 1-800-820-1283

Plan C-8865-S

PRICES AND DETAILS
ON PAGES 2-5

379

Brimming with Charm

- This charming luxury residence is brimming with all the right stuff for today's busy executive family!
- Exterior features like half-round windows, soldier coursing, shake siding and multiple repeated gables hint at the wonders within.
- From the foyer, the living areas unfold beautifully. To the left is the sunken living room, which boasts a fireplace and overlooks one of several lovely outdoor planters.
- A second gathering place is the huge sunken family room, where you'll find a corner fireplace, two built-in plant shelves and access to a patio in back.
- Just up the stairs, in the nice-sized library, you'll find a third fireplace.
- A wet bar and the island kitchen are ready for formal entertaining in the grand dining room.
- The incredible master suite offers a sitting area, an exercise area, a private deck, dual walk-in closets and a secluded bath with a whirlpool tub.

Plan B-87137	
Bedrooms: 4	**Baths:** 3 full, 2 half
Living Area:	
Upper floor	1,244 sq. ft.
Main floor	3,798 sq. ft.
Total Living Area:	**5,042 sq. ft.**
Standard basement	3,600 sq. ft.
Garage	590 sq. ft.
Exterior Wall Framing:	2x4

Foundation Options:

Standard basement

(All plans can be built with your choice of foundation and framing. A generic conversion diagram is available. See order form.)

BLUEPRINT PRICE CODE:	I

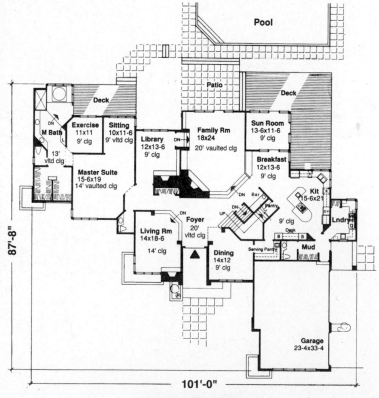

MAIN FLOOR

UPPER FLOOR

ORDER BLUEPRINTS ANYTIME!
CALL TOLL-FREE 1-800-820-1283

Plan B-87137

PRICES AND DETAILS
ON PAGES 2-5

Tall Two-Story

- This gorgeous two-story is introduced by a barrel-vaulted entry and supporting columns. Inside, a spectacular curved staircase leads to a balcony overlook.
- Off the two-story-high foyer, a library with a 16-ft.-high vaulted ceiling is perfect for reading or study.
- A formal dining room opposite the library opens to the fabulous island kitchen. The kitchen offers an angled serving bar to the bayed breakfast area and adjoining living room.
- The spacious living room, with an 18-ft. vaulted ceiling, opens to a backyard patio. A fireplace flanked by built-in shelving warms the whole family area.
- The master bedroom boasts a 10-ft. gambrel ceiling, a sunny bay window and patio access. The spacious master bath offers his-and-hers walk-in closets, an oval tub and a separate shower.
- A second stairway near the utility room leads to the upper floor, where there are three more bedrooms, two baths and a bonus room above the garage. The bonus room could be finished as a game room, a media center or a hobby area.

Plan DD-3125

Bedrooms: 4+	Baths: 3½
Living Area:	
Upper floor	982 sq. ft.
Main floor	2,147 sq. ft.
Total Living Area:	**3,129 sq. ft.**
Unfinished Bonus	196 sq. ft.
Standard basement	1,996 sq. ft.
Garage	771 sq. ft.
Exterior Wall Framing:	2x4

Foundation Options:
Standard basement
Crawlspace
Slab
(All plans can be built with your choice of foundation and framing. A generic conversion diagram is available. See order form.)

BLUEPRINT PRICE CODE: E

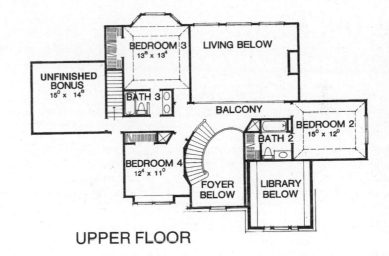

UPPER FLOOR

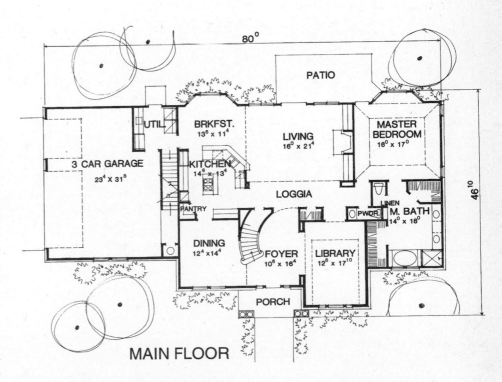

MAIN FLOOR

ORDER BLUEPRINTS ANYTIME!
CALL TOLL-FREE 1-800-820-1283

Plan DD-3125

PRICES AND DETAILS ON PAGES 2-5

Five-Bedroom Traditional

- This sophisticated traditional home makes a striking statement both inside and out.
- The dramatic two-story foyer is flanked by the formal living spaces. The private dining room overlooks the front porch, while the spacious living room has outdoor views on two sides.
- A U-shaped kitchen with a snack bar, a sunny dinette area and a large family room flow together at the back of the home. Sliding glass doors in the dinette access the backyard terrace.
- The second floor has five roomy bedrooms and two skylighted baths. The luxurious master suite has a dressing area, a huge walk-in closet and a high ceiling with a beautiful arched window. The private bath offers dual sinks and a whirlpool tub.

Plan AHP-9392

Bedrooms: 5	Baths: 2½
Living Area:	
Upper floor	1,223 sq. ft.
Main floor	1,193 sq. ft.
Total Living Area:	**2,416 sq. ft.**
Standard basement	1,130 sq. ft.
Garage	509 sq. ft.
Storage	65 sq. ft.
Exterior Wall Framing:	2x4 or 2x6

Foundation Options:
Standard basement
Crawlspace
Slab
(All plans can be built with your choice of foundation and framing. A generic conversion diagram is available. See order form.)

BLUEPRINT PRICE CODE:	C

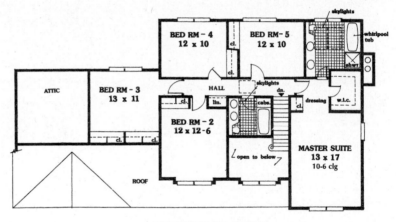

UPPER FLOOR

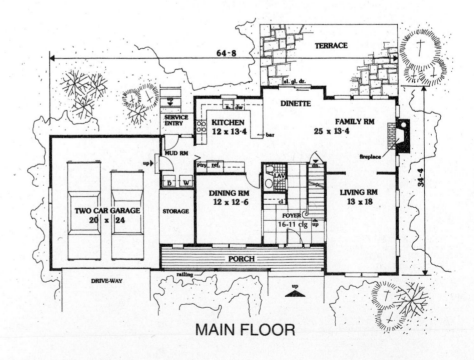

MAIN FLOOR

ORDER BLUEPRINTS ANYTIME!
CALL TOLL-FREE 1-800-820-1283

Plan AHP-9392

PRICES AND DETAILS
ON PAGES 2-5

Fun for the Whole Family

- This home will serve as the backdrop for years of fun for your family. An idyllic porch offers a nice spot to relax.
- Inside, the foyer leads into the secluded living room. With a beautiful bayed dining room nearby, this space is perfect for formal affairs.
- The walk-through kitchen is well suited for preparing bountiful holiday feasts. A 14½-ft. vaulted ceiling and a sunny bay window brighten the breakfast area.
- A serving bar joins the breakfast area to the family room, where a handy built-in desk allows students to finish homework under a parent's eye. You'll also love the adjacent screened porch.
- The master suite is a great retreat at day's end. The master bath's garden tub gives you the treatment you deserve.
- Upstairs, a sitting area is the ideal place for a computer or reading nook.

Plan C-8409

Bedrooms: 4	Baths: 2½
Living Area:	
Upper floor	1,063 sq. ft.
Main floor	2,005 sq. ft.
Total Living Area:	**3,068 sq. ft.**
Storage room	205 sq. ft.
Screened porch	381 sq. ft.
Daylight basement	1,653 sq. ft.
Garage	452 sq. ft.
Exterior Wall Framing:	2x4

Foundation Options:

Daylight basement

Crawlspace

Slab

(All plans can be built with your choice of foundation and framing. A generic conversion diagram is available. See order form.)

BLUEPRINT PRICE CODE: E

UPPER FLOOR

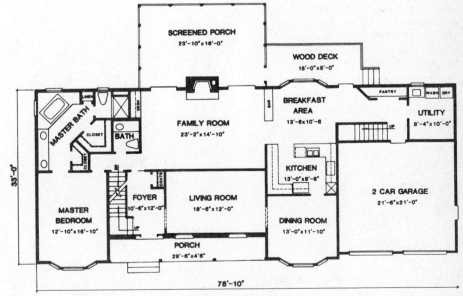

MAIN FLOOR

ORDER BLUEPRINTS ANYTIME!
CALL TOLL-FREE 1-800-820-1283

Plan C-8409

PRICES AND DETAILS
ON PAGES 2-5

383

Live in Luxury

- This luxurious home is introduced by a striking facade. Arched windows and a majestic entry accent the stucco finish. An alternate brick exterior is included with the blueprints.
- A graceful curved stairway is showcased in the grand two-story foyer, which is flanked by the formal rooms. The spacious living room flaunts an inviting fireplace. Double doors at the rear close off the adjoining study, which has functional built-in shelves.
- The central family room boasts a second fireplace and two sets of French doors that open to the backyard.
- A full pantry and a range island with an eating bar offer extra storage and work space in the roomy kitchen. The attached breakfast room is dramatically surrounded by windows.
- The spacious master suite and three secondary bedrooms are located on the upper floor. The master bedroom offers dual walk-in closets and a skylighted private bath with twin vanities and an oval spa tub. A second bath services the secondary bedrooms. The laundry room is conveniently located on the upper floor as well.

Plan CH-360-A

Bedrooms: 4	Baths: 2½
Living Area:	
Upper floor	1,354 sq. ft.
Main floor	1,616 sq. ft.
Total Living Area:	**2,970 sq. ft.**
Basement	1,616 sq. ft.
Garage	462 sq. ft.
Exterior Wall Framing:	2x4

Foundation Options:

Daylight basement
Standard basement
Crawlspace

(All plans can be built with your choice of foundation and framing. A generic conversion diagram is available. See order form.)

BLUEPRINT PRICE CODE: **D**

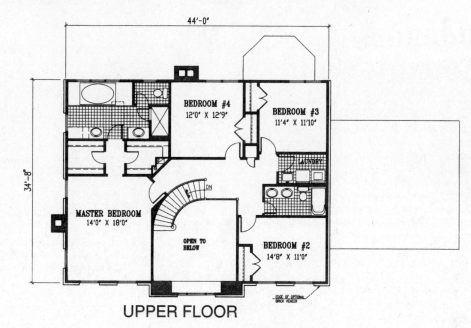

UPPER FLOOR

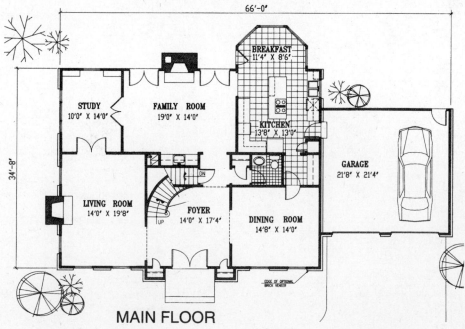

MAIN FLOOR

ORDER BLUEPRINTS ANYTIME!
CALL TOLL-FREE 1-800-820-1283

Plan CH-360-A

PRICES AND DETAILS
ON PAGES 2-5

Stunning Country-Style

- A lovely front porch that encases bay windows provides a friendly welcome to this stunning country-style home.
- Inside, the main living areas revolve around the large country kitchen and dinette, complete with an island worktop, a roomy built-in desk and access to a backyard deck.
- A raised-hearth fireplace, French doors and a 12-ft., 4-in. cathedral ceiling highlight the casual family room.
- The formal dining room is open to the living room and features an inviting window seat and a tray ceiling. A French door in the bay-windowed living room opens to the relaxing porch.
- A quiet den and a large laundry area/mudroom complete the main floor.
- The upper floor showcases a super master suite with a bay window, an 11-ft., 8-in. tray ceiling, two walk-in closets and a private bath with a garden tub and its own dramatic ceiling.
- Three additional bedrooms share a full bath designed for multiple users.

Plan A-538-R

Bedrooms: 4+	Baths: 2½
Living Area:	
Upper floor	1,384 sq. ft.
Main floor	1,755 sq. ft.
Total Living Area:	**3,139 sq. ft.**
Standard basement	1,728 sq. ft.
Garage	576 sq. ft.
Exterior Wall Framing:	2x4

Foundation Options:

Standard basement

(All plans can be built with your choice of foundation and framing. A generic conversion diagram is available. See order form.)

BLUEPRINT PRICE CODE:	E

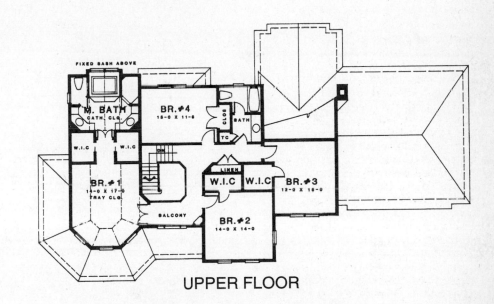

UPPER FLOOR

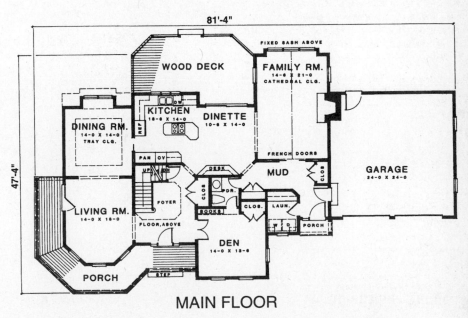

MAIN FLOOR

ORDER BLUEPRINTS ANYTIME!
CALL TOLL-FREE 1-800-820-1283

Plan A-538-R

PRICES AND DETAILS
ON PAGES 2-5

385

Time-Tested Traditional

- Multi-paned windows, shutters, lap siding and a gracious entrance combine in this home to create a time-tested traditional design.
- The sidelighted foyer is flanked by a charming study to the left and the formal dining room to the right.
- A raised-hearth fireplace and double doors that access a large rear patio highlight the spacious living room.
- Neatly tucked between the formal and casual eating areas, the U-shaped kitchen is a model for efficiency. The adjoining breakfast nook is a perfect spot to begin the day.
- Upstairs, the deluxe master bedroom unfolds in splendor. The private bath boasts an 11-ft. vaulted ceiling, a garden tub, a separate shower, a roomy walk-in closet and a dual-sink vanity.
- Two additional bedrooms are generously sized, and share a full bath.

Plan C-8350

Bedrooms: 3+	Baths: 2½
Living Area:	
Upper floor	1,146 sq. ft.
Main floor	1,214 sq. ft.
Total Living Area:	**2,360 sq. ft.**
Daylight basement	1,214 sq. ft.
Garage	452 sq. ft.
Storage	68 sq. ft.
Exterior Wall Framing:	2x4

Foundation Options:
Daylight basement
Crawlspace
(All plans can be built with your choice of foundation and framing. A generic conversion diagram is available. See order form.)

BLUEPRINT PRICE CODE:	C

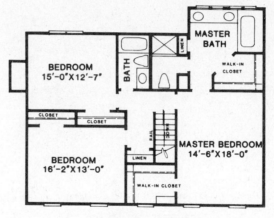

UPPER FLOOR

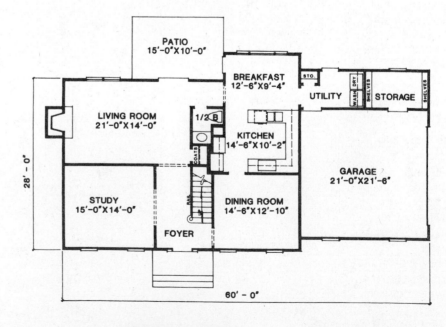

MAIN FLOOR

ORDER BLUEPRINTS ANYTIME!
CALL TOLL-FREE 1-800-820-1283

Plan C-8350

PRICES AND DETAILS
ON PAGES 2-5

Classic Cape

- Staggered exterior rooflines and distinguished interior ceilings add character to this spacious two-story.
- A 15-ft. vaulted foyer soars to the upper level. Its central location offers access to the 11-ft. tray-ceilinged living room, the formal dining room, a versatile den with an 11-ft. tray ceiling, and informal living areas to the rear of the home.
- The sunny dinette, the U-shaped kitchen and the large family room open to each other, creating a comfortable space for casual times. The family room features a charming fireplace, a box-beam ceiling and a cozy boxed-out window. The dinette's sliding glass doors open to a wood deck.
- A handy laundry room and a half-bath are tucked between the kitchen and the three-car garage.
- Two bedrooms and a bath share the upper level with the large master suite, which boasts a huge walk-in closet and a private bath with a garden whirlpool tub, a separate shower, twin sinks and a compartmentalized toilet.

Plan A-2231-DS

Bedrooms: 3	Baths: 2½
Living Area:	
Upper floor	1,086 sq. ft.
Main floor	1,600 sq. ft.
Total Living Area:	**2,686 sq. ft.**
Standard Basement	1,600 sq. ft.
Garage	768 sq. ft.
Exterior Wall Framing:	2x6

Foundation Options:

Standard basement
(All plans can be built with your choice of foundation and framing. A generic conversion diagram is available. See order form.)

BLUEPRINT PRICE CODE:	D

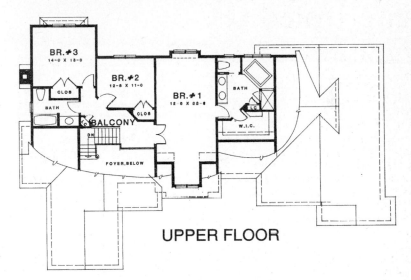

UPPER FLOOR

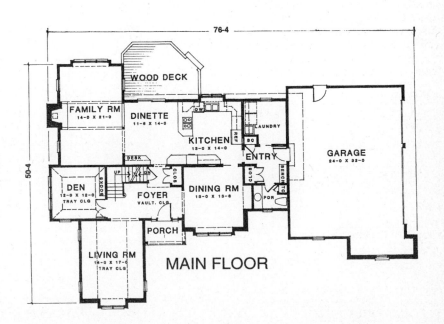

MAIN FLOOR

ORDER BLUEPRINTS ANYTIME!
CALL TOLL-FREE 1-800-820-1283

Plan A-2231-DS

**PRICES AND DETAILS
ON PAGES 2-5**

387

Contemporary Colonial

- A Palladian window and a half-round window above the entry door give this Colonial a new look. Inside, the design maximizes space while creating an open, airy atmosphere.
- The two-story-high foyer flows between the formal areas at the front of the home. Straight ahead, the exciting family room features a built-in wet bar and a fireplace framed by French doors.
- A bay window brightens the adjoining breakfast nook and kitchen. An angled counter looks to the nook and the family room, keeping the cook in touch with the family activities.
- The four bedrooms on the upper floor include a luxurious master suite with an 11-ft. vaulted ceiling and a skylighted bathroom. The upper-floor laundry also makes this a great family home.
- The basement plan (not shown) has room for an optional den or bedroom, a recreation room with a fireplace, a storage room and a utility area.

Plan CH-320-A

Bedrooms: 4+	Baths: 3
Living Area:	
Upper floor	1,164 sq. ft.
Main floor	1,293 sq. ft.
Total Living Area:	**2,457 sq. ft.**
Basement	1,293 sq. ft.
Garage	462 sq. ft.
Exterior Wall Framing:	2x4

Foundation Options:

Daylight basement

Standard basement

Crawlspace

(All plans can be built with your choice of foundation and framing. A generic conversion diagram is available. See order form.)

BLUEPRINT PRICE CODE: C

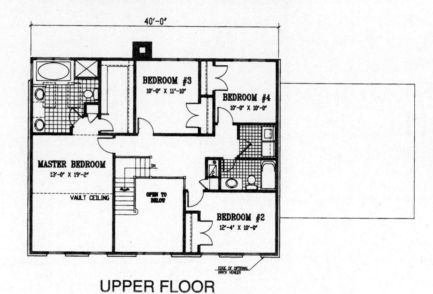

UPPER FLOOR

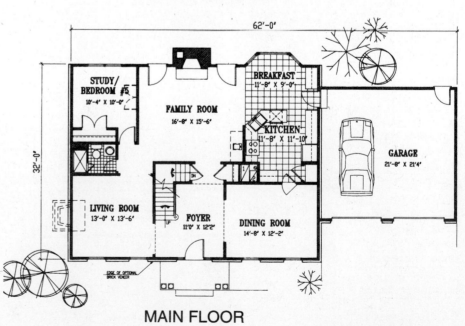

MAIN FLOOR

ORDER BLUEPRINTS ANYTIME!
CALL TOLL-FREE 1-800-820-1283

Plan CH-320-A

PRICES AND DETAILS
ON PAGES 2-5

Traditional Elegance

- This home's stately traditional exterior is enhanced by a stunning two-story entry and brick with quoin corner details.
- The formal living and dining rooms flank the entry foyer.
- The informal living areas face the rear yard and include an island kitchen, a dinette bay and a sunken family room with a fireplace.
- The main floor also includes a handy mudroom that opens to the garage and flows back to a laundry room, a powder room and a sunny den or fifth bedroom.
- The upper floor houses four spacious bedrooms and two full baths, including a lavish master bath with a corner spa tub and a separate shower.

Plan A-2230-DS

Bedrooms: 4+	Baths: 2½
Living Area:	
Upper floor	1,455 sq. ft.
Main floor	1,692 sq. ft.
Total Living Area:	**3,147 sq. ft.**
Standard basement	1,692 sq. ft.
Garage	484 sq. ft.
Exterior Wall Framing:	2x6

Foundation Options:

Standard basement

(All plans can be built with your choice of foundation and framing. A generic conversion diagram is available. See order form.)

BLUEPRINT PRICE CODE:	E

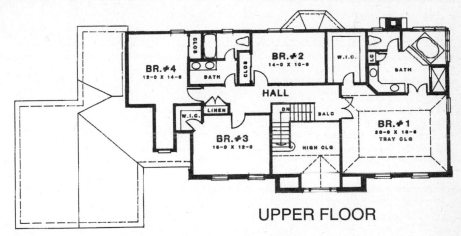

UPPER FLOOR

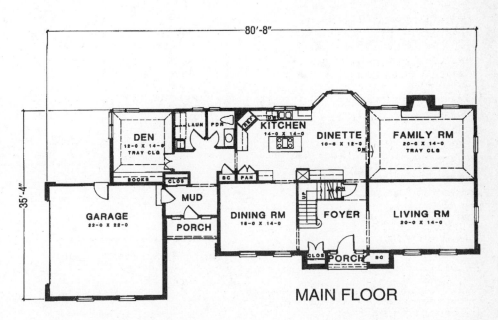

MAIN FLOOR

ORDER BLUEPRINTS ANYTIME!
CALL TOLL-FREE 1-800-820-1283

Plan A-2230-DS

PRICES AND DETAILS
ON PAGES 2-5

389

Grand Colonial Home

- This grand Colonial home boasts a porch entry framed by bay windows and gable towers.
- The two-story foyer flows to the dining room on the left and adjoins the bayed living room on the right, with its warm fireplace and flanking windows.
- At the rear, the family room features a 17-ft. ceiling, a media wall, a bar and terrace access through French doors.
- Connected to the family room is a high-tech kitchen with an island work area, a pantry, a work desk and a circular dinette.
- A private terrace, a romantic fireplace, a huge walk-in closet and a lavish bath with a whirlpool tub are featured in the main-floor master suite.
- Three bedrooms and two full baths share the upper floor.

Plan AHP-9120

Bedrooms: 4	Baths: 3½
Living Area:	
Upper floor	776 sq. ft.
Main floor	1,551 sq. ft.
Total Living Area:	**2,327 sq. ft.**
Standard basement	1,580 sq. ft.
Garage	440 sq. ft.
Exterior Wall Framing:	2x4 or 2x6

Foundation Options:
Standard basement
Crawlspace
Slab
(All plans can be built with your choice of foundation and framing. A generic conversion diagram is available. See order form.)

BLUEPRINT PRICE CODE:	C

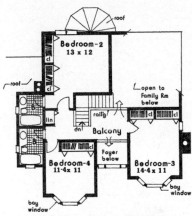

UPPER FLOOR

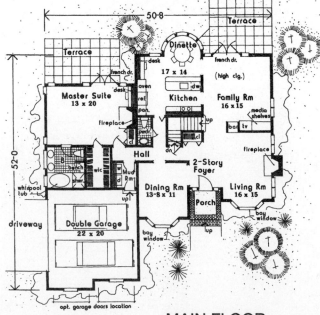

MAIN FLOOR

ORDER BLUEPRINTS ANYTIME!
CALL TOLL-FREE 1-800-820-1283

Plan AHP-9120

PRICES AND DETAILS
ON PAGES 2-5

European Elegance

- This traditional home's steep roof, stucco trim and copper-topped bay windows present an elegant, European-style appearance.
- A handsome bay-windowed library and a formal dining room flank the foyer.
- The central family room features a high ceiling, an exciting fireplace and large windows that offer a view of the backyard patio.
- An oversized bay window encircles the sunny morning room and overlooks the patio. The adjoining island kitchen boasts a pantry closet, lots of counter space and a nearby laundry room.
- Another bay window accents the master bedroom, which includes a private garden bath.
- A versatile den and a bonus room share the upper floor with two additional bedrooms and a full bath.

Plan DD-2703	
Bedrooms: 4+	**Baths:** 3
Living Area:	
Upper floor	728 sq. ft.
Main floor	2,024 sq. ft.
Bonus room	262 sq. ft.
Total Living Area:	**3,014 sq. ft.**
Standard basement	2,024 sq. ft.
Garage	583 sq. ft.
Exterior Wall Framing:	2x4

Foundation Options:

Standard basement

Crawlspace

Slab

(All plans can be built with your choice of foundation and framing. A generic conversion diagram is available. See order form.)

BLUEPRINT PRICE CODE:	E

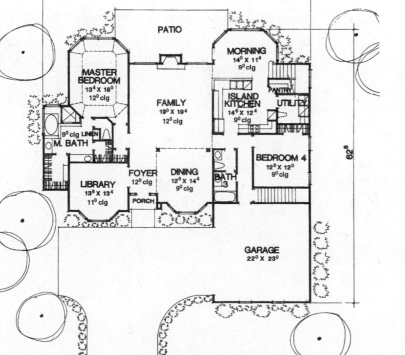

MAIN FLOOR

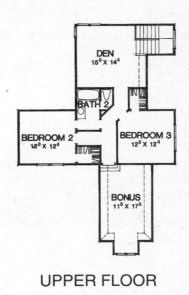

UPPER FLOOR

ORDER BLUEPRINTS ANYTIME!
CALL TOLL-FREE 1-800-820-1283

Plan DD-2703

PRICES AND DETAILS
ON PAGES 2-5

391

Great Areas for Family Living

- This home holds lots of appeal both inside and out. Charming window treatments and brick accents mark the exterior. Inside, great family living areas are the rule.
- Open to the adjoining kitchen and dinette, the huge family room is highlighted by an inviting fireplace and a wide bay window.
- The dinette offers a built-in desk, while the kitchen includes an island cooktop/snack counter, a windowed sink and a large pantry closet.
- The formal living and dining areas are natural extensions of the less formal spaces. Both rooms boast sparkling bay windows, and the living room is enhanced by a 16-ft. cathedral ceiling.
- The second level hosts four generously sized bedrooms and two baths. The master bedroom is a real showpiece, with a 10½-ft. cathedral ceiling and a sumptuous bath.

Plan A-2216-DS

Bedrooms: 4	Baths: 2½
Living Area:	
Upper floor	1,126 sq. ft.
Main floor	1,440 sq. ft.
Total Living Area:	**2,566 sq. ft.**
Standard basement	1,440 sq. ft.
Garage	528 sq. ft.
Exterior Wall Framing:	2x6

Foundation Options:

Standard basement

(All plans can be built with your choice of foundation and framing. A generic conversion diagram is available. See order form.)

BLUEPRINT PRICE CODE:	D

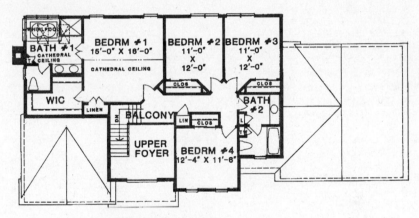

UPPER FLOOR

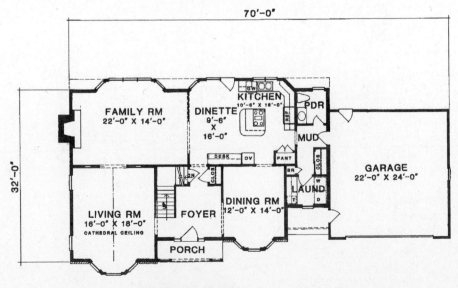

MAIN FLOOR

ORDER BLUEPRINTS ANYTIME! CALL TOLL-FREE 1-800-820-1283   Plan A-2216-DS   **PRICES AND DETAILS ON PAGES 2-5**

Sprawling French Country

- A hip roof and gable accents give this sprawling home a country, French look.
- To the left of the entry, the formal dining room is illuminated with a tall arched window arrangement.
- The spectacular living room stretches from the entry of the home to the rear. A vaulted ceiling in this expansive space rises to 19 ft., and windows at both ends offer light and a nice breeze.
- Angled walls add interest to the roomy informal areas, which overlook the covered lanai. The island kitchen opens to the adjoining morning room and the sunny family room.
- The spacious main-floor master suite is highlighted by a 13-ft. vaulted ceiling and a bayed sitting area. The master bath features dual walk-in closets, a large spa tub and a separate shower.
- Three extra bedrooms and two more baths share the upper level.

Plan DD-2889

Bedrooms: 4	Baths: 3½
Living Area:	
Upper floor	819 sq. ft.
Main floor	2,111 sq. ft.
Total Living Area:	**2,930 sq. ft.**
Standard basement	2,111 sq. ft.
Garage	622 sq. ft.
Exterior Wall Framing:	2x4

Foundation Options:

Standard basement

Crawlspace

Slab

(All plans can be built with your choice of foundation and framing. A generic conversion diagram is available. See order form.)

BLUEPRINT PRICE CODE: D

UPPER FLOOR

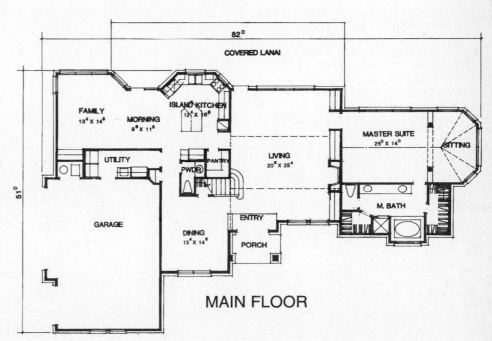

MAIN FLOOR

ORDER BLUEPRINTS ANYTIME!
CALL TOLL-FREE 1-800-820-1283

Plan DD-2889

PRICES AND DETAILS
ON PAGES 2-5

393

Satisfaction by Design

- Unique angles, skylights, French doors, plant shelves, fireplaces, bookshelves, a marble pedestal and a wet bar top a long list of features distinctly designed to satisfy any homeowner.
- A strong brick and stucco exterior creates a practical, pleasing image.
- Inside, the foyer presents a clear view into the gorgeous living room, with its stepped ceiling, fireplace, media center and French doors leading to the huge, skylighted back porch.
- The master bedroom provides a lush, pampering retreat at the end of a busy day. It boasts lots of space, private access to the back porch, a large walk-in closet, and a secluded bath complete with a luxurious plant shelf.
- A bay-windowed breakfast nook also has access to the back porch, and is just steps from the kitchen. Efficient and spacious, the kitchen easily handles formal meals in the nearby dining room.
- Upstairs, a game room easily doubles as a guest bedroom.

Plan L-707-EMB

Bedrooms: 3+	Baths: 3
Living Area:	
Upper floor	386 sq. ft.
Main floor	2,319 sq. ft.
Total Living Area:	**2,705 sq. ft.**
Garage and storage	756 sq. ft.
Exterior Wall Framing:	2x4

Foundation Options:

Slab

(All plans can be built with your choice of foundation and framing. A generic conversion diagram is available. See order form.)

BLUEPRINT PRICE CODE:	D

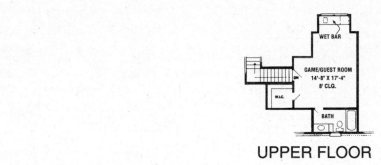

UPPER FLOOR

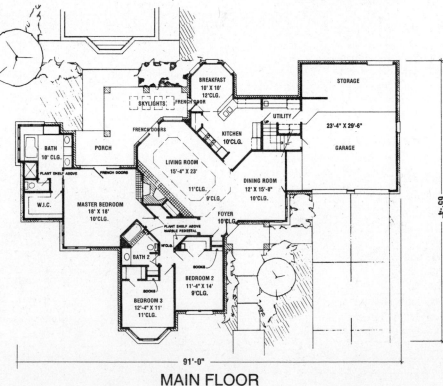

MAIN FLOOR

ORDER BLUEPRINTS ANYTIME! CALL TOLL-FREE 1-800-820-1283   Plan L-707-EMB   PRICES AND DETAILS ON PAGES 2-5

Meant to Impress

- From the exquisite exterior detailing, reminiscent of a stately English manor, to the elegant yet comfortable interior living spaces, this home is sure to impress.
- The kitchen is at the core of the design, featuring a breakfast bar that faces the bayed dinette and an island work center that provides extra space while directing traffic flow. A built-in desk, a deluxe walk-in pantry and a lazy Susan are other features.
- The sunken family room boasts a fireplace, a 12-ft. tray ceiling and French doors to the backyard.
- French doors also open to the charming living room and the cozy study.
- The stairway and the 17-ft. vaulted foyer are illuminated by a clerestory window above the front door.
- The master bedroom offers a 12-ft. tray ceiling, and a sumptuous spa bath. Three more bedrooms share another full bath.

Plan A-2210-DS

Bedrooms: 4+	Baths: 2½
Living Area:	
Upper floor	1,208 sq. ft.
Main floor	1,634 sq. ft.
Total Living Area:	**2,842 sq. ft.**
Standard basement	1,634 sq. ft.
Garage	484 sq. ft.
Exterior Wall Framing:	2x6

Foundation Options:

Standard basement

(All plans can be built with your choice of foundation and framing. A generic conversion diagram is available. See order form.)

BLUEPRINT PRICE CODE:	D

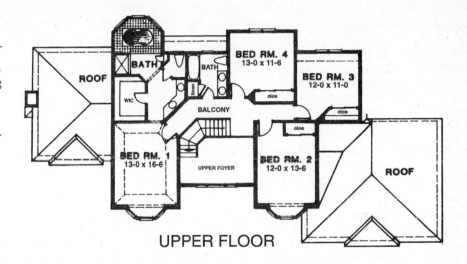

UPPER FLOOR

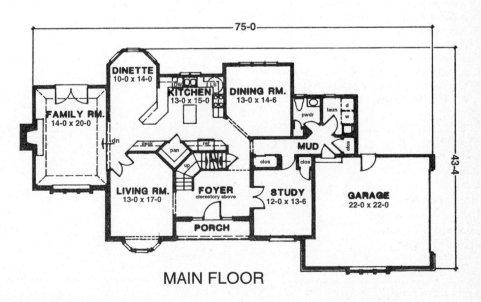

MAIN FLOOR

ORDER BLUEPRINTS ANYTIME!
CALL TOLL-FREE 1-800-820-1283

Plan A-2210-DS

PRICES AND DETAILS
ON PAGES 2-5

395

REAR VIEW

Take It Outside

- The layout of this beautiful home wraps around a veranda and an upstairs deck, taking full advantage of beautiful backyard views and privacy.
- Out front, the dazzling entrance will wow visitors as they are ushered inside to an equally impressive two-story foyer. On the left, the dining room awaits those special occasions—like an anniversary or a much-anticipated job promotion–when you bring out your best silver and china.
- In the living room, ample space is available for visiting with friends. In the corner, a wet bar saves steps to the kitchen, while beautiful windows on either side of the fireplace allow gorgeous views of the outside. With such a great setting, lively conversation will flow readily.
- The combined kitchen and breakfast area boasts an efficient, casual design. By the breakfast nook, a curved wall of glass block draws in sunshine, while a built-in hutch displays fine wares.
- With a fireplace and a private deck, the master suite upstairs is well suited to romantic nights. In the bath, more glass block embraces the raised tub.

Plan L-810-SHB

Bedrooms: 3+	Baths: 3½
Living Area:	
Upper floor	1,206 sq. ft.
Main floor	1,602 sq. ft.
Total Living Area:	**2,808 sq. ft.**
Exterior Wall Framing:	2x4

Foundation Options:

Slab

(All plans can be built with your choice of foundation and framing. A generic conversion diagram is available. See order form.)

BLUEPRINT PRICE CODE:	D

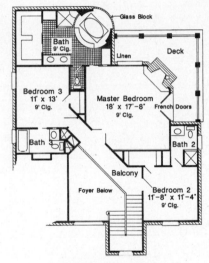

UPPER FLOOR

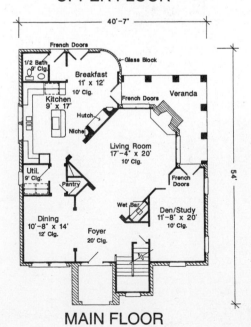

MAIN FLOOR

ORDER BLUEPRINTS ANYTIME!
CALL TOLL-FREE 1-800-820-1283   Plan L-810-SHB   *PRICES AND DETAILS*
ON PAGES 2-5

Family Time

- Designed with the family in mind, this lovely town-and-country home provides a relaxed, informal living environment.
- The covered front porch leads into the inviting two-story-high foyer. Off the foyer, the sunken living room offers a 16-ft., 8-in. sloped ceiling and a bright boxed-out window.
- The adjacent formal dining room is conveniently close to the spacious island kitchen, which features a pantry, a planning desk and a lazy Susan. Sliding glass doors in the adjoining dinette open to the backyard.
- The bright and airy family room is open to the dinette and kitchen, creating a huge informal entertaining expanse. A fireplace adds character to the area.
- Double doors off the foyer lead into a quiet study, which would be ideal for use as a home office or extra bedroom.
- Upstairs, the roomy master suite includes a private bath and a separate dressing area with a walk-in closet.
- A second full bath services the two remaining bedrooms, each of which offers a walk-in closet.

Plan A-2181-DS

Bedrooms: 3+	Baths: 2½
Living Area:	
Upper floor	1,015 sq. ft.
Main floor	1,356 sq. ft.
Total Living Area:	**2,371 sq. ft.**
Standard basement	1,356 sq. ft.
Garage	508 sq. ft.
Exterior Wall Framing:	2x4

Foundation Options:

Standard basement

(All plans can be built with your choice of foundation and framing. A generic conversion diagram is available. See order form.)

BLUEPRINT PRICE CODE:	C

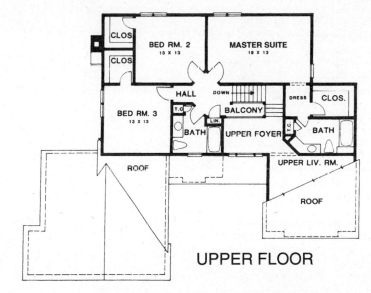

UPPER FLOOR

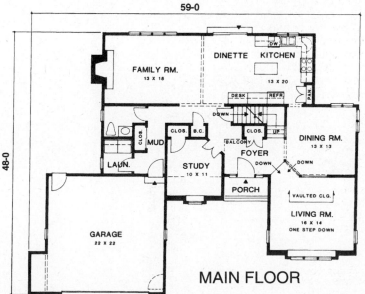

MAIN FLOOR

ORDER BLUEPRINTS ANYTIME!
CALL TOLL-FREE 1-800-820-1283

Plan A-2181-DS

PRICES AND DETAILS
ON PAGES 2-5

397

Executive Excellence

- This executive home with a stucco exterior has a bright interior with flowing spaces and lots of windows.
- The two-story-high entry opens to the formal living and dining rooms, which are defined by decorative columns and enhanced by a shared 11-ft. ceiling.
- The island kitchen, bayed morning room and family room merge together at the rear of the home. A fireplace warms the area, and plenty of glass provides views of a large back deck.
- A guest bedroom/study is perfect for visiting relatives.
- Upstairs, the master suite boasts an enormous walk-in closet and a lavish master bath with a boxed-out window, a spa tub and a separate shower.
- Two more bedrooms share another full bath. The third bedroom is expanded by an 11-ft. cathedral ceiling.
- Ceilings in all main-floor rooms are at least 9 ft. high for added spaciousness.

Plan DD-2725

Bedrooms: 3+	Baths: 3
Living Area:	
Upper floor	1,152 sq. ft.
Main floor	1,631 sq. ft.
Total Living Area:	**2,783 sq. ft.**
Standard basement	1,631 sq. ft.
Garage	600 sq. ft.
Storage	100 sq. ft.
Exterior Wall Framing:	2x4

Foundation Options:

Standard basement
Crawlspace
Slab

(All plans can be built with your choice of foundation and framing. A generic conversion diagram is available. See order form.)

BLUEPRINT PRICE CODE: D

UPPER FLOOR

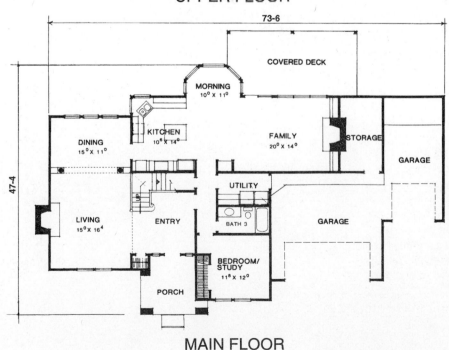

MAIN FLOOR

Dignified and Stately

- Decorative corner quoins and a symmetrical hip roofline give a distinct European flavor to this dignified and stately brick home.
- Brightened by a high window, the two-story foyer bridges the formal dining room and living room and unfolds to the informal living areas at the rear.
- The spacious sunken family room has a large bay window and a cozy fireplace. An open rail separates the family room from the dinette and the island kitchen.
- The dinette's sliding glass doors open to the backyard and let the sun shine in. A pantry is convenient to the kitchen, as are a nice-sized laundry room and a powder room.
- Upstairs, the master suite boasts a walk-in closet and a separate dressing area with a vanity. The private bath has a garden tub and a towel closet.
- Three additional bathrooms share a second full bath. The balcony area overlooks the foyer below.

Plan A-2166-DS

Bedrooms: 4	Baths: 2½
Living Area:	
Upper floor	1,156 sq. ft.
Main floor	1,224 sq. ft.
Total Living Area:	**2,380 sq. ft.**
Standard basement	1,224 sq. ft.
Garage	484 sq. ft.
Exterior Wall Framing:	2x4

Foundation Options:

Standard basement

(All plans can be built with your choice of foundation and framing. A generic conversion diagram is available. See order form.)

BLUEPRINT PRICE CODE: C

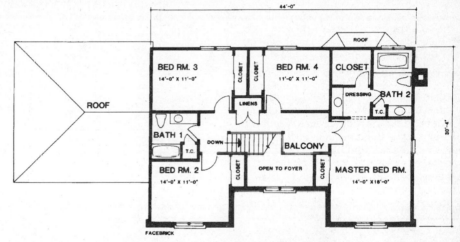

UPPER FLOOR

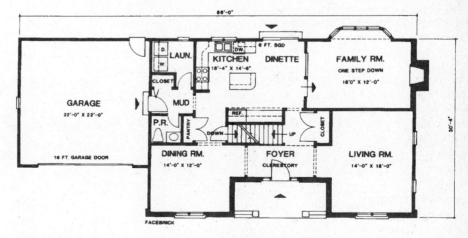

MAIN FLOOR

ORDER BLUEPRINTS ANYTIME!
CALL TOLL-FREE 1-800-820-1283

Plan A-2166-DS

PRICES AND DETAILS
ON PAGES 2-5
399

Picture of Style

- With keystone-topped arches, front-facing gables and a decorative balcony above the entry, this beautiful two-story home is truly a picture of style.
- Inside, entertaining will take on added elegance in the formal dining and living rooms. A butler's pantry off the dining room simplifies serving, while a porch off the living room lets guests step outside to enjoy a view of the stars.
- Built-in shelves and a graceful arch lead the way to the family room. When the kids gather for a bedtime story, the fireplace serves as a toasty backdrop.
- In the breakfast nook, morning coffee revives sleepy souls. The family chef will delight in the kitchen, which boasts an island cooktop with a serving bar. Built-in shelves hold cookbooks.
- Upstairs, the master suite provides a great setting for quiet times. A romantic see-through fireplace lends ambience to the bedroom and the bath. Half-walls anchored by elegant columns define the sitting room, where you will love to settle in and savor the Sunday *Times*.

Plan FB-5477-CARM

Bedrooms: 4	Baths: 3½
Living Area:	
Upper floor	1,844 sq. ft.
Main floor	1,418 sq. ft.
Total Living Area:	**3,262 sq. ft.**
Daylight basement	1,418 sq. ft.
Garage	820 sq. ft.
Exterior Wall Framing:	2x4

Foundation Options:

Daylight basement

(All plans can be built with your choice of foundation and framing. A generic conversion diagram is available. See order form.)

BLUEPRINT PRICE CODE:	E

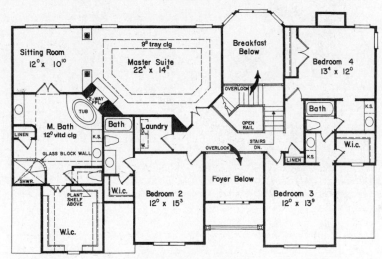

UPPER FLOOR

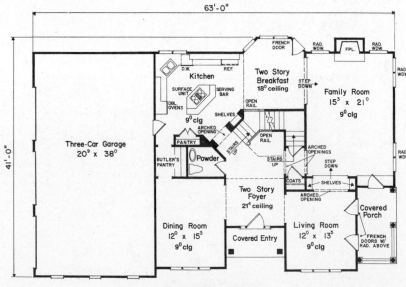

MAIN FLOOR

ORDER BLUEPRINTS ANYTIME!
CALL TOLL-FREE 1-800-820-1283

Plan FB-5477-CARM

PRICES AND DETAILS
ON PAGES 2-5

Victorian Farmhouse

- Fish-scale shingles and horizontal siding team up with the detailed front porch to create a look of yesterday. Brickwork enriches the sides and rear of the home.
- The main level features 10-ft.-high ceilings throughout the central living space. The front-oriented formal areas merge with the family room via three sets of French doors.

- The island kitchen and skylighted eating area have 16-ft. sloped ceilings.
- A breezeway off the deck connects the house to a roomy workshop. A two-car garage is located under the workshop and a large utility room is just inside the rear entrance.
- The main-floor master suite offers an opulent skylighted bath with a garden vanity, a spa tub, a separate shower and an 18-ft.-high sloped ceiling.
- The upper floor offers three more bedrooms, two full baths and a balcony that looks to the backyard.

Plan E-3103

Bedrooms: 4	Baths: 3½
Living Area:	
Upper floor	1,113 sq. ft.
Main floor	2,040 sq. ft.
Total Living Area:	**3,153 sq. ft.**
Daylight basement	2,040 sq. ft.
Tuck-under garage and storage	580 sq. ft.
Workshop and storage	580 sq. ft.
Exterior Wall Framing:	2x6

Foundation Options:

Daylight basement
Crawlspace
Slab
(All plans can be built with your choice of foundation and framing. A generic conversion diagram is available. See order form.)

BLUEPRINT PRICE CODE:	E

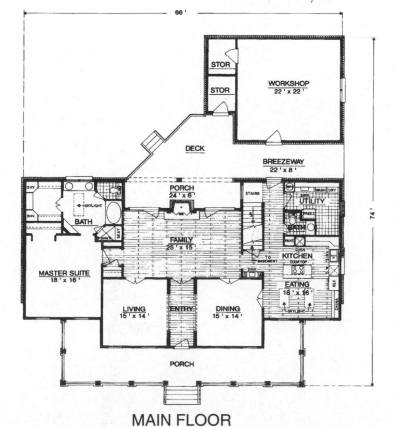

MAIN FLOOR

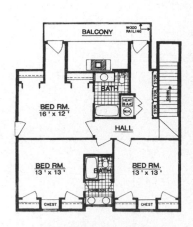

UPPER FLOOR

ORDER BLUEPRINTS ANYTIME!
CALL TOLL-FREE 1-800-820-1283

Plan E-3103

PRICES AND DETAILS
ON PAGES 2-5

401

Photo by Kevin Robinson

Striking Hillside Home Design

- This striking home is designed for a sloping site. The two-car garage and sideyard deck are nestled into the hillside, while cedar siding and a shake roof blend in nicely with the terrain.
- Clerestory windows brighten the entry and the living room, which unfold from the covered front porch. The huge living/dining area instantly catches the eye, with its corner fireplace, 17-ft. sloped ceiling and exciting window treatments. The living room also offers an inviting window seat, while the dining room has sliding glass doors to the large deck.
- The adjoining nook and kitchen also have access to the deck, along with lots of storage and work space.
- The isolated bedroom wing includes a master suite with his-and-hers closets and a private bath. The two smaller bedrooms share a hall bath.
- The daylight basement hosts a laundry room, a recreation room with a fireplace and a bedroom with two closets, plus a large general-use area.

Plan H-2045-5

Bedrooms: 4	Baths: 3
Living Area:	
Main floor	1,602 sq. ft.
Daylight basement	1,133 sq. ft.
Total Living Area:	**2,735 sq. ft.**
Tuck-under garage	508 sq. ft.
Exterior Wall Framing:	2x4

Foundation Options:

Daylight basement
(All plans can be built with your choice of foundation and framing. A generic conversion diagram is available. See order form.)

BLUEPRINT PRICE CODE: D

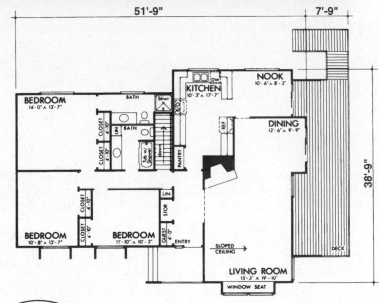

MAIN FLOOR

**NOTE:
The above photographed home may have been modified by the homeowner. Please refer to floor plan and/or drawn elevation shown for actual blueprint details.

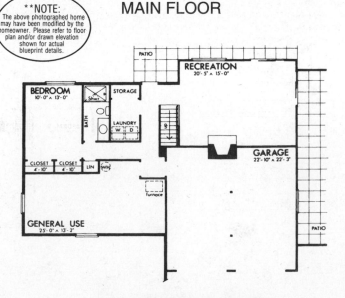

DAYLIGHT BASEMENT

ORDER BLUEPRINTS ANYTIME!
CALL TOLL-FREE 1-800-820-1283

Plan H-2045-5

PRICES AND DETAILS
ON PAGES 2-5

Luxurious Interior

- This luxurious home is introduced by an exciting tiled entry with a 17½-ft. vaulted ceiling and a skylight.
- The highlight of the home is the expansive Great Room and dining area, with its fireplace, planter, 17½-ft. vaulted ceiling and bay windows. The fabulous wraparound deck with a step-up hot tub is the perfect complement to this large entertainment space.
- The kitchen features lots of counter space, a large pantry and an adjoining bay-windowed breakfast nook.
- The exquisite master suite flaunts a sunken garden tub, a separate shower, a dual-sink vanity, a walk-in closet and private access to the deck area.
- The game room downstairs is perfect for casual entertaining, with its warm woodstove, oversized wet bar and patio access. Two bedrooms, a full bath and a large utility area are also included.

Plan P-6595-3D

Bedrooms: 3	Baths: 2½
Living Area:	
Main floor	1,530 sq. ft.
Daylight basement	1,145 sq. ft.
Total Living Area:	**2,675 sq. ft.**
Garage	462 sq. ft.
Exterior Wall Framing:	2x6

Foundation Options:

Daylight basement

(All plans can be built with your choice of foundation and framing. A generic conversion diagram is available. See order form.)

BLUEPRINT PRICE CODE:	D

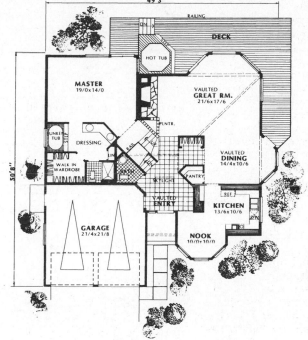

MAIN FLOOR

DAYLIGHT BASEMENT

ORDER BLUEPRINTS ANYTIME!
CALL TOLL-FREE 1-800-820-1283

Plan P-6595-3D

PRICES AND DETAILS
ON PAGES 2-5

403

You Asked for It!

- Our most popular plan in recent years, E-3000, has now been downsized for affordability, without sacrificing character or excitement.
- Exterior appeal is created with a covered front porch with decorative columns, triple dormers and rail-topped bay windows.
- The floor plan has combined the separate living and family rooms available in E-3000 into one spacious family room with corner fireplace, which flows into the dining room through a columned gallery.
- The kitchen serves the breakfast room over an angled snack bar, and features a huge pantry.
- The stunning main-floor master suite offers a private sitting area, a walk-in closet and a dramatic, angled bath.
- There are two large bedrooms upstairs accessible via a curved staircase with bridge balcony.

Plan E-2307

Bedrooms: 3	Baths: 2½
Living Area:	
Upper floor	595 sq. ft.
Main floor	1,765 sq. ft.
Total Living Area:	**2,360 sq. ft.**
Standard basement	1,765 sq. ft.
Garage	484 sq. ft.
Storage	44 sq. ft.
Exterior Wall Framing:	2x6

Foundation Options:
Standard basement
Crawlspace
Slab
(All plans can be built with your choice of foundation and framing. A generic conversion diagram is available. See order form.)

BLUEPRINT PRICE CODE: C

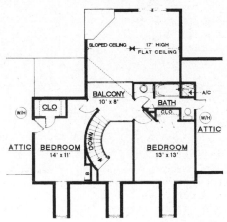

UPPER FLOOR

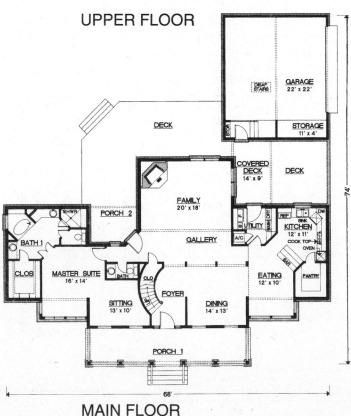

MAIN FLOOR

ORDER BLUEPRINTS ANYTIME!
CALL TOLL-FREE 1-800-820-1283

Plan E-2307

PRICES AND DETAILS
ON PAGES 2-5

Elegant Interior

- An inviting covered porch welcomes guests into the elegant interior of this spectacular country home.
- Just past the entrance, the formal dining room boasts a stepped ceiling and a nearby server with a sink.
- The adjoining island kitchen has an eating bar that serves the breakfast room, which is enhanced by a 12-ft. cathedral ceiling and a bayed area of 8- and 9-ft.-high windows. Sliding glass doors lead to a covered side porch.
- Brightened by a row of 8-ft.-high windows and a glass door to the backyard, the spacious Great Room features a stepped ceiling, a built-in media center and a corner fireplace.
- The master bedroom has a tray ceiling and a cozy sitting area. The skylighted master bath boasts a whirlpool tub, a separate shower and a walk-in closet.
- A second main-floor bedroom, or optional study, offers private access to a compartmentalized bath. Two more bedrooms share a third bath on the upper floor. Generous storage space is also included.

Plan AX-3305-B

Bedrooms: 3+	Baths: 3
Living Area:	
Upper floor	550 sq. ft.
Main floor	2,017 sq. ft.
Total Living Area:	**2,567 sq. ft.**
Upper-floor storage	377 sq. ft.
Standard basement	2,017 sq. ft.
Garage	415 sq. ft.
Exterior Wall Framing:	2x4

Foundation Options:

Standard basement
Crawlspace
Slab

(All plans can be built with your choice of foundation and framing. A generic conversion diagram is available. See order form.)

BLUEPRINT PRICE CODE: D

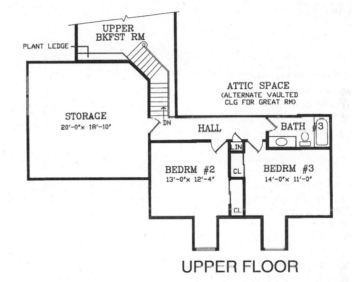

UPPER FLOOR

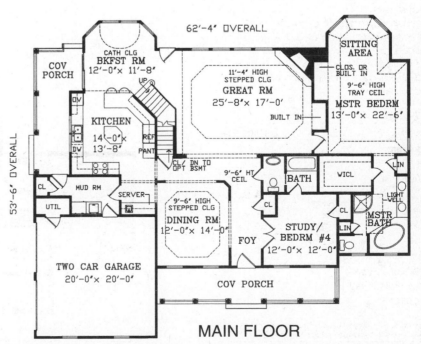

MAIN FLOOR

ORDER BLUEPRINTS ANYTIME!
CALL TOLL-FREE 1-800-820-1283

Plan AX-3305-B

PRICES AND DETAILS
ON PAGES 2-5

405

Innovative Floor Plan

- The wide, covered front porch, arched windows and symmetrical lines of this traditional home conceal the modern, innovative floor plan found within.
- A two-story-high foyer guides guests to the front-oriented formal areas, which have views to the front porch.
- The hotspot of the home is the Great Room, with one of the home's three fireplaces and a media wall. Flanking doors open to a large backyard deck.
- The island kitchen and glassed-in eating nook overlook the deck and access a handy mudroom. High 9-ft. ceilings add to the aura of warmth and hospitality found on the main floor of this home.
- Another of the fireplaces is offered in the master suite. This private oasis also boasts a 13-ft.-high cathedral ceiling and a delicious bath with a garden tub.
- Upstairs, one bedroom has a sloped ceiling and a private bath. Three more bedrooms share another full bath.

Plan AHP-9360

Bedrooms: 5	Baths: 3½
Living Area:	
Upper floor	970 sq. ft.
Main floor	1,735 sq. ft.
Total Living Area:	**2,705 sq. ft.**
Standard basement	1,550 sq. ft.
Garage and utility area	443 sq. ft.
Exterior Wall Framing:	2x6

Foundation Options:

Standard basement
Crawlspace
Slab

(All plans can be built with your choice of foundation and framing. A generic conversion diagram is available. See order form.)

BLUEPRINT PRICE CODE: D

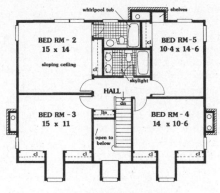

UPPER FLOOR

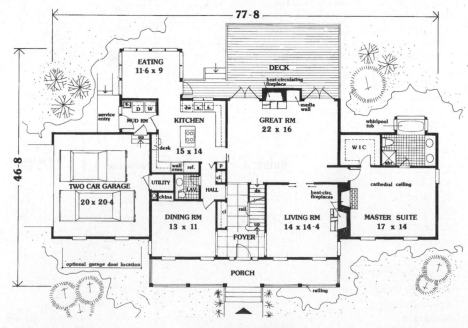

MAIN FLOOR

ORDER BLUEPRINTS ANYTIME!
CALL TOLL-FREE 1-800-820-1283

Plan AHP-9360

PRICES AND DETAILS
ON PAGES 2-5

Photo by Mark Englund/HomeStyles

Ornate Design

- This exciting home is distinguished by an ornate facade with symmetrical windows and a columned entry.
- A beautiful arched window highlights the two-story-high foyer, with its open-railed stairway and high plant shelf. The foyer separates the two formal rooms and flows back to the family room.
- With an 18-ft. ceiling, the family room is brightened by corner windows and warmed by a central fireplace.
- Columns introduce the sunny breakfast area and the gourmet kitchen, which features an angled island and serving bar, and a butler's pantry that serves the nearby dining room.
- Ceilings in all main-floor rooms are 9 ft. high unless otherwise specified.
- Upstairs, a dramatic balcony overlooks the family room and the foyer.
- The master suite boasts a 10-ft. tray ceiling, a sitting room and an opulent garden bath with a 12-ft. vaulted ceiling. Three more bedrooms, each with a walk-in closet and private bath access, complete the upper floor.

Plan FB-5347-HAST

Bedrooms: 4+	Baths: 4
Living Area:	
Upper floor	1,554 sq. ft.
Main floor	1,665 sq. ft.
Total Living Area:	**3,219 sq. ft.**
Daylight basement	1,665 sq. ft.
Garage	462 sq. ft.
Exterior Wall Framing:	2x4

Foundation Options:

Daylight basement
Crawlspace

(All plans can be built with your choice of foundation and framing. A generic conversion diagram is available. See order form.)

BLUEPRINT PRICE CODE:	E

NOTE:
The above photographed home may have been modified by the homeowner. Please refer to floor plan and/or drawn elevation shown for actual blueprint details.

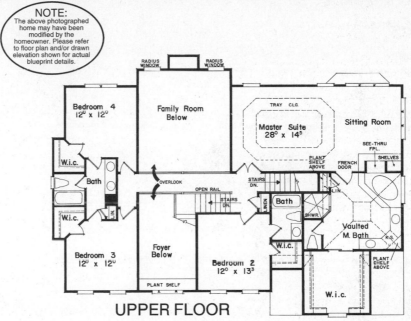

UPPER FLOOR

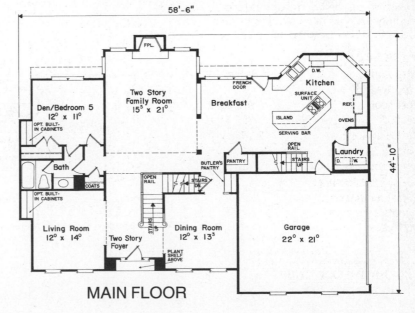

MAIN FLOOR

ORDER BLUEPRINTS ANYTIME!
CALL TOLL-FREE 1-800-820-1283

Plan FB-5347-HAST

PRICES AND DETAILS
ON PAGES 2-5

407

Photos courtesy of Larry Garnett and Associates

REAR VIEW

Vivacious Victorian

- The facade of this classic Victorian home is enhanced by a covered veranda bordering three sides.
- Inside, the modern interior begins with an airy two-story foyer that flows directly into a cozy bayed parlor.
- Past a bright window wall and a door to the side yard, the bay-windowed formal dining room boasts a wonderful built-in china hutch.
- Behind bifold doors, the island kitchen sports a nifty built-in desk and a cheery

bayed morning room with speedy access to the veranda.
- Beautiful views are also offered from the family room, which flaunts a handsome fireplace, a wet bar and a wine rack.
- French doors access a bayed study that may be used as an extra bedroom.
- An angled staircase leads up to three secondary bedrooms, one of which has a 13-ft. ceiling. A compartmentalized bath and a laundry room are nearby.
- At the end of the hall, the master bedroom features a long, private deck. The gorgeous master bath offers a stunning, bay-windowed bathing area.
- Unless otherwise noted, each room has a 9-ft. ceiling.

Plan L-3163

Bedrooms: 4+	**Baths:** 2½
Living Area:	
Upper floor	1,598 sq. ft.
Main floor	1,565 sq. ft.
Total Living Area:	**3,163 sq. ft.**
Garage (detached)	576 sq. ft.
Exterior Wall Framing:	2x4

Foundation Options:

Slab
(All plans can be built with your choice of foundation and framing. A generic conversion diagram is available. See order form.)

BLUEPRINT PRICE CODE: E

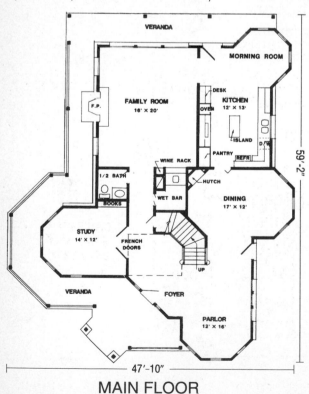

NOTE:
The above photographed home may have been modified by the homeowner. Please refer to floor plan and/or drawn elevation shown for actual blueprint details.

MAIN FLOOR

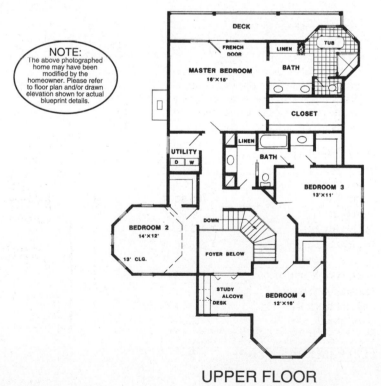

UPPER FLOOR

Photo by Karlis Grants

Dramatic Interior Spaces

- This home's design utilizes unique shapes and angles to create a dramatic and dynamic interior.
- Skylights brighten the impressive two-story entry from high above, as it flows to the formal living areas.
- The sunken Great Room features a massive stone-hearthed fireplace with flanking windows, plus a 19-ft. vaulted ceiling. Sliding glass doors open the formal dining room to a backyard patio.
- The spacious kitchen features an oversized island, plenty of counter space and a sunny breakfast nook.
- A den or third bedroom shares a full bath with another secondary bedroom to complete the main floor.
- An incredible bayed master suite takes up the entire upper floor of the home. The skylighted master bath features a bright walk-in closet, a dual-sink vanity, a sunken tub and a separate shower.

Plans P-6580-3A & -3D

Bedrooms: 2+	Baths: 2
Living Area:	
Upper floor	705 sq. ft.
Main floor	1,738 sq. ft.
Total Living Area:	**2,443 sq. ft.**
Daylight basement	1,738 sq. ft.
Garage	512 sq. ft.
Exterior Wall Framing:	2x4
Foundation Options:	**Plan #**
Daylight basement	P-6580-3D
Crawlspace	P-6580-3A

(All plans can be built with your choice of foundation and framing. A generic conversion diagram is available. See order form.)

BLUEPRINT PRICE CODE:	C

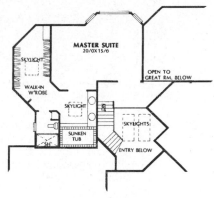

UPPER FLOOR

**NOTE:
The above photographed home may have been modified by the homeowner. Please refer to floor plan and/or drawn elevation shown for actual blueprint details.

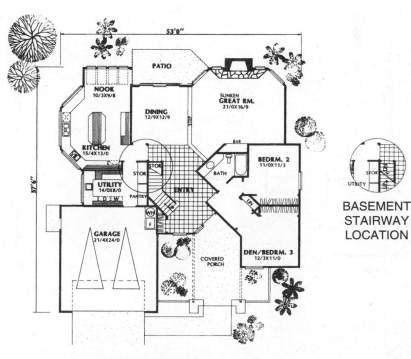

MAIN FLOOR

BASEMENT STAIRWAY LOCATION

Panoramic Porch

- A gracious, ornately rounded front porch and a two-story turreted bay lend Victorian charm to this home.
- A two-story foyer with round-top transom windows and a plant ledge above greets guests at the entry.
- The living room enjoys a 13-ft.-high ceiling and a panoramic view overlooking the front porch and yard.
- The formal dining room and den each feature a bay window for added style.
- The sunny kitchen incorporates an angled island cooktop with a eating bar to the bayed breakfast room.
- A step down, the family room offers a corner fireplace that may be enjoyed throughout the casual living spaces.
- The upper floor is highlighted by a stunning master suite, which flaunts an octagonal sitting area with a 10-ft. tray ceiling and turreted bay. The master bath offers a corner spa tub and a separate shower. Two additional bedrooms share another full bath.

Plan AX-90307

Bedrooms: 3+	Baths: 3
Living Area:	
Upper floor	956 sq. ft.
Main floor	1,499 sq. ft.
Total Living Area:	**2,455 sq. ft.**
Standard basement	1,499 sq. ft.
Garage	410 sq. ft.
Exterior Wall Framing:	2x4

Foundation Options:

Standard basement
Slab

(All plans can be built with your choice of foundation and framing. A generic conversion diagram is available. See order form.)

BLUEPRINT PRICE CODE:	C

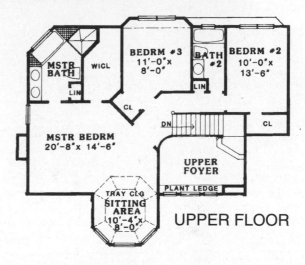

UPPER FLOOR

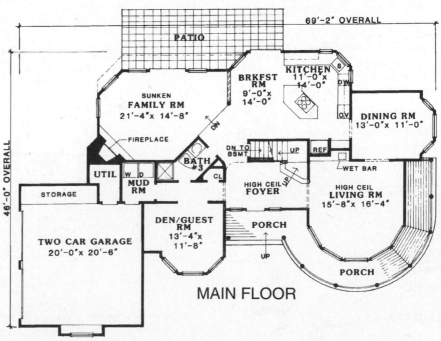

MAIN FLOOR

Photo by Mark Englund/HomeStyles

Stately Colonial

- This stately Colonial features a covered front entry and a secondary entry near the garage and the utility room.
- The main foyer opens to a comfortable den with elegant double doors.
- The formal living areas adjoin to the left of the foyer and culminate in a lovely bay window overlooking the backyard.
- The open island kitchen has a great central location, easily accessed from each of the living areas. Informal dining can be extended to the outdoors through sliding doors in the dinette.
- A half-wall introduces the big family room, which boasts a high 16-ft., 9-in. vaulted ceiling, an inviting fireplace and optional built-in cabinets.
- The upper floor is shared by four bedrooms, including a spacious master bedroom with a large walk-in closet, a dressing area for two and a private bath. An alternate bath layout is included in the blueprints.
- A bonus room may be added above the garage for additional space.

Plan A-2283-DS

Bedrooms: 4+	Baths: 2½
Living Area:	
Upper floor	1,137 sq. ft.
Main floor	1,413 sq. ft.
Total Living Area:	**2,550 sq. ft.**
Optional bonus room	280 sq. ft.
Standard basement	1,413 sq. ft.
Garage	484 sq. ft.
Exterior Wall Framing:	**2x6**

Foundation Options:

Standard basement

(All plans can be built with your choice of foundation and framing. A generic conversion diagram is available. See order form.)

BLUEPRINT PRICE CODE: D

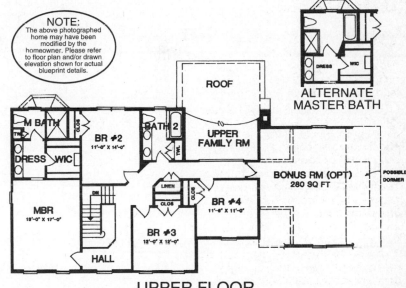

NOTE:
The above photographed home may have been modified by the homeowner. Please refer to floor plan and/or drawn elevation shown for actual blueprint details.

ALTERNATE MASTER BATH

UPPER FLOOR

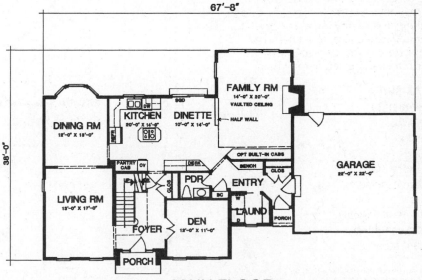

MAIN FLOOR

ORDER BLUEPRINTS ANYTIME!
CALL TOLL-FREE 1-800-820-1283

Plan A-2283-DS

PRICES AND DETAILS
ON PAGES 2-5

411

Deluxe Master Suite

- This traditional home has an enticing style all its own, with a deluxe main-floor master suite.
- In from the covered porch, the front entry flows into the main living areas.
- Straight ahead, the family room features a handsome fireplace flanked by doors to a screened back porch.
- The kitchen easily services the formal dining room and offers a snack bar to the bayed breakfast nook. A nice utility room with a pantry and a half-bath is just off the nook and the garage entry.
- The secluded master suite boasts a 9-ft. tray ceiling and a luxurious bath with a garden tub, a separate shower and two vanities, one with knee space.
- Upstairs, each of the two additional bedrooms has a walk-in closet and a private bath. The optional bonus room can be finished as a large game room, a bedroom or an office.

Plan C-8915

Bedrooms: 3+	Baths: 3 full, 2 half
Living Area:	
Upper floor	832 sq. ft.
Main floor	1,927 sq. ft.
Bonus room	624 sq. ft.
Total Living Area:	**3,383 sq. ft.**
Daylight basement	1,674 sq. ft.
Garage	484 sq. ft.
Exterior Wall Framing:	2x4

Foundation Options:

Daylight basement

Crawlspace

(All plans can be built with your choice of foundation and framing. A generic conversion diagram is available. See order form.)

BLUEPRINT PRICE CODE: E

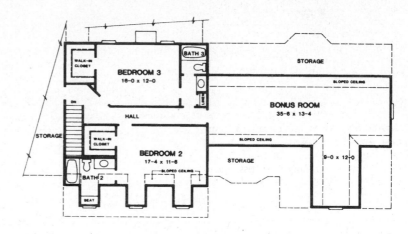

UPPER FLOOR

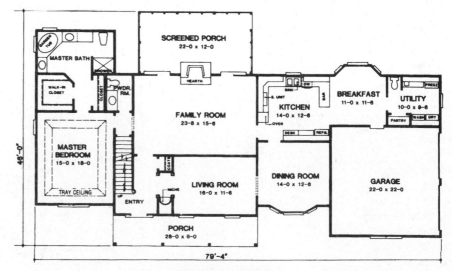

MAIN FLOOR

Large-Scale Living

- Eye-catching windows and an appealing wraparound porch highlight the exterior of this outstanding home.
- Inside, high ceilings and large-scale living spaces prevail, beginning with the foyer, which has an 18-ft. ceiling.
- The spacious living room flows into the formal dining room, which opens to the porch and to an optional rear deck.
- The island kitchen extends to a bright breakfast room with deck access. The family room offers an 18-ft. vaulted ceiling and a corner fireplace.
- Unless otherwise noted, every main-floor room boasts a 9 ft. ceiling.
- Upstairs, the lush master bedroom boasts an 11-ft. vaulted ceiling and two walk-in closets. The skylighted master bath features a spa tub, a separate shower and a dual-sink vanity.
- Three more bedrooms are reached by a balcony, which overlooks the family room. In one bedroom, the ceiling jumps to 10 ft. at the beautiful window.

Plan AX-93309

Bedrooms: 4	Baths: 2½
Living Area:	
Upper floor	1,180 sq. ft.
Main floor	1,290 sq. ft.
Total Living Area:	**2,470 sq. ft.**
Basement	1,290 sq. ft.
Garage and storage	421 sq. ft.
Exterior Wall Framing:	2x4

Foundation Options:

Daylight basement

Standard basement

Slab

(All plans can be built with your choice of foundation and framing. A generic conversion diagram is available. See order form.)

BLUEPRINT PRICE CODE:　　　C

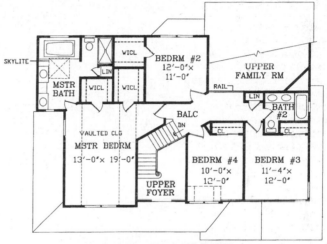

UPPER FLOOR

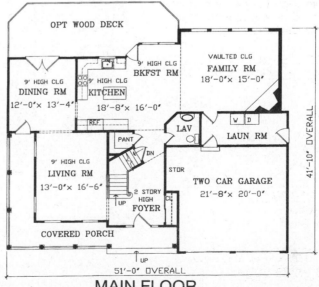

MAIN FLOOR

Photo by Mark Englund/HomeStyles

Elegant Country

- This stately country home is filled with high elegance.
- Round-top windows brighten the living and dining rooms on either side of the long entry.
- Straight ahead, an 18-ft. ceiling crowns the family room, which is warmed by a handsome fireplace. Two sets of French doors flanking the fireplace lead to a huge deck.
- The secluded master suite boasts a stunning bath, with a step-up quarter-circle Jacuzzi tub under a columned

pergola, an arched window and a 12-ft. sloped ceiling!
- A peninsula cooktop/snack bar highlights the marvelously open kitchen. In one window-lined corner, a breakfast nook lies bathed in sunlight. A convenient porte cochere is nice for unloading groceries on rainy days.
- Unless otherwise specified, all main-floor rooms have 9-ft. ceilings.
- A game room at the top of the stairs may also be used as an extra bedroom.
- Along the balcony hall, two good-sized bedrooms enjoy private bath access. A third bedroom has a full bath nearby.

Plan E-3501	
Bedrooms: 4+	**Baths:** 3½
Living Area:	
Upper floor	1,238 sq. ft.
Main floor	2,330 sq. ft.
Total Living Area:	**3,568 sq. ft.**
Standard basement	2,348 sq. ft.
Garage and storage	848 sq. ft.
Exterior Wall Framing:	2x6

Foundation Options:

Standard basement
Crawlspace
Slab
(All plans can be built with your choice of foundation and framing. A generic conversion diagram is available. See order form.)

BLUEPRINT PRICE CODE: F

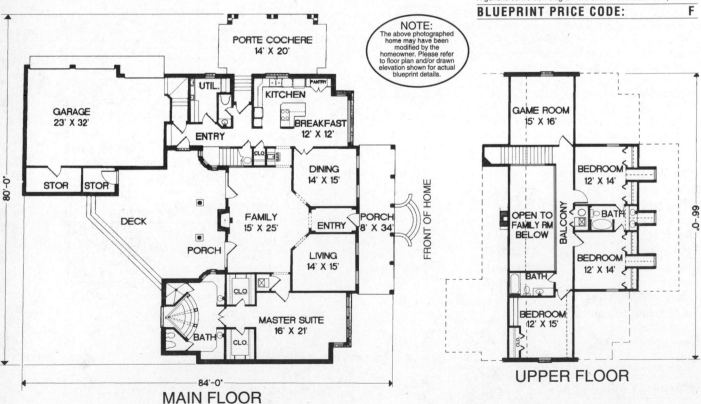

NOTE:
The above photographed home may have been modified by the homeowner. Please refer to floor plan and/or drawn elevation shown for actual blueprint details.

MAIN FLOOR

UPPER FLOOR

ORDER BLUEPRINTS ANYTIME!
CALL TOLL-FREE 1-800-820-1283

Plan E-3501

PRICES AND DETAILS
ON PAGES 2-5

Dramatic
Rear Views

- Columned front and rear porches offer country styling to this elegant two-story.
- The formal dining room and living room flank the two-story-high foyer.
- A dramatic array of windows stretches along the informal, rear-oriented living areas, where the central family room features a 17-ft.-high vaulted ceiling and a striking fireplace.
- The modern kitchen features an angled snack counter, a walk-in pantry and a work island, in addition to the bayed morning room.
- The exciting and secluded master suite has a sunny bayed sitting area with its own fireplace. Large walk-in closets lead to a luxurious private bath with angled dual vanities, a garden spa tub and a separate shower.
- The centrally located stairway leads to three extra bedrooms and two full baths on the upper floor.

Plan DD-2912

Bedrooms: 4	Baths: 3½
Living Area:	
Upper floor	916 sq. ft.
Main floor	2,046 sq. ft.
Total Living Area:	**2,962 sq. ft.**
Standard basement	1,811 sq. ft.
Garage	513 sq. ft.
Exterior Wall Framing:	2x4

Foundation Options:

Standard basement

Crawlspace

Slab

(All plans can be built with your choice of foundation and framing. A generic conversion diagram is available. See order form.)

BLUEPRINT PRICE CODE:	D

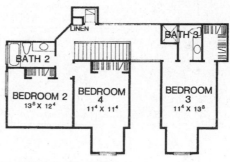

UPPER FLOOR

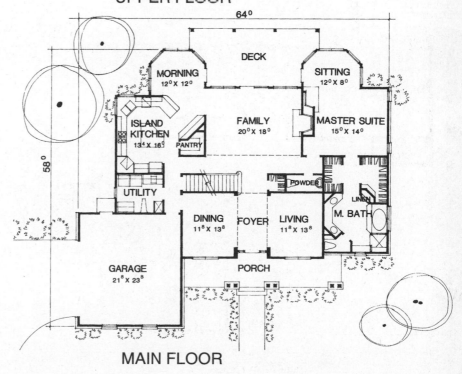

MAIN FLOOR

ORDER BLUEPRINTS ANYTIME!
CALL TOLL-FREE 1-800-820-1283

Plan DD-2912

PRICES AND DETAILS
ON PAGES 2-5

415

REAR VIEW

Fantastic Facade, Stunning Spaces

- Matching dormers and a generous covered front porch give this home its fantastic facade. Inside, the open living spaces are just as stunning.
- A two-story foyer bisects the formal living areas. The living room offers three bright windows, an inviting fireplace and sliding French doors to the Great Room. The formal dining room overlooks the front porch and has easy access to the kitchen.
- The Great Room is truly grand, featuring a fireplace and a TV center flanked by French doors that lead to a large deck.
- A circular dinette connects the Great Room to the kitchen, which is handy to a mudroom and a powder room.
- The main-floor master suite boasts a 14-ft. cathedral ceiling, a walk-in closet and a private bath with a whirlpool tub.
- Upstairs, four large bedrooms share another whirlpool bath. One bedroom offers a 12-ft. sloped ceiling.

Plan AHP-9397

Bedrooms: 5	Baths: 2½
Living Area:	
Upper floor	928 sq. ft.
Main floor	1,545 sq. ft.
Total Living Area:	**2,473 sq. ft.**
Standard basement	1,545 sq. ft.
Garage and storage	432 sq. ft.
Exterior Wall Framing:	2x4 or 2x6

Foundation Options:

Standard basement

Crawlspace

Slab

(All plans can be built with your choice of foundation and framing. A generic conversion diagram is available. See order form.)

BLUEPRINT PRICE CODE: C

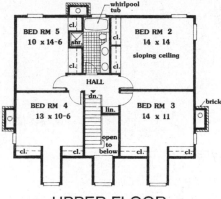

UPPER FLOOR

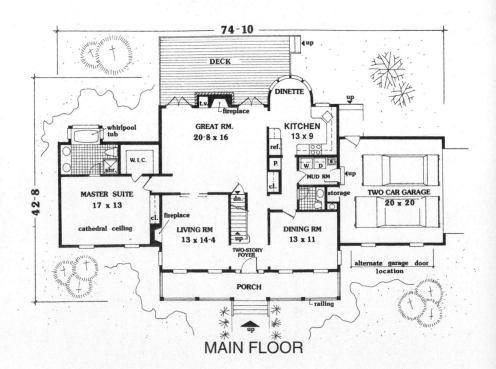

MAIN FLOOR

ORDER BLUEPRINTS ANYTIME! *CALL TOLL-FREE 1-800-820-1283*   Plan AHP-9397   *PRICES AND DETAILS* *ON PAGES 2-5*

Exquisite Home

- This home's curved front steps and stately two-story-high entry introduce its exquisite interior design.
- The two-story-high foyer shows off a sweeping stairway and is flanked by the formal living areas.
- Straight ahead is the family room, with its 19-ft. vaulted ceiling, spectacular window wall and masonry fireplace.
- The roomy island kitchen includes a bayed breakfast area. A nearby wet bar is open to the dining room.
- A skylighted screened porch boasts a handy built in barbecue grill.
- The beautiful master suite showcases a 12-ft. coffered ceiling and a spacious private bath with a huge garden tub and a curved shower.
- Upstairs, two skylighted baths serve three bedrooms, one with a window seat and the other two with 12-ft. cathedral ceilings. A balcony overlooks the foyer and family room below.
- Ceilings in all main-floor rooms are at least 10 ft. high for added spaciousness.

Plan DD-4458

Bedrooms: 4	Baths: 3½
Living Area:	
Upper floor	1,067 sq. ft.
Main floor	3,391 sq. ft.
Total Living Area:	**4,458 sq. ft.**
Standard basement	3,391 sq. ft.
Garage	774 sq. ft.
Exterior Wall Framing:	2x4

Foundation Options:

Standard basement
Crawlspace
Slab

(All plans can be built with your choice of foundation and framing. A generic conversion diagram is available. See order form.)

BLUEPRINT PRICE CODE: G

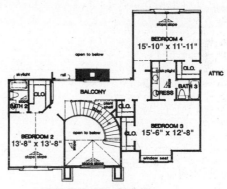

UPPER FLOOR

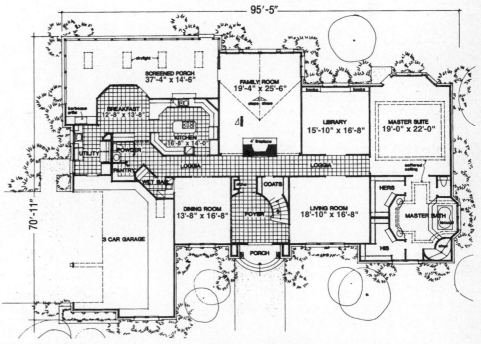

MAIN FLOOR

ORDER BLUEPRINTS ANYTIME!
CALL TOLL-FREE 1-800-820-1283

Plan DD-4458

PRICES AND DETAILS
ON PAGES 2-5

417

Classic Country-Style

- Almost completely surrounded by an expansive porch, this classic plan exudes warmth and grace.
- The foyer is liberal in size and leads guests to a formal dining room to the left or the large living room to the right.
- The open country kitchen includes a sunny, bay-windowed breakfast nook. A utility area, a full bath and garage access are nearby.
- Upstairs, the master suite is impressive, with its large sleeping area, walk-in closet and magnificent garden bath.
- Three secondary bedrooms share a full bath with a dual-sink vanity.
- Also note the stairs leading up to an attic, which is useful for storage space.

Plan J-86134

Bedrooms: 4	Baths: 3
Living Area:	
Upper floor	1,195 sq. ft.
Main floor	1,370 sq. ft.
Total Living Area:	**2,565 sq. ft.**
Standard basement	1,370 sq. ft.
Garage	576 sq. ft.
Exterior Wall Framing:	2x4

Foundation Options:

Standard basement
Crawlspace
Slab

(All plans can be built with your choice of foundation and framing. A generic conversion diagram is available. See order form.)

BLUEPRINT PRICE CODE:	D

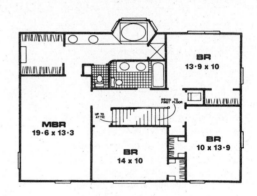

UPPER FLOOR

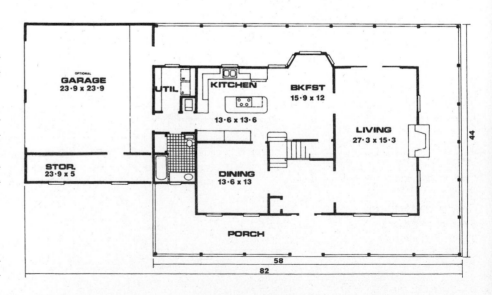

MAIN FLOOR

ORDER BLUEPRINTS ANYTIME!
CALL TOLL-FREE 1-800-820-1283

Plan J-86134

PRICES AND DETAILS
ON PAGES 2-5

Dramatic Contemporary

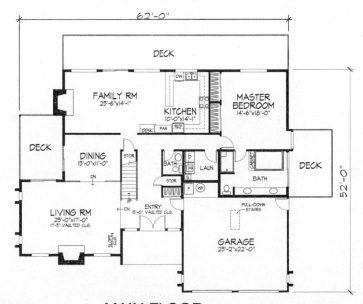

REAR VIEW

- Dramatic rooflines and appealing outdoor spaces combine with a functional floor plan to create this comfortable contemporary home.
- Skylights shed light on the soaring entry, which offers views of the living room and the distinctive staircase.
- A striking fireplace accents the sunken living room. Together with the dining room, this space is ideal for entertaining large or small gatherings.
- The sprawling family room features its own fireplace, and shares a snack bar with the U-shaped kitchen.
- With its own deck and a sumptuous private bath, the master bedroom is sure to please.
- Upstairs, three identically sized bedrooms share a spacious full bath. A balcony area accesses a covered deck, and overlooks the living room.

Plans H-3708-1 & -1A

Bedrooms: 4	Baths: 2½
Living Area:	
Upper floor	893 sq. ft.
Main floor	2,006 sq. ft.
Total Living Area:	**2,899 sq. ft.**
Daylight basement	2,006 sq. ft.
Garage	512 sq. ft.
Exterior Wall Framing:	2x6
Foundation Options:	**Plan #**
Daylight basement	H-3708-1
Crawlspace	H-3708-1A

(All plans can be built with your choice of foundation and framing. A generic conversion diagram is available. See order form.)

BLUEPRINT PRICE CODE:	D

UPPER FLOOR

MAIN FLOOR

ORDER BLUEPRINTS ANYTIME!
CALL TOLL-FREE 1-800-820-1283

Plans H-3708-1 & -1A

PRICES AND DETAILS
ON PAGES 2-5

419

Gentle Breezes

- With or without palm trees, this design invokes a breezy sense of tropical relaxation. A unique front porch and upper- and lower-level rear verandas embrace the open outdoors.
- From the foyer, an arched opening sweeps guests into the expansive Grand Room, which boasts a fireplace, a 14-ft. tray ceiling and an optional aquarium.
- The breakfast nook flows into the kitchen, which shares an eating bar with the Grand Room. A large pantry and easy access to the formal dining room add to its practicality.
- A versatile study, to the left of the foyer, provides the perfect haven for you and

your favorite books. It can also be converted to an extra bedroom.
- The master suite encompasses the entire left wing of the home. Its fantastic features treat you as though you are at a spa resort!
- When you wake, throw open the French doors to the veranda for a breath of fresh air. Large walk-in closets connect the bedroom to its opulent private bath. Here, a garden tub, a separate shower, a dual-sink vanity and a compartmentalized toilet keep you feeling sane.
- Two additional bedrooms across the home share another full bath.
- Unless otherwise specified, all main-floor rooms feature 9-ft., 4-in. ceilings.

Plan SG-6622	
Bedrooms: 3+	**Baths: 2**
Living Area:	
Main floor	2,190 sq. ft.
Lower floor	1,383 sq. ft.
Total Living Area:	**3,573 sq. ft.**
Tuck-under garage	583 sq. ft.
Exterior Wall Framing:	2x6
Foundation Options:	

Slab
(All plans can be built with your choice of foundation and framing. A generic conversion diagram is available. See order form.)

BLUEPRINT PRICE CODE:	F

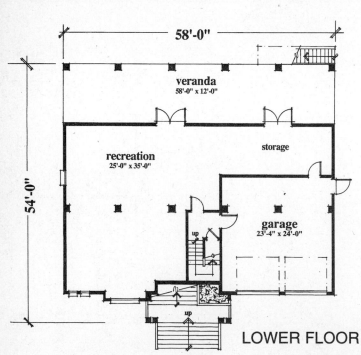

LOWER FLOOR

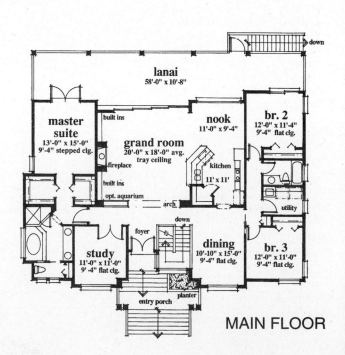

MAIN FLOOR

Comfortable Contemporary

- This home's contemporary facade and roofline give way to an impressive Great Room for ultimate comfort.
- The sidelighted two-story foyer unfolds directly to the spectacular sunken Great Room, which is highlighted by a 10-ft., open-beam ceiling. A wood-burning stove, a pair of ceiling fans and two French doors that open to a rear wraparound deck are also showcased.
- Sharing the Great Room's 10-ft. ceiling, the open kitchen boasts an eating bar and a pass through to the dining area.
- The secluded master bedroom features a TV wall with his-and-hers dressers. A French door provides access to a covered deck. The master bath flaunts a relaxing whirlpool tub and two vanities.
- Where not otherwise noted, the main-floor rooms have 9-ft. ceilings.
- A long balcony on the second level overlooks the foyer. Two good-sized bedrooms offer nice views of the backyard and share a full bath.

Plan LRD-22994

Bedrooms: 3	Baths: 2½
Living Area:	
Upper floor	692 sq. ft.
Main floor	1,777 sq. ft.
Total Living Area:	**2,469 sq. ft.**
Standard basement	1,655 sq. ft.
Garage	550 sq. ft.
Exterior Wall Framing:	2x6

Foundation Options:
Standard basement
Crawlspace
Slab
(All plans can be built with your choice of foundation and framing. A generic conversion diagram is available. See order form.)

BLUEPRINT PRICE CODE: C

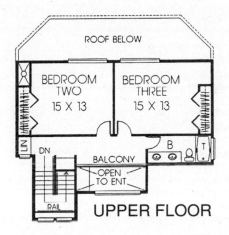

UPPER FLOOR

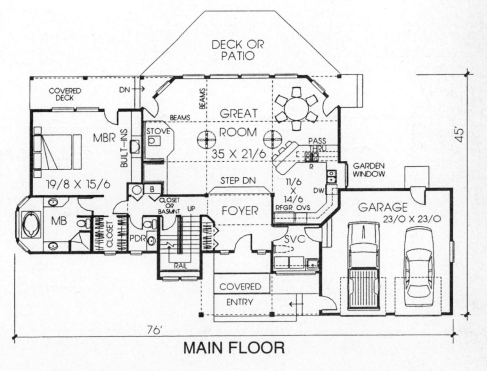

MAIN FLOOR

ORDER BLUEPRINTS ANYTIME!
CALL TOLL-FREE 1-800-820-1283

Plan LRD-22994

PRICES AND DETAILS
ON PAGES 2-5

421

Life in Action

- There's oodles of opportunity for a vigorous lifestyle in this delightful design. The upper-floor game room is large enough to host your Ping-Pong, air-hockey and Foosball tables!
- When you wish to stimulate your mind, the raised loft area is a prime spot for a library; it comes complete with built-in bookshelves.
- Downstairs, a mammoth family room and a breathtaking living room satisfy your need for casual and formal entertainment. Around the corner from the family room, a French door introduces a stunning covered veranda.
- Warmly connecting the bayed breakfast room and the island kitchen, a cheery fireplace brightens each new day.
- The master bedroom provides a cozy haven for those who need to retreat every now and then. A boxed-out window beckons you to read and relax, and the private access to the veranda allows you to bask in the glow of a full moon and its palette of stars.
- A cavernous walk-in closet and a gorgeous raised tub highlight the master bath. The separate shower and dual-sink vanity nicely complete the scene.

Plan L-727-HC

Bedrooms: 4+	Baths: 3 full, 2 half
Living Area:	
Upper floor	1,453 sq. ft.
Main floor	2,272 sq. ft.
Total Living Area:	**3,725 sq. ft.**
Garage	809 sq. ft.
Exterior Wall Framing:	2x4

Foundation Options:

Slab

(All plans can be built with your choice of foundation and framing. A generic conversion diagram is available. See order form.)

BLUEPRINT PRICE CODE:	F

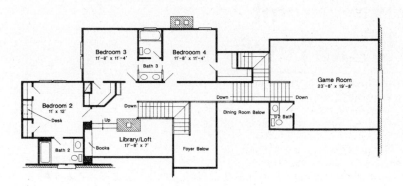

UPPER FLOOR

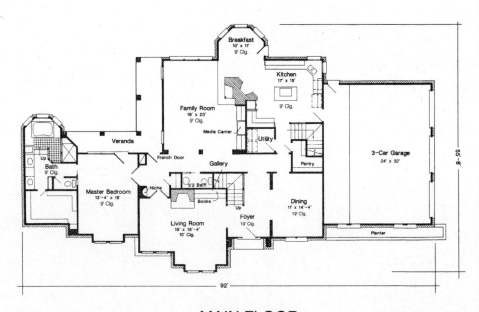

MAIN FLOOR

Magnificent Masonry Arch

- This beautiful brick home attracts the eye with its magnificent arch high above the recessed entry.
- The two-story-high foyer is highlighted by a huge half-round transom as it radiates between a bayed study and the elegant formal dining room.
- The fabulous kitchen boasts a walk-in pantry, a snack bar and a sunny bayed breakfast nook with backyard access.
- A fireplace flanked by windows brings comfort to the adjoining family room, which is set off from the main foyer by a stately architectural column.
- The main-floor master suite includes a private bath enhanced by a 13-ft. cathedral ceiling, a walk-in closet, a garden tub, a separate shower and two roomy vanities.
- Another full bath serves the study, which may be used as a bedroom.
- The upper-floor balcony leads to two secondary bedrooms, each with a tidy walk-in closet and private access to a shared split bath.

Plan KLF-9309

Bedrooms: 3+	Baths: 3
Living Area:	
Upper floor	574 sq. ft.
Main floor	1,863 sq. ft.
Total Living Area:	**2,437 sq. ft.**
Garage and tool storage	519 sq. ft.
Exterior Wall Framing:	2x4

Foundation Options:

Slab

(All plans can be built with your choice of foundation and framing. A generic conversion diagram is available. See order form.)

BLUEPRINT PRICE CODE: C

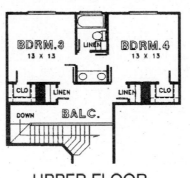

UPPER FLOOR

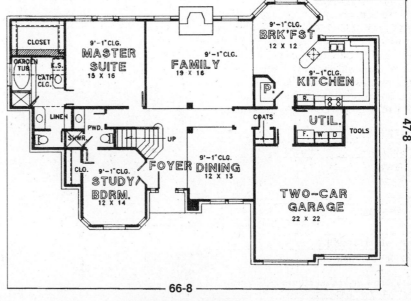

MAIN FLOOR

Enticing Estate

- This breathtaking estate entices you with its sweeping stature and gorgeous interior environment.
- Entry is granted at an intriguing angle; guests are immediately greeted by the sight of the home's elegant dining room and parlor.
- An archway ushers them into the family room, where a regal fireplace crackles and media shelves make for exciting nights. Sliding glass doors open to a covered patio that extends nearly the entire width of the home. An outdoor kitchen and a half-bath make this the perfect spot for a pool!

- Your family's budding chef will fall in love with the kitchen. It boasts an island cooktop and plenty of storage space. The breakfast nook offers a French door, through which you can sneak out to the front porch for a sun-blessed bowl of yogurt and granola.
- The secluded master suite is, in a word, grandiose. It boasts private access to the back patio, plus a juice bar in the sleeping chamber. The master bath features a shower built for two and a roman tub in the corner.
- Detached guest quarters let you sleep overnight visitors or provide a fitting place for in-laws to spend their retirement years with privacy.

Plan HDS-99-300	
Bedrooms: 3+	**Baths:** 3 full, 2 half
Living Area:	
Main floor	2,816 sq. ft.
Bonus room	290 sq. ft.
Guest quarters	330 sq. ft.
Total Living Area:	**3,436 sq. ft.**
Two-car garage	463 sq. ft.
One-car garage	384 sq. ft.
Exterior Wall Framing:	8-in. concrete block

Foundation Options:

Slab
(All plans can be built with your choice of foundation and framing. A generic conversion diagram is available. See order form.)

BLUEPRINT PRICE CODE:	E

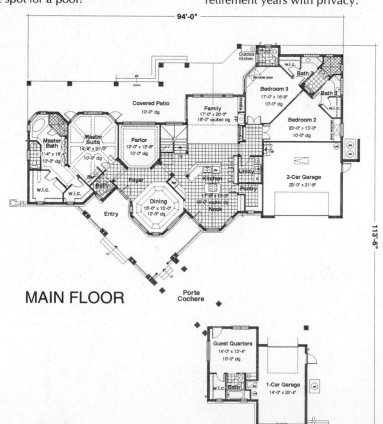

MAIN FLOOR

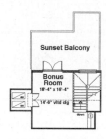

BONUS ROOM

Rapt in Country Memories

- This beautiful home's wraparound porch will carry you away to a time when all was right with the world.
- Triple dormers and nostalgic shuttered windows combine with gorgeous oval glass in the front door to make the facade charming indeed!
- Looks can be deceiving, however. The interior of the home is thoroughly up-to-date, with every conceivable feature.
- Straight back from the foyer, a fireplace and tall windows under a 19 ft. high cathedral ceiling make the living room a thing to behold.
- The roomy kitchen serves formal or casual meals with minimal effort. A breakfast nook and a serving counter host quick snacks.
- Two corner porches are easily accessible for thoughtful moments.
- Or, refresh yourself in the master suite's garden tub. A good book will keep you there for hours.
- Upstairs, the game room's balcony offers sweeping views; two big bedrooms share a nice bath.

Plan L-2449-VC

Bedrooms: 3	Baths: 2½
Living Area:	
Upper floor	780 sq. ft.
Main floor	1,669 sq. ft.
Total Living Area:	**2,449 sq. ft.**
Exterior Wall Framing:	2x4

Foundation Options:

Slab

(All plans can be built with your choice of foundation and framing. A generic conversion diagram is available. See order form.)

BLUEPRINT PRICE CODE: C

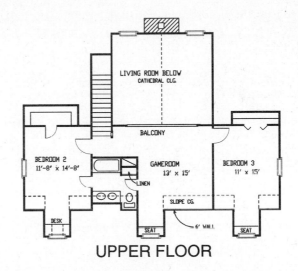

UPPER FLOOR

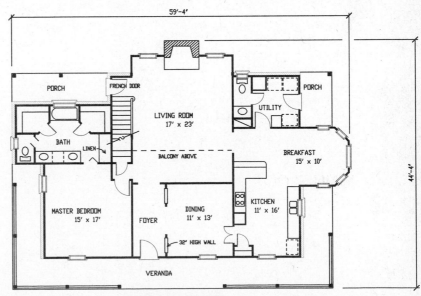

MAIN FLOOR

ORDER BLUEPRINTS ANYTIME!
CALL TOLL-FREE 1-800-820-1283

Plan L-2449-VC

PRICES AND DETAILS
ON PAGES 2-5

425

True Grit

- Traditional Arts and Crafts styling gives this bungalow grit and durability. Its bold, low-maintenance exterior combines natural stone and cedar.
- Inside, skylights and transom windows produce plenty of natural light for the thoroughly modern floor plan.
- A lofty 20-ft.-high ceiling soars above the foyer and the Great Room, which are separated by a dramatic stone fireplace and a railed balcony.
- A decorative arch and wood-framed glass doors surround the Great Room's large-screen media center, while skylights overhead radiate sunshine.
- The functional island kitchen enjoys an ideal location near the busy living spaces and the laundry room. You won't miss your favorite TV show as you're washing the dinner dishes!
- A compartmentalized private bath with a delightful garden tub keeps the owners of this home pampered in style.
- Two more bedrooms share the upper floor with a versatile bonus room that can be tailored to your needs.

Plan GA-9601

Bedrooms: 3+	Baths: 2½
Living Area:	
Upper floor	594 sq. ft.
Main floor	1,996 sq. ft.
Total Living Area:	**2,590 sq. ft.**
Unfinished bonus room	233 sq. ft.
Standard basement	1,996 sq. ft.
Garage	576 sq. ft.
Exterior Wall Framing:	2x6

Foundation Options:

Standard basement
(All plans can be built with your choice of foundation and framing. A generic conversion diagram is available. See order form.)

BLUEPRINT PRICE CODE: D

UPPER FLOOR

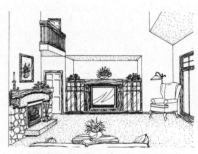

VIEW INTO GREAT ROOM

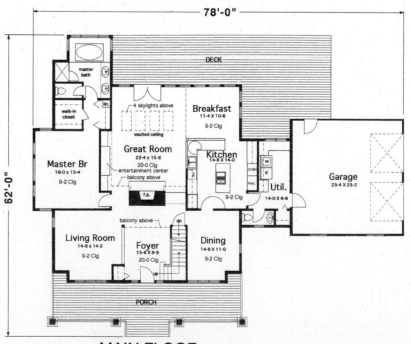

MAIN FLOOR

ORDER BLUEPRINTS ANYTIME!
CALL TOLL-FREE 1-800-820-1283

Plan GA-9601

PRICES AND DETAILS
ON PAGES 2-5

Think Big

- For those who demand nothing but the best in their lives and their homes, this grand two-story design promises an elegant setting for every type of affair.
- Soaring columns dominate the facade as they usher guests inside with an impressive formality. Once inside, the beautiful curved staircase in the two-story foyer recalls a more regal era.
- For your most important gatherings, the two-story living room fosters a dignified air. Built-in cabinets on either side of the fireplace display fine works of art, while two sets of French doors create a pretty picture on the far wall.
- For day-to-day activities, the home's casual area fits the bill. Here, the busiest rooms in the home—the kitchen, the family room and the breakfast nook—are located close to one another.
- When you need some time to call your own, retreat to your private oasis in the master suite. Here, a bayed sitting area offers you a spot for contemplation. In the bath, the luxurious raised tub will take all your worries away.
- Upstairs, a loft overlooking the family room serves nicely as a reading nook.

Plan FB-5497-CAST

Bedrooms: 4	Baths: 3½
Living Area:	
Upper floor	1,598 sq. ft.
Main floor	2,764 sq. ft.
Total Living Area:	**4,362 sq. ft.**
Daylight basement	2,764 sq. ft.
Garage	743 sq. ft.
Exterior Wall Framing:	2x4

Foundation Options:

Daylight basement

(All plans can be built with your choice of foundation and framing. A generic conversion diagram is available. See order form.)

BLUEPRINT PRICE CODE: G

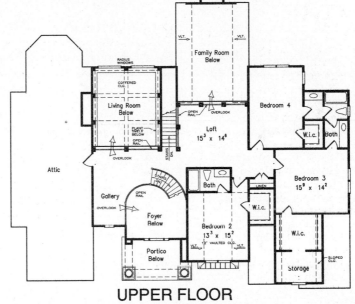

UPPER FLOOR

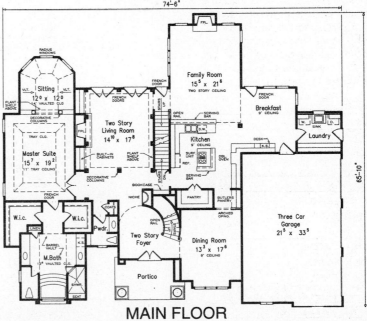

MAIN FLOOR

ORDER BLUEPRINTS ANYTIME!
CALL TOLL-FREE 1-800-820-1283

Plan FB-5497-CAST

PRICES AND DETAILS
ON PAGES 2-5

427

Large as Life

- With its impressive stucco exterior and amenity-packed interior, this elegant home will serve as a constant reminder of your many successes.
- Double doors usher guests inside, where a stunning 21½-ft. ceiling in the foyer and the parlour will draw compliments. A view of the parlour's series of French doors topped by high arched windows completes the grand entrance.
- During dinners, the pretty dining room ensures the perfect setting. A pass-through ale bar under a graceful arch saves steps to and from the kitchen.
- For life's less formal occasions, retreat to the gathering room. Here, a 14½-ft. vaulted ceiling visually enlarges the space, while an entertainment niche neatly holds media equipment. A serving bar by the kitchen keeps chips and soda nearby during movie nights.
- Across the home, a 12-ft. tray ceiling lends style to the master suite. Late at night, read your favorite novel by the fireplace in the sitting room.
- Upstairs, a good-sized loft can be closed in to serve as an additional bedroom.
- Unless otherwise noted, all rooms include 10-ft. ceilings.

Plan EOF-11

Bedrooms: 3+	Baths: 4
Living Area:	
Upper floor	882 sq. ft.
Main floor	2,844 sq. ft.
Total Living Area:	**3,726 sq. ft.**
Garage	538 sq. ft.
Exterior Wall Framing:	2x6

Foundation Options:

Slab

(All plans can be built with your choice of foundation and framing. A generic conversion diagram is available. See order form.)

BLUEPRINT PRICE CODE: F

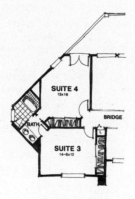

ALTERNATE UPPER FLOOR

UPPER FLOOR

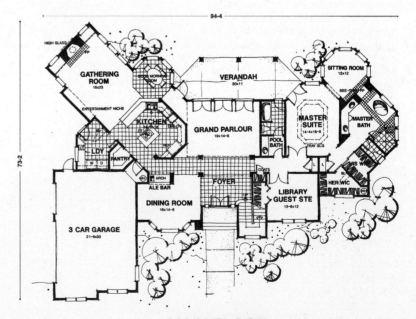

MAIN FLOOR

ORDER BLUEPRINTS ANYTIME!
CALL TOLL-FREE 1-800-820-1283

Plan EOF-11

PRICES AND DETAILS
ON PAGES 2-5

Attractive Stone

- A stone facade gives this cozy country home an attractive countenance.
- Serving as the focal point of the foyer, a graceful staircase curves up to three secondary bedrooms and a huge game room that is perfect for wild weekends!
- The formal areas lie to the right of the foyer, within easy serving distance of the kitchen, where an island cooktop and a serving counter make meal preparation truly enjoyable.
- An adjacent bayed breakfast nook flows into the sprawling family room, where a handsome fireplace spreads warmth. Three sets of beautiful French doors open to a huge covered deck.
- Bayed and boxed-out windows liven the secluded master bedroom, which boasts a lovely stepped ceiling. The master bath is enhanced by a luxurious whirlpool tub tucked into a bayed window, plus a separate shower and twin walk-in closets.
- Near a handy powder room, a quiet study or extra bedroom overlooks the covered front porch.

Plan DD-3820-C

Bedrooms: 4+	Baths: 3 full, 2 half
Living Area:	
Upper floor	1,350 sq. ft.
Main floor	2,530 sq. ft.
Total Living Area:	**3,880 sq. ft.**
Standard basement	2,530 sq. ft.
Garage	830 sq. ft.
Exterior Wall Framing:	2x4

Foundation Options:
Standard basement
Crawlspace
Slab
(All plans can be built with your choice of foundation and framing. A generic conversion diagram is available. See order form.)

BLUEPRINT PRICE CODE: F

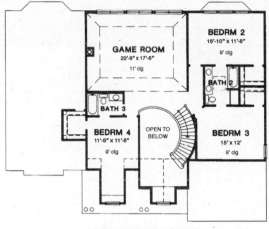

UPPER FLOOR

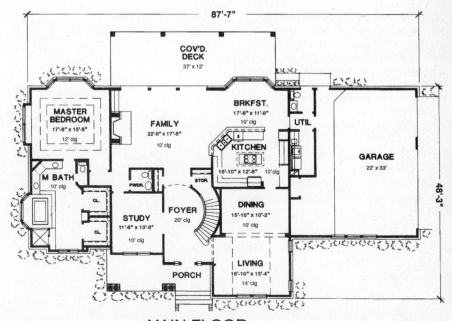

MAIN FLOOR

ORDER BLUEPRINTS ANYTIME!
CALL TOLL-FREE 1-800-820-1283

Plan DD-3820-C

PRICES AND DETAILS
ON PAGES 2-5

429

Loaded with Amenities

- This beautiful home offers a stunning interior that is loaded with amenities.
- The sidelighted entry gives way to a terrific two-story-high foyer, which is brightened from above by a charming clerestory window arrangement.
- The large living room flows into the formal dining room for plenty of entertaining space.
- The open kitchen offers a wonderful work island and a handy lazy Susan. The adjacent dinette features a planning desk, a pantry closet and outdoor access through sliding glass doors.
- An 11-ft., 9-in. cathedral ceiling presides over the sunken family room, which boasts a nice fireplace and a generous view of the backyard.
- The quiet study would make a great den, home office or guest room.
- Upstairs, the big master suite includes a private bath and a walk-in closet. Three additional bedrooms share a hall bath.

Plan A-2165-DS

Bedrooms: 4+	Baths: 2½
Living Area:	
Upper floor	980 sq. ft.
Main floor	1,362 sq. ft.
Total Living Area:	**2,342 sq. ft.**
Standard basement	1,362 sq. ft.
Garage	484 sq. ft.
Exterior Wall Framing:	2x4

Foundation Options:

Standard basement

(All plans can be built with your choice of foundation and framing. A generic conversion diagram is available. See order form.)

BLUEPRINT PRICE CODE: C

UPPER FLOOR

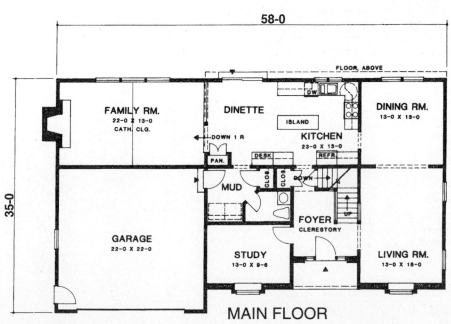

MAIN FLOOR

ORDER BLUEPRINTS ANYTIME!
CALL TOLL-FREE 1-800-820-1283

Plan A-2165-DS

PRICES AND DETAILS
ON PAGES 2-5

Clearly Country

- This country-style home boasts beautiful columns and plenty of glass on its facade for great front views.
- The sidelighted 18-ft.-high entry leads nicely into the living room, which features a handsome fireplace.
- To the right of the entry, the formal dining room is perfect for special meals.
- Close by, the island kitchen is well placed for entertaining. Bay windows brighten the cheery breakfast nook; a French door leads to a sprawling backyard patio.
- Another fireplace graces the family room, with its entertainment center and French-door access to the patio.
- The master bedroom flaunts a gorgeous bay window. The master bath is enhanced by a garden tub and a high plant shelf.
- All main-floor rooms have 9-ft. ceilings.
- Upstairs, walk-in closets highlight the secondary bedrooms. One bedroom boasts a private bath; another bath is shared by the other two bedrooms.

Plan DD-2779

Bedrooms: 4	Baths: 3½
Living Area:	
Upper floor	825 sq. ft.
Main floor	1,954 sq. ft.
Total Living Area:	**2,779 sq. ft.**
Standard basement	1,954 sq. ft.
Garage	422 sq. ft.
Exterior Wall Framing:	2x4

Foundation Options:

Standard basement
Crawlspace
Slab

(All plans can be built with your choice of foundation and framing. A generic conversion diagram is available. See order form.)

BLUEPRINT PRICE CODE:	D

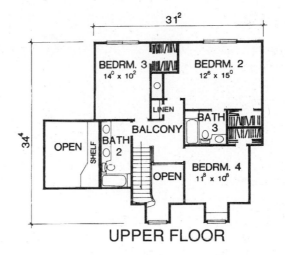

UPPER FLOOR

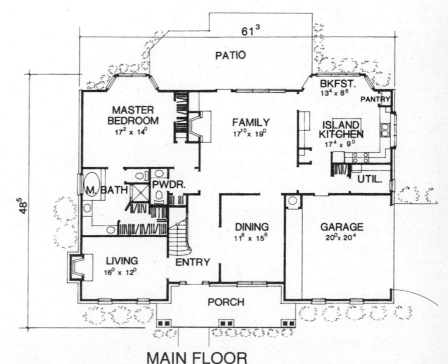

MAIN FLOOR

ORDER BLUEPRINTS ANYTIME!
CALL TOLL-FREE 1-800-820-1283

Plan DD-2779

PRICES AND DETAILS
ON PAGES 2-5
431

Home at Last!

- Whether you're returning from a business trip or a personal vacation, you'll never get tired of coming home to this spectacular stucco delight.
- Breezy outdoor spaces parade around the home, starting with a nostalgic front porch and ending at a relaxing spa tub on a sprawling backyard deck.
- The spacious interior is bright and open. Past the entry, a gallery with French doors leads to the superb kitchen.
- The family can discuss the day's news over breakfast at the big snack bar or in the sunny bayed morning room.
- For activities of a larger scale, the living room offers an engaging fireplace, exciting views and enough space to house your entertainment equipment.
- A two-sided fireplace adds a romantic glow to the master bedroom and private sitting area. The elegant, skylighted master bath promises luxury for two!
- All main-floor rooms have 9-ft. ceilings.
- The upper-floor bedrooms are furnished with a shared bath and their own walk-in closets and sunny sitting spaces.

Plan DD-2617

Bedrooms: 4	Baths: 3
Living Area:	
Upper floor	609 sq. ft.
Main floor	2,034 sq. ft.
Total Living Area:	**2,643 sq. ft.**
Standard basement	2,034 sq. ft.
Garage and storage	544 sq. ft.
Exterior Wall Framing:	2x4

Foundation Options:

Standard basement
Crawlspace
Slab

(All plans can be built with your choice of foundation and framing. A generic conversion diagram is available. See order form.)

BLUEPRINT PRICE CODE:	D

UPPER FLOOR

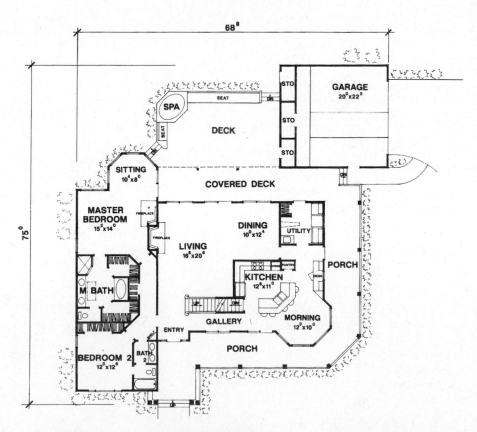

MAIN FLOOR

ORDER BLUEPRINTS ANYTIME!
CALL TOLL-FREE 1-800-820-1283

Plan DD-2617

PRICES AND DETAILS
ON PAGES 2-5

Eye-Catching Exterior

- This attractive home boasts a warm blend of wood, brick and stone on the outside and plenty of space for a big, busy family inside.
- A clerestory-brightened foyer flows into the large living room, which includes an impressive fireplace as it joins the dining room to create a gorgeous space for entertaining.
- The sunny kitchen offers a dinette that opens to the backyard. A step down from the dinette, the bayed family room boasts another fireplace.
- A library with built-in bookshelves makes a great home office.
- Upstairs, the master suite features a spacious sleeping area, two large windows, a dressing area, a large walk-in closet and a private bath with an enticing whirlpool tub.
- The three remaining bedrooms are roomy and share a convenient hall bath that has a dual-sink vanity.

Plan A-130	
Bedrooms: 4	**Baths:** 2½
Living Area:	
Upper floor	1,305 sq. ft.
Main floor	1,502 sq. ft.
Total Living Area:	**2,807 sq. ft.**
Standard basement	1,502 sq. ft.
Garage	576 sq. ft.
Exterior Wall Framing:	2x4
Foundation Options:	

Standard basement
(All plans can be built with your choice of foundation and framing. A generic conversion diagram is available. See order form.)

BLUEPRINT PRICE CODE:	D

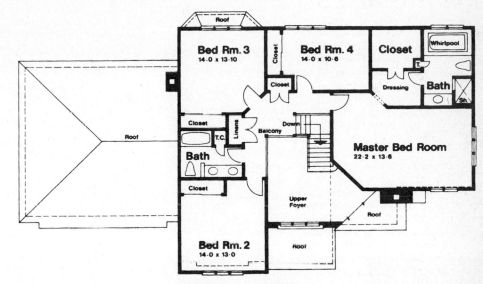

UPPER FLOOR

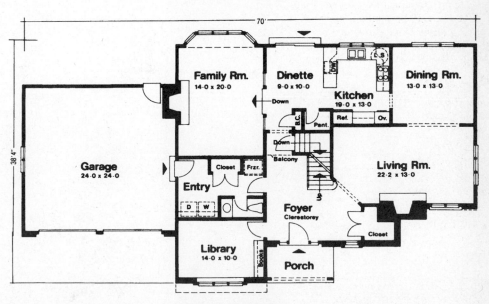

MAIN FLOOR

ORDER BLUEPRINTS ANYTIME!
CALL TOLL-FREE 1-800-820-1283

Plan A-130

PRICES AND DETAILS
ON PAGES 2-5

433

A Gallant Effort

- A wrought-iron balcony, stylish arches and striking stucco lend a European flair to this home's gallant facade.

- Beyond the exquisite entry, a 19-ft.-high foyer shows off a sweeping stairway that climbs to the "Romeo" balcony high above.

- Columned arches introduce the dining room and the central Great Room, which also has a soaring 19-ft. ceiling.

- An island cooktop, a convenient snack bar and two pantries keep the spacious kitchen neat and organized. Relax with your morning coffee in the breakfast room or the adjacent Keeping Room.

- If you prefer privacy, the master suite's sunny sitting area and luxurious whirlpool tub are just steps away from your bed. After you've chosen your clothes from your personal closet, get ready for the day at the vanity's handy knee space.

- Two more baths, three secondary bedrooms and a great game room for the kids occupy the upper floor. The game room can also be accessed from a stairway near the kitchen.

Plan BOD-42-1A

Bedrooms: 4+	Baths: 3½
Living Area:	
Upper floor	1,625 sq. ft.
Main floor	2,639 sq. ft.
Total Living Area:	**4,264 sq. ft.**
Garage and storage	511 sq. ft.
Exterior Wall Framing:	2x4

Foundation Options:
Crawlspace
Slab
(All plans can be built with your choice of foundation and framing. A generic conversion diagram is available. See order form.)

BLUEPRINT PRICE CODE:	G

REAR VIEW

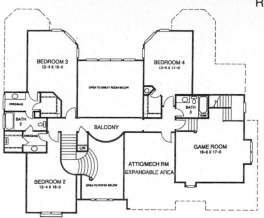

UPPER FLOOR

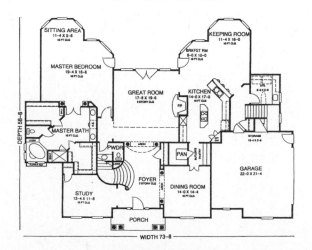

MAIN FLOOR

ORDER BLUEPRINTS ANYTIME!
CALL TOLL-FREE 1-800-820-1283

Plan BOD-42-1A

PRICES AND DETAILS
ON PAGES 2-5

Feature-Packed

- This comfortable design combines every feature on your wish list, for a perfectly stunning addition to any neighborhood.
- Transom and sidelight windows brighten the stylish, open foyer.
- Tasteful entertaining begins in the living room, with its boxed-out window and 18-ft. ceiling. Not to be outdone, the dining room's ceiling soars to 22 feet.
- The family chef will love the kitchen, which boasts an island cooktop, a big pantry and a menu desk. Defined by a 36-in.-high wall, the breakfast nook offers a casual spot for enjoying everyday meals.

- The large family room's wet bar, fireplace and media niche set you up for a relaxing evening at home.
- Available for changing family needs, the swing suite would make a perfect spot for an aging parent or a home office.
- All main-floor rooms offer 9-ft. ceilings, unless otherwise noted.
- The upper floor hosts a fabulous master suite with an 11-ft. ceiling and a great exercise area. Three more bedrooms complete the plan.

Plan B-93020	
Bedrooms: 4+	Baths: 4
Living Area:	
Upper floor	1,590 sq. ft.
Main floor	1,890 sq. ft.
Total Living Area:	**3,480 sq. ft.**
Standard basement	1,890 sq. ft.
Garage and storage	629 sq. ft.
Exterior Wall Framing:	2x6

Foundation Options:

Standard basement
(All plans can be built with your choice of foundation and framing. A generic conversion diagram is available. See order form.)

BLUEPRINT PRICE CODE:	E

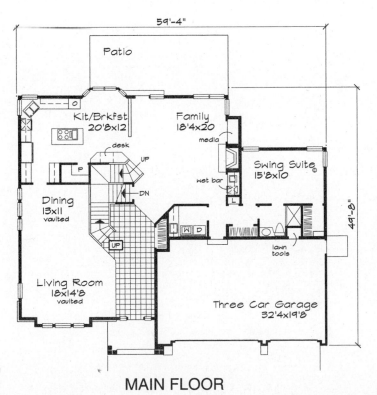

MAIN FLOOR

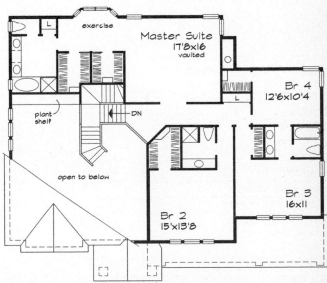

UPPER FLOOR

ORDER BLUEPRINTS ANYTIME!
CALL TOLL-FREE 1-800-820-1283

Plan B-93020

PRICES AND DETAILS
ON PAGES 2-5

435

Gracious Days

- As it brings a touch of Victorian flair to this country-style home, a charming gazebo provides a gracious spot for afternoon visits and lemonade.
- Inside, the living and dining rooms flank the foyer, creating an elegant setting for parties. With a closet and private access to a bath, the living room could also be used as a bedroom or a home office.
- Straight ahead, handsome columns frame the Great Room, where puddles of sunshine will form under the two skylights. Sliding glass doors let in the fresh scent of spring blooms. A corner fireplace warms chilled fingers after an afternoon of raking leaves.
- In the kitchen, a sizable island doubles as a workstation and a snack bar. The sunny bay in the breakfast nook will rouse the sleepiest child.
- Across the home, the owners receive some extra special treatment in the master suite. Features here include a pair of walk-in closets, a linen closet and a bath with a dual-sink vanity.

VIEW INTO GREAT ROOM

Plan AX-95349

Bedrooms: 3+	Baths: 3
Living Area:	
Upper floor	728 sq. ft.
Main floor	2,146 sq. ft.
Total Living Area:	**2,874 sq. ft.**
Unfinished loft	300 sq. ft.
Standard basement	2,146 sq. ft.
Garage	624 sq. ft.
Exterior Wall Framing:	2x6

Foundation Options:

Standard basement
Crawlspace
Slab

(All plans can be built with your choice of foundation and framing. A generic conversion diagram is available. See order form.)

BLUEPRINT PRICE CODE:	D

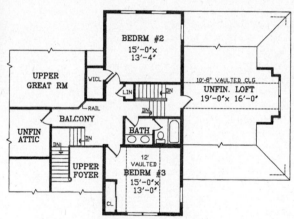

UPPER FLOOR

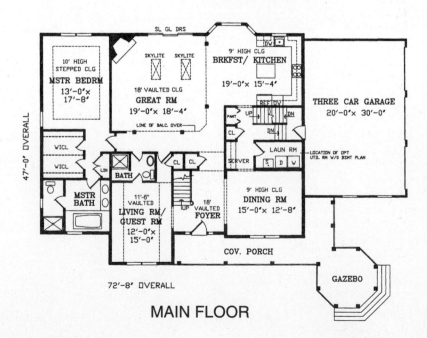

MAIN FLOOR

ORDER BLUEPRINTS ANYTIME!
CALL TOLL-FREE 1-800-820-1283

Plan AX-95349

PRICES AND DETAILS
ON PAGES 2-5

Stately Style

- Classic columns and half-round windows enhance the facade of this beautiful two-story home.
- The bright, sidelighted foyer offers views across a columned half-wall into the living room, which boasts a 17-ft. vaulted ceiling and a cozy fireplace.
- Decorative columns also flank the entrance to the formal dining room.
- Close by, the gourmet kitchen adjoins a charming breakfast nook. French doors set into a wall of windows open to a spacious backyard deck.
- The nearby sunken family room with a 17-ft. vaulted ceiling promises fun-filled evenings. Its amenities include a wet bar, a cheery fireplace and French doors to the deck.
- Adjacent to the family room, a swing suite with private bath access can be tailored to meet changing needs.
- Upstairs, the luxurious master bedroom features a 12-ft. vaulted ceiling and a quiet sitting room for private reflection in comfort. The master bath is enhanced by a walk-through closet, a platform tub and a dual-sink vanity.

Plan B-93019

Bedrooms: 4+	Baths: 3
Living Area:	
Upper floor	1,190 sq. ft.
Main floor	1,433 sq. ft.
Total Living Area:	**2,623 sq. ft.**
Standard basement	1,433 sq. ft.
Garage	450 sq. ft.
Exterior Wall Framing:	2x4

Foundation Options:

Standard basement

(All plans can be built with your choice of foundation and framing. A generic conversion diagram is available. See order form.)

BLUEPRINT PRICE CODE: D

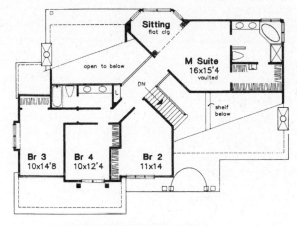

UPPER FLOOR

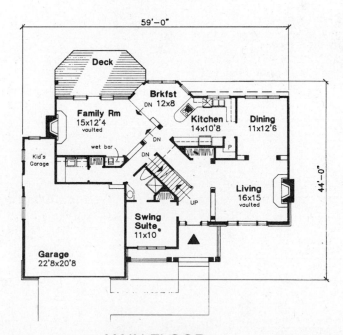

MAIN FLOOR

ORDER BLUEPRINTS ANYTIME!
CALL TOLL-FREE 1-800-820-1283

Plan B-93019

**PRICES AND DETAILS
ON PAGES 2-5**

437

Sweet Nostalgia

- This two-story design conjures up sweet memories of simpler days, when home served as grand central for the family.
- A covered porch out front whispers a quiet welcome to visitors. On summer nights, pull up a chair to listen to the pitter-patter of the raindrops.
- Inside, the Great Room acts as home base for daily activities. An 18-ft. vaulted ceiling opens up the space, while a fireplace adds cheer.
- Finding someone to cook will be a snap once the family sees the kitchen. Even a master chef would envy the island cooktop and workstation.
- Across the home, a stylish 13½-ft. vaulted ceiling makes the master suite extra special. After a day of hiking, sink into the whirlpool tub to rejuvenate.
- Unless otherwise noted, every room on the main floor has a 9-ft. ceiling.
- Upstairs, the bath and front bedrooms include dormers under 10½-ft. ceilings. The family's students can turn these dormers into neat reading nooks.

Plan AHP-9550

Bedrooms: 4	Baths: 2½
Living Area:	
Upper floor	762 sq. ft.
Main floor	1,689 sq. ft.
Total Living Area:	**2,451 sq. ft.**
Standard basement	1,689 sq. ft.
Garage and storage	484 sq. ft.
Exterior Wall Framing:	2x4 or 2x6

Foundation Options:

Standard basement

Crawlspace

Slab

(All plans can be built with your choice of foundation and framing. A generic conversion diagram is available. See order form.)

BLUEPRINT PRICE CODE: C

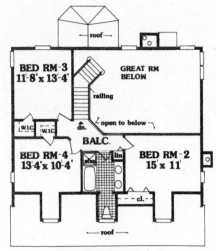

UPPER FLOOR

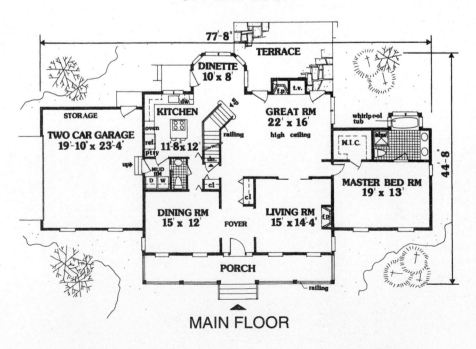

MAIN FLOOR

 ORDER BLUEPRINTS ANYTIME!
CALL TOLL-FREE 1-800-820-1283

Plan AHP-9550

PRICES AND DETAILS
ON PAGES 2-5

Creative Curves

- A creative floor plan adds excitement to this elegant European-inspired estate.
- Brightened by high windows, the two-story-high foyer features a curved staircase. Visible from the foyer past a columned half-wall, the formal dining room is serviced by a uniquely shaped wet bar in the island kitchen.
- The designer kitchen, enhanced by a 12-ft. domed ceiling, has wraparound windows over the corner sink, a panoramic breakfast area and a built-in media center with a computer desk.
- The family room, which has an 18-ft. ceiling and sliding glass doors to a rear deck, is separated from the two-story-high living room by a warming see-through fireplace.
- The master suite has a 9-ft. tray ceiling and a stylish bow window. The master bath boasts a spa tub, a separate shower, dual vanities and a walk-in closet.
- Upstairs, a railed balcony overlooks the foyer and the living room. Ideal for use as guest quarters, one of the three upstairs bedrooms has a private bath.

Plan B-91029

Bedrooms: 4	Baths: 3½
Living Area:	
Upper floor	909 sq. ft.
Main floor	2,194 sq. ft.
Total Living Area:	**3,103 sq. ft.**
Standard basement	2,194 sq. ft.
Garage	692 sq. ft.
Exterior Wall Framing:	2x6

Foundation Options:

Standard basement

(All plans can be built with your choice of foundation and framing. A generic conversion diagram is available. See order form.)

BLUEPRINT PRICE CODE:	E

UPPER FLOOR

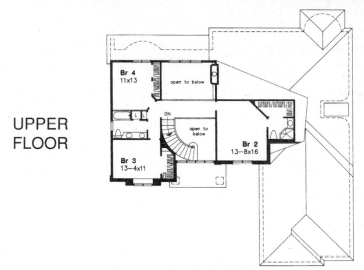

MAIN FLOOR

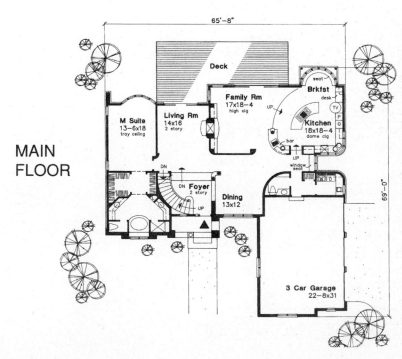

CALL TOLL-FREE 1-800-820-1283

Plan B-91029

PRICES AND DETAILS ON PAGES 2-5

439

Place of Peace

- This elegant home's covered front and back porches promise moments of sweet tranquility.
- A vaulted turret dominates the home's facade, which serves as a sophisticated introduction to the interior.
- Straight ahead through the two-story foyer, the Great Room boasts a window wall overlooking the back porch and a fine fireplace for warmth and romance.
- The large breakfast room is the perfect complement to the walk-through kitchen. The path from the kitchen to the prowed dining room passes through a tidy butler's pantry.
- Solitude is the operative word in the master bedroom, which drapes you in warmth from its fireplace and grants passage to the back porch through sliding glass doors. The opulent bath delivers a whirlpool tub, a separate shower and a walk-in closet.

REAR VIEW

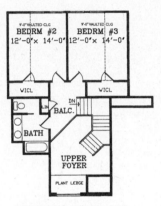

UPPER FLOOR

Plan AX-94329

Bedrooms: 3	Baths: 2½
Living Area:	
Upper floor	570 sq. ft.
Main floor	1,808 sq. ft.
Total Living Area:	**2,378 sq. ft.**
Standard basement	1,808 sq. ft.
Garage, storage and utility	461 sq. ft.
Exterior Wall Framing:	**2x4**

Foundation Options:

Standard basement
Crawlspace
Slab
(All plans can be built with your choice of foundation and framing. A generic conversion diagram is available. See order form.)

BLUEPRINT PRICE CODE:	**C**

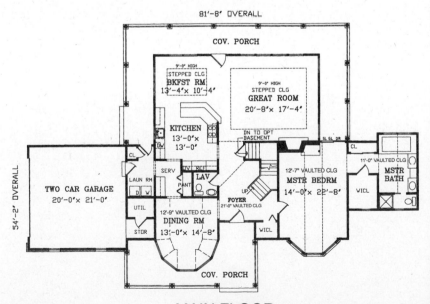

MAIN FLOOR

ORDER BLUEPRINTS ANYTIME!
CALL TOLL-FREE 1-800-820-1283

Plan AX-94329

PRICES AND DETAILS
ON PAGES 2-5

Picture-Perfect

- Those tall, cold glasses of summertime lemonade will taste even better when enjoyed on the shady front porch of this picture-perfect home.

- Inside, the two-story, sidelighted foyer unfolds to the formal living areas and the Great Room beyond.

- Fireplaces grace the living room and the Great Room, which are separated by French pocket doors. A TV nook borders the fireplace in the Great Room, letting the kids catch their favorite show while Mom and Dad fix dinner in the kitchen. Two sets of French doors swing wide to reveal a backyard deck.

- A glassy dinette with an 8-ft. ceiling makes breakfasts cozy and comfortable.

- Restful nights will be the norm in the master suite, which boasts a 14-ft. cathedral ceiling. Next to the walk-in closet, the private bath has a whirlpool tub in a fabulous boxed-out window.

- Unless otherwise noted, all main-floor rooms are topped by 9-ft. ceilings.

- At day's end, guests and children may retire to the upper floor, where four big bedrooms and a full bath await them.

Plan AHP-9512

Bedrooms: 5	Baths: 2½
Living Area:	
Upper floor	928 sq. ft.
Main floor	1,571 sq. ft.
Total Living Area:	**2,499 sq. ft.**
Standard basement	1,571 sq. ft.
Garage and storage	420 sq. ft.
Exterior Wall Framing:	2x4 or 2x6

Foundation Options:

Standard basement

Crawlspace

Slab

(All plans can be built with your choice of foundation and framing. A generic conversion diagram is available. See order form.)

BLUEPRINT PRICE CODE: **C**

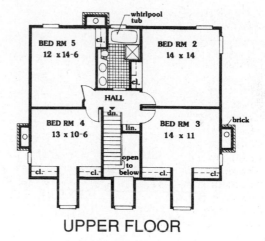

UPPER FLOOR

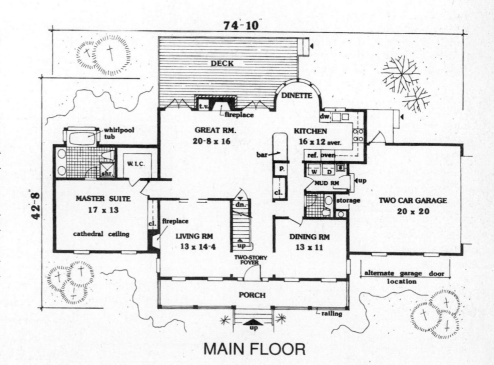

MAIN FLOOR

ORDER BLUEPRINTS ANYTIME!
CALL TOLL-FREE 1-800-820-1283

Plan AHP-9512

**PRICES AND DETAILS
ON PAGES 2-5**

441

Distinct Design

- This home's distinct design is seen from the curvature of its covered porch to its decorative wrought-iron roof rail.
- The 17-ft.-high foyer is lighted in an oval theme, through the clerestory window, the front door and its flanking sidelights. The broad foyer stretches between the vaulted formal living areas and a casual TV room across from a full bath.
- With its unique corner design, the fireplace in the Great Room also warms the unusual rounded dining room and the breakfast area.
- The dining room boasts a 14-ft-high ceiling, while the kitchen features an angled sink, a nearby pantry and a handy wet bar facing the Great Room.
- The master suite, with its 13-ft.-high tray ceiling, offers a bath with a spa tub and a designer shower, both brightened by glass blocks.
- Upstairs, a balcony hall leads to a turreted recreation room, two bedrooms and a full bath.

Plan AX-92326

Bedrooms: 3+	Baths: 3
Living Area:	
Upper floor	736 sq. ft.
Main floor	1,960 sq. ft.
Total Living Area:	**2,696 sq. ft.**
Standard basement	1,915 sq. ft.
Garage	455 sq. ft.
Exterior Wall Framing:	2x4

Foundation Options:

Standard basement
Crawlspace
Slab

(All plans can be built with your choice of foundation and framing. A generic conversion diagram is available. See order form.)

BLUEPRINT PRICE CODE:	D

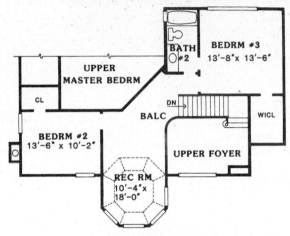

UPPER FLOOR

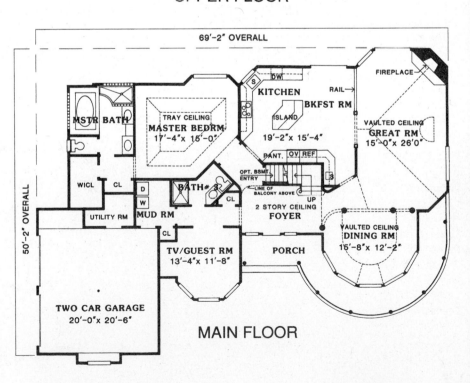

MAIN FLOOR

ORDER BLUEPRINTS ANYTIME!
CALL TOLL-FREE 1-800-820-1283

Plan AX-92326

PRICES AND DETAILS
ON PAGES 2-5

Striking Facade

- Flattering windows and a striking roofline grace the facade of this comfortable and appealing home.
- Down the short hallway to the right of the two-story foyer, the living room offers a cozy atmosphere. The adjoining den, with attractive window seats, may be converted into a bedroom, if desired.
- Directly ahead of the foyer, the large family room sports a 16-ft., 8-in. tray ceiling and a crackling fireplace.
- Around the corner, the island kitchen flows into a dinette with a built-in desk and sliding doors to the backyard. The nearby garage entrance has a cute changing bench.
- All main-floor rooms have 9-ft. ceilings.
- Beautiful balcony views highlight the upstairs sleeping area.
- The master bedroom is enhanced by a 10-ft. tray ceiling and a large walk-in closet. The master bath boasts a platform tub, a separate shower and a private toilet.
- Three secondary bedrooms and an optional bonus room round out the upper floor.

Plan A-2353-DS

Bedrooms: 4+	**Baths:** 2½
Living Area:	
Upper floor	1,135 sq. ft.
Main floor	1,411 sq. ft.
Total Living Area:	**2,546 sq. ft.**
Bonus room (unfinished)	312 sq. ft.
Standard basement	1,411 sq. ft.
Garage	549 sq. ft.
Exterior Wall Framing:	2x6

Foundation Options:

Standard basement

(All plans can be built with your choice of foundation and framing. A generic conversion diagram is available. See order form.)

BLUEPRINT PRICE CODE: D

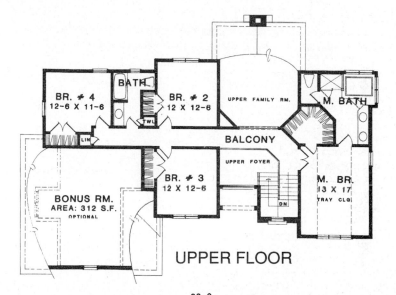

UPPER FLOOR

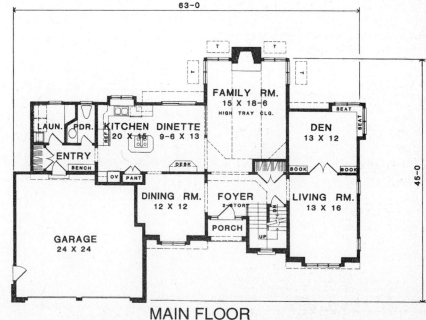

MAIN FLOOR

ORDER BLUEPRINTS ANYTIME!
CALL TOLL-FREE 1-800-820-1283

Plan A-2353-DS

PRICES AND DETAILS
ON PAGES 2-5

443

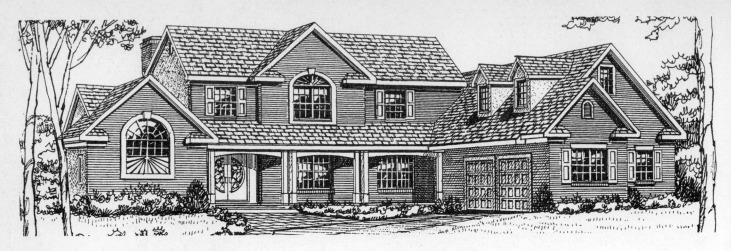

Rites of Passage

- As your family's life passes from stage to stage, you'll appreciate how this warm country home remains flexible.
- When the kids are robust and rowdy, there's plenty of room to roam in the central Great Room. On warm days, if they're not content in their upper-floor bedrooms, you can shoo them to the home's huge front porch.
- Mornings will find you in the island kitchen, the smell of bacon wafting over the adjoining breakfast nook.
- Your circle of friends will change from time to time; entertaining them is easy in the formal living and dining rooms, which are open to each other, but defined by eye-catching columns.
- A fabulous oasis awaits you in the master bedroom, which basks in natural sunlight from its bayed window. The master bath includes a whirlpool tub beneath a 12-ft. ceiling.
- As your parents pass into the autumn of their lives, they can live with dignity in their secluded suite, which pampers them with private access to a porch, plus a walk-in closet and a full bath.

Plan AX-5372

Bedrooms: 4	Baths: 3½
Living Area:	
Upper floor	581 sq. ft.
Main floor	2,182 sq. ft.
Total Living Area:	**2,763 sq. ft.**
Future attic expansion	437 sq. ft.
Standard basement	2,180 sq. ft.
Garage and storage	594 sq. ft.
Exterior Wall Framing:	2x4

Foundation Options:

Standard basement

Crawlspace

Slab

(All plans can be built with your choice of foundation and framing. A generic conversion diagram is available. See order form.)

BLUEPRINT PRICE CODE: D

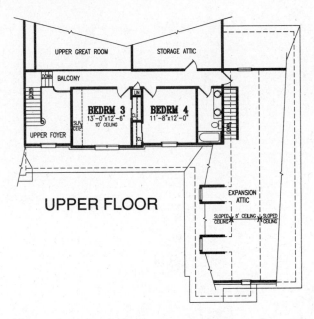

UPPER FLOOR

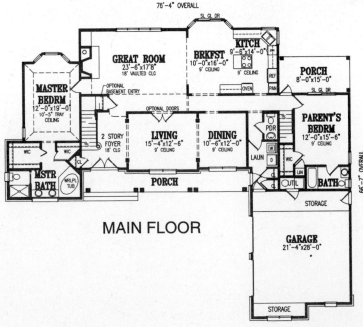

MAIN FLOOR

Fill Your Life with Sunshine

- This home is as warm and inviting on the inside as it is on the outside. Two fireplaces, lots of sunny living spaces and a superb master suite are among its many attributes.
- The master suite claims one of the fireplaces, plus offers a luxurious bath and twin walk-in closets. French doors lead both to the rear garden and to the relaxing front porch.

- The living room hosts the remaining fireplace and also has French doors opening to the front porch. The adjoining dining room includes an elegant bow window.
- The kitchen and the breakfast room overlook an inviting sun room. A half-bath and a utility room are close by.
- The main floor has 9-ft. ceilings throughout, while the upper floor has 8-ft. ceilings. The blueprints include a choice of three bedrooms on the second floor or two bedrooms separated by a game room.

Plan J-91068

Bedrooms: 3+	Baths: 2½
Living Area:	
Upper floor	893 sq. ft.
Main floor	1,947 sq. ft.
Total Living Area	**2,840 sq. ft.**
Standard basement	1,947 sq. ft.
Garage	441 sq. ft.
Exterior Wall Framing	2x4

Foundation options:

Standard basement, crawlspace, slab
(All plans can be built with your choice of foundation and framing. A generic conversion diagram is available. See order form.)

BLUEPRINT PRICE CODE:	D

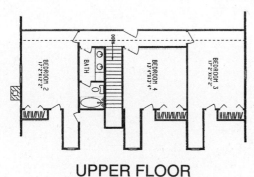

UPPER FLOOR
WITH THREE BEDROOMS

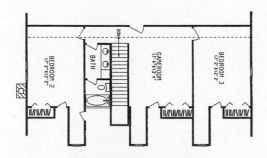

UPPER FLOOR
WITH TWO BEDROOMS AND GAME ROOM

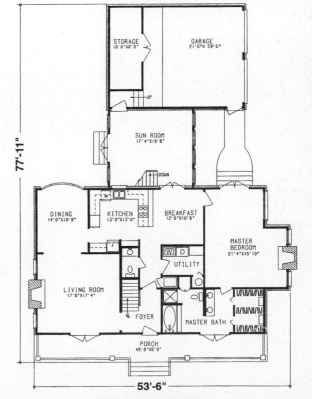

MAIN FLOOR

ORDER BLUEPRINTS ANYTIME!
CALL TOLL-FREE 1-800-820-1283

Plan J-91068

PRICES AND DETAILS
ON PAGES 2-5

445

Ultimate Elegance

- The ultimate in elegance and luxury, this home begins with an impressive foyer that reveals a sweeping staircase and a direct view of the backyard.
- The centrally located parlor, perfect for receiving guests, has a two-story-high ceiling, a spectacular wall of glass, a fireplace and a unique ale bar. French doors open to a covered veranda with a relaxing spa and a summer kitchen.
- The gourmet island kitchen boasts an airy 10-ft. ceiling, a menu desk and a walk-in pantry. The octagonal morning room has a vaulted ceiling and access to a second stairway to the upper level.
- A pass-through snack bar in the kitchen overlooks the gathering room, which hosts a cathedral ceiling, French doors to the veranda and a second fireplace.
- Bright and luxurious, the master suite has a 10-ft. ceiling and features a unique morning kitchen, a sunny sitting area and a lavish private bath.
- The curved staircase leads to three bedroom suites upstairs. The rear suites share an enchanting deck.

Plan EOF-3

Bedrooms: 4+	Baths: 5½
Living Area:	
Upper floor	1,150 sq. ft.
Main floor	3,045 sq. ft.
Total Living Area:	**4,195 sq. ft.**
Garage	814 sq. ft.
Exterior Wall Framing:	2x6

Foundation Options:

Slab

(All plans can be built with your choice of foundation and framing. A generic conversion diagram is available. See order form.)

BLUEPRINT PRICE CODE: G

UPPER FLOOR

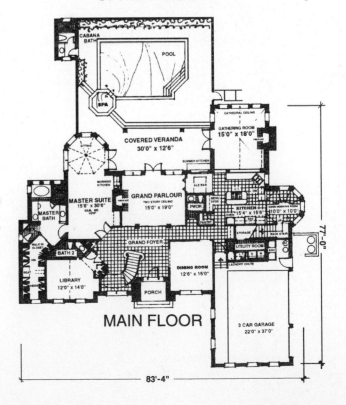

MAIN FLOOR

Stately Flair

- Stately columns, an arched entry and dramatic rooflines give this home its distinguished flair.
- Inside, the two-story foyer is flanked by the formal dining room and a quiet library with a 19-ft. cathedral ceiling and a tall arched window.
- The spacious central living room offers an 18-ft., 4-in. ceiling, a nice fireplace and access to a backyard patio.
- The modern island kitchen and bayed breakfast area merge with the living room, creating a flowing, open feel.
- The large main-floor master suite boasts a 10½-ft. ceiling, a sunny bay window, private patio access and an elegant bath with a spa tub, a separate shower and a dual-sink vanity with knee space.
- Unless otherwise specified, all main-floor rooms have 9-ft. ceilings.
- On the upper floor, a versatile media room and a computer room provide plenty of space for work and play. Two of the three bedrooms are enhanced by 10-ft. gambrel ceilings.
- The large workshop off the garage is great for do-it-yourselfers and hobbyists.

Plan DD-3583

Bedrooms: 4+	Baths: 3½
Living Area:	
Upper floor	1,436 sq. ft.
Main floor	2,147 sq. ft.
Total Living Area:	**3,583 sq. ft.**
Standard basement	2,147 sq. ft.
Garage and workshop	594 sq. ft.
Exterior Wall Framing:	2x4

Foundation Options:
Standard basement
Crawlspace
Slab
(All plans can be built with your choice of foundation and framing. A generic conversion diagram is available. See order form.)

BLUEPRINT PRICE CODE: F

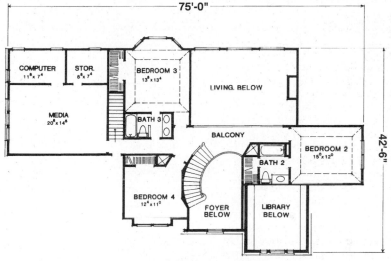

UPPER FLOOR

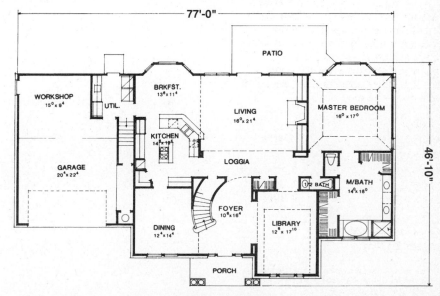

MAIN FLOOR

ORDER BLUEPRINTS ANYTIME!
CALL TOLL-FREE 1-800-820-1283

Plan DD-3583

***PRICES AND DETAILS
ON PAGES 2-5***

447

Symmetrical Bay Windows

- This home's ornate facade proudly displays a pair of symmetrical copper-topped bay windows.
- A bright, two-story-high foyer stretches to the vaulted Great Room, with its fireplace and backyard deck access.
- The island kitchen offers a snack bar and a breakfast nook that opens to the deck and the garage.
- The main-floor master suite features private deck access, dual walk-in closets and a personal bath with a corner garden tub. A laundry room and a bayed study are nearby.
- Upstairs, three secondary bedrooms and another full bath are located off the balcony bridge, which overlooks both the Great Room and the foyer.
- A second stairway off the breakfast nook climbs to a bonus room, which adjoins an optional full bath and closet.

Plan C-9010

Bedrooms: 4+	Baths: 2½-3½
Living Area:	
Upper floor	761 sq. ft.
Main floor	1,637 sq. ft.
Bonus room	347 sq. ft.
Optional bath and closet	106 sq. ft.
Total Living Area:	**2,851 sq. ft.**
Daylight basement	1,637 sq. ft.
Garage	572 sq. ft.
Exterior Wall Framing:	2x4

Foundation Options:

Daylight basement
Crawlspace
(All plans can be built with your choice of foundation and framing. A generic conversion diagram is available. See order form.)

BLUEPRINT PRICE CODE: D

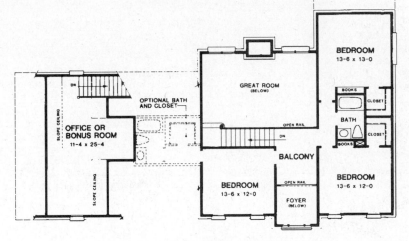

UPPER FLOOR

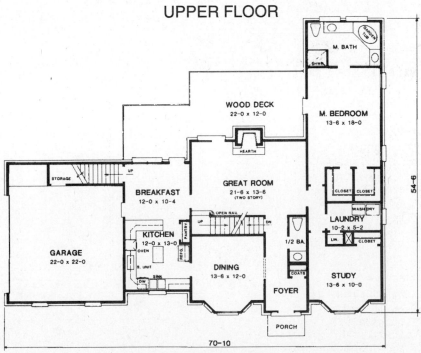

MAIN FLOOR

 ORDER BLUEPRINTS ANYTIME!
CALL TOLL-FREE 1-800-820-1283   Plan C-9010   *PRICES AND DETAILS ON PAGES 2-5*

Formal Yet Friendly

- The formal yet friendly atmosphere of this elegant two-story home draws immediate attention from casual passers-by and welcome guests.
- The two-story entry extends a warm greeting, with its columned court, gabled roof and exciting windows. Inside, the raised, 20-ft. vaulted entry focuses on the 20-ft. soaring family room, with its fireplace and surrounding two-story-high windows.
- A cozy den and the spacious living room flank a full main-floor bathroom on one wing of the home, while a roomy kitchen and formal dining area fill out the other.
- The eat-in kitchen is open to the family room and has a bay window viewing out to the deck.
- The upstairs is highlighted by a bridge that is flooded with light and overlooks the family room and entry. The master suite enjoys a 9-ft. coffered ceiling, a walk-in closet and a full private bath.
- A bonus room lies above the garage.

Plan B-91011

Bedrooms: 3+	Baths: 3
Living Area:	
Upper floor	961 sq. ft.
Main floor	1,346 sq. ft.
Bonus room	186 sq. ft.
Total Living Area:	**2,493 sq. ft.**
Standard basement	1.346 sq. ft.
Garage	480 sq. ft.
Exterior Wall Framing:	2x4

Foundation Options:
Standard basement
(All plans can be built with your choice of foundation and framing. A generic conversion diagram is available. See order form.)

BLUEPRINT PRICE CODE: C

REAR VIEW

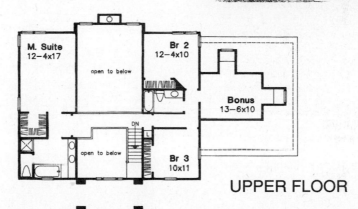

UPPER FLOOR

M. Suite 12-4x17
open to below
Br 2 12-4x10
Bonus 13-6x10
DN
open to below
Br 3 10x11

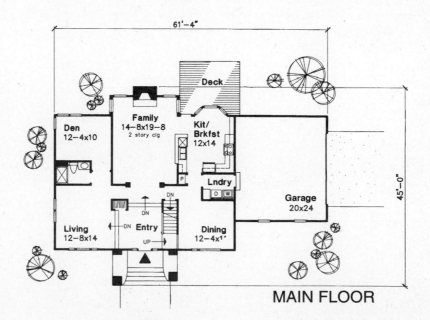

MAIN FLOOR

61'-4"
45'-0"

Deck
Den 12-4x10
Family 14-8x19-8 2 story clg
Kit/Brkfst 12x14
Lndry
Garage 20x24
Entry
Living 12-8x14
Dining 12-4x1"

ORDER BLUEPRINTS ANYTIME!
CALL TOLL-FREE 1-800-820-1283

Plan B-91011

PRICES AND DETAILS
ON PAGES 2-5

449

Nostalgic Exterior Appeal

- A covered front porch, large half-round windows and Victorian gable details give this nostalgic home classic appeal.
- A stunning two-story foyer awaits guests at the entry, which is flooded with light from the half-round window above.
- The central island kitchen is brightened by the bay-windowed breakfast room, which looks into the family room over a low partition.
- Highlighted by a skylight and a corner fireplace, the cathedral-ceilinged family room is sure to be a high-traffic area. Sliding glass doors allow activities to be extended to the backyard patio.
- Upstairs, the master bedroom boasts a unique sloped ceiling and a lovely boxed-out window. The master bath has a spa tub, a corner shower and a dual-sink vanity. A dressing area and a walk-in closet are also offered.
- Three more upstairs bedrooms share two linen closets and a hallway bath. A railed balcony bridge overlooks the foyer and the family room.

Plan AX-90305

Bedrooms: 4	Baths: 2½
Living Area:	
Upper floor	1,278 sq. ft.
Main floor	1,237 sq. ft.
Total Living Area:	**2,515 sq. ft.**
Standard basement	1,237 sq. ft.
Garage	400 sq. ft.
Exterior Wall Framing:	2x4

Foundation Options:

Standard basement

Slab

(All plans can be built with your choice of foundation and framing. A generic conversion diagram is available. See order form.)

BLUEPRINT PRICE CODE:	D

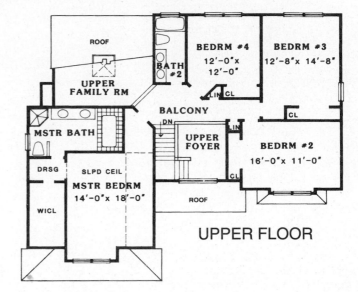

UPPER FLOOR

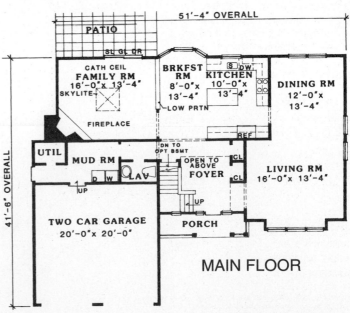

MAIN FLOOR

ORDER BLUEPRINTS ANYTIME!
CALL TOLL-FREE 1-800-820-1283

Plan AX-90305

PRICES AND DETAILS
ON PAGES 2-5

An Eye-Catcher

- An intriguing roofline, arched windows and a stucco finish highlight this home's eye-catching exterior design.
- The vaulted foyer leads directly into an impressive sunken and vaulted living room, outlined with columns that echo the exterior treatment.
- The formal dining room is visually joined to the living room to create an expansive area for entertaining.
- The gourmet kitchen opens to a large family room, which boasts a vaulted ceiling, a corner fireplace and access to a sizable rear deck.
- The front-facing bedroom is expanded by a 9-ft. ceiling that vaults to 12½ feet. A coved ceiling enhances the den or fourth bedroom.
- A sweeping staircase, brightened by a feature window, leads to the upper floor. Here, the terrific master suite includes a built-in TV center, a gas fireplace, a huge walk-through closet and a splendid bath with a raised spa tub and a separate shower.
- Another bedroom with a private bath is also found on the upper floor.

Plan LRD-11388

Bedrooms: 3+	Baths: 3
Living Area:	
Upper floor	1,095 sq. ft.
Main floor	2,125 sq. ft.
Total Living Area:	**3,220 sq. ft.**
Standard basement	2,125 sq. ft.
Garage	802 sq. ft.
Exterior Wall Framing:	2x6

Foundation Options:

Standard basement

Crawlspace

Slab

(All plans can be built with your choice of foundation and framing. A generic conversion diagram is available. See order form.)

BLUEPRINT PRICE CODE: E

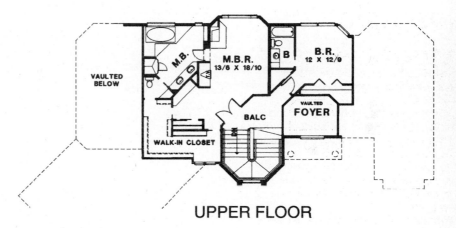

UPPER FLOOR

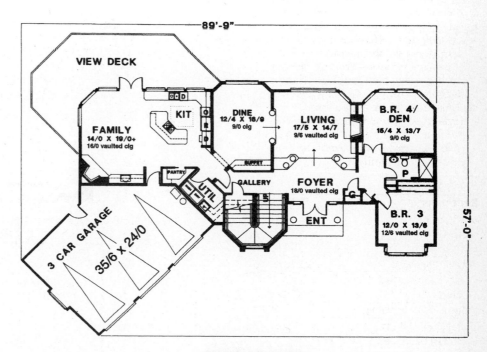

MAIN FLOOR

Very Victorian

- Distinctive characteristics reminiscent of the Queen Anne era are evident in this home's exterior: a rounded tower, a curved wraparound veranda and steeply pitched intersecting rooflines.
- Front doors of leaded glass open to a grand foyer with an elegant stairway and overlooking balcony. Beautiful and durable hardwood floors extend throughout the main floor.
- The spacious living room's circular sitting area has panoramic views of the veranda, which is arrived at through French doors. Pedestal columns set off the adjoining formal dining room.
- With a warm fireplace, a media center, a wet bar and twin serving counters, the family room, breakfast and kitchen areas lavishly fulfill your casual entertaining needs.
- Among the four upper-floor bedrooms is a romantic master suite with a private sitting area, balcony and skylighted bath; space for a sauna and an optional exercise loft atop a spiral stairway is also available.
- Each of the secondary bedrooms has a walk-in closet and its own bath.

Plan L-437-VSC

Bedrooms: 4	Baths: 4½
Living Area:	
Upper floor	1,818 sq. ft.
Main floor	1,617 sq. ft.
Total Living Area:	**3,435 sq. ft.**
Garage and storage	638 sq. ft.
Exterior Wall Framing:	2x4
Foundation Options:	

Slab
(All plans can be built with your choice of foundation and framing. A generic conversion diagram is available. See order form.)

BLUEPRINT PRICE CODE:	E

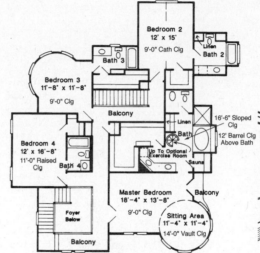

UPPER FLOOR

VIEW INTO DINING ROOM AND
LIVING ROOM BEYOND

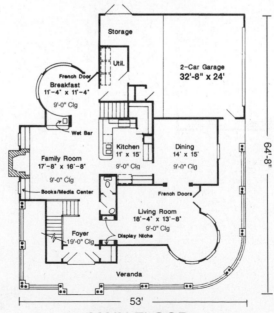

MAIN FLOOR

ORDER BLUEPRINTS ANYTIME!
CALL TOLL-FREE 1-800-820-1283

Plan L-437-VSC

PRICES AND DETAILS
ON PAGES 2-5

Outstanding Options

- This terrific two-story was designed with oodles of outstanding options.
- The 17-ft.-high foyer is flanked by the columned dining room and the formal living room, which offers optional doors to the family room.
- The oversized family room features a built-in desk, an inviting fireplace and French-door access to a backyard patio.
- The focal point of the L-shaped kitchen is its versatile island cooktop and snack bar. The bay-windowed nook hosts casual meals.

- Upstairs, a skylight brightens the railed hallway that leads to the bedrooms.
- The sizable master suite includes optional doors to a corner den or extra bedroom. The skylighted master bath boasts a spa tub, a separate shower, a dual-sink vanity and a private toilet.
- Two front bedrooms share a hall bath.
- The skylighted bonus room features an 11-ft., 6-in. vaulted ceiling and an optional bath. This area would make a nice office or hobby room and could accommodate overnight guests.
- Good-sized laundry facilities may be located upstairs off the bonus room or downstairs off the kitchen.
- The two-car garage includes ample space for a storage area or a workshop.

Plan S-41693	
Bedrooms: 3+	**Baths:** 2½-3½
Living Area:	
Upper floor	1,087 sq. ft.
Main floor	1,164 sq. ft.
Bonus room	400 sq. ft.
Total Living Area:	**2,651 sq. ft.**
Basement	1,104 sq. ft.
Garage	644 sq. ft.
Exterior Wall Framing:	2x6
Foundation Options:	

Daylight basement
Standard basement
Crawlspace
Slab
(All plans can be built with your choice of foundation and framing. A generic conversion diagram is available. See order form.)

BLUEPRINT PRICE CODE:	D

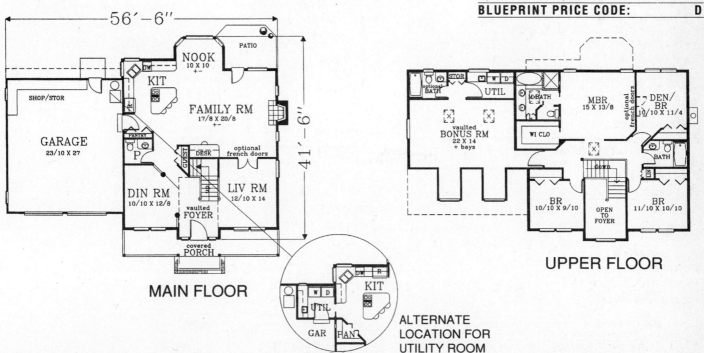

MAIN FLOOR

ALTERNATE LOCATION FOR UTILITY ROOM

UPPER FLOOR

ORDER BLUEPRINTS ANYTIME!
CALL TOLL-FREE 1-800-820-1283

Plan S-41693

PRICES AND DETAILS
ON PAGES 2-5

453

Contemporary Elegance

- This striking contemporary design combines vertical siding with elegant traditional overtones.
- Inside, an expansive activity area is created with the joining of the vaulted living room, the family/dining room and the kitchen. The openness of the rooms creates a spacious, dramatic feeling, which extends to an exciting two-story sun space and a patio beyond.

- A convenient utility/service area near the garage includes a clothes-sorting counter, a deep sink and ironing space.
- Two bedrooms share a bright bath to round out the main floor.
- Upstairs, the master suite includes a sumptuous skylighted bath with two entrances. The tub is positioned on an angled wall, while the shower and toilet are secluded behind a pocket door. An optional overlook provides views down into the sun space, which is accessed by a spiral staircase.
- A versatile loft area and a large bonus room complete this design.

Plan LRD-1971	
Bedrooms: 3+	**Baths:** 2
Living Area:	
Upper floor	723 sq. ft.
Main floor	1,248 sq. ft.
Sun space	116 sq. ft.
Bonus room	225 sq. ft.
Total Living Area:	**2,312 sq. ft.**
Standard basement	1,248 sq. ft.
Garage	483 sq. ft.
Exterior Wall Framing:	2x6

Foundation Options:
Standard basement
Crawlspace
(All plans can be built with your choice of foundation and framing. A generic conversion diagram is available. See order form.)

BLUEPRINT PRICE CODE:	C

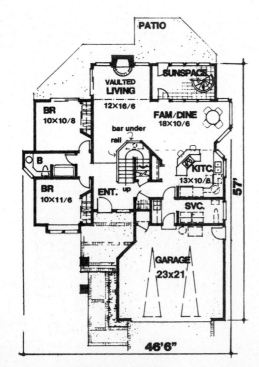

MAIN FLOOR

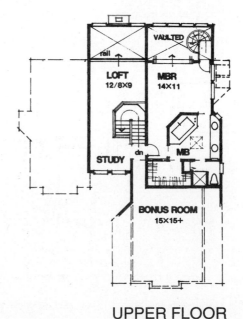

UPPER FLOOR

ORDER BLUEPRINTS ANYTIME!
CALL TOLL-FREE 1-800-820-1283

Plan LRD-1971

PRICES AND DETAILS
ON PAGES 2-5

Wonderful Expectations

- This home's huge wraparound porch creates wonderful expectations about what awaits inside; and its remarkable design doesn't disappoint!
- Large, open areas work great for gathering family and friends. The family room and the living room each offer lots of space, and both are cheered by a friendly fireplace.

- A third fireplace is found in the heartwarming master suite, which also boasts dual walk-in closets, a secluded bath and access to the backyard via a lovely French door.
- The outstanding kitchen has lots of nooks and crannies for storage—including a corner pantry. Located between the dining and morning rooms, it's convenient for any meal.
- Upstairs, you'll find three nice-sized bedrooms and an entertainment/study area that can convert to a fifth bedroom if necessary.

Plan L-182-FCC

Bedrooms: 4+	Baths: 3½
Living Area:	
Upper floor	943 sq. ft.
Main floor	2,237 sq. ft.
Total Living Area:	**3,180 sq. ft.**
Garage and work area	603 sq. ft.
Exterior Wall Framing:	2x4

Foundation Options:

Slab
(All plans can be built with your choice of foundation and framing. A generic conversion diagram is available. See order form.)

BLUEPRINT PRICE CODE: E

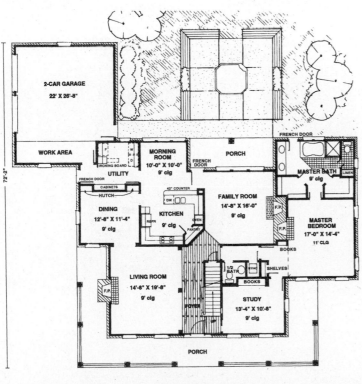

MAIN FLOOR

UPPER FLOOR

ORDER BLUEPRINTS ANYTIME!
CALL TOLL-FREE 1-800-820-1283

Plan L-182-FCC

PRICES AND DETAILS
ON PAGES 2-5

455

Natural Attraction

- It's only natural that you should be attracted to this appealing home. With its timeless brick facade and Victorian touches, it may seem reminiscent of the pastoral countrysides that inhabit your fondly remembered dreams.
- For your sophisticated nature, oversized formal rooms reside just off the raised foyer. What pleasure you'll feel as you usher your guests into these elegant yet inviting spaces!

- When it's time to unwind with your loved ones, head for the family room. If the evening calls for quiet, select a book from the built-in shelves and lose yourself in its pages. If your mood is just a tad more rambunctious than that, step into the media alcove, light a fire and catch the latest blockbuster movie.
- Warm summer days are the perfect excuse to step through the family room's fabulous French doors and enjoy an afternoon in the sun.
- How about a kiss in the sitting area of the master bedroom before turning in for the night? Or perhaps bubbles for two in the private bath's splashy tub!

Plan L-649-HB	
Bedrooms: 4	**Baths:** 2½
Living Area:	
Upper floor	1,284 sq. ft.
Main floor	1,363 sq. ft.
Total Living Area:	**2,647 sq. ft.**
Garage	504 sq. ft.
Exterior Wall Framing:	2x4
Foundation Options:	

Slab

(All plans can be built with your choice of foundation and framing. A generic conversion diagram is available. See order form.)

| **BLUEPRINT PRICE CODE:** | **D** |

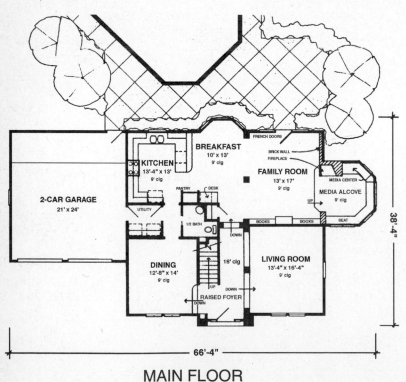

MAIN FLOOR

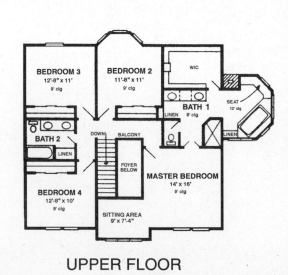

UPPER FLOOR

ORDER BLUEPRINTS ANYTIME!
CALL TOLL-FREE 1-800-820-1283

Plan L-649-HB

PRICES AND DETAILS ON PAGES 2-5

Hot Tub, Deck Highlighted

- Designed for indoor/outdoor living, this home features a skylighted spa room with a hot tub and a backyard deck that spans the width of the home.
- A central hall leads to the sunny kitchen and nook, which offer corner windows, a snack bar and a pantry.
- Straight ahead, the open dining and living rooms form one huge space, further pronounced by expansive windows. The 16-ft. vaulted living room also features a fireplace and sliding glass doors to the deck.
- The master suite includes a cozy window seat, a large walk-in closet, a private bath and access to the tiled spa room. The spa may also be entered from the deck and an inner hall.
- Upstairs, two more bedrooms share a full bath and a balcony that overlooks the living room below.
- The optional daylight basement offers a deluxe sauna, a fourth bedroom, a laundry room and a wide recreation room with a fireplace. A large game room and storage are also included.

REAR VIEW

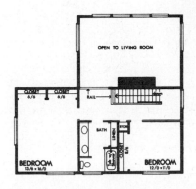

UPPER FLOOR

DAYLIGHT BASEMENT

Plans H-2114-1A & -1B

Bedrooms: 3+	Baths: 2½-3½
Living Area:	
Upper floor	732 sq. ft.
Main floor	1,682 sq. ft.
Spa room	147 sq. ft.
Daylight basement	1,386 sq. ft.
Total Living Area:	**2,561/3,947 sq. ft.**
Garage	547 sq. ft.
Exterior Wall Framing:	2x6
Foundation Options:	**Plan #**
Daylight basement	H-2114-1B
Crawlspace	H-2114-1A

(All plans can be built with your choice of foundation and framing. A generic conversion diagram is available. See order form.)

BLUEPRINT PRICE CODE:	**D/F**

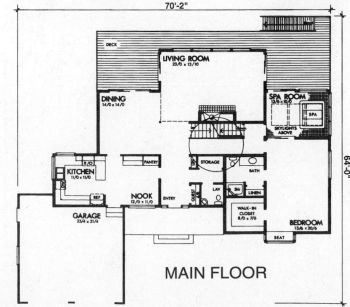

MAIN FLOOR

STAIRWAY AREA IN CRAWLSPACE VERSION

All-American Country Home

- The covered wraparound porch of this popular all-American home creates an old-fashioned country appeal.
- Off the entryway is the generous-sized living room, which offers a fireplace and French doors that open to the porch.
- The large adjoining dining room further expands the entertaining area.
- The country kitchen has a handy island and flows into the cozy family room, which is enhanced by exposed beams. A handsome fireplace warms the entire informal area, while windows overlook the porch.
- The quiet upper floor hosts four good-sized bedrooms and two baths. The master suite includes a walk-in closet, a dressing area and a private bath with a sit-down shower.
- This home is available with or without a basement and with or without a garage.

Plans H-3711-1, -1A, -2 & -2A

Bedrooms: 4	Baths: 2½
Living Area:	
Upper floor	1,176 sq. ft.
Main floor	1,288 sq. ft.
Total Living Area:	**2,464 sq. ft.**
Standard basement	1,176 sq. ft.
Garage	505 sq. ft.
Exterior Wall Framing:	2x6
Foundation Options:	**Plan #**
Basement with garage	H-3711-1
Basement without garage	H-3711-2
Crawlspace with garage	H-3711-1A
Crawlspace without garage	H-3711-2A

(All plans can be built with your choice of foundation and framing. A generic conversion diagram is available. See order form.)

BLUEPRINT PRICE CODE: C

PLANS H-3711-1 & -1A
WITH GARAGE

PLANS H-3711-2 & -2A
WITHOUT GARAGE

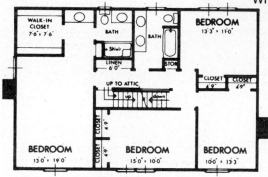

UPPER FLOOR

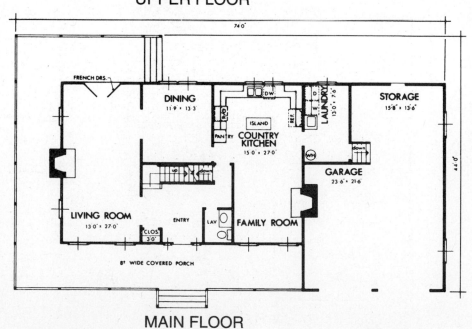

MAIN FLOOR

ORDER BLUEPRINTS ANYTIME!
CALL TOLL-FREE 1-800-820-1283

Plans H-3711-1, -1A, -2 & -2A

PRICES AND DETAILS
ON PAGES 2-5

Dramatic Dimension

- With a soaring chimney, sharp peaks and high brick arches, this two-story projects dramatic vertical dimension.
- Once inside, your eye remains skyward as you behold the sweeping stairway to the two upper-floor bedrooms.
- Bold block columns to the left set off the sunken living room, which features a striking fireplace centered between decorative transom windows.
- Over a half-wall, the formal dining room is closed off from the busy kitchen with bifold doors. The attached morning room accesses the backyard.
- Adjacent guest quarters house returning family members or late-night friends.
- A stunning window wall in the central game room overlooks a courtyard with a splashy fountain and brick planters.
- The sprawling master suite also offers views of the inviting outdoor spaces.

Plan L-3177-C	
Bedrooms: 4	**Baths:** 3
Living Area:	
Upper floor	680 sq. ft.
Main floor	2,497 sq. ft.
Total Living Area:	**3,177 sq. ft.**
Garage	678 sq. ft.
Exterior Wall Framing:	2x4
Foundation Options:	
Slab	

(All plans can be built with your choice of foundation and framing. A generic conversion diagram is available. See order form.)

BLUEPRINT PRICE CODE:	E

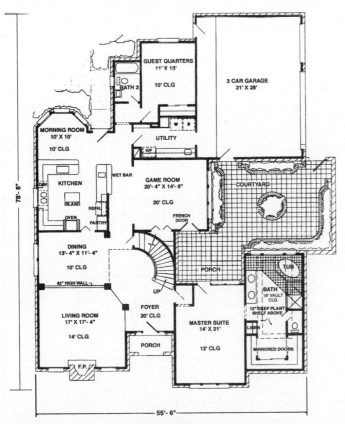

MAIN FLOOR

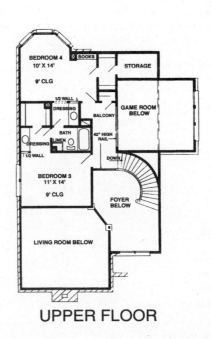

UPPER FLOOR

ORDER BLUEPRINTS ANYTIME!
CALL TOLL-FREE 1-800-820-1283

Plan L-3177-C

PRICES AND DETAILS
ON PAGES 2-5

459

Vote for Grace

- Dressed in a noble suit of brick and copper highlights, this elegant home casts a convincing vote for gracious and comfortable living.
- Below the raised foyer, a downright aristocratic air fills the living room, where a soothing fireplace resides.
- French doors and an arched walkway lead to the long family room, where dazzling windows throw a natural spotlight on family gatherings. Another

French door swings open to allow passage to an angled backyard patio.
- Casual and formal eating spaces flank the wide-open kitchen, where you'll find oodles of counter space for fixing those late-night monster sandwiches!
- Upstairs, a fabulous master bedroom awaits to coddle you with a soothing sitting area and two walk-in closets at the entrance to the bath.
- Of the remaining upper-floor bedrooms, the rearmost boasts a bayed window for admiring the fall colors.

Plan L-574-HB	
Bedrooms: 4	**Baths:** 2½
Living Area:	
Upper floor	1,218 sq. ft.
Main floor	1,354 sq. ft.
Total Living Area:	**2,572 sq. ft.**
Garage	504 sq. ft.
Exterior Wall Framing:	2x4
Foundation Options:	

Slab
(All plans can be built with your choice of foundation and framing. A generic conversion diagram is available. See order form.)

BLUEPRINT PRICE CODE:	D

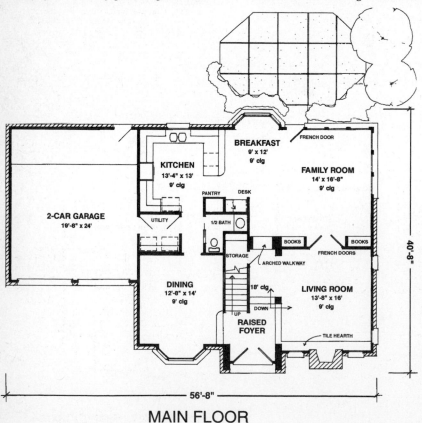

MAIN FLOOR

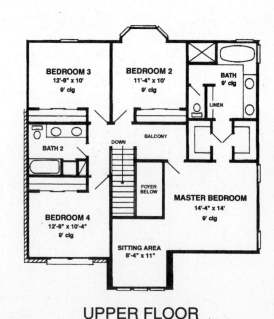

UPPER FLOOR

Gracious Traditional

- This traditional home is perfect for a corner lot, with a quaint facade and an attached garage around back.
- Tall windows, elegant dormers and a covered front porch welcome guests to the front entry and into the foyer.
- Just off the foyer, the formal dining room boasts a built-in hutch and views to the front porch.
- The expansive, skylighted Great Room features a wet bar, a 16-ft. vaulted

ceiling, a stunning fireplace and access to the screened back porch.
- The kitchen includes a large pantry and an eating bar to the bayed breakfast nook. A large utility room with garage access is nearby.
- The master bedroom offers a walk-in closet and a bath with a large corner tub and his-and-hers vanities.
- Two additional bedrooms have big walk-in closets, built-in desks and easy access to another full bath.
- Upstairs, a loft overlooks the Great Room and is perfect as an extra bedroom or a recreation area.

Plan C-8920

Bedrooms: 3+	Baths: 3
Living Area:	
Upper floor	305 sq. ft.
Main floor	1,996 sq. ft.
Total Living Area:	**2,301 sq. ft.**
Daylight basement	1,996 sq. ft.
Garage	469 sq. ft.
Exterior Wall Framing:	2x4

Foundation Options:

Daylight basement
Crawlspace
(All plans can be built with your choice of foundation and framing. A generic conversion diagram is available. See order form.)

BLUEPRINT PRICE CODE:	C

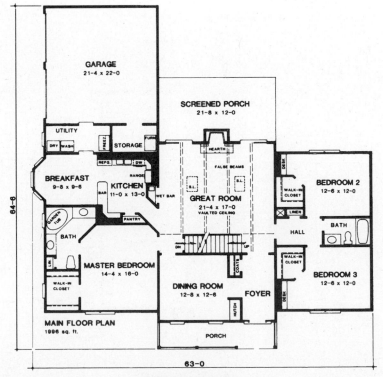

MAIN FLOOR

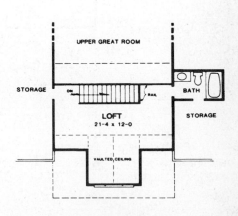

UPPER FLOOR

ORDER BLUEPRINTS ANYTIME!
CALL TOLL-FREE 1-800-820-1283

Plan C-8920

PRICES AND DETAILS
ON PAGES 2-5

461

Return to Yesterday

- Bold rooflines complemented by crisply angled windows blend the traditional with the new, a theme that is increasingly popular with today's home builders. Rough-sawn corner trim and vertical cedar siding give this home an unusual and dramatic look.
- Fireplaces warm the formal living room and the good-sized family room.
- An inviting patio is accessible from the family room and the dining room.
- The master bedroom offers a private deck and a walk-in closet. The master bath features a dual-sink vanity, a raised tub platform in a bay window and a separate shower.
- Two corner bedrooms share a compartmentalized bath; the front-facing bedroom has an 11½-ft. vaulted ceiling.
- Note the balcony library situated above the 16½-ft vaulted entry, plus the skylighted bonus space that could be a fourth bedroom or a rec room.

Plan LRD-2180

Bedrooms: 3+	Baths: 2½
Living Area:	
Upper floor	1,051 sq. ft.
Main floor	1,184 sq. ft.
Bonus room	232 sq. ft.
Total Living Area:	**2,467 sq. ft.**
Standard basement	1,184 sq. ft.
Garage	374 sq. ft.
Exterior Wall Framing:	2x6

Foundation Options:
Standard basement
Crawlspace
(All plans can be built with your choice of foundation and framing. A generic conversion diagram is available. See order form.)

BLUEPRINT PRICE CODE:	C

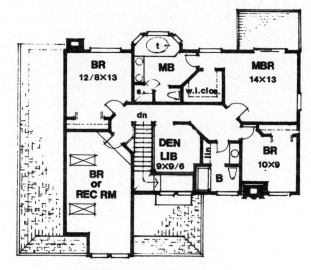

UPPER FLOOR

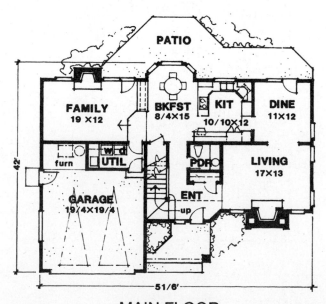

MAIN FLOOR

Absolute Luxury

- This home's folksy, Victorian facade conceals absolute luxury within.
- A metal-roofed front porch introduces the sidelighted, 19-ft.-high foyer. The foyer spills into the living room, which expands past columned half-walls to the bayed formal dining room.
- Steps away, the open kitchen flaunts an angled serving bar that faces the family room and a cute breakfast nook.
- The family room's fireplace spreads warmth throughout the home. French doors open to a study with built-in shelves and cabinets.

- In the breakfast nook, French doors open to the backyard. A sunken media room with a 10-ft. ceiling promises raucous fun, while a hobby room with a sewing table offers solitude.
- Upstairs, the posh master bedroom has a central fireplace, built-in cabinets, a 9-ft. coffered ceiling and French doors to a private deck.
- The master bath enjoys a Jacuzzi tub beneath a 12½-ft. gazebo ceiling, and an exciting exercise room.
- Three more bedrooms boast private access to two full baths.
- Unless otherwise noted, all rooms are topped by 9-ft. ceilings.

Plan L-841-VSC	
Bedrooms: 4+	**Baths:** 3½
Living Area:	
Upper floor	1,891 sq. ft.
Main floor	1,948 sq. ft.
Total Living Area:	**3,839 sq. ft.**
Garage and storage	600 sq. ft.
Exterior Wall Framing:	2x4
Foundation Options:	

Slab
(All plans can be built with your choice of foundation and framing. A generic conversion diagram is available. See order form.)

BLUEPRINT PRICE CODE:	**F**

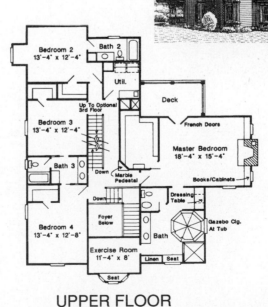

REAR VIEW

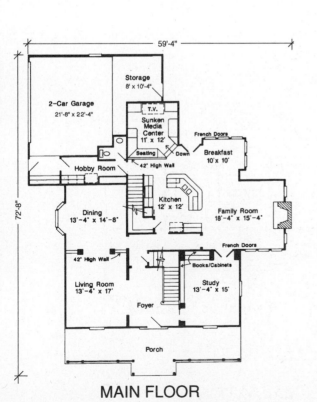

MAIN FLOOR

UPPER FLOOR

A Taste of Perfection

- Dignified and distinctive, this executive home's paned glass windows, steeply pitched roof and arched entrance create a sweet taste of perfection.
- The raised foyer offers a commanding view of the dining room and living room. The living room's all-glass wall and 11-ft. sloped ceiling add to the interesting sensation.
- Ten-foot ceilings are featured throughout the rest of the first floor, with the exception of the kitchen, which vaults up to a story-and-a-half.
- French doors open to a rear porch from the master bedroom, which also boasts a double-sided fireplace.
- The upper floor features three additional bedrooms and a large game room.
- Plans for an optional attached three-car garage, a bonus room and a sun room between the garage and the morning room are included with the blueprints.

Plan L-232-TCC

Bedrooms: 4+	**Baths:** 3½
Living Area:	
Upper floor	1,116 sq. ft.
Main floor	2,114 sq. ft.
Total Living Area:	**3,230 sq. ft.**
Optional sun room	270 sq. ft.
Optional bonus room	728 sq. ft.
Optional attached garage	865 sq. ft.
Exterior Wall Framing:	2x4

Foundation Options:

Slab

(All plans can be built with your choice of foundation and framing. A generic conversion diagram is available. See order form.)

BLUEPRINT PRICE CODE: **E**

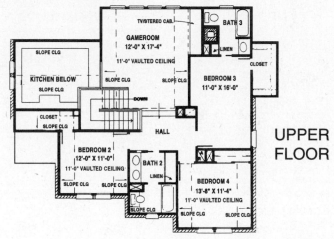

UPPER FLOOR

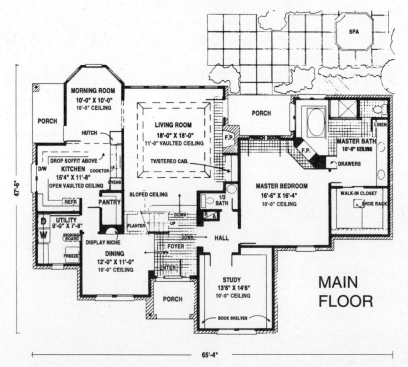

MAIN FLOOR

Quiet Vibrance

- The distinctive charm of this vibrant two-story design makes it an easy place to come home to.
- A two-story foyer provides a dramatic entrance for guests, while the living room and dining room, both with 14-ft. vaults, make a great place for you to entertain them.
- The gourmet kitchen boasts a large center island to make meal preparation easy and fun.
- Defrost the kids after a day of tobogganing, or retire for a romantic evening, in front of the family room's heartwarming fireplace.
- Unless otherwise noted, all main-floor rooms are enhanced by 9-ft. ceilings.
- The exquisite master bedroom suite is the feature attraction on the second floor. It includes a skylighted reading room, a walk-in closet and a secluded bath with a corner spa tub.
- Two secondary bedrooms, a skylighted hall bath and two handy linen closets complete the upper floor. The front bedroom has a 14-ft. vaulted ceiling.

Plan SUN-3215

Bedrooms: 3+	Baths: 3
Living Area:	
Upper floor	1,097 sq. ft.
Main floor	1,373 sq. ft.
Total Living Area:	**2,470 sq. ft.**
Garage	706 sq. ft.
Exterior Wall Framing:	2x6

Foundation Options:

Crawlspace

Slab

(All plans can be built with your choice of foundation and framing. A generic conversion diagram is available. See order form.)

BLUEPRINT PRICE CODE:	C

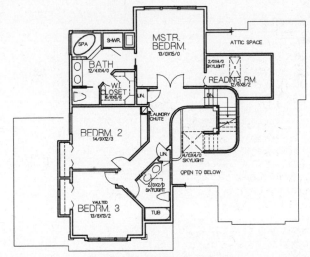

UPPER FLOOR

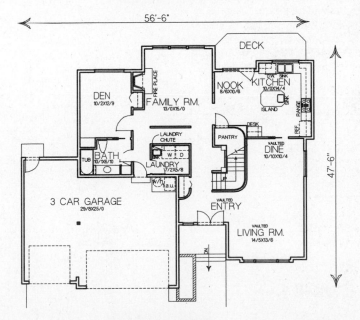

MAIN FLOOR

ORDER BLUEPRINTS ANYTIME!
CALL TOLL-FREE 1-800-820-1283

Plan SUN-3215

PRICES AND DETAILS
ON PAGES 2-5

465

Luxury and Originality

- Rich brick detailing, arched windows and a combination of hipped and gabled roofs mark the exterior of this luxurious traditional home.
- The two-story foyer focuses on the formal living and dining rooms and the winding staircase.
- The gourmet kitchen faces the spectacular triangular-shaped family room, highlighted by a gambrel ceiling, a central fireplace and lots of windows. Another stairway off the breakfast area leads to the upstairs game room, which also sports a gambrel ceiling.
- The master suite offers a bayed sitting area, private access to the rear porch and a dynamite bath with a cathedral ceiling, a U-shaped vanity and a spa tub embraced by overhead plant shelves. Two walk-in closets and an oversized shower complete this magnificent suite.
- All three bedrooms on the upper floor include walk-in closets and enjoy private access to one of two full baths.

Plan KLF-9217

Bedrooms: 4	Baths: 3½
Living Area:	
Upper floor	1,194 sq. ft.
Main floor	2,209 sq. ft.
Total Living Area:	**3,403 sq. ft.**
Garage	519 sq. ft.
Exterior Wall Framing:	2x4

Foundation Options:

Slab

(All plans can be built with your choice of foundation and framing. A generic conversion diagram is available. See order form.)

BLUEPRINT PRICE CODE: E

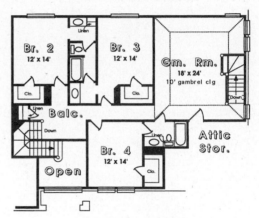

UPPER FLOOR

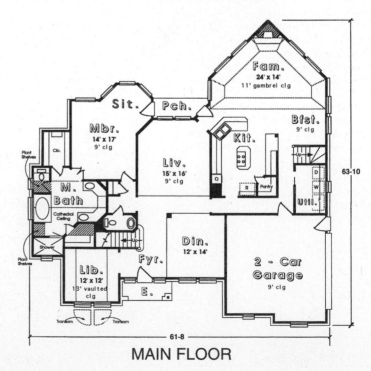

MAIN FLOOR

ORDER BLUEPRINTS ANYTIME!
CALL TOLL-FREE 1-800-820-1283

Plan KLF-9217

PRICES AND DETAILS
ON PAGES 2-5

Formal, Casual Entertainment

- This charming home has plenty of space for both formal and casual entertaining.
- On the main floor, the huge central living room will pamper your guests with an impressive fireplace, a wet bar and two sets of French doors that expand the room to a backyard porch.
- The large formal dining room hosts those special, sit-down dinners.
- There's still more space in the roomy island kitchen and breakfast nook to gather for snacks and conversation.
- For quiet evenings alone, the plush master suite offers pure relaxation! A romantic two-way fireplace between the bedroom and the bath serves as the focal point, yet the whirlpool garden tub is just as inviting.
- The main-floor rooms are enhanced by 10-ft. ceilings; the upper-floor rooms have 9-ft. ceilings.
- The kids' recreation time can be spent in the enormous game room on the upper floor. Private baths service each of the vaulted upper-floor bedrooms.

Plan L-105-VC

Bedrooms: 4+	Baths: 4
Living Area:	
Upper floor	1,077 sq. ft.
Main floor	1,995 sq. ft.
Total Living Area:	**3,072 sq. ft.**
Garage	529 sq. ft.
Storage	184 sq. ft.
Exterior Wall Framing:	2x4

Foundation Options:

Slab

(All plans can be built with your choice of foundation and framing. A generic conversion diagram is available. See order form.)

BLUEPRINT PRICE CODE:	E

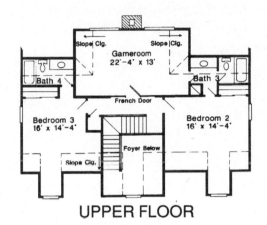

UPPER FLOOR

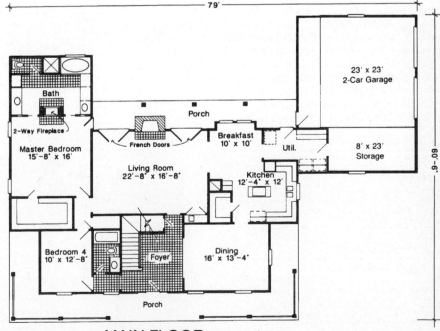

MAIN FLOOR

ORDER BLUEPRINTS ANYTIME!
CALL TOLL-FREE 1-800-820-1283

Plan L-105-VC

PRICES AND DETAILS
ON PAGES 2-5

467

Gracious, Open Living

- A wonderfully open floor plan gives this gracious country-style home a feeling of freedom. A full wraparound porch extends the openness to the outdoors.
- The sidelighted foyer offers views into the formal dining room and the study, and displays a unique two-way staircase to the upper floor.
- The quiet study, which would make a great den or guest room, is the perfect spot for reading your favorite novel or catching up on correspondence.
- The serene dining room is large enough to host a turkey dinner for the relatives.
- At the rear of the home, the Great Room, breakfast nook and island kitchen combine for an informal setting.
- The Great Room's fireplace warms the entire area on cold winter evenings. On

either side of the bayed breakfast nook, French doors open to the porch.
- A laundry/utility room and a full bath flank the hallway to the two-car, side-entry garage, which includes a wide storage room.
- Three bedrooms, two baths and an exciting playroom are located on the upper floor.
- The railed playroom is brightened by a beautiful Palladian window. The kids will enjoy this room for hours on end, playing cards or video games. The playroom is large enough to be finished as a bedroom if needed.
- The master bedroom boasts a huge sleeping area and a walk-in closet. The luxurious private bath features a nice oval tub housed in a beautiful window bay. A separate shower, a dual-sink vanity and a private toilet are other notable amenities.
- Two secondary bedrooms share a roomy hall bath.

Plan J-9289	
Bedrooms: 3+	**Baths:** 3
Living Area:	
Upper floor	1,212 sq. ft.
Main floor	1,370 sq. ft.
Total Living Area:	**2,582 sq. ft.**
Standard basement	1,370 sq. ft.
Garage and storage	720 sq. ft.
Exterior Wall Framing:	2x4
Foundation Options:	
Standard basement	
Crawlspace	
Slab	

(All plans can be built with your choice of foundation and framing. A generic conversion diagram is available. See order form.)

BLUEPRINT PRICE CODE:	D

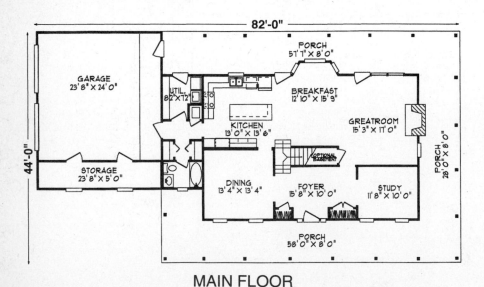

MAIN FLOOR

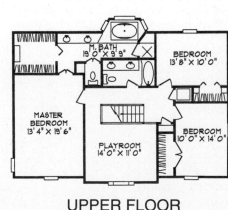

UPPER FLOOR

ORDER BLUEPRINTS ANYTIME!
CALL TOLL-FREE 1-800-820-1283

Plan J-9289

PRICES AND DETAILS
ON PAGES 2-5

Rich Victorian Comes to Life

- With a veranda wrapped around an octagonal turret, decorative shingle siding and double posts atop brick pedestals, this design brings to life the rich Victorian-style home.
- The covered entry provides a pretty place to greet arriving guests.
- A bay window, a built-in bookcase and a handsome fireplace are three of the features found in the huge family room.
- French doors lead from the family room to a playful game room, which can quickly be turned into a spare bedroom for overnight visitors.
- The efficient kitchen is ready to serve the formal dining room and the casual breakfast nook with equal ease.
- Three upper-floor bedrooms are highlighted by the master suite, where you'll find a walk-in closet, a skylighted private bath and a nice sitting area.
- Each secondary bedroom boasts a walk-in closet and a built-in bookcase.
- Plans for a two-car detached garage are included with the blueprints.

Plan L-2368

Bedrooms: 3+	Baths: 3
Living Area:	
Upper floor	1,069 sq. ft.
Main floor	1,299 sq. ft.
Total Living Area:	**2,368 sq. ft.**
Detached garage	576 sq. ft.
Exterior Wall Framing:	2x4

Foundation Options:
Slab
(All plans can be built with your choice of foundation and framing. A generic conversion diagram is available. See order form.)

BLUEPRINT PRICE CODE:	C

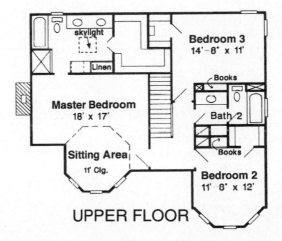

UPPER FLOOR

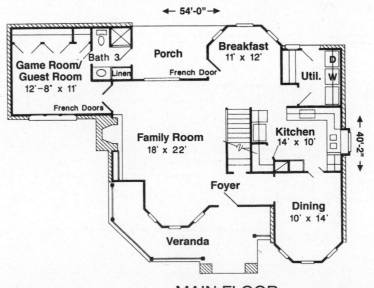

MAIN FLOOR

ORDER BLUEPRINTS ANYTIME!
CALL TOLL-FREE 1-800-820-1283

Plan L-2368

PRICES AND DETAILS
ON PAGES 2-5

469

Nice Angles

- This award-winning design utilizes angular spaces to create a logical and functional flow of traffic.
- Dramatic rooflines and lovely window treatments adorn the brick exterior.
- Inside, the two-story foyer reveals a graceful curved stairway. Columns set off the adjacent dining room.
- On the left, a secluded study is enhanced by a 12-ft. ceiling.
- An 11-ft. coffered ceiling presides over the central living room, with its corner fireplace and angled window wall.
- The island kitchen boasts a large pantry, an eating bar and a sunny breakfast nook with access to a rear porch.
- In the inviting family room, a 14-ft. ceiling embraces a stunning window arrangement. Built-in shelves flank a second fireplace.
- The master bedroom shows off a bow window. A 12-ft., 3-in. cathedral ceiling soars above the posh master bath, with its oval tub, separate shower, two sinks and knee space for a makeup table.
- Upstairs, a raised game room with an 11-ft., 8-in. ceiling is surrounded by three more bedrooms. The ceiling in the front bedroom slopes up to 10½ feet.

Plan KLF-921

Bedrooms: 4+	Baths: 3½
Living Area:	
Upper floor	1,150 sq. ft.
Main floor	2,383 sq. ft.
Total Living Area:	**3,533 sq. ft.**
Exterior Wall Framing:	2x4

Foundation Options:

Slab

(All plans can be built with your choice of foundation and framing. A generic conversion diagram is available. See order form.)

BLUEPRINT PRICE CODE:	**F**

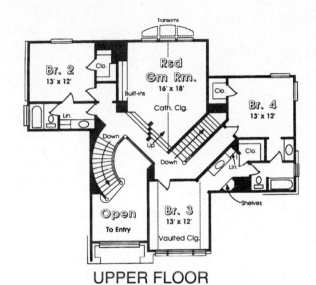

UPPER FLOOR

MAIN FLOOR

ORDER BLUEPRINTS ANYTIME!
CALL TOLL-FREE 1-800-820-1283

Plan KLF-921

PRICES AND DETAILS
ON PAGES 2-5

Innovative Use of Space

- This fascinating design is recognized for its innovative use of space.
- You can't help feeling the draw of its inviting exterior layout.
- The central formal spaces separate the master suite and the den or study from the informal spaces. The rear window wall in the living room allows a view of the outdoors from the oversized foyer.

- The unique arrangement of the master suite lets traffic flow easily from the bedroom to the dressing areas, to the garden tub and to a walk-in closet that you could get lost in.
- The spacious two-story family room, kitchen and breakfast room open to one another, forming a large family activity area with corner fireplace, snack counter and surrounding windows.
- A second main-floor bedroom, two upper-floor bedrooms and three extra baths complete the floor plan.

Plan HDS-99-166	
Bedrooms: 4+	**Baths:** 4
Living Area:	
Upper floor	540 sq. ft.
Main floor	2,624 sq. ft.
Total Living Area:	**3,164 sq. ft.**
Garage	770 sq. ft.
Exterior Wall Framing:	2x4

Foundation Options:

Slab
(All plans can be built with your choice of foundation and framing. A generic conversion diagram is available. See order form.)

BLUEPRINT PRICE CODE:	E

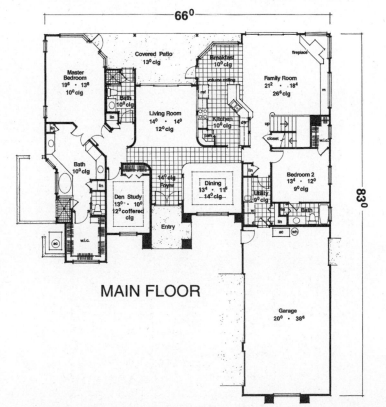

MAIN FLOOR

UPPER FLOOR

ORDER BLUEPRINTS ANYTIME!
CALL TOLL-FREE 1-800-820-1283

Plan HDS-99-166

PRICES AND DETAILS
ON PAGES 2-5

471

Rich Victorian

- The deep, rich tradition of Queen Anne Victorian homes is easily understood after close inspection of this marvel.
- Oohs and aahs and envious sighs will come from passersby upon viewing its columned, railed veranda, turrets and fishscale shingles.
- Equally impressive is the interior. The enormous family room anchors the main floor, and features a bay window, a media/book center by a mighty fireplace and windows overlooking the back porch.
- Carefully positioned to serve the bay-windowed breakfast nook and the

formal dining room, the island kitchen stands ready for any sort of meal.
- Separated somewhat from the main living area is the recreation room; enter via French doors and enjoy its special sense of privacy. It includes a bay window and access to a third bath which walks out to the back porch.
- Upstairs, the master bedroom will take you back to some noble, romantic era. The dome ceiling in the sitting area, the skylighted bath and the roomy walk-in closet treat you like royalty.
- The two nice-sized secondary bedrooms each boast bookshelves and walk-in closets, and also share a full-sized bath.

Plan L-2412	
Bedrooms: 3+	**Baths:** 3
Living Area:	
Upper floor	1,086 sq. ft.
Main floor	1,326 sq. ft.
Total Living Area:	**2,412 sq. ft.**
Detached garage	576 sq. ft.
Exterior Wall Framing:	2x4
Foundation Options:	

Slab
(All plans can be built with your choice of foundation and framing. A generic conversion diagram is available. See order form.)

BLUEPRINT PRICE CODE: C

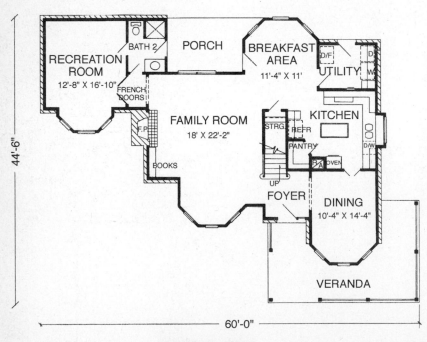

MAIN FLOOR

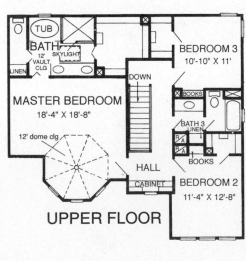

UPPER FLOOR

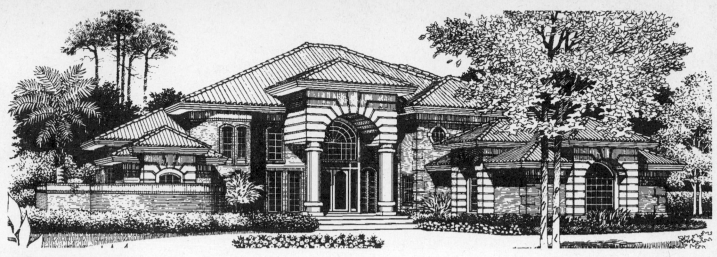

Elegance Perfected

- The grand style of this luxurious home brings elegance and grace to perfection.
- The contemporary architecture exudes an aura of grandeur, drawing the eye to its stately 2½-story entry portico.
- The interior is equally stunning with open, flowing spaces, high ceilings and decorative, room-defining columns.
- The formal zone is impressive, with a vast foyer and a sunken living room highlighted by dramatic window walls and a 20½-ft. ceiling. Round columns set off a stunning octagonal dining room with a 19-ft., 4-in. ceiling. A curved wet bar completes the effect!
- The informal areas consist of an island kitchen, a breakfast nook, a large family room and an octagonal media room. Activities can be extended to the covered back patio through doors in the breakfast nook and the family room.
- The fabulous master suite shows off a romantic fireplace, a 12-ft. ceiling, an enormous walk-in closet and a garden bath with a circular shower!
- Two more main-floor bedrooms, an upper-floor bedroom and loft area, plus two more baths complete the plan.

Plan HDS-90-819

Bedrooms: 4+	Baths: 3½
Living Area:	
Upper floor	765 sq. ft.
Main floor	3,770 sq. ft.
Total Living Area:	**4,535 sq. ft.**
Garage	750 sq. ft.
Exterior Wall Framing:	2x4

Foundation Options:

Slab

(All plans can be built with your choice of foundation and framing. A generic conversion diagram is available. See order form.)

BLUEPRINT PRICE CODE: H

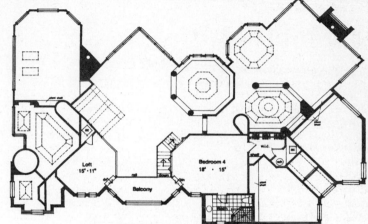

UPPER FLOOR

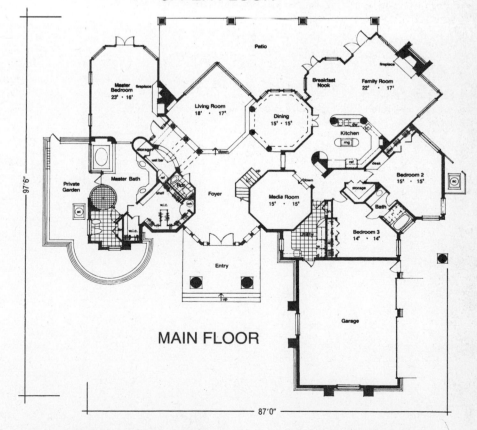

MAIN FLOOR

ORDER BLUEPRINTS ANYTIME!
CALL TOLL-FREE 1-800-820-1283

Plan HDS-90-819

***PRICES AND DETAILS
ON PAGES 2-5***

473

Colonial Spirit

- This elegant two-story captures the spirit of the French Colonial home, with its brick exterior, columned entry, attic dormers and arched transom windows.
- The stately mood continues into the foyer, where a sweeping stairway and a high plant shelf complement the soaring 18-ft. ceiling.
- Straight ahead, an abbreviated gallery leads to the high-traffic kitchen, which is intersected by each of the home's main living spaces; doors to the living room and dining room keep formal occasions quiet.
- Your guests will also appreciate the living room's inviting fireplace and refreshing wet bar.
- High half-round transoms beautifully frame the home's second fireplace in the relaxing family room.
- In the opposite wing resides a secluded study and a luxurious master suite with dual closets and vanities, plus a step-up tub under a dramatic arched window.
- An exciting game room serves the four secondary bedrooms upstairs.
- Also included in the blueprints is an optional two-car garage (not shown), which attaches at the utility room.

Plan L-505-GC

Bedrooms: 5+	Baths: 3½
Living Area:	
Upper floor	1,346 sq. ft.
Main floor	2,157 sq. ft.
Total Living Area:	**3,503 sq. ft.**
Garage	592 sq. ft.
Exterior Wall Framing:	2x4

Foundation Options:

Slab

(All plans can be built with your choice of foundation and framing. A generic conversion diagram is available. See order form.)

BLUEPRINT PRICE CODE: F

UPPER FLOOR

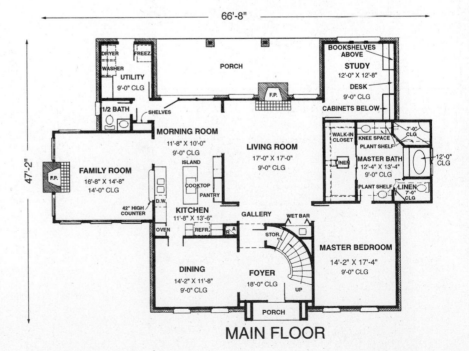

MAIN FLOOR

ORDER BLUEPRINTS ANYTIME!
CALL TOLL-FREE 1-800-820-1283

Plan L-505-GC

PRICES AND DETAILS
ON PAGES 2-5

Large Deck Wraps Home

- A full deck and an abundance of windows surround this exciting two-level contemporary.
- The brilliant living room boasts a huge fireplace and a 14-ft.-high cathedral ceiling, plus a stunning prow-shaped window wall.

- Skywalls brighten the island kitchen and the dining room. A pantry closet and laundry facilities are nearby.
- The master bedroom offers private access to the deck. The master bath includes a dual-sink vanity, a large tub and a separate shower. A roomy hall bath serves a second bedroom.
- A generous-sized family room, another full bath and two additional bedrooms share the lower level with a two-car garage and a shop area.

Plan NW-579	
Bedrooms: 4	**Baths:** 3
Living Area:	
Main floor	1,707 sq. ft.
Daylight basement	901 sq. ft.
Total Living Area:	**2,608 sq. ft.**
Tuck-under garage	588 sq. ft.
Shop	162 sq. ft.
Exterior Wall Framing:	2x6
Foundation Options:	
Daylight basement	

(All plans can be built with your choice of foundation and framing. A generic conversion diagram is available. See order form.)

BLUEPRINT PRICE CODE:	**D**

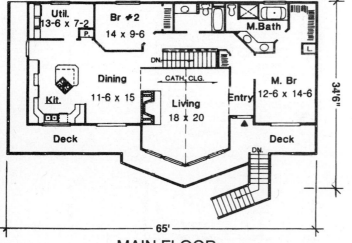

MAIN FLOOR

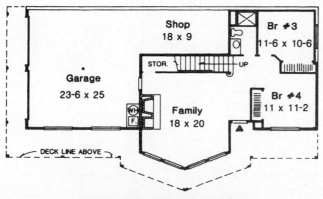

DAYLIGHT BASEMENT

VIEW INTO LIVING ROOM

ORDER BLUEPRINTS ANYTIME!
CALL TOLL-FREE 1-800-820-1283

Plan NW-579

PRICES AND DETAILS
ON PAGES 2-5

475

Blend of Old and New

- In this design, a traditional wraparound porch encompasses an interior filled with the best features in today's homes.
- Inside, columns and bookshelves introduce the living room, which hosts gatherings in style. A sunny garden room shares the living room's two-way fireplace, and would be a quiet, pleasant spot for reading.
- For most activities, the family room at the rear will suit you well, as it interacts nicely with the kitchen and the breakfast nook.
- In the master suite, a number of perks offer special treatment. The secluded patio provides a private spot for coffee, while twin vanities and bountiful closet space easily accommodate two.
- The bedrooms upstairs also include neat features like built-in shelves, private bath access and good-sized closets. In the two front-facing bedrooms, pretty dormers would serve well as cozy places to sit and reflect on the day.
- Every main-floor room boasts a 10-ft. ceiling, while each of the upper-floor rooms features a 9-ft. ceiling.

Plan L-3050-C

Bedrooms: 4	Baths: 3½
Living Area:	
Upper floor	787 sq. ft.
Main floor	2,263 sq. ft.
Total Living Area:	**3,050 sq. ft.**
Exterior Wall Framing:	2x4

Foundation Options:

Slab

(All plans can be built with your choice of foundation and framing. A generic conversion diagram is available. See order form.)

BLUEPRINT PRICE CODE: E

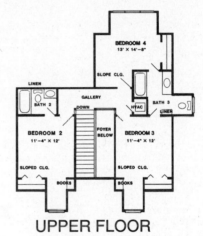

UPPER FLOOR

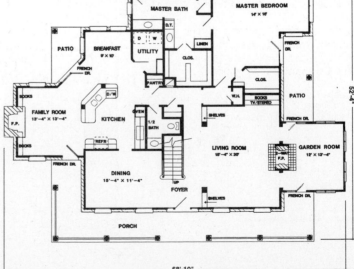

MAIN FLOOR

Plan L-3050-C

Wonderful Blend

- Handsome boxed-out windows with arched transom glass, repeated above the front entry, enhance the traditional exterior. Combined with a contemporary interior that offers features such as vaulted and tray ceilings and open, flowing room arrangements, this home is a wonderful blend of styles.
- The vaulted living room merges with the formal dining room to give plenty of space for entertaining.
- An island worktop is found in the kitchen, which opens to the family room and the octagonally bayed breakfast nook, which accesses to the rear yard.
- A den or guest room has double doors and private access to the main-floor bath with a shower.
- The upstairs master suite offers a lovely cathedral ceiling, a large walk-in closet and a private bath with dual sinks, a separate shower and a luxury tub.

Plan GL-2429

Bedrooms: 3+	Baths: 3
Living Area:	
Upper floor	913 sq. ft.
Main floor	1,516 sq. ft.
Total Living Area:	**2,429 sq. ft.**
Standard basement	1,516 sq. ft.
Garage	484 sq. ft.
Exterior Wall Framing:	2x6

Foundation Options:

Standard basement

(All plans can be built with your choice of foundation and framing. A generic conversion diagram is available. See order form.)

BLUEPRINT PRICE CODE: C

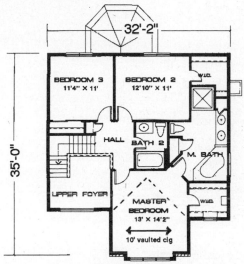

UPPER FLOOR

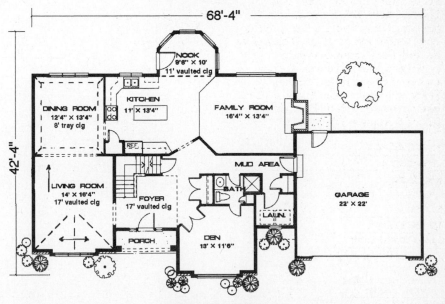

MAIN FLOOR

Hit the Heights

- Soaring ceilings top the central gathering areas in this stunningly accented home.
- A sophisticated facade ushers guests into the two-story foyer. Here, the formal living and dining rooms are introduced as the main attractions.
- Ahead, a sunken family room provides a prime spot for your loved ones to grow closer. On Friday nights, the fireplace adds a definite romantic air after the kids have gone to bed.
- The walk-through kitchen boasts an island cooktop/serving bar combo and a radiant window sink. A French door between the kitchen and the breakfast area leads the way to the backyard. Wouldn't an aromatic cedar deck look great on the other side of that door?
- The dining room is a quick step away, just past the handy butler's pantry.
- Upstairs, double doors open to the big master suite. Its private bath features a plant shelf overlooking a garden tub, a sit-down shower and a dual-sink vanity with knee space. The cavernous walk-in closet is a pleasant extra.

Plan FB-5049-EVER

Bedrooms: 4	Baths: 3½
Living Area:	
Upper floor	1,308 sq. ft.
Main floor	1,575 sq. ft.
Total Living Area:	**2,883 sq. ft.**
Daylight basement	1,575 sq. ft.
Garage and storage	532 sq. ft.
Exterior Wall Framing:	2x4

Foundation Options:

Daylight basement

(All plans can be built with your choice of foundation and framing. A generic conversion diagram is available. See order form.)

BLUEPRINT PRICE CODE:	**D**

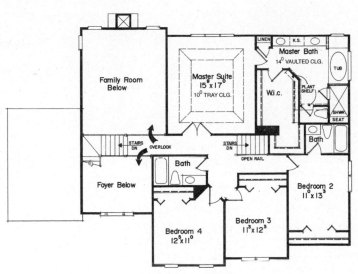

UPPER FLOOR

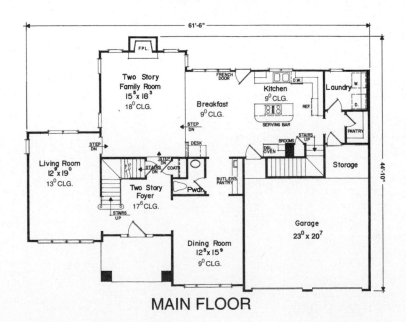

MAIN FLOOR

ORDER BLUEPRINTS ANYTIME!
CALL TOLL-FREE 1-800-820-1283

Plan FB-5049-EVER

PRICES AND DETAILS
ON PAGES 2-5

Design Leaves Out Nothing

- This design has it all, from the elegant detailing of the exterior to the exciting, luxurious spaces of the interior.
- High ceilings, large, open rooms and lots of glass are found throughout the home. Nearly all of the main living areas, as well as the master suite, overlook the veranda.
- Unusual features include an ale bar in the formal dining room, an art niche in the Grand Room and a TV niche in the Gathering Room. The Gathering Room also features a fireplace framed by window seats, a wall of windows facing the backyard and a half-wall open to the sunny morning room.
- The centrally located cooktop-island kitchen is conveniently accessible from all of the living areas.
- The delicious master suite includes a raised lounge, a three-sided fireplace and French doors that open to the veranda. The spiral stairs nearby lead to the "evening deck" above. The master bath boasts two walk-in closets, a sunken shower and a Roman tub.
- The upper floor hosts two complete suites and a loft, plus a vaulted bonus room reached via a separate stairway.

Plan EOF-61

Bedrooms: 3+	Baths: 4½
Living Area:	
Upper floor	877 sq. ft.
Main floor	3,094 sq. ft.
Bonus room	280 sq. ft.
Total Living Area:	**4,251 sq. ft.**
Garage	774 sq. ft.
Exterior Wall Framing:	2x6

Foundation Options:

Slab

(All plans can be built with your choice of foundation and framing. A generic conversion diagram is available. See order form.)

BLUEPRINT PRICE CODE: G

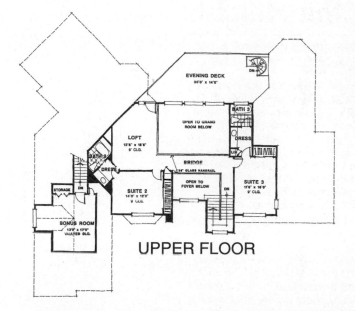

UPPER FLOOR

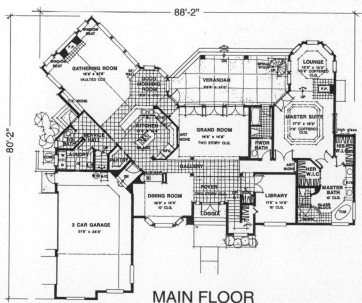

MAIN FLOOR

ORDER BLUEPRINTS ANYTIME!
CALL TOLL-FREE 1-800-820-1283

Plan EOF-61

PRICES AND DETAILS
ON PAGES 2-5

479

One More Time!

- The character and excitement of our most popular plan in recent years, E-3000, have been recaptured in this smaller version of the design.
- The appealing facade is distinguished by a covered front porch and accented with decorative columns, triple dormers and rail-topped corner windows.
- Off the foyer, a central gallery leads to the spacious family room, where a corner fireplace and a 17-ft. vaulted ceiling are highlights. Columns in the gallery introduce the kitchen and the dining areas.
- The kitchen showcases a walk-in pantry, a built-in desk and a long snack bar that serves the eating nook and the dining room.
- The stunning main-floor master suite offers a quiet sitting area and a private angled bath with dual vanities, a corner garden tub and a separate shower.
- A lovely curved stairway leads to a balcony that overlooks the family room and the foyer. Two large bedrooms, a split bath and easily accessible attics are also found upstairs.

Plan E-2307-A

Bedrooms: 3	Baths: 2½
Living Area:	
Upper floor	595 sq. ft.
Main floor	1,765 sq. ft.
Total Living Area:	**2,360 sq. ft.**
Standard basement	1,765 sq. ft.
Garage	484 sq. ft.
Storage	44 sq. ft.
Exterior Wall Framing:	2x6

Foundation Options:
Standard basement
Crawlspace
Slab
(All plans can be built with your choice of foundation and framing. A generic conversion diagram is available. See order form.)

BLUEPRINT PRICE CODE: C

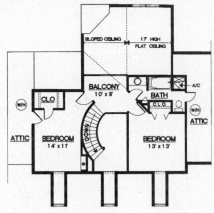

UPPER FLOOR

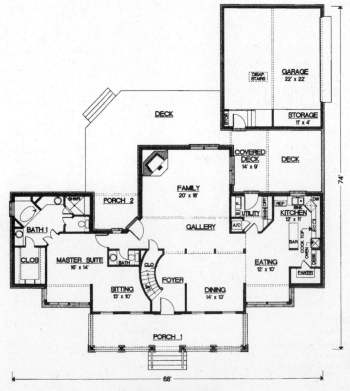

MAIN FLOOR

ORDER BLUEPRINTS ANYTIME!
CALL TOLL-FREE 1-800-820-1283

Plan E-2307-A

PRICES AND DETAILS
ON PAGES 2-5

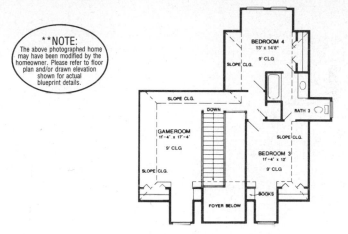

Country Masterpiece!

- A handsome railed veranda punctuated by colonial columns bids a warm welcome to this French Country home.
- Historic hardwood floors in the foyer and dining room coupled with an abundance of windows, glass doors and 9-ft. ceilings give the interior the style and character of a masterpiece!
- Pocket doors isolate the study or guest room from the noise of incoming traffic.
- At the core of the informal spaces is an airy kitchen that interacts with the family room and the breakfast area over a 42-in.-high snack counter.
- The sprawling master suite basks in the comfort of a garden bath and a sunny sitting area that opens to the backyard.
- A window seat is centered between built-in bookshelves in the second main-floor bedroom.
- The upper-floor bedrooms share the use of a full bath and a huge game room.
- A detached three-car garage is included with the blueprints.

Plan L-308-FC

Bedrooms: 4+	Baths: 3
Living Area:	
Upper floor	787 sq. ft.
Main floor	2,519 sq. ft.
Total Living Area:	**3,306 sq. ft.**
Detached three-car garage	942 sq. ft.
Exterior Wall Framing:	2x4

Foundation Options:
Slab
(All plans can be built with your choice of foundation and framing. A generic conversion diagram is available. See order form.)

BLUEPRINT PRICE CODE:	E

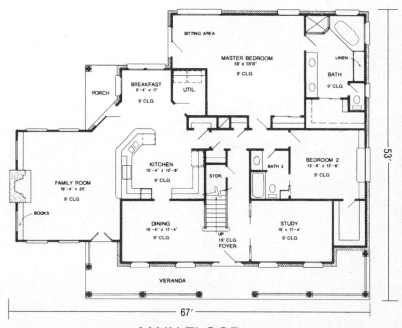

UPPER FLOOR

MAIN FLOOR

ORDER BLUEPRINTS ANYTIME!
CALL TOLL-FREE 1-800-820-1283

Plan L-308-FC

PRICES AND DETAILS
ON PAGES 2-5

481

Photo by Mark Englund/HomeStyles

Old-Fashioned Charm

- A trio of dormers add old-fashioned charm to this modern design.
- Both the living room and the dining room offer 12-ft.-high vaulted ceilings and flow together to create a sense of even more spaciousness.
- The open kitchen/nook/family room features a sunny alcove, a walk-in pantry and a woodstove.
- A first-floor den and a walk-through utility room are other big bonuses.
- Upstairs, the master suite includes an enormous walk-in closet and a deluxe bath with a refreshing spa tub and a separate shower and water closet.
- Two more bedrooms, each with a window seat, and a bonus room complete this stylish design.

Plan CDG-2004

Bedrooms: 3+	Baths: 2½
Living Area:	
Upper floor	928 sq. ft.
Main floor	1,317 sq. ft.
Bonus area	192 sq. ft.
Total Living Area:	**2,437 sq. ft.**
Partial daylight basement	780 sq. ft.
Garage	537 sq. ft.
Exterior Wall Framing:	2x6

Foundation Options:

Partial daylight basement

Crawlspace

(All plans can be built with your choice of foundation and framing. A generic conversion diagram is available. See order form.)

BLUEPRINT PRICE CODE: C

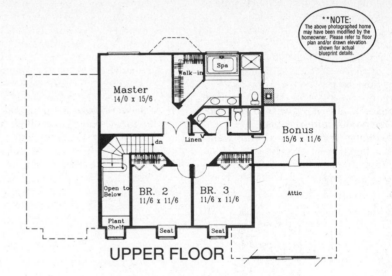

**NOTE: The above photographed home may have been modified by the homeowner. Please refer to floor plan and/or drawn elevation shown for actual blueprint details.

UPPER FLOOR

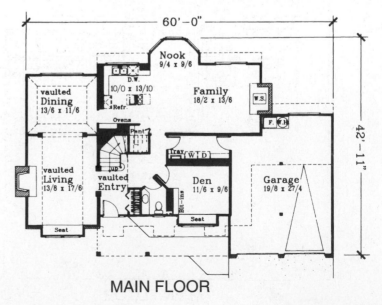

MAIN FLOOR

ORDER BLUEPRINTS ANYTIME!
CALL TOLL-FREE 1-800-820-1283

Plan CDG-2004

PRICES AND DETAILS ON PAGES 2-5

Photo by Mark Englund/HomeStyles

Take the Plunge!

- From the elegant portico to the striking rooflines, this home's facade is magnificent. But the rear area is equally fine, with its spa, waterfall and pool.
- Double doors lead from the entry into the open foyer, where a 12-ft. ceiling extends into the central living room beyond. A sunken wet bar juts into the pool area, allowing guests to swim up to the bar for refreshments.
- The dining room boasts window walls and a tiered pedestal ceiling that steps up from 10 ft. at the center to 12 ft. at the outside edges. The island kitchen

easily services both the formal and the informal areas of the home.
- A big breakfast room flows into a family room with a fireplace and sliding glass doors to the patio and pool.
- The master suite offers an opulent bath, patio access and views of the pool through a curved window wall. A 12-ft. ceiling tops both the master suite and the nearby den or study.
- A railed staircase leads to the upper floor, where there are two bedrooms, a continental bath and a shared balcony deck overlooking the pool area.
- The observatory features high windows to accommodate an amateur stargazer's telescope. This room could also be used as a nice activity area for hobbies or games.

Plan HDS-99-154	
Bedrooms: 3+	**Baths:** 3
Living Area:	
Upper floor	675 sq. ft.
Main floor	2,212 sq. ft.
Total Living Area:	**2,887 sq. ft.**
Garage	479 sq. ft.
Exterior Wall Framing:	2x4
Foundation Options:	
Slab	
(All plans can be built with your choice of foundation and framing. A generic conversion diagram is available. See order form.)	
BLUEPRINT PRICE CODE:	**D**

＊＊NOTE:
The above photographed home may have been modified by the homeowner. Please refer to floor plan and/or drawn elevation shown for actual blueprint details.

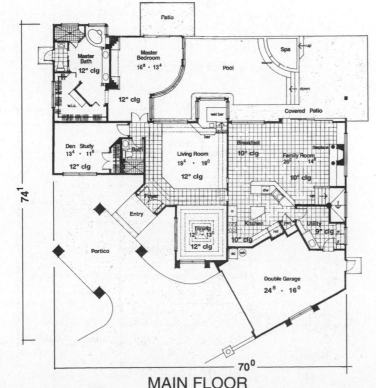

MAIN FLOOR

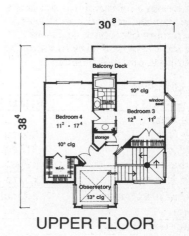

UPPER FLOOR

Photo by Mark Englund/HomeStyles

Creative Spaces

- This expansive home uses vaulted ceilings and multiple levels to create a functional, airy floor plan.
- The broad, vaulted entry foyer leads to the bayed living room, which is warmed by a striking fireplace. A few steps down, the dining room opens to a wide backyard deck.
- The island kitchen features a sunny sink area and a breakfast nook with deck access. A laundry room, a half-bath and a den or extra bedroom are also found on this level.
- Adjacent to the nook, the sunken family room boasts a wet bar, a second fireplace and a bright window wall with sliding glass doors to a lovely patio.
- Upstairs, the master suite includes a sunken bedroom with a private deck. The lavish master bath offers a sunken garden tub, a dual-sink vanity and a skylight near the private shower.
- Three large secondary bedrooms share another skylighted bath. Each bedroom has its own unique design feature.

Plans P-7664-4A & -4D

Bedrooms: 4+	Baths: 2½
Living Area:	
Upper floor	1,301 sq. ft.
Main floor	1,853 sq. ft.
Total Living Area:	**3,154 sq. ft.**
Daylight basement	1,486 sq. ft.
Garage	668 sq. ft.
Exterior Wall Framing:	2x4
Foundation Options:	**Plan #**
Daylight basement	P-7664-4D
Crawlspace	P-7664-4A

(All plans can be built with your choice of foundation and framing. A generic conversion diagram is available. See order form.)

BLUEPRINT PRICE CODE:	E

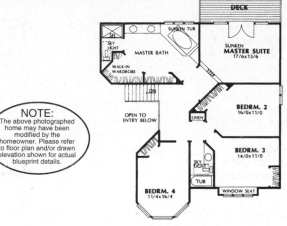

NOTE: The above photographed home may have been modified by the homeowner. Please refer to floor plan and/or drawn elevation shown for actual blueprint details.

UPPER FLOOR

BASEMENT STAIRWAY LOCATION

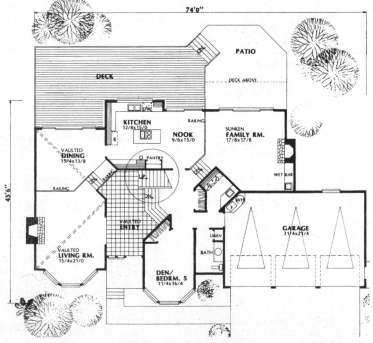

MAIN FLOOR

ORDER BLUEPRINTS ANYTIME!
CALL TOLL-FREE 1-800-820-1283

Plans P-7664-4A & -4D

PRICES AND DETAILS
ON PAGES 2-5

Photo courtesy of Breland and Farmer Designers, Inc.

Shaded Kiss

- Columned porches give this brick and stucco home a shaded kiss of Old World charm and grace. Dormer windows and a soaring roofline complete the facade.
- The magic continues inside, with a massive living room that boasts a cozy fireplace to satisfy your passion for romance. French doors grant passage to a secluded porch.
- Privacy reigns in the isolated master suite, which offers a sitting area and a built-in desk. Double doors introduce the luxurious bath with style. There, you'll find a marvelous oval tub, a separate shower, and a walk-in closet and vanity for each of you.
- Like to entertain? Give your meals that personal touch in the formal dining room! For casual cuisine, try the eating nook at the other end of the kitchen, or gather around the island for munchies.
- Upstairs, a balcony hall lets the kids enjoy the porch before heading to bed. The upper porch is railed for their safety and your peace of mind.

Plan E-2604

Bedrooms: 4	Baths: 2½
Living Area:	
Upper floor	855 sq. ft.
Main floor	1,750 sq. ft.
Total Living Area:	**2,605 sq. ft.**
Standard basement	1,655 sq. ft.
Garage and storage	569 sq. ft.
Exterior Wall Framing:	2x6

Foundation Options:

Standard basement
Crawlspace
Slab

(All plans can be built with your choice of foundation and framing. A generic conversion diagram is available. See order form.)

BLUEPRINT PRICE CODE: D

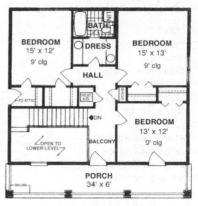

NOTE:
The above photographed home may have been modified by the homeowner. Please refer to floor plan and/or drawn elevation shown for actual blueprint details.

UPPER FLOOR

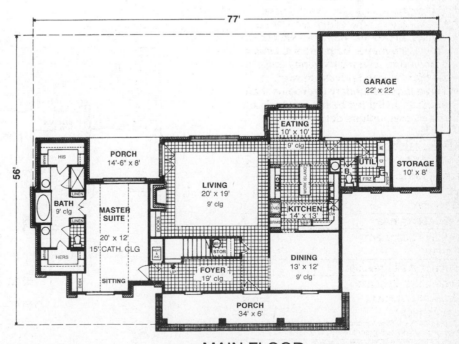

MAIN FLOOR

ORDER BLUEPRINTS ANYTIME!
CALL TOLL-FREE 1-800-820-1283

Plan E-2604

PRICES AND DETAILS
ON PAGES 2-5

485

Home with Sparkle

- This dynamite design simply sparkles, with the main living areas geared toward a gorgeous greenhouse at the back of the home.

- At the front of the home, a sunken foyer introduces the formal dining room, which is framed by a curved half-wall. The sunken living room boasts a 17-ft. vaulted ceiling and a nice fireplace.

- The spacious kitchen features a bright, two-story skywell above the island. The family room's ceiling rises to 17 feet. These rooms culminate at a solar greenhouse with an indulgent hot tub and a 12-ft. vaulted ceiling. The neighboring bath has a raised spa tub.

- Upstairs, the impressive master suite includes its own deck and a stairway to the greenhouse. A vaulted library with a woodstove augments the suite. Ceilings soar to 16 ft. in both areas.

Plan S-8217

Bedrooms: 3+	Baths: 2
Living Area:	
Upper floor	789 sq. ft.
Main floor	1,709 sq. ft.
Bonus room	336 sq. ft.
Total Living Area:	**2,834 sq. ft.**
Partial basement	1,242 sq. ft.
Garage	441 sq. ft.
Exterior Wall Framing:	2x6

Foundation Options:

Partial basement
Crawlspace
Slab
(All plans can be built with your choice of foundation and framing. A generic conversion diagram is available. See order form.)

BLUEPRINT PRICE CODE: D

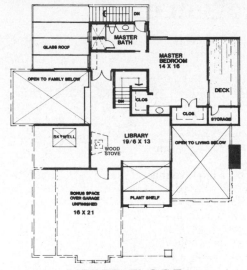

UPPER FLOOR

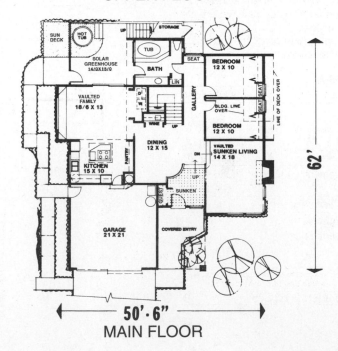

MAIN FLOOR

ORDER BLUEPRINTS ANYTIME!
CALL TOLL-FREE 1-800-820-1283

Plan S-8217

PRICES AND DETAILS
ON PAGES 2-5

Photo by Mark Englund/HomeStyles

Stately Elegance

- The elegant interior of this home is introduced by a dramatic barrel-vaulted entry with stately columns.
- Double doors open to the 19-ft.-high foyer, where a half-round transom window brightens an attractive open-railed stairway.
- Off the foyer, the living room is separated from the sunny dining room by impressive columns.
- The island kitchen offers a bright corner sink, a walk-in pantry and a bayed breakfast area with backyard views.
- The adjoining family room offers a door to a backyard patio, while a wet bar and a fireplace enhance the whole area.
- Upstairs, the master suite boasts a private bath with two walk-in closets, a garden spa tub and a separate shower.
- Three secondary bedrooms have private bathroom access.
- Ceilings in all rooms are 9 ft. high for added spaciousness.

Plan DD-2968-A

Bedrooms: 4+	Baths: 3½
Living Area:	
Upper floor	1,382 sq. ft.
Main floor	1,586 sq. ft.
Total Living Area:	**2,968 sq. ft.**
Standard basement	1,586 sq. ft.
Garage	521 sq. ft.
Exterior Wall Framing:	2x4

Foundation Options:

Standard basement

Crawlspace

Slab

(All plans can be built with your choice of foundation and framing. A generic conversion diagram is available. See order form.)

BLUEPRINT PRICE CODE: D

NOTE:
The above photographed home may have been modified by the homeowner. Please refer to floor plan and/or drawn elevation shown for actual blueprint details.

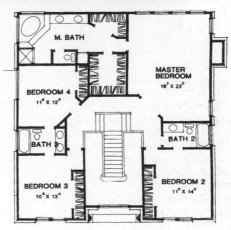

UPPER FLOOR

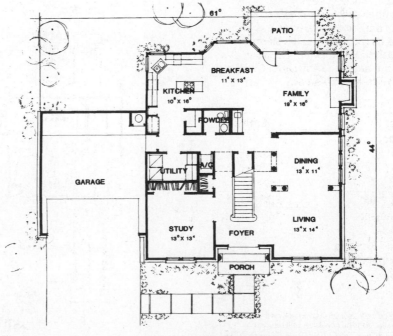

MAIN FLOOR

ORDER BLUEPRINTS ANYTIME!
CALL TOLL-FREE 1-800-820-1283

Plan DD-2968-A

PRICES AND DETAILS
ON PAGES 2-5

487

Truly Nostalgic

- Designed after "Monteigne," an Italianate home near Natchez, Mississippi, this reproduction utilizes modern stucco finishes for the exterior.
- Columns and arched windows give way to a two-story-high foyer, which is accented by a striking, curved stairwell.
- The foyer connects the living room and the study, each boasting a 14-ft. ceiling and a cozy fireplace or woodstove.
- Adjacent to the formal dining room, the kitchen offers a snack bar and a bayed eating room. A unique entertainment center is centrally located to serve the main activity rooms of the home.
- A gorgeous sun room stretches across the rear of the main floor and overlooks a grand terrace.
- The plush master suite and bath boast his-and-hers vanities, large walk-in closets and a glassed-in garden tub.
- A main-floor guest bedroom features a walk-in closet and private access to another full main-floor bath.
- Two more bedrooms with private baths are located on the upper level. They share a sitting area and a veranda.

Plan E-3200

Bedrooms: 4	Baths: 4
Living Area:	
Upper floor	629 sq. ft.
Main floor	2,655 sq. ft.
Total Living Area:	**3,284 sq. ft.**
Standard basement	2,655 sq. ft.
Garage	667 sq. ft.
Exterior Wall Framing:	2x6

Foundation Options:

Standard basement
Crawlspace
Slab

(All plans can be built with your choice of foundation and framing.
A generic conversion diagram is available. See order form.)

BLUEPRINT PRICE CODE: E

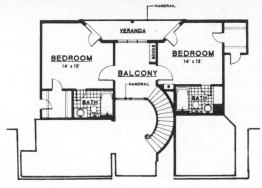

UPPER FLOOR

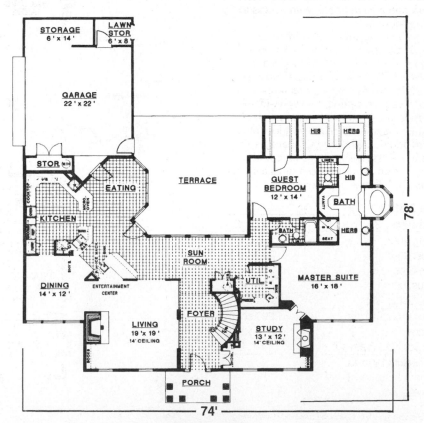

MAIN FLOOR

Plan E-3200

Tasteful Style

- Traditional lines and a contemporary floor plan combine to make this home a perfect choice for the '90s.
- The two-story-high entry introduces the formal living room, which is warmed by a fireplace and brightened by a round-top window arrangement. The living room's ceiling rises to 13 ft., 9 inches.
- A handy pocket door separates the formal dining room from the kitchen for special occasions. The U-shaped kitchen features an eating bar, a work desk and a bayed nook with access to an outdoor patio.
- The spacious family room includes a second fireplace and outdoor views.
- Cellings in all main floor rooms are at least 9 ft. high for added spaciousness.
- Upstairs, the master suite features a 12-ft. vaulted ceiling, two walk-in closets and a compartmentalized bath with a luxurious tub in a window bay.
- Two additional bedrooms share a split bath. A versatile bonus room could serve as an extra bedroom or as a sunny area for hobbies or paperwork.

Plan S-8389

Bedrooms: 3+	Baths: 2½
Living Area:	
Upper floor	932 sq. ft.
Main floor	1,290 sq. ft.
Bonus room	228 sq. ft.
Total Living Area:	**2,450 sq. ft.**
Standard basement	1,290 sq. ft.
Garage	429 sq. ft.
Exterior Wall Framing:	2x6

Foundation Options:

Standard basement

Crawlspace

Slab

(All plans can be built with your choice of foundation and framing. A generic conversion diagram is available. See order form.)

BLUEPRINT PRICE CODE: C

UPPER FLOOR

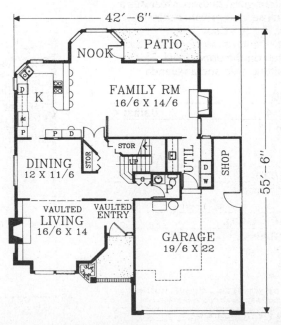

MAIN FLOOR

ORDER BLUEPRINTS ANYTIME!
CALL TOLL-FREE 1-800-820-1283

Plan S-8389

PRICES AND DETAILS
ON PAGES 2-5

489

Classic Cape Cod

- Six eye-catching dormer windows and a charming front porch create a stately, dignified look for this handsome home.
- An elegant open staircase is the focal point of the inviting foyer, which is set off from the formal dining room by decorative wood columns.
- A swinging door leads to the exciting kitchen, which includes an angled counter overlooking the breakfast room.
- The spectacular skylighted family room boasts a soaring 17-ft.-high ceiling. A cozy fireplace is flanked by tall windows and a set of French doors to the backyard.
- The deluxe master bedroom offers a 13-ft. vaulted ceiling and a charming bay window. The skylighted master bath has a gaden spa tub, a separate shower, two walk-in closets and a dual-sink vanity.
- Upstairs, a railed balcony overlooks the family room and foyer. Three bright bedrooms share a hallway bath.

Plan CH-445-A

Bedrooms: 4	Baths: 2½
Living Area:	
Upper floor	988 sq. ft.
Main floor	1,707 sq. ft.
Total Living Area:	**2,695 sq. ft.**
Partial basement	1,118 sq. ft.
Garage	802 sq. ft.
Exterior Wall Framing:	2x4

Foundation Options:

Partial daylight basement
Partial basement
Crawlspace
(All plans can be built with your choice of foundation and framing. A generic conversion diagram is available. See order form.)

BLUEPRINT PRICE CODE: D

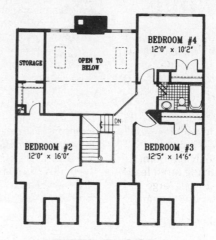

UPPER FLOOR

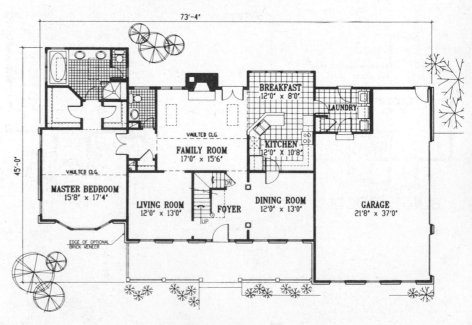

MAIN FLOOR

Photo by Mark Englund/HomeStyles

Room to Move

- Large rooms and high ceilings give this French-style home an expansive feel; ceiling fans lend atmosphere and grace to the main living spaces.
- Accessed from the 12-ft.-high entry, the dining and living rooms boast 11-ft. ceilings. Lovely windows with arched transoms flood each room with natural light, while a fireplace and built-in bookshelves highlight the living room.
- Double doors from the dining room lead into the kitchen, which sports a large serving bar, a built-in desk and a central work island with cabinets. Two boxed-out windows above the sink let in the sun, while the breakfast nook basks in the light from a bay window.
- A 10-ft. stepped ceiling rises over the secluded master suite, which offers private access to the covered backyard porch. Behind double doors, the luxurious garden bath enjoys the bedrooms' warm see-through fireplace.
- The secondary bedrooms have 10-ft. ceilings and share a skylighted bath.
- The bonus room above the garage may be designed as an additional bedroom or a quiet office space.

Plan RD-2240

Bedrooms: 4+	Baths: 2½
Living Area:	
Main floor	2,240 sq. ft.
Bonus room	349 sq. ft.
Total Living Area:	**2,589 sq. ft.**
Garage	737 sq. ft.
Exterior Wall Framing:	2x4

Foundation Options:

Crawlspace
Slab
(All plans can be built with your choice of foundation and framing. A generic conversion diagram is available. See order form.)

BLUEPRINT PRICE CODE: **D**

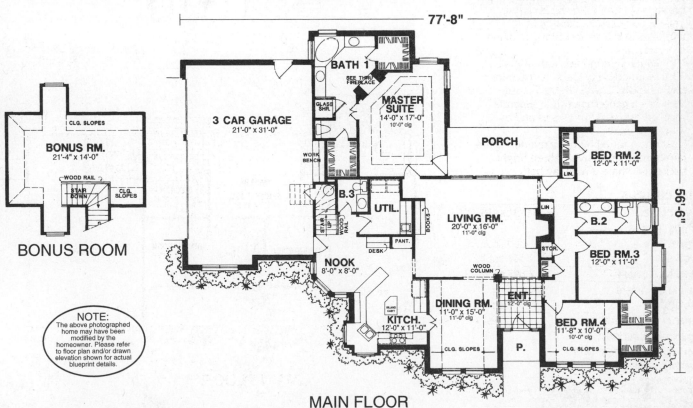

BONUS ROOM

MAIN FLOOR

NOTE: The above photographed home may have been modified by the homeowner. Please refer to floor plan and/or drawn elevation shown for actual blueprint details.

Photo by Mark Englund/HomeStyles

Good Sense

- This home's stone facade and unique metal roof add appeal, while the interior layout contributes good sense.
- Inside, the entry flows past bookshelves to the living room; a 20-ft. sloped ceiling soars over both areas.
- In the living room, a warm fireplace and a neat media center topped by an attractive arch serve as fun diversions.
- The breakfast nook, which opens to a patio through a French door, shares a snack bar with the island kitchen. A pass-through between the kitchen and the dining room simplifies meal service.
- Across the home, a bayed sitting area and an entertainment center make the master bedroom an exciting retreat. The master bath leads to a double walk-in closet, where shoe shelves and a bench make the most of the space.
- Unless otherwise mentioned, every main-floor room includes a 9-ft. ceiling.
- Upstairs, two bedrooms and a study, all with sloped 10-ft. ceilings, share a hall bath. The study has a private balcony, and the rear bedroom has its own deck.

Plan DD-2703-1

Bedrooms: 3+	Baths: 2½

Living Area:	
Upper floor	727 sq. ft.
Main floor	1,921 sq. ft.
Total Living Area:	**2,648 sq. ft.**
Standard basement	1,921 sq. ft.
Garage and storage	600 sq. ft.
Exterior Wall Framing:	2x4

Foundation Options:
Standard basement
Crawlspace
Slab
(All plans can be built with your choice of foundation and framing. A generic conversion diagram is available. See order form.)

BLUEPRINT PRICE CODE: D

NOTE:
The above photographed home may have been modified by the homeowner. Please refer to floor plan and/or drawn elevation shown for actual blueprint details.

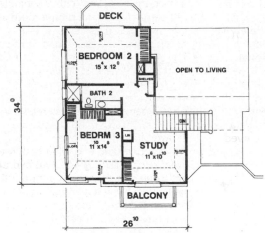

UPPER FLOOR

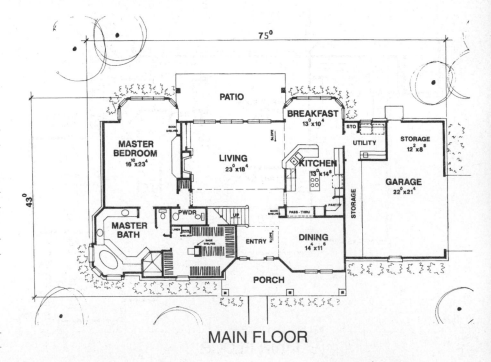

MAIN FLOOR

ORDER BLUEPRINTS ANYTIME!
CALL TOLL-FREE 1-800-820-1283

Plan DD-2703-1

PRICES AND DETAILS
ON PAGES 2-5

Award Winner!

- A successful combination of a traditional exterior and modern interior spaces makes this home a winner.
- A winning entry in a recent national design competition, this design has a facade that is filled with character and free of overbearing garage doors. The focus instead goes to the front entry, with decorative columns supporting a covered porch highlighted by a curved shed roof.

- A two-story foyer greets guests. Graceful arched openings and pillars separate the foyer from the formal dining room and the Great Room, which boasts a fireplace and views of a backyard patio.
- The gourmet kitchen features an island cooktop, a walk-in pantry and a snack bar to the sunny breakfast room.
- The main-floor master suite offers a private porch and a spacious personal bath with a garden tub, a separate shower and a large walk-in closet.
- Another bedroom and a full bath round out the main floor. Two more bedrooms are located upstairs, with a third full bath and a loft reading area under a dormer. A central game room features access to a sunny corner deck.

Plan BOD-26-8A

Bedrooms: 4	Baths: 3
Living Area:	
Upper floor	792 sq. ft.
Main floor	1,904 sq. ft.
Total Living Area:	**2,696 sq. ft.**
Garage	528 sq. ft.
Exterior Wall Framing:	2x4

Foundation Options:

Crawlspace
Slab
(All plans can be built with your choice of foundation and framing. A generic conversion diagram is available. See order form.)

BLUEPRINT PRICE CODE:	D

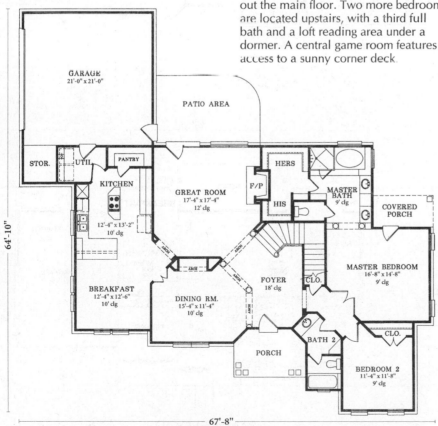

MAIN FLOOR

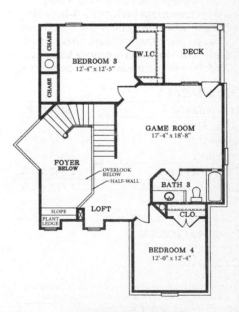

UPPER FLOOR

ORDER BLUEPRINTS ANYTIME!
CALL TOLL-FREE 1-800-820-1283

Plan BOD-26-8A

PRICES AND DETAILS
ON PAGES 2-5

493

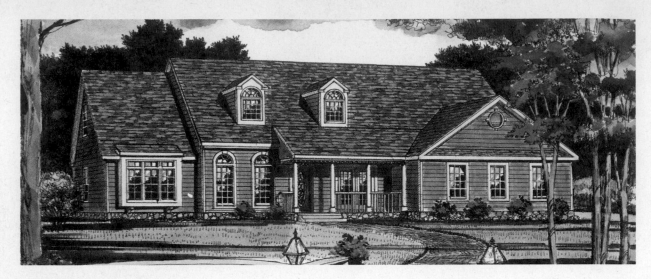

Country Charm

- While the facade of this home features country details, the interior includes many up-to-date amenities.
- Inside, a stepped ceiling crowns the dining room, where French doors allow guests to enjoy the sounds of raindrops. A wet bar makes serving easy.
- With a closet and private access to a split bath, the office near the entry would also serve well as a bedroom. A 9-ft. ceiling here adds a spacious feel.
- An 18-ft., 5-in. vaulted ceiling soars over the Great Room, which will be the setting for many family meetings.
- In the kitchen, an island counter makes room for baking sprees. A 12-ft. vaulted ceiling tops the breakfast nook, where sliding French doors lead to a porch.
- Across the home, a window seat in the master suite is perfect for relaxing.
- Upstairs, a raised loft would be a neat place to set up the kids' computer nook.
- The foyer, the master suite, the dining room and the two bedrooms upstairs include 9½-ft. ceilings.

Plan AX-94314

Bedrooms: 3+	Baths: 3
Living Area:	
Upper floor	646 sq. ft.
Main floor	2,118 sq. ft.
Total Living Area:	**2,764 sq. ft.**
Storage/future space	400 sq. ft.
Standard basement	2,118 sq. ft.
Garage and storage	497 sq. ft.
Exterior Wall Framing:	2x4

Foundation Options:

Standard basement
Crawlspace
Slab
(All plans can be built with your choice of foundation and framing. A generic conversion diagram is available. See order form.)

BLUEPRINT PRICE CODE: D

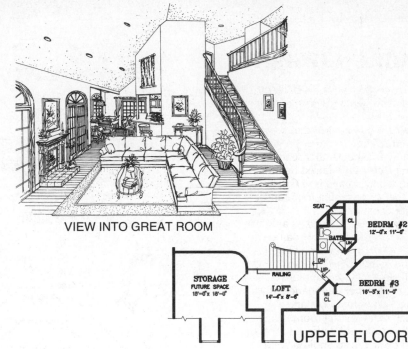

VIEW INTO GREAT ROOM

UPPER FLOOR

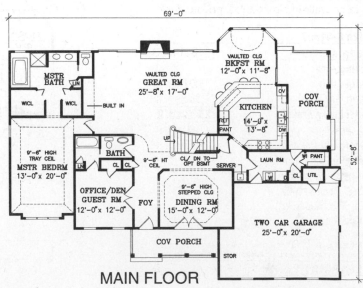

MAIN FLOOR

ORDER BLUEPRINTS ANYTIME!
CALL TOLL-FREE 1-800-820-1283

Plan AX-94314

PRICES AND DETAILS
ON PAGES 2-5

Dynamic Design

- Angled walls, vaulted ceilings and lots of glass set the tempo for this dynamic home.
- The covered front entry opens to a raised foyer and a beautiful staircase with a bayed landing.
- One step down, a spectacular see-through fireplace with a raised hearth and built-in wood storage is visible from both the bayed dining room and the stunning Great Room.
- The Great Room also showcases an 18-ft.-high vaulted ceiling, wraparound windows and access to a deck or patio.
- The adjoining nook has a door to the deck and is served by the kitchen's snack bar. The kitchen is enhanced by a 9-ft. ceiling, corner windows and a pass-through to the dining room.
- Upstairs, the master suite offers a 10-ft.-high coved ceiling, a splendid bath, a large walk-in closet and a private deck.

Plan S-41587

Bedrooms: 3+	Baths: 3
Living Area:	
Upper floor	1,001 sq. ft.
Main floor	1,550 sq. ft.
Total Living Area:	**2,551 sq. ft.**
Basement	1,550 sq. ft.
Garage (three-car)	773 sq. ft.
Exterior Wall Framing:	2x6

Foundation Options:

Daylight basement
Standard basement
Crawlspace
Slab

(All plans can be built with your choice of foundation and framing. A generic conversion diagram is available. See order form.)

BLUEPRINT PRICE CODE: D

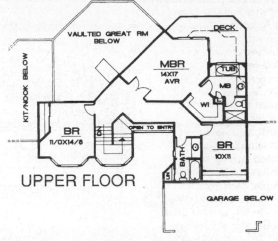

UPPER FLOOR

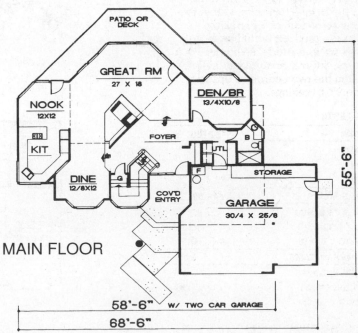

MAIN FLOOR

58'-6"
68'-6"
55'-6"
W/ TWO CAR GARAGE

ORDER BLUEPRINTS ANYTIME!
CALL TOLL-FREE 1-800-820-1283

Plan S-41587

PRICES AND DETAILS
ON PAGES 2-5

495

Photo by Gil Ford

Spacious and Stately

- This popular home design boasts a classic Creole exterior and a symmetrical layout, with 9-ft.-high ceilings on the main floor.
- French doors lead from the formal living and dining rooms to the large family room. The central fireplace is flanked by French doors that open to a covered rear porch and an open-air deck.
- The kitchen is reached easily from the family room, the dining room and the rear entrance. An island cooktop and a window-framed eating area are other features found here.
- The real seller, though, is the main-floor master suite with its spectacular bath. Among its many extras are a built-in vanity, a spa tub and a 16-ft. sloped ceiling with a skylight.
- Three upstairs bedrooms, each with double closets and private bath access, make this the perfect family-sized home.

Plan E-3000

Bedrooms: 4	Baths: 3½
Living Area:	
Upper floor	1,027 sq. ft.
Main floor	2,008 sq. ft.
Total Living Area:	**3,035 sq. ft.**
Standard basement	2,008 sq. ft.
Garage	484 sq. ft.
Storage	96 sq. ft.
Exterior Wall Framing:	2x6

Foundation Options:

Standard basement

Crawlspace

Slab

(All plans can be built with your choice of foundation and framing. A generic conversion diagram is available. See order form.)

BLUEPRINT PRICE CODE: E

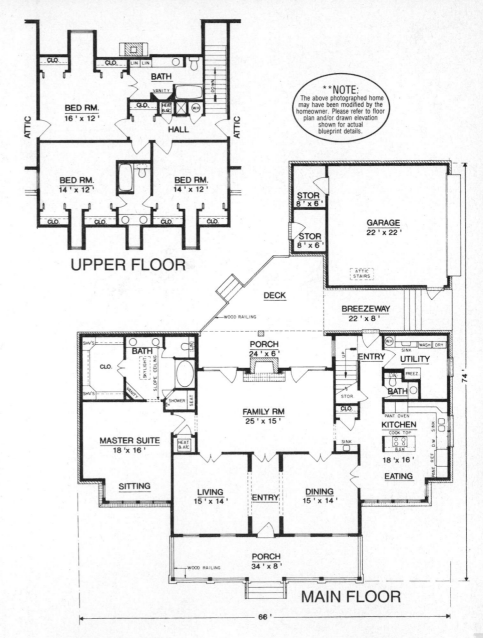

**NOTE: The above photographed home may have been modified by the homeowner. Please refer to floor plan and/or drawn elevation shown for actual blueprint details.

UPPER FLOOR

MAIN FLOOR